The Harlem Renaissance
1920–1940

Series Editor

Cary D. Wintz
Texas Southern University

A Garland Series

Contents of the Series

Analysis and Assessment, 1980–1994

Edited with introductions by

Cary D. Wintz
Texas Southern University

GARLAND PUBLISHING, INC.
New York & London
1996

Library of Congress Cataloging-in-Publication Data

Analysis and assessment, 1980–1994 / edited with introductions by
    Cary D. Wintz.
        p.   cm. — (The Harlem Renaissance, 1920–1940 ; 7)
    Includes bibliographical references.
    ISBN 0-8153-2218-6 (alk. paper)
        1. American literature—Afro-American authors—History and
criticism.   2. American literature—20th century—History and criticism.   3. Harlem (New York, N.Y.)—Intellectual life—20th century.   4. Afro-Americans—Intellectual life.   5. Harlem Renaissance.
I. Wintz, Cary D., 1943–   .   II. Series.
PS153.N5A54   1996
810.9'896073'09041—dc20   96-17088
                                                      CIP

Printed on acid-free, 250-year-life paper
Manufactured in the United States of America

Contents

The Harlem Renaissance: An International Perspective

The Politics and Aesthetics of the Harlem Renaissance

Series Introduction

The Harlem Renaissance was the most significant event in African American literature and culture in the twentieth century. While its most obvious manifestation was as a self-conscious literary movement, it touched almost every aspect of African American culture and intellectual life in the period from World War I to the Great Depression. Its impact redefined black music, theater, and the visual arts; it reflected a new more militant political/racial consciousness and racial pride that was associated with the term "New Negro"; it embodied the struggle for civil rights that had been reinvigorated by the founding of the N.A.A.C.P. and the ideology of W.E.B. Du Bois; and it was an aspect of the urbanization of African Americans that first attracted public attention in the early twentieth century with the black migration.

Within this context it is difficult to pinpoint the chronological limits of the Harlem Renaissance. Generally the consensus among scholars is that the Harlem Renaissance was an event of the 1920s, bounded on one side by World War I and the race riots of 1919 and on the other side by the 1929 stock market crash. Some, however, have either greatly expanded or sharply restricted the time span of the movement. In 1967 Abraham Chapman wrote that he saw elements of the Renaissance in Claude McKay's poetry of 1917 and even in W.E.B. Du Bois's poem, "The Song of the Smoke," which was published in 1899.[1] Nathan Huggins argued that the Renaissance began during the years between the beginning of World War I and 1920, when the center of power in the African American community shifted from Tuskegee to Harlem, and he saw the Harlem Riots of 1935 as the end of the movement.[2] John Hope Franklin, on the other hand, wrote as late as 1980 that the Harlem Renaissance extended into the 1960s; more recently he has modified that concept, and now speaks of a first and second phase of the Harlem Renaissance, with the latter phase extending into the 1940s and beyond; he also observes that African American literary creativity was not confined to Harlem, but spread across the entire country[3] Benjamin Brawley, the preeminent African American literary historian contemporary to the Harlem Renaissance, downplayed the concept of the "so-called Negro literary renaissance," which he felt was centered around the publication of Carl Van Vechten's *Nigger Heaven* in 1926 and which he argued had no significant positive influence on African American literature.[4] Finally, Sterling Brown, one of the Harlem Renaissance poets and later a literary scholar, denied that Harlem was ever the center of a black literary movement.[5]

For the purposes of this collection the Harlem Renaissance is viewed primarily as a literary and intellectual movement. While theater, music, and the visual arts are looked at briefly, the focus is on African American literature, the assessment and criticism of this literature, and the relation of this literature to the political and social issues confronting African Americans in the early twentieth century.

The Harlem Renaissance was a self-conscious movement. That is, the writers and poets who participated in the movement were aware that they were involved in a literary movement and assumed at least partial responsibility for defining the parameters and aesthetics of the movement; black scholars and intellectuals were also aware of the Harlem Renaissance (even if they railed against it) and attempted to define the movement in terms both of literature and the political and social implications of that literature. While it was self-conscious, the Harlem Renaissance lacked a well-defined ideological or aesthetic center. It was more a community of writers, poets, critics, patrons, sponsors, and publishers than a structured and focused intellectual movement. It may be best conceptualized as an attitude or a state of mind—a feeling shared by a number of black writers and intellectuals who centered their activities in Harlem in the 1920s and early 1930s. The men and women who participated in the movement shared little but a consciousness that they were part of a common endeavor—a new awakening of African American culture and creativity; other than that what bound them together was a pride in their racial heritage, an essentially middle-class background, and the fact that all, to a greater or lesser degree, were connected to Harlem at the time that Harlem was emerging as the cultural, intellectual, and political center of black America.

Within this context, the Harlem Renaissance may best be conceptualized as a group of black writers and poets, orbiting erratically around a group of black intellectuals positioned in the N.A.A.C.P., the Urban League, and other African American political and educational institutions. These older intellectuals supported the movement, criticized it, attempted with varying success to define it, and served as liaison between the writers and the white publishers, patrons, and critics who dominated the business of literature in the United States in the 1920s. Complicating and enriching this mix was the fact that the lines between the various types of participants were not clearly drawn. James Weldon Johnson, for example, was a major promoter of the movement and a poet and novelist in his own right; Jessie Fauset, the most prolific novelist of the period, also served as literary editor of *The Crisis* and actively promoted the careers of young black writers; Countee Cullen, Sterling Brown, and Gwendolyn Bennett wrote regular literary columns, while Wallace Thurman, Langston Hughes, and several other writers attempted to publish literary magazines; and Carl Van Vechten, a white promoter of African American literature, worked closely with the Knopfs to publish black literature, authored the best-known novel of Harlem life, and almost singlehandedly created the white fascination with Harlem and African American life that characterized the 1920s.

With this definition it becomes a little easier to define the parameters of the movement. The Harlem Renaissance began in the early 1920s, when Jean Toomer published *Cane* and African American writers and intellectuals began to realize that something new was happening in black literature. The movement extended well into the 1930s and included the works of Zora Neale Hurston, Claude McKay, and Langston Hughes that were published in that decade. As long as they and other writers consciously identified with the Renaissance, the movement continued. It did not, however, encompass the younger writers like Richard Wright, Frank Yerby, or Ralph Ellison, who emerged in the 1930s and 1940s. Like so much else, these boundaries are not exact. Antecedents to the Harlem Renaissance are clear in the first two decades of the twentieth century; likewise it is easy to place some of Langston Hughes's work from the 1940s and 1950s in the Renaissance.

The goal of this series is to reprint articles and other materials that will delineate a clear picture and foster an understanding of the Harlem Renaissance. Three types of materials are included in this series. First, and most important, are the critical and interpretive materials on the Harlem Renaissance written by participants in and contemporaries of the movement. These firsthand accounts will assist readers in understanding the efforts of Harlem Renaissance writers, poets, and critics to define the movement and enable readers to glimpse the dynamics of the movement. Second, this series includes a retrospective look at the Harlem Renaissance through the eyes of participants and contemporaries, as well as by writers and critics who were involved in post-Renaissance black literature. Finally, the series presents a sample of the scholarly analysis and criticism of the movement from the 1950s through the early 1990s. The selections come from articles, essays, columns, and reviews in periodical literature; selections from memoirs, novels, histories, and books of criticism; and essays from scholarly journals. These materials are supplemented by a selection of previously unpublished materials, including letters, speeches, and essays. Not included are the literary works of the Harlem Renaissance. There are a number of anthologies of African American literature that already serve that purpose well.

This series also reflects one of the major problems confronting the study of the Harlem Renaissance in particular and African American history in general—the difficulty of accessing needed source materials. For years the study of African American history was handicapped by the fact that many of its primary sources had not been preserved or were not made available to scholars. If they had been preserved, they were housed in scattered collections and often incompletely processed and catalogued. The sharp increase in interest in African American history during the last thirty years has improved this situation enormously, but problems still persist. This series is in part an effort to make material related to one aspect of African American history more available to students and scholars. Unfortunately, it also suffers from the problem that some resources, even when located, are not readily available. For this reason a number of items by James Weldon Johnson had to be excluded; likewise, a very valuable retrospective on the Harlem Renaissance that was published initially in *Black World* is missing here. In the future, perhaps these and other barriers that impede research in African American history will be lifted.

As in any project of this nature there are scores of persons who have provided valuable support and assistance; it is impossible to name them all here. I want to especially thank Leo Balk and Carole Puccino of Garland Publishing. Leo with patience and firmness guided this series to completion; Carole worked diligently to arrange permissions for the publication of the material that appears here. In addition, I want to thank Paul Finkelman, who played a key role in helping me conceptualize the scope and nature of this project. Wolde Michael Akalou, Howard Beeth, Merline Pitre, and my other colleagues and students at Texas Southern University provided valuable feedback as the project developed. I also had wonderful assistance from the staff at the libraries

I visited while collecting the material for this series. I want to especially acknowledge the staff at the Harry Ransom Humanities Research Center at the University of Texas at Austin, the Beinecke Library at Yale University, and the Heartman Collection at the Robert J. Terry Library at Texas Southern University; in addition, librarians at the Fondren Library at Rice University, the M.D. Anderson Library at the University of Houston, the Perry Casteñeda Library at the University of Texas at Austin, and the library at the University of Houston, Clear Lake helped me track down the copies of the more elusive journals and periodicals used for this collection. I also want to thank Kathy Henderson and and Barbara Smith-Labard, who helped arrange for permission to publish previously unpublished materials from the collections at the Harry Ransom Humanities Research Center. Finally, research for this project was supported in part by a Travel to Collections grant from the National Endowment for the Humanities.

Cary D. Wintz

Notes

1. Abraham Chapman, "The Harlem Renaissance in Literary History," *CLA Journal* 11 (September 1967): 44–45.

2. Nathan Irvin Huggins, ed., *Voices from the Harlem Renaissance* (New York: Oxford University Press, 1976), 6–10.

3. John Hope Franklin, *From Slavery to Freedom: A History of Negro Americans*, 5th ed. (New York: Alfred Knopf, 1980), 383; John Hope Franklin and Alfred A. Moss, Jr., *From Slavery to Freedom: A History of African Americans*, 7th ed. (New York: McGraw–Hill, Inc., 1994), 379–80.

4. Benjamin Brawley, *The Negro Genius: A New Appraisal of the American Negro in Literature and the Fine Arts* (New York: Dodd, Mead, 1937), 231–68.

5. Sterling Brown, "The New Negro in Literature (1925–1955)." In *The New Negro Thirty Years Afterward*, ed. by Rayford W. Logan, Eugene C. Holmes, and C. Franklin Edwards (Washington, D.C.: Howard University Press, 1955).

Further Reading

Cooper, Wayne F. *Claude McKay: Rebel Sojourner in the Harlem Renaissance*. Baton Rouge: Louisiana State University Press, 1987.

Douglas, Ann. *Terrible Honesty: Mongrel Manhattan in the 1920s*. New York: Farrar, Straus, and Giroux, 1995.

Ferguson, Blanche E. *Countee Cullen and the Negro Renaissance*. New York: Dodd, Mead, 1966.

Hemenway, Robert E. *Zora Neale Hurston: A Literary Biography*. Urbana: University of Illinois Press, 1977.

Huggins, Nathan Irvin. *Harlem Renaissance*. New York: Oxford University Press, 1971.

———, ed. *Voices from the Harlem Renaissance*. New York: Oxford University Press, 1976.

Hull, Gloria T. *Color, Sex, and Poetry: Three Women Writers of the Harlem Renaissance*. Bloomington: Indiana University Press, 1987.

Kerman, Cynthia Earl, and Richard Eldridge. *The Lives of Jean Toomer: A Hunger for Wholeness*. Baton Rouge: Louisiana State University Press, 1987.

Levy, Eugene. *James Weldon Johnson: Black Leader, Black Voice*. Chicago: University of Chicago Press, 1973.

Lewis, Dadid Levering. *W.E.B. Du Bois: Biography of a Race, 1868–1919*. New York: Henry Holt, 1993.

———. *When Harlem Was in Vogue*. New York: Vintage Books, 1981.

Marable, Manning. *W.E.B. Du Bois: Black Radical Democrat*. Boston: Twayne Publishers, 1986.

Rampersad, Arnold. *The Life of Langston Hughes*. Vol 1. *I, Too, Sing America: 1902–1941*. New York: Oxford University Press, 1986.

———. *The Life of Langston Hughes*. Vol 2. *I Dream a World: 1942–1967*. New York: Oxford University Press, 1988.

Singh, Amritjit. *The Novels of the Harlem Renaissance: Twelve Black Writers, 1923–1933*. University Park: The Pennsylvania State University Press, 1976.

Sundquist, Eric J. *To Wake the Nations: Race in the Making of American Literature*. Cambridge: Harvard University Press, 1993.

Tillery, Tyrone. *Claude McKay: A Black Poet's Struggle for Identity*. Amherst: The University of Massachusetts Press, 1992.

Wintz, Cary D. *Black Culture and the Harlem Renaissance*. Houston: Rice University Press, 1988.

Volume Introduction

In the 1980s and early 1990s, the sophistication of the scholarly analysis of the Harlem Renaissance increased, reflecting the increasing sophistication of and increasing interest in the field of African American studies. While black journals continued to publish material on the Harlem Renaissance, more and more of this material found its way into mainstream journals. Major changes in the scholarship of the Harlem Renaissance included the increased emphasis on the role of women in the movement and the application of the methodologies and insights of race and gender studies to this topic. In addition, the last fifteen years witnessed an increased interest in the Harlem Renaissance on the part of European and African scholars. This international perspective focused attention on the relationship between the Harlem Renaissance and the literature of African and Caribbean writers, as well as the writers of other colonized or oppressed peoples.

This volume is organized into four sections. The first is a selection of criticism and analysis of African American literature in general as well as criticism of the work of specific Harlem Renaissance writers. The second section examines the Harlem Renaissance from an international perspective. While there is still some interest in the links between African and African American literature during the Harlem Renaissance, most of the essays in this section examine the Renaissance from the perspective of European literary scholarship. The third section contains selections that focus on the politics and aesthetics of the Harlem Renaissance. Material in this section focuses on the relationship between black writers and their black and white patrons, promoters, and publishers and also relates the Renaissance to the racial and political currents of the 1920s. This volume concludes with an assessment of the work and careers of individual Harlem Renaissance writers. While much of this material focuses on the work of writers like Jean Toomer, Langston Hughes, Claude McKay, and Zora Neale Hurston, there is also an effort to rediscover and interpret in terms of the Harlem Renaissance the work of lesser-known black writers, especially black women writers.

Home in Harlem, New York: Lessons from the Harlem Renaissance Writers

SIDNEY H. BREMER earned her doctorate in English from Stanford University and teaches literatures and cultures of the United States at the interdisciplinary University of Wisconsin, Green Bay, where she is associate professor of Urban and Public Affairs, Literature, and Women's Studies. She has published essays on women as characters and authors in literature, on urban literature and its biographical and cultural contexts, and especially on the gender differences in turn-of-the-century Chicago literature. "Home in Harlem, New York" is part of her book-length study, tentatively entitled Urban Intersections, *on the informing influence of gender, ethnicity, and region on United States authors' urban experiences and imagery.*

America's mainstream culture has long lodged "home" in the mythic permanency of a rural cottage. There the kinship circle, sense of belonging, and implicit responsibilities that define "home" are tended by a purely white, motherly wife. As an imaginary bulwark against industrial urbanization, this mythic image of home took shape in the nineteenth century's mass periodicals. It later expanded into the small-town Main Streets of Hollywood movies and the privatized suburban fantasies of television. It is an unrealistic, even dangerously deceptive image, as many American authors—from Mark Twain and Charles Chesnutt to Sinclair Lewis to Joyce Carol Oates—have shown. Few of us are wived and familied white men commuting to some privileged space apart. Even for those few, the cottage front hides the complexities of familial and social relations. The rural rootedness of our mythic home ignores, moreover, the predominantly mobile, urban realities of modern American life. Indeed, "movement over a variety of county" may well be Americans' "largest common background," as a wise though little remembered Chicago novelist named Edith Wyatt affirmed as early as 1914; and most of us have been doing our moving and working and living in cities since the 1930 census.

If we are to feel at home in our changing urban world, we need images of home that are more fitting to our experience—not for reasons of sentiment but in order to feel realistically grounded, belonging, and responsible there. We need specifically urban images of home to be able to see ourselves at home with—even when at odds with—our own experience, with others, and with our dreams in cities. First, we need to know the city as a physical home place, with the power to evoke sensory memory, what William Faulkner calls the "memory [that] knows before knowing remembers" (111). Second, we need to recognize that, like it or not, we belong to urban home communities—those families and neighborhoods and birthright groups with which we share our history, images, social circumstances, and physical experience. Third, we need to be able to find a symbolic home for our aspirations in the city, as F. Scott Fitzgerald once could in Edmund

Wilson's book-lined New York apartment.

But that homelike "apartment [where] life was mellow and safe" was a city whose *loss* Fitzgerald lamented in his 1932 essay "My Lost City" (25). Just when cities were becoming de facto home for most Americans, much American literature despaired of an urban "home." It conceded to ethnic minority writers the imaginative home that Walt Whitman had offered for mobile urban Americans when he "loved well those cities" of Manhattan and Brooklyn, with their sensory vitality, embracing crowds, and visionary unities, in "Crossing Brooklyn Ferry" (160–62). The wake of World War I swamped the Progressive dream of a "civic family" that turn-of-the-century Chicago's residential writers like Henry Blake Fuller, Edith Wyatt, and Elia Peattie had shared with Jane Addams (Bremer 39). It also upset the thrust toward realistic comprehension and technological progress that had mitigated the newcomer's reaction to the city's strangeness in turn-of-the-century works by William Dean Howells, Theodore Dreiser, Upton Sinclair, Henry James, and others. Only the latter group's alienating images survived in the Euro-American vision of the living-dead megalopolis—its physical landscape reduced to a "valley of ashes," its society and psyches to grotesque "fragmentation," and its dreams to "gruesomely preserved" artifacts and mass-produced clichés (Fitzgerald, *Great Gatsby* 23; Dos Passos, qtd. in Wagner 63; Wharton 50; West). The megalopolitan world epitomized by these images of Greater New York offers no home to the human body, social spirit, or soul.

But our literature does include an alternative stream of urban imagery. During those same megalopolitan 1920s, some of New York's most powerful ethnic minority writers bravely claimed the city—at least, their neighborhood microcosm of the city—as a home for the transient outcasts of American society. Like the Jewish immigrants crowded into the Lower East Side before them, Harlem's African American newcomers constituted a critical mass large enough to sustain a subculture and to achieve high visibility. Harlem, too, had its own cultural resources of language, folkways, and ritual aesthetic forms. Although seriously compromised by poverty, undependable white patronage, and a colonized color consciousness, Harlem also had its own cultural institutions—political organizations, clubs and cafés and theaters, newspapers, and places of worship. Like the Lower East Side, it was touted as a "city within a city" (Cahan 51; White 187; see also Ellison 122). Like Jewish immigrants from the pogroms of Eastern Europe, too, Harlem's migrants from the Jim Crow South viewed the city as a "promised land"—as Jewish American Mary Antin also proclaimed Boston in the title of her 1912 autobiography and as Claude Brown, a second-generation Harlem autobiographer, confirmed even in 1965 in *Manchild in the Promised Land*. Brown referred to that vision with some conscious irony, however. For Harlem's African Americans, like the Jews before them, were also subject to continuing minority exclusions—not only from American society's daily goods and powers but also from such common dreams as the sentimental, rural-cottage image of home. So they were predisposed to a critical perspective on the dominant cultural values that World War I had bankrupted. Indeed, as in Jewish American literature, a strong tension between hope and oppression grounds the Harlem Renaissance vision of urban neighborhood-ghetto as a home away from home.

The writers of the Harlem Renaissance were an extremely mobile crew, who felt joined, not estranged, by their wanderings, because they were part of the great migration of black people to the urban Northeast around World War I. Collectively they developed a vision of an urban home that was at once an organic place, a birthright community, and a cultural aspiration. In all three of these dimensions, the vitality of their home reached out even across continents joined in oppression. And Harlem, New York, their capital city within a city, was the center. Whether or not they happened to be living there at any particular time, the Harlem Renaissance writers regarded Harlem as their primary, symbolic home. Thus their Harlem focused an exemplary attempt to make a home for modern urban transients.[1] Their lives and works tried Harlem's strengths as well as its limitations as home place, community, and aspiration. Their Harlem Renaissance was a civic, as well as an aesthetic, enterprise.

Nearly all the Harlem Renaissance writers were urban wanderers. Even those who were raised in small towns came to Harlem via other cities—Northerner W. E. B. Du Bois from the faculty of Atlanta University, Southerner Zora Neale Hurston from service as a manicurist in Washington, DC, Westerner Wallace Thurman from the post office in Los Angeles. Young Langston Hughes arrived from Cleveland, Nella Larsen from Chicago, Rudolph Fisher from Washington, DC, Dorothy West from Boston; and before them, James Weldon Johnson came from Jacksonville, Walter White from Atlanta, Jessie Fauset from Philadelphia, and Claude McKay from Kingston, Jamaica. They were from cities and on the move.

In fact, the best publicized "New Negro" leaders of the Harlem Renaissance were more often away than in residence during the 1920s: Claude McKay took off in 1922 for a twelve-year vagabondage through major cities of Europe and Africa; loyal Langston Hughes just kept coming back from sea or college for Harlem weekends, vacations, and special occasions; and Countee Cullen, the only leader of the Harlem Renaissance raised in New York City, was away over half the time at Harvard, then in Paris. So many Renaissance Harlemites flocked to Paris that Alain Locke once called it a "transplanted Harlem."[2] Even for the senior writers who were also political organizers, editors, and its most stable residents, Harlem was a rather brief hegira. Nearly all, young and old alike, had moved on by 1932, as the Depression stripped away the Jazz Age excess to expose Harlem's underlying poverty.

The writers' urban wanderlust, however, only increased their identification with Harlem as the hub of a dynamic world. Harlem was the goal of many African American migrants in the 1910s and 1920s, collecting over 200,000 black residents by 1930. Because the city's economy was service-oriented rather than industrial, Manhattan did not draw the predominantly rural, unskilled blacks who migrated to other Northern cities. The new Harlemites, like their writers, came mostly from other cities—one-fourth from the West Indies, like McKay and Arthur Schomburg (J. W. Johnson, *Black Manhattan* 14–53; C. S. Johnson 279). And they came because Harlem was the symbolic center of African America generally—the "Negro Capital" or "Mecca" or "Promised Land," as it was variously dubbed.

Indeed, Harlem's symbolic status knew few circumstantial limits. Wherever they might be, the wandering citizens of Harlem felt its presence whenever they came into contact with its characteristic textures, persons, or arts. Distance could even increase African Americans' sense of identification with Harlem, as a place to go to or aspire to or think toward. McKay published his superb 1928 novel, *Home to Harlem*, from abroad, then wrote Hughes in 1930, "I am thinking of coming home next fall or winter. I write of America as home [although] I am really a poet without a country."[3] Longing from abroad for the "refuge" of an American city's Black Belt (*Long Way* 304), McKay could see a home in America where he had previously seen only imperial oppression. And he identified America-as-home specifically with Harlem, whereas he had previously associated America-as-oppressor with the surrounding city of New York—for instance, in his 1922 poem "The White City" (*Harlem Shadows* 23). Thus in tension with the oceanic reach of Harlem's symbolic home, New York implicitly defined Harlem's limits for McKay. In this imagistic distinction between Harlem and New York, he was profoundly visionary, as we shall see.

McKay was typical in his use of sensory images to present Harlem as home place. In Harlem Renaissance literature, African America's capital city is organic, not mechanical. It is fleshy—and embodied in lively colors, tastes, and sounds. This basic organicism is the first noteworthy strength of Harlem as home. Its sensory elements are basic enough to be found anywhere and portable enough to go anywhere, although they concentrate most vividly in Harlem's streets. The organicism of Harlem's street life is life-giving, too. More earthy than its perversions in Anglo-American exotica, this Harlem is nurturing as well as sexually exciting. When McKay's fictional double in *Home to Harlem*, Jake Brown, longs back to Harlem from abroad, he longs for the sexual edibles that its streets offer: "Fifth Avenue, Lenox Avenue, and One Hundred and Thirty-fifth Street, with their chocolate-brown and walnut-brown girls, were calling him" (5). While McKay's masculinist fantasy of women as food offers a troubling glimpse into the sexual politics of the Harlem Renaissance, its sensory intensity was embraced by his female

compatriots, too. Another major work also published in 1928, Nella Larsen's novel *Quicksand*,
similarly describes its heroine's "magic sense of
having come home" in Harlem "as if she were tasting some agreeable, exotic food . . . " (65). So
Harlem's street life excites and feeds its homecoming participants—as it also gave life's breath to
Langston Hughes on his arrival there in 1921: "At
every subway station I kept watching for the sign:
135TH STREET. When I saw it, I held my breath.
. . . I went up the steps and into the bright September sunlight. Harlem! I looked around. Negroes everywhere! . . . I took a deep breath and
felt happy again" (*Big Sea* 81). A rather basic equation: Harlem's streets = sex + food + breath =
life-giving home.

In its organic embodiedness, Harlem as home
denies the mainstream American image of the city
as a machine boxed off from nature. Its urban
streets are continuous with Walt Whitman's "Song
of the Open Road" (1855)—just as sensory and dynamic, connecting rural with urban folk life and
generating new life in the city. The Harlem Renaissance writers simply did not share in America's
standard idealization of the countryside—as a rural home to be held especially dear and apart from
the alien city. Few of the Harlem Renaissance writers had had childhood homes in any rural places
or small towns, nostalgic memories of which they
might find hard to shake. Conversely and collectively, the historical memory of slavery had soured
all of them on America's rural past. It is perhaps
not surprising, then, that they challenged America's cultural habit of rural nostalgia.

But it is surprising that they affirmed the pastoral values of organic energy and Edenic belonging that the pastoral tradition associated with rural
settings, that they brought those values into the urban setting of Harlem, and that, in the process,
they undercut assumptions about urban artificiality and alienation. Those assumptions were
undoubtedly reinforced by the personal and
historical experience of many African Americans
under the domination of whites in urban as well
as rural America. Nonetheless the countercultural
experience of organic vitality in Harlem was
powerful—and reinforced by two academic movements, which Du Bois and Alain Locke led and
younger renaissance writers like Hurston, Hughes,

and Cullen followed: the aesthetic cult of African
primitivism and the anthropological exploration
of African American folklore. Each of these
schools of thought located organic vitality not in
a particular setting but in the people themselves,
in a racial heredity of primitivism or in an ethnic
heritage of song and story. Together with the
Harlem Renaissance writers, they simultaneously
extended and challenged the pastoral tradition by
suggesting that its values of organic energy and belonging are more a matter of inner human development than of external environments. Thus
the vision of Harlem as home brings the transcendent power of the pastoral to bear on city life.

The very streets of Harlem come to life with human personalities in the third great Harlem Renaissance novel of 1928, *The Walls of Jericho*, by
Rudolph Fisher. Fifth Avenue is a "fallen" aristocrat above 125th Street; Seventh Avenue is a
"promenade" of "triumphant" Sunday church-
goers in all their "self-righteousness"; and ficti-
tious Court Avenue, where "dicty" middle-class
Harlemites live, is "a straight, thin spinster" (3–4,
44–45, 188–89). In all their variety, these streets are
both home to Harlem residents and Harlem residents themselves, at home there. "Such skillful hu-
manization of inanimate objects" (Singh 86)
breaks down the distinction between human beings and their urban environment. It envelops people in an organic vitality that is compatible, even
coterminous with their physical and emotional
life.

The streets of the Harlem Renaissance are indeed magical in their sensory life-force. Like
totems, they are repeatedly invoked by name and
imbued with transcendent power in Harlem
Renaissance literature. Gathering together the life
of the folk, parading it, and publicizing it abroad,
they transcend limits of place—making Harlem an
"[i]sland within an island, but not alone," as
Hughes later wrote in a poem he sent to McKay
in 1943 ("Broadcast to the West Indies"). Harlem's
streets transcend time and weather, too. Seventh
Avenue especially accomplishes this feat. The parade of dark skins on Seventh Avenue makes "the
frigid midwinter night . . . warmer," while the
"rainbow" hues of its costumes make the noon-
time "sun grin . . . more brightly" at two important points in the first black mystery novel, *The*

Conjure-Man Dies, written by Rudolph Fisher and published in 1932 (3, 86–87). A Seventh Avenue parade of organic, colorful vitality appears in almost every Harlem Renaissance novel. In other Harlem streets, too, children's dances promise future life and inspire art, as Jessie Fauset's novel *There Is Confusion* (1924) and Wallace Thurman's short story "Terpsichore in Harlem" (1930?) both insist.

Filled with children as well as adults, women as well as men, Harlem's streets are a neighborhood extension of family life and generation. That does not mean that the Harlem streets are happy—any more than families are always happy. But they are alive, generative. In explicit, repeated contrast to the deadening subway machines and dwarfing skyscraper streets of Anglo New York, Harlem's streets are defined by people walking. They are a "stream of life" in Fauset's 1929 novel, *Plum Bun* (97; cf. 87), "rivers" in Larsen's *Quicksand* (253). Even death confirms the generativity of life, as blues spawn the laughter of jazz and street life spills into the cabarets in Langston Hughes's first book of poems, *The Weary Blues* (1925).

Beyond Hughes's lyrics, however, the openended vitality of the streets rarely breaks into Harlem's interior spaces, those overcrowded containers where sensory richness becomes sensory overload. In the cabaret and rent-party scenes that are standard as street parades in Harlem Renaissance literature, the many colors and edibles and sounds become kaleidoscopic, dizzying, explosive. Harlem's churches, too, can get caught up in this confusion. They regularly mix spiritual with sensory vitality—dangerously so in Nella Larsen's deep *Quicksand.* There the heroine is self-divided—both Danish American and African American—and unable to express her full life in the race pride that Harlem's streets celebrate. Accelerating into a "torrent" of passion, the streets' "rivers" of organic life sweep her into a storefront church, where she is welcomed as a "scarlet 'oman" and lured into wild "rites" that drain her spiritual resources for merely physical ends (253–63).

Perhaps the Harlem Renaissance women saw most clearly the power of Harlem's organic vitality of place to enslave people in merely sensory existence (see Carby 170–75). But the men reluctantly

recognized, too, that Harlem was finally not openended but materially bound—a promised land in a ghetto. As their white fellow traveler Carl Van Vechten spelled it out in the title of his 1926 novel, Harlem's sensory surfaces might seem like "nigger heaven," but "nigger heaven" was slang for the segregated back balconies that African Americans had to occupy in theaters. So Van Vechten's hero protests:

> Nigger Heaven! That's what Harlem is. We sit in our places in the gallery of this New York theatre and watch the white world sitting down below in the good seats in the orchestra. Occasionally they turn their faces up towards us, their hard, cruel faces, to laugh or sneer, but they never beckon. It never seems to occur to them that Nigger Heaven is crowded, that there isn't another seat, that something has to be done. (149)

Enforced crowding: that was the prison in which the Harlem Renaissance paraded its colors and music, the ghetto that was the "Negro Capital" of America, the source of the tears in Harlemites' laughter.

Van Vechten's black friends objected that he was giving away "family secrets."[4] And so he was. The Harlem Renaissance writers walked a delicate line. While emphasizing the fertile dirt in which their dreams grew, they resisted recognizing the extent to which white ghettoization limited the spread of Harlem's sensory vitality, even turned it back on itself. Instead they asserted the magic of that vitality and its sole dependence on their own community.

For that sensory power could be carried wherever—albeit only where—black people could congregate. It was part and parcel of their birthright community. And Harlem as home was as much a locus of communal association—its second noteworthy strength—as a place of residence for them. As a community to which they belonged by right of birth, Harlem anchored the personal contacts and the institutions that linked its artists to its political activists, librarians, partygoers, even gangsters, and just plain folks. Those communal associations were what kept them coming back to be grounded in its sensory life. Human community was the germ of that life. So the Southern-born author of its first generation, James Weldon Johnson, implied in 1931 when he proclaimed himself "a New Yorker" by a kind of "blood tie," because his "father and mother met in this city" (Speech 2).

Especially did street blues and jive and jazz and sermons express that community. Johnson, Hughes, and Fisher made these rhythms into the central stuff of their literary art. Many Harlem Renaissance writers appended glossaries of "Harlemese" to their novels as regularly as they included Seventh Avenue parades and cabarets and rent parties. But *The Walls of Jericho* showed that the lively idiom of Harlem's community also hid Harlem's full humanity. As Fisher's text explained, "[b]eneath the jests, the avowed fear, the merriment, was a characteristic irony, a markedly racial tendency to make light of what actually was grave" (29)—namely, the social separation of blacks from whites, of Harlem from the rest of New York City, of a part of humanity from the whole. This separation was the most serious limitation on Harlem as home.

The walled city is Fisher's synthesizing metaphor for these communal limits. It stands for both the divided city of Harlem, New York, and for the divided self. Fisher's streetwise hero, Joshua Jones, brashly yet stereotypically nicknamed Shine, describes the biblical outlines of the story:

> Well, this Joshua thought he was the owl's bowels, till one day he run up against a town named Jericho. Town—This place was a flock o' towns. It was the same thing to that part o' the country that New York is to this. . . . But try and get in. This burg has walls around it so thick that the gals could have their jazzhouses on top. . . . And here this red hot papa, Joshua, who's never had his damper turned down yet—here he is up against that much wall—and the damn thing don't budge.   (181–82)

He continues his namesake's story until the walls come tumbling down, but he doesn't report to his street buddies the still deeper lesson drawn from it in the church service he attended with his fiancée. There the minister explained:

> You, my friend, are Joshua. You have advanced through a life of battle. . . . And then you find your-

self face to face with a solid blank wall—a wall beyond which lies the only goal that matters—the land of promise.
> Do you know what that goal is? It is the knowledge of man's own self.   (186–87)

Wrapped up in Harlem's jive, Joshua had been walled off from himself. The segregation of one part of humanity from another is not just an external division, then; it divides each part internally too. Not only is Harlem divided from Greater New York, Fisher reveals; Harlem is self-divided as well. And so, by implication, is the rest of New York.

That canker at the root of this home community also limits Harlem's effectiveness as a home of dreams. Zora Neale Hurston explained the aspirations of the Harlem Renaissance in specifically urban terms in 1934: it sought to find the "fabulous cities of artistic concepts . . . within the mind and language of some humble Negro." As itself a "fabulous city of artistic concepts," Harlem was also home to its writers in this sense: it expressed African America's cultural aspirations in public voice. As a literary center, the wellspring of a creative movement its writers proclaimed a renaissance, and as a recurring, central subject in their art, Harlem offered them this third, spiritual home strength. In celebrating the organic place and community of Harlem in fiction, poetry, plays, autobiographies, and histories, they were simultaneously realizing, and reflecting on, Harlem as an expression of their creative spirit.

As Harlem's sensory life and communal rituals were both expressive and ghettoized, however, so its dreams were both profound and deceptive. For the most part, Harlem Renaissance writers accepted the ambiguities of make-believe. Rather than aspire to some unvarnished truth, the renaissance writers offered Harlem's own self-dramatization in place of racist stereotypes imposed from without. They considered the make-believe of the "signifying monkey" (Gates 286–88) part of Harlem's home power to generate art and symbolize aspiration. *Quicksand, The Walls of Jericho,* and most other Harlem Renaissance novels explicitly embrace the fusions of truth and pretense—even of paradise and damnation—in the rites of storefront churches and the rhythms of cabarets. It seems as wonderful as it is awful that Wallace Thurman's heroine in *The Blacker the Berry* (1929) could not "tell whether the cast was before or behind the proscenium arch" in the Lafayette Theater, what with all "the spontaneous monkey shines" of the audience and "stereotyped antics of the hired performers" (202–03). Such Harlem Renaissance literature presents Harlem as a masquerade.

In some sense, any art is a masquerade—the more deceptive the more profound, as Vladimir Nabokov argues over and over in his expatriate novels. Insofar as Harlem Renaissance literature recognizes and even celebrates the mix of sex and soul, of jazz and blues, of promise and limitation, of truth and deception in the heart of Harlem, it offers an image of home wondrously adequate to the ambiguities of human life. Insofar as the Harlem Renaissance writers recognize that they are both a divided and a connected people—and ritualize that tragicomedy in their art—they are closer to the home truth of modern life than are other Americans who think that home is undivided, simple, and pure.

But that home truth needs its special place in the human community. As aspiration gave boundary-breaking meaning to Harlem as sensory place and birthright community, so the place and community legitimized Harlem as home vision in Harlem Renaissance art. Not to be rescued *from* poverty or the people, Harlem's aspirations were viewed as living *in* its poverty and people. Indeed, painter Aaron Douglass proclaimed the primary goal of the Harlem Renaissance to achieve the "spiritually earthy" quality of "mediating between dung and God."[5] In their Harlem home, dreams were rooted in the dirt and grit of physical and communal life—and could be ruined there, too, as Douglass's close friend Langston Hughes would dramatize forty years later, in his most famous poem, by figuring forth "a dream deferred" as spoiled food and broken skin.

The three dimensions of Harlem as home—place, community, aspiration—needed one another. And unfortunately, Harlem as place, community, and aspiration was finally limited by Greater New York. A civic as well as an aesthetic moment, the Harlem Renaissance realized both the strengths and the limitations of home in Harlem, New York. But its Anglo-American com-

patriots did not. And that Anglo-American failure was both civic and aesthetic, too. In particular, the artistic aspirations of the Harlem Renaissance were often denied place and citizenship in Greater New York—even by friends, and even in the name of art itself. Such civic denial was the outcome when Carl Van Vechten had his way with money raised to memorialize James Weldon Johnson.

James Weldon Johnson had already written the first black New York novel, *The Autobiography of an Ex-Coloured Man* (1912), coauthored African America's "national anthem," "Lift Every Voice," and served as United States consul to Venezuela and Nicaragua, when he moved north from Jacksonville, Florida, in 1914 to "become a citizen of New York." He came to regard the city as "home," and he continued to do so even after he moved on to Nashville in 1931. He felt related to the city as a godson might or as if the bond were even "closer to a blood tie" (J. W. Johnson, Speech 2). In New York he assumed leadership of the NAACP—as its first black executive secretary—in time to help act out the "cherished belief" he shared with so many others of the renaissance, that African American art could "destroy race prejudice" by presenting "the Negro as a creator and a contributor to American civilization."[6] As he had written Walter White a few years earlier, art "is the approach that offers the least friction" (qtd. in Waldron 116). But Harlem Renaissance art may have gone so far so smoothly only because, in the last analysis, as Angela Davis has also recently argued (21), Anglo-Americans continue to separate art from civics—and in the process, continue to deny art's full power.

When Johnson died in 1938, Van Vechten, his literary executor, formed the James Weldon Johnson Memorial Committee, including Johnson's honorary pallbearers and other luminaries like Mayor La Guardia, W. E. B. Du Bois, Eleanor Roosevelt, Langston Hughes, Duke Ellington, and Marian Anderson. They adopted an idea proposed by Harlem sculptor Augusta Savage, that a statue be erected at Seventh Avenue and 110th Street—at the corner of Central Park "where Harlem meets the rest of Manhattan," Hughes later explained in a 1941 fund-raising appeal.[7]

Johnson's widow, Grace Nail Johnson, was particularly emphatic about this "large N. Y. idea," "this civic expression," and she proposed that the monument be inscribed with a poem that Johnson had sent his dear friend Van Vechten back in 1925, "wonder[ing]," as he put it then, "if we love the city in about the same way." "My City," his widow now wrote, was the poem in which he had "declared" New York his "home."[8] "My City" is typical of the Harlem Renaissance in locating the organic energy and belonging associated with "home" in an urban, as contrasted with a rural, setting. It is unusual in extending that imagery beyond the city's black neighborhoods to embrace all Manhattan:

My City

When I come down to sleep death's endless night,
The threshold of the unknown dark to cross,
What to me then will be the keenest loss,
When this bright world blurs on my fading sight?
Will it be that no more I shall see the trees
Or smell the flowers or hear the singing birds
Or watch the flashing streams or patient herds?
No. I am sure it will be none of these.

But, ah! Manhattan's sights and sounds, her
    smells,
Her crowds, her throbbing force, the thrill that
    comes
From being of her a part, her subtle spells,
Her shining towers, her avenues, her slums—
O God! the stark, unutterable pity,
To be dead, and never again behold my city!

(*Saint Peter* 37)

But Van Vechten proposed instead that the monument be inscribed with Johnson's sonnet to African American artists, "O Black and Unknown Bards"; and the Committee for a James Weldon Johnson Memorial adopted that idea at a meeting attended by only six committee members, all men.[9] The same meeting endorsed the Harlem-Manhattan location proposed by Augusta Savage but chose African American Richmond Barthé to sculpt an allegorical statue quite different from the representational death mask of Johnson that Savage had already completed. These decisions limited the civic dimensions of the project and turned it toward more abstract aesthetic ends. And it is quite possible that the men who made the decisions lacked some more profound respect for

embodiment—in place and in human form—that Grace Johnson and Augusta Savage shared as women. Toni Morrison has recently suggested such a gendered sensitivity by describing her own "strong sense of place . . . [of] the mood of the community":

> I think some of it is just a woman's strong sense of being in a room, a place, or a house. Sometimes my relationship to things in a house would be a little different from, say, my brother's or my father's or my sons'. I clean them and I move them and I do very intimate things "in place": I am sort of rooted in it. . . .
>
> (167–68)

In any case, New York City's powerful park commissioner, Robert Moses, jammed the whole works. In 1941 he rejected the proposal to site Barthé's allegorical nude at Seventh Avenue and 110th Street—because, he proclaimed, the statue would be a bad influence on the children of Harlem. In 1942 Moses suggested placing the statue inside Central Park—near a Puerto Rican and black area where "no white man or dicty Negro has ever set foot," Van Vechten objected. Then Moses suggested saving the statue for a proposed postwar housing project deep inside Harlem, since World War II had made it impossible to divert metal from guns to statues anyhow. When Moses finally did agree to the original proposal in late 1945, the costs of casting had increased far beyond the funds that had been raised before the war.[10] That blow sounded the death knell for the statue. It would have been the first public monument to a black person in the city of New York.

But that is not the end of the story. In 1941, just before the committee approached Moses, Van Vechten took up another, related cause. He discovered that Yale University did not have "any Negro books at all"; and Yale, he wrote the memorial committee's secretary, Walter White, was "in the thickest part of the collegiate world." When Van Vechten later concurred with Moses that a statue was "rather a waste of time" and finally "decided to do something else" himself—as he recalled in a 1960 Columbia oral-history interview ("Reminiscences" 344–45)—he chose not only to endow a literary archive rather than a public statue but also to separate what became the James Weldon Johnson Memorial Collection from the thickest part of the African American world, a Harlem home. Van Vechten determined that Harlem's Schomburg Collection, purchased by the New York Public Library in 1926, was "already . . . outstanding" and not in need of help (unlike poor Yale?). He also opted for Yale's commitment to archival preservation to perpetuate "the fame of the Negro" and against the Schomburg Center's commitment to "dissemination and widespread use" of black literature (Hutson 17) in "the largest Negro city in the world"—where "the black masses can read and follow in [their forebears'] footsteps," as Arthur Schomburg put the case for the New York Public Library's Harlem branch.[11]

The decisions of Anglo-Americans Robert Moses and Carl Van Vechten, then, finally denied Johnson's public citizenship—his home—in greater New York. So his statue was not built, and he was memorialized in an academic library away from the city he claimed as home. Similarly, the Harlem Renaissance itself has been treated more often as a merely aesthetic moment rather than as a civic enterprise, too—and its image of home has consequently been ignored. Cut off from the surrounding island of New York, Harlem could only be an imperfect home to African Americans—and no home at all to other mobile, urban Americans. Segregated from and subordinated to Greater New York, the sensory place, the birthright community, and the cultural aspirations that Harlem expressed as home could not be fully joined. When New York lost the 110th Street statue of James Weldon Johnson, it lost a complex symbol for celebrating Harlem's uniqueness and Harlem's connection to Greater New York. Today, too, when we treat Harlem's art apart from that art's place and community, we obscure the power and poignancy of its vision of Harlem as home.

The Harlem of renaissance literature and life nonetheless offers us important suggestions for making our cities home for mobile Americans. Its street forms dramatize the power of crowded open-ended spaces—of continuities and possibilities, rather than of separations and end points. Filled with the generative energy of people of both sexes and all ages, its central streets overflow with sensory accents too—vivid colors, tastes, and sounds that celebrate pedestrian interaction. That sensory base helps to enhance and celebrate group identities—in ways that are transferable to other places. The community includes artists as self-dramatizing, masquerading participants in all this—and encourages them to reflect on its meaning. Harlem's opening and enriched place, its celebrant community groups, and its arts all interconnect, moreover. For the Harlem Renaissance writers essayed to make Harlem their home in all these ways at once. If not in their own segregated lives, then at least within the works of their civic art, Harlem did give its people "that magic sense of having come home."

Notes

[1] See Houston Baker's admiring description of *The New Negro* as an "inscription of Afro-American modernity in mass, urban, national, and international terms" (83).

[2] Alain Locke, letter to Langston Hughes, 2 Sept. 1926, Hughes Papers, James Weldon Johnson Memorial Collection, Beinecke Library, Yale U.

[3] Claude McKay, letter to Langston Hughes, 30 Aug. 1930, Hughes Papers, Johnson Memorial Collection.

[4] Charles S. Johnson, letter to Carl Van Vechten, 10 Aug. 1926, Van Vechten Correspondence–*Opportunity*, Johnson Memorial Collection.

[5] Aaron Douglass, letter to Langston Hughes, [21 Dec. 1925], Hughes Papers, Johnson Memorial Collection.

[6] J. W. Johnson, letter to Carl Van Vechten, 6 Mar. 1927, Van Vechten Correspondence, Johnson Memorial Collection.

[7] List, 15 Dec. 1938; Augusta Savage, letter to Walter White, 14 Apr. 1940, Van Vechten Correspondence–Johnson Memorial, Johnson Memorial Collection. Langston Hughes, "In Memory of a Man," ms., 4 Apr. 1941, Hughes Mss. Collection 529, Johnson Memorial Collection.

[8] Grace Nail Johnson, letters to Carl Van Vechten, 19 Dec. 1938 and 4 Jan. 1939; James Weldon Johnson, letter to Van Vechten, 28 Feb. 1925, Van Vechten Correspondence–Johnson Memorial, Johnson Memorial Collection.

[9] Minutes, 12 Dec. 1939, Van Vechten Correspondence–Johnson Memorial Collection.

[10] Robert Moses, letter to Walter White, n.d., enclosed in White, letter to Carl Van Vechten, 2 Apr. 1942; Van Vechten, letter to White, 9 May 1942; minutes, 4 Dec. 1942; White, letters to Johnson Memorial Committee, 25 Oct. 1945 and 5 Feb. 1947, Van Vechten Correspondence–Johnson Memorial, Johnson Memorial Collection.

[11] Carl Van Vechten, letter to Walter White, 14 Aug. 1941, Van Vechten Correspondence, Johnson Memorial Collection; Arthur Schomburg, letter to Langston Hughes, 16 Feb. 1933,

and letter to Nancy Cunnard, 23 Oct. 1935, Schomburg Papers 7: 3, 8, Schomburg Center for Research in Black Culture, New York Public Library.

Works Cited

Antin, Mary. *The Promised Land*. Boston: Houghton, 1912.
Baker, Houston A., Jr. *Modernism and the Harlem Renaissance*. Chicago: U of Chicago P, 1987.
Bremer, Sidney H. "Lost Continuities: Alternative Urban Visions in Chicago Novels, 1890–1915." *Soundings* 64 (1981): 29–51.
Brown, Claude. *Manchild in the Promised Land*. New York: Macmillan, 1965.
Cahan, Abraham. *Yekl*. New York: Appleton, 1896.
Carby, Hazel V. *Reconstructing Womanhood*. New York: Oxford UP, 1987.
Davis, Angela. "'Strong beyond all definitions. . . .'" *Women's Review of Books* 4 (July-Aug. 1987): 1, 21.
Ellison, Ralph. *Invisible Man*. New York: Random, 1952.
Faulkner, William. *Light in August*. New York: Random, 1932.
Fauset, Jessie Redmon. *Plum Bun*. New York: Stokes, 1929.
——. *There Is Confusion*. New York: Boni, 1924.
Fisher, Rudolph. *The Conjure-Man Dies: A Mystery Tale of Dark Harlem*. 1932. Facsim. ed. New York: Arno and New York Times, 1971.
——. *The Walls of Jericho*. New York: Knopf, 1928.
Fitzgerald, F. Scott. *The Great Gatsby*. New York: Scribner's, 1925.
——. "My Lost City." *The Crack-Up*. Ed. Edmund Wilson. 1934. New York: New Directions, 1945. 23–33.
Gates, Henry Louis, Jr. "The Blackness of Blackness: A Critique of the Sign and the Signifying Monkey." *Black Literature and Literary Theory*. New York: Methuen, 1984. 285–321.
Hughes, Langston. *The Big Sea: An Autobiography*. New York: Knopf, 1940.
——. "Broadcast to the West Indies." Letter to Claude McKay. 23 July 1943. McKay Papers. James Weldon Johnson Memorial Collection. Beinecke Library, Yale Univ.
——. *The Weary Blues*. New York: Knopf, 1925.
Hurston, Zora Neale. "Race Cannot Become Great until It Recognizes Its Talent." Clipping from *Washington Tribune*. 29 Dec. 1934. Julius Rosenwald Fund Archives 423: 9. Fisk Univ.

Hutson, Jean. Interview. With Barbara Kline. 16 Mar. and 5 May 1978. Oral History Collection. Butler Library, Columbia Univ.
Johnson, Charles S. "The New Frontage on American Life." *The New Negro: An Interpretation*. Ed. Alain Locke. New York: Boni, 1925. 278–98.
Johnson, James Weldon. *The Autobiography of an Ex-Coloured Man*. Blue Jade Ed. New York: Knopf, 1927.
——. *Black Manhattan*. 1930. Facsim. ed. New York: Atheneum, 1958.
——. *Saint Peter Relates an Incident*. New York: Viking, 1935.
——. Speech of Resignation, NAACP. 1931. Johnson Papers 103. James Weldon Johnson Memorial Collection. Beinecke Library, Yale Univ.
Larsen, Nella. *Quicksand*. New York: Knopf, 1928.
McKay, Claude. *Harlem Shadows: The Poems of Claude McKay*. New York: Harcourt, 1922.
——. *Home to Harlem*. New York: Harper, 1928.
——. *A Long Way from Home*. New York: Furman, 1937.
Morrison, Toni. "'Intimate Things in Place': A Conversation with Toni Morrison." With Robert Stepto. 19 May 1976. *The Third Woman*. Ed. Dexter Fisher. Boston: Houghton. 167–82.
Singh, Amritjit. *The Novels of the Harlem Renaissance*. University Park: Pennsylvania State UP, 1976.
Thurman, Wallace. *The Blacker the Berry*. 1929. Facsim. ed. New York: Arno and New York Times, 1969.
——. "Terpsichore in Harlem." *Aunt Hagar's Children*. Ms. N.d. Thurman Collection I-16. James Weldon Johnson Memorial Collection. Beinecke Library, Yale Univ.
Van Vechten, Carl. *Nigger Heaven*. New York: Knopf, 1926.
——. "The Reminiscences of Carl Van Vechten." Interviews. With William T. Ingersoll. Mar.-May 1960. Oral History Collection. Butler Library, Columbia Univ.
Wagner, Linda W. *Dos Passos: Artist as American*. Austin: U of Texas P, 1979.
Waldron, Edward W. *Walter White and the Harlem Renaissance*. Port Washington: Kennikat, 1978.
West, Nathanael. *Miss Lonelyhearts*. New York: New Directions, 1933.
Wharton, Edith. *The Age of Innocence*. 1920. New York: Modern Library-Random, 1943.
White, Walter. *Flight*. New York: Knopf, 1926.
Whitman, Walt. *Leaves of Grass*. Comprehensive Reader's Ed. Ed. Harold W. Blodgett and Sculley Bradley. New York: New York UP, 1965.
Wyatt, Edith Franklin. "Overland." Newspaper clipping. 27 June [1914]. Scrapbook 1914-16. Wyatt Mss. (1873-1958). Newberry Library, Chicago.

Myth and History: Discourse of Origins in Zora Neale Hurston and Maya Angelou

Elizabeth Fox-Genovese

Dust Tracks on a Road. It does not take much imagination to glimpse the traces of the South in Zora Neale Hurston's title. Roads on which feet leave dust tracks are dusty roads—hot, sun-baked, dirt roads that comb the Southern heartland from South Carolina to Texas. Dusty roads link Eatonville, Florida, to Stamps, Arkansas. These are the roads that bare-footed black Southern women have traveled since slavery days. These are the roads that cheaply shod black Southern women still travel on foot, or on dilapidated buses. Trains now link these Southern towns, if not to each other, to the rest of the country. But the roads remain, like a faded tracing on the face of the South. The roads of black folks delineate the topography of those centuries of oppression which emancipation could not eradicate. The roads of black folks, like a grid of veins and arteries, join disparate communities and scattered women in the throbbing center of a common past.

I Know Why the Caged Bird Sings. The fracturing of slavery's shackles formally freed individuals, but left blacks as a people caged. Unbreakable bars closed black communities in upon themselves, denying both the communities and the individuals who composed them access to the surrounding white world. Within those cages, black communities developed their own vibrant life, black women raised up black girls in the way that they should go. Singing in the face of danger, singing to thwart the stings of

Elizabeth Fox-Genovese is Eléonore Raoul Professor of Humanities and Director of Women's Studies at Emory University in Atlanta, Georgia. Her most recent book is *Within the Plantation Household: Black and White Women of the Old South* (U of North Carolina P, 1988); her *Feminism Without Illusions: A Critique of Individualism* will be published by the University of North Carolina Press in 1991.

Black American Literature Forum, Volume 24, Number 2 (Summer 1990)
© 1990 Elizabeth Fox-Genovese

insolence, singing to celebrate their Lord, singing to testify to a better future, singing with the life blood of their people, black women defied their imprisonment. The cages constrained, but did not stifle them. The songs of confinement grounded the vitality of their tradition, launched the occasional fledgling to freedom.

The collective identity of African-American women sinks its roots in the roads and fields, the towns and villages of the South. In the pages of white Southern women, the South frequently figures as a natural wonder. For them, towering oaks, dusky cypresses, resplendent magnolias embody the splendor of their region—its distinct physical presence.[1] For black women, that landscape wears a more ominous face, for its splendors belong to the whites. For black women, the South wears a human face, with the face of danger always shadowing the face of love. Above all, however conflictedly, the South remains home—the wellspring of self.

Slavery days are long gone, but their traces linger, shooting up like those uncontrollable weeds that can eat up a garden in the course of a summer. Even during slavery, free black communities flourished in the North and in pockets of the South. But the very name "free black" belies those communities' freedom from the heavy hand of slavery as a social system and indexes their ties to the South. The tradition of African-American autobiography began, in William L. Andrews's phrase, as the determination "to tell a free story."[2] The obsession with freedom betokened the indissoluble, if submerged, obsession with slavery. Race grounded the association. In a country in which only black people were enslaved, blackness and unfreedom merged in a shadowy negation of the virtues of freedom. Slavery grounded and guaranteed racism. Slavery confirmed the association between freedom and virtue, between freedom and whiteness, between whiteness and virtue. Slavery negated the individualism of blacks singly, negated the autonomy of blacks as a community. And these very negations ineluctably bound "free" blacks to the history of their enslaved brothers and sisters. In dissociating themselves from the condition of their enslaved people, they risked dissociating themselves from their people—from their race.

In the roads and cages of the South, during slavery times as thereafter, lay the history—the pre-history—of each and every black self. These roads and cages embodied the specific history that made the black self a singular self, rather than an accidental exemplar of some archetypical self. Only through recuperation of that history could African-American men and women represent their discrete selves as whole and free. The challenge of representing a metaphysically free yet historically specific self proved daunting, although never insurmountable.[3] And if daunting for black men, how much more so for black women? For if black men confronted the specific challenge of demonstrating their manhood in a culture that viewed enslavement as the negation not only of freedom but of manly virtue, black women remained torn between demonstrating their virtuous womanhood and their individualism. The pressures to opt for the demonstration of true womanhood were strong. Many black men accepted the values of white society that held that a dependent and subservient woman offered stellar proof of a man's manhood. Many white women expected black women faithfully to adhere to white culture's images of true womanhood as retiring and self-abnegating. But professed dependence and self-denial threw black women back into the arms of slavery, even if now in the service of their own people.

Gender, race, and condition wove a tight web around black women's possibilities for self-representation, especially since for them, as for their men, any understanding of the self led back over dusty roads to Southern cages.[4] Worse, the conventions of womanhood that whites had developed and middle-class blacks apparently embraced branded the very act of authorship as pushy and unfeminine. As women and as blacks, African-American women autobiographers were, in some measure, bound to construct their self-representations through available discourses, and in interaction with intended readers. For them, as for white women and for white and black men, the self had to be represented in the (recognizable) discourses of one or more interpretive communities. To be sure, their self-representations could variously—and even simultaneously—comply with, subvert, or transform prevailing discourses. But the abiding danger persisted of seeing themselves through the prism of a (white) androcentric discourse, literally through men's eyes, through white eyes.

At the beginning of the twentieth century, American culture knew no black discourse of Southern roads and cages. The discourses existed, but did not figure prominently—and certainly not independently—in the dominant discourses of the country. Here and there a bit of dialect would surface, here and there a trace of song, but almost always through the objectifying consciousness of a white observer. The music, the tales, the speech of black communities remained largely confined to the Southern oral culture in which it flowered.[5] In *Caged Bird*, Maya Angelou recalls the double language of her teens:

My education and that of my Black associates were quite different from the education of our white schoolmates. In the classroom we all learned past participles, but in the streets and in our homes the Blacks learned to drop *s*'s from plurals and suffixes from past-tense verbs. We were alert to the gap separating the written word from the colloquial. We learned to slide out of one language and into another without being conscious of the effort. At school, in a given situation, we might respond with "That's not unusual." But in the street, meeting the same situation, we easily said, "It be's like that sometimes" (219).

It required education in the dominant (white) speech for her to recognize the black language of the streets, and beyond it the language of Stamps, as distinct. Without immersion in white culture, she would never have recognized the distinctiveness of the speech of her people, would simply have accepted it as a given. Similarly, Hurston remembered the chinaberry blossoms of Eatonville and that, as a child, she had "loved the fleshy, white fragrant blooms" but had not made too much of them. "They were too common in my neighborhood." But when she got to New York she "found out that the people called them gardenias, and that the flowers cost a dollar each" and was impressed (18). Black American speech has penetrated the dominant culture through the writings of literate blacks who have recuperated the oral culture of their people through the prism of that dominant culture, which has suggested new ways of seeing, writing, interpreting that culture. And, for African-American autobiographers in particular, the culture of their people has remained the seedbed of their origins as selves. But when they have written of that culture, they inescapably have written as exiles. Their very writing betokens the chasm that separates them from folk culture as oral culture.

In different ways, Zora Neale Hurston and Maya Angelou broke ground for new representations of the African-American female self. *Dust Tracks*, published in 1942, and *Caged Bird*, published in 1969, explicitly reclaim the Southern past as the grounding of their authors' identities. Both explicitly reject white norms of womanhood as models. In Hurston's pages, the Southern past reemerges as a mythic past suitable for the unique self; in Angelou's pages, it acquires a historical and sociological specificity that helps to account for the modern strength of the female self as survivor.

"Like the dead-seeming, cold rocks, I have memories within that came out of the material that went to make me. Time and place have had their say." Hurston thus opens *Dust Tracks* by explicitly reclaiming her concrete origins, by tying her memories to the permanence of cold rocks.[6] She was "born in a Negro town," not, she insists, "the black back-side of an average town." And she

likens the town, Eatonville, Florida, to "hitting a straight lick with
a crooked stick." Never in anyone's plans, the town was "a by-
product of something else. It all started with three white men on
a ship off the coast of Brazil" (3). A tale of adventure, daring, and
happenstances resulted, on August 18, 1886, in that Negro town's
becoming "the first of its kind in America, and perhaps in the world"
(10). And the spirit of those unique founders "has reached beyond
the grave"—implicitly to Hurston herself. Hurston underscores the
mythical origins by concluding the chapter, "It was in the late
eighties that the stars fell, and many of the original settlers date their
coming 'just before, or just after the stars fell' " (11). Thus the place
that had its say in her origins was unlike any other the world has
known, and the time was the time of falling stars.

In later days, Hurston's Mama "exhorted her children at every
opportunity to 'jump at de sun' " (20-21). If they did not land there,
they would at least "get off the ground." By then, her Papa "did
not feel so hopeful. Let well enough alone. It did not do for Negroes
to have too much spirit." And he always threatened "to break mine
or kill me in the attempt," insisting that sooner or later Hurston
would fall victim to white "posses with ropes and guns." But Mama,
unruffled, merely responded " 'Zora is my young'un' " and
predicted that she would " 'come out more than conquer' " (21).
By which she meant, Hurston translates for her readers, that Zora's
disposition was like her mother's, not her father's.

Hurston's discussion of her parents laces the star-falling magic
of Eatonville with unmistakable traces of the harsh realities of black
Southern life. Her father, reputedly the offspring of a white man,
and thus possibly the offspring of a rape, conjures up in his
wonderful looks the price that such a "buck" would have fetched
under slavery. His "over-the-creek" origins temper his ambition,
even in all-black Eatonville, with the fearsome knowledge of white
folks' power. Uppityness, impudence, a tongue can only bring Zora
retribution. And if talking back can wreak these horrors, what can
be expected of writing back, or simply writing about? The will to
aspire comes from her mother, that slip of a girl who had the
imagination to defy her successful family by marrying the man who
captured her fancy. Thus Hurston, like Angelou a generation later,
links her own resolve to the grit and courage of Southern black
women. But Hurston translates her mother's words for her literate
readers.

Turning to her own birth, Hurston admits that her account "is all
hear-say."[7] Her father, she muses, probably never "got over the
trick he felt that I played on him by getting born a girl" (27), thus

suggesting by her wording that her having been born a girl at all was an accident—that her femaleness is separable from her self, her "I." Such play on gender—and even race—as distinct from the essence of her self pervades the account. In describing her father's abiding disgust at her femaleness she remarks, "A little of my sugar used to sweeten his coffee right now." And then translates, "That is a Negro way of saying his patience was short with me" (27). She thus reminds her readers that she speaks white as well as "Negro" and thereby distances herself from the father who, she claims, had not wanted her. And turning the tables on him, Hurston replaces him at the scene of her birth with a "white man of many acres and things" who, knowing that her father was away, stopped by to bring her mother sweet potatoes and, seeing "how things were, and, being the kind of man he was, . . . took out his Barlow Knife and cut the navel cord" (29). Thus, on a mythically storming night, Zora came into the world "grannied" by a white man, who, in contrast to her father, proudly pronounced her a "God-damned fine baby." As she owed her birth, so did Zora owe her name, to an extraordinary intervention. Her mother had promised a friend, a Mrs. Neale, that she could name the baby if it were a girl. Mrs. Neale had picked Zora up somewhere and thought it very pretty. "Perhaps she had read it somewhere, or somebody back in those woods was smoking Turkish cigarettes" (30). From the start, Hurston suggests, that name brought her under the sign of literacy or exotic fantasy.

The play on identity pervades Hurston's account of her early life, which she depicts largely as the development of her "inside search." Time and again her ceaseless, searching questions ran up against the wall of old folks' impatience. The old folks—the black community—had been told how things were "and that had been enough for them, or to put it in Negro idiom, nobody didn't tell 'em, but they heard" (33). The collective wisdom of the oral culture did not satisfy Zora, who kept straining for something beyond the horizon. In particular, the young Zora yearned to "find out about the end of things. I had no doubts about the beginnings. They were somewhere in the five acres that was home to me. Most likely in Mama's room" (36-37).

Her father, who had opposed her birth, opposed her in her quests as well. He especially opposed her desire for a " 'fine black riding horse with white leather saddle and bridles' " with which to ride to the horizon. In his outraged opinion, the mere desire for such a horse was " 'a sin and a shame!' " Who did she think she was? She certainly was not like any of his other children. " 'Lemme tell you something right now, my young lady; you ain't white.' " "That,"

Hurston annotates, "is a Negro saying that means 'Don't be too ambitious. You are a Negro and they are not meant to have but so much'" (38). But she did want a horse, and if she could not have one, she wanted nothing else. Since he would not give her one, she made one up: She would have her horse by her own efforts. So, implicitly, in her mind she would be white. Zora did not meet the expectations of her community much better than she met those of her father. "So I was driven inward. I lived an exciting life unseen" (40). The only person she pleased was the white man who had grannied her and who admiringly and affectionately enjoined her, " 'Snidlits, don't be a nigger . . . . Niggers lie and lie!'" "The word Nigger," Hurston explains, "used in this sense does not mean race. It means a weak, contemptible person of any race" (41). Even as a child, she claims, she "knew without being told that he was not talking about my race when he advised me not to be a nigger. He was talking about class rather than race" (43). For, as he explained to her, people who lie are scared of something. She must never lie. " 'Nothing can't lick you if you never get skeered'" (41). She had only to keep on fighting.

Zora's inner life received fresh material from school, which she loved, and, especially, from reading, which fed her imagination and disillusioned her with the world she knew. "My soul was with the gods and my body in the village. People just would not act like gods" (56). In this frame of mind, Zora experienced the twelve visions that mapped the stations of her future life and cut her off from her community. Longing to be like everybody else, she stood alone "in a world of vanished communion with my kind, which is worse than if it had never been. Nothing is so desolate as a place where life has been and gone" (59). And, Hurston intervenes, "I consider that my real childhood ended with the coming of the pronouncements" (60). Zora's visions were rapidly succeeded by the death of her mother, which in turn was succeeded by the beginnings of her wanderings. Zora's mother's death brought the early chapter of her life to a close: "Mama died at sundown and changed a world"; "that moment was the end of a phase in my life." Thenceforward, she was adrift. "That hour began my wanderings. Not so much in geography, but in time. Then not so much in time as in spirit" (89). Her adult journey is another story, although bits of it figure in the later chapters of *Dust Tracks*.

All of *Dust Tracks* must be taken with caution. Hurston became an accomplished "liar" who also spun her tales to suit her purposes, became an accomplished artist who also crafted her work to satisfy her imagination. Poised between two worlds—the black South of her childhood and the white North of her education and adulthood—, she constructed the statue of herself that she permitted the world to see. The Northern education and, in its wake, membership in the literate culture of the nation shaped her expectations of her readers and, in some measure, shaped her representation of herself. But she never completely weeded out her Southern roots. As she herself maintained, "In the first place, I was a Southerner, and had the map of Dixie on my tongue" (135). And then, she was always "Mama's child" (91), even if she notes that her Mama, alarmed by Zora's tendency to wander, could not understand that some "children are just bound to take after their fathers in spite of women's prayers" (32).

Like Janie in *Their Eyes Were Watching God*, Hurston returns from the horizon transformed to establish herself in the male preserve of tale-telling. As the teller of her tale, she transcends her gender-specific discourse in her interpretive community. To the extent that she speaks in the language of that community, she does so as an outsider rather than a member. Her trip to the horizon has given her new eyes and ears. She speaks her native tongue as an interpreter. We might say that only her exposure to another discourse has permitted her to tell her story. Without that exposure, the story would have been a life, not a story at all. The same could be said of *Dust Tracks*. But, recognizing *Dust Tracks* as a story, we must also recognize it as, in some measure, a lie. A frequently glorious, frequently disquieting lie, but a lie nonetheless. And somewhere in *Dust Tracks* lies buried the fear that, as her white godfather told her, prompts people to lie.

"I hadn't so much forgot as I couldn't bring myself to remember" (3). *I Know Why the Caged Bird Sings* begins with memory and its lapses. Maya Angelou represents her young self as unable to remember the remainder of a poem. The poem that the younger self could not remember began, "What are you looking at me for? / I didn't come to stay . . ." (3). The line she could not remember went, "I just come to tell you, it's Easter Day" (5). Angelou thus opens *Caged Bird* under the aegis of memory, truth, and passing through. The "n[o]t stay[ing]" of the poem recited by the children in the Colored Methodist Episcopal Church in Stamps, Arkansas, referred to the reality of resurrection from the brevity and immateriality of life on this troubled earth to a better life. Yet in Angelou's hands, the poem also evokes a secular meaning. Surely, her younger self had not come to Stamps to stay. Was she not merely passing time before rejoining her parents, claiming her birthright, embarking on a better life?

For the young Marguerite, the birthright she would one day claim is her own whiteness. Watching her grandmother make her dress for that Easter day, she had known "that once I put it on I'd look like a movie star," would "look like one of the sweet little white girls who were everybody's dream of what was right with the world." But the light of Easter morning harshly reveals the magic dress to be only "a plain ugly cut-down from a white woman's once-was-purple throwaway." Yet Marguerite clings to the truth of her own resurrection: "Wouldn't they be surprised when one day I woke out of my black ugly dream . . . ?" (4). It was all a dreadful mistake. "Because I was really white and because a cruel fairy stepmother, who was understandably jealous of my beauty, had turned me into a too-big Negro girl, with nappy black hair, broad feet and a space between her teeth that would hold a number two pencil" (4-5). And Angelou, the narrator, notes, bringing her adult knowledge to bear on the memories, "If growing up is painful for the Southern Black girl, being aware of her displacement is the rust on the razor that threatens the throat. It is an unnecessary insult" (6).

In *Caged Bird*, Angelou sifts through the pain to reappropriate— on her own terms—that Southern past and to undo the displacement. Her highly crafted, incandescent text selectively explores the intertwining relations of origins and memory to her identity. The unrecognized whiteness of the child she represents herself as having been gives way to the proud blackness of the woman she has become. The pride is the pride of a survivor, of history repossessed. That "the adult American Negro female emerges a formidable character," she insists, should be "accepted as an inevitable outcome of the struggle won by survivors" (265).

In her brief opening prologue, Angelou establishes both her perspective as adult narrator—the survivor of the memories of which she is writing—and the perspective of the child she recollects herself as having been. As child she presumably experienced the world around her in a seamless flow, punctuated by disconnected fragments, like a young girl's traumatic inability to control her urine. The adult narrator captures the emblematic memories, vivid and compelling in themselves, and weaves them together to illustrate and anchor the truth of the story as a whole. The prologue thus offers a concrete identification of the protagonist as black, Southern female—the interpreter of her own experience, the teller of her own story.

The "I"—Marguerite Johnson, nicknamed My (later expanded to Maya) by her beloved brother Bailey—was not born in the South. When she was three and Bailey four they arrived there wearing tags,

" 'To Whom It May Concern' " (6). Uprooted by the collapse of their parents' "calamitous" marriage, they had been shipped home to their father's mother, whom they called "Momma" (6-7). Angelou locates that trip in relation to the experience of the other frightened black children who must also have crossed the United States thousands of times, in relation to the social consequences of some blacks' migration northward during the early decades of the twentieth century. The consequences of that migration wrested Maya and Bailey, like countless others, from their mother, who remained in the North to attempt to make a living amidst the debris of the fractured expectations of easy affluence. But it hardly left them "motherless," as the black women who befriended them on the Southern lap of their journey would have had it. For their grandmother closed the gap in the generations by becoming their Momma, and her town, after recognizing them as "harmless (and children)," responded to them by closing "in around us, as a real mother embraces a stranger's child. Warmly, but not too familiarly" (7).

Angelou represents the ten years (interrupted by a brief and fateful period with her mother in St. Louis), from three to thirteen, that she spent under Momma's care in Stamps as the core of her childhood and, implicitly, as the wellspring of her adult identity. Through her evocations of Stamps she links herself to the Southern roots and history of her people—to a succession of American Negro female survivors whom she implicitly credits with laying the foundations for her own survival. But that core includes an inescapable harshness that weaves through Angelou's text, structuring the memories, containing the faith, gentleness, and mutual concern that kept its worst consequences at bay, even as it sorely tried them. Stamps, for all its black core of loving security, bred paranoia. "Stamps, Arkansas, was Chitlin' Switch, Georgia; Hang 'Em High, Alabama; Don't Let the Sun Set on You Here, Nigger, Mississippi; or any other name just as descriptive." The people of Stamps "used to say that whites in our town were so prejudiced that a Negro couldn't buy vanilla ice cream. Except on July Fourth. Other days he had to be satisfied with chocolate" (47). Stamps also bred the deep solidarity of the black community that gathered in Momma's store to listen to the broadcast of Joe Louis's fight with Carnera, listen without breathing, without hoping, just waiting. Life-defying, suspenseful minutes later Louis had won. "Champion of the world. A Black boy. Some Black mother's son." But the triumphant crowd disperses slowly, with caution. "It wouldn't do for a Black man and his family to be caught on a lonely country road on a night when Joe Louis had proved that we were the strongest people in the world" (132).

Nor would it do for a black woman to ask a white dentist, who owes her the money that had saved his practice during the Depression, to treat her suffering granddaughter. " 'Annie,' " he met Momma's desperate plea, " 'my policy is I'd rather stick my hand in a dog's mouth than in a nigger's' " (184). Nor would it do for black children to aspire to any but a utilitarian education. Marguerite's graduation from eighth grade—a momentous occasion for the community as well as the graduates—dawns with the promise of perfection, but its perfection shatters with the appearance of the visiting white commencement speaker from Texarkana. Promising the white children (of whom there were none in the audience) the most advanced educational opportunities, he praises the black children (the graduating class that he is addressing) for having sent a "first-line football tackler" to Arkansas Agricultural and Mechanical College, a terrific basketball player to Fisk. "The white kids were going to have a chance to become Galileos and Madame Curies and Edisons and Gauguins, and our boys (the girls weren't even in on it) would try to be Jessie Owenses and Joe Louises" (174). Marguerite and her classmates, drawers of meticulous maps, spellers of decasyllabic words, memorizers of the whole of *The Rape of Lucrece*, have been exposed as "maids and farmers, handymen and washerwomen" (175-76). How, amidst such ugliness, could Henry Reed even think of delivering his valedictory address, "To Be Or Not To Be?" Hadn't he understood anything? Henry, "the conservative, the proper, the A student," has understood everything. Completing his prepared address as if dreams still have meaning, he turns his back to the audience, faces his class, and singing, nearly speaking, he intones, " 'Lift ev'ry voice and sing / Till earth and heaven ring / Ring with the harmonies of Liberty . . . .' " Henry understands. "It was the poem written by James Weldon Johnson. It was the music composed by J. Rosamond Johnson. It was the Negro national anthem. Out of habit we were singing it" (178). And singing the song that she, like every other black child had learned with her ABCs, Marguerite hears it for the first time. By the close of the singing, they "were on top again. As always, again. We survived. The depths had been icy and dark, but now a bright sun spoke to our souls. I was no longer simply a member of the proud graduating class of 1940; I was a proud member of the wonderful, beautiful Negro race" (179).

Shortly after graduation, Momma decides that Marguerite and Bailey are to join their mother in California. Stamps is no place for an ambitious black boy, no place, although she never says so, for an ambitious black girl. Marguerite's previous trip away from Stamps, her previous stay with her mother, offered no grounds for believing that the world beyond Stamps is safer. During that stay in Saint Louis, Marguerite had been raped by the man with whom her mother was living. Withal, Angelou does not represent that rape, which racked the eight-year-old girl's body with unbearable pain, as the worst. The worst occurred during the subsequent trial of the rapist at which Marguerite, forced to testify, lied. Under examination she felt compelled to say that Mr. Freeman had never tried to touch her before the rape, although he had and she believed she had encouraged him to. That lie "lumped in my throat and I couldn't get air" (82). On the basis of that lie Mr. Freeman was convicted. In fact, the lie did not cause Mr. Freeman to serve time; his lawyer got him released. It did cause his death. No sooner had he been released than her mother's brothers killed him. To Marguerite, "a man was dead because I lied. . . . Obviously I had forfeited my place in heaven forever . . . . I could feel the evilness flowing through my body and waiting, pent up, to rush off my tongue if I tried to open my mouth. I clamped my teeth shut, I'd hold it in" (84).

In the wake of the trial, Marguerite and Bailey were sent back to Stamps, where for nearly a year Marguerite persisted in her silence. Then, Mrs. Bertha Flowers, "the aristocrat of Black Stamps," threw her a life line. Mrs. Flowers "was one of the few gentlewomen I have ever known, and has remained throughout my life the measure of what a human being can be" (91). From the start, Mrs. Flowers appealed to her because she was like "women in English novels who walked the moors (whatever they were) with their loyal dogs racing at a respectful distance." Above all, "she made me proud to be a Negro, just by being herself" (92). Mrs. Flowers joined the world of Stamps to the world of literature, embodied in her person the dreams that shaped Marguerite's imagination. For Marguerite, under Mrs. Flower's tutelage, formal education became salvation. But even as she introduced Marguerite to the delights of *Tale of Two Cities*, Mrs. Flowers enjoined her to recognize the beauties and sense of black folk culture. Ignorance and illiteracy, she insisted, should not be confused. "She encouraged me to listen carefully to what country people call mother wit. That in those homely sayings was couched the collective wisdom of generations" (97). Language, the human form of communication, alone separate man from the lower animals. Words, she insisted, have a life beyond the printed page. Words, even written words, acquire meaning by being spoken. Books should be read aloud. Angelou thus represents Mrs. Flowers as bridging the gap between oral and literary culture, between the black community of Stamps and *Jane Eyre*.[8] Under Mrs. Flowers's influence, Marguerite again began to speak.

Southern roads and cages. Hurston and Angelou knew them well, but represented them differently. The differences reflect differences in generation—the Harlem Renaissance, the 1960s—but also something more. Hurston apparently did not find it easy to connect her Southern past to her Northern present, to connect the little black girl to the adult author. To reclaim her past, Hurston, much like a performer or a trickster, had to dish it up as a fable for others' consumption. The Eatonville of her youth became, in her hands, a mythic land immune to time and place, became an Atlantis, a garden of Eden. But by so reconstructing Eatonville, Hurston confessed her own exile. With her mother's death and the beginnings of her wanderings, that earlier world ended. Hurston thus represents herself as cut free from her moorings, which she could only repossess through the foreign tongue of the literati.

Angelou depends no less than Hurston on that foreign tongue. But unlike her, she insists upon the connections. Less afraid than Hurston of the burden of her people's history, she anchors herself in that history. Less afraid than Hurston of her own anger at racism and oppression, she insists upon their persistence. Openly proclaiming the "lifelong paranoia" that Stamps forced upon her, she can also claim her kinship with generations of black female survivors. No less a denizen of the Republic of Letters than Hurston, Angelou claims her rightful place as a woman—a black woman. For Hurston's myth, she substitutes history and thereby claims her specific identity.

It all comes back to the South. But it also comes back to lies. For Hurston, lying represented the magic of men's tales, the delights of crafted deception, even if, on her own telling, lying also masked fear. No less than Hurston, Angelou recognized lying as the mask of fear, but for her lying led not to stories but to imposed silence. To write her story—to speak at all—she had to conquer the fear, repudiate the lie. Hurston's South instructed her in the necessity of lying to preserve the self from violence, denial, and death, but in her glorious "lies" she denied the knowledge, transformed the fearful reality into a death-defying myth. To be heard at all she felt obliged to represent herself in black face—a spoofing, harmless minstrel. The lessons of Angelou's South were no less harsh, but including as they did the faith of Momma, the courage of Henry Reed, and the teachings of Mrs. Flowers, they also taught her that the South need not be wrapped in mythical denial. It could be claimed as the legacy of the people—especially the women—who had taught her how to survive and to sing.

Notes

[1]Excellent examples of white Southern women's devotion to the Southern landscape can be found in Augusta J. Evans's novels *Beulah* (1859) and *Macaria* (1862).

[2]Andrews, in *To Tell a Free Story*, emphasizes nineteenth-century African-Americans' concern with freedom in their self-representations, but the relation between freedom and the independent self figures in most discussions of the slave narrative. See, for example, Sekora and Turner; Davis and Gates; Foster; Smith, *Where I'm Bound*; Baker; and Stepto. The theme of freedom and selfhood was unquestionably important to Frederick Douglass and Harriet Jacobs. See Martin; Yellin's introduction to Jacobs's *Incidents*; and my epilogue to *Within the Plantation Household*.

[3]Barbara McCaskill offers a pioneering exploration of the relations between African-American women's self-representations and the expectations of their readerships. Henry Louis Gates's welcome 30-volume *Schomburg Library* offers a newly coherent picture of African-American women's writings, and the authors of the introductions to the discrete volumes offer important discussions of the specific texts.

[4]I have offered a fuller discussion of the nature of African-American women's experience and self-representations in relation to gender, especially their sense of gender identity, in "To Write My Self" and *Within the Plantation Household*.

[5]For a thorough and thoughtful discussion of black folk culture, see Levine. For examples of white evocation of black dialect, see Harriet Beecher Stowe's *Uncle Tom's Cabin* (1852). Significantly, Jacobs, in *Incidents*, represents slave women on the plantation as speaking in dialect, but herself as speaking perfect "white" English.

[6]Throughout, I am distinguishing between Hurston, the narrator or autobiographer, and Zora, her former self; between Angelou, narrator or autobiographer, and Marguerite, her former self. For one of the many discussions of the problem of the autobiographical narrator, see Smith's *A Poetics of Women's Autobiography*. For my own views on the general problem of autobiography and additional references, see my edition of *The Autobiography of Du Pont de Nemours*.

[7]On Hurston's notorious inaccuracy, see Hemenway's introduction to the second edition of *Dust Tracks*; on some of the problems of that inaccuracy, see my essay "My Statue, My Self"; on Hurston's ambiguous forms of address, see Johnson; and on Hurston's life, see Hemenway's *Zora Neale Hurston*.

[8]*Jane Eyre* was Marguerite's favorite novel, as *Huckleberry Finn* was Bailey's, and Angelou mentions it frequently in *Caged Bird*.

Works Cited

Andrews, William L. *To Tell a Free Story: The First Century of Afro-American Autobiography, 1760-1865*. Urbana: U of Illinois P, 1986.
Angelou, Maya. *I Know Why the Caged Bird Sings*. New York: Random, 1969.

Baker, Houston A., Jr. *The Journey Back: Issues in Black Literature and Criticism*. Chicago: U of Chicago P, 1980.

Davis, Charles, and Henry Louis Gates, Jr., eds. *The Slave's Narrative*. New York: Oxford UP, 1985.

Foster, Frances Smith. *Witnessing Slavery: The Development of Ante-Bellum Slave Narratives*. Westport: Greenwood, 1979.

Fox-Genovese, Elizabeth, ed. & trans. *The Autobiography of Du Pont de Nemours*. Wilmington: Scholarly, 1984.

——. "My Statue, My Self: Autobiographical Writings of Afro-American Women." *The Private Self: Theory and Practice of Women's Autobiographical Writings*. Ed. Shari Benstock. Chapel Hill: U of North Carolina P, 1988. 63-89.

——. "To Write My Self: The Autobiographical Writings of Afro-American Women." *Feminist Issues in Literary Scholarship*. Ed. Shari Benstock. Bloomington: Indiana UP, 1987. 161-80.

——. *Within the Plantation Household: Black and White Women of the Old South*. Chapel Hill: U of North Carolina P, 1988.

Gates, Henry Louis, Jr., ed. *The Schomburg Library of Nineteenth-Century Black Women Writers*. 30 vols. New York: Oxford UP, 1988.

Hemenway, Robert E. *Zora Neale Hurston: A Literary Biography*. Urbana: U of Illinois P, 1978.

Hurston, Zora Neale. *Dust Tracks on a Road: An Autobiography*. Ed. Robert E. Hemenway. 2nd ed. Urbana: U of Illinois P, 1984.

Jacobs, Harriet. *Incidents in the Life of a Slave Girl*. Ed. Jean Fagin Yellin. Cambridge: Harvard UP, 1987.

Johnson, Barbara. *A World of Difference*. Baltimore: Johns Hopkins UP, 1987.

Levine, Lawrence. *Black Culture and Black Consciousness: Afro-American Folk Thought from Slavery to Freedom*. New York: Oxford UP, 1977.

Martin, Waldo E., Jr. *The Mind of Frederick Douglass*. Chapel Hill: U of North Carolina P, 1984.

McCaskill, Barbara. "An Eternity for Telling: Topological Traditions in Afro-American Women's Writing." Diss. Emory U, 1988.

Sekora, John, and Darwin T. Turner, eds. *The Art of Slave Narrative: Original Essays in Criticism and Theory*. Macomb: Western Illinois U, 1982.

Smith, Sidonie. *A Poetics of Women's Autobiography: Marginality and the Fictions of Self-Representation*. Bloomington: Indiana UP, 1987.

——. *Where I'm Bound: Patterns of Slavery and Freedom in Black American Autobiography*. Westport: Greenwood, 1974.

Stepto, Robert B. *From Behind the Veil: A Study of Afro-American Narrative*. Urbana: U of Illinois P, 1979.

25

THE TALKING FRAME OF ZORA NEALE HURSTON'S TALKING BOOK: STORYTELLING AS DIALECTIC IN *THEIR EYES WERE WATCHING GOD*

By Cathy Brigham

Zora Neale Hurston's *Their Eyes Were Watching God* is a celebration of the oral tradition central to African-American literature and culture. The narrative engages in a variegated dialectic of storytelling, signifying, sounding, declamation contests, preaching, and song. The rich diversity of oral forms and narrative voices in *Their Eyes Were Watching God* both enhances the realistic characterization of individuals and communities portrayed in the novel and serves as a vehicle for the running commentary that tells the stories of those characters and communities. Some critics have found the novel's narrative structure—which divides the narrative task between the omniscient narrator, Janie, and Pheoby—and Janie's refusal to tell her own story, problematic.[1] This essay argues that many of the "problems" with the novel's narrative structure and voice disappear if we view the narrative structure as a multivocal storytelling dialectic and reexamine the stance that equates a character's political empowerment with her "finding" a first-

---

[1] Robert B. Stepto represents this perspective in his assessment of the novel's "one great flaw" as "not the framing dialogue, but Janie's tale itself." Stepto argues that "Hurston's curious insistence on having Janie's tale . . . told by an omniscient third person, rather than by a first-person narrator, implies that Janie has not really found her voice and self after all" (Robert B. Stepto, "Ascent, Immersion, Narration," *Behind the Veil: A Study of Afro-American Narrative* [Urbana: U of Illinois P, 1979] 7; see rpt. in Harold Bloom, ed., *Zora Neal Hurston's Their Eyes Were Watching God*, Modern Critical Series [New York: Chelsea House, 1987] 9-18). Bernard Bell concurs with Stepto, calling "the awkward handling of point of view" a "major problem in the narrative" (*The Afro-American Novel and Its Tradition* [Amherst: U of Massachusetts P, 1987] 123; hereafter cited parenthetically in the text by page reference only).

person voice with which to tell her tale. In talking to a tale that talks back, Janie partakes of the talking cure which she has sought in returning to Eatonville, and Hurston creates a complex multivocal narrative structure that speaks from, to, and about Janie's cultural perspective, as well as to itself.

Hurston celebrates a culture and a storytelling tradition that Bernard Bell terms "residually oral":

> Whereas an oral culture relies primarily on sound, the spoken word, and a literate culture primarily on sight, the written word, residually oral cultures rely on the interplay or dialectic between the two. (20, 21)

Bell identifies five categories of the residually oral that have played a primary role in the evolution of the African-American novel: Oratory, Myth, Legend, Tale, and Song. All five are well represented in *Their Eyes Were Watching God*, but tale-telling is especially significant. Nearly every character is at some point a boisterous tale-teller vying with the narrator for the reader's ear. The novel is concerned with both the act of storytelling—*Their Eyes* displays its narrative structure by passing the task of tale-telling from one narrator to another, with each commenting on the role of the storyteller—and with the function of storytelling: Hurston, Bell writes, "empowers Janie Crawford to liberate herself and her friend Pheoby through storytelling" (25). Glynis Carr, in her study of *Their Eyes* as bildungsroman, notes that

> while Hurston the artist tells the story of Janie's coming of age, the terms of this bildungsroman are in the heroine's increasing verbal competence and final mastery of storytelling, both as artistic performance and as affirmation of personal and cultural identity.[2]

Henry Louis Gates, Jr., writes that Hurston's most important innovations in *Their Eyes* are the "rhetorical struc-

---

[2] Glynis Carr, "Storytelling as *Bildung* in Zora Neale Hurston's *Their Eyes Were Watching God*," *CLA Journal* 31.2 (1987): 189-90.

tures and verbal rituals" that "signify the sheer play of black language."[3] In a close reading that develops a theory of the African-American "speakerly text," Gates explores the chorus of residually oral forms that make up the novel's talking frame and discusses their thematic importance in terms similar to those stated by Carr (above). This essay diverges from Gates's reading to explore the manner in which the voices in the talking frame talk to each other, creating a dialectic on gender and power.

Janie's story is situated within a frame narrative featuring an omniscient narrator who introduces the novel's principal concerns on the first page: male "dreams mocked to death by time," and the female will to act, to make "the dream . . . the truth." These concerns are taken up by a succession of tale-tellers who create a dialectic within the novel's narrative structure—a talking frame—by responding to one another's central arguments about gender and male-female relationships. The tale-tellers resemble—in the dialectic created by their exchange—the tale-telling sitters on the porch of Joe Starks's store. Chief among the gender and power issues they raise is what Bell Hooks calls "the false notion that if Black women are being heard, Black men's voices are necessarily silenced, and if Black men's voices are heard, Black women must assume a voiceless position."[4] The novel's tale-tellers, verbal gameplayers, and chorus all comment on the truth or falsity of this notion, and it is central to Janie's struggle for a voice in her three romantic relationships.

The omniscient narrator frames the narrative in expansive visual imagery—"Ships at a distance . . . come in with

[3] Henry Louis Gates, Jr., *The Signifying Monkey* (New York: Oxford UP, 1988) 194. Hereafter cited parenthetically in the text by page reference only.

[4] Bell Hooks and Cornel West, *Breaking Bread: Insurgent Black Intellectual Life* (Boston: South End Press, 1991) 3. Hooks is exploring issues in contemporary culture, not discussing *Their Eyes* in this passage. Here, and in the passages I quote from Cornel West's dialogue with Hooks in *Breaking Bread*, I apply Hook's and West's words to Hurston's work.

the tide . . . sail forever on the horizon. . . . [T]he sun was gone, but he had left his footprints in the sky"[5]—imagery that yields to the ordinary and the everyday as Janie enters the novel preceded by a crowd of curious ill-wishers who "pass notions through their mouths" and sit "in judgment" as Janie walks back into town in her overalls (1-2). The crowd functions as a chorus, introducing the questions that the narrative will answer:

> "What she doin' coming back here in dem overalls? Can't she find no dress to put on?—Where's dat blue satin dress she left here in?—Where all dat money her husband took and died and left her?—What dat ole forty year ole 'oman doin' wid her hair swinging down her back lak some young gal?—Where she left dat young lad of a boy she went off here wid?—Thought she was going to marry?—Where he left *her*?" (2)

Janie immediately passes the task of answering the chorus's questions to Pheoby, insisting that " 'tain't worth the trouble. You can tell 'em what Ah say if you wants to. Dat's just de same as me 'cause mah tongue is in mah friend's mouf" (6). In an act of sisterhood that has been both maligned and celebrated, Janie, "full of that oldest human longing—self-revelation," indicates to Pheoby that she seeks a talking cure rather than a larger audience: "Pheoby, we been kissin'-friends for twenty years, so Ah depend on you for a good thought. And Ah'm talking to you from dat standpoint" (7).[6] Audience, however, is of primary impor-

---

[5] Zora Neale Hurston, *Their Eyes Were Watching God* (New York: Harper, 1990) 1. Hereafter cited parenthetically in the text by page reference only.

[6] For arguments against the centrality of sisterhood in *Their Eyes Were Watching God*, see Darwin T. Turner, *In a Minor Chord: Three Afro-American Writers and Their Search for Identity* (Carbondale: Southern Illinois UP, 1971); see also Bell 125 and Stepto (fn 1, above). For analyses which argue for the centrality of sisterhood, see Glynis Carr (fn 2, above); Alice Walker, *In Search of Our Mothers' Gardens: Womanist Prose* (New York: Harcourt, 1983); Marjorie Pryse, "Zora Neale Hurston, Alice Walker, and the 'Ancient Power' of Black Women," *Conjuring: Black Woman, Fiction, and Literary Tradition*, ed. Marjorie Pryse and Hortense J. Spillers (Bloomington: Indiana UP, 1985); Claire Crabtree, "The Confluence of Folklore, Feminism, and Black Self-Determination in Zora Neale Hurston's *Their Eyes Were Watching God*," *Southern Literary Journal* 17.2

tance in this novel. As Gates notes, "throughout this narrative, the word *voice* recurs with great frequency. Who speaks, indeed, proves to be of crucial import to Janie's quest for freedom, but who sees and who hears at all points in the text remain fundamental as well" (200). With the preface that " 'tain't no use in me telling you somethin' unless Ah give you de understandin' to go 'long wid it" (7), Janie reaches back into her childhood, retrieves early events that fixed her racial and sexual identity, and shares them with Pheoby. Her subject matter, her role as messenger from the world outside of Eatonville, and the nature of communications within Eatonville guarantee her a larger audience.

Janie tells the novel's first story, the story of her discovery of her racial identity, in the first-person voice. Her story responds directly to the omniscient narrator's framing comment: "Women forget all those things they don't want to remember and remember everything they don't want to forget" (1). Janie's earliest memory is of the discovery of her otherness. She tells us that she failed to recognize herself in a photo because she did not realize that she was different from the white children with whom she grew up. She is alienated from the black community as well. The black children tease her " 'bout livin' in de white folks' backyard," and "make out they couldn't play wid nobody dat lived on premises" (9). The omniscient narrator has framed this story as a woman's reminiscence about women who act to realize their dreams. Janie introduces the subject of these actions (dreaming, remembering, acting): a quest for individual identity and a place in a community.

At the close of Janie's narrative, the omniscient narrator intervenes, frames the tale-telling, and establishes the pri-

(1985); 54-66; and Lorraine Bethel, " 'This Infinity of Conscious Pain': Zora Neale Hurston and the Black Female Literary Tradition," *All the Women Are White, All the Blacks are Men, But Some of Us Are Brave: Black Women's Studies*, ed. Gloria T. Hull, Patricia Bell Scott, and Barbara Smith (Old Westbury, New York: The Feminist Press, 1982), rpt. in Bloom 9-18.

macy of audience: "Pheoby's hungry listening helped Janie to tell her story. . . . The night time put on flesh and blackness" (10). At this point, the omniscient narrator ostensibly begins to relate the tale that Janie tells to Pheoby, but as Barbara Johnson and Henry Louis Gates point out, the voice we hear is not a truly omniscient voice. Neither is it the voice of Pheoby, with a few brief exceptions. The narrative voice engages in "free indirect discourse," which Johnson and Gates define as

> not the "voice" of *both* a character *and* a narrator; rather, it is a bivocal utterance, containing elements of both direct and indirect speech. It is an "utterance" that no one could have spoken, yet which we recognize because of its characteristic "speakerlyness," its paradoxically *written* manifestation of the aspiration to the *oral*.[7]

The dual roles of involved storyteller and omniscient narrator enable the same voice to observe: "Joe Starks hadn't been dead but nine months and here she goes sashaying off to a picnic in pink linen. Done quit attending church like she used to" (105), and "she saw a dust-bearing bee sink into the sanctum of a bloom; the thousand sister-calyxes arch to meet the love embrace and the ecstatic shiver of the tree from root to tiniest branch creaming in every blossom and frothing with delight" (11). The latter utterance situates Janie firmly in the "flesh and blackness" which the

---

[7] Barbara Johnson and Henry Louis Gates, Jr., "A Black and Idiomatic Free Indirect Discourse," *Reading Zora: Discourse and Rhetoric in Their Eyes Were Watching God* (New York: Methuen, 1987) 75-76; see rpt. in Bloom 73-86. Johnson and Gates address a "black and idiomatic free indirect discourse." Gates discusses free indirect discourse in *Their Eyes* in *The Signifying Monkey* as well (170-215). Earlier discussions and definitions of free indirect discourse include Roy Pascal, *The Dual Voice: Free Indirect Discourse and Its Functioning in the Nineteenth-Century European Novel* (Totowa, N.J.: Rowman and Littlefield, 1977); Michel Peled Ginsberg, "Free Indirect Discourse: Theme and Narrative Voice in Flaubert, George Eliot, and Verga," diss., Yale U, 1977; Brian McHale, "Free Indirect Discourse: A Survey of Recent Accounts," *Journal for Descriptive Poetics and Theory* 3 (1978): 249-87; and Stephen Ullman, *Style in the French Novel* (Cambridge: Cambridge UP, 1957).

narrator has just ascribed to the night: it is the story of her awakening sexuality and her vision beneath the pear tree.

Nanny, the next tale-teller in the novel's talking frame, responds immediately to Janie's/Pheoby's/the omniscient narrator's poetic vision of sexual discovery. Nanny's vision of sexuality, grounded in her experience of slavery and its aftermath, is anything but poetic. She responds to Janie's pear tree vision story by "desecrating the pear tree" with her insistence on Janie's immediate marriage to Logan Killicks (13). If Janie's vision is entirely grounded in a romantic ideal, Nanny's is grounded in the material. Claire Crabtree argues that "while Nanny encourages Janie's aspirations for a better life, she insists on defining what those aspirations should be. She defines them only in terms of economic security [Killick's sixty acres], a definition which belies the rich imagery of her language."[8] Bernard Bell presents an opposing point of view: "Janie and the implied author reject not only Nanny's dream of what a woman ought to be and do . . . but also never really understand or share the 'ancient power' of her love and sacrifice to provide a better life for her family" (125). If we address Nanny's and Janie's tales as elements of the novel's talking frame, the question of who is rejecting what becomes less important than the question of audience. Nanny's story of her sexual exploitation under slavery and her advice to her granddaughter function as a moral fable responding to Janie's romance tale—the pear tree vision. Nanny and Janie shout about their stories at each other across an unnavigable void: a generation gap that separates Nanny's experiences under slavery from Janie's childhood "on prem-

---

[8] Crabtree 60-61. Crabtree is not the first or the only critic to offer a cultural/materialist critique of Nanny's story. See, for example, Bethel (fn 6, above); John F. Callahan, " 'Mah Tongue Is in Mah Friend's Mouff': The Rhetoric of Intimacy and Immensity in *Their Eyes Were Watching God*, Bloom 87-113; and Elizabeth Meese, "Orality and Texuality in *Their Eyes Were Watching God*," *Crossing the Double Cross: The Practice of Feminist Criticism* (Chapel Hill: U of North Carolina P, 1986), rpt. in Bloom 59-72.

ises." In a discussion of contemporary culture, Bell Hooks and Cornel West point out that the gap between generations has reached a point of critical rupture in many African-American communities that is "often tragically expressed in gender relations," a situation foreshadowed in *Their Eyes* (11). Janie's and Nanny's stories address each other, but the tale-teller's histories and their different conceptions of gendered identity prevent mutual understanding. Both tales, however, engage in a dialogue with the novel's framing assertion that "the dream is the truth" (1). Unrealized dreams are central to both. Nanny was "born back in slavery, so it wasn't for me to fulfill my dreams of whut a woman oughta be and do. . . . Ah wanted to preach a great sermon about colored women sittin' on high, but they wasn't no pulpit for me. . . . Ah said Ah'd save de text for you" (15-16).

Janie takes up Nanny's text and revises it. She accepts Nanny's plans to situate her "on high" as queen of Logan Killick's sixty acres and discovers the constricting nature of a purely materialist definition of elevation. She then confuses the "high chair" that Joe Starks wishes her to occupy with the position of power Nanny envisioned, but it too reveals its limitations (58). Janie is taken in by Starks's story—a story that presents the dream as readily accessible, "down heah in Floridy . . . dis place dat colored folks [is] buildin' theyselves" (15). She soon realizes, however, that she is no closer to "sittin' on high" as Joe Starks's wife than she was on Logan Killicks's. Janey left Killicks's farm with Joe to disprove Nanny's assertion that "de nigger woman is de mule uh de world," but she finds herself as free in Eatonville as her symbolic counterpart, the mule that Starks "emancipates" and displays as evidence of his benevolent rulership (14).

The mule stories and tall-tales exchanged on Starks's porch contribute to the multivocality of the tale's talking frame, but they add more than voice. Gates writes that "the plays of language . . . seem to be present essentially to re-

veal the complexity of black oral forms of narration" (195)
and that the extended ritualized vernacular contests "seem
to be present in the text more for their own sake than to
develop the plot" (199). These complex verbal exchanges do
not develop the plot in any recognizable linear fashion.
They do, however, serve rhetorical purposes beyond the display of verbal accuity that is inherent in both the vernacular forms themselves and in Hurston's use of them. The ritualized vernacular contests in *Their Eyes* address relations
of power and gender. The sitters on Starks's porch "use
storytelling or 'lying' . . . to sublimate their white-provoked
feelings of aggression to achieve mastery of words and their
world" (Bell 21). Hurston emphasizes their mastery of their
world in her depiction of Eatonville as outside of white time
and space. There is no white side of town; there are no
white employers, no Jim Crow laws. Hurston has written
white society out of Eatonville's text. Only outside of Eatonville, in the courtroom scene, does white law intrude. In
the ritualized courtship exchanges in which Charlie Jones,
Jim, and Dave vie for the attention of Bootsie, Teadi, Big
'oman, and Daisy Blunt, the men claim the power and
wealth to buy anything the women want and to stage the
most outlandish situations to prove their devotion. The
women are empowered to choose a suitor, and everybody
realizes "it's not courtship. It's acting-out courtship and
everybody is in the play" (63). Everybody has equal access
to the ritual and the power it confers. The power of the
verbal ritual has another dimension as well. Within a mainstream society where, as Cornel West observes, "[w]hite su-
premacist discourse associat[es] Black being with Black
bodies, as if we have no minds, no intelligence, are only the
sum total of our visible physicality,"[9] the ritualized verbal
exchanges emphasize intellect and wit, even as they are employed in the service of "acting-out courtship."
Given the power of the storyteller to create alternative

[9] Hooks and West 86.

realities, to create worlds in which the oppressed are politically empowered, Starks's insistence on excluding Janie from the porch-sitters' tale-telling is a repressive political act: "Janie loved the conversation and sometimes she thought up good stories on the mule, but Joe had forbidden her to indulge" (50). In a novel where storytelling functions as both frame and subject, its suppression is significant. Janie's storytelling impulse is not fulfilled until she leaves Eatonville with Tea Cake and becomes a part of the community on the muck.

When Tea Cake enters the novel, the multivocal talking frame fades into the background. Tea Cake enters *Their Eyes* as a storyteller: " 'Good evenin' Mis' Starks,' he said with a sly grin as if they had a good joke together. She was in favor of the story that was making him laugh before she even heard it" (90). His appeal to Janie is based at least in part on his skill with oratory and storytelling. Janie must find her voice before she can enter into the ideal male/female relationship she has envisioned. In a dialogue with Pheoby that interrupts the omniscient narrator's story soon after Tea Cake's entry, Janie confides, "In the beginnin' new thoughts had tuh be thought and new words said. After Ah got used tuh dat, we gits 'long jus' fine. He done taught me the maiden language all over" (109).

In addition to being a skilled orator, singer, and tale-teller, Tea Cake embodies a black folk hero-type with a long history in African-American fiction: the Bad Nigger.[10] Bell discusses the Bad Nigger as both "the white American myth of the depraved emancipated black Southerner" and a black heroic model (159). In the white American myth, "as popularized in the post-Reconstruction fiction of Thomas Nelson Page and Thomas Dixon, the Bad Nigger is bestial

---

[10] Bell addresses the Bad Nigger as a product of and a response to white fears and myths of black bestiality (159, 160, 164, 165, 186, 217). SallyAnn Ferguson treats Tea Cake as an embodiment of Stackolee, "whose prototype is the antebellum 'bad nigger' " ("Folkloric Men and Female Growth in *Their Eyes Were Watching God*," *Black American Literature Forum* 21 (1987): 191.

and criminal in nature" (Bell 159). The black heroic model revises this myth and responds to white society's fear of those it oppresses:

> Deprived of the opportunity to live free and full lives because they are black and poor, some radical black individuals who heroically defy the power of whites, ambivalently called Bad Niggers by fellow blacks, use rebellion as an act of self-affirmation. (Bell 159)

Like Native-American and other trickster figures, the Bad Nigger is especially adept at gambling and sexual exploits. Tea Cake's escapades include the theft of Janie's secret savings, which he uses to host an all-night barbecue, during the course of which he pays ugly women not to enter and he knocks out two of a guest's front teeth. Tea Cake's voice breaks into the narrator's account of his Bad Nigger exploits at the barbecue. He narrates his second Bad Nigger story himself: "Ah won de money jus' lak Ah told yuh." And when a fellow gambler accuses him of cheating and pulls a razor: "Ah wuz all over 'im jus' lak gravy over rice .. . he wuz hollerin' for me tuh turn him loose, but baby, Ah turnt him every way *but* loose" (121).

The community chorus interrupts the narrator several times during the Tea Cake segments and asserts that Tea Cake is nothing more than the two-dimensional degenerate Bad Nigger of white mythology, and that he will exhaust Janie's savings and desert her. The chorus offers as evidence the story of Annie Tyler and Who Flung. Annie Tyler is a fifty-two-year-old widow "with a good home and insurance money" who has the unfortunate habit of becoming romantically involved with younger men who bilk her of funds and then disappear. Who Flung is the final bilker. He takes Annie for everything she is worth and sends her limping back to Eatonville with nothing but the clothes on her back, "all the capers that cheap dye could cut . . . showing in her hair," and "hanging bosom and stomach and buttocks and legs that drooped down over her ankles" (114). Annie Tyler is constructed in opposition to Janie, whose physical beauty is the object of envy and the subject of gossip. The Annie Tyler and Who Flung tale is a free-floating narrative that comes to "pay [Janie] a visit" when she is wondering where Tea Cake and her money are on the night of the barbecue, making "itself into pictures [that] hung around Janie's bedside all night long" (113, 114). As an element of the talking frame, the Annie Tyler and Who Flung tale speaks to the narrative in much the same manner as Nanny's materialist analysis of Janie's romantic fantasy. It cautions against marrying for any reason other than financial gain, and it warns of the public scorn that a woman who seeks sexual gratification outside of marriage may expect. The omniscient narrator talks back to the chorus—by developing Janie and Tea Cake's relationship in opposition to the Annie Tyler and Who Flung model. Tea Cake returns to Janie and returns her money, plus interest, after prospering in the gambling/knife fight episode.

They go off together to the muck, where the narrator depicts their relationship as comparatively egalitarian and playful. They are situated at the center of a close-knit community that lends its own voice to the novel's talking frame: a rich and boisterous storytelling, guitar-picking, signifying orality that nurtures Janie's voice to the point where "she got so she could tell big stories herself from listening to the rest" (128). It is, however, in the midst of this transformational working-class setting that we encounter what is to feminist critics the novel's most disturbing scene: the episode in which Tea Cake beats Janie and in which the omniscient narrator comments, "No brutal beating at all. He just slapped her around a bit to show he was boss" (140). There is perhaps no satisfying explanation for the presence of this incident and the narrator's dismissal of woman abuse as trivial in what is otherwise a narrative of black female empowerment. A reading that takes into account the chapter's talking frame and the larger narrative frame to which it speaks does, however, shed some light on this difficult segment. The narrative voice that describes the inci-

37

dent is the one we have come to associate with the omniscient narrator. But it is a voice that is more truly omniscient, in the purely descriptive sense of the word, than we have come to expect in this novel. It is the voice of an impartial narrator familiar with the inner workings of characters' minds (excluding Janie's, in this scene), but it is simultaneously the voice of at least four different speakers in the talking frame: Tea Cake, Sop-de-Bottom, the community chorus, and a commentator I shall call the Psychologist. To indicate the narrators in the talking frame, I have inserted labels in the excerpt below.

> [OMNISCIENT NARRATOR:] Before the week was over he had whipped Janie. [PSYCHOLOGIST:] Not because her behavior justified his jealousy, but it relieved that awful fear inside him. Being able to whip her reassured him in possession. [TEA CAKE/COMMUNITY CHORUS:] No brutal beating at all. He just slapped her around a bit to show who was boss. [OMNISCIENT NARRATOR:] Everybody talked about it next day in the fields. It aroused a sort of envy in both men and women. The way he petted and pampered her as if those two or three face slaps had nearly killed her made the women see visions and the helpless way she hung on him made men dream dreams.
> [SOP-DE-BOTTOM:] "Tea Cake, you sho is a lucky man. . . . Uh person can see every place you hit her. Ah bet she never raised her hand tuh hit yuh back, neither. Take some uh dese ol' rusty black women and dey would fight yuh all night long and next day nobody couldn't tell you ever hit 'em. Dat's de reason Ah done quit beatin' mah woman. You can't make no mark on 'em at all. Lawd! wouldn't Ah love tuh whip uh tender woman lak Janie!" (140-41)

The Psychologist explains, but does not excuse, Tea Cake's behavior. In the "no brutal beating" sentence, and the sentence that follows it, we get Tea Cake's explanation. It is a perspective on woman's place in society that we have come to associate with the community chorus, a perspective that is reflected in the chorus of questions that follows Janie down the street upon her return to Eatonville. The comments on women's visions and men's dreams in the omniscient narrator's "response," refer back to, and engage in a dialectic with, the first page of the novel. The irony in this choice of words becomes apparent when we recall that men's dreams, according to the novel's opening passage, will be "mocked to death by Time"—and here the narrator refers to men's dreams of controlling women through the use of violence.

Sop-de-Bottom reiterates Tea Cake's desire to "show [women] [who] was boss," in a manner that the Psychologist would find richly symbolic. Sop-de-Bottom describes a desire to vent his impotent rage on the only being who is lower than the black man in the social structure imposed upon him by white society—the black woman—and he expresses his desire to inscribe male domination on the female body, to make a "mark on 'em." In Tea Cake's actions and Sop-de-Bottom's lines, Hurston addresses what Bell Hooks and Cornel West call the "tremendous sense of inadequacy and . . . often suppressed rage [that] takes the form of Black male violence against Black women." [11] West addresses the root of the problem: "The very notion that Black people are human beings is a new notion in Western Civilization and is still not widely accepted in practice."[12] In a discussion of "Black women's agency and . . . the problems Black men have when asked to acknowledge Black women's humanity," West continues, "it must be remembered that this refusal to acknowledge one another's humanity is a reflection of the way we are seen and treated in the larger society."[13]

The first line in the beating segment that I attribute to the Psychologist is an important one to my reading of the segment. The voice maintains that Tea Cake's beating of Janie "relieved that awful fear inside him" (140). West writes that the "fear and failure . . . . imposed upon [black people] by a larger racist society" is the "fundamental problem" in situations of black male violence against black

[11] Hooks and West 55-56.

[12] Hooks and West 12.

[13] Hooks and West 12.

women. Tea Cake's fear is produced by Mrs. Turner's attempts to convince Janie, in the chapter preceding the beating segment, that marrying a man as dark as Tea Cake was a mistake. In beating Janie, Tea Cake thinks that he is showing Mrs. Turner, and the white hierarchies of beauty and social standing she has internalized, that he is the "boss" (140).

Janie's voice is notably absent. Although the distance which she places between herself and her narrative, along with her analytical, philosophical perspective on her story, places her closest, perhaps, to the voice of the Psychologist, she does not speak for herself as Tea Cake does in the passage following the one quoted above. Her silence and Sop-de-Bottom's macabre remark about marking the bodies of women speak for her. Janie's powerlessness and victim-status in this scene are signified by the absence of her voice. From this point in the text forward, Janie follows West's prescription for the healing of violent rifts between black men and women" she "assert[s] herself boldly and defiantly as [a] human being" throughout Tea Cake's illness and death, at her murder trial, and in her return to Eatonville.[14]

Janie tells the biggest story of all, in the courtroom after Tea Cake's death. It is the kind of story that this novel privileges, a story rooted in experience. She has had "to *go* there tuh *know* there" (183), and she tells the story to save her life. The courtroom story is told to a white male jury and an audience of white women whom Janie wishes "she could make . . . know how it was instead of those menfolks" (176). The black community of migrant laborers who had been Janie's friends are an "anonymous herd" (177) in the back of the courtroom ready to condemn Janie for Tea Cake's murder, "their tongues cocked and loaded" (176). When they attempt to offer evidence against Janie, they are silenced by the prosecuting attorney, who would rather see Janie found innocent than hear a black voice speak for his

[14] Hooks and West 56.

side. At the center of this complex rhetorical situation, Janie is in the same predicament that she was in when she discovered her blackness in the photograph: she is an outsider to both the black and the white communities, and she wishes to tell her tale to a female audience. The white women in the courtroom, although they are demurely sympathetic, with their polite applause and tears when Janie is found innocent, do not represent a community that Janie can or wants to become a meaningful part of. They are there to condemn black manhood. They have come to hear about Tea Cake the rabid animal, and Janie's innocence has meaning for them only in the context of Tea Cake's validating their beliefs about the animalistic and dangerous nature of the black man. Janie naively thanks them for "realiz[ing] her feelings" (179) and makes her way to a boarding house on the black side of town before darkness falls.

Although we do not hear Janie's courtroom story in the first-person voice, the entire novel is, in effect, the story that Janie tells in court, the story that goes "way back to let them know how she and Tea Cake had been with one another so they could see she could never shoot Tea Cake out of malice" (178). If we view the narrative structure of *Their Eyes* as a talking frame for Janie's story, it becomes apparent that the audience, for all of the tales that have contributed to the narrative's dialectic up to the point of the courtroom scene, has been a black audience, an audience that might be found sitting on the porch of Joe Starks's store. If we were to hear Janie speak in the first-person voice in the courtroom, she would be speaking outside of the talking frame, because she would be speaking primarily to a white audience rather than entering into a dialogue with the talking frame—a black audience that, unlike the black audience in the courtroom, talks back. We do not hear Janie's voice until she is back in Eatonville, "satisfied tuh be heah," providing closure in her tale to Pheoby and giving instructions for the tale's retelling:

41

"Ah done been tuh de horizon and back. . . . Ah knows all dem sitters-and-talkers gointuh worry they guts into fiddle strings till dey find out whut we been talkin' 'bout. Dat's all right, Pheoby, tell 'em, . . . tel 'em dat love ain't somethin' lak uh grindstone dat's de same thing everywhere and do de same thing tuh everything it touch. Love is lak de sea." (182)

When Janie brings the horizon and the sea into her final conversation with Pheoby, she signals closure to the tale's talking frame, which opened with the omniscient narrator's discourse on ships on the horizon as a metaphor for the dreams of men and women.

In telling her tale to Pheoby, Janie—and Hurston—affirm what Lorraine Bethel refers to as "Black Woman Identification":

The idea of Black women seeking their own identity and defining themselves through bonding on various levels—psychic, intellectual, and emotional, as well as physical—with other Black women. . . . [is] the process and struggle of choosing a hated identity: choosing to be a Black woman, not only in body, but in spirit as well. It is the process of identifying one's self and the selves of other Black women as inherently valuable.[15]

Pheoby affirms the text's black woman identification as well, and she establishes the importance of her character as audience in her final lines: "Lawd! . . . Ah done growed ten feet higher from jus' listenin' tuh you, Janie, Ah ain't satisfied wid mahself no mo'. Ah means tuh make Sam take me fishin' wid him after this. Nobody better not criticize yuh in mah hearin' " (183). Pheoby also signals closure to the talking frame: In her reference to fishing, and in her statement of her intention to act, to "make Sam take me fishin'," she responds to the omniscient narrator's opening discourse on the sea and commentary on women "act[ing]" "to make the dream . . . the truth" (1). The omniscient narrator responds, in the novel's concluding paragraph, bringing the talking frame full circle, from the ships "sail[ing] forever on the horizon, never out of sight, never landing . . ." (1) to the image of Janie "pull[ing] in her horizon like a great fish-net

[15] Bethel 17.

. . . from around the waist of the world" (184). This image of female empowerment, emphasized by its strategic position as structuring device in the talking frame and privileged as the primary topic in the narrative's multivocal discourse, completes the reconstruction of Eatonville as an egalitarian, black nationalist utopia. The Eatonville that Janie returns to is black-owned and black-controlled, as it was under Joe Starks's stewardship, but it is now a community in which one woman has taken up the challenge of the first framing paragraph and made "the dream . . . the truth," and in which her sisters, like Pheoby, won't be satisfied with themselves until, as the opening paragraph suggested, they "act and do things accordingly." At the novel's close, the celebration of orality in which Joe Starks had "forbidden [Janie] to indulge" (50) is now the shared province of Eatonville's male and female residents. With the device of the talking frame, Hurston affirms Janie's speakerly subjectivity and creates an egalitarian discourse community that finds its voice and its audience in traditional residually oral forms.

Pennsylvania State University
University Park, Pennsylvania

REREADING CLAUDE MCKAY

By P. S. Chauhan

If McKay's conflicting views were an enigma to his friends, the ambiguities of his work are a bafflement to his critics. Naturally, the variant readings of the man and his fiction today constitute the central problem of McKay scholarship. Wayne Cooper, McKay's biographer, trying to find an acceptable solution, locates the source of all ideological paradoxes in the personal pathology of a personality "characterized always by a deep-seated ambivalence" that was caused mainly by "dependence upon a succession of father figures."[1]

There is another way, however, to explain the presence of incongruous elements in McKay's work. It is more than likely that his work seems paradoxical because it has been read in an inappropriate context. Beginning with James Weldon Johnson's *Black Manhattan* (1930), critics have concluded, certainly to their satisfaction, that McKay was "of the Harlem group,"[2] indeed that he was "one of the movement's ornaments."[3] In the latest study of the Harlem School, *The Harlem Renaissance: Revaluations* (1989), Geta LeSeur affirms that "Claude McKay remains today part of the acknowledged literary triumvirate of the Harlem Renaissance. He shares this prestigious position with Langston Hughes and Jean Toomer."[4] Her view is typical of the current scholarship's understanding of McKay's affiliations.

[1] Wayne F. Cooper, *Claude McKay, Rebel Sojourner in the Harlem Renaissance: A Biography* (Baton Rouge: Louisiana State Univ. Press, 1987), pp. ix-x.

[2] James Weldon Johnson, *Black Manhattan* (New York: Knopf, 1930), p. 264.

[3] George E. Kent, "Patterns of the Harlem Renaissance," in Arna Bontemps, ed., *The Harlem Renaissance Remembered* (New York: Dodd, 1972), p. 34.

[4] Geta LeSeur, "Claude McKay's Marxiusm," in *The Harlem Renaissance Revaluations*, ed. Amritjit Singh, William S. Shiver, and Stanley Brodwin (New York: Garland, 1989), p. 219.

One fruitful close reading of McKay's work—a reading heretofore denied him—however, forces us to the conclusion that to anchor his consciousness in Harlem is to dislocate his true emotional geography; it is, indeed, to misread the map of his political awareness. If we would account for all the elements of his thought, we might have to take McKay for what he really was in life: a colonial writer who happened to stop over in Harlem on his lifelong quest for a spiritual home, on a quest, incidentally, that no colonial writer has ever effectively escaped. His association with Harlem, it can be affirmed, was no more than what Harlem itself has been to Afro-American letters: "a moment in renaissancism."[5] Such being the case, by continuing to identify his work exclusively with Harlem's ethos, we have not only robbed it of its uniqueness but also denied it the central place it deserves in the global discourse of black writers that McKay so ably initiated. Arbitrary points of reference have led us only to skewed inferences.

Unable, or unwilling, to read McKay as a writer from Jamaica, then a British colony, and hence as one with a mindset entirely different from that of the Harlemite, many critics have landed themselves in a puzzle. James Weldon Johnson, a person whom McKay in the dedicatory note to *Harlem: Negro Metropolis* (1940) calls a "friend and wise counselor," finds McKay's lifelong nostalgia for Jamaica intriguing. "Reading McKay's poetry of rebellion," says Johnson, "it is difficult to conceive of him dreaming of his native Jamaica and singing,"[6] Such perplexity results, obviously, from an ignorance of, or from ignoring, a basic fact about the colonial sensibility: that it straddles two worlds—the one of its origin, the other of its adoption. Politically, its values and attitudes derive from, and swing between, the two sets. It sides, at once, with each of the two antagonists:

[5] Houston A. Baker, Jr., *Modernism and the Harlem Renaissance* (Chicago: Univ. of Chicago Press, 1987), p. 106.

[6] Johnson, p. 219.

the victim and the victimizer.

That McKay should have been assimilated into the Harlem Renaissance looks rather natural in retrospect. For one thing, noticed when literary history understood artistic works in terms of schools or movements, Claude McKay was bound to be read as part of the Harlem Renaissance, especially since to be black and to have a powerful literary voice was considered nothing less than miraculous. After all, "If We Must Die," written in response to the scarlet riots of the summer of 1919, not only "expressed the feelings of a great many Negros" of America,[7] but also "became almost a tribal litany of Negroes in the twenties."[8] His poems truly served as a clarion call to the New Negro, "the younger generation [that was] vibrant with a new psychology."[9] But to credit McKay with the boom and bloom of black art and literature, or with the general growth of interest in Harlem, is to be guilty of the *post hoc, ergo propter hoc* fallacy. That the birth of the Renaissance followed McKay's departure from Harlem need not argue for his paternity of the movement.

McKay's own comments about the Harlem Renaissance, distant and mocking, would argue against his incorporation into the movement. Invited by James Weldon Johnson "to return to America to participate in the Negro renaissance movement," McKay found himself loathe to return to Harlem, for, he explained years later, "if I did return I would have to find a new orientation among the Negro intelligentsia."[10] This is hardly the sentiment of an author who is said to have been the progenitor of the Renaissance. Even when he did devote a book to the Negro Metropolis, McKay could not bring himself to say anything more sympathetic

[7] John Hope Franklin, *From Slavery to Freedom: A History of Negro Americans*, 4th ed. (New York: Knopf, 1974), p. 360.

[8] Blyden Jackson, "Essential McKay," *Phylon*, 14 (1953), 217.

[9] Alain Locke, *The New Negro: An Interpretation* (New York: Boni, 1925), p. 3.

[10] Claude McKay, *A Long Way from Home* (1937; rpt. New York: Arno, 1969), pp. 306-07.

about the Renaissance than the following:

> New Yorkers had discovered the existence of a fashionable
> clique, and an artistic and literary set in Harlem. The big racket
> which crepitated from this discovery resulted in an enormously
> abnormal advertisement of bohemian Harlem. And even solid
> real estate values were affected by the fluid idealistic art values
> of Harlem.[11]

The truth is that McKay was even less responsible for
the Harlem Renaissance than Pound had been for the Chicago School of Poetry. He was *for* the Harlem Renaissance,
but certainly not *of* it.

Yet to stress McKay's colonial heritage is by no means to
minimize his value to the movement or the overall worth of
his work. To the contrary, his work did, indeed, carve out a
path which black writers all over the world, not only the
Harlemite, could, if they would, follow. Some of them, like
Alain Locke, who altered the title of McKay's poem "The
White House" to "White Houses," and thus destroyed the
symbolic statement intended by the poet, dared not follow
McKay's lead. But a few others did. Aimé Césaire, according to the interview published in *Discourse on Colonialism*
(1955), was inspired by McKay's novel *Banjo* (1930), which
for him was "really one of the first works in which an author spoke of the Negro and gave him a certain literary dignity."[12] That McKay's self-assurance, like his passionate
devotion to the cause of the black race, did a yeoman's service to the advancement of African American literature is a
fact widely, and correctly, accepted.

What is little suspected, however, is the pervasive presence of the colonial sensibility in his work. This essay seeks
to identify only a few of the traits distinguishing the colonial strain. But even a small sample of a new evidence
should serve as a sufficient warrant to call for a fresh reading of Claude McKay. What follows here, then, is a brief

---

[11] Claude McKay, *Harlem: Negro Metropolis* (New York: Dutton, 1940), p. 26.

[12] Aimé Césarie, interview, *Discourse on Colonialism*, by Réne Depestre, trans.
Maro Riofrancos (New York: Monthly Review Press, 1972), p. 71.

analysis of his work and then a demonstration of how its structure and its tone can be explained only with reference to McKay's colonial heritage.

Linguistically, his work bears the mark all too common to the writing done in colonies. It is pulled by two gravitational forces: the one of his native tongue, the other of the language of the colonizer. In his first book of poems published in the United States, *Harlem Shadows* (1922), McKay confesses to the linguistic tension that had been part of his upbringing. "The speech of my childhood and early youth," he writes, "was the Jamaica dialect . . . which still preserves a few words of African origin, and which is more diffcult of understanding than the American Negro dialect. But the language we wrote and read in school was England's English."[13] The dual versions of the language, like those of the island culture, internalized during the period of his cognitive development, haunt McKay's work to the very end and affect its tone and texture in various ways.

His earliest poems, *Songs of Jamaica* (1912), were proclaimed to be dialect poetry, which, in the main, they were. In the poetic pieces there is, however, something besides dialect at work, as is seen, for example, in his poem "Whe' Fe Do?" Note the fifth stanza of the poem:

> We've go to wuk wid might an' main,
> To us we ha' an' use we brain,
> To toil an' worry, 'cheme and 'train
> Fe t'ings that bring more loss dan gain;
> To stan' de sun an' bear de rain,
> An' suck we bellyful o'pain
> Widouten cry not yet complain—
> For dat caan' [won't] do.[14]

It is significant that if there is a vernacular grammar at work in the line "widouten cry nor yet complain," there is a literary and a balanced line as well ("to toil and worry,

[13] Claude McKay, *Harlem Shadows* (New York, Harcourt, 1922), p. xix.

[14] Claude McKay, *Songs of Jamaica* (Kingston, Jamaica: Aston W. Gardner, 1912), p. 23.

scheme and train"), a line, by the way, with a caesura, too. A purely native expression, "to suck a bellyful of pain," is similarly relieved by a perfectly English phrase, "to work with might and main."

The split between the two versions of English goes deeper, however, than it may appear at first. The fourth line has, for example, a perfectly good English "that," but the eighth line reverts to the dialectal "dat." And there is another word, too, which in its journey through the stanza undergoes a similar transformation between the fourth and the eighth lines. Whereas the fourth begins with "Fe," the eighth opens with the normal "For." Lexical loyalties of the poet, the stanza bears out, are about evenly divided between the native dialect and the metropolitan English. Even as he seeks to embody the experience of a farm laborer, McKay gets enticed by the idiom of the Master, by the privileged language of the dominant group, betraying the inroads of the colonizer's influence.

The argument of McKay's later poetry, like the diction of his earlier poems, is disposed around two poles: the vernacular and the metropolitan. The progression of his well-known poems readily reveals the bipolar tensions that underlie the conceptual design of his verses. Whether it be "To One Coming North," "North and South," or "The Tropics in New York," the absent landscape of Jamaica is so powerfully present in the poems as to displace the New York scene, the immediate locale and the subject of the poem. The pattern is best illustrated by "When Dawn Comes to the City." The name of the city, let it be said, does not matter, for the City is the "other" of Jamaica, consistently symbolized by McKay as the Country.

If the first stanza of the poem creates the urban street where "the tired cars go grumbling by, / The moaning, groaning cars," the second recalls the picture of a pastoral paradise, "the heart of the island of the sea, / Where the cocks are crowing, crowing, crowing, / And the hens are cackling in the rose-apple tree." If the third stanza details how the city "milk carts go rumbling by / Under the dying stars," the fourth nostalgically pictures "the tethered cow [which] is lowing, lowing, lowing" and why "there, oh there, on the island of the sea, / There would I be at dawn."[15] The thesis and the antithesis of space, like the contrapuntal arrangement of verses, represent the bipolar sites that pervade the imaginary world of Claude McKay, one of them forever anchored in the Caribbean.

It is remarkable in this context that McKay, as Eugenia W. Collier points out, uses "the highly 'artisitic' forms of Western lyrics," and not "the surging rhythms of African music,"[16] which, say, Langston Hughes and Edward Braithwaite have used. James Weldon Johnson was the first to point to the incongruity that for "pouring out cynicism, bitterness, and invective," McKay "took the sonnet form as his medium."[17]

Yet for a poet grounded in British education and well versed in Milton, Wordsworth, Keats, and Hopkins, it was as natural that he should use the disciplined form of a sonnet as it was that he should possess "the classical feeling" which Frank Harris discovered in his poetry.[18] Just as McKay's cynicism and invective came from his experience as a subaltern in an imperial colony, the sonnet form came from his formal education in the classics of the colonizer.

Even when McKay had managed to slough off the Jamaica dialect, he continued to be possessed by the memories of the Jamaican flora and fauna. It is only by reconginizing McKay's unconscious proclivity towards Jamaican animals that one may explain why his imagery militates against the texture of the traditional narrative. His yarn, spun with the staple of the English idiom, sets up expecta-

[15] McKay, *Harlem Shadows*, pp. 60-62.

[16] Eugenia W. Collier, "The Four-Way Dilemma of Claude McKay," *CLA Journal*, 15 (1972), 345-53.

[17] Johnson, p. 264.

[18] McKay, *A Long Way from Home*, p. 11.

tions associated with the tenor of the average English novel. But before the reader has a chance to settle down, he is suddenly jolted as tropical imagery leaps at him. Describing, in *Home to Harlem*, the fight between the two boys in Susie's parlor, the narrator says: "Biff! Square on the mouth. The chocolate leaped up like a tiger-cat at his assailant. . . . Like an enraged ram goat, he held and butted the light-brown boy twice, straight on the forehead."[19] Later on, the account of Jerco's suicide by razor reads: "Jerco had cut his throat and was lying against the bowl of the water-closet. . . . And he sprawled there like a great black boar in a mess of blood" (p. 309).

Now the tiger-cat, the ram goat, and the black boar do not stray from Central Park in New York, even though the story is located on its fringes. Indeed, they are as alien to the American topography as is the violence of these images to the tenor of the English novel. It seems that McKay's mind, harking back to the tropical landscape of his native island, quietly ushers its beasts into the parlors of Manhattan and the restaurants of Marseilles. Even as the author negotiates the surge and rhythm of the English sentence, his memory drags in the native creatures, populating, in consequence, the metropolitan English narrative with strange birds, beasts, and flowers.

His punctuating the English prose with the bestiary of Jamaica creates resonances that travel beyond the fictional narrative. A few examples of his iconography may well establish their alien origins: "Kojo Jeems' face was as jolly as a pot bubbling with Congo peas and a chunk of salted beef";[20] or "some couples were dancing, thick as maggots in a vat of sweet liquor, and as wriggling" (*HH*, p. 14). The vernacular imagery, alien to much of the English novel, may

[19] Claude McKay, *Home to Harlem* (New York: Harper, 1928), p. 72. Hereafter cited parenthetically in the text by the abbreviation *HH*, followed by the page number(s).

[20] Claude McKay, *Banana Bottom* (New York: Harper, 1933), p. 79.

well seem to be an interloper in this tributary of the English fiction until one recalls that it comes from the mind
where two topographies meet, one of the Caribbean island
and the other of the Northern continent.

McKay's iconography becomes the more revealing because the revolting images have been reserved, probably unconsciously, for black characters alone. And they tend to
degrade, nay dehumanize, the very people they vivify for
us. Of the two characters that receive the full endorsement
and respect of the author, only one—Ray—for instance, is
black. In fact, he enjoys the singular distinction of serving
as the author's political spokesperson and as his philosophic
persona. But odd are the terms in which a crucial decision
of this important character is couched. Like Henry James's
Lambert Strether, Ray decides to abandon his guiding an-
gel, Agatha. For if he does not depart from her and from
Harlem, he reasons, "soon he would become one of the con-
tented hogs in the pigpen of Harlem, getting ready to litter
little black piggies." It is natural to assume that one affectionately disposed towards Harlem infants would not conceive of them as "little black piggies" or describe their delivery as a "littering." The spokesperson, clearly, bears the
disdain of an outsider to the community and, possibly, of a
superior. An unconscious slip such as this betrays, at the
same time, the insidious influence of the white colonizer's
thinking upon the colonial's attitude towards his own
people.

Clearly, McKay's imagery reveals two things: one, that
his tropes brutally undercut the stature of the black characters whom the author would have us celebrate; the other,
that the ostensible effort to win respect for his community
is constantly sabotaged by the author's disdain for the representatives of that community.

Now each of these inferences points to a deep rift in the
mind of the writer. At the very least, it is symptomatic of
what Freud calls the "defensive identification" of the oppressed with the oppressor. Bruno Bettleheim reports that

some of the victims of the Nazis so identified themeselves with their victimizers that they would pick up bits and rags of the captors to decorate themselves with. McKay seems, similarly, to have picked up bits and pieces of the white colonizer's disdain for the native black community, for it is the Master's stance that comes through in the colonial author's unguarded moments.

One reason why McKay's attitude towards black characters is less than respectful is that, unlike Harlem writers—Jean Toomer, Zora Neale Hurston, and Rudolph Fisher, who went to their folk roots—McKay went for literary inspiration to Anglo-Saxon masters, to Dickens, Shaw, Whitman, and Lawrence. As a person raised in a colony, it was impossible for him totally to divest his mind of the literature and the attitudes of the colonizer and to adopt the literary genealogy of the African-American peers of his generation.

Nothing in McKay's writing so powerfuly registers his ambivalence towards the interest of the Harlem community as his shifting attitude towards the Harlem prostitute. If the narrator of the poem "Harlem Shadows" is the rueful patriarch bemoaning the corruption of the "little dark girls who in slippered feet / Go prowling through the night from street to street," that of the novel *Home to Harlem* gloats in the depredations of Jake and his associates who, like predators, go stalking through the night, always "hungry foh a li'l brown honey" (*HH*, p. 23). The poem and the novel, read together, suggest an author running with the hare and hunting with the hound.

The speaker of the poem is so revolted by the carnal barter forced upon the "lass"of his race that he can speak of her only as a dismembered thing, as "the slippered feed," "the little gray feet," "of tired feet," "the timid little feet of clay," "the sacred brown feet," and "the weary, weary feet." Here is a compassionate father totally undone by the dishonor of his little ones, whose feet are helplessly propelled by poverty from street to street.

The novel *Home to Harlem*, on the other hand, so unre-
servedly parades free sex that it drives the reader into a
shockingly different latitude of McKay's psychic landscape.
Here one comes upon a Laurentian celebration of sex,
where Jake, a deserter of the U.S. Army, gambols through
black Manhattan like an unrepentant Mellors. Sexual in-
dulgence is not only permitted in the fictional version of
Harlem but virtually the only activity permitted in this
Harlem. The McKay who, as an insider, felt the shame of
"the sacred brown feet of [his] fallen race," mocks, as an
outsider, the promiscuity of Harlem, exercising a freedom
available only to the colonial, who at once dwells in two
worlds—one of his own people, the other of his Master.

Now, these bipolar pulls have consequences for McKay's
narrative structure as well. *Home to Harlem*, for instance,
in opening windows on sensuous aspects of Harlem life, follows the tradition of literary realism. But by refraining
from an attempt at a holistic picture of Harlem existence, it
seeks to modify these conventions, concentrating, instead,
on portraits of middle-class frolics enacted in parlors,
streets, and night clubs. The novel, at one level, offers a
glimpse of the gaiety of Harlem existence. But Jake and
Ray, who, together, form the composite protagonist of the
tale, are so alien to the spirit of the Harlem community
that they can hope to preserve their personal integrity and
sanity only when they put some distance between Harlem,
which they had considered their home, and themselves,
which, thanks to their experiences there, they now understand a little better.

The very plot of the novel is at war with the title *Home
to Harlem*. For while the title promises a tale of relief at
Jake's finally making it to the home port, the progression of
the plot uncovers a terrible irony inasmuch as the subsequent developments lead the principals away from Harlem
in search of a home elsewhere.

Jake, who comes rushing to Harlem hoping to land there
in a sweet and secure haven, must escape it to save his hide,

for he discovers that as Zeddy had forewarned him, there were treacherous people in Harlem who would squeal to the police about his desertion from the Army. "Without any natural reason, they would go vomitting out their guts to the ofays about one another." (*HH*, p. 23). Therefore, even if there is "a rather basic equation: Harlem's streets = sex + food + breath = life-giving home,"[21] Jake must bid goodbye to the dream of finding a home in Harlem. Hence, as the novel closes, the reader finds Jake and his newfound love, Felice, on the move again, "walking to the subway station along Lennox Avenue" (*HH*, p. 340), on their way out to Chicago, to another uncertainty.

Thus ends the search for home, and thus ends the rover's tale, creeping towards another station. Such, however, is the destiny of most children of the colonial imagination: continually searching for a home while perpetually moving into exile. Naipaul's Mr. Biswas is not the only character who will never attain a home for himself.[22] His tale is prefigured in McKay's fiction, in the colonial version of the Sisyphean myth which McKay so cleverly fashions in *Home to Harlem* and in *Banjo*. The only character of McKay's who ever finds a home is Bita (*Banana Bottom*, 1933), but such arrival for a fictional character becomes possible only when the writer's fancy returns to settle in his native land, as, for once, it did. The home for McKay was never Harlem, but Jamaica, where alone his characters could regain their integrity.

It can well be argued that McKay's vacillation between alternating preferences for the native culture and the metropolitan, like his pull between the pastoral and the urban, between an allegiance to Marxism and a desire for free peasantry, can be satifactorily explained only in terms of the colonial's attachment to the simple rhythms of his na-

[21] Sidney H. Bremer, "Home in Harlem, New York: Lessons from the Harlem Renaissance Writers," *PMLA*, 105 (1990), p. 50.

[22] See V. S. Naipaul, *A House for Mr. Biswas* (London: Deutsch, 1961).

tive world and to a fascination for the metropolitan systems
of the West, whose cruelty and inequity would constantly
drive his thoughts back to the security of a remembered
community. A creature of colonial experience, McKay was
condemned to dwell in the limbo of the imagination of the
colonized, unable forever to state a clear-cut preference.
That is the primary reason why his work seems so paradoxical, why it bears the print of the journeys between the polarities of a divided mind.

To comprehend him satisfactorily, therefore, one must
approach McKay not from one direction alone, but from
two. One must read McKay, indeed one must re-read Mc-
Kay, in a context different from that of the Harlem Renaissance, the context he has long been relegated to. In order to
appreciate the nature of his ambiguities, one must recognize
the intellectual baggage he brought with him to Harlem—the English attitudes, a European sensibility, and the
general impedimenta of a colonial mind, congnitive elements altogether unknown to most Harlemites.

University of Pennsylvania
Philadelphia, Pennsylvania

Constructing and Reconstructing Afro-American Texts: The Critic as Ambassador and Referee

Wahneema Lubiano

1

Reconstructing Womanhood: The Emergence of the Afro-American Woman Novelist
By Hazel Carby
Oxford University Press
1987

Self-Discovery and Authority in Afro-American Narrative
By Valerie Smith
Harvard University Press
1987

In the midst of a burgeoning critical interest in Afro-American literature, we ought to consider both the place of that criticism within Afro-American literary history and its problematic entry into a larger discursive domain. One of the effects of a racial (and racist) discourse is to inscribe in literary discourse a two-tiered system of "required" knowledge. Members of the dominant group can assume that the criticism of a specific literary period of British or American literature will be meaningful to those with similar interests. Yet the same cannot be said for the discourses of marginalized literature. Critics of Afro-American literature, for instance, speak to each other—and have done so for decades within the pages of journals such as *Callaloo, CLA, Black American Literature Forum, Phylon, Obsidian,* and *Black World,* among others—but as Afro-American literary discourse attracts an increasing, but still largely uninformed, attention from the dominant group, such critics confront the limitations of this new audience and the concomitant pressure to make particular discussions more generally available.[1]

Unlike other specialists, critics of Afro-American literature must try to speak to each other even as they must realize that they are also addressing other interested readers who may not feel, or may never have felt, that it is within the scope of their own critical or pedagogic agendas to know very much about current debates within Afro-American literature. Du Bois's "double consciousness" returns with a vengeance: we critics of Afro-American literature feel the need to speak to each other with the uninformed audience constantly in mind, a dilemma that often results in producing criticism that of necessity rein-

58

vents certain wheels of our discourse instead of focusing on the complexities of history and interpretation.

Speaking out of this double consciousness means simplifying—a restriction that inheres in the discourse of a marginalized literature. The single greatest difficulty facing Afro-American scholars is the need to figure out, in the space of an article or a book, how to convey the full complexity of periods or genres or intertextual relationships. Yet few scholars are obliged to write an essay or book on the entire tradition of British literature, except along the most particular methodological, thematic, or specifically problematic lines; in such an instance a critic charts instead some pieces of a broader territory or negotiates the territory so that while much might be engaged, no one expects that everything will be addressed. This is not the case for the Afro-Americanists who regularly make themselves responsible for charting very large pieces of the ground: "the Afro-American novel" "narrative strategy in Afro-American fiction," "the black American woman writer," "Afro-American literature in the twentieth century," among other things. Books written by Afro-Americanists are frequently structured to engage, explain, account for, redefine, or reconstruct a "tradition" of Afro-American literature and to offer representative close readings. But the use of the word "tradition" is itself charged with ambiguity, one not always explicitly addressed by the critic.

The word "tradition" is as slippery as "culture." Tradition can refer either to a process or to a collection of objects described as part of a definable group. As a collection, a tradition is reduced to the inscription of absolute, coherent, and cohesive qualities on a set of discrete texts. An abstract and exceedingly complex set of overdetermined relationships are thus made concrete. Nonetheless, the ongoing debates over the amorphous and dynamic processes by which a definable (after a fashion) group, Afro-Americans, has generated a collection of writings is drawing our attention to the ways in which such collections are constituted—the means of the texts' production—as well as the objects of interpretation, the texts themselves.

The debate is not peculiar to Afro-American literature. According to Rita Copeland: "From antiquity onwards, the distinction between textual production and textual interpretation is ambiguous at best. . . . more broadly, the Ciceronian and late Greek traditions erected a theory of style on a systematic evaluation of the textual legacy of past authors, so that new authors might measure themselves against traditional models" (1). Copeland refers to a historical problem not customarily given an explicit discursive space in medievalist vernacular circles, an unstated yet dynamic preoccupation. I deliberately raise that issue here in order to set Afro-American literature in the context of issues engaged in the most canonical of circles. The relationship of textual production to textual interpretation in Afro-American literary discourse is not necessarily more explicitly engaged, but it is necessarily a political relationship because of the larger history of Afro-Americans themselves in the United States, and because Afro-American texts inevitably come to any reading public to some extent via the dominant culture's publishing apparatus and via a literary discourse that is influenced by the dominant culture.

What is an Afro-American tradition of literature? It is the concrete samples of written material available that critics of Afro-American literature have decided to include: slave narratives, essays, autobiographies, political speeches, stories, romances, novels, poetry, dramas, and position papers. It is also the carefully researched account of the means of producing these items. And, finally, it is also a carefully historicized theorizing about the writings that yields information for negotiating a more productive and useful interpretation of Afro-American texts.

Although textual production and textual interpretation are politicized in Afro-American literary discourse by virtue of that literature's relationship to Anglo-American literary discourse, this relationship is not always self-consciously articulated. Afro-Americanists have often interpreted those texts as if the relationship of a text to its production was an always already known quantity that could be referred to as a casually explicit or implicit reflection of the racism of the dominant culture. Such references suggest that racism operates always under a set of conditions that anyone could recognize. But what of the specificities of the relationship of Afro-American texts to models of textual production outside of the field? And what are we to make of the texts that seem to be aberrant texts within this field? For most of the period between its publication in 1937 and the early 1970s, for example, Zora Neale Hurston's *Their Eyes Were Watching God* was excluded by the movers and shakers of the Harlem Renaissance and then by Richard Wright's agenda. Now it is taken for granted that Hurston is part of the Afro-American tradition.

Is a tradition always the most stable and conservative reading assigned to a process, arguing for forces engaged in a specific set of texts in specific ways? The problem with defining a tradition—whether one speaks to it as process and production, or as collection of objects, or in a way that elucidates the overlap between the two—is that summarizing a dynamic comprehensible to a largely uninformed audience means reconstructing that dynamic in reductionist terms. The summarizing that is so much a part of the work of an Afro-Americanist is information organization that concretizes the amorphous at the cost of simplifying. Furthermore, because we are speaking of and to a discourse that is racialized and marginalized, the summaries construct essentialist categories. The abuse of "the Afro-American tradition . . ." is continual and assured.

But if the potential for such abuse is present, so is the impulse to preserve and resurrect the material and to describe how the material has made its way in the world. Frantz Fanon described this impulse as the work of the native intellectual asserting, in the face of the colonizer's big lies about the history and the culture of the natives, the "real" history of the natives (215). He speaks of recreating a glorious past as a weapon against colonialism, which "has never ceased to maintain that the Negro is a savage" (211). Thus, the politically motivated native intellectual constitutes him- or herself as a champion of his or her culture (218).

Within the context of racial marginalization then, the political nature of Afro-American literature and its discourse is a foregone conclusion. Afro-American writing has gone on in the midst of, and as a contribution to, a debate that has its own always already context: Afro-American literature inserts itself as proof of the equality of Afro-Americans (Gates, *Figures in Black* xv–xxxii, 3–58). The underlying assumption of many Afro-American scholars, intellectuals, and writers over the course of the eighteenth, nineteenth, and twentieth centuries, was that art, especially written art, would make us free. This literature records the primary racial American "other" as confronting, subverting, or co-opting the dominant group's political, economic, and social power. Regardless of how fervently a black American writer demands or begs for the right to be just "a poet—not a Negro poet" (Hughes 692)—this is, as Houston Baker tropes it, AMERICA (66). And in AMERICA no marginalized writer writes alone; Afro-Americans—as *Invisible Man* asserts—live a public life (563), always interpolated by their marginalization. Afro-American writers live their lives not only in the gaze of the external dominating culture—a sense of which, Du Bois and Fanon assert, Afro-Americans carry always—but with the weight of their own group's unrelenting, if not always articulated, concern over what any Afro-American writer says or writes, anywhere and under whatever conditions.

The summarizing that is so much a part of the work of an Afro-Americanist is information organization that concretizes the amorphous at the cost of simplifying. Furthermore, because we are speaking of and to a discourse that is racialized and marginalized, the summaries construct essentialist categories. The abuse of "the Afro-American tradition . . ." is continual and assured.

Ron Karenga, joining Leopold Senghor, insisted that black art is collective (32). At different times critics of Afro-American literature have argued about whether Karenga refers to writing by committee, writing out of a collective and consensual consciousness, or whether he meant that Afro-American writing intended to speak always for the group. He could very well have been describing the political and historical impossibility of any member of a group—that is finally more a social construction than any other essentialist gathering of folk—speaking with an individual voice *and being heard by the dominant group as a single voice.*

That the interpretation of these texts cannot be cleanly separated from a consideration of their production explains the importance that critics of Afro-American literature attach to discussions of tradition. Reference to tradition nods in the direction of textual production—even for those critics more interested in the formal qualities of the texts—and contextualizes a project of close readings. Despite the increasing attention given to Afro-American writing from the dominant culture, despite even the project, currently undertaken by Henry Louis Gates, Jr., of creating a Norton anthology of Afro-American literature, the concept of Afro-American belles lettres remains unlikely. It remains unlikely because of the political relationship of Afro-American writers and their books to the dominant culture, and because the collection of texts, regardless of how the Afro-American tradition is explained, includes so many important works whose primary purpose could never be described as simply engaging aesthetic attention. All of this is old news to Gates: more important is making available representative texts and the literary history that will go into the headnotes of Gates's anthology, which may help to assure that the ignorance of the dominant culture need not continue to pressure critics of Afro-American literature into simplifying complex issues.

Given the vexed nature of the issues at stake in any act of Afro-American criticism, what are the additional stakes inherent in the fact that more women critics of Afro-American literature are currently writing and being read both within and outside Afro-American literary discourse? If we are to consider, as Gates, Alain Locke, Houston Baker, among others, have stated, that the Harlem or New Negro Renaissance marks the first moment of explicitly articulated Afro-American concern with critical activity, then the scarcity of women's representation in Afro-American metacommentary is at least sixty years old.[2] Those women who wrote criticism were marginalized by the men who dominated the discourse and who argued almost exclusively with each other. And so it has remained. Women, especially Afro-American women, have criticized Afro-American texts for decades—the table of contents pages of *CLA, Black World, The Crisis, Black American Literature Forum, Callaloo,* and others tells us so—but until the past few years, women critics have not been as visible, nor has their writing been considered as important as it is now. The presence at this time of Hortense Spillers, Mary Helen Washington, Gloria Hull, Hazel Carby, Valerie Smith, Deborah McDowell, Barbara Christian, and others, has meant that "tradition" is being critiqued along gender lines to correct previous assumptions. Moreover, their presence complicates a tradition that is also currently being defined by the male critics of Afro-American literature with high public profiles: Gates, Baker, Robert Stepto, and William Andrews, among others (Hull 7–8).

The conflicted nature of the relationship between the discourse of a marginalized literature and that of the dominant culture, and the complex interstices between the means of textual production and textual interpretation form the context for two recent books by women critics of Afro-American literature.[3] One takes up only Afro-American women writers, while the other focuses on the writing of both genders within the field. The studies converge on problems of tradition, production, and interpretation, and for these critics—as for others who write in the Afro-American discourse—there is the ever-present pressure to make the arguments within the terms set equally by a specialized group (other such critics) and by the dominant culture.

2

Speaking to a "tradition" of Afro-American writing is a task fraught with difficulties. Addressing the text, and the means of its production, including both the political realities of its time (with all the advantages of hindsight) for the group and the writer, makes a work such as Hazel Carby's immensely valuable. In making her project the historicizing of a group of texts and their writers, the complexities of tradition as a process are maintained and examined more fully.

Carby's undertaking, *Reconstructing Womanhood: The Emergence of the Afro-American Woman Novelist,* engages the very specific situations of Afro-American women writers working from the middle of the nineteenth century to the early part of the twentieth at the nexus of history, politics, and social relationships between white and black Americans and among black Americans.[4] Her work would be useful if for no other reason than its introduction, which sets out the magnitude of Carby's tasks: a cogent "rethinking of black feminist criticism and theory." The introduction lays bare the shortcomings of black feminist theory to date and juxtaposes that discourse against Anglo-American feminist theory in order to illuminate both bodies of thought. Carby proposes that this study (a) will trace the ideologies of womanhood as "they were adopted, adapted, and transformed to effectively represent the material conditions of black women" and (b) will examine the ways in which "black women intellectuals reconstructed the sexual ideologies of the nineteenth century to produce an alternative discourse of black womanhood"; (c) will question "contemporary feminist historiography and literary criticism which seek to establish the existence of an American sisterhood between black and white women"; (d) will reconstitute the late nineteenth and early twentieth centuries as epochs of political contributions from black women; (e) and will provide "a literary history of the emergence of black women as novelists" (6–7). Carby focuses on specific confrontations with general history on the part of specific black women writers and intellectuals as a way both to excavate the buried past of those writers and to establish paradigms for gender-determined political interventions into the literary and political discourses of the time.

Reconstructing Womanhood includes a thorough account of the projects of Frances E. W. Harper and Pauline Hopkins and how they embodied the tensions inherent in the presence of black women in the landscape of American racism and their relationship to the ideology of "womanhood." As part of the frame for her close readings and her study of the means of production of texts, Carby describes the complex relationship between slave and mistress. And she measures the achievement of black women writers on the basis of their co-optation of the conventions of the sentimental novel in regard to their own politically corrective projects.

Across the terrain of historians (male and female, black and white), Carby's first two chapters engage both the history of the period and the relationship of that history to the texts. Her knowledge of the lines of argument from John Blassingame, who chartered the "dialectical existence of two male slave stereotypes" but who ignored the "complex and contradictory nature of figurations of the black woman as slave," to Catherine Clinton's reconstruction of the function of the Southern planters' patriarchal control over all reproduction and its effect on *all* women, is a solid grounding for the ways in which that control and its restrictions became the battlefield for the specificity of Harper and Hopkins's projects. It is, however, her discussion of the shift from slave narrative to fiction as it is embodied in Harper's *Iola Leroy* that surveys the changing and unchanging terrain of slavery and the postslavery period in a manner that the tradition of black women writers will follow. For Carby, the migration of a particular woman, and the places in which that woman's journey brings her into contact with the governing constraints of the dominant group, stands in for the migration of the entire group.

This study explores, additionally and most pertinently, the relationship of black women's texts and white women's texts along the lines of feminist theory and genre. In these terms, *Iola Leroy* is discussed as both part of and a departure from the conventions of the nineteenth-century woman's novel. Furthermore, the text's marginalization by male Afro-American scholars—as early as Sterling Brown's dismissal of it as derivative of William Wells Brown's *Clotel*—is deconstructed and presented in a necessary prehistory for an informed reading of this text, and, by extension, other texts by black women of the same period.

Carby's argument about the mulatto/a as a racial construction opens up narrative possibilities in far more complex terms than have been discussed previously in black literary history. She sees the mulatto as simultaneously exploring and explaining the relationship between the races: "The figure of the mulatto should be understood and analyzed as a narrative device of mediation. . . . In relation to the plot, the mulatta figure allowed for movement between two worlds, white and black, and acted as a literary displacement of the actual increasing separation of the races" (89–90). Barbara Christian's dismissal of the mulatta as a mere marker of appeal to whites, Carby argues, is predicated on the assumption that "social conventions totally determine the creation and use of literary conventions" (89). That is to say, such a misunderstanding of the narrative use of the mulatta reinforces the notion that black texts are "transparent" (Gates, "Criticism" 6).

This study also restores, in all of their complexity, the canonical place of texts by Pauline Hopkins and Nella Larsen. But it more than sets the tone for a reevaluation of two individual writers; her discussion enriches our understanding of the writing of black women as political engagement—especially as it lays out the ways in which such fiction challenges the use of racial ideology as a cover for the domestic economy of imperialism.

65

Carby ends by showing the constraints on Nella Larsen's participation in the Harlem Renaissance. In Larsen's novels "sexual politics tore apart the very fabric of the romance form" (168). Her attention to Larsen's novels entails a more close reading than is apparent anywhere else in this book. This close reading is based on a critique of the black social constructions of the Harlem Renaissance and reveals the intragroup tensions, contradictions, and internalizations of the dominant group's social constructions—the interstices between race and the aesthetics of sexuality.

3

Valerie Smith's work, on the other hand, is engaged in another kind of historical project but one which also considers the idea of an Afro-American tradition. Her introduction sees the tradition as a dynamic process, one that takes into some account the means of production, but of primary importance to Smith is textual production as the way tradition begins: the result of individual writers of a marginalized group co-opting or subverting a particular technology in order to realize themselves imaginatively and then acting in the world on the basis of the strength of that imagination-borne autonomy.

Her study, *Self-Discovery and Authority in Afro-American Narrative,* sets itself the task of exploring, through individual writers' encounters with their specific histories, the function of the idea of literacy within the Afro-American tradition. Smith makes clear that her definition of literacy follows the work of Robert Patterson and its insistence on a cognitive dynamic more than a specific activity. Her construction of the relationship of literacy and narrative focuses on the intentionality of Afro-American narrative: "fictionalizing one's life . . . bestows a quality of authenticity on it" and "plot construction, characterization, and designation of beginnings and endings" provide a measure of authority (2). Through the process of authorship, narrators earn authority.

The tradition that Smith discusses is how particular texts are borne out of a humanistic determination to attest to one's place in the world and how certain strategies make that determination possible. She asserts an argument for writers of both genders, and her book focuses on texts by both men and women, but she also argues that the result of the use of writing technology is, to some extent, overdetermined by gender. For Smith, writers are craftspeople functioning autonomously. She begins with the early writers as self-conscious participants in an individually motivated collectivity to which they commit themselves, but she also represents their individuality as politically purposeful; these writers are writing themselves as individuals into power both out of their realization of their group's condition and as a means to change that condition.

Her analysis is most useful in her chapter on slave narratives. Her reading of Olaudah Equiano's text, for example, focuses on his use of voice variations to register varying degrees of self-consciousness as well as to engage in shifting but always subversive critiques of the ideology of Christianity. She juxtaposes his more distanced critique of Christianity with Frederick Douglass's direct confrontation and denunciation of the ideology, and draws the line of difference between their more solitary *bildungs* and Harriet Jacobs's narrative. She states that Jacobs's text is a critique based on the self in relation to others and argues convincingly that this difference is one that gender inflects.

The last half of the book focuses on later texts and their relationship to the idea of history—both personal and group history. She moves ahead to James Weldon Johnson's *Autobiography of an Ex-Coloured Man* and reads that novel as a possible mediation of an alternative to Johnson's own life. She considers Richard Wright's fiction along the same axis, but departs from a consideration of actual autobiography to theoretical autobiography for Ralph Ellison's *Invisible Man.* Both texts foreground the larger history of Afro-Americans. By the final chapter of her work, which focuses on Toni Morrison, Smith has more directly invoked the idea of history as the ground on which she builds her reading of Morrison's *The Bluest Eye, Sula,* and *Song of Solomon.* The tie to the idea of autobiography as the paradigm for Afro-American narrative is her reading of the text as an implied autobiography of Milkman Dead. She argues that the narrative process is the means of self-knowledge, and her thematic analysis of the context of the Morrison texts is a chronicle of the construction of a self in relation to a community. Here, at the end of her text, Smith's concept of the self-empowering function of authorship is strongest.

The force of Smith's confession that her book "lacks the analysis of broad historical and political forces" is most evident in the structure of her study: she places her readings of the Equiano, Douglass, and Jacobs slave accounts in genre context, but she constructs, in her readings of later fictional narratives, biographical models for her close readings. Fascinating as these are, they limit the usefulness of her study as literary history. The implicit problem of her theory is the limitation of the idea of autobiography as the organizing principle for Afro-American narrative, and it is autobiography more than the idea of literacy that eventually takes over as the organizing principle for her close readings.

In her Morrison chapter, however, her analysis is least linked to a formal or structural exegesis, a type of exegesis that she had suggested in her introduction as a way of reclaiming the Afro-American narratives from the false "transparency" assigned to them by reading such texts as one-way mirrors on history or biography (7). Substituting for the biography or history of Morrison is the biography of the character Milkman Dead. On the other hand, Smith's reading of Milkman Dead's increasingly complex narration of himself extends the possibilities of theorizing about autobiography as a way of opening up the language of the fictional text. And, finally, her reading of Morrison also argues that consideration of the continuum of an author's work is necessary. For Smith then, texts exist as objects of interpretation with the use of authorial biography as a way to address the means of the text's production, although this connection is not explicitly stated. Her work is nonetheless useful in other inadequately addressed areas of concern for the scholar and teacher of Afro-American narrative: the need to understand the relationship of such narratives to the dominant parameters of genre and the necessity for historically informed and interesting close readings.

The pressures against which critics of Afro-American literature find themselves working, however, are much apparent in the weakness of Smith's study. Her title, *Self-Discovery and Authority in Afro-American Narrative,* forces her to deliver too big a paradigm: a theory to account for the possibilities of something as big, potentially, as the whole of Afro-American narrative. Moving from Equiano to Morrison means covering too much ground, and in the space of fewer than 200 pages, that presentation, inevitably, ends up a totalizing argument. While Smith's explanations for the uses of literacy—especially the differences gender makes—are compelling, the attempt to account for "Afro-American narrative" manifests yet again the impulse to say everything to the large, less informed mainstream audience.

The close reading of slave narratives juxtaposed against the parameters of historically specific genres is a strength that Carby's work shares. But Carby's strength—historical specificity and its part in the appropriating and exploiting of genre convention—is not put to use in her brief, decidedly truncated discussion of Zora Neale Hurston. She addresses Hurston in this study's concluding paragraph and in a matter almost peripheral to her own particular endeavor, but one with extended ramifications for the larger study of Afro-American textual production and cultural studies, and the overlap between such studies and textual interpretation. In her last paragraph, Carby refers to a pattern "established from Alice Walker back through Zora Neale Hurston which represents the rural folk as bearers of Afro-American history and preservers of Afro-American culture," a pattern that has "marginalized the fictional urban confrontations of race, class, and sexuality . . ." (175).

While Hurston has been described and at times has described herself as writing from an impulse to *represent* the rural folk as a source of Afro-American history and culture, neither her self-representation nor her representation by critics amounts to a privileging that marginalized other writers of the "urban" Afro-American scene. Hurston never presented the folk as an ideal or utopian monolith; her work with the folk accentuated the ongoing dynamic of folk life, the folk's dialectical relationship to the constraints of their existence. And she did this work at a time when the pressure for the presentation of the urban scene, as well as the discomfort felt by most of the male writers and critics with female sexuality, was farther marginalizing an already politically, economically, and educationally marginalized subset of Afro-American culture.

While the lack of attention to the prose of Ann Petry, Dorothy West, and Gwendolyn Brooks is a fact, it is not the result of privileging Hurston or Walker as ruralists. Petry, Brooks (as prose writer), and West's reception by the literary gatekeepers of their historical and textual moments is itself a confluence of several issues, including gender and the backlash against naturalism and social realism. That is not something that can be blamed on Hurston; even at the time that they were being ignored, so was she.

Furthermore, the steadily increasing interest in Morrison indicates that at least one of the urbanists is holding her own.[5] It is important to remember also that while *feminist* use of Alice Walker's texts and Zora Neale Hurston's texts has increased general awareness of those two writers certainly, and while that use has generated a narrow canon of "feminist Afro-American writers" in *some* places, in other places other feminists have also involved themselves in the study of Morrison, Bambara, and other Afro-American women writers of the urban, including the less-read Brooks, Petry, and West, among others. It is

important to remember that the teaching of Afro-American
literature goes on also in the historically black college circuit,
with attention to a more representative number of texts. As an
undergraduate at Howard University, I read and was taught (by
Arthur Davis) all of the writers about whom Carby writes.

Much of the recent work on Hurston has tried to offset her
marginalization by writers and critics, preeminently Richard
Wright, who saw her as mired in a Southern, rural, black minstrelsy precisely because her work suggested that poor, Southern
blacks could also participate in Afro-American culture and that
their participation was being overlooked, buried under another
(and I think equally important) political and artistic imperative
that was privileged in that time: the importance of focusing
attention on the presentation of those who had migrated from
the South to the North and the Midwest, the newly urban black
proletariat and middle class. W. E. B. Du Bois, Alain Locke,
Langston Hughes, and George Schuyler, among other intellectuals and critics, were busily fighting over which *urban* black
group was to be considered the carriers of black culture. Furthermore, Hurston, as W. Lawrence Hogue argues in *Discourse
and the Other: The Production of the Afro-American Text* (26-
29), was marginalized by the dominance of naturalism as the
preferred mode of fictional narrative, a dominance established
by the literary standard-bearers of the time. Hurston was marginalized additionally because of her insistence on recreating
and representing black southern dialect and folklore within her
work. Hurston's focus on that language and folklore flew in the
face of the prevailing wisdom. By the time she published *Their
Eyes Were Watching God,* James Weldon Johnson had already
delimited the use of dialect; at the same time, both politically
conservative and Marxist critics were condemning the use of
folklore materials as opportunistic and regressive—politically
incorrect. For those critics the representation of folklore was a
recourse to exploitation of the most oppressed segment of the
black American group. Implicit and often explicit in their condemnation was an admission that there was nothing in black
southern culture worth representing and that the people of that
group existed only as objects of the most abject oppression.
June Jordan challenged that perception of Hurston in her article
"On Richard Wright and Zora Neale Hurston" in *Black World*
in 1974, and others have challenged it since, including Gates
in *The Signifying Monkey.*

I address this issue at such length because to refer to Hurston's work as a "romantic evocation of the rural and the folk"
(Carby 175) leaves out a necessary historicizing of Hurston and

her deliberate interventionary project, the historicizing that Carby does so ably for Harper, Hopkins, and Larsen. It is not necessary that Carby do that work for Hurston; but it is important that she not reduce Hurston in a nonhistoricized way. To refer to Hurston as Carby does is to recreate an unhelpful dichotomy between those writers who explore the political possibilities in representations of urban Afro-America and those who explore the same possibilities in rural Afro-America.

The problem that Carby has with Hurston might well come from that pressure that I describe at the beginning of this essay. And that is the pressure to account for everything. Carby cannot account for all of the elements of whatever might be the tradition of Afro-American novelists; she does not even have to account entirely for "the emergence of the Afro-American woman novelist"—and she does not. She performs a more useful service. She accounts for the textual production, the political problematic of race and gender in an age previously thought of, as she puts it, as the age of great black men. She uncovers the overlapping areas of textual production, political intervention, and interpretation of texts written by specific writers within a specific frame of time. It is finally the kind of project that offers itself as resistance against the pressure on critics of Afro-American literature to deliver everything each time one of us speaks.

Notes

1. Here I follow the language that Henry Louis Gates, Jr., uses to describe scholars working with Afro-American texts (*Figures in Black* 43). Saying "critics of Afro-American literature" or Afro-Americanists makes it clear that I do not intend to racialize individuals who work with texts written by Afro-American writers. When it is necessary for me to refer to a certain subset of the category of critics of Afro-American literature, I say so directly, e.g., "Black critics of nineteenth-century Afro-American literature. . . ."

2. One can read this in the pages of Alain Locke's *New Negro,* and in James Weldon Johnson's *The Book of American Negro Poetry,* where he asserts: "No people that has produced great literature has ever been looked upon by the world as distinctly inferior" (vii). One need only think about the Irish to know how wrong Johnson was in recommending the production of "great" literature as the way out of a political, economic, and military disempowerment.

3. No doubt the increased availability of Afro-American women's texts as well as the participation of Afro-American women in feminist organizing, practice, and theorizing has something to do with the increased visibility of women Afro-American scholars, but throughout the nineteenth century Afro-American women were represented in those kinds of activities; in fact,

some of the Afro-American women writers we read now were part of nineteenth-century feminist discourse. One could argue that women critics of Afro-American literature are more visible because they have done much of the work of making Afro-American women writers available. Whatever the origins of their recent visibility, the means of production of Afro-American women critics, it seems to me, is at least as complicated as the means of production of Afro-American women writers and a study of the intricacies of the emergence of the Afro-American woman critic may be a timely project.

4. Carby's text uses "black" to refer to Afro-Americans and in my discussion of her work I follow her usage.

5. The body of Morrison criticism now includes one book (recently released, Holloway's—to my knowledge the first book devoted entirely to an Afro-American woman prose writer that is not simply a collection of essays), a book of essays forthcoming from Cambridge UP, dissertations (written in the United States and abroad), chapters in major books of Afro-American criticism, and numerous articles.

Works Cited

Baker, Houston. *Blues, Ideology and Afro-American Literature: A Vernacular Theory*. Chicago: U of Chicago P, 1984.

Copeland, Rita. "Academic Discourses and Literary Production: Defining the Genres." New Chaucer Society. Vancouver, 11 Aug. 1988.

Ellison, Ralph. *Invisible Man*. New York: Random House, 1972.

Fanon, Frantz. *The Wretched of the Earth*. New York: Grove, 1968.

Gates, Henry Louis, Jr. "Criticism in the Jungle." *Black Literature and Literary Theory*. New York: Methuen, 1984.

———. *Figures in Black: Words, Signs and the "Racial" Self*. New York: Oxford UP, 1987.

———. *The Signifying Monkey: A Theory of Afro-American Literary Criticism*. New York: Oxford UP, 1988.

Hogue, W. Lawrence. *Discourse and the Other: The Production of the Afro-American Text*. Durham: Duke UP, 1986.

Holloway, Karla, and Stephanie Demetrakopoulos. *New Dimensions of Spirituality: A Biracial and Bicultural Reading of the Novels of Toni Morrison*. New York: Greenwood P, 1987.

Hughes, Langston. "The Negro Artist and the Racial Mountain." *The Nation* CXXII (June 1926): 692.

Hull, Gloria. *Color, Sex, and Poetry: Three Women Writers of the Harlem Renaissance*. Bloomington: Indiana UP, 1984.

Johnson, James Weldon. *The Book of American Negro Poetry*. New York: Harcourt, 1922.

Jordan, June. "On Richard Wright and Zora Neale Hurston." *Black World* 24 (Aug. 1974): 4–8.

Karenga, Ron. "Black Cultural Nationalism." *The Black Aesthetic.* Ed. Addison Gayle. New York: Doubleday, 1971.

Locke, Alain. *The New Negro.* New York: Atheneum, 1977.

Nellie McKay

Black Theater and Drama in the 1920s: Years of Growing Pains

Drama more than any other art form except the novel embodies the whole spiritual life of a people; their aspirations and manners, their ideas and ideals, their fantasies and philosophies, the music and dignity of their speech—in a word, their essential character, and it carries this likeness of a people down the centuries for the enlightenment of remote times and races.[1]

Our ideal is a national Negro Theater where the Negro playwright, musician, actor, dancer, and artist in concert shall fashion a drama that will merit the respect and admiration of America. Such an institution must come from the Negro himself, as he alone can truly express the soul of his people . . . in . . . the rich veins of folk-tradition of the past and the portrayal of the authentic life of the Negro masses of today.[2]

THESE STATEMENTS, THE FIRST by Theophilus Lewis, and the, second by Montgomery Gregory, both made in 1926, underline the importance that Afro-Americans place on the role of drama in the development of culture, and the predominant attitudes of black critics of the form in the 1920s. In a heritage that spans centuries, from Africa through the Middle Passage, and permeating the diaspora—from the slave community to the rituals of contemporary religious ceremonies—drama has been at the center of day-to-day black activities, meeting the demands of black spiritual life in the face of multiple oppressions.

---

[1]Theophilus Lewis, "Survey of the Negro Theater—III," *The Messenger*, Vol. VIII, no. 10 (October 1926), p. 302.

[2]Montgomery Gregory, "The Drama of Negro Life," *The New Negro, An Interpretation*, ed. Alain Locke (New York: Albert and Charles Boni, 1925), p. 159.

615

Little wonder, then, that literary and cultural historians, as well as critics of black theater and drama unanimously bemoan the poverty of Afro-American formal theater and drama in the first two decades of the twentieth century. Black intellectuals, conscious of the need to strengthen all areas of cultural influences, tried hard but failed to bring a vibrant black theater to birth, and to make that theater a significant part of the history of the Harlem Renaissance. Serious, authentic black theater that attracted public attention did not emerge from the Afro-American community until the 1930s and 1940s with such playwrights as Owen Dodson and Langston Hughes. With the benefit of hindsight, we can point to some of the reasons for the slow progress of black dramaturgical/theatrical development in comparison to other branches of the arts. One was the fact that theater and drama required the collaboration of many people; another, the persistence of negative racial stereotypes of black people; and a third, the economics of theater production. At the same time, concerned critics did their bit to overcome these obstacles by vigorously proposing active directions in which black theater and drama could develop. This essay examines ideas that three such critics expressed between 1926 and 1927: W. E. B. DuBois, editor of the *Crisis;* Alain Locke, another central figure of the Harlem Renaissance; and Theophilus Lewis, drama critic of *The Messenger.* It concludes with a brief look at some achievements of the period. In the case of DuBois, in particular, his views on all areas of Afro-American art evolved through earlier uncertainties to a fixed and stable position by 1925.

Among others, historian/critic Nathan Huggins has noted that while there was no black tradition of theater in America at the turn of the century, for almost a hundred years prior, Afro-Americans "had a very substantial [if distorted and grotesque] place in the American theatrical tradition."[3] Put another way, Clinton Oliver wrote that the black American "was in American theater long before he was a genuine part of it."[4] "Black" characters—as stereotypes that were the butt of white ridicule—appeared on the American stage as early as 1769, while, for more than half a century, white-originated black minstrelsy was the most popular form of

[3]Nathan Huggins, *Harlem Renaissance* (New York: Oxford University Press, 1971), p. 286.

[4]Clinton Oliver and Stephanie Sills, eds. *Contemporary Black Drama from* A Raisin in the Sun *to* No Place to Be Somebody (New York: Scribner's Sons, 1971), p. 4.

616

mass entertainment in the country. The black character (on and off stage), defined in the white American mind by minstrelsy—lazy, comic, pathetic, childlike, idiotic, etc.—embodied an image that was disastrous to the advancement of serious black theater, and one not easily reversed. For openers, although there were nineteenth century Afro-American entertainers who repudiated it, many blacks, at all levels in turn-of-the-century theater, continued to accommodate themselves to minstrelsy because it was lucrative. Those like Bob Cole tried to alter that form through various creative innovations, including shows that were organized, written, produced and managed by blacks. By adding African themes to the form in 1902, the Williams and Walker show, *Dahomey*, achieved another step away from the stock qualities of minstrelsy. The black musical comedy reached its highest watermark in 1921 with *Shuffle Along*, also written, produced, and performed by blacks, and initially opening to black audiences in Washington, D.C. and Philadelphia before its smashing success on Broadway. One of the great ironies of the minstrel tradition is the manner in which contemporary black playwrights have transformed the "old form into a vehicle for anger and satire" in such plays as Douglas Turner Ward's *Day of Absence* and Ed Bullins' *Gentleman Caller*.[5]

A large part of the controversy that black intellectuals, dramatists and actors argued in the years leading up to and through the 1920s was connected to disagreements surrounding a definition of black theater, its cultural role and function, and the relationship between black playwrights, producers, actors, and black audiences. Loften Mitchell illustrated the dimensions of the first question in his essay, "Harlem Has Broadway on Its Mind," in which he indicated that more than a dozen major theater groups were formed there between 1910 and 1930. Some groups, like the Lafayette and Lincoln Players, wanted the freedom to perform plays unrelated to the black experience. Others, like DuBois' Krigwa Players and the Negro People's Theater, championed "dignified" plays of Negro life; and a number, like the Rose McClendon Players and the Pioneer Drama Group, wanted to illustrate that, given similar circumstances, blacks and whites reacted alike.[6] Such fundamental differences of opinion do not

[5] Oliver and Sills, p. 8.

[6] Loften Mitchell, "Harlem Has Broadway On Its Mind," *Theater Arts*, Vol. XXXVII (June 1953), pp. 68–69.

617

blur the evidence of ferment, and clearly indicate the interest that many Afro-Americans had in the establishment of "black" theater—however they perceived the nature of the productions they offered their audiences.

From its beginning in 1910, the *Crisis,* under DuBois's editorship, although deeply involved in the politics of race, made clear its support of the arts, including theater and drama. Its influence was large, appealing to a wide black readership with information not otherwise readily available to them. Beginning in 1910 with a circulation of 1,000 copies, by 1919 it reached a peak of 95,000. DuBois set the literary tone in his editorials and essays, blending stories, travel accounts, and character portraits into these different forms, and often using sarcasm, satire, and irony to make his point. In addition, he made the journal easily accessible by publishing works by new as well as already known writers. From 1925 through 1927 the *Crisis* ran annual literary and artistic competitions for first, second, and third place winners in five categories: stories, plays, poetry, essays and illustrations. In 1928, when the readership of the *Crisis* had declined substantially, the contests were discontinued, and instead small prizes were given for the best contributions of each month.

There is little question that the bias of the *Crisis* was toward race pride, and DuBois' attitudes were toward the primacy of the role and function of black art within the Afro-American community. In 1926 he made his now-famous declaration that "all Art is propaganda, and ever must be . . . for gaining the right of black folk to love and enjoy."[7] Not everyone agreed with DuBois, and the differences of opinions on art and propaganda became the legacy for intellectuals of every succeeding generation to debate. The issue for us may be a reconciliation with DuBois's definition of propaganda, and its relationship to Beauty, Truth, and Justice.

Not the least of DuBois' artistic concerns was the representation of Afro-Americans in drama. "As the renaissance of art comes among American Negroes" he wrote, "the theater calls for new birth."[8] He felt that, as minstrels, comedians, singers, etc., Afro-American performers had been trained to entertain white audiences, and black audiences had not demanded authentic black

[7]W. E. B. DuBois, "Criteria of Negro Art," *Crisis,* Vol. 32, no. 6 (October 1926), p. 296.
[8]DuBois, "Krigwa Players Little Negro Theater," *Crisis,* Vol. 32, no. 3 (July 1926), p. 134.

618

drama of them. Black actors would only do their "best" he noted, when that best was "evoked" by black people who wanted to see their own lives accurately depicted by their own writers and performers.

To this end, in 1926 he organized the first of the Krigwa Players Little Negro Theater groups, one-act black play groups that performed plays of black life in black schools and churches across the country. In the philosophy behind these groups we have his definition of black theater and drama:

> The plays of a real Negro theater must be: 1. *About us*. That is, they must have plots which reveal Negro life as it is. 2. *By us*. That is, they must be written by Negro authors who understand from birth and continual association just what it means to be a Negro today. 3. *For us*. That is, the theater must cater primarily to Negro audiences and be supported and sustained by their entertainment and approval. 4. *Near us*. The theater must be in a neighborbood near the mass of ordinary Negro people.[9]

DuBois saw the Krigwa groups as building blocks in the foundation of a folk-play movement in America. He pointed to the appropriateness for the Krigwa movement of many of the plays that surfaced in the literary contests sponsored by the *Crisis* and other agencies (underlining the cultural contribution that the *Crisis* made by initiating these competitions); and to the need for interested persons to identify dramatic talent. In New York, the Harlem branch of the New York Public Library offered one of its basement lecture rooms to the Krigwa Players, built a stage and dressing rooms for the actors, and supplied them with lighting equipment. The players furnished the props and secured their own audiences. Krigwa premiered with two tragedies (one a first prize winner in a *Crisis* competition) and a comedy (also a *Crisis* prizewinner). The players gave three performances, each to a full house of approximately 200 people, and they cleared "something over $240." DuBois concluded that the venture met with undisputed success, and proved the rightness of his program for an authentic Afro-American theater. A central issue here was a theater sufficiently inexpensive to permit its support by black audiences. He plunged ahead to encourage the organization of the second group in Washington, D.C.

The 1920s controversy among intellectuals and writers over the

---

[9]DuBois, "Krigwa Players Little Negro Theater," p. 134.

619

merits of propaganda as a function of art is clear in the separate position that DuBois and Alain Locke took on this issue. Still, both men were partly responsible for nurturing the flowering of Afro-American arts in that period. DuBois followed up his strong 1926 statement on black theater by implementing his theories with the Krigwa Players Little Negro Theater. Locke helped to establish a dramatic laboratory at Howard University in Washington, D.C. His position on black theater and drama is clear in his 1927 essay, "The Negro and the American Theater," originally published in *Theater: Essays on the Arts of the Theater,* edited by Edith J. R. Isaacs.[10]

Like DuBois, Locke called for new directions in the development of an Afro-American tradition in drama, but where the first gave scant information on the steps of the process, Locke unveiled a detailed agenda. Like DuBois, he felt that the "likeliest soil" for an American "dramatic renascence" as in the folk art of Afro-America, but he went farther to suggest the path "should lead back over the trail of the group tradition to an interest in things African. . . . [For] African life and themes," he said, "apart from any sentimental attachment, offer a wonderful field and province for dramatic treatment." In general, he thought, the white American stage was bereft of action, instinct and emotion, qualities that black performers would bring to black drama if it existed as "expression and artistic interpretation," outside of "propaganda," which he called the "drama of discussion and social analysis."

Like DuBois, Locke's blueprint for a new black drama wedded playwrights and actors to the roots of black culture and the black idiom. He challenged both groups to break with already established dramatic conventions, and to strike out on new experimental ground. Black drama had to "grow in its own soil and cultivate its own intrinsic elements; . . . [in order to] become truly organic, and cease being a rootless derivative." He identified the "art of the Negro actor" as "the free use of body and voice as instruments of feeling," and urged its liberation from old ways (e.g., minstrelsy and buffoonery) in the interests of vibrant artistic revelations. He envisioned the evolution of a truly "great" black drama in two stages. The first, he thought, should look to the folk play, which,

---

[10]Alain Locke, "The Negro in the American Theater," *The Black Aesthetic* (New York: Doubleday, 1971), pp. 263–71. The quotations from Locke that follow are from this essay.

620

realistically and imaginatively, was "drama of free expression and imaginative release . . . with no objective but to express beautifully and colorfully race folk life. . . . " He suggested that "more . . . poetic strain . . . more of the joy of life even when life flows tragically, . . . more of the emotional depth of pity and terror" would give it the vitality it needed. The technical model of this drama would become the foundations for serious black theater.

Locke's second stage in the development of a dramatic tradition was the point at which he broke with DuBois. While both men dismissed the musical comedies as buffoonery and pathos, Locke's disenchantment with Afro-American playwriting revolved around the social problem plays—with what he called their tendency toward "moralistic allegories or melodramatic protests as dramatic correctives and antidotes for race prejudice." Admitting that black dramatists had the advantage of "psychological intimacy" with their subject, he denied them the objectivity that "great art" requires in dealing with these issues, and decried their counter partisanship and propagandistic attitudes. The black playwright, he said, needed to "achieve mastery of a detached, artistic point of view, and reveal the inner stresses and dilemmas of these situations." In time, he hoped for a "race" drama that served as an imaginative channel of escape and spiritual release, and by some process of emotional re-enforcement to cover life with the illusion of happiness and spiritual freedom."

DuBois, who, as noted above, championed the folk-play as the starting point for authentic black drama, and who was also deeply concerned with the refinements of art, was not in accord with Locke's views on objectivity and emotional detachment in art. Among other things, his *Crisis* writings were, on one hand, propagandistic; on the other, often intimate and self-revelatory. In 1926 he wrote that Locke's new book, *The New Negro*,[11] articulated

> better than any book that has been published in the last ten years the present state of thought and culture among American Negroes and it expresses it so well and so adequately, with such ramification into all phases of thought and attitude, that it is a singularly satisfying and inspiring thing.[12]

---

[11] Locke, *The New Negro, An Interpretation* (New York: Albert and Charles Boni, 1925).

[12] DuBois, Review of Locke, *The New Negro, Crisis*, Vol. 31, no. 3 (January 1926), p. 140.

621

But he criticized Locke's position on art and propaganda, pointing out that the book, "filled and bursting with propaganda," proved Locke's thesis wrong. He noted that its propaganda was "for the most part beautifully and painstakingly done," and he (DuBois) doubted if "in any renaissance there can be a search for disembodied beauty which is not really a passionate effort to do something tangible, accompanied and illumed and made holy by the vision of eternal beauty." DuBois's now famous survey on the role and function of black art, "The Negro in Art, How Shall He Be Portrayed," which took place in the *Crisis* between February and October 1926, brought many reactions from white and black writers and critics, but did little to resolve a dilemma in which opinions were so firmly fixed.

Theophilus Lewis had an entirely different background from Harvard-educated DuBois and Locke, recognized men of great refinement, erudition and letters. In contrast to them, Lewis had little formal education, no claims to fame, and worked in the Post Office. However, even as a child he loved theater, and when he arrived in New York after the war he patronized the Harlem houses. His career as drama critic for *The Messenger* began unexpectedly when he submitted an essay on the subject to that journal and it was accepted (without remuneration). But A. Phillip Randolph, the editor, invited him to join the company of *The Messenger's* regular contributors, and he agreed.[13]

Unlike the *Crisis* and *Opportunity*, with which Locke was closely associated, in its early years (1917–23) the general editors of *The Messenger* had somewhat of a bias against "art." They published verse, but only if it served the social and economic ends of the journal.[14] However, between 1923 and 1928, when Lewis and George Schuyler took over many of the editorial prerogatives of the publication, socialist verse disappeared from its pages in favor of more artistic works by well-known litterateurs like Countee Cullen, Langston Hughes, and Georgia Johnson. From July 1923 to July 1927 Lewis contributed a regular monthly column under the title, "The Theater, The Souls of Black Folks" (echoing

[13] Theodore Kornweibel, Jr., "Theophilus Lewis and the Theater of the Harlem Renaissance," *The Harlem Renaissance Remembered*, ed. Arna Bontemps (New York: Dodd, Mead and Company, 1972), p. 171.

[14] Abby Arthur Johnson and Ronald Mayberry Johnson, *Propaganda and Aesthetics, The Literary Politics of Afro-American Magazines in the Twentieth Century* (Amherst: University of Massachusetts Press, 1979), p. 58.

622

DuBois's famous work although never showing any reverence for the older man). In so doing he was not only the first but the only regular black drama critic of that era. As others have noted, he did not simply review plays; like DuBois and Locke he also attempted to evolve an ideology for a national black theater.[15] Unlike them, he based his theories not only on philosophical concepts of a tradition in black drama, but also on analyses of close observations of what was occurring at the grassroots level of popular Harlem theater of the day.

In the 1926 July, September, and October issues of *The Messenger,* Lewis' columns analyzed current conditions of black theater and drama. His most precise definition of black theater did not come until his final "Theater" column in July 1927 in "Main Problems of the Negro Theater." His prescription for black theater and drama was less rigid than DuBois', but somewhat less flexible than Locke's:

> Negro drama, reduced to a simple statement, is . . . the body of plays written by Negro authors. The kind of life represented in the play is immaterial. The scene may be in Norway or Spain, and the characters presumably natives of one or the other country. Nevertheless it will be a Negro play if it is the product of a Negro mind. Hamlet is not a Danish play. . . . The Phaedra of Euripides is Greek, while the Phaedra of Racine is French. . . . A play is a work of art and . . . to maintain that Negro drama consists merely of plays about Negro life, regardless of who writes them, is to alter the accepted meaning of terms.[16]

DuBois, Locke and Lewis agreed that the responsibility for vital authentic black theater rested with dramatists, players and audiences, perhaps in different proportions, but with each group assuming weighty responsibilities. The stage, said Lewis, was the "vehicle for two important arts—drama and acting," and the black stage "should be a vital force in the spiritual life of the race," delighting and exalting the audience at the same time.[17] But while DuBois and Locke essentially attacked past traditions in which they saw contemporary Afro-American drama mired, and promoted visionary theories for change, Lewis first looked more

---

[15] Johnson and Johnson, p. 60; Kornweibel, Jr., p. 171.

[16] Lewis, "Main Problems of the Negro Theater," *The Messenger,* Vol. IX, no. 7 (July 1927), p. 229.

[17] Lewis, "Bird's Eye View of the Negro Theater," *The Messenger,* Vol. VIII, no. 7 (July 1926), p. 214.

closely at the reasons behind the failures of each element of the theater of his day. He examined the roles of dramatists, actors, and audience in the light of the economics of black theater in a way that neither Locke nor DuBois came close to doing. He realized that while the audience, through its financial support, influenced the type of theater that existed, that the dramatist gave it enduring features and actors made it what it was, there was an economic structure that pre-determined the outcome of the whole.

Lewis blamed the black middle class for three areas of negligence toward promoting authentic Afro-American theater. The first was for its non-support of existing black dramatic activities. While the group freely criticized black theater, it did not support possibilities for change through its presence or financial resources. As a result, the lesser educated audience kept black theater alive. Equally irresponsible was the middle-class lack of critical insight into the economic politics of theater. Theater took on the character of those who supported it, and in this case, since most black theater was economically controlled by whites interested only in profits, promoters catered to those who supported their ends by their presence, applause, and money. In addition, Lewis accused the middle class of ambivalence toward authentic black theater. Instead of promoting serious black drama, the educated classes often demanded a theater that imitated the white American stage. Such a demand, Lewis said, fostered artificiality and did nothing to create a tradition in Afro-American theater. At the same time, black actors and dramatists, anxious for work, often accommodated themselves to the travesty of the economic exploitation of their talents and were also responsible for contributing to the abysmal state of black theater. In the final analysis, it was the lower classes who kept black theater alive, assuring, on some level, an evolution of a tradition. Lewis warned that without economic autonomy the black theater would never become the "medium for the expression of the spirit of Negro people" that everyone wanted it to be.[18] In its failure to develop indigenous drama, said Lewis, black theater contributed nothing to the culture of the race, nor gave it anything to pass on as a gift to the general culture of humanity.[19]

His solution to the problems echoed DuBois and Locke. He called for a national theater and a repertory system that, isolated

---

[18]Lewis, "Survey of the Negro," *The Messenger*, Vol. VIII, no. 9 (September 1926), p. 279.
[19]Lewis, "Survey of the Negro Theater—III," p. 302.

624

from the white stage, addressed its appeal to colored audiences. In this theater dramatists would be at home creating race character, which he said was "the real meaning of Negro drama"; and actors would lift their audiences to a "beauty they were not previously conscious of . . . gradually creat[ing even in the lower classes] a demand for a higher standard of entertainment."[20] It is interesting to note that all three critics found most to be optimistic about in the craft of the performers, especially in the energy of their dancing and the rich ribaldry of their comedy.

Yet, in spite of the bleak picture of the state of the art that emerges from these reports, the situation was not as barren as they suggest. The promotion of all branches of literary endeavor by the *Crisis* and *Opportunity* yielded a number of one-act dramas, including many folk plays. Before the end of the decade, anthologies of drama on black life also appeared, including *Plays of Negro Life* (works not exclusively by black playwrights) edited by Alain Locke and Montgomery Gregory (1923), and *Plays and Pageants from the Life of the Negro,* edited by Willis Richardson (1930). At the University of North Carolina, the *Carolina Magazine* did a "Negro Play Number" with plays of black life in 1929. Notably too, several black women were prominent among the new dramatists of the time. Between 1918 and 1930 eleven black women published twenty-one plays between them, in comparison to no more than half-a-dozen men who saw their works in print during these years. However, this count does not include plays that were performed although never published. Most of those that ended up in print were one-act in length and suitable to the Little Theater Movement. Themes varied from conflicts of race, class, and gender (the latter in women's plays), to struggles for self within the black community, and comedy on black folk life.

Among the most interesting playwrights of this period of experimentation were Marita Bonner, Jean Toomer, and Willis Richardson. Richardson, who wrote more than twenty one-act dramas and several longer ones, mostly folk-plays, won first prizes in the Krigwa Players and the Amy Spingarn *Crisis* magazine contests, and was the first black dramatist whose work appeared on Broadway, with *The Chip Woman's Fortune* (1923). His 1935 anthology, *Negro History in Thirteen Plays* is the first such collection devoted exclusively to black playwrights. Richardson's plays

---

[20]Lewis, "Survey of the Negro Theater—III," p. 301.

were performed in New York, in Washington, D.C., and in St. Paul as well.

Both Marita Bonner and Jean Toomer also wrote folk-plays, but are most interesting to contemporary scholars because of their experimentations with expressionist drama. Bonner's *The Purple Flower* used symbol, dance, and rhythm, with characters who are representations of qualities of human nature—good and bad— that depict various people of color joining efforts to overthrow white supremacy. The drama is impressive both for its technical apparatus, which was then known only to a small number of American playwrights, as well as for its ideas. The play concludes with the characters of color resigned to the inevitability of a race war, ready to shed their blood for freedom and human dignity. Toomer wrote three expressionist plays, *Natalie Mann, The Sacred Factory*, and *The Gallonwerps. Natalie Mann* concentrates on the loss of black identity that occurs among middle-class Afro-Americans who imitate white European cultural habits. The other two plays, written after Toomer became involved with the mystic George Gurdjieff, address the sterility of the world at large from the perspective of the philosophy that informed the teachings of that man.

The 1920s were years of growing pains in the development of a tradition in Afro-American theater and drama. As it is often the case, the intellectuals and others who determine trends are often much more advanced in their vision than those who make them come true. By the 1920s there was a solid, urban, educated, sophisticated black middle class, and men like DuBois and Locke felt the responsibility to help to direct the group away from narrow self-interests and into directions that would raise the cultural aspirations of the black masses. Fiction, poetry, painting, music, and sculpture flourished as drama seemed not to, largely because, unlike other areas of the arts, it was not an individualistic venture, but one that required the involvement of many people for its success. The goals of the critics were ambitious: to overturn the almost century-old black public performance tradition as the majority of white and some black people had conceived it. This was the task that they set about to accomplish. If their successes were slow in coming, they were no less significant. It is heartening to know that first they turned to the black experience—to the folk-play, the spirit life of black people—for the model on which to lay the foundations of authentic Afro-American drama. This is a heritage of which we can well be proud.

626

Passing for What? Aspects of Identity in Nella Larsen's Novels

Cheryl A. Wall*

True, she was attractive, unusual, in an exotic, almost savage way, but she wasn't one of them.

—*Quicksand* (124)

". . . I was determined . . . to be a person and not a charity or a problem, or even a daughter of the indiscreet Ham. Then, too, I wanted things. I knew I wasn't bad-looking and that I could 'pass.' "

—*Passing* (56)

At the height of the Harlem Renaissance, Nella Larsen published two novels, *Quicksand* (1928) and *Passing* (1929). They were widely and favorably reviewed. Applauded by the critics, Larsen was heralded as a rising star in the black artistic firmament. In 1930 she became the first Afro-American woman to receive a Guggenheim Fellowship for Creative Writing. Her star then faded as quickly as it had risen, and by 1934 Nella Larsen had disappeared from Harlem and from literature.[1] The novels she left behind prove that at least some of her promise was realized. Among the best written of the time, her books comment incisively on issues of marginality and cultural dualism that engaged Larsen's contemporaries, such as Jean Toomer and Claude McKay, but the bourgeois ethos of her novels has unfortunately obscured the similarities. However, Larsen's most striking insights are into psychic dilemmas confronting certain black women. To dramatize these, Larsen draws characters who are, by virtue of their appearance, education, and social class, atypical in the extreme. Swiftly viewed, they resemble the tragic mulattoes of literary convention. On closer examination, they become the means through which the author demonstrates the psychological costs of racism and sexism.

For Larsen, the tragic mulatto was the only formulation historically available to portray educated middle-class black women in fiction.[2] But her protagonists subvert the convention consistently. They

*Cheryl Wall is a member of the English department at Rutgers, the State University of New Jersey. She has been a contributor to *American Women Writers*, *Notable American Women*, and *Phylon*.

are neither noble nor long-suffering; their plights are not used to symbolize the oppression of blacks, the irrationality of prejudice, or the absurdity of concepts of race generally. Larsen's deviations from these traditional strategies signal that her concerns lie elsewhere, but only in the past decade have critics begun to decode her major themes. Both *Quicksand* and *Passing* contemplate the inextricability of the racism and sexism which confront the black woman in her quest for a wholly integrated identity. As they navigate between racial and cultural polarities, Larsen's protagonists attempt to fashion a sense of self free of both suffocating restrictions of ladyhood and fantasies of the exotic female Other. They fail. The tragedy for these mulattoes is the impossibility of self-definition. Larsen's protagonists assume false identities that ensure social survival but result in psychological suicide. In one way or another, they all "pass." Passing for white, Larsen's novels remind us, is only one way this game is played.

Helga Crane, the protagonist of *Quicksand*, never considers racial passing, but she is keenly aware of playing a false role. Her inability to assume it comfortably leads her to ponder her "difference." As the novel opens, Helga is teaching at Naxos, a Southern black college where she is doomed to be an outsider, unable to conform or to be happy in her nonconformity. Initially, the self-righteous, stultifying atmosphere of the school seems to be at fault. Clearly modeled on Tuskegee Institute where Larsen herself was once employed, Naxos tolerates neither innovation nor individualism. Moreover, the institution, for all its rhetoric of race consciousness and race pride, seems intent on stamping out in its students those qualities which Helga characterizes as racial. On reflection, however, Helga realizes that her problems go deeper than conditions at Naxos. She understands that her battles with school authorities and snobbish co-workers are symptomatic of her personal struggle to define herself.

Helga recognizes that, superficially, her more sophisticated taste in clothing and furnishings sets her apart at Naxos and conditions the way in which others respond to her. For example, when she mentions resigning, a colleague urges her to stay because " 'we need a few decorations to brighten our sad lives' " (43). The dark-skinned young woman making this statement reveals not only a negative self-image, but the expectation that light-skinned "pretty" women like Helga should assume an ornamental role. Helga's interracial parentage—her father is black and her mother white—troubles her too, but it is not the primary cause of her unease. Her real struggle is against imposed definitions of blackness and womanhood. Her "difference" is ultimately her refusal to accept society's terms even in the face of her inability to define alternatives.

In the class-conscious community of Naxos, however, her heritage is a practical liability, and Helga is concerned lest it jeopardize her engagement to James Vayle, the son of prominent black Atlantans. Vayle, whose name evokes the "veil" of Du Bois's famous metaphor, lives shrouded by the narrow, petty ideas of the college; his only ambition is to rise within its ranks. He is as impatient with Helga's inability to win the acceptance of their peers as she is contemptuous of his self-satisfaction. She analyzes their relationship thus: "She was, she knew, in a queer indefinite way, a disturbing factor. She knew too that something held him, something against which he was powerless. The idea that she was in but one nameless way necessary to him filled her with a sensation amounting almost to shame. And yet his mute helplessness against that ancient appeal by which she held him pleased her and fed her vanity—gave her a feeling of power" (34). Here is an incipient realization that sexuality is political; it is "power." But Helga mistakenly assumes it is hers to wield. Actually she is trapped by the need to repress her sexuality, to assume the ornamental, acquiescent role of "lady," which not only Vayle but the entire Naxos community expects. Her reflection that "to relinquish James Vayle would most certainly be social suicide . . ." is followed by a scene in Helga's rather ornately furnished room in which "faintness closed about her like a vise" (35). Revealingly, the words which force Helga's actual departure are not spoken by Vayle, but by the "apparently humane and understanding" administrator, Robert Anderson, who argues that she is needed there because she is "a lady."[3]

The next important setting of the novel is Harlem, where, in happy contrast to Naxos, Helga Crane meets people who share her tastes and ideas. "Their sophisticated cynical talk, their elaborate parties, the unobtrusive correctness of their clothes and homes, all appealed to her craving for smartness, for enjoyment" (84-85). Better yet, they are extremely scornful of institutions like Naxos, and Helga feels her own actions have been vindicated. Even Robert Anderson has traded Naxos for New York. Then there is the "continuously gorgeous panorama of Harlem," which to Helga is so fascinating that she rarely finds occasion to venture to other areas of the city. In short, she feels a sense of freedom in Harlem, she is accepted there, and she chooses not to risk the rejection of the white world. Besides, she is convinced that Harlem offers a complete, self-contained life. "And she was satisfied, unenvious. For her this Harlem was enough" (87).

Of course, Larsen's point is that Harlem is not enough. Life there is "too cramped, too uncertain, too cruel" (163). Shallow and provincial, Helga's Harlemites are possessed of a race consciousness at once consuming and superficial, proud and ineffectual. They immerse themselves in the race problem, scanning newspapers to tabulate every injustice against the race, yet they keep their distance from the suffering masses. Indeed, though they proclaim their love of blackness, they imitate the values and ways of white folks down to the smallest detail. They dislike Afro-American songs and dances, the rhythms of black speech, and "like the despised people of the white race, . . . preferred Pavlova to Florence Mills, John McCormack to Taylor Gordon, Walter Hampden to Paul Robeson" (92). Floundering in this maze of contradictions, these New Negroes are unable to confront themselves and their situation honestly.

The peculiar demands of the Jazz Age further complicated matters for the Harlem bourgeoisie. As more and more white New Yorkers, like Americans generally, were drawn to black culture—or at least what they believed to be black culture—, the New Negroes felt compelled to increase their own identification with their traditions. Unfortunately, they were often as ignorant of these traditions as anyone else and embraced the popular imitations instead. Larsen uses a nightclub scene, an almost obligatory feature in Harlem novels, to examine the packaging of manufactured blackness:

> For the while, Helga was oblivious of the reek of flesh, smoke, and alcohol, oblivious of the oblivion of other gyrating pairs, oblivious of the color, the noise, and the grand distorted childishness of it all. She was drugged, lifted, sustained by the extraordinary music, blown out, ripped out, beaten out, by the joyous, wild, murky orchestra. The essence of life seemed bodily motion. And when suddenly the music died, she dragged herself back to the present with a conscious effort; and a shameful certainty that not only had she been in the jungle, but that she had enjoyed it, began to taunt her. She hardened her determination to get away. She wasn't, she told herself, a jungle creature. (107-08)

Of course Helga is correct about not being a jungle creature, but then neither are any of the club's other patrons. This image was nonetheless foisted on blacks as Harlem barrooms were refurbished to resemble African jungles, and as bands, even the best ones, like that of Duke Ellington, began advertising the latest in "jungle music." It all made Harlem a more exotic tourist attraction while it increased the confusion of some local residents. In Larsen's interpretation, the ersatz culture marketed to blacks as their own was clearly insufficient. It borrowed enough of the authentic traditions to retain some power, but it existed dysfunctionally in a vacuum. The reference to the "grand distorted childishness of it all" applies to the spectacle of these urbane, middle-class New Yorkers attempting to find their cultural roots in the basement of a Harlem speakeasy. For Helga, the artifice is repelling.[4]

Both Vayle and Anderson reappear in the Harlem sequences of the novel, thereby demonstrating that the expectations for women remain the same there. Helga's meeting with Vayle confirms the wisdom of her decision to reject him, social suicide being preferable to spiritual death. For his part, he wants to resume the engagement and tries to impress upon Helga her obligation as a member of the Talented Tenth to marry and have children. " 'Don't you see that if we—I mean people like us—don't have children, the others will still have. That's one of the things that's the matter with us. The race is sterile at the top' " (173). This is a responsibility Helga neither recognizes nor accepts, and she is happy to leave Vayle to Naxos. Robert Anderson is another matter, however. On seeing him again, she becomes aware of a strong and mutual sexual attraction. Taught too well to repress any sexual feelings, she denies them. Anderson's behavior is equally circumspect.

Larsen introduces a minor character named Audrey Denney to highlight the psychic cost of Helga's self-denial. Audrey is glamorous and bold, ignoring the outraged reactions her appearance and behavior elicit from respectable Harlemites like Anne Grey, the wealthy young widow with whom Helga lives. Most objectionable is her refusal to limit her socializing to Harlem; Audrey has white friends and possibly white lovers. However disreputable her character, she is the object of eager attention from black men as well. In the nightclub scene Robert Anderson joins her circle of admirers. When he does, Helga's envious approbation gives way to jealousy. Larsen concludes the scene with well-placed references to asphyxiation, as her heroine escapes the smoke-filled cabaret for the brisk night air.

Helga is emerging too from the restricting definitions of ladyhood so accepted in the middle-class black world. She does not consider chastity the supreme virtue the women at Naxos insist it to be, though she notes that, as "sophisticated" as Anne Grey is, she has preferred a passionless marriage. Helga is also aware of the energy black women waste trying to conform to a white standard of beauty. Straightened hair, she reflects, does not beautify, though as her own is naturally straight, she cannot voice this opinion. Ever conscious of clothes, she resents the prohibition of bright colors by those who want it understood that black women do not love red. She does. She further seeks the adventure that color usually symbolizes. That is what makes Audrey Denney so appealing to her. Audrey is unencumbered by the norms that define Negro ladies. Having white friends is the least of her daring. More to the point, Audrey has declined to play the husband-hunting game. She need not marry to find someone to pay for all those tasteful, elegant things with which real ladies surround themselves.

Eventually, Harlem becomes as oppressive an environment as Naxos. The constant, superficial race consciousness seems to demand that Helga deny a part of herself, and when a white uncle gives her five thousand dollars she uses his conscience money to escape to Copenhagen. Denmark promises "no Negroes, no problems, no prejudice" (103), though Helga is slightly wary of the reception she will receive from relatives there. Her fears prove unfounded, her well-to-do aunt and uncle welcome her warmly, but the kind reception is proffered with an eye to the role the young woman can play in advancing the couple's social fortunes. Immediately, they inform Helga that she should capitalize on her "difference." She should wear " 'striking things, exotic things' " (120) so she will make an impression. They are more than happy to supply the necessary wardrobe. Though she recognizes their motives and resents being a decoration, a curio with which her relatives hope to capture the notice of influential people, Helga enjoys, as always, the expensive clothes, the physical freedom, and the fact that her dark skin, so despised in America, makes her the source of endless fascination to the Danes. Forced to discover and parade her own beauty, she feels new confidence and self-acceptance.

Her satisfaction does not last. Not only does she tire of being continuously exhibited, but she finds that she is much more race conscious than she had realized. One telling incident occurs at a theater, where a minstrel act featuring two black Americans upsets her greatly. By turns moved and embarrassed by their "stage Negro" antics, she is infuriated by the audience's gleeful response to the performance. Without fully understanding why, she returns to the vaudeville house again and again. The reason is clear to the reader who sees the extent to which Helga has become a "stage Negro" herself. After this experience, her thoughts of America are filled with outrage at the way blacks are abused; in fact, she never thinks of the United States except in relation to race.

In Copenhagen, no one requires that Helga be a lady; instead she is made into an exotic female Other—symbol of the unconscious, the unknowable, the erotic, and the passive.[5] Although her aunt and uncle are among those who conspire to this end, by dressing her in batik dresses, leopard-skin coats, and glittering jewelry, it is Axel Olsen who most fervently wants to recreate her. Olsen is a fashionable portrait painter and an odd man, given to overwrought, theatrical gestures. It is he who demonstrates most sharply the confluence of racism and sexism, in both the way he paints Helga and the way he courts her. In their first meeting he examines the specimen before him and pronounces her " 'amazing' " and " 'marvelous' "; her smile becomes a "mask" as he announces his findings to his audience (125). Larsen borrows vocabulary from anthropology throughout the Copenhagen section, but never to greater effect than when Olsen is present. Helga's role, as she realizes, is to be exhibited, to "incite" a voluptuous impression in sedate Danish drawing rooms. Soon she finds herself enjoying "the fascinating business of being seen, gaped at, desired" (130). When she sees the resulting impression reproduced on Olsen's canvas, she disowns the image. "It wasn't, she contended, herself at all, but some disgusting sensual creature with her features" (152). Olsen is, of course, sure that he has captured the essential Helga; but although he has discerned the sensuality she had concealed in America, his portrait is not the mirror of Helga's soul he believes it to be. He has confused the image and the woman. He is so in love with her image that, after Helga ignores his insinuations that they have an affair, he proposes marriage. He is mystified by her refusal.

Critic Hortense Thornton has suggested that because Helga stresses their racial differences in her rejection of Olsen, perhaps "her acknowledgment of race is used as a mask for her sexual repression" (299). In my view, this scene more than any other shows how inextricably bound sexual and racial identity are. Olsen follows his marriage proposal with a frank admission that he would have preferred that she be his mistress. At that point she protests, " '. . . in my country the men, of my race at least, don't make such suggestions to decent girls' " (148). Olsen cannot hear her objection. He rants instead about her " 'deliberate lure,' " and declares that for him marrying her will be " 'an experience.' " And finally, he sums up her character:

> "You know, Helga, you are a contradiction. You have been, I suspect, corrupted by the good Fru Dahl, which is perhaps as well. Who knows? You have the warm impulsive nature of the women of Africa, but, my lovely, you have, I fear, the soul of a prostitute. You sell yourself to the highest buyer. I should of course be happy that it is I. And I am." (149)

Only the spell of racial mythology could lead a man to mistake such insults for gallantry. Olsen knows nothing of African women, but that does not shake his belief in their exotic primitivism. Black women, he feels, are completely sentient, sexual beings. Helga Crane should confirm that belief. When she does not, it proves she has been contaminated by the West, has suffered the primordial female corruption. Yet even so damaged, she is the closest approximation of the exotic female Other he is likely to find. He is willing to settle.

Olsen makes explicit the connection between prostitution and marriage Larsen had earlier implied in the scene with Audrey Denney and in Helga's musings about marriage as a means to acquire things. His words evoke a declaration of independence from Helga which is echoed in any number of current novels. " 'But you see, Herr Olsen, I'm not for sale. Not to you. Not to any white man. I don't care at all to be owned' " (150). Shortly after this confrontation, Helga leaves Denmark. Olsen's accusations linger, however, and influence her behavior upon her return to Harlem. Determined not to sell herself, she gives herself away.

Unwilling to repress her sexuality any longer, she misconstrues Robert Anderson's intentions when he drunkenly kisses her. She is ready to have an affair, but Anderson, now married to Anne Grey, declines. Helga's subsequent turmoil is marked by an increasing number of asphyxiation metaphors. Nella Larsen, like many women writers, found rooms to be appropriate symbols of female confinement and frustration.[6] She uses Helga's room in Naxos, a Chicago subway car, and a Harlem cabaret among other examples. With the narrowing of choices available to Helga, such references redouble and intensify. A Harlem church becomes, for example, a kind of transcendent women's room. In its heightened emotional atmosphere, the predominantly female congregation purges itself of discontent and despair. The church sisters attend Helga until she too achieves a temporary catharsis. As drawn by Larsen, this scene resembles that of the cabaret, except this time Helga has lost the ability to be critical. Despite some badly overwritten and patronizing description of the service, the scene as a whole is credible.

The calm that descends upon the restless Helga and the promise of serenity bulwarked by faith presents an alternative to the materially rich but spiritually impoverished life she has led in Harlem and Copenhagen; it seems to offer a resolution. This resolution, more accurately a retreat, is personified by the aptly named Reverend Pleasant Green, whom she hurriedly marries. In rural Alabama Rev. Green's female parishioners assume the role played by the women in the Harlem mission. But their ministrations cannot sustain her. Neither can the sexual release she finds in marriage. Reality is too harsh, and the confinement of the birthing room is inescapable. Her five children tie her permanently to a life she loathes.[7]

Helga has fought against the white world's definition of a Negro, knowing she is neither exotic nor primitive, neither "savage" nor sharecropper. At the same time she has resisted male definitions of her womanhood. Having no foundation on which to base one, Helga never achieves true self-definition. If her quest ends in defeat, her struggle is nonetheless admirable. Larsen's depiction of a memorable protagonist, her adept narration, and her skillful development of the central metaphor expressed by the novel's title have all won praise. Most critics agree that *Quicksand* is one of the best novels of the Harlem Renaissance.

Response to Larsen's second novel, *Passing*, has been less favorable. From one perspective, critics argue that *Passing* fails to exploit fully the drama of racial passing and declines instead into a treatment of sexual jealousy. If, from another perspective, the novel is the best treatment of its subject in Afro-American literature, then the topic of blacks passing for white is dated and trivial.[8] In Larsen's novel, however, "passing" does not refer only to the sociological phenomenon of blacks crossing the color line. It represents instead both the loss of racial identity and the denial of self required of women who conform to restrictive gender roles. Like "quicksand," "passing" is a metaphor of death and desperation, and both central metaphors are supported by images of asphyxiation, suffocation, and claustrophobia. Unlike "quicksand," "passing" provokes definite associations and expectations that Larsen is finally unable to transcend. Looking beyond these associations, one sees that *Passing* explores the same themes as its predecessor. Though less fully developed than Helga Crane, the main characters of this novel likewise demonstrate the price black women pay for their acquiescence and, ultimately, the high cost of rebellion.

Two characters, Irene Redfield and Clare Kendry, dominate the novel: Both are attractive, affluent, and able to "pass." Irene identifies with blacks, choosing to "pass" only for occasional convenience, while Clare has moved completely into the white world. Each assumes a role Helga Crane rejects: Irene is the perfect lady, and Clare, the exotic Other. A chance meeting in the tearoom of an exclusive Chicago hotel, on an occasion when both women are "passing," introduces the action of the novel. Clare recognizes the childhood friend she has not seen in twelve years, and she is eager to renew the acquaintance. Irene, assured and complacent in her life as the wife of a Harlem physician, is more cautious. Reluctantly, she accepts Clare's invitation to tea, where they are joined by another school friend, Gertrude, who is married to a white man, and by Clare's husband Jack Bellew. Bellew proves to be a rabid racist, and Irene vows never to see Clare again. Two years later, her resolve is shaken. While visiting New York, and partly in response to her husband's bigotry, Clare longs for the company of blacks. She presents herself at Irene's home uninvited and, over Irene's objections, makes increasingly frequent jaunts to Harlem. Distressed by the unsettling effect produced by Clare's presence, Irene begins to suspect that Clare is having an affair with Dr. Redfield. But before Irene can act on her suspicions, Bellew follows Clare to Harlem and confirms his. Clare Kendry falls through a sixth-story window to her death.

Although her death is typical of the tragic mulatto's fate, the Clare Kendry character breaks the mold in every other respect.[9] Her motives for "passing" are ambiguous. Though she seeks the freedom to define herself, she also wants the material comforts the white world offers. As she explains, " '. . . I was determined to get away, to be a person and not a charity or a problem, or even a daughter of the indiscreet Ham. Then, too, I wanted things. I knew I wasn't bad-looking and that I could "pass" ' " (56). The psychic rewards are few, but at first Clare is sure the money is worth its price. Bellew is an international banking agent, apparently as rich as Croesus, who indulges his wife's love of luxury. Clare can chat glibly of travels to pre-War Paris and post-War Budapest. She can also refer to herself as a " 'deserter,' " yet Irene looks in vain for traces of pain, fear, or grief on her countenance. Even when Clare begins to doubt the wisdom of her choice, she claims no noble purpose, merely loneliness and a vague yearning for " 'my own people.' " In fact, her trips to Harlem involve more pleasure-seeking than homecoming. At one point, she confesses to Irene: " 'Why, to get the things I want badly enough, I'd do anything, hurt anybody, throw anything away. Really, 'Rene, I'm not safe' " (139). In drawing such an unsympathetic character, Larsen seems initially merely to flout the tragic-mulatto convention.

Rather than emphasize the pathos of the "passing" situation, Larsen stresses its attractive veneer. Clare Kendry always looks exquisite, whether wearing a "superlatively simple cinammon-brown frock" with a "little golden bowl of a hat" or a stately black taffeta gown. Clothes, furnishings, notepaper—all the accoutrements of Clare's life are painstakingly described. At times Larsen's intentions seem definitely satirical, as when on one occasion Clare chooses a dress whose shade not only suits her but sets off her hotel room's decor! But at other points Larsen seems to solicit the reader's admiration for the graceful, elegant Clare.

Annis Pratt's analysis of patterns in women's fiction offers a tenable explanation for such inconsistency: "It is as if the branch of women's fiction that deals most specifically with society were incapable of either fully rejecting it or fully accommodating to it, the result being the disjunction of narrative structure, ambivalence of tone, and inconclusive characterizations typical of this category" (168). *Passing* displays all of these features with its abrupt and unearned ending, its often arch and stilted dialogue, and the author's wavering response to her characters. To be sure, Larsen's own social world was mirrored in her novel, and she evidently found it difficult to reject it out of hand. Nevertheless, what seems at first an annoying preoccupation with "minutiae" (to borrow Hoyt Fuller's apt term [18]) becomes instead a statement on the condition of women in the book.

Clare's survival depends literally on her abiltity to keep up appearances. She must look like the white society matron she pretends to be. But her looks, clothes, and facile conversation are the envy of the other female characters. They too spend an inordinate amount of time shopping and preening. In their lives, maintaining the social niceties is an obligation, and pouring tea is, in the words of one, " 'an occupation.' " Each of these characters, like Clare, relies on a husband for material possessions, security, identity. Each reflects and is a reflection of her husband's class status. Clare's is merely an extreme version of a situation all share.

An analysis of the Irene Redfield character supports this reading. The novel is told from her point of view, and she consistently calls attention to the differences between herself and Clare. More often than not, Nella Larsen minimizes these differences to great effect. For example, Irene craves stability and abhors the risks Clare thrives on; she is a devoted mother, whereas Clare professes little interest in the welfare of her daughter, and she prides herself on her loyalty to the race. However, Irene's world is barely more secure than that of her friend, and when it is threatened, she is every bit as dangerous. The parallels are established in the first encounter described above, when, because both are "passing," they are playing the same false role. Indeed it is Irene who fears detection; her alarmed, defensive reaction contrasts ironically with the cool demeanor assumed by Clare, whose only concern is recognizing an old friend. In the subsequent meeting with Bellew, Irene is horrified that Clare, whom he jokingly calls "Nig," tolerates her husband's bigotry; but Irene herself listens to his insults. She even imagines that "under other conditions" she could like the man. Her attempt to excuse her cowardice by claiming to have acted out of loyalty to race and to Clare as a member of the race is entirely specious. Although Irene does volunteer work for the "Negro Welfare League," the race is important to her only insofar as it gives the appearance of depth to a shallow life.

What Irene does value is her marriage, not out of any deep love for her husband Brian, but because it is her source of security and permanence. Much like Anne Grey's in *Quicksand*, the Redfields' marriage is passionless; the couple sleep in separate bedrooms, and Brian argues that the sooner their children learn that sex is " 'a grand joke,' " the better off they will be. The Redfields' life is one Irene has "arranged." She has dissuaded Brian from pursuing his dream of a new life in Brazil. She has spun a cocoon around her sons, forbidding discussion of racism and of sex as too disagreeable, and she plans someday to send the boys to European boarding schools (like the one Clare's daughter attends in Switzerland). Nothing is allowed to encroach upon the sanctuary of home and family.

When Clare enters this safe harbor, she upsets the order Irene cherishes. She visits unannounced, plays with the children, and chats with the servants. She poses other threats as well. Typically, Irene bolsters her self-image by defining herself in relation to her "inferiors": Her comments on women whose husbands are less successful than hers evidence this snobbery. When, for example, Gertrude expresses her anger at Bellew's racism—a deeper anger than Irene can muster—Irene dismisses her. After all, Gertrude looks like the butcher's wife she is; her feelings could not matter. Clare is too clearly Irene's equal, in many respects her superior, to be neutralized in this way. Compared to Clare, Irene feels at times "dowdy and commonplace" (128). Partly in self-defense and partly because Clare invites the role, Irene begins to view her friend as an exotic Other. Watching her, she has the sensation of "gazing into the eyes of some creature utterly strange and apart" (77). Then again, Clare's look was "unfathomable, utterly beyond any comprehension" of Irene's (85). Irene invents for Clare a complex inner life. But she is not responding to the person before her so much as to her own notions of Otherness. Clare's "Negro eyes" symbolize the unconscious, the unknowable, the erotic, and the passive. In other words, they symbolize those aspects of the psyche Irene denies within herself. Her confused sense of race becomes at last an evasion by which she avoids confronting her deepest feelings.

Clare's repeated assertions of her own dangerousness reinforce Irene's fears and allow her to objectify Clare completely. When her suspicions grow that Clare is interested in Brian, Clare becomes a menace she must eliminate; for without Brian, Irene believes she is nothing. Her opportunity comes during the confusion surrounding Bellew's unexpected appearance at a Harlem party. Although the evidence is all circumstantial, Larsen strongly implies that Irene pushes Clare through the window.[10] She is certainly capable of it, for by the end of the novel Irene is indeed Clare's double, willing to " 'do anything, hurt anybody, throw anything away' " to get what she wants. A psychological suicide, if not a murderer, she too has played the game of "passing" and lost.

Passing, like *Quicksand*, demonstrates Larsen's ability to explore the psychology of her characters. She exposes the sham that is middle-class security, especially for women whose total dependence is morally debilitating. The absence of meaningful work and community condemn them to the "walled prison" of their own thoughts. In this cramped enclosure, neurosis and fantasy breed. She exposes as well the fears and self-contempt experienced by those, like Helga, who seek to escape the constrictions of middle-class life. Helga is an admirable character because she recognizes early on that "passing" is not worth the price. Her integrity earns her no victory; her rebellion is as ineffectual as the dishonorable Clare's. As these characters deviate from the norm, they are defined—indeed too often define themselves—as Other. They thereby cede control of their lives. But, in truth, the worlds these characters inhabit offer them no possibility of autonomy or fulfillment.

Nathan Huggins has observed that of the Harlem Renaissance writers "Nella Larsen came as close as any to treating human motivation with complexity and sophistication. But she could not wrestle free of the mulatto condition that her main characters had been given" (236). I would argue that Larsen achieves a good measure of complexity and sophistication, yet Huggins' point has merit, especially in regard to *Passing*. Much more than *Quicksand*, this novel adheres to the pattern: the victim caught forever betwixt and between until she finds in death the only freedom she can know. The inevitable melodrama weakens the credibility of the narrative and diverts attention from the author's real concerns. Still, the plot reveals something of the predicament of the middle-class black woman, and the book itself illuminates problems facing the black woman novelist.

Among the images of black women presented in fiction before the Harlem Renaissance, the tragic mulatto character was the least degrading and the most attractive, which partly explains its prominence in Jessie Fauset's novels and in those of her predecessors, dating back to Harriet Wilson and Frances Watkins Harper. Nella Larsen's personal history doubtless increased the character's appeal for her, as the reality behind the image was her own story. Besides, depicting the tragic mulatto was the surest way for a black woman fiction writer to gain a hearing. It was also an effective mask. In a sense Nella Larsen chose to "pass" as a novelist; not surprisingly, readers who knew what they were seeing—that is, reading—missed the point.

Notes

[1]Biographical material may be found in my entry on Larsen in *American Women Writers*; in Adelaide Cromwell Hill's "Introduction" to *Quicksand*; and in Mary Helen Washington's "Nella Larsen: Mystery Woman of the Harlem Renaissance."

[2]For a full discussion of the tragic mulatto convention in novels by black women, see Barbara Christian's *Black Women Novelists* (35-61).

[3]Sexism as an issue in the novel was first explored at length by Hortense Thornton in "Sexism As Quagmire: Nella Larsen's *Quicksand*." My reading of the novel owes much to Thornton's essay.

[4]Nathan I. Huggins notes Larsen's rejection of black primitivism in his *Harlem Renaissance* (160-61). See also Addison Gayle's *The Way of the New World* (130-35).

[5]A classic statement on female Otherness is found in Simone de Beauvoir's *The Second Sex* (viii-xxix).

[6]See, for example, Annis Pratt's *Archetypal Patterns in Women's Fiction* (41-70), and Sandra Gilbert's and Susan Gubar's *The Madwoman in the Attic* (83-92).

[7]The novel illustrates the pattern in women's fiction whereby the confinement of pregnancy replicates the confinement of society for women (see Gilbert and Gubar 88).

[8]These conclusions reflect the views, respectively, of Amaritjit Singh in *The Novels of the Harlem Renaissance* (99), of Robert Bone in *The Negro Novel in America* (102), and of Hoyt Fuller in his "Introduction" to *Passing* (14).

[9]Most commentators have read *Passing* as a tragic-mulatto story, but two critics offer sharply different views. Mary Mabel Youmans argues in "Nella Larsen's *Passing*: A Study in Irony" that Irene is the one who actually "passes" because she gives up her racial heritage for middle-class security. And in "Nella Larsen's *Passing*: A Problem of Interpretation," Claudia Tate argues that *Passing* is an intriguing romance in which Irene Redfield is the heroine and the unreliable center of consciousness.

[10]Tate insists that the evidence is adequate to determine Irene's guilt or innocence (145).

Works Cited

Beauvoir, Simone de. *The Second Sex*. 1949. New York: Bantam, 1961.

Bone, Robert. *The Negro Novel in America*. Rev. ed. New Haven: Yale UP, 1965.

Christian, Barbara. *Black Women Novelists: The Development of a Tradition, 1892-1976*. Westport: Greenwood, 1980.

Fuller, Hoyt. "Introduction." *Passing*. By Nella Larsen. New York: Collier, 1971. 11-24.

Gayle, Addison, Jr. *The Way of the New World: The Black Novel in America*. New York: Anchor, 1975.

Gilbert, Sandra M., and Susan Gubar. *The Madwoman in the Attic: The Woman Writer and the Nineteenth-Century Literary Imagination*. New Haven: Yale UP, 1979.

Hill, Adelaide Cromwell. "Introduction." *Quicksand*. By Nella Larsen. New York: Collier, 1971. 9-17.

Huggins, Nathan I. *Harlem Renaissance*. New York: Oxford UP, 1971.

Larsen, Nella. *Passing*. 1929. New York: Collier, 1971.

———. *Quicksand*. 1928. New York: Collier, 1971.

Pratt, Annis. *Archetypal Patterns in Women's Fiction*. Bloomington: Indiana UP, 1981.

Singh, Amaritjit. *The Novels of the Harlem Renaissance: Twelve Black Writers, 1923-1933*. University Park: Pennsylvania State UP, 1976.

Tate, Claudia. "Nella Larsen's *Passing*: A Problem of Interpretation." *Black American Literature Forum* 14 (1980): 142-46.

Thornton, Hortense. "Sexism As Quagmire: Nella Larsen's *Quicksand*." *CLA Journal* 16 (1973): 285-301.

Wall, Cheryl. "Nella Larsen." *American Women Writers: A Critical Reference Guide from Colonial Times to the Present*. Ed. Lina Mainero. New York: Frederick Ungar, 1980. 2: 507-09.

Washington, Mary Helen. "Nella Larsen: Mystery Woman of the Harlem Renaissance." *MS*. Dec. 1980: 44-50.

Youmans, Mary Mabel. "Nella Larsen's *Passing*: A Study in Irony." *CLA Journal* 18 (1974): 235-41.

RACE AND GENDER IN THE SHAPING OF THE AMERICAN LITERARY CANON: A CASE STUDY FROM THE TWENTIES

PAUL LAUTER

The map of American literature which most of us have used was drawn fifty years ago. Its moutains, bumps and flats were charted; its deserts certified unfit for cultural habitation. Only during the past decade, in response to the movements for change of people of color and of women, have we begun to face the task—not systematically undertaken since the 1920s—of resurveying the territory.

That task, the revision of the literary canon, has been necessary because in the twenties processes were set in motion that virtually eliminated black, white female, and all working-class writers from the canon. Institutional as well as theoretical and historiographic factors were involved in that exclusion, and I shall describe some of these shortly. But why is the literary canon of importance and what precisely was the history of its development in the twenties?

I mean by the "American literary canon" that set of authors and works generally included in basic American literature college courses and textbooks, and those ordinarily discussed in standard volumes of literary history, bibliography, or criticism. Many such books are also available in widely marketed paperback series of "classics." Obviously, no conclave of cultural cardinals establishes a literary canon, but for all that it exercises substantial influence. For it encodes a set of social norms and values; and these, by virtue of its cultural standing, it helps endow with force and continuity. Thus, although we cannot ascribe to a literary canon the decline in attention to the concerns of women in the 1920s, the progressive exclusion of literary works by women from the canon suggested that such concerns were of lesser value than those inscribed in canonical books and authors. The literary canon is, in short, a means by which culture validates social power.

Feminist Studies 9, no. 3 (Fall 1983). © by Paul Lauter.

A study of the origins of the American literary canon, then, is not simply an antiquarian exercise. Changing the canon has over the past decade become a major objective of literary practitioners of women's studies, black studies, and other "ethnic" studies— the academic wings of the social movements of the 1960s and 1970s. Fundamental alteration of the canon to include significant numbers of minority and white female writers will both reflect and help spur a widening revaluation of the significance of the experiences with which such writers are often concerned. But the American literary canon will be changed only by conscious literary and organizing efforts. This study is, therefore, part of the groundwork for that effort, an attempt to understand the processes which created the literary canon as most of us know it even today.

What was the history of the canon in the twenties? In his 1916 preface to *The Chief American Prose Writers*, Norman Foerster wrote that "the nine writers represented in this volume have become, by general consent, the American prose classics."[1] Over forty years later, with—I must believe—a certain sense of irony, Foerster wrote in the preface to *Eight American Writers*: "In the consensus of our time eight writers—Poe, Emerson, Thoreau, Hawthorne, Melville, Whitman, Mark Twain, and Henry James— constitute our 'American Classics.'"[2] Only Poe, Emerson, and Hawthorne were common to both lists. We are relatively familiar with the changes of taste that, largely in the decade following World War I, devalued Benjamin Franklin, Washington Irving, James Fenimore Cooper, William Cullen Bryant, James Russell Lowell, Henry Wadsworth Longfellow, Oliver Wendell Holmes, as well as John Greenleaf Whittier, Sidney Lanier, William Dean Howells, to name but a few. Those changes of taste also rescued Melville from obscurity, elevated Twain and James, as well as Thoreau—particularly certain of their works—and eventually focused serious attention on Emily Dickinson. Less familiar is the literary or canonical history of white women and black and working-class writers of both sexes.[3]

The twenties witnessed, as we know, a flourishing of literary work by black as well as by white writers. African Americans, as is often forgotten, had previously produced a substantial body of literary art, in the form of songs, tales, and slave narratives, as well as in more "formal" styles.[4] Newly crowded into urban ghettos, pushed back from the activism of a decade of struggle for civil and political rights, subjected to white curiosity about their supposed "exotic" qualities, black authors and singers generated a significant literary renaissance in the twenties. Substantial collections of black writings were issued in that decade and during the thirties,[5] and at least some black writers managed to make a living from their trade. These facts were in no way reflected in the teaching of American literature, in general anthologies, or in most critical discussions by whites of the literature of the United States.

It would have been no great revolution to include black writers; even Edmund Clarence Stedman had printed five spirituals and six poems by Paul Lawrence Dunbar in his *American Anthology, 1787-1900* (Boston: Houghton Mifflin Co., 1900). Nevertheless, of twenty-one major classroom anthologies (and their numerous revised editions) produced between 1917 and 1950, nine contained no works by black artists; three included only a few spirituals; four contained one black writer each (Dunbar; Phillis Wheatley, twice; Richard Wright); two printed some spirituals and one black writer (W.E.B. Dubois; Countee Cullen—who is dropped in a revised edition). Only three somewhat unusual anthologies included the work of more than one black writer—never more than three—as well as a few spirituals or work songs.[6] General and classroom poetry anthologies reveal a similar pattern. Conrad Aiken's Modern Library volumes, *Twentieth-Century American Poetry* (1927, 1944) and *A Comprehensive Anthology of American Poetry* (1929, 1944) included no black poets, although the latter was advertised as "a newly edited anthology that includes every American poet of note from the 17th century to the present day. . . ." Oscar Williams's "Little Treasuries" (Scribner's) of *Modern Poetry* and of *American Poetry* (1946, 1952) similarly omitted black poets, although the latter did include a section devoted to "American Indian Poetry." F.O. Matthiessen's 1950 version of the *Oxford Book of American Verse* eliminated the one black poet, Dunbar, who had been included in Bliss Carman's 1927 version.

The most notable exceptions to this pattern are Alfred Kreymborg's 1930 *Lyric America* (Tudor Publishing; also called *An Anthology of American Poetry*), which included the work of seven black men, and Louis Untermeyer's *Modern American Poetry* (Harcourt, Brace & Co.). Untermeyer's editing exemplifies the rise and fall of interest in black writers. His first two editions (1919 and 1921) contained poems by Dunbar, joined in the 1925 version by Countee Cullen, James Weldon Johnson, Claude McKay, and Alex

Rogers, and then later by Langston Hughes and Jean Toomer. By the 1942 sixth edition, however, only Dunbar, Johnson, Cullen, and Hughes remained; the seventh edition witnessed the elimination of Dunbar. The general and poetry anthologies uniformly omitted all black women with the solitary and rare exception of Phillis Wheatley.

Similarly, Jay Hubbell's 987-page history, *The South in American Literature: 1607-1900,* consciously excludes black writers as "northern" and outside the book's chronology, although it includes other distinctly northern and twentieth-century writers. The index conveys the operative view of African-American writing: apart from a few miscellaneous entries, the index is limited to "See also Abolitionists, folk songs, folklore, and slavery."[7] More recent anthologies and critical works do, of course, include some black writers, but fundamental organizing principles have seldom been altered to accommodate the fact that the significant literary work of African Americans cannot be understood as an expression of "European culture" in an "American environment"—to use Norman Foerster's formulation.[8]

The position of white women writers in the formation of the canon is rather more complex: some perspective is gained by examining the work of one of the earliest professors of American literature, Fred Lewis Pattee. Pattee's anthology, *Century Readings for a Course in American Literature,* first published in 1919, reflects his appreciation of women writers; it includes work by Harriet Beecher Stowe, Mary Wilkins Freeman, Sarah Orne Jewett, Helen Hunt Jackson, Rose Terry Cooke, Constance Fenimore Woolson, and even Emma Lazarus, among many other women writers. In *The New American Literature* (1930), Pattee praised Willa Cather, Edith Wharton, Ellen Glasgow, and Zona Gale, in particular. "The work of these women marks the highest reaches to which the novel of characterization and manners has attained in America during our period. Perhaps no literary phenomenon in our history," he continued, "has been more noteworthy than this feminine assumption of leadership. The creation of fiction in most of its areas has proven to be an art adapted peculiarly for the powers of women. Feminine success has, however, come also from another peculiar fact: woman has surpassed her male competitors in workmanship, in artistry, in the quality of work toiled over and finished—she has been compelled to do this because of an age-old conception or prejudice. Her success," Pattee concludes, "has raised fiction-writing during the period to the rank of a new regular profession for women."[9] A few years later, another member of the older generation of professors, Arthur Hobson Quinn, in his 1936 *American Fiction,* devoted chapters to Gale, Mary Austin, Dorothy Canfield, and Susan Glaspell, as well as substantial sections to Cooke, Stowe, Elizabeth Stoddard, Rebecca Harding Davis, and Elizabeth Stuart Phelps.[10]

Nevertheless, the first edition of Howard Mumford Jones and Ernest E. Leisy's *Major American Writers,* which was issued in 1935, contains no work by women whatsoever, although it includes such luminaries as William Byrd, Philip Freneau, Bret Harte, and Sidney Lanier, as well as all the traditional schoolroom poets of New England. In later editions, Jones and Leisy admitted Dickinson to their canon, joined in solitude by Glasgow.[11] By 1948, when the National Council of Teachers of English (NCTE) reviewed American literature in the college curriculum, only three women appeared in the ninety syllabi of survey courses studied. Dickinson appeared in twenty-four of these courses; that placed her seventeenth on the list, tied with Holmes and Cooper, but behind Whittier, Lowell, Bryant, Longfellow, and others. The other women were the last two writers listed; Wharton (number thirty-six) appeared in five courses of the ninety surveyed; Cather (number thirty-seven) appeared four times. Before both of them came Frank Norris, Hamlin Garland, Theodore Dreiser, Mather (presumably Cotton), William Bird, Abraham Lincoln, Bret Harte, and Jonathan Edwards.[12] Ben W. Fuson's 1952 study of twenty-seven American literature anthologies shows significant representation of only six women among seventy authors whose works are substantially covered. In all, women represent no more than 13.7 percent and as little as 3.2 percent of the writers in these anthologies, on average about 8 percent. The proportion of women is often related to the proportion of what Fuson calls "borderline" or non-*belles lettres* items.[13] One 1950 collection, edited by Lyon Norman Richardson, G.H. Orians, and H.R. Brown, recognized that a need already existed for giving "special attention to a reconsideration of the works of our women authors."[14]

These academic opinions and statistics reflect a cultural reality which had developed perhaps a decade before. Interest in many of the novelists praised by Pattee and Quinn had begun to decline some time before the critics of the twenties wrote about them. After all, to cite a reversed instance of the lag between social change, cultural consciousness, and academic revision, it took fifteen years after *Brown v. Board of Education* and a decade after the sit-ins began to achieve even token representation of black writers in contemporary anthologies.[15] The essentially nineteenth-century tastes of Pattee and Quinn and their concerns for gentility did not survive the 1920s.[16] Since women were seen as the preservers of gentility and women writers as its promoters, the change in literary taste helped ensure their exclusion from the canon.

Thus, as the NCTE survey accurately shows, by the end of the fifties, one could study American literature and read no work by a black writer, few works by women except Dickinson and perhaps Marianne Moore or Katherine Anne Porter, and no work about the lives or experiences of working-class people.

How can we account for such a development? Three important factors may be responsible: the professionalization of the teaching of literature, the development of an aesthetic theory that privileged certain texts, and the historiographic organization of the body of literature into conventional "periods" and "themes."

The proliferation of American literary anthologies that began in the twenties was a product of the expansion of higher education generally. More particularly the anthologies reflected that American literature had become a legitimate subject for academic study only after the First World War. Courses in American literature had seldom been taught in schools and colleges before the last decade of the nineteenth century; classroom anthologies and American literature texts began to appear only after the turn of the century. The dominant view of the cultivated was that American letters were a branch—a shaky one at that—of the British stock.[17] In the decade prior to 1915, there were 4 articles on American literature out of perhaps 250 in *The Publications of the Modern Language Association (PMLA)*. The American Literature Group, now one of the Modern Language Association's largest, began in 1921 with a meeting attended by only a handful of professors. By 1928, however, that group had been responsible for publishing the influential *Reinterpretation of American Literature*; and by 1929, for starting the magazine *American Literature*. Although the subject remained something of an academic stepchild, it was a major topic of concern for literati from H.L. Mencken to Virginia Woolf.

The survey courses, the anthologies, the professional specialization all contributed to the academic institutionalization of reading choices. What had been the function of individuals, of families, or of literary clubs and certain magazines—choosing books to be remembered and read, building culture and taste— became the purview of the classroom. Even on college campuses prior to 1920, and certainly in communities, a good deal of literary study, particularly of contemporary authors, was carried on within literary societies, mainly female. (The campus men's societies were concerned primarily with debating and oratory; off campus men's clubs, whatever else they were, were *not* literary.) My own research indicates that on campus in the 1920s reading choices were increasingly "suggested" by professors; indeed, formal courses began to absorb what had earlier been talked about "in society." By the thirties, if they still existed, campus literary societies met to play bridge and to get up theatre parties. Community literary societies continued, much diminished, but the taste of participants was likely to have already been formed in college. Thus, in significant measure, influence over reading shifted before the thirties from women who were not academic professionals to academics, the great majority of whom were white and male. And reading choices moved significantly away from the range of female writers—Mary Austin to Sigrid Undset—who had been a staple of most women's literary clubs.[18]

Demographic factors were also at work, as historian Laurence Veysey has pointed out. The proportion "of the mature working-age population in America" who were college and university professors and librarians was rising "spectacularly" in the decades leading to 1920—especially in relation to older, static learned professionals, like doctors, lawyers, and the clergy. Although they constituted only a tiny portion of people at work, professors had enormously larger impact "as the universities increasingly took over training for a wide variety of prestigious occupations. . . ." In fact, Veysey writes that

the social effect of intellectual specialization [occurring in universities among other areas of American life] was to transfer authority, most critically over the printed word and what was taught in colleges to sons and daughters of the elite, away from the cultivated professions considered as an entirety and toward a far smaller, specially trained segment within them, those who now earned Ph.D. degrees. . . . Concretely, this meant vesting such authority in a group that, as of 1900, numbered only a few hundred persons spread across the humanistic fields. The immediate effect was thus the intensification of elitism as it was transferred onto a new academic basis. A double requirement was now imposed—intellectual merit, at least of a certain kind, defined far more rigorously, as well as a continuing expectation of social acceptability.[19]

In short, the professoriat exercised increasing control of the definition of a "literate" reader, including those who were to become the next generation's writers.[20]

The social base of that professoriat was small. The professors, educators, critics, the arbiters of taste of the twenties, were, for the most part, college-educated white men of Anglo-Saxon or northern European origins. They came, that is, from that tiny, elite portion of the population of the United States which, around the turn of the century, could go to college. Through the first two decades of the new century, this dominant elite had faced a quickening demand for some power and control over their lives from Slavic, Jewish, Mediterranean, and Catholic immigrants from Europe, as well as from black immigrants from the rural South. Even women had renewed their demand for the vote, jobs, control over their bodies. The old elite and their allies moved on a variety of fronts, especially during and just after the First World War, to set the terms on which these demands would be accommodated. They repressed, in actions like the Prohibition Amendment and the Palmer raids, the political and social, as well as the cultural, institutions of immigrants and of radicals. They reorganized schools and professionalized elementary and secondary school curriculum development, in significant measure as a way to impose middle-class American "likemindedness" on a heterogeneous, urban, working-class population.[21] Similarly, calling it "professionalization," they reorganized literary scholarship and teaching in ways that not only asserted a male-centered culture and values for the college-educated leadership, but also enhanced their own authority and status as well.[22]

The Modern Language Association, for example, underwent a major reorganization just after the First World War, the effect of which was to concentrate professional influence in the hands of groups of specialists, most of whom met at the annual convention. The convention thus took on much greater significance, practically and symbolically in terms of defining professional leadership. As professionalism replaced gentility, the old all-male "smoker" at the convention was discontinued. With it also disappeared a female and, on occasion, modestly feminist institution: the ladies' dinner. We do not fully know how, or even in this instance whether, such institutions provided significant support for women scholars, nor do we know what was lost with their disappearance in the 1920s.[23] Clearly, women were left without any significant organizational base within the newly important convention. For when, in 1921, specialized groups were established for MLA conventions, women's roles in them were disproportionately small, minor, and largely confined.[24] If the men gave up the social institution that had helped sustain their control, they replaced it with professional authority in the new groups. Not only were women virtually excluded from leadership positions in them and given few opportunities to read papers, but they also appear to have been pushed toward—as men were certainly pushed away from—subject areas considered "peripheral" to the profession. For example, folk materials and works *by* women became particularly the province *of* women—as papers, dissertation topics, and published articles illustrate.[25]

As white women were excluded from the emerging scholarly power structures, and blacks—female or male—were kept almost entirely ghettoized in black colleges, "their subjects," women and blacks, remained undeveloped in a rapidly developing profession. For example, in the first ten years of its existence, *American Literature* published 24 full articles (as distinct from Notes and Queries or Reviews) by women scholars out of a total of 208. Nine of those appeared in the first two volumes, and a number of women published more than once. An article on Dickinson appeared in volume 1, and others in volumes 4 and 6. These apart, the *only* article on a woman writer until volume 10 was one on American comments, mostly by men, on George Sand. In volume 10 one finds a piece, by a male scholar, on Cather, as well as another trying to show that Ann Cotton derived her material from husband John. It is not, I should add, that the journal confined itself to "major" writers or to authors from the early or mid-nineteenth century. Quite the contrary, it ran pieces on stalwarts like John Pendleton Kennedy, not to speak of *Godey's Ladies' Book,* as well as articles dealing with a number of twentieth-century male authors.

While professionalization was thus erecting institutional barriers against women, their status was being attacked in other ways. Joan Doran Hedrick has shown how the ideology of domesticity and the bogey of "race suicide," which reemerged around the turn of the century, was used during the next thirty years to attack women teachers, both the proverbial spinster schoolmarm and the female college professor.[26] The extent to which such attacks arose from the pressure of job competition, general political conservatism, antisuffrage backlash, or other factors is not yet clear. It was true, however, that women had not only been competing more and more effectively for positions in the humanities, but also that the predominance of women students in undergraduate literature courses had long worried the male professoriat. In 1909, for example, the chairman of the MLA's Central Division had devoted his address to the problem of "Coeducation and Literature." He wondered whether the predominance of women taking literary courses "may not contribute to shape the opinion that literature is preeminently a study for girls, and tend to discourage some men. . . . This is not yet saying," he continued, "that the preference of women turns away that of men. There are many factors to the problem. But it looks that way." How, he asked, can we deal with the problem that the "masculine ideal of culture" has largely rejected what the modern languages, and we as its professors, have to offer? "What may we teachers do more or better than we have done to gain for the humanities as represented by literature a larger place in the notion of masculine culture?"[27]

Something of an answer is provided in an unusually frank way in the *Annual Reports* of Oberlin College for 1919-20. In the section on the faculty, Professor Jelliffe, on behalf of Bibliography, Language, Literature, and Art, urged the hiring of an additional teacher of composition. He writes: "In my opinion the new instructor, when appointed, should be a man. Of sixteen sections in Composition only three are at present being taught by men instructors. This is to discredit, in the opinion of our students, the importance of the subject, for despite the excellent teaching being done by the women of the English faculty, the students are quick to infer that the work is considered by the faculty itself of less importance than that to which the men devote their time."[28]

Such ideas, the institutional processes I have described, and other historical forces outside the scope of the paper, gradually eroded the gains women had made in higher education in the decades immediately following the turn of the century. By the early 1920s, women were earning 16 percent of all doctorates; that proportion gradually declined (except for the war years) to under 10 percent in the fifties. Similarly, the proportion of women in the occupational category of college presidents, professors, and instructors rose from 6.4 percent in 1900 to 32.5 percent around 1930, but subsequently declined to below 22 percent by 1960.[29] The proportion of women earning advanced degrees in the modern languages and teaching these subjects in colleges was, of course, always somewhat higher, but the decline affected those fields in a similar way. Because more women were educated in these fields, they were particularly vulnerable in the thirties to cutbacks ostensibly instituted to preserve jobs for male "bread-winners" or to nepotism regulations newly coined to spread available positions among the men. Not surprisingly, by the 1950s only 19 percent of the doctorates being earned in the modern languages were awarded to women,[30] a proportion higher than in fields like sociology, history, or biology, but significantly lower than it had been thirty years earlier. As a result, the likelihood of one's encountering a female professor even in literature—and especially at elite male or coeducational institutions—was perhaps even slighter than the chances of encountering a female writer.

Blacks, female or male, faced a color line that professional-ization did nothing to dispel. Black professors of literature were, for the most part, separated into their own professional organiza-tion, the College Language Association, and into positions at segregated black colleges. The color line persisted in *American Literature* so far as articles on black writers were concerned, until 1971, when the magazine printed its first piece, on James Weldon Johnson. The outlook apparently shared by *American Literature's* editors comes clearest in a brief review (10 [1938]: 112-113) by Vernon Loggins, then at Columbia, of Benjamin Brawley's collec-tion of *Early Negro American Writers.* "The volume . . . gives a hint of American Negro literature before Dunbar, but scarcely more than a hint. Yet it should be of practical value in American literature courses *in Negro colleges.* Professor Brawley obviously had such an aim in mind in making the compilation" (emphasis added). Over the years a few articles appeared on images of blacks in the writings of white authors, but in general, as such reviews and notes on scholarly articles make clear, those interested in black writers were effectively referred to the *Journal of Negro History* or to the *College Language Association Journal.*[31]

Although the existence of such black professional organizations and periodicals reflected the pervasiveness of institutional racism in American life, such black-defined groups and magazines like the *Crisis* had at least the advantage of providing to black writers and scholars outlets for and encouragement of their work. Women, especially white professional writers, faced rather a different problem in this period: one can observe a significant shift in cultural authority from female-defined to male-defined institutions—in symbolic terms, one might say, from women's literary societies to *Esquire* magazine. The analogy may, at first, seem farfetched, but it is probably more accurate than the cartoon view of women's clubs with which we have lived since the twenties. In fact, the taste of the older generation of "genteel" professors and magazine editors largely accorded with that of the female literary clubs; the outlook of the new professoriat and *Esquire,* the *Playboy* of its day, largely coincided, at least with respect to the subjects and writers of fiction, as well as to certain conceptions of male camaraderie and culture.[32] To understand why, we must now turn to the aesthetic theories which helped to shape the canon.

Two aesthetic systems, ultimately in conflict, came to dominate literary thought in the twenties and thirties. One set of critics viewed literature—or at least some books—as important to reconstructing a "usable past" consonant with the new role of the United States as a dominating world power. To one degree or another, all the scholars who developed American literature as a field of study were devoted to this objective. Another critical school emphasized the "aesthetic" or formal qualities of literature—literature as *belles lettres*—above whatever historical interest it might have, or even the values presumably conveyed by it. Indeed, later formalist critics came to disparage the very idea that art—or even criticism—"conveyed" anything at all. Both nationalist and formalist aesthetics, however disparate, produced a *narrowing* of the canon.

The American literature professors of the twenties were, as I have suggested, a serious group that asserted national responsibilities. And they presented the tasks of American literature in broad moral terms. In his introduction to *The Reinterpretation of American Literature,* Norman Foerster posed the work of literary professionals in the context of the international role of the United States. "The power of America renders it perilous to remain in the dark as to what she really is." Literature would reveal our culture, for, as Harry Hayden Clark added, "in the life of the past, as mirrored in literature, there exists a reasonable and dependable guide for a troubled present. . . ."[33] For such aspirations, a focus on domesticity and family, on education and marriage, even on "love and money," to use Jane Austin's formula, would not do, they felt. The tension for the "new woman" between work life and family life would also not suffice as a topic of high national seriousness. Women were liberated, it was said, by the vote, a relaxed style of dress, labor-saving devices, a new sexual openness. They could enter most male professions—it was up to them. So the concerns of "feminist fiction" were no longer relevant.

Besides, a central problem with American literature, or so some seemed to feel, was its "feminization." Joseph Hergesheimer, a then-popular if rapidly dated novelist, had attacked "The Feminine Nuisance in American Literature" in a *Yale Review* article of 1921. Literature in the United States, he claimed (pp. 719-20), "is being strangled with a petticoat," written primarily for women, without a "grain of masculine sand." Hergesheimer's definition of the truly masculine hero provides, in its crude exaggerations, a useful reflection of a developing literary ideal.

I must return to the word vitality, for that alone explains my meaning: such men have perceptibly about them the air, almost the shock, of their force. It is a quality, at bottom, indescribable, without definition, subconscious; and we can do no more than recognize its presence. Such men are attended by a species of magic; they go in direct lines through the impotent turnings of sheep-like human tracks; and as their stay, they have principally that unshakable self-confidence which is condemned as conceit by lesser spirits. It is, therefore, unavoidable that the man I am describing should be, from the absolute standard of normality, abnormal; any wide imagination, any magical brain, is abnormal, with necessities, pressures, powers, altogether beyond the comprehension of the congenital clerk. . . . Does anyone think that, laying an arm across the shoulders of his devoted wife, he would explain how he had repudiated the dishonest offer of the Mikado of Japan? Can you see him playing auction bridge in a room twittering like an aviary?[34]

The Bookman, more than any other periodical responsive to the interests of women readers and literary clubs, quickly ran a response from "the feminine nuisance."[35] Frances Noyes Hart chided Hergesheimer as ungrateful, in view of his large female readership, and pointed out that she knew of

no group of masculine authors who deal less in manufactured sunshine or specious sweetness and light than the large group of women who are now at the head of their profession in England and America—Ethel Sidgwick, Willa Sibert Cather, Rebecca West, May Sinclair, Edith Wharton, Katharine Fullerton Gerould, Dorothy Richardson, Anne Douglas Sedgwick, Sheila Kaye-Smith, Clemence Dane—I take the names at random; there are at least a score more. They face life in varied ways—some nervewracked and tense, some grateful and ironic, some lusty and ruthless, some shadowed and mysterious, some bitter and defiant—but unquestionably they all face it, with scant truckling to any public thirsting for spurious joy and the conventional happy ending.

By the end of the decade, however, even *The Bookman* had joined the antifemale parade, featuring in its March, 1929 (vol. 69), issue a piece by another forgotten novelist, Robert Herrick, somewhat more subtly called "A Feline World." Herrick begins with what he conceives to be a discovery: that younger women novelists have come to "disregard the tradition that this is primarily a man's world and have taken to describing boldly their own primary interests, among themselves, for themselves." He does not, he claims, "deplore" the tendency; rather, he misses "the stir of the old-time, standard fiction" of men, "above all, the talk about politics and bawdy and religion and the reorganizing of our bad, old world. . .mature talk even when the characters were very young" (p. 2). George Meredith, Herrick argues, did not confine his fiction "to the tea table or boudoir or night club. . .,"and Hardy was not solely preoccupied "with emotional subtleties, subjective illusions. Certainly never with purely social reactions and complications. . . ." With [Arnold] Bennett, Herrick continues on page 3, "we have moved farther along toward feminization. . . .even the males are feminized; they act and usually talk like women and their chief preoccupations are the petty daily affairs belonging in general to the home."

Herrick's final argument, in a magazine read mainly by women, takes an ugly turn. Women novelists are, he claims, particularly occupied with sex, not bluntly, like their brothers, but with more erotic effect. "Women," he continues, "know the neurotic sides of sex, which do not eventuate in either marriage or maternity, as well as what once was called (with a hush) the perverted side, the wooing of one's own sex. A disturbing number of recent stories by women deal with this taboo and are not overly vague in the handling of it. We must assume that it interests many of their readers." Thus the interest of women in women novelists becomes primarily a manifestation of lesbianism. It is only a short step from there to using the label "feline" to cover everything that manly intellectuals and activists must deplore; the female, "feline" world becomes identified with intellectual and social reaction, with a rejection of idealism and experimentation, and even with militarism. To be sure, the absurdities of Hergesheimer and Herrick, can be dismissed along with Hawthorne's competitive jealousy of that "damned mob of scribbling women." Yet they express a widely held set of attitudes, both about women generally and about art. They reflect the other side of the professoriat's concern that a truly American art be attractive to, embody the values of, masculine culture. For, as professors and male novelists seemed to perceive it, the problems of the United States were not to be encountered over the cup of proverbial tea, in reading novelists at once genteel and sensual, or in fretting over village life in Maine or Louisiana. America needed the grand encounters with nature of Melville or even Thoreau, the magical abnormalities of Ahab, the deeper possibilities for corruption Twain and even James in their different ways established. I do not want to overdraw the picture. But as Hergesheimer and Herrick illustrate, I am afraid that I could not. The strenuous nationalism of even the most professional scholars, the masculinist attitudes of otherwise refined novelists, defined the issues for the art of the time as fundamentally distinct from the concerns of the domestic sphere which, it was insisted, were to occupy most women, including most female writers.

These attacks on "gentility" and "domesticity" centered, for the most part, on the subject matter of an earlier generation and sought to substitute a more "masculine" content for art. Still, academic scholars continued to view art as a guide to conduct, although the conduct and values being extolled were quite changed. On the other hand, the generation of literary critics who, following T.S. Elliot, began to come to prominence in the 1920s, were doubtful—if not altogether suspicious—of the power of art to shape behavior at all. Indeed, these writers, led by the American "New Critics," felt that civilized values were well on the way to being overwhelmed by "mass society," and that the functions of the artist and the "man of letters" in the modern world were much more defensive than shaping, protective of the remnants of culture rapidly being ground under. What could be defended, if anything, was the value of art itself, and what needed emphasis was not the behavior a work of art promoted, or its subject matter as such, but its language and form, which represented and sustained the best achievements of human creativity.

On the face of it there appears to be no reason why such a formalist aesthetic should narrow the canon in the ways I have indicated. But there are a number of reasons why that was in fact the result. There is, first, the basis on which the "best" achievements of human creativity are defined. Allen Tate, for example, argues that the presence of "tension"—"the full organized body of all the extension and intension that we can find in it"—accounts for the quality of great poetry.[36] Such a definition sets at a discount art which strives for simplicity, transparency, and unity in its effects.[37] Obviously, it leads to the preference of "A Valediction: Forbidding Mourning" over "Roll, Jordan." No doubt, the spiritual lacks the complex language and ambiguity of John Donne's poem; but then "A Valediction" has never inspired many thousands to survive tyranny. Formalist criteria of excellence developed in the 1920s by critics like John Crowe Ransom, Cleanth Brooks, R.P. Blackmur, and Tate, have emphasized complexity, ambiguity, tension, irony, and similar phenomena; such standards are by no means casual. They place a premium on the skills of the literary interpreter: *He* shall unpack the ambiguities and tensions to the uninitiated students, the products of a degraded "mass education." Such criteria are thus directly related to the status of the literary critic. To say it another way: what the American Scholar may have lost with the decline of the ability of the educated classes to establish standards of conduct shall be rescued by reinvesting "the man of letters in the modern world" with authority at least over standards of language. "His critical responsibility is thus. . .the recreation and the application of literary standards. . . . His task is to preserve the integrity, the purity, and the reality of language wherever and for whatever purpose it may be used. . . . The true province of the man of letters is nothing less (as it is nothing more) than culture itself. . . . It is the duty of the man of letters to supervise the culture of language, to which the rest of culture is subordinate, and to warn us when our language is ceasing to forward the ends proper to man. The end of social man is communion in time through love, which is beyond time."[38] Such critical "authority" over culture has, to be sure, proved illusory, but with respect to the canon it did play a significantly narrowing role.

A second and closely related factor leading to a narrowed canon derives from the critical emphasis upon "masterpieces," rather than "tendencies," to use Van Wyck Brooks's 1918 formulation. Focusing on the formal qualities of discrete works of art gradually eroded the earlier scholars' concern for tendencies, for the social and cultural context within which all art is born.[39] In the late thirties, anthologies like Jones and Leisy's *Major American Writers* began to reflect the narrowing focus to fewer "major" works by fewer "major" writers. Successive editions of the highly successful anthology edited by Norman Foerster also show the influence of this trend: between the second and third editions such writers as Stowe, Richard Henry Dana, William Gilmore Simms, Mary Noailles Murfree, Wharton, and Dorothy Canfield Fisher were eliminated, as were most of the "cultural" pieces, including excerpts from the Bay Psalm Book and the New England Primer. Obviously, critics did not propose as a dictum that only white men could be "major" writers, but it was preeminently the works of white males like themselves that they selected.[40] Further, the tide toward certain "masterpieces," once it set in, could hardly be reversed except through the intervention of forces from outside the literary profession. For two generations or more, literary professionals, brought up under the influence of formalist criticism, knew little or nothing of the work of writers outside the hardening canon and thus had few alternative models—or standards—for determining noncanonical masterpieces, much less for understanding tendencies.

Both critics and scholars of the period would no doubt have joined in rejecting such an argument on the grounds that literary masterpieces have the ability to create their own audiences, to break through existing limits of taste and perception and to open readers to new experience. In some measure they would be correct in this rather Romantic conception of the power of art. Yet people survive, in part, by excluding from awareness much of what presses on their senses. They selectively screen out these most recent victims of starvation, that student's persistent difficulties, this critic's passion for Gwendolyn Brooks, that writer's evocation of plantation or domestic experience. It is natural to do so—one cannot physically or psychologically respond to all stimuli. But *what* one screens away is by no means natural or inevitable. Rather, it is a product of particularities of nationality and time, of class and race and gender, as well as of elements of private life.

The arbiters of taste, scholars and critics alike, were as I have pointed out, drawn from a narrow stratum of American society. Their experience seldom included the lives and work about which black writers, for example, wrote. Indeed, upper-class white Americans in the twenties acknowledged the lives of black people, and the work of black writers, only in "their place"—as "exotic," like a taste for Pernod or jazz, a quaint expression of the "folk." It was very well to visit Harlem, but decidedly inappropriate to include blacks in the anthology or the classroom, much less in the Modern Language Association. As we have come

to learn with the overthrow of the doctrine of "separate, but
equal," if people need not be dealt with physically, socially,
seriously, their experiences are not likely to be seen as providing a
basis for significant art.[41] The literary canon does not, after all,
spring from the brow of the master critic; rather, it is a social construct. As our understanding of what is trivial or important alters
in response to developments in the society, so our conception of
the canon will change. But that perception has itself been forced
on us only by the movements for social change of the sixties and
seventies. Fifty years ago, the dominant scholars and critics were
able to dismiss lives and art beyond their experience, concentrating instead on scrutinizing with considerable ingenuity a narrow range of work. But part of the price was a constricted canon.

The third factor on which I shall touch is historiographic: the
conventional definitions of periods in American literature, which
were, in the twenties, formulated by men such as Foerster, Brooks,
and Clark. Many generations of their students were trained in a se-
quence involving the "Puritan Mind," "Romanticism," the
"Frontier Spirit," the "Rise of Realism"—categories which provide the basis for *The Reinterpretation of American Literature*.
Such phrases have been widely, if loosely, used, both as historical
frameworks and as cultural classifications, and while their
popularity diminished in some respects with the rise of formalist
criticism and the decline of literary history after the 1930s, they
have remained surprisingly influential. They shape significantly
the ways in which we think about culture, emphasizing works
that fit given frameworks, obscuring those which do not.

In the twenties, literary historians acknowledged that their
work was perhaps a decade behind that of American historians;
they used the historians' structures to frame the study of literature
and thus the canon. A similar situation exists today: feminist and
Third World historians have demonstrated that historical epochs
are experienced differently by women and men, by whites and by
people of color. To quote Gerda Lerner, for example: "neither
during or after the American revolution nor in the age of Jackson
did women share in the broadening out of opportunities and in
the political democratization experienced by men. On the contrary, women in both periods experienced status loss and a
restriction of their choices as to education or vocation, and had
new restraints imposed upon their sexuality, at least by prescrip-

tion.''[42] The usual divisions of history according to wars or political events turn out to be more relevant to the lives of men than of women; moreover, such divisions are often used less to understand the dynamics of history than as convenient pigeonholes in which to place works in syllabi or anthologies. To review the canon, we must create a usable past, as Brooks advised in 1918. Simply eliminating historical frameworks, as some anthologists and scholars have done in response to the inadequacies of traditional categories, leaves us viewing discrete works in a historical void. New categories can bring into focus, rather than obscure, the experience and culture of people of color and of white women. They allow us to illuminate the interrelationships of culture and other historical forces. And from a practical standpoint, they help us construct new courses and anthologies—like that being developed by The Feminist Press project on Reconstructing American Literature, designed to present and to validate the full range of the literatures of America. Finally, alternative categories provide useful perspectives on the limitations of the traditional formulations by suggesting how different a canon posed in their terms would be. But in a way, we have little choice about proposing different literary categories, for the seams of the old ones simply cannot contain the multitude of previously ignored literary works.

As a historical category, "Puritanism" has been used to exaggerate the significance of New England, and particularly the male, theocratic portion of it, within the complex tableau of American colonial experience. Focusing on Puritanism, a socioreligious construct, seems largely to have led to the study of the ideology by which a narrow group of male divines construed and confirmed their dominant roles in New England society. Implicitly, the category did not readily lend itself to exploration of the broader contexts of New England family, political and business life, much less to comparisons with cultural development in other English as well as non-English settlements. Emphasizing Puritanism as religious ideology distorted understanding of the witchcraft trials, Anne Hutchinson, colonial family and sex life, and the systematic extermination of "Indians." Imposing the label of "Puritanism" on the culture of early New England also obscures the important dynamic of colonization and decolonization, possibly a more helpful tool for framing colonial American history, as V.F. Calverton pointed out fifty years ago.[43]

The colonies embodied many now-familiar aspects of settler

societies. These included exploitative, if not altogether genocidal, attitudes toward the indigenous population, provincial exaggerations of imported social patterns, and increasingly ambivalent relationships to the parent society. These aspects were reflected in colonial culture, from the myths about the native Americans and the captivity narratives, to the terrors of Charles Brockden Brown, and the late-coming calls for literary decolonization contained in works like Emerson's "The American Scholar" and Margaret Fuller's "American Literature."[44] I do not pose colonization and decolonization as the only "correct" historical frameworks for analyzing seventeenth- and eighteenth-century white culture. The terms do seem to me, though, a useful way to understand the general development of culture in the young United States, as well as to illuminate the social origins and functions of Puritan intellectual writings generally examined only in relation to one another. And the concept of colonization and decolonization contains, I think, some inherent intellectual safeguards against the abuses to which the concept of "Puritanism" seems to have been open.

As an ahistorical cultural category, Puritanism also came in the twenties to represent a legacy of repression embodied in grim Salem shades and proper Cambridge ladies. Critics like Ludwig Lewisohn celebrated Freudianism as a liberating ideology, enabling a natural sexuality to flourish in life as in literature. The counterposition of Puritanism to Freudianism not only distorted history—for the Puritans were hardly celibate—but often emphasized a finally puerile issue of libido: "Does she or doesn't she?" That may give prominence to Henry Miller or some of the sillier parts of Hemingway; but it obscures books like Kate Chopin's *The Awakening,* Edith Summers Kelley's *Weeds,* Agnes Smedley's *Daughter of Earth*[45] more broadly concerned with the contexts for and consequences of sexuality, with the implications of contraception and abortion, the problems of childbearing, the tension between sexuality and work.

Both as a category of history and of culture, then, "Puritanism" helped produce a distorted canon. A similar problem exists with respect to the category of the "Frontier Spirit." The phrase came to be defined in terms exalting male individualism, physical courage, and the honor code of the "lone cowhand" heroically confronting and triumphing over savagery. Although literary historians achieved some distance on this image of the frontier, they continued to focus on books that described human relationships with nature in terms of confrontation, conquest, and exploitation; that omitted what was left back east, where most people still lived; and that produced distorted images of native American "savages," and white female bearers of "civilization." They canonized works that obscured the historical reality of the "trail of tears," of Indian starvation, of women's loneliness and self-sufficiency. Although recent feminist and native American scholarship has quite altered understanding of the history of the frontier, it is not at all clear that a category like the "Frontier Spirit" could, even now, be freed of its chauvinist cultural baggage and be used to validate a significantly different canon.

By contrast, "urbanization" provides a still-relevant historical focus. The major period of urbanization in the United States stretched over the 80 to 100 years during which European and Asian immigrants came to this country, contributing, along with native-born emigrants from the South and other rural areas, to the swelling population of its cities. That process continues today, as Puerto Rican, Haitian, Dominican, Vietnamese, other Hispanic and Asian immigrants come to the United States. The life-styles, values, and family structures of rural peoples have been and continue to be challenged and changed as they attempt to assimilate to more homogeneous, sophisticated urban styles and to survive economically in an urban industrial environment. That clash of values, that struggle for survival is a central subject of some of this country's best (yet noncanonical) books: Upton Sinclair's *The Jungle,* William Attaway's *Blood on the Forge,* Harriette Arnow's *The Dollmaker,* and Tillie Olsen's *Yonnondio.*[46] Further, although an emphasis on the frontier helps submerge the lives and roles of women (one escapes them to "light out" for the "territory"), urbanization is a lens that brings into clear focus the doubly changing roles of women in the family and in work. It provides a fuller vision than the twenties' emphasis on the frontier, which may have served the purpose of distinguishing the United States from Europe but which also obscured the experience of women, as well as of urbanized immigrant and minority men.

I have suggested two different categories of historical and cultural coherence—colonization/decolonization and urbanization. I wish to add a third cultural category that has characterized all of American history; it is embodied in W.E.B. DuBois's comment that "the problem of the twentieth century is the problem of the color line." To focus on the color line is to recognize, in the first place, that among the earliest indigenous literary forms in the United States were those produced by people not of European but of African origins: namely, slave narratives, work and "sorrow" songs, dialect and other oral tales. These literary works were based in particular historic contexts—slavery, reconstruction, northern migration. That they continue to live is not only a measure of their artistic vitality, but also an indication that the struggles brought alive in Frederick Douglass's *Narrative* of his life, in Charles Chesnutt's stories, and in Gwendolyn Brooks's Bronzeville continue. The art of the color line also produces an especially rich and recurrent image—invisibility. The central metaphor of Ralph Ellison's *Invisible Man,* it is also the theme of Chesnutt's "The Passing of Grandison," and important to Nella Larsen's fiction.

The canon that might have developed from categories like colonization and decolonization, urbanization, and the color line differs substantially from the one that did, in fact, emerge from the categories of the twenties. Although a few of the books and authors I mention as illustrations, like *The Awakening,* have been incorporated into the canon—or at least into anthologies—most have not; some works are even out of print. But the major issue is not assimilating some long-forgotten works or authors into the existing categories; rather, it is reconstructing historical understanding to make it inclusive and explanatory instead of narrowing and arbitrary.

To the extent that the categories I have criticized are historically valid, they raise another issue; the very conception of periodicity. Dividing experience chronologically tends to accentuate the discontinuities rather than the continuities of life. It is something like imagining the world as it is presented in a tabloid newspaper, with its emphasis on the exceptional, rather than upon the commonplace, the ongoing. In some measure, women's lives in patriarchal society have been more fully identified with continuities—birthing, rearing, civilizing children; maintaining family and cultural stability. Indeed, there is some evidence to suggest that the rituals of female experience—regular, periodic, sustained—are culturally distinguishable from those of males. In this regard, emphasizing distinct chronological or literary periods may be one-dimensional, obscuring what is ongoing, continued. The color line persists, although its conventions and the forms of its literary expression are different in colonial and in modern, urbanized society. Urbanization is surprisingly similar over time. The point is simply that social and cultural continuities need to be understood as clearly as the periodic categories that seem to remain useful if the canon is not to be distorted in yet another way.

I have tried to outline a number of the factors that shaped the American literary canon into the rather exclusive form it had even as late as the 1960s. Certain other significant forces—for example, publishing decisions and changes in the publishing industry or the shorter-term impact of popular critics—remain to be examined in detail. But I have found nothing thus far that conflicts with the patterns I have sketched. Indeed, the one dissertation that has examined processes shaping the canon viewed literary scholars in their roles as teachers and anthologists as far more influential than publishers or critics.[47]

It is also important to understand that processes of institutionalization such as I have discussed, development of heavily capitalized anthologies and national marketing of texts—not to speak of academic tradition and inertia—all contribute to the difficulty of changing a canon once it has been formed. For well over a decade now feminist scholars and scholars of color, participants in broad social movements for human rights, have tried to reconstitute the canon. From one point of view, certain progress has been made: the Norton anthology, for example, now includes part of Frederick Douglass's *Narrative* and Kate Chopin's *The Awakening,* among other previously buried works. But it is not so clear that the institutional, aesthetic, and historiographic factors which had once served to exclude such works have yet been sufficiently scrutinized, much less fundamentally altered. Thus, what is here presented must be seen as part of a work in progress toward not only a more representative and accurate literary canon, but also toward basic changes in the institutional and intellectual arrangements that shape and perpetuate it.

NOTES

1. Norman Foerster, ed., preface to *The Chief American Prose Writers* (Cambridge, Mass.: Riverside Press, 1916), iii.
2. Norman Foerster and Robert P. Falk, eds., preface to *Eight American Writers* (New York: W.W. Norton & Co., 1963), xv.
3. I will not, primarily for reasons of space, deal with working-class literature in this article. Some of the earlier anthologies contained sections of popular songs and ballads of the Revolution and the Civil War, an occasional work song, and perhaps a selection

from Jack London or Upton Sinclair. But little or nothing of working-class or socialist culture of the nineteenth and early twentieth centuries was taken seriously as art. Not until the 1930s, with the resurgence of left-wing cultural institutions in the United States and the development of theories of "proletarian literature," were the real experiences of working people validated as a basis for literature. And even then, much of what working-class writers themselves produced, in the way of songs and other occasional writings, for example, remained marginal even to progressive literary theorists. Questions concerning the basic characteristics, value, and functions of working-class literature remain vexed today. They are discussed in Raymond Williams, *Culture and Society, 1780-1950* (New York: Harper, 1960); Martha Vicinus, *The Industrial Muse* (New York: Barnes & Noble, 1974); Paul Lauter, "Working-Class Women's Literature: An Introduction to Study," *Women in Print 1,* ed. Joan Hartman and Ellen Messer-Davidow (New York: Modern Language Association, 1982), 109-34; and Dan Tannacito, "Poetry of the Colorado Miners, 1903-1905," *Radical Teacher,* no. 15 (1980).

4. See, for example, the useful but not exhaustive "Select Chronology of Afro-American Prose and Poetry, 1760-1970" in *Afro-American Writing,* ed. Richard A. Long and Eugenia W. Collier (New York: New York University Press, 1972) 1: xix-xlii; Dorothy B. Porter, *North American Negro Poets: A Bibliographical Check-List of Their Writing (1760-1944)* (1945; reprint, New York: Burt Franklin, 1963); and Ora Williams, *American Black Women in the Arts and Social Sciences: A Bibliographical Survey,* rev. and enl. ed. (Metuchen, N.J.: Scarecrow Press, 1978).

5. For example, Robert T. Kerlin, *Contemporary Poetry of the Negro* (1921; reprint, Freeport, N.Y.: Books for Libraries Press, 1971); James Weldon Johnson, ed., *The Book of American Negro Poetry* (New York: Harcourt, Brace & Co., 1922); Robert T. Kerlin, *Negro Poets and Their Poems* (Washington, D.C.: Associated Publishers, 1923); Newman Ivey White and Walter Clinton Jackson, eds., *An Anthology of Verse by American Negroes* (Durham, N.C.: Trinity College Press, 1924); Countee Cullen, ed., *Caroling Dusk* (New York: Harper & Row, 1927); Alain Locke, ed., *Four Negro Poets* (New York: Simon & Schuster, 1927); V.F. Calverton, ed., *An Anthology of American Negro Literature* (New York: Modern Library, 1929); Otelia Cromwell, Lorenzo Dow Turner, and Eva B. Dykes, eds., *Readings from Negro Authors* (New York: Harcourt, Brace & Co., 1931).

6. The anthologies consulted are the following: W.R. Benét and N.H. Pearson, eds., *The Oxford Anthology of American Literature* (New York: Oxford University Press, 1938); Walter Blair, Theodore Hornberger, and Randall Stewart, eds., *The Literature of the United States* (Glenview, Ill.: Scott, Foresman, 1946); Percy H. Boynton, ed., *Milestones in American Literature* (Boston and New York: Ginn & Co., 1923); Oscar Cargill, Robert E. Spiller, Tremaine McDowell, Louis Wann, and John Herbert Nelson, eds., *American Literature: A Period Anthology,* 5 vols. (New York: Macmillan Co., 1933); Joe Lee Davis, John T. Frederich, and Frank L. Mott, eds., *American Literature* (New York: Charles Scribner's Sons, 1948); Milton Ellis, Louise Pound, and George Weida Spohn, eds., *A College Book of American Literature* (New York: American Book Co., 1939); Norman Foerster, ed., *American Poetry and Prose* (Boston: Houghton Mifflin, 1923, 1934, 1947, 1962); James D. Hart and Clarence Gohdes, eds., *American Literature* (New York: Dryden Press, 1955); Jay B. Hubbell, ed., *American Life in Literature* (New York: Harper & Brothers, 1936, 1949); Howard Mumford Jones and E.E. Leisy, eds., *Major American Writers* (New York: Harcourt, Brace & Co., 1939, 1945); Ludwig Lewisohn, ed., *Creative America* (New York: Harper & Brothers, 1933); Alfred E. Newcomer, Alice E. Andrews, and Howard Judson Hall, eds., *Three Centuries of American Poetry and Prose* (Chicago: Scott, Foresman, 1917); Fred Lewis Pattee, ed.,

Century Readings for a Course in American Literature (New York: Century Co., 1919, 1922, 1926, 1931); L.W. Payne, Jr., ed., *Selections from Later American Writers* (Chicago: Rand McNally, 1926); Henry A. Pochmann and Gay Wilson Allen, eds., *Masters of American Literature* (New York: Macmillan, 1949); Arthur Hobson Quinn, Albert Baugh, and W.D. Howe, eds., *The Literature of America* (New York: Odyssey, 1926); Franklyn B. Snyder and Edward D. Snyder, eds., *A Book of American Literature* (New York: Macmillan, 1927, 1935); William Thorp, Merle Curti, and Carlos Baker, eds., *The Library Record,* vol. 2 of *American Issues* (New York: Lippincott, 1941); Harry R. Warfel, Ralph Henry Gabriel, and Stanley T. Williams, eds., *The American Mind* (New York: American Book Co., 1937); W. Tasker Witham, ed., *Masterpieces of American Literature,* vol. 2 of *Living American Literature* (New York: Stephen Daye Press, 1947).

By contrast, Bernard Smith's *The Democratic Spirit* (New York: Knopf, 1941) includes work by Frederick Douglass, W.E.B. DuBois, James Weldon Johnson, Claude McKay, Countee Cullen, Langston Hughes, and Richard Wright. Smith, who was active on the Left, saw "democratic writers" as constituting the central literary tradition of the United States.

7. Jay Hubbell also devotes ten pages to that eminent "southerner," Ralph Waldo Emerson, as well as chapters to Stowe and the white dialect "humorists." *The South in American Literature, 1607-1900* (Durham, N.C.: Duke University Press, 1934). The seventeen-volume *Library of Southern Literature,* ed. Edwin A. Alderman, Joel Chandler Harris, and Charles W. Kent (Atlanta: Martin and Hoat, 1907-23) contains many "dialect stories" by white writers like Harris, Thomas Dixon, and Thomas Nelson Page, but no work by a black person. Frederick Douglass is included in the "Biographical Dictionary of Authors," but not in the bibliography of works or in the Historical Chart. The index contains references to "Negro Dialect, Life, Character, and Problems (see also Slavery)" and "Negro Song (verse)," which turns out to be a single poem, but no other reference to a black author.

8. Norman Foerster, "American Literature," *Saturday Review of Literature* 2 (3 April 1926): 678.

9. Fred Lewis Pattee, *The New American Literature* (New York: Century Co., 1930), 268.

10. Arthur Hobson Quinn, *American Fiction* (New York: D. Appleton-Century Co., 1936). Quinn had been working on this book for many years; it thus reflects a taste formed some decades earlier.

11. Howard Mumford Jones and Ernest E. Leisy, eds., *Major American Writers,* rev. and enl. ed. (New York: Harcourt, Brace & Co., 1945). It was suggested privately to me by a person who knew the editors that the choice of Glasgow was influenced by an editor's friendship with her.

12. Committee on the College Study of American Literature and Culture, William G. Crane, chairperson, *American Literature in the College Curriculum* (Chicago: National Council of Teachers of English, 1948), 27.

13. Ben W. Fuson, *Which Text Shall I Choose for American Literature? A Descriptive and Statistical Comparison of Currently Available Survey Anthologies and Reprint Series in American Literature* (Parkville, Mo.: Park College Press; distributed in cooperation with the College English Association, 1952).

14. Lyon Norman Richardson, G.H. Orians, and H.R. Brown, eds., *The Heritage of American Literature* (Boston: Ginn & Co., 1951).

15. The lag in secondary schools, where bureaucratic forms and political control were established early and elaborately, is far greater, as was attested by the three or even

four generations of American schoolchildren for whom "the modern novel" was represented by *Silas Marner, The Rise of Silas Lapham,* and *Ethan Frome.*

16. In reviewing Carl Van Doren's *American Literature: An Introduction* (Los Angeles: U.S. Library Association, 1933), for example, Pattee writes: "It seems to be the fashion now to exclude from the roll of American authors of major importance all who were not . . . shockers of *hoi polloi* readers who are old-fashioned in taste and morals. Van Doren's little volume excludes Bryant, Longfellow, Whittier, Holmes, Lowell, Stowe, Harte, and the like, and fills one fourth of his space with Emily Dickinson, Henry Adams, Mencken, Cabell, Dreiser, Lewis, Paine, Poe, Melville, Thoreau, Whitman, Mark Twain, and Emerson . . . ." See Pattee, *American Literature* 5 (January 1934): 379-80.

17. American letters, wrote Henry S. Pancoast (in *An Introduction to American Literature* [New York, 1898], p. 2) are only "the continuation of English literature within the limits of what has become the United States, by people English in their speech, English to a considerable extent by inheritance, and English in the original character of their civilization." Pancoast quoted in Howard Mumford Jones, *The Theory of American Literature,* rev. ed. (Ithaca: Cornell University Press, 1965), 98. Even Virginia Woolf pointed out that Emerson, Lowell, and Hawthorne "drew their culture from our books." See Woolf, "American Fiction," *Saturday Review of Literature* 2 (1 August 1925); 1. On the early development of courses in American literature, and the resistance to them, see, for example, Fred Lewis Pattee, *Tradition and Jazz* (New York: Century Co., 1925), 209-19.

18. These generalizations are based upon research I have been conducting for a book on the origins of the American literary canon. At this writing, I have examined the papers of over a dozen such literary societies as well as materials from and for such clubs provided by periodicals such as *Bookman.*

19. Laurence Veysey, "The Humanities, 1860-1920," typescript of paper for volume on the professions, c. 1974, 21, 24.

20. Pattee remarks that "American literature today is in the hands of college-educated men and women. The professor has molded the producers of it." See Pattee, *Tradition and Jazz,* 237.

21. Barry M. Franklin, "American Curriculum Theory and the Problem of Social Control, 1918-1938" (Paper presented at the Annual Meeting of the American Educational Research Association, Chicago, 15-19 April 1974), ERIC, ED 092 419. Franklin quotes Edward A. Ross, *Principles of Sociology* (New York: Century Co., 1920): "Thoroughly to nationalize a multitudinous people calls for institutions to disseminate certain ideas and ideals. The Tsars relied on the blue-domed Orthodox church in every peasant village to Russify their heterogeneous subjects, while we Americans rely for unity on the 'little red school house.'"

22. Whatever its ostensible objectives, in practice, professionalization almost invariably worked to the detriment of female practitioners—and often female "clients" as well. The details of this argument have been most fully worked out for medicine; see, for example, Barbara Ehrenreich and Deirdre English, *Complaints and Disorders: The Sexual Politics of Sickness* (Old Westbury, N.Y.: Feminist Press, 1973), and *For Her Own Good: One Hundred and Fifty Years of the Experts' Advice to Women* (New York: Pantheon, 1979). See also Janice Law Trecker, "Sex, Science, and Education," *American Quarterly* 26 (October 1974): 352-66; and Margaret W. Rossiter, *Women Scientists in America: Struggles and Strategies to 1940* (Baltimore: Johns Hopkins University Press, 1982), especially the chapters titled "A Manly Profession," pp. 73-99, which includes a wonderful discussion of the professionally exclusionary function of the male

"smoker," and "Academic Employment: Protest and Prestige," 160-217.

23. The ladies' dinner had disappeared by 1925. A good deal of work on female cultures of support has recently been published, beginning with Carroll Smith-Rosenberg, "The Female World of Love and Ritual: Relations between Women in Nineteenth-Century America," *Signs* 1 (Autumn 1975): 1-27. In another professional field, history, women apparently felt so excluded from the mainstream and in need of mutual support that in 1929 they formed the Berkshire Conference of Women Historians, an institution extended in the 1970s to include sponsorship of a large conference on women's history. In most academic fields, however, while the proportion of *individual* women obtaining doctorates might have increased or been stable during the 1920s, female-defined *organizations* seem virtually to have disappeared—and with them, I suspect, centers for women's influence.

24. From 1923 on, the MLA gathered in what was called a "union" meeting, rather than in separate conventions of the Eastern, Central, and Pacific divisions—another indication of the new importance of the convention. That year 467 registered as attending the session. Fifty-nine women attended the ladies' dinner; some of the women were probably wives and other women members probably did not attend. About 24 percent of the MLA members were female; very likely a smaller proportion attended the convention. Among the divisions and sections there were 37 male chairpersons, and 1 female, Louise Pound, who chaired the Popular Culture section. There were 29 male secretaries, and 1 woman, Helen Sandison, served as secretary for two sections. Of the 108 papers, 6 were delivered by women.

In 1924, 978 persons registered, and 121 women went to the ladies' dinner. There continued to be 1 female chairperson, Louise Pound, and now 43 men. The female secretarial corps had increased to 5, Helen Sandison still serving twice, and "Mrs. Carleton Brown" now serving as secretary for the Phonetics section. Of the 128 papers, 7 were by women.

In *PMLA*, the proportion of women remained, relatively, much higher. In 1924, women were 7 of 47 authors; in 1925, 9 of 47; and in 1926, 11 of 55.

25. For example, of those seven papers delivered by women in the 1924 MLA meeting, two were in Popular Literature, two on Phonetics—where, perhaps not incidentally, women were officers—one in American Literature. Similarly, the entry for American Literature prepared by Norman Foerster for the 1922 American Bibliography (*PMLA*, 1923) contains one paragraph devoted to works about Indian verse, black writers, and popular ballads. Four of the scholars cited in this paragraph are women, 5 are men. Otherwise, 58 men and 9 women scholars are cited in the article. Of the 9 women, 2 wrote on women authors, 2 are cobibliographers, and 1 wrote on Whittier's love affair.

26. Joan Doran Hedrick, "Sex, Class, and Ideology: The Declining Birthrate in America, 1870-1917," unpublished *MS,* c. 1974. Hedrick demonstrates that many of the sociologists and educators who developed the idea of utilizing curriculum for social control were involved with the supposed problem of "race suicide" and active in efforts to restrict immigration as well as to return women to the home.

27. A.G. Canfield, "Coeducation and Literature," *PMLA* 25 (1910): lxxix-lxxx, lxxxiii.

28. *Annual Reports of the President and the Treasurer of Oberlin College for 1919-20* (Oberlin, Ohio: Oberlin College, 10 December 1920), 231-32.

29. Rudolph C. Blitz, "Women in the Professions, 1870-1970," *Monthly Labor Review* 97 (5 May 1974): 37-38. See also Pamela Roby, "Institutional Barriers to Women Students in Higher Education," in *Academic Women on the Move,* ed. Alice S. Rossi and Ann Calderwood (New York: Russell Sage Foundation, 1973), 37-40; and Michael J.

Carter and Susan Boslego Carter, "Women's Recent Progress in the Professions, or, Women Get a Ticket to Ride after the Gravy Train Has Left the Station," *Feminist Studies* 7 (Fall 1981): 477-504.

30. Laura Morlock, "Discipline Variation in the Status of Academic Women," in *Academic Women on the Move,* 255-309.

31. In 1951, the Committee on Trends in Research of the American Literature Group circulated a report on research and publications about American authors during 1940-50, together with some notes on publications during the previous decade. For the 1885-1950 period, the report (basing itself on categories established by the *Literary History of the United States*) provided information on ninety-five "major authors." Of these, four were black: Charles Chesnutt, Paul Laurence Dunbar, Langston Hughes, Richard Wright—in context a surprisingly "large" number. Chesnutt is one of the few of the ninety-five about whom no articles are listed for either period; for Dunbar, one three-page article is listed and a "popular" book; for Hughes, there are four articles, two by Hughes himself. Only Wright had been the subject of a significant number of essays. Among "minor authors," as defined by *LHUS,* Countee Cullen had two articles, totaling five pages, written about him; W.E.B. DuBois nothing; and James Weldon Johnson, Claude McKay, and Jean Toomer, among others, were not even listed. Available in Modern Language Association, American Literature Group Files, University of Wisconsin Memorial Library Archives, Madison, Wisconsin.

32. One suggestive illustration.

I was pleased to get your letter and hear about the hunting. I don't know whether you realize how fortunate you people are to live where the game is still more plentiful than the hunters. It is no fun up here where hunting frequently resembles a shooting duel.

I am vastly amused by the report of the situation of the good and important woman who thought we should have more women on our committees in the American Literature Group. . . . Beyond . . . [Louise Pound and Constance Rourke] I cannot think of another woman in the country who has contributed sufficiently to be placed on a par with the men on our Board and committees. If you can think of anyone, for heaven's sake jog up my memory. We must by all means keep in the good graces of the unfair sex.

Sculley Bradley to Henry A. Pochmann, 12 January 1938, Modern Language Association, American Literature Group Files, University of Wisconsin Memorial Library Archives, Madison, Wisconsin.

33. Norman Foerster, ed., introduction to *The Reinterpretation of American Literature* (New York: Harcourt, Brace & Co., 1928), vii; Henry Hayden Clark, "American Literary History and Amerian Literature," in *The Reinterpretation of American Literature,* 213.

34. Joseph Hergesheimer, *Yale Review,* n.s., 10 (July 1921): 716-25.

35. Frances Noyes Hart, "The Feminine Nuisance Replies," *The Bookman* 54 (September 1921): 31-34.

36. Allen Tate, "Tension in Poetry," *The Man of Letters in the Modern World* (New York: Meridian Books, 1955), 71.

37. Susan Sniader Lanser and Evelyn Beck make the same point in "[Why] Are There No Great Women Critics?" in *The Prism of Sex: Essays in the Sociology of Knowledge,* ed. Julia A. Sherman and Evelyn T. Beck, (Madison: University of Wisconsin Press, 1979). Deborah Rosenfelt adds: "Because the New Criticism valued works that could be analyzed as autonomous, self-contained structures without reference to the artist or to the historical era, certain genres (like poetry and fiction) became more highly regarded than others (like autobiography or essay)." See Rosenfelt, "The Politics of Bibliography," *Women in Print 1,* p. 21.

38. Allen Tate, "The Man of Letters in the Modern World," in *The Man of Letters in the Modern World,* 20-22.

39. Frank Lentricchia develops a similar analysis in *After the New Criticism* (Chicago: University of Chicago Press, 1980), especially p. 202: "Whether it comes from Harold Bloom or traditional historians of American poetry like Hyatt Waggoner and Roy Harvey Pearce, the isolation of Emerson and an Academic 'tradition' . . . running through Whitman, Stevens, Roethke, and Ginsberg produces a repetitious continuity which celebrates the individual authorial will ('tradition and the individual talent') and which dissolves, in the process, the myriad, changing forces, poetic and otherwise, that shaped the identities of figures as culturally separated as Emerson and Roethke."

40. Compare Rosenfelt's analysis of Perry Miller's introduction to his 1962 anthology in "The Politics of Bibliography," 19-23.

41. A similar problem existed with respect to art that focused on the lives of working-class people. See Alice Kessler-Harris and Paul Lauter's introduction to the books in the Feminist Press series of 1930s' women writers. And Joseph Freeman's introduction to *Proletarian Literature in the United States* (New York: International Publishers, 1935), 9-19.

42. Gerda Lerner, "Placing Women in History: A 1975 Perspective," in *Liberating Women's History*, ed. Berenice A. Carroll (Urbana: University of Illinois Press, 1976), 363.

43. V.F. Calverton, *The Liberation of American Literature* (New York: Octagon Books, 1973), 1-6. The original edition was published in 1932.

44. Two key sentences catch the essence of Emerson's and Fuller's outlooks in this respect. Emerson: "We have listened too long to the courtly muses of Europe." Fuller: "Books which imitate or represent the thoughts and life of Europe do not constitute an American literature."

45. Kate Chopin, *The Awakening* (Chicago and New York: H.S. Stone & Co., 1899); the revived edition was edited by Kenneth Eble (New York: Carpicorn Books, 1964). Edith Summers Kelley, *Weeds* (New York: Harcourt, Brace & Co., 1923); a revived edition was first edited by Matthew J. Bruccoli in 1972; it has been reedited, with a previously omitted scene of childbirth, by Charlotte Goodman (Old Westbury, N.Y.: Feminist Press, 1982). Agnes Smedley, *Daughter of Earth* (New York: Coward-McCann, 1929); revived edition edited by Paul Lauter (Old Westbury, N.Y.: Feminist Press, 1973). Chopin's book was out of print from about 1906, Kelley's from about 1924, and Smedley's from about 1937.

46. Upton Sinclair, *The Jungle* (New York: Vanguard, 1905); the book has been available in popular editions since publication. William Attaway, *Blood on the Forge* (Garden City: Doubleday, Doran, 1941); the book is available new only from The Chatham Bookseller, Chatham, New Jersey. Harriette Arnow, *The Dollmaker* (New York: MacMillan, 1954). Tillie Olsen, *Yonnondio: From the Thirties* (New York: Dell, 1974).

47. The only detailed study of the formation of the canon I have come across concludes that scholars, because they are the teachers of the tradition, are the prime influences on the shaping of the canon. See Joseph Darryl McCall, "Factors Affecting the Literary Canon" (Ph.D. diss., University of Florida, 1958).

MODERNISM AND THE HARLEM RENAISSANCE

HOUSTON A. BAKER, JR.
University of Pennsylvania

> Harlem is vicious
> modernism. Bangclash.
> Vicious the way its made.
> Can you stand such Beauty?
> So violent and transforming.
> —Amiri Baraka, "Return of the Native"

THE TERM "MODERNISM" HAS SOMETHING OF THE CHARACTER OF KEAT'S COLD pastoral. Promising a wealth of meaning, it locks observers into a questing indecision that can end in unctious chiasmus. Teased out of thought by the term's promise, essayists often conclude with frustratingly vague specifications. Harry Levin's essay "What Was Modernism?", for example, after providing lists, catalogues, and thought problems, concludes with the claim that modernism's distinguishing feature is its attempt to create "a conscience for a scientific age" (630).[1] Modernism's definitive act, according to Levin, traces its ancestry to "Rabelais, at the very dawn of modernity."

Such an analysis can only be characterized as a terribly general claim about scientific mastery and the emergence of the modern. It shifts the burden of definition from "modernism" to "science," without defining either enterprise.

Robert Martin Adams, in an essay bearing the same title as Levin's offers a key to modernism's teasing semantics.[2] Adams writes:

> Of all the empty and meaningless categories, hardly any is inherently as empty as "the modern." Like "youth," it is a self-destroying concept; unlike "youth," it has a million and one potential meanings. Nothing is so dated as yesterday's modern, and nothing, however dated in itself, fails to qualify as "modern" so long as it enjoys the exquisite privilege of having been created yesterday. (31-32)

This essay is, in part, a direct excerpt from a book-length study of the same title that will be issued by the University of Chicago Press in the fall of 1987, and, in part, an abbreviated summary of claims argued at some length in that book. The principal aim of both the essay and the book is to suggest a problematic, or an analytical model, that will enable a useful reassessment of the Harlem Renaissance. Such an analysis would escape the pitfalls of a period analysis of Afro-American expressivity and take Harlem as a moment not in a developing and exclusive literary enterprise, but as a moment in a general and distinctive Afro-American discursive history comprised of a definable array of strategies. The presentation that follows will, hopefully, give impetus to such a reassessment. Versions of this essay were prepared and delivered as lectures for the English Institute (August 1985) and the Afro-American Studies Department at Yale University (November 1985). At Yale, I had the privilege of delivering the Richard Wright Lecture.

132

Adams implies that bare chronology makes modernists of us all. The latest moment's production—by definition—instantiates "the modern." And unless we arbitrarily terminate modernism's allowable tomorrows, the movement is unending. Moreover, the temporal indeterminacy of the term allows us to select (quite randomly) structural features that we will call distinctively "modern" on the basis of their chronological proximity to us. We can then read these features over past millennia. Like Matthew Arnold in his Oxford inaugural lecture entitled "On the Modern Element in Literature," we can discover what is most distinctively modern in works a thousand years old.

As one reads essay after essay, one becomes convinced that Ihab Hassan's set of provocative questions in a work entitled "POSTmodernISM A Paracritical Bibliography" are apt and suggestive for understanding the frustrating persistence of "modernism" as a critical sign. Hassan queries:

> When will the Modern Period end?
>
> Has ever a period waited so long? Renaissance? Baroque? Neo-Classical? Romantic? Victorian?
>
> When will Modernism cease and what comes thereafter?
>
> What will the twenty-first century call us? and will its voice come from the same side of our graves?
>
> Does Modernism stretch merely to stretch out our lives? Or, ductile, does it give a new sense of time? The end of periodization? the slow arrival of simultaneity?
>
> If change changes ever more rapidly, and the future jolts us now, do men, paradoxically, resist both endings and beginnings?[3](7)

Certainly it is the case that scholars resist consensus on everything—beginnings, dominant trends, and endings—where *modernism* is concerned.

Yet, for Anglo-American and British traditions of literary and artistic scholarship there is a tenuous agreement that some names and works *must* be included in any putatively comprehensive account of modern writing and art. Further, there seems to be an identifiable pleasure in listing features of art and writing that begin to predominate (by Virginia Woolf's time line) on or about December, 1910.

The names and techniques of the "modern" that are generally set forth constitute a descriptive catalogue resembling a natural philosopher's curiosity cabinet. In such cabinets disparate and seemingly discontinuous objects share space because that is the very function of the cabinet—to house or give order to varied things in what appears a rational, scientific manner. Picasso and Pound, Joyce and Kandinsky, Stravinsky and Klee, Brancusi and H. D. are made to form a series. Collage, primitivism, montage, allusion, "dehumanization," and leitmotifs are forced into the same field. Nietzsche and Marx, Freud and Frazier, Jung and Bergson become dissimilar bedfellows. Such naming rituals have the force of creative works like *Ulysses* and *The Waste Land*. They substitute a myth of unified purpose and intention for definitional certainty. Before succumbing to the myth, however, perhaps we should examine the "change" that according to Woolf's calendar occurred on or about December, 1910.

Surely that change is most accurately defined as an acknowledgment of radical uncertainty. Where precisely anyone or anything was located could no longer be charted on old maps of "civilization," nor could even the most microscopic observation tell the exact time and space of day. The very conceptual possibilities of both time and space had been dramatically refigured in the mathematics of Einstein and the physics of Heisenberg. A war of barbaric immensity combined with imperialism, capitalism and totalitarianism's subordination or extermination of tens of millions to produce a reaction to human possibilities quite different from Walt Whitman's joyous welcoming of the modern. Whitman in the nineteenth century exalted: "Years of the modern! years of the unperform'd!"

For T. S. Eliot, the completed and expected performance of mankind scarcely warranted joy. There was, instead, the "Murmur of maternal lamentation" presaging:

> Cracks . . . and bursts in the violet air
> Falling towers
> Jerusalem Athens Alexandria
> Vienna London
> Unreal.[4]

Eliot's speaker, however, is comforted by the certainty that there are millennia of "fragments" (artistic shrapnel) constituting a *civilization* to be mined, a cultured repertoire to act as a shore against ruins. That is to say, Fitzgerald's Tom Buchanan in *The Great Gatsby* seems to be a more honestly self-conscious representation of the threat that some artists whom we call "modern" felt in the face of a new world of science, war, technology, and imperialism. "Civilization's going to pieces," Tom confides to an assembled dinner party at his lavish Long Island estate while drinking a corky (but rather impressive) claret. "I've gotten to be a terrible pessimist about things," he continues.[5]

Now, I don't mean to suggest that Anglo-American, British, and Irish moderns did not address themselves with seriousness and sincerity to a changed condition of humankind. Certainly they did. But they also mightily restricted the province of what constituted the tumbling of the towers, and they remained eternally self-conscious of their own pessimistic "becomings." Tom's pessimism turns out to be entirely bookish. It is predicated upon Stoddard's (which Tom remembers as "Goddard's") racialistic murmurings. What really seems under threat are not the towers of civilization, but rather an assumed supremacy of boorishly racist, indisputably sexist, and unbelievably wealthy Anglo-Saxon males. One means of shoring up one's self under perceived threats of "democratization" and a "rising tide" of color is to resort to elitism—to adopt a style that refuses to represent any *thing* other than the stylist's refusal to represent (what Susan Sontag refers to as an "aesthetics of silence").

Another strategy is to claim that one's artistic presentations and performances are quintessential renderings of the unrepresentable—human subconsciousness, for example, or primitive structural underpinnings of a putatively civilized mankind, or the simultaneity of a space-time continuum. Yet another strategy—a somewhat tawdry and dangerous one—is advocacy and allegiance to authoritarian movements or institutions that promise law and order. Regardless of their strategies for confronting it, though, it was *change*—a profound shift in what could be taken as unquestionable assumptions about the meaning of human life—that moved those artists whom we call "moderns." And it was only a rare one among them who did not have some formula—some "ism"—for checking a precipitous toppling of man and his towers. Futurism, imagism, impressionism, vorticism, expressionism, cubism—all offered explicit programs for the arts *and* the salvation of humanity. Each in its turn yields to other formulations of the role of the writer and the task of the artist in a changed and always, ever more rapidly changing world.

Today, we are "postmodern." Rather than *civilization*'s having gone to pieces, it has extended its sway in the form of a narrow and concentrated group of power brokers scarcely more charming, humane or informed than Tom Buchanan. To connect the magnificent achievements, breakthroughs and experiments of an entire panoply of modern intellectuals with fictive attitudes of a fictive modern man (Fitzgerald's Tom) may seem less than charitable. For even though Tom evades the law, shirks moral responsibility, and still ends up rich and in possession of the fairest Daisy of them all (though he ends, that is to say, as the capitalist triumphant, if not the triumphant romantic hero of the novel), there are still other modes of approach to the works of the moderns.

Lionel Trilling, for example, provides one of the most charitable scholarly excursions to date.[6] He describes modern literature as "shockingly personal," posing "every question that is forbidden in polite society" and involving readers in intimate interactions that leave them uneasily aware of their personal beings in the world. One scholarly reaction to Trilling's formulations, I'm afraid, is probably like that of the undergraduates whom he churlishly suggests would be "rejected" by the efforts of Yeats and Eliot, Pound and Proust. It is difficult, for example, for an Afro-American student of literature like me—one unconceived in the philosophies of Anglo-American, British, and Irish moderns—to find intimacy in either the moderns' hostility to *civilization* or in their fawning reliance on an array of images and assumptions bequeathed by a *civilization* that, in its prototypical form, is exclusively Western, preeminently bourgeoisie, and optically white.

Alas, Fitzgerald's priggishly astute Nick has only a limited vocabulary when it comes to a domain of experience that I, as an Afro-American, know well: "As we crossed Blackwell's Island a limousine passed us, driven by a white chauffeur, in which sat three modish negroes, two bucks and a girl. I laughed aloud as the yolks of their eyeballs rolled toward us in haughty rivalry" (69). If only Fitgerald had placed his "pale well-dressed negro" in the limousine or if Joseph Conrad[7] had allowed his Africans to actually be articulate or if D. H. Lawrence[8] had not suggested through Birkin's reflection on African culture that:

> Thousands of years ago, that which was imminent in himself must have taken place in these Africans: the goodness, the holiness, the desire for creation and productive happiness must

have lapsed, leaving the single impulse for knowledge through the senses, knowledge arrested
and ending in the senses, mystic knowledge in disintegration and dissolution, knowledge such
as the beetles have, which live purely within the world of corruption and cold dissolution.
(245-46)

Or if O'Neill[9] had only bracketed the psycho-surreal final trappings of his
Emperor's world and given us the stunning account of colonialism that remains
implicit in his quip at the close of his list of dramatis personae: "The action of the
play takes place on an island in the West Indians, as yet un-self-determined by white
marines." If any of these moves had been accomplished, then perhaps I might feel,
at least, some of the intimacy and reverence Trilling suggests.

But even as I recall a pleasurable spring in New Haven when I enjoyed cracking
Joycean codes in order to teach *Ulysses*, I realize that the Irish writer's grand
monument is not a work to which I shall return with reverence and charitably
discover the type of inquisition that Trilling finds so engaging: "[Modern literature]
asks us if we are content with our marriages, with our family lives, with our
professional lives, with our friends"(7-8). I am certain that I shall never place
Ulysses in a group of texts that I describe, to use Trilling's words, as "spiritual" if not
"actually religious." Perhaps, the reason I shall not is because the questions Trilling
finds—correctly or incorrectly—intimately relevant to his life are descriptive only
of a bourgeois, characteristically twentieth-century, white Western mentality. As
an Afro-American, a person of African descent in the United States today, I spend a
great deal of time reflecting that in the world's largest geographies the question
"Where will I find water, wood, or food for today?" is (and has been for the entirety
of this century) the most pressing and urgently posed inquiry.

In "diasporic," "developing," "Third World," "emerging"—or whatever adjective one chooses to signify the non-Western side of Chenweizu's title "The West
and the Rest of Us"—nations or territories there is no need to pose, in ironical
Audenesque ways, questions such as: Are we happy? Are we content? Are we
free?[10] Such questions presuppose, at least, an adequate level of sustenance and a
faith in human behavioral alternatives sufficient to enable a self-directed
questioning. In other words, without food for thought, all modernist bets are off.
Rather than reducing the present essay to a discourse on underdevelopment,
however, or invoking a different kind of human being, what I want to evoke by
emphasizing concerns other than those of "civilization" and its discontents is a
discursive constellation that marks a change in Afro-American nature that
occurred on or about September 18, 1895. The constellation that I have in mind
includes Afro-American literature, music, art, graphic design, and intellectual
history. It is *not* confined to a traditionally defined belles lettres, or, to Literature
with a capital and capitalist "L".

In fact, it is precisely the confinement (in a very Foucaultian sense discovered in
Madness and Civilization) of such bourgeois categories (derivatives of Kantian
aesthetics) that the present essay seeks to subvert.[11] Hence, there will be few sweeps
over familiar geographies of a familiar Harlem Renaissance conceived as an

enterprise of limited accomplishment and limited liability—"Harlem Renaissance, Ltd." Instead, I shall attempt to offer an account of discursive conditions of possibility for what I define as "renaissancism" in Afro-American expressive culture as a whole. I am, thus, interested less in *individual* "artists" than in areas of expressive production. It is my engagement with these areas of Afro-American production (intellectual history, music, graphic design, stage presence, oratory, etc.) that provides intimacy and that leads me, through a specifically Afro-American modernism, to blues geographies that are still in search of substantial analysis—and liberation.

* * *

The affinity that I feel for Afro-American modernism is not altogether characteristic. Scholars have been far from enthusiastic in their evaluation of the "Harlem Renaissance" of the 1920s—an outpouring of Afro-American writing, music, and social criticism that includes some of the earliest attempts by Afro-American artists and intellectuals to define themselves in "modern" terms. Few scholars would disagree that the Harlem Renaissance marks a readily identifiable "modern" movement in Afro-American intellectual history, and most would concede that the principal question surrounding the Harlem Renaissance has been: "Why did the renaissance fail?"

Scarcely four years after "Black Tuesday," that awful moment which plummeted American into depression, a prominent intellectual and contemporary of the renaissance wrote:

> It is a good thing that [the editor] Dorothy West is doing in instituting a magazine [*Challenge*] through which the voices of younger Negro writers can be heard. The term "younger Negro writers" connotes a degree of disillusionment and disappointment for those who a decade ago hailed with loud huzzas the dawn of the Negro literary millennium. We expected much; perhaps, too much. I now judge that we ought to be thankful for the half-dozen younger writers who did emerge and make a place for themselves.[12]

James Weldon Johnson's disillusionment that the Harlem Renaissance "failed" finds its counterparts and echoes in the scholarship, polemics, and popular rhetoric of the past half-century. An avatar of Johnson's disillusionment, for example, is the scholarly disapprobation of Nathan Huggins' provocative study *Harlem Renaissance* (1971).[13]

Huggins charges that the *Harlem Renaissance* failed because it remained provincial. Its spokespersons unfortunately accepted the province of "race" as a domain in which to forge a New Negro identity. Mired in this ethnic provincialism, writers like Countee Cullen, Claude McKay, Langston Hughes, Alain Locke and others failed to realized that they did not have to battle for a defining identity in America. They needed only, in Huggins' view, to claim "their *patria*, their nativity" as American citizens (309). The Harvard historian believes that Afro-Americans are—and have always been—inescapably implicated in the warp and woof of the American fabric. In fact, he holds that they are nothing other than "Americans" whose darker pigmentation has been appropriated as a liberating mask by their lighter complexioned fellow citizens. Hence, Afro-Americans are fundamentally bone of the bone—if not flesh of the flesh—of the American people, and the intricacies of minstrelsy and the aberrations of the Harlem Renaissance are both misguided, but deeply revelatory, products of the way race relations have stumbled and faltered on the boards of progressive optimism in the United States.

While Huggins adduces provinciality and narrowness as causes for a failed Harlem Renaissance, his contemporary and fellow Afro-American historian David Levering Lewis takes a contrary view.[14] Lewis ascribes Harlem's failings to a tragically wide, ambitious, and delusional striving on the part of renaissance intellectuals. Writing ten years after Huggins, Lewis describes the appearance of Alain Locke's compendium of creative, critical, and scholarly utterances *The New Negro* (1925) as follows:

> its thirty-four Afro-American contributors (four were white) included almost all the future
> Harlem Renaissance regulars—an incredibly small band of artists, poets, and writers upon
> which to base Locke's conviction that the race's "more immediate hope rests in the revaluation
> by white and black alike of the Negro in terms of his artistic endowments and cultural
> contributions, past and prospective." To suppose that a few superior people, who would not
> have filled a Liberty Hall quorum or Ernestine Rose's 135th Street library, were to lead ten
> million Afro-Americans into an era of opportunity and justice seemed irresponsibly
> delusional. (117)

Lewis suggests that this delusional vision was a direct function of a rigidly segregated United States. Unlike Huggins, who assumes *patria* as a given, Lewis claims that Afro-Americans turned to art during the twenties precisely because there was no conceivable chance of their assuming *patria*—or anything else in white America. Art seemed to offer the only means of advancement because it was the *only* area in America—from an Afro-American perspective—where the color line had not been rigidly drawn. Excluded from politics and education, from profitable and challenging areas of the professions, and brutalized by all American economic arrangements, Afro-Americans adopted the arts as a domain of hope and an area of possible progress.

Lewis' stunningly full research reveals the merits of his thesis. He provides a grim look at dire economic and social restrictions that hedged blacks round everywhere in the United States during the 1920s. Exceptional art—like effective and liberating social strategies—was, perhaps, a quite illusory Afro-American goal. In the end, all of Harlem's sound and flair could not alter the indubitably American fact that black men and women, regardless of their educational or artistic accomplishments, would always be poorer, more brutally treated, and held in lower esteem than their white American counterparts. The renaissance, thus, reveals itself in retrospect, according to Lewis, as the product of middle-class black "architects [who] believed in ultimate victory through the maximizing of the exceptional. They [members of the 'talented tenth'] deceived themselves into thinking that race relations in the United States were amenable to the assimilationist patterns of a Latin country" (305-06).

The gap between the Afro-American masses and the talented tenth could not have been manifested more profoundly than in the latter's quixotic assimilationist assumptions. For, ironically, the most acute symbol of Harlem's surge at the wall of segregation is not poems nor interracial dinner parties, according to Lewis, but rather the Harlem riot of 1935, in which thousands took to the streets and unleashed their profound frustrations by destroying millions of dollars' worth of white property. The riot, for Lewis, offers the conclusive signal that the strivings of the twenties were delusional and that the renaissance was fated to end with a bang of enraged failure.

Johnson, Huggins, and Lewis are all scholars who merit respect for their willingness to assess an enormously complex array of interactions spanning more than a decade of Afro-American artistic, social, and intellectual history. Thanks to their efforts, we have far more than a bare scholarly beginning when we attempt to define one of the seminal moments of Afro-American "modernism." Yet, the scholarly reflections that we possess are, unfortunately, governed by a problematic—a set of questions and issues—that makes certain conclusions and evaluations inevitable. For if one begins with the query that motivates Johnson and others, then one is destined to provide a derogatory account of the twenties. "Why did the Harlem Renaissance fail?" is the question, and the query is tantamount to the unexpected question sprung by a stranger as one walks a crowded street: "When, Sir, did you stop beating your wife?" Both questions are, of course, conditioned by presuppositions that restrict the field of possible responses. To ask "why" the renaissance failed is to agree, at the very outset, that the twenties did not have profoundly beneficial effects for areas of Afro-American discourse that we have only recently begun to explore in depth. Willing compliance in a problematic of "failure" is equivalent, I believe, to efforts of historians—black and otherwise— who seek causal explanations for the "failure" of the Civil Rights Movement.

It seems paradoxical that a probing scholar of Lewis' caliber—an investigator who implies strongly that he clearly understands the low esteem in which Afro-Americans will *always* be held—devotes three hundred pages to proving the "failure" of a movement that in the eyes of white America could never have been a success—precisely because it was "Afro-American." The scholarly double bind that forces Afro-Americanists to begin with *given* assessments of black intellectual history and thus laboriously work their way to dire conclusions is, quite simply, an unfortunate result of disciplinary control and power politics. The purely hypothetical injunction to an Afro-Americanist from the mainstream might be stated as follows:

> Show me, by the best scholarly procedures of the discipline, why the Harlem Renaissance was a failure, and I will reward you. By explaining this *failure*, you will have rendered an "honest" intellectual service to the discipline, to yourself, and to your race.

The primary evaluation where such an injunction is concerned remains, of course, that of the dominating society whose axiological validity and aptitude are guaranteed by its dictation of the governing problematic.

If, for the moment, we return to Anglo-American and British modernism, it is difficult to conceive of scholars devoting enormous energy to explicating the "failure" of modernism. Surely it is the case that the various "isms" of the first decades of British and American modernism did not forestall wars, feed the poor, cure the sick, empower coal miners in Wales (or West Virginia), or arrest the spread of bureaucratic technology. Furthermore—though apologists will not thank me for saying so—the artistic rebels and rebellions of British and American modernism were often decidedly puerile and undeniably transient. The type of mind-set that has governed a Harlem Renaissance problematic would be in force vis-à-vis British and American modernism, I think, if a scholar took Ranier Marie Rilke's evaluation in a letter to a friend as the indisputable truth of modernism's total effect on the world. Writing at the outbreak of World War I, Rilke laments:

> that such confusion, not-knowing-which-way-to-turn, the whole sad man-made complication of this provoked fate, that exactly this incurably bad condition of things was necessary to force out evidence of whole-hearted courage, devotion and bigness? While we, the arts, the theater, called nothing forth in these very same people, brought nothing to rise and flower, were unable to change anyone.[15]

A too optimistic faith in the potential of art may, in fact, be as signal a mark of British and American modernism's "failure" as of the Harlem Renaissance. I suspect, however, that no group of British or white American scholars would take *failure* as their watchword and governing sign for an entire generation and its products. The predictable corollary of my suspicion is my belief that a new problematic is in order for the Harlem Renaissance. What is needed, I believe, is a reconceptualization of the questions we will ask in order to locate the efforts of the 1920s.

* * *

The new problematic that I am attempting to formulate begins with turn-of-the-century Afro-American discursive strategies and their motivation. My claim is that Afro-American spokespersons in late nineteenth-century America were primarily interested in a form of discourse—of public address and delivery—that would effectively articulate the needs, virtues, and strengths of a mass of Afro-Americans stranded by Jim Crow discrimination and violent lynch law in the "country districts" of the South. Both Booker T. Washington and W. E. B. DuBois set forth statements that define strategies of discourse—a black "discursive field," as it were—that are southern in focus and revolutionary in implication. For in *Up From Slavery* (1901) and *The Souls of Black Folk* (1903) alike, we find that the "subject" is the black masses of southern country districts; the goal of both works is the effective liberation of this mass group from feudal subsistence economies and legally reinforced conditions of ignorance and illiteracy. In order to be recognized and heard as Afro-American spokespersons, however, both Washington and DuBois had to assume a discursive stance in relationship to the signal white American *form* for representing blacks—the minstrel mask.

Briefly, minstrelsy is a perduring legacy and strategy of representation when blacks appear in white discourse. It offers a form of appropriation, a domestic space for taking, hearing, and containing the black OTHER. Only by assuming a posture relative to this space could turn-of-the-century, Afro-American spokespersons become effectively articulate.

While the options of such spokespersons were not as clear-cut as a simple duality would suggest, I claim that Washington and DuBois, in their deployment of a "mastery of form" and a "deformation of mastery," respectively, set the contours of a field of Afro-American phonics that marks the birth of Afro-American modernism.

"Mastery" is such a common term in colleges and universities with the MA and MPhil degrees that the first strategy—"mastery of form"—is easily understood. But "deformation" is a more difficult concept.

What I intend by the term is akin to what the deconstructionist Jacques Derrida calls the "trace." The deformative sounds of Afro-America are the group phonics and common language of the masses, sounds that are traditionally labelled "sub-standard," "nonsensical," or "unlearned" by white speakers. But such commonly understood sounds, under a linguist's scrutiny, reveal themselves as normal, standard, literate components of one dialect. The provisional and dialectical character of Black English infects, as it were, assumptions by all speakers in the United States that their language variety is anything other than a quite provisional dialect. It is impossible to sustain a master, standard, or absolute position in the face of the radically demonstrated provisionality of one's position. When Caliban knows himself as a usurped king, it is time for Prospero to depart the island.

Deformation, then, is the putative bondsperson's assured song of his or her own exalted, expressive status in an always coequal world of sounds and soundings. Anecdotally, one can image Paul Whiteman trying to sustain the title "King of Jazz" in the presence of Louis Armstrong. In the context of the present discussion, it is very difficult to imagine ninety-nine percent of the Anglo-American population of the years between 1899 and 1920 attempting to convince itself that it sounded in any way as brilliant as W. E. B. DuBois, who takes apart—or de-forms—illusions of such equality through the lyrical brilliance of his prose and his deliberately ironical and satirical mockeries of such illusion.

Washington intersperses *Up From Slavery* with outrageous darky jokes, caricatures of elderly black southern men and women, aspersions against overly ambitious northern blacks, and insulting stereotypes of the race, including a portrait of his own mother as a CHICKEN THIEF. But he also devotes a quarter of his autobiography to the art of public speaking, and his outlandish portrayals of the folk of the "country districts" reveal themselves, finally, as means of holding the attention of an audience that knows but one sound—minstrelsy—of the Negro. In effect, Washington employs sounds of the minstrel mask, or form, to create a space and audience for black public speaking. That public speaking, in turn, is employed to secure philanthropic funds for a black vocational educational institution that constitutes a moral skills center for the black folks of the country districts. Tuskegee Institute is the ultimate result of Washington's sounding on, and mastery of, the minstrel form. His mastery of form is, in fact, signified by the transcendence of minstrel *non-sense* represented by Tuskegee.

In contrast to Washington's mastery of form is DuBois' deformation of mastery. Refusing the sounds of minstrelsy, DuBois instituted black song, specifically the Afro-American spiritual, as the carrier of a black folk energy from southern country districts. Fisk University, built, in part, by monies obtained from concerts of spirituals presented by the Fisk Jubilee Singers, becomes a symbol of the type of educational centers that are needed to move Afro-Americans into the first ranks of twentieth-century life. For DuBois, the black university is the site where black folk energies and Western high culture merge, producing a sound that surpasses all traditional American music, or minstrelsy. In its emphasis on the symbolic weight of black folk spirituality and spiritual singing, *The Souls of Black Folk* stands as a singing book.

The defining discursive models of mastery and deformation provided by Washington and DuBois produce not a binary opposition, but, rather, a type of Cartesian plane—a system of coordinates in which any point on, say, a horizontal axis of mastery implies a coexistent point on a vertical axis of deformation. Hence, the notion of a discursive field.

Alain Locke, a key Afro-American spokesperson of the 1920s, seems to have possessed a brilliant comprehension of this field. For his anthology *The New Negro* (1925) represents Afro-American discourse in its myriad stops and resonances. Locke's collection is a blend of business-like mastery and lyrical and intrepid deformation. It is a public document geared toward specifically in-group and distinctively racial ends. Its purpose is to sound a comprehensive Afro-American voice, one capable of singing in the manner of spirituals (Locke himself wrote the very centerpiece essay on the Afro-American spirituals), yet adept in the ways of southern education and vocation. There are essays devoted both to Hampton-Tuskegee vocationalism and to black business enterprise in the South. Moreover, *The New Negro* employs a rich array of African and Afro-American graphics in order to frame its claims for the emergence of a "New Negro" with venerable visuals drawn from centuries-old traditions. The result is a landmark in Afro-American discourse: a collection that sounds a resonantly new note as both a public speaking manual and a deeply racial (and vernacular) singing book.

High cultural and vernacular expressivity merge in the office of moving Afro-America from subservience, low esteem, and dependency to the status of respected and boldly outspoken nation. What is signal in Locke's venture is the unabashed coalescence of mass and class, "standard" dialect and black vernacular, aesthetic and political concerns. A long and probing essay addressed to the cause of African decolonization and written by DuBois is the concluding section of Locke's work.

If *The New Negro* is representative of efforts of Harlem Renaissance spokes-persons (and I believe it is), then the discursive results of Harlem in black intellectual history can scarcely be deemed failures. For Locke's work both enjoins and represents a successful expressive moment in the field constituted by a mastery of form and a deformation of mastery. *The New Negro* is a kind of manual of maroonage, a voice of a northern, urban black population that has radically absented itself from the erstwhile plantations and devastated country districts of the South. Combining a panoply of folk sounds with traditional artistic forms and entrepreneurial and practical concerns of black liberation, *The New Negro* projects an articulate, nationalistic, and independent black voice. That voice—if at times too sanguine, overly self-conscious and self-confident—constitutes a high point for energies set in motion at the turn of the century.

Further, the voice of the New Negro comprised a model for subsequent generations. When Sterling Brown, who is preeminently a poet and critic of the 1930s, assumed the mantle of "folk poet" as a natural wrap, he demonstrated the efficacy and effects of a successful Afro-American modernism. For what the Harlem Renaissance, as a masterfully achieved space within a black discursive field, enabled was a speaking or sounding place where a middle-class, Phi Beta Kappa, college-bred poet like Brown could responsibly play a distinctive note. DuBois' black, country folk as university pupils find their voice and representation in the Jubilee Singers of Nashville. The urbane Sterling Brown met the blues singer Gertrude "Ma" Rainey in Nashville (home of Fisk University). He was in the company of the famous black musicologist and Fisk faculty member John Work when they encountered Rainey at a Nashville club. What the two men drew from the tradition of folk sound represented by Rainey is now a matter of black discursive history.

Brown's *Southern Road* (1932) is one of the most outstanding collections of modern, black verse in existence. Work's collections and analyses of black song (*Folk Song of the American Negro, Jubilee, Ten Spirituals*) are unsurpassed. The productions of the two men not only guaranteed their own recognition, reward, and employment, but also brought new perspective to the group portrait of the Afro-American that had been in formation since the turn of the century. This perspective was a usable construction for writers like Richard Wright and Zora Neale Hurston who had their maturation in the thirties.

* * *

The success of the Harlem Renaissance as Afro-American modernism's defining moment is signalled by *The New Negro*'s confidently voiced plays within a field marked by the mastery of form and the deformation of mastery. Only by reconstructing or re-membering a discursive history of Afro-America and its socioeconomic and sociopolitical motivations and objectives can one see Harlem and its successors as articulations that carry a population not away from querulous literary ancestors, but rather *up from slavery*. Modernism for Afro-America finds impetus, empowerment, and inspiration in the black city (Harlem). No cracks and bursts in the violet air here, only soundings designed to secure the highest available social, economic, and artistic rewards for a generation that moved decisively beyond the horrors of old country districts.

A blues sound rolled forth, producing the sense of a moment's speaking, an augury of possibilities for finance and even fusion (jazz) that surely became orchestrated during the 1960s and 1970s, the period of a Black Arts Movement that referred to itself in energetically self-conscious ways as "Renaissance II."

Perhaps the eternally modern in Afro-American discursive and intellectual history is not so much signalled by the single "Harlem Renaissance" as by a more inclusive "renaissancism" defined as an ever-present, folk or vernacular drive that moves always up, beyond, and away from whatever forms of oppression a surrounding culture next devises. "Renaissancism" is, finally, the sign of the modern that joins Harlem and the *Indigene* movement of Haiti and African Negritude. One might say that the success of Afro-American renaissancism consists in its heralding of a countermodernism, as it were, a drive unlike the exquisite disillusionment and despair of Britain and Jazz Age U.S.A. I use "counter" just as advisedly as I earlier employed "modernism" alone, for now I believe the complexities—a very peculiar set of expressive manifestations and critical and theoretical issues—of Afro-American twentieth-century expression should be comprehensible. Recognition of such complexities leads to the recognitions of a trace, a something not accounted for in traditional, Anglo-American definitions of modernism. One definition of what can be recognized is a "countermodernism."

This countertradition found its socioeconomic and sociopolitical groundings in what the sagacious Franz Fanon called "dying colonialism." *The New Negro*, as stated earlier, concludes with an essay by DuBois that sings, figuratively, this death of colonialism and sounds a note of liberation to which hundreds of millions of formerly colonized, darker peoples of the world can march. This note from Harlem, as any scan of the global scene today will reveal, is, perhaps, the most thoroughly modern sound the United States has yet produced.

NOTES

[1]Harry Levin, "What Was Modernism?", *Massachusetts Review* 1 (1960): 609-30. All citations are marked by page numbers in parentheses.

[2]Robert Martin Adams, "What Was Modernism?", *Hudson Review* 31 (1978): 19-33. Hereafter in my notes, I will list the full reference. Subsequent cites will be marked by page numbers in parentheses.

[3]Ihab Hassan, "POSTmodernISM A Paracritical Bibliography," *New Literary History* 3 (1971): 5-30.

[4]T. S. Eliot, "The Waste Land," in *Modern Poetry*, ed. Maynard Mack et al., 2nd ed. (Englewood Cliffs, N.J.: 1961), 157-58.

[5]F. Scott Fitzgerald, *The Great Gatsby* (New York, 1953), 13.

[6]Lionel Trilling, "On the Teaching of Modern Literature," in *Beyond Culture* (New York, 1965), 327.

[7]I refer, of course, to Conrad's "Heart of Darkness."

[8]D. H. Lawrence, *Women in Love* (New York, 1974).

[9]The reference is to Eugene O'Neill's *The Emperor Jones*.

[10]Wystan Hugh Auden's ordinary citizen as "Modern Man" is coldly described by the speaker of "The Citizen (To JS/07/M/378 This marble Monument Is Erected by the State)," a 1940 poem, as "in the modern sense of an old-fashioned word, he was a saint." Quoted from Mack, *Modern Poetry*, 206. The speaker is not undone when his/her report is broken by someone's question about such exemplary conduct: "Was he free? Was he happy?" The speaker answers: "...The Question is absurd:/Had anything been wrong, we should certainly have heard."

[11]In *Madness and Civilization*, Michel Foucault argues that it is *de rigueur* for a rational, bourgeois, capitalist state to "confine" the poor, the criminal, and the insane in order to know the boundaries of affluence, sanity, and innocence. It is, however, *confinement* in itself that enforces the categories; if you are an inmate of a "total institution" (like a prison, or, American Slavery as the "Prisonhouse of Bondage"), then you are automatically classified according to the defining standards of that institution. The Kantian reference is, of course, to the *Critique of Judgement* (1790). Once "ART" and "AESTHETICS" are distinguished from "popular culture" and "low taste," then one has effected a confinement that can be enforced merely by mentioning a word. Such distinctions—resting on Western metaphysics—can be used to defend and preserve canons of literature and to protect "artistic" masterpieces from all criticism. Only "*men* of Taste" are held to possess the developed "aesthetic sense" and sensibility requisite to identification and judgment of genuine works of "art." If such men declare that a product is *not* ART but a product of some other category, there is no escape from their authority of confinement—except subversion.

[12]"Foreword," *Challenge* 1 (1934):1.

[13]Nathan Huggins, *Harlem Renaissance* (New York, 1971). Subsequent citations appear in text.

[14]David Levering Lewis, *When Harlem Was in Vogue* (New York, 1981). Subsequent citations appear in text. The phrase "when Harlem was in vogue" is drawn from the section of Langston Hughes' autobiography *The Big Sea* (1940) devoted to the Harlem Renaissance. Hughes writes of the renaissance as a mere "vogue" set in motion and largely financed by white downtowners while Negroes played minstrel and trickster roles in it all. A time of low-seriousness and charming highjinks is what Highes (one hopes ironically) portrays. In fact, I think Hughes' characterization is as much a product of the dreadful disappointment he suffered when his patron (Mrs. R. Osgood Mason) dumped him because he decided to write an "engaged" poem, a "socialist" response to the opening of a luxury hotel in New York when so many were starving. He reads treacherous patronage over the entire Harlem Renaissance. Further, to say, as Hughes does, that you were "only funning" is to dampen the pain that results if *you* were really serious and your patron was "funning" all along. In any case, I believe Hughes' account (partially because he lived and produced wonderful work through subsequent generations) has had an enormous effect on subsequent accounts of the renaissance. In many ways, this effect has been unfortunate.

[15]Quotes from Miklos Szabolcsi, "Avant-garde, Neo-avant-garde, Modernism: Questions and Suggestions," *New Literary History* 3 (1971): 75.

The Harlem Renaissance: A Revisionist Approach

In the decade following the Great War, there emerged a group of writers, musicians, dramatists, and visual artists who gathered in the exciting and burgeoning Harlem section of Manhattan. These young black intellectuals took as one of their major themes the development of a new type of Negro, one who stood in strong contrast to the one portrayed in eighteenth and nineteenth century literature. Such a polemic is presented in the various essays and pieces of fiction found in the seminal text of the period, Alain Locke's anthology, *The New Negro*, published in 1925.

One extremely interesting aspect of Locke's text is that of the thirty-six contributors to the collection of essays, poems, short stories, and novel excerpts, only eight contributors were women. And what is troubling about these contributions is that, with one exception, he only included women writers whose works supported *his* notion of the development of a "New Negro" in early twentieth century America. Only two of the critical pieces included in the anthology are by women, and one of those two essays articulates an idea of female negritude which stands in sharp contrast to Locke's polemic.

Not only did Locke's anthology exclude many of his black female contemporaries, so did many of the major anthologies of the period. In 1922, James Weldon Johnson edited *The Book of American Negro Poetry*. He included seven women in his collection of a total of forty contributors. Three years later, Locke published his collection; and in 1927, Countee Cullen published *Caroling Dusk: An Anthology of Verse by Negro Poets*. Cullen's text contains the works of thirteen women poets. In 1929, a white man, Victor Francis Calverton, edited Anthology of American Negro Literature and included six major women poets, a novelist, and a playwright.

A close examination of Alain Locke's *The New Negro* provides an interesting description of exactly who this "new" Negro is. Locke defines him one way in his essay, " The New Negro," while Elise Johnson McDougald characterizes him quite differently in "The Task of Negro Womanhood."

> The Negro today is inevitably moving forward under the
> control largely of his own objectives. What are these
> objectives? Those of his outer life are happily already well
> and finally formulated, for they are none other than the ideals
> of American institutions and democracy. Those of his inner
> life are yet in process of formation, for the new psychology
> at present is more of a consensus of feeling than of opinion,
> of attitude rather than of program. (*New Negro* 10)

25

According to Locke's definition of the "new Negro," the persona is male, forward-moving, integrationist, and in possession of a new sense of spirituality and creativity. He is acutely aware of his divided self, one side Negro, one side American, and is determined that if the "more intelligent and representative elements of the two race groups" get in "vital touch with one another," (9) surely the group in power will concede that the historically oppressed group is worthy of tasting American democracy. Moreover, the "new" Negro stands in contrast with the "old" Negro who was a savage member of a dark, segregated ghetto; he was, in effect, a naive child.

The "new" Negro woman, on the other hand, looks very differ-ent. In her essay, Elise Johnson McDougald outlines this "new" Negro woman's arduous difficulties. (369) She curiously begins her essay by encouraging the reader to look to the Harlem woman because she is supposedly free from sex and race discrimination and unencumbered with the hardships of household duties. However, her argument that follows fails to convince the reader adequately that such glowing conditions exist, even in Harlem. The "new" Negro woman is first concerned with black and white society's failure to recognize her multiplicity of problems in America; since the problems are varied in nature, they cannot be treated en masse. Secondly, she is portrayed in society as having low morals, values, and standards, and her beauty is typified by "Aunt Jemima." (370) Finally, she faces terrible hardships in industry where she is doubly discriminated against for her race and sex. The "new" Negro woman is vastly different from the self-satisfied "new" Negro man described by Locke. She is no less assertive, competent, or visionary than he, but she is forced to grapple with the twofold quandary of sexual and racial discrimination as it is manifested in social, familial, and economic oppression.

It is perhaps here that answers might be gleaned as to why so few women are included in the male-edited anthologies of the time. Since in reality such a great discrepancy exists between the "new" Negro man and woman, it becomes difficult to show fairly the plight of the black woman while effectively arguing for the "in control" black man. As such, it is beneficial to support such a polemic using narrowly interpreted non-fiction and fiction. Secondly, since the close group of male and female writers centered in Harlem created an intimate inner circle for creativity and publication, women (and perhaps some men) not directly involved could not hope to have their work recognized. Moreover, there is the issue of sexism with which the ponderer of post-war literature must reckon. It is interesting to observe how someone like Charles S. Johnson, editor of *Opportunity Magazine* during the 1920's, notes his contributors. He provides brief personal and professional sketches for each of his male contributors but groups all the female artists together with a "thanks," When observed from this perspective, it is no wonder that the "new" Negro is depicted as having a particular character with particular interests.

But when the darkened definition of the "new" Negro is viewed in the light of the sensible inclusion of the "new" Negro woman, the "who" of the Harlem Renaissance must then be redefined as an early twentieth century American man and woman who

26

are painfully aware of historical oppression, inaccurate representation, and unjust exclusion from American institutions. They must also deal with the present society's inability to welcome them graciously as competent, deserving members. Finally, he and she possess an enlightened understanding of their race and seek to educate their counterparts as to the evolution of a new black aesthetic and political ideal in America.

There were, without doubt, more women publishing during the 1920's in Harlem who, for various reasons, were not being included in male-edited anthologies. Because of their exclusion from the black mainstream vehicles, their works were relegated to even more marginalized journals and poorly distributed publications. In light of that fact, their works have not been consistently included in courses in American literature. Subsequently, the exclusion of many early twentieth century Black women's works from the existing canon of American literature facilitates the further truncation of an Afro-American literary ancestry.

Such an understanding leads to a threefold project of recovering and collecting these forgotten women's works and then rewriting them into the existing canon of American literature. The first stage of reevaluation of the Harlem Renaissance with respect to gender is attempted above. When the period is reinterpreted in terms of the women who were contributing to the outpouring of literary creativity, notions of when the Renais-sance took place begin to change as well *(Gender and the Politics of History)*.

Thus the second phase of reevaluating the Renaissance with respect to gender centers around the determination of when the period begins and ends. Many scholars arbitrarily outline the immediate decade following the First World War as the official Renaissance period, with the end being the stock market crash of 1929. Such an arbitrary depiction only affords scholars the ability to examine the height of creativity during this time. Yet, one can argue that a better understanding of these works, particularly the works of the female artists, can be gained through an examination of the work leading up to and away from the Renaissance apex. As such, the period delineation must continue into the second post-war decade.

Given this expansive time period, one can gauge the progress and quality of artists' works by reading through the period's beginning, middle, and end. Moreover, it is clear from the above discussion of Locke's text that the editor and contributors were vividly aware of the development of a black American characterized by "twoness." However, since Locke's anthology, as Johnson's, was published in the early part of the decade, while Cullen's was toward its end, it would seem that the beginning of the decade serves as a point of reference to examine the developmental stages of such a renaissance with its height in the 1920's.

To continue, 1937 marks the publication year of Zora Neale Hurston's *Their Eyes Were Watching God*. Hurston is often seen by critics as the writer whose works close this period of a recognizable harvesting of black artistry. A 1929 closing date excludes all of Hurston's novels, autobiography, and folklore, and specifically *Their Eyes Were Watching God*, a text which in many ways exemplifies the Harlem Renaissance ideal

27

of assertion of independence. Furthermore, most of the artists included in the Renaissance continued to publish well after 1929. In many cases, their best and more significant works were published afterward. Such an expansion also aids in fair evaluation of the development of the artists' careers.

The task of redefining the "when" of the Harlem Renaissance with respect to gender must be seen from its proper view point. It is not that the period must be extended to include women who were publishing in the 1930's, and thereby expand the pool of eligible artists. On the contrary, rightful admission and full examination of the female artists' contributions necessarily expand the period. The artists influence the period, as opposed to the period being artificially extended to include the artists.

Finally, in terms of the redefinition of the "where" of the Renaissance, recovery, collection, and inclusion of the works of black women publishing in Harlem during the 1920's and 1930's exclude many women who may not have been publishing in Harlem at that time but were nonetheless making great contributions to an exciting outpouring of aesthetic creativity which had its base in Harlem (*New Negro* 301-11). It might be that the Harlem group was influencing the rest of the country's artistic production, but it might be equally interesting to evaluate the reverse influence of the influx of outsiders on the Harlem group.

A closer examination of the creative works of blacks throughout the United States during that time would yield evidence that the country was experiencing more than a "Harlem" Renaissance but a black American Renaissance with a very visible concentration in Harlem. The omission of mid-western black females, for example, would exclude an artist like Marita O. Bonner, publishing in Chicago, Illinois. Zora Neale Hurston, whose wealthy white patrons made their homes in New York City, was doing her collecting and writing of folklore in Florida. Artists like Dorothy West and Helene Johnson had their beginnings in Boston, Massachusetts, and subsequently were contributors to the Boston-based *Saturday Evening Quill*. Furthermore, the Washington, D.C. group of artists, which at critical points in the period's development included Georgia Douglas Johnson, Alain Locke, Zora Neale Hurston, and Beatrice Murphy, offered significant and essential contributions to the creation of a new aesthetic. Further research would favorably prove that exciting artistic production was occurring in areas immediately north, south, and further west of New York City. A discussion of this nature might logically lead to a greater understanding of literary canon formation as it functions in American literature.

28

WORKS CITED

Calverton, Victor Francis, ed. *Anthology of American Negro Literature.* New York: The Modern Library, 1929.

Cullen, Countee, ed. *Caroling Dusk: An Anthology of Verse by Negro Poets.* New York: Harper & Row Publishers, 1955 (1927).

Johnson, James Weldon, ed. *The Book of American Negro Poetry.* New York: Harcourt Brace Jovanovich, Inc., 1931 (1922).

Locke, Alain, ed *The New Negro.* New York: Atheneum, 1986 (1925)

Scott, Joan. *Gender and the Politics of History.* New York: Columbia University Press, 1988.

Crystal J. Lucky
New Haven
Connecticut, USA

29

AFRICAN AND BLACK AMERICAN LITERATURE: THE "NEGRO RENAISSANCE" AND THE GENESIS OF AFRICAN LITERATURE IN FRENCH ⸻

Mbulamwanza Mudimbe-Boyi

Translated by J. Coates

THE AMERICAN CONTEXT

One of the most important moments of self-assertion and emergence for the black personality in the world was the Negro Renaissance or, as it is also called, the Harlem Renaissance. It was the reflection and the remarkable expression not only of a peculiar culture but also the living proof of a particular cultural longing. This literary movement demonstrates the integration of black American culture with American society and, to a very great degree, with the black world as a whole.

It was Margaret Butcher who noted with some force that:

By setting up an inveterate tradition of racial differences in the absence of any fixed or basic differences of culture and tradition on the Negro's part, American slavery introduced into the very heart of American society a crucial dilemma whose resultant problems, with their progressive resolution, account for many fateful events in American history and for some of the most characteristic qualities of American culture. On all levels, political, social, and cultural, this dilemma has become the focal point, disruptive as well as constructive, of major issues in American history. In the pre-Civil War period, the issue was slavery versus anti-slavery; in the Reconstruction era it was discrimination and bi-racialism versus equalitarian nationalism. In the contemporary era, it is segregation and cultural separatism versus integration and cultural democracy.[1]

Summed up in this passage we find the most important points of contradiction in American society, which essentially boil down to certain basic modes of life and dynamics in the American context.

My thanks to Dr. V. Y. Mudimbe and Dr. Ngandu for the help they have given me towards the completion of this work. My thanks also to the translator of this paper.

Yet what was the point of making appeals if one was black and living in the America of Lothrop Stoddard and Madison Grant, who were adopting and revising the racial theories of Gobineau, Schultz, Wagner, and Chamberlain? And what was the point of making demands if, just at the very moment when the purity and power and beauty of New Orleans music was bursting upon the world, the ideas and the violence of a regenerated Ku Klux Klan were being paraded and spread about? For during the 1920s, as during the final quarter of the last century, black musicians and black writers, like all black people who "were trying to make their voices heard, carried a heavy burden marked with all the signs of inferiority which every single black bore, no matter which tradition had lent its character to his plays or poetry or novels."[2]

It was in this climate of derision toward anything black that the Negro Renaissance in America emerged to give some direction and significance to the black personality both in literature and in the culture as a whole.

THE HARLEM RENAISSANCE AND THE BLACK PERSONALITY

The Harlem Renaissance movement which Arna Bontemps brought to life in 1921 is, in fact, the philosophical, spiritual, and artistic result of a number of movements and actions beginning at the turn of the century.[3] Among them we should note: W. E. B. Du Bois's organization of the National Association for the Advancement of Colored People (NAACP), his editing of the *Crisis*, and his organization of several Pan-African congresses; Marcus Garvey's creation of the Black Star Steamship Line and the founding of the review the *Negro World*; and Carter G. Woodson's founding of the Association for the Study of Negro Life and History. All these projects and creations, with their fair share of generosity and radicalism (and sometimes, of utopia), directly helped the rehabilitation of black Americans.

The "Black Renaissance" was thus brought about by blacks for blacks. It was himself that the American black put forward as a subject for his own literary creations, and he went to great lengths to express for himself his own particular problems and his own aspirations and rights in a form which seemed to correspond best with his own fate.

Jean Wagner has summed up this new perspective: "The Black Renaissance rises as a whole from a new vision of the past which the whole race shares together."[4]

The movement was composed of many themes: there was revolt against the injustices suffered by blacks; the demand for a new personality and for a cultural identity; and finally there was nostalgia and fascination for the far-off land of Africa. The movement expressed the feelings and thoughts of blacks. And thus where literature is concerned one may speak of a realistic, engaged literature, yet it was also romantic. The nostalgia for Africa appears in fact as a wish to return to roots, coupled with a great love for the history and life of the African people. Africa also appears as a mythical continent, a lost paradise; but at the same time it is also a representation of a black past before all the denials and distortions of slavery. So by turning back and resurrecting Africa there was a possibility for self-assertion: the extent to which black Americans could feel certain about their past governed the extent to which they could place their hope in the future.

This movement for self-assertion, racial rehabilitation, and recognition of the links of solidarity with Africa was centered in Harlem and crystallized around three writers—Claude MacKay, Countee Cullen, and Langston Hughes—to which one should add the voices of Jean Toomer, James W. Johnson, Sterling Brown, Jessie Fausset, Nella Larsen, and others.

These writers produced an eminently American, but also an explicitly black, literature. The writing reflects the material conditions of existence of black writers, as well as the ideological and spiritual expression of a special group in American society. There are two principal themes: first, the rehabilitation of black history and of blacks in contact with "white" and "Anglo-Saxon" culture; and second, the reappraisal of the black race and its art in a world of cultural interaction.

This unique revolution was to be achieved through the efforts and work of the *exiles*. Although effectively exiled from their fatherlands like other blacks, the blacks in America who were to rise up were also exiles within their own culture. Many of them came from places other than Harlem: Claude MacKay was Jamaican; E. Wabrond was Guyanese; Langston Hughes came from Missouri; and Arna Bontemps was from California. And several of these poets were not from the black middle class. They were academics who, through learning, had moved away from their origins: Claude MacKay came from the State University of Kansas; Jean Toomer from Wisconsin and City College; Jesse Fausset from Cornell; Langston Hughes from Lincoln University; Rudolph Fisher was a professor from Howard University.[5] So they were a minority within a minority; first, because on the level of social relations, they were black in a white-dominated country; and second, because they were the privileged among the blacks. What they began to shout out was: "I am different because I'm Black" and "I, too, am America." These shouts were to launch an important literary movement which was to have considerable influence in the United States and in other parts of the world.

THE NEGRO RENAISSANCE AND NEGRITUDE

During the 1920s there appeared in Paris a series of publications on Africa: in 1920 there was *L'Anthologie Nègre* ("The Negro Anthology") by Blaise Cendrars, a collection of stories, legends, fables, poems, and songs from black Africa; in 1921 there was *Batouala, Véritable Roman Nègre* ("Batouala, A True Negro Novel") by Réne Maran; and finally in 1927 there was *Le Voyage au Congo* ("Journey to the Congo") by André Gide, followed by *Retour du Tchad* ("Return from Chad") in 1928.[6] In these last two books, as Jean Wagner notes, "Black America thought it had found confirmation of its idea that France was turning back toward genuine life forces. Postwar American writers, rebels against both the system and the Victorian prudery that dominated small-town life, thought they had found in the black man a kind of noble savage whose primitive spontaneity had somehow been left untouched by the horrors of the civilization which they were surveying."[7]

It was a period in which among the intellectuals and liberals in Europe there was a distinct interest developing in Africa and African people. The black man, in his innocence and splendor, became a kind of curiosity. This approach pervaded both the colonial administration and applied anthropology. There was a search, on the one hand, for the most efficient means of colonizing Africa and, on the other hand, to fill in the gaps in the ancient history of European man which meant describing "African savages" in terms based upon models taken from Western prehistorical accounts.[8] Yet at the same time, the West was discovering that it was no longer the norm in history and thought, that it was not the prime incarnation of either civilization or culture, and that rational thought as an absolute value and major reference was nothing but a myth. The subjective philosophies set off by German romanticism in the eighteenth and nineteenth centuries were beginning to spread, while the notion of relativity on which specialists in the exact and natural sciences were working began to invade the social sciences and the humanities. The human and spiritual misery at the end of the 1914 to 1918 war also led to a serious questioning of the values of that Western culture which in practice could so effectively set the instruments of death in motion.

It was at this moment that white Europe discovered the American black, jazz, African art and, above all, masks. Certain ethnologists (Frobenius, Delafosse, Monod and so on) kept a wary distance from the ideology of applied anthropology and described a sympathetic, dynamic, and original African culture quite different from the mistaken images put out by colonial propaganda. At the same time there also started to be some deep questioning in the works of African scholars who had felt only satisfaction and pride up to then: what actually was African culture?

Leopold Senghor, in an excellent little book entitled *Pierre Teilhard de Chardin et la Politique Africaine* ("Pierre Teilhard de Chardin and African Politics") has described the astonishment of young black students in Paris and elsewhere in Europe who suddenly discovered good reasons for feeling pride in being Africans.[9] And Lilyan Kesteloot has shown in her book that one of the main causes of this confidence was being in touch with black American writers.[10]

Whenever they speak about the beginnings of their literary movement, the poets of Negritude (or, more precisely, the three apostles Césaire, Senghor, and Damas) give recognition to the leading role that the black American writers played in arousing their general sense of awareness and the sense of racial awareness that was worked out in the Negro Renaissance. Therefore it was with good reason that Senghor, in his paper to the Colloquium on Negritude held in Dakar in 1971, rightly called them the "fathers of Negritude."

To understand the influence of the black American writers on France, it should be remembered that they brought their rebellion to Paris. There, like other writers such as Ernest Hemingway and Gertrude Stein in this period, they had fled from the dehumanizing system of racial segregation and the dryness and conformity of American culture during the 1920s. There were three focal points to their demands—rebellion, violence (both literary and political), and racial awareness.

First, they rebelled against the structure of American society (see, for instance, Banjo by Claude MacKay), a society into which they had been thrust but yet one which disowned them ("I, too, am America," exclaimed Langston Hughes). They made claims for their rights; for the rights of American citizens; for their human dignity (as in "If we must die," for example, a poem by Claude MacKay); for the right to live; and for the recognition of Africa (as in Countee Cullen's poem "Heritage"). And they denounced racial hatred by both blacks and whites.

Second, one can understand why their tentative gropings would often be toward a sort of religious mystique in which evil (sin, the devil, hell) would be symbolized by the fall of man (especially in the work of Countee Cullen, but also in that of Claude MacKay). They were tempted by communism as a social system, as an ideology, and as an epistemology, insofar as communism claimed to resolve all contradictions, to end man's alienation, and to give freedom not just to the proletariat but to blacks—crushed through exploitation, destroyed through racial discrimination, and denied through poverty.

Third, there was the inner assertion of the exile, which is to say the intense existential anxiety that without doubt sprang from the rejection suffered by the black in American society, but which was equally caused by the very fact of Americanism. This can be seen in the rebellion and misery and bitterness which had been sung about ever since the first Negro spirituals, such as "Nobody Knows the Trouble I've Seen." This torn black conscience ("the shock of Americanism on the Negro conscience," in Chester Himes's words) would only find itself properly by going over all the psychological conflicts, frustrations, and traumas that had been endured by blacks since slavery.

The poets of the Negro Renaissance were the first to show signs of a wish to discover and develop their own culture: American jazz erupted in Europe and brought with it a new violence in art and, more particularly, in music. The phenomenon of Josephine Baker made a deep impression on the French ballet in 1925 with the dazzling spectacles that she made, for example, at the Folies Bergères. This had prompted the majority of observers to think that the black African poets involved in the Negritude movement had only taken up the Negro Renaissance rebellion in order to assert the "African Presence."

First of all, there was *La Revue du Monde Noir* ("The Black World Review") published in Paris (1931-1932) which established a point of focus for all the blacks in the French capital. Previous meetings had been organized where most black writers had worked toward one goal: the reappraisal of black culture.

What we want to do is offer to the intellectual elite of the Black race and to the friends of the Blacks an organ in which they may publish works of art, literature and science; to study and make known through newspapers, books, conferences or classes, everything that concerns *Negro civilization* and the natural riches of Africa—the fatherland that is three times sacred to the Black Race; to forge amongst Blacks throughout the world, drawing no distinctions between nationalities, an intellectual and moral link that will help them to know themselves better, to love each other as brothers, to defend their collective interests more effectively and to lend honour to their Race.

This statement was directly inspired by the manifesto of the Negro Renaissance. The contribution made by poets such as Claude MacKay and Langston Hughes is by no means negligible.

Thus *La Revue*, in wishing to identify Negro values and reappraise black culture with an eye on historical truth, brought about a kind of cultural awakening through justifying its own myths. It talked about the "cultural unity of the black world" which was a unity presented as a belief in oneself and as a force acting in the face of the colonial powers. It should, however, be noted that in *La Revue*, in contrast to the Negro Renaissance, there was to be neither aggressiveness nor polemics, but rather the demand for a return to oneself—a demand made with greater serenity through writing that was sometimes not so much racist as rather conciliatory. There remained nevertheless something of the atmosphere of Alain Locke's "New Negro Movement" in the attitude of understanding and sympathy and responsibility in respect to blacks.

In 1932, when *La Revue du Monde Noir* ceased to appear, the young people from the Antilles who were studying at the universities of Paris declared themselves "suffocated" by the system of exploitation and denial which was making the black man "less than his master's object." They founded the review *Légitime Défense* ("Self Defense") which in one single issue effectively inaugurated the "New Negro" movement. Against the great alienation that the black writer experienced (because of his "borrowed personality"), protesting over the muddled poet (for whom "being a good copy of light-skinned man is meant to stand for social as well as poetic reason"), the authors of *Légitime Défense* in their own way took up the aims of the Negro Renaissance. Speaking about the militant function of the literature that they were trying to start up, E. Lero stated: "The wind that is rising from Black America will, we hope, swiftly sweep our Antilles clean of the fruits fallen from a decayed culture. Langston Hughes and Claude MacKay, the two black revolutionary poets, have brought to us, steeped in red alcohol, the African love of life, the African joy in love and the African dream of death. And already the young poets from Haiti are beginning to bring us verses inspired with the dynamics of the future."

The development of the black rebellion can be traced from Negro Renaissance to "Haitian Indigenism," and from *Légitime Défense* to Negritude. But in this journey of suffering and exaltation, the writers of the Negro Renaissance were establishing the paradigm for the conscience of the race. This is why an extract of MacKay's novel *Banjo* is given in *Légitime Défense* as a model for the New Negro's literary work, as the principal objective in *Banjo* was to resist European culture by turning back to African culture.

Black American literature already contained the germs of the principle themes for Negritude, and in this respect one can claim that the real fathers of the Black cultural Renaissance in France were neither the writers in the Antillian tradition nor the surrealist poets nor the French novelists between the wars but the Black writers from the United States! They had left a deep stamp on our writers in the way they had tried to represent the whole race, and had let up a cry in which every single Black recognized himself: it was the first cry of rebellion.[11]

Indeed when black students from Africa and those from the Antilles came together in Paris it was a meeting of exiles, for they were in a double exile: both from their native countries and equally from their social and cultural context.

This experience of the black writers from Africa and the Antilles was set within a framework of colonization and cultural assimilation. Their poetry, for example, was composed of refusal and rebellion. Rebellion was made on a social level by their denunciation of the abuses of colonization and the exploitation and humiliation of the Negro. This can be seen in Senghor's *Chants d'Ombre* (''Songs from Darkness''), in this poem "May Khoras and Balafongs Go with Me," in *Hosties Noires* ("Black Victims"), and in the poems "To the Call from Saba's Race," "A Preliminary Poem," "Prayer of Peace," and finally "Letter to a Prisoner." On the cultural level there was also rebellion against white culture and assimilation and toward an authentic culture drawn from African roots. This rebellion had the corollary of rehabilitation and reappraisal of precolonial Africa, as in Senghor's poem "May Khoras and Balafongs Go with Me." This may also be found in later African writers such as Paul Hazoumé in *Doguicimi*, Laye Camara in *l'Enfant Noir* ("The Dark Child"), Nazi Boni in *le Crépuscule des Temps Anciens* ("Twilight of Ancient Times"), in Djibril Tamsir Niane's *Soundjata ou l'Epopee Mandingue* ("Soundjata or the Epic of Mandingue"), and Seydou Badian's *La Mort de Chaka*. All of these authors were either trying to bring to life personages from historic times or to recreate a life of tradition complete with rites and customs, the daily life in a village.

Recognition of their own values led black African writers to start questioning the West and its norms as well. This questioning is shown in novels such as *Un Vie de Boy* ("Boy's Life"), *Le Vieux Nègre et la Médaille* ("The Old Negro and the Medal") and *Chemins d'Europe* (Paths of Europe") by Ferdinand Oyono; *Ville Cruelle* ("Cruel Town"), *Mission Terminee* ("Mission to Kula"), *Le Pauvre Christ de Bomba* ("The Poor Christ of Bomba"), and *Le Roi Miraculé* (The Miraculous King") by Mongo Beti; and *Les Bouts de Bois de Dieu* ("God's Bits of Wood") by Sembene Ousmane.

This challenge to the West, together with the situation he found himself in, finally led the African to start questioning himself. And in the end there was a meeting with the West, which is what we find in Ousmane Soce's *Les Mirages de Paris* ("Mirages of Paris"), Bernard Dadie's *Un Nègre à Paris* ("A Negro in Paris"), and Ake Loba's *Kocoumbo l'Etudiant Noir* ("Kocoumbo the Black Student"). From this inner questioning there arose an existential anxiety: the translation of frustration and the rending schism between loyalty to the race and culture of the blacks and entry into a world dominated by new and strange values. This is admirably illustrated by Cheik Hamidou Kane in *L'Aventure Ambiguë* ("Ambiguous Adventure"), and in V. Y. Mudimbe's *Entre les Eaux* ("Between the Waters"). Samba Diallo, the hero of *L'Aventure Ambiguë*, sums up this painful quest of his own: "I am not a distinct country of Diallobes, facing a West that is distinct, and understanding with a cool head what I can take from it and what I am supposed to leave behind in exchange. I have become both of them. There is no one clear way between these two choices. There is only one strange nature—one in distress at not being two."[12] This situation of conflict was clearly summed up by W. E. B. Du Bois, though in different terms:

It is a peculiar sensation, this double-consciousness, this sense of always looking at one's self through the eyes of others, of measuring one's soul by the tape of a world that looks on in amused contempt and pity. One ever feels his two-ness: an American, a Negro; two souls, two thoughts, two unreconciled strivings; two warring ideals in one dark body, whose dogged strength alone keeps it from being torn asunder.[13]

Similarly in African poetry this expression came as a liberation that can be seen in the use of free verse and breaks in rhythm similar to the jumping rhythm of the blues, which is a special expression licensed by the sensibilities and sentiments of blacks. Senghor, David Diop, and others provide eminent examples of this kind of liberty and spontaneity of form. As Senghor wrote, black poetry is a "poetry of flesh and earth; if one is to talk like Hughes, peasant poetry which has not lost contact with the telluric forces. And this explains its cosmic rhythm, its music and its imagery of running water, rustling leaves, beating wings and twinkling stars."[14]

After *Légitime Défense*, and especially after *La Revue du Monde Noir*, the meeting together of the blacks from America, Africa, and the Antilles encouraged the dawn and rising of the great Negro poetry in French and, in a general way, the birth and development of what we today call Negro-African writing.[15] Since then the constant exchange and circulation of ideas have been established, so that the movement can be described in three stages.[16] First Africa was the point of departure for black ideas that spread from Europe to America. Second, during the decade from 1920 to 1930, Harlem-America became the center of a series of new ideas which, passing first through Paris, spread into the black world in Africa and the Caribbean. Finally today there has been established a bipolar route between Africa and the black diaspora in America and the Caribbean.

African literature, having found its examples in black American literature, takes on the same ideological character. In fact from the ideological point of view, it becomes clear that this writing has only one single aim, namely to show how black people really are, or, to take the voluntarist terms of W. E. B. Du Bois to show: "the feeling of being in at the birth of a new criterion for happiness, a new desire to be creative, a new will to exist; as if in this dawn of life of the Black group we have been woken up from some sort of sleep." The problems, the history of black Africa, its beginnings and its mythic splendors are all brought out, but on a romantic pretext, as if to contrast all the more starkly with the misery and limitations of blacks in the modern world. Both African and American writers tend in this way to insist rather strongly upon a blockage of an ideological nature, yet they do at the same time note the essential meaning of this blockage, which is both historical and sociological in nature—the history of blacks and their status and role in the contemporary world.[17]

This consideration can be reformulated with the help of a concept from literary realism, in order to indicate the importance and relevance of Negro Renaissance and Negritude.

Any society which has enjoyed a certain stability tends to corrupt those who are sensitive to the need to speak up for the groups least favored and for those in the greatest minority. Once corrupted, unionized bureaucracies and writers become integrated into the bourgeoisie, allying themselves with the interests of the dominant class which is glad to know them well and to see reflections of itself mirrored in them. But once these groups have performed their tasks their work should become a permanent questioning, a constant search for coherence, and, in the case of American society as in that of colonized Africa, there should be awkward questions raised about nationhood and law. This search would be, if Trotsky is to be believed, the essential direction of art itself, "it being fundamentally a function of the nerves demanding total sincerity."[18]

Seen in this perspective, the writer appears as a man engaged in the construction of a better world and could not in any way be a neutral observer, whether he be critical or skeptical. (Langston Hughes as well as Aimé Césaire and Lilyan S. Lenghor are examples.) The propositions put forward by the writer involved in the construction of a better world do not come from nowhere: they are born in the ups and downs of the socioeconomic world and cannot, for fear of being in contradiction with the real world, try to be original themselves. The fact is that all positive action ought to take into account both the past experience of society and contemporary norms. All great movements, wrote Trotsky, started on the "garbage dump."[19]

Here we have confirmation that an artistic movement, like any other movement, does not start at the bottom. That is to say, it does not begin with the mass of the people but is born and takes its life from the questioning of an avant-garde elite or a group—the group here being the Harlem group and the Negritude group. This questioning has both the strength and the promise of fresh action. It gets established during the process of searching, while also drawing lessons from past experience.

It is the small groups that have made the progress of art. Once the creative resources of the dominating artistic trend have been exhausted, the "garbage dump" people remain, and it is they who know how to look at the world with new eyes. The greater the daring of their conceptions and methods, the more they will be opposed to the established authorities who rely upon support from the conservative base of the masses, and the more the conventional, the skeptical and the snobs are inclined to see in them merely impotent originals or "heaps of anaemic garbage."[20]

The critical-realist approach, like the one founded by the Negro Renaissance and the Negritude movement, is characterized by this active perspective, which represents an advance for humanity. Thus when one ideology is criticized it is bound to be replaced by another ideology.

To be more precise, the only proper base to work from is from an actual acquaintance with social realities. But this is where the opposition between critical realism and social realism arises: for this acquaintance "defines a concrete perspective which above all else implies in a writer a full awareness of society as much as the reality of the contemporary world."[21] Hence no doubt the success of sociohistorical writers such as Jessie Fausset (*Iola-Leroy, There Is Confusion, The Chinaberry Tree*, and *Comedy*), and of Nella Larsen (*Quicksand*) and Langston Hughes (*Sandy*). And by the same token the bitter writing of Leon Damas, Aimé Césaire, and F. Fanon on the Negritude side. These writers have had the advantage of taking concrete facts as their pretext and this has allowed them in principle to make an analysis that may seem objective and realistic, as well as to sketch in a solution relatively close to the actual march of events.

There may be the problem of the specific features of these writings. Purely theoretical knowledge will not inspire the creation of a literary work unless it agrees with the aesthetic categories of the author.

A literary work should rest upon a correct conception of social and historical realities, and this is what allows it on the one hand to acquire an authentically realistic value and, on the other hand, what constitutes a particular and irreplaceable factor in the influence which it normally should exercise; but in the one point of view as in the other, no theoretical knowledge of the world, nor of mankind will ever inspire a writer, without it being totally incorporated into or allowed to be completely absorbed by his aesthetic categories.[22]

In what exactly does the peculiarity of literary categories consist, when these categories turn a work into an entity relatively independent of theoretical knowledge? For surely this perspective leads one to believe that any philosophical theory can inspire a literary work, which is equally true for all other kinds of social action; and this poses the precise problem of these actions regarded as reflections or effects of the evolution and structure of a society.

The writer himself is, as the evidence shows, conditioned by society and by the contradictions of the group or social class that he belongs to. But at the same time this conditioning may be drastically reduced by careful use of the rules of "authentic realism." Indeed the ideological world would, thus, no longer be a simple reflection of the economic organization of society.[23]

This call for a kind of comprehensive and radical analysis of literature is satisfactory proof that in the case of the Negro Reniassance literature, as in that of Negritude, we may find a literature that is really involved. This literature is the reflection of the material conditions of existence of black writers. It is also the ideological and spiritual expression of a group in society: the blacks.

It is fundamentally characterized by two main themes: the rehabilitation of black history; the condition of the black in contact with a white culture. On the American side there are W. E. B. Du Bois, Marcus Garvey and Carter G. Woodson; and there are Cheik Anta Diop, Th. Obenga, and J. Kizerbo on the African side.

This is a group which, because it feels itself badly integrated into another group, is clamoring for its "right to cry out and speak." It bursts out and, in declaring its differences, declares as well its right to the sun and to life. It also rises up against all received wisdom by demanding fresh judgment, by rewriting the history of the past, by interpreting in its own way the present time and its conflicts, and finally by projecting its own particular dreams into a future where it seeks to escape the dogmatism and violence of the dominant white classes in America, while in Africa it seeks to escape the white power of colonization.

The struggle of black Americans strongly attracted the first black writers from the Antilles and from Africa. The myth created around African unity which had suggested a utopian vision of Pan-Africanism (in the writing of Padmore, for example) was constantly being reactivated throughout the struggle for political and cultural liberation in Africa. It had even inspired ideas of the most violent kind, like those of Cheik Anta Diop. The emergence of the New Negro in America lies in the political and cultural awakening of black Africa, and vice versa.

The first texts of Negro-African writing bore the influence of the poets of the Negro Renaissance, with *Pigments* by Damas, opening with an epigraph by Claude MacKay: "Be not deceived, for every deed you do I could match, outmatch: Am I not Africa's son. Black of that black land where black deeds are done." While some poems were dedicated to Mercer Cook and Louis Armstrong, Senghor also dedicated poems to Claude MacKay and Langston Hughes and translated Countee Cullen. Later these same black-American writers participated in the Congresses of Black Writers and Artists in Paris in 1956 and in Rome in 1959. They published literary texts and analytical articles in the review, *Présence Africaine*, and founded the African Society for Culture. One can perhaps now understand why so large a number of studies have been carried out about them and why one whole issue of *Présence Africaine* was published in honor of Langston Hughes. In this fact lies recognition of the important contribution made by the American Negro Renaissance toward the promotion and expression of blacks in Africa and throughout the world.

NOTES

1. Margaret Butcher, *Les Noirs dans la Civilisation Américaine* (Paris: Buchet-Chástel, 1959), p. 13. Translated into French by F. Vernan and J. Rosenthal from *The Negro in American Culture* (New York: Knopf, 1956). Based on materials left by A. Locke. The best general account is Nathan I. Huggins, *Harlem Renaissance* (New York: Oxford University Press, 1971).

2. Jean Wagner, *Les Poètes Noirs des Etats-Unis* (Paris: Librairie Istra, 1963), p. 42.

3. Arna Bontemps, *La Renaissance de Harlem* (Paris: Collection Nouveaux Horizons, 1975), p. 10.

4. Wagner, *Poètes Noirs*, p. 103.

5. *See* Bontemps, *Renaissance*, p. 55.

6. *Batouala* received the Prix Goncourt. It was quickly translated into English and had a real influence among blacks in the United States.

7. Wagner, *Poètes Noirs*, p. 105.

8. *See*, for example, V. Y. Mudimbe, *L'Autre Face du Royaume: Une introduction à la critique des langages en folie* (Lausanne: L'Age d'Homme, 1973).

9. (Paris: Editions de Seuil), 1962.

10. Lilyan Kesteloot, *Les Ecrivains Noirs de Langue Francaise: naissance d'une littérature* (Brussels: Institut Solvay, 1966), p. 63.

11. Kesteloot, *Ecrivains Noirs*, p. 64.

12. *L'Aventure Ambiguë* (Paris: Julliard, 1961), p. 175.

13. W. E. B. Du Bois, *The Souls of Black Folk* (Chicago: A. C. McLurg and Co., 1903), p. 3.

14. Kesteloot, p. 81.

15. *See* J. Jahnheiz, *A History of Neo-African Literature* (London: Faber and Faber, 1968).

16. George Shepperson, "Notes on the Negro-American Influences on the Emergence of African Nationalism," *Journal of African History* 1, no. 2 (1960): 299-312.

17. *See also* Gh. Gouraige, *La Diaspora d'Haïti et l'Afrique* (Ottawa: Ed. Naaman, 1974).

18. Leon Trotsky, *Littérature et Révolution* (Paris: Union Générale d'Editions, 1964), pp. 467-70.

19. Ibid., p. 468.

20. Ibid., p. 469.

21. Gyorgy Lukacs, *La Signification Présente du Réalisme Critique* (Paris: Gallimard, 1960), p. 176.

22. Lukacs, *Signification Présente*, p. 178.

23. *See* Lukacs, *Thomas Mann* (Paris: Maspero, 1967), p. 198.

Survival and song: Women poets of the Harlem Renaissance

MAUREEN HONEY

Department of English, University of Nebraska

This paper concerns Black women poets of the Harlem Renaissance. Considered by modern critics to have adopted anachronistic subject matter and to be out of step with the militant race-consciousness of the period, these poets have been largely neglected in discussions of the 1920's, despite the fact that this was the most significant flowering of Black women's writing until the 1960's. I provide an interpretive model that reveals the rebellious messages in this verse, one that helps explain the poets' imaginative choices by placing them in their historical context and linking them to a female poetic tradition. This approach makes clear the affirming nature of Renaissance poetry by women and makes it accessible to us today, anticipating as it does contemporary issues and forging a modern sensibility.

WRITERS OF the Harlem Renaissance occupy a crucial place in the history of Afro-American literature for the high artistic quality of such works as *Cane* by Jean Toomer and Nella Larsen's *Quicksand*, for the distinctive voices of Langston Hughes and Zora Neale Hurston, and for the defiant pride which their movement came to represent. With the exceptions of Hurston and possibly Larsen, however, the women writers of the period have been largely overlooked, at best accorded a minor status in this important literary episode. I wish to urge retrieval of their work from the obscurity into which it has fallen and suggest an interpretive approach that reveals its value for contemporary study.

I am focusing on poetry as it was the chosen genre of an overwhelming majority of Black women publishing during the 1920's.[1]

Women's Studies. 1989
Vol. 16. pp. 293-315
Reprints available directly from the publisher
Photocopying permitted by licence only

Well known in Black intellectual circles of their day and widely published, women poets achieved the respect of their peers and were popular with a Black middle-class audience. Scholars who lived through the Renaissance generally write favorably of them. Sterling Brown, for instance, compares Anne Spencer to Emily Dickinson and calls Georgia Douglas Johnson's poetry "skillful and fluent."[2] James Weldon Johnson praises Gwendolyn Bennett for her "delicate, poignant" lyrics while calling attention to Jessie Fauset's "light and neat" touch.[3] Later critics, however, have tended to see women's verse as conventional and sentimental, out of step with the militant, rebellious race-consciousness of the period.[4] Those who accord it some artistic value nevertheless agree that most women poets remained within the genteel school of "raceless" literature, having largely confined themselves to the realm of private experience, love lyrics, and nature poetry reminiscent of the nineteenth century.[5] I wish to argue that the full import of women's imaginative choices has been obscured for most modern readers by their seemingly anachronistic subject matter. When placed in its historical context, however, women's poetry comes alive and its significance as the first modern Black female voice becomes clear. Furthermore, a new reading reveals that it is animated, not by an imitative implulse, but rather stems from a defiant sensibility reflective of the Black women who wrote it.

In his discussion of Renaissance poetry, Sterling Brown characterizes Gwendolyn Bennett, Helene Johnson, Carrie Clifford, and Allison Davis as "race conscious" writers.[6] By this he means that they exhibit the qualities most often associated with "New Negro" writing: identification with the race, a miltant proud spirit, overt anger at racism, rejection of white culture, an attempt to reconstruct a now invisible heritage, and determination to fight oppression. Bennett and Johnson appear frequently in early anthologies represented by selections that declare their independence from white standards. Johnson uses playful, bold street language to praise Black urban style as in this poem about male beauty: "Gee, boy, I love the way you hold your head, high sort of and a bit to one side, like a prince, a jazz prince."[7] Bennett, in "Hatred," one of the most widely reprinted of Renaissance poems, lays a curse on her enemies, the implacability of which is matched only by its assurance: "I shall hate you like a dart of singing steel ... while rekindled fires in my eyes shall wound you like swift arrows."[8] Both were known for their poetry exalting Black pride. In

Bennett's "To A Dark Girl," for example, the speaker sees "something of old forgotten queens" in the way a young girl walks, while Johnson admires a "disdainful and magnificent" Black man sauntering down a Harlem street, his laughter "arrogant and bold."[9]

Two things are noteworthy about Brown's remarks. The first is that, until recently, women were considered part of the Renaissance mainstream and used as examples of modern "Black pride" writers. Indeed, fully half of the poetry by women in the pages of *Opportunity* and *The Crisis* from 1920 through 1931 dealt explicitly with race issues.[10] Prejudice, lynching, stereotypes, white cultural imperialism, finding strength in one's ancestors and culture, the beauty of Blackness, and the assertion of rights were all popular subjects during the decade for both men and women. Moreover, nearly as many women's poems were published as those by men.[11] Yet as time went on, the image of women's poetry grew to be that of the pastoral or romantic lyric with only occasional references to the vast amount of race poems produced.[12]

Second, in mentioning well known poets Anne Spencer and Georgia Douglas Johnson, Brown fails to indicate that they wrote on race themes even though they composed powerful pieces about political and racial issues. While the majority of their work is comparatively private, they were clearly interested in and supportive of the new militance. Spencer addressed lynching, female oppression, and racism in her writing.[13] Johnson reflected often on the ironies of race prejudice and imperialism, berating white men for being "weak-kneed ... afraid to face the counsel of their timid hearts."[14] Similarly, nature poet Effie Lee Newsome wrote of African boys as pathfinders for a new world while Mae V. Cowdery, known for her love poetry, ventured occasionally into political areas.[15] Conversely, the "race poets" tried their hand at personal topics.[16]

From looking at the output of each poet, it is clear that while a given woman might have preferred one kind of subject over another, she generally did not confine herself to it. As a group, these women shared a sensibility that transcended the categories into which they were placed. In part because the race poets were overshadowed by Langston Hughes, Claude McKay, and Sterling Brown, later criticism would focus on the lyricists, obscuring the implicit connection between the social and personal writing most of them did.

Jessie Fauset is one of the writers who concentrated on the private world of romantic love in her poetry yet she stated in 1922 that the issue of race was always with her: "I cannot if I will forget the fact of color in almost everything I do or say ..."[17] Anne Spencer, who excelled at lush descriptions of her garden, fought against racial discrimination in her small Virginia town and declared in the headnote to her verse in Countée Cullen's anthology: "I proudly love being a Negro woman."[18] Angelina Weld Grimké chose to write imagistic nature poems and at the same time admired her activist father and abolitionist aunt, Charlotte Forten Grimké. The seeming contrast between these women's personal struggles against racism and the nonracial quality of their writing is a characteristic shared by many female poets of the time and has been interpreted as an escapist impulse, evidence of a self-denying identification with white culture, or a declaration of independence from the role Black writers were expected to fill. Feeling constrained by the label "race writer," they opted for what they considered more universal themes appropriate to the art of poetry and insisted on the freedom to follow their individual muse.[19]

When viewed in the context of what women produced as a whole during the Renaissance, however, a more complex picture emerges of this nonracial poetry. Because the total work of each writer was small (with the exception of Georgia Douglas Johnson), the pattern of metaphors and themes characteristic of women's writing is not evident when looking at individual poets. The impulse behind the poetry, therefore, is unclear since the framework from which it emerged is invisible. Artistic choices were made repeatedly that give definition to individual poems seemingly divorced from a Black sensibility and that make it accessible to us today. Rather than representing a split consciousness, one that denies the Afro-American heritage of the writer, this poetry uses the landscape of nature and romantic love to affirm the humanity of women rendered invisible by the dominant culture. As will be explained later, these were areas with which Black women felt comfortable and that provided opportunities to counter the destructive effects of racism and sexism.

Erlene Stetson is one of the few critics to place these poets in a tradition of art characterized by subversive allusion to an oppressive social framework. In Black women's attempt to create a voice of their own, she maintains, they have addressed two key questions through subtle exploration of a personal landscape: "How do we assert ... our identities in a world that prefers to believe we do not exist? How do we balance and contain our anger and pain?"[20] It is in reference to these questions that the pattern of metaphors and subjects used by writers of the twenties takes on new meaning.

In the early years of this century, as now, Black women struggled to find images of themselves in a culture that glorified whiteness. Ridiculed by ministrel stereotypes, objectified as beasts of burden or docile servants, found wanting when measured against white standards of beauty or achievement, they attempted to counterpose a reality that affirmed their worth. The celebration of Africian heritage, folklore, and the deracinated personality were among the major strategies used by Renaissance writers of all kinds for asserting a self ignored or condemned by Anglo-Saxon civilization. Yet, as Nathan Huggins concludes, the focus on Africa and participation in a movement that came to be known as "primitivism" posed problems for Black artists, especially women.[21] Prevailing knowledge of Africa was one-dimensional and it was limited as a source of ethnic identity for a group native to America. Distorted into humiliating parodies by whites, rural folk culture, with a few notable exceptions, was something from which the mostly urban generation creating the new art wished to distance itself.[22] In addition, most of the women writing at the time did not live in Harlem, the inspirational source of new urban poetry being turned to by men.[23] Finally, celebration of the instinctual and "primitive" threatened to emprison Blacks in another stereotype, particularly women, who had long suffered from being identified with their sexuality. As the following lines indicate, white fascination with Black sensuality was suspect and perceived as objectifying by women: "Emerges now a hero new, a soul unknown to claim the horizon of your fancy ... souls of lust embroidered to your liking — not shaming gazing eyes but feeding them."[24]

While women did celebrate their nonEuropean roots and lifestyle, they found their primary symbols of identity in nature. Africa and Harlem appear in their writing yet the impulse was to turn away from these settings toward a garden, field, hill, horizon, or forest. Aside from affording them an alternative to subjects dimly glimpsed, focus on the natural world in part grew out of attitudes shared by Black women writers with other artists of the period. One of these was rebellion against the idea of progress as the principle moving force in history, an optimistic belief prevalent in the prewar period that the

world was getting better through technological and moral advancement.[25] Accelerated by World War I, disillusionment with the notion
that material and spiritual advancement coincided in America was
characteristic of white intellectuals in the 1920's, so much so that
many of them took up residence in Europe to escape what they saw as
a poisonous malaise in their native land.[26] Despite writers' beliefs that
art could humanize America, Blacks had even more compelling
reasons for rejecting faith in the modern industrial world as a force for
enlightenment since racism had viciously exploded on the scene in the
immediate postwar years with a rash of lynchings and attacks on
urban Black communities.[27] As a pristine counterpoint to the manmade
machinery of an industrialized society, nature could provide an alternative vision and language.

The city was a symbol of freedom for these writers, but their poetry
indicated that it also resonated with a power that felt alien and intru-
sive. In this poem, for example, the speaker likens skyscrapers to behe-
moths that block her vision: "Skylines are marking me in today, like
huge arms ... locking out the world's eye, forgetting all about the
stars."[28] A sense of the city as barrier to a female voice is also present
in Marjorie Marshall's "Nostalgia," where she yearns for "fresh-
blown winds that roam through silent hills" and declares: "I shall go
forth from here; these burning streets shall know my songs no more —
and I shall guard my ears against the rigid cry of steel on stones."[29]
Similarly, Anne Spencer speaks of releasing her poetic song and
thereby escaping manmade structures: "My thought leans forward ...
quick! you're lifted clear of brick and frame to moonlit garden
bloom."[30] Black women poets were inspired by and echo the nineteenth century English romanticists they studied in school in part
because placing nature at the center of the imagination allowed them
to get some distance on an urban world that attracted them yet represented a reality not of their making.

It is instead in a landscape untouched by man that these poets
found mirrors. "My soul is like a tree lifting its face to the sun, flinging
wide its branches ... to breathe into itself a fragrance of far-off fields of
clover" (Mae Cowdrey).[31] "The river is a decrepit old woman shiver-
ing in her sombre shawl of fog" (Ethel Caution).[32] "I would be one
with the morning to hold in my throat soft ecstasies of bird notes ... I
would be one with the evening to clasp in my hands strange brilliancy
of star dust" (Majorie Marshall).[33] This poetry locates the self in a sett-

ing not only of continual regeneration but one that has also suffered damage at the hands of men seeking to remake the world in their likeness. This connection is made explicit in Anne Spencer's "White Things," where the oppression of Blacks is seen as part of a long genocidal history wherein their tormentors destroy life in order to rule: "Most things are colorful things — the sky, earth and sea. Black men are most men; but the white are free! White things are rare things; so rare, so rare — They stole from out a silvered world — somewhere. Finding earth-plains fair plains, save greenly grassed, they strewed white feathers of cowardice, as they passed; The golden stars with lances fine, the hills all red and darkened pine, they blanched with their wand of power; and turned the blood in a ruby rose to a poor white poppy-flower."[34]

The connection between women and the land is clear in nature poetry with references to female-like valleys, hills, "the sable breast of earth," and soft ground pregnant with life. Whiteness, in contrast, is associated with power, control, and death. The poem "Chalk-dust," for example, concerns the desire of a teacher to escape her classroom and "roll in wet, green grass, plunge headfirst into youth, and music, and laughter." The dust permeates the air, her hair, and clothing and symbolizes the dry lifeless facts written in chalk on her blackboard: "It has the relentless persistence of the long dead. It gets between me and the rays of the sun . . . It will strangle me slowly, quietly; and sift over my body when I, like it, am so dead as to be merely useful."[35] The world of book knowledge, figures, formal education is white and suffocating while colorful nature releases a life-giving joyous sensuality.

Similarly, the white light of the moon is portrayed as a force that will steal the soul of a mother's baby in African writer Aqua Laluah's poem "Lullaby": "Close your sleepy eyes, or the pale moonlight will steal you. Else in the mystic silence, the moon will turn you white, Then you won't see the sunshine, nor smell the open roses, nor love your Mammy any more, whose skin is dark as night. Wherever moonlight stretches her arms across the heavens, you will follow . . . till you become instead a shade in human draperies."[36] Here, Laluah creates an allegory for the process by which Black people become separated from their roots, culture, and true selves through using the moon as a symbol of white culture and appreciation of nature as a concomitant of self-love. If you gaze too long at images of whiteness, the mother warns her child, you will reject your racial heritage and conform to alien standards thereby becoming a shadow self living in the corners of people's minds.

The moon is a central element in two poems that link it to themes of destruction. Heba Jannath likens the moon to a nun in death who is impervious to the "bedeviled" comets dancing around her grave. She is for the speaker a reflection of her deadened spirit rendered lifeless in self-protection against the pain of lost passion: "O Moon, thy face is a frozen mirror wherein our Sun and Satellites behold themselves; and I, myself — and the chilling breath from off thy silent wastes relieves our passion fires."[37] While the poem expresses gratitude for this beacon of serenity, it is a calm dearly bought as the speaker is "self-lost in nothingness." A more complicated use is made of white metaphors in Esther Popel's "Theft."[38] The moon is described as an old woman looking in vain for her children, afraid of and taunted by the elements as she hurries home. She creeps along, huddled in an old black cape and tries to escape the wind who pelts her with snowballs "filling her old eyes with the flakes of them." Suddenly, she falls and is buried by the snow while jewels fall from their bag onto the earth where they are seized by tall trees which then sparkle with their "glittering plunder." The trees are uncharacteristically malevolent in this poem, but the usage of moon and snow are typical. The snow blinds this old woman, trips and envelopes her; it causes her to lose a small treasure carefully guarded. Finally, its companion, the wind, laughs at her piteous moans and turns her own children against her who, though found, prove to be an enemy. Negative white elements are present in a double sense here, for not only is the desperate mother defeated by them, she is herself white, or rather yellow, the color of old white paint. Popel's central figure is ambiguous in that she evokes pity, modifying the image of the moon as dangerous. At the same time, she represents weakness, debilitation, and devastating loss.

Allusions to white domination and danger abound yet the predominant message is that it can be resisted. Alice Dunbar Nelson's reflections on a snow-covered autumn tree, for instance, focus on its resilience to a force trying to claim it: "Today I saw a thing of arresting poignant beauty: a strong young tree, brave in its Autumn finery ... bending beneath a weight of early snow which ... spread a heavy white chilly afghan over its crested leaves./Yet they thrust through, defiant, glowing, claiming the right to live another fortnight."[39] The assertion of vitality against deathly stillness appears again in "Late

Afternoon": "She snowshowed by ... following the hush that called her from the wood, finding in whiteness deep on leaves and sod a soundlessness she somehow understood./The wood seemed waiting for the falling snow, breathless and still and lovely in its sure welcoming of further white, and so she found a beauty she could not endure. Her quick hand shut her eyes out from the sight: the woods would take the kiss of snow all night."[40]

Initially drawn by the soft still beauty of the snowfall, the wanderer is captivated by the silence with which it blankets the wood she is tempted to enter. The poem calls attention to the soundlessness of "whiteness deep on leaves and sod," the "breathless" welcoming posture of the trees, and the "hush" that beckons to the woman on snowshoes. While beautiful, the snowfall has a sinister quality as it silences and covers a motionless stand of trees. Nearly seduced into stillness herself, the woman continues her journey: "her quick hand shut her eyes out from the sight." Both poems link whiteness to the covering of life with a suffocating pall, no less deathlike for its loveliness. Yet each poet places within her scene an act of resistance, one that preserves vibrancy and movement in the midst of a threatening storm.

Angelina Weld Grimké's well known piece, "Tenebris," echoes this subtle assertion of self against a white power: "There is a tree, by day, that, at night, has a shadow, a hand huge and black, with fingers long and black. All through the dark against the white man's house, in the little wind, the black hand plucks and plucks at the bricks. The bricks are the color of blood and very small. Is it a black hand, or is it a shadow?"[41] Grimké's poetry is deceptively free of direction in that she presents, without comment, a string of images connected by a logic outside the poem. One of her strengths is that her selection of elements seems to allude to a larger reality and lends itself to a variety of interpretations. In this case, by likening the branches of a tree to a hand "huge and black," whose shadow rests against "the white man's house," Grimké invites us to find in her image a statement about the relationship of Blacks to white society. One reading of the poem is that it sees Black struggle as a subterranean, persistent chipping away at white structures. The black hand "plucks and plucks" at the bricks which are "the color of blood and very small" at night, when the occupant is sleeping, falsely secure that the image on his house is only the shadow of a harmless tree. Yet the last line asks: 'Is it a black hand, or is it a shadow?" and we are left sensing that the white man's house is in danger.

These poems center on trees, a common motif of the period. The tree offered an attractive symbol for the enduring self in its quest for growth, in its proud dignity, and in its will to survive. These are qualities hinted at in another Grimké poem, "The Black Finger." Here the speaker marvels at the silhouette of a cypress at sunset: "I have just seen a most beautiful thing: slim and still, against a gold, gold sky, ... sensitive, exquisite, a black finger pointing upwards." Leading the eye toward a vast open space, symbolically pointing the way to a world where the soul can soar, the tree in this poem can in some sense symbolize the miraculous survival of Black aspiration as the poet ends by asking: "Why, beautiful still finger, are you black? And why are you pointing upwards?"[42]

Helene Johnson makes somewhat the same allusion in "Trees at Night" where she draws an image of vibrant wonder for her crystallized by the interplay of light and shadow on a moonlit night: "Slim sentinels stretching lacy arms about a slumberous moon; ... Black quivering silhouettes, tremulous, ... Fragile pinnacles of fairy castles; Torn webs of shadows; and printed 'gainst the sky — The trembling beauty of an urgent pine."[43] It is the silhouette of the tree that attracts the poet's eye, the intricate pattern of branches against a sky, the stillness of a solid trunk anchored by sure roots and pushing against the force of gravity. The trunk's rich brownness is starkly highlighted in silhouette, devoid of obscuring foliage and beautiful in its hardy survival of harsh conditions, a quality connected to toughness of Black people in a poem by Anita Scott Coleman: "Black men are the tall trees that remain standing in a forest after a fire. Flames strip their branches ... yet stand these trees for their roots are thrust deep in the heart of the earth."[44]

Another common metaphor is night which is both portrayed as protector and personified as a Black woman. While night offers the obvious parallel of color as a source of self-imagery, it also has been feared as a time of danger, a place inhabited by scary supernatural beings in white culture. Night symbolizes the unknown, the absence of reason and control, the antithesis of conscious awareness. These are also properties assigned to Black people and, having felt the sting of "otherness," it makes sense that women identified with a dark power, feared and maligned. In rescuing night from white fantasies and imbuing it with creative force, the poet could symbolically remove from herself the stigma of distorted perceptions.

"What do I care for morning," asks Helene Johnson, "for the color of rising sun? ... Give me the beauty of evening, the cool consummation of night."[45] The preference for nighttime over daylight expressed in Johnson's poem is marked in women's poetry and served a variety of functions. One of these was to assert the primacy of Blackness in a world that highlighted white things: "What does it matter if white light can boast their rays before — Brightest days burn out themselves, and night rules evermore."[46] Quieter, calmer, less dramatic than the day, night was nevertheless an essential force in life, the contemplation of which brought serenity to a restless discontented spirit. Gwendolyn Bennett's imagist portrait, "Street Lamps in Early Spring," is typical in its tone of sensitive appreciation. "Night wear a garment all velvet soft, all violet blue ... and over her face she draws a veil as shimmering fine as floating dew ... And here and there in the black of her hair the subtle hands of Night move slowly with their gem-starred light."[47] Insensitively overlooked, the beauty of Blackness and femaleness is here brought to center stage from its background role and praised for its steady subtle force.

Bennett's poem captures another aspect of night's usefulness as an image for Black women. Personified as female, she is said to draw over her face a veil "shimmering fine as floating dew." Cast as a goddess whose features are hidden from view by the absence of light, night stands for the masked self, obscured by the fears and projected fantasies of gazers with the power to define. Yet although night is veiled in mystery, she escapes the distorted negative images of those who fail to see her clearly. Self-assured, she parades through poetry of the twenties with regal grace: "Night comes walking out our way in a velvet gown. Soft she steps to music gay, as only lovely ladies may ... and in her hair, wind-tossed and free, a million stars are tucked away — the glint of silver carelessly encrusting polished ebony."[48] The donning of a mask for self-protection, then, does not forever cut one off from the vital beautiful person underneath who possesses powers unrecognized by the world.

Not only is she is a vibrant woman of great spirit who rules her domain wisely, but night offers respite from the daily struggle to survive, for in the dark world, Blackness cannot be used as a marker of difference. Since there is no need to dissemble, the poet can come alive in her presence: "Last night I danced on the rim of the moon delirious and gay, quite different from the mood I wear about by day ... And

177

oh! my feet flew madly! My body whirled and swayed! My soul danced in its ecstacy untrammeled, unafraid!" (Ethel Caution)[49] "Within the shadow of the moon you danced ... Your dark flame-beauty challenging a glance, you flung a sob-caught laugh and leaped afar into the arms of night, with upturned face that mocked the waning beauty of the moon, its fragile curves ... lacked your Nile-born grace" (Majorie Marshall).[50] "To dance — in the light of the moon, a platinum moon poised like a slender dagger on the velvet darkness of night" (Mae Cowdery).[51] "In Alabama stars hang down so low, so low they purge the soul with their infinity" (Jessie Fauset).[52] While poets looked to natural settings in general for space in which to savor the abandonment of confining roles, night was sought most frequently as it was a time when the objectifying gaze was covered by sleep and the freedom to be at one with darkness could be safely enjoyed.

It is to night also that the poet turns for solace and restoration. Here, Mae Cowdery soothes her wounded heart by communing with the stars and moon: "I want to take down with my hands the silver stars that grow in heaven's dark blue meadows and bury my face in them./I want to wrap all around me the silver shedding of the moon to keep me warm."[53] Georgia Douglas Johnson also seeks the darkness when gripped by sorrow in "Escape:" "Shadows, shadows, hug me round in your solitude profound."[54] The reference to night as comforter can be seen as an affirmation of Black resilience. It also transforms the night from a setting of terror, a time when Black people were tormented by white vigilantes, into one of peace. Poems centered on lynching victims, for instance, commonly close on a note of relief wherein night mercifully descends to remove a man's soul from his tortured body.

The images of softness linked to night indicate its association with maternal caresses and a mother's comforting embrace. In the poem "Dark Madonna," for example, night is described as "an old Negro woman hovering above her sleeping children ... Along their brows she draws cool hands./Her breasts yearn for the hunger of their waking."[55] Consoler of the bruised and even broken spirit, guardian of the soul at rest, night serves as a metaphor for the restorative powers within to which the poet can turn when feelings of despair overwhelm her. Just as the death of each day is followed by a healing period of quiet repose, so too does the battered spirit find sustenance in womb-like suspension of interaction with the outside world.

The impulse to protect oneself from a hurtful reality is not an admission of defeat, but rather an acknowledgement that the forces arrayed against a Black woman's dignity and development of her powers are formidable. Much of the poetry characterizes these forces as male as well as white. Blanche Taylor Dickinson, for instance, identifies with an icicle's short-lived brilliance in sunlight: "Chilled into a serenity as rigid as your pose you linger trustingly, but a gutter waits for you. Your elegance does not secure you favors with the sun. He is not to pity fragileness. He thinks all cheeks should burn and feel how tears can run."[56] Similarly, in "Magalu," Helene Johnson warns her African sister against a missionary's attempts to convert her: "Do not let him lure you from your laughing waters."[57] Finally, Gwendolyn Bennett relates the fate of a woman seduced by a man in "silvern armour" with "silver spurs and silken plumes a-blow" who finds that under his visor lies the face of death.[58]

Anne Spencer's poem, "Letter to My Sister," provides insight into the motif of retreat found in poetry concerning night and links it to these warnings about male destruction. Though the gods she mentions are not identified as male, it is made clear that women battle a common enemy and share a kind of bondage that sets them apart from men. "It is dangerous for a woman to defy the gods," she begins, "to taunt them with the tongue's thin tip ... or draw a lined daring them to cross." The speaker adds, however, that appeasement will not protect women from harm: "Oh, but worse still if you mince along timidly — dodge this way or that, or kneel, or pray." Instead, she recommends deftly removing one's treasured secrets from view and revealing them only under strict conditions of privacy: "Lock your heart, then quietly, and, lest they peer within, light no lamp when dark comes down. Raise no shade for sun."[59] Although the day's piercing light destroys, it can be thwarted by guarding the innermost recesses of the self in periodic flights to invisibility.

Another Spencer poem, "Lady, Lady," brings to the surface the three major themes of nature poetry: equation of Blackness and femaleness with strength, resistance to white and male oppression, and survival of the core self. Typical of Renaissance poetry, it studies a member of the working class made invisible by racism and classism. "Lady, Lady, I saw your face, dark as night withholding a star ... The chisel fell, or it might have been you had borne so long the yoke of men. Lady, Lady, I say your hands, twisted, awry, like crumpled roots, bleached poor white in a sudsy tub, wrinkled and drawn from your rub-a-dub. Lady, Lady, I saw your heart, and altared there in its darksome place were the tongues of flames the ancients knew, where the good God sits to spangle through."[60] The washerwoman's external appearance bears the stamp of her oppressor. Her face has been chiseled by pain borne from carrying "the yoke of men;" her hands are twisted "like crumpled roots" by the labor she does for white people, symbolizing the stunting of her growth and crippling of her true posture. They are also "bleached poor white," a mirror of the degree to which her race has consigned her to a draining exploited existence controlled by whites. Despite the harsh life she has led, however, there remains a sacred inviolable place within where her spirit burns brightly "altared there in its darksome place," host to a transcendent guiding force.

Nature furnished women with an objective correlative to articulate their aspirations, fears, wounds, and struggles to define themselves in a patriarchal racist society. Through exploring properties of the natural world, they found images that spoke to their condition and dreams. In a society with insufficient mirrors, poets constructed an imaginary reality which reflected their beauty, worth, and strength.

Another major subject of women's poetry was romantic love. Largely devoid of references to race or gender oppression, it concentrates on private affairs of the heart, the pain of loss, the ecstacy of union with another. Seemingly unconnected to the poet's relation to her society, it appears at first glance to be an anomalous feature of a literary movement to record authentically the Afro-American experienced and break free of stereotypes. Yet the love poetry reverberates with emotions that implicitly challenge the dehumanizing flat caricatures of Black people found in American culture.

One of the many misconceptions held by white people about Blacks at the time was that they were a happy race, perpetually childlike in their ability to laugh at woe and shrug off cares. Such an image served important psychological functions for whites, among them relief from guilt, avoidance of fears about rebellion, and escape from a sober model of propriety.[61] A laughing Black face put whites at ease and seemingly offered a world where troubles could be left behind. New Negro writers addressed this issue by making public their rage at the various forms racism took and exposing as a lie Black contentment with servility. These aspects of twenties militance are present in women's poetry. Anita Scott Coleman, for example, sees a beautiful anger in her people: "I love black faces ... They are full of smould'ring fire."[62] Others declare the era of smiling docility to be over: "Sambo's laugh used to ring out ... But now Sambo has lost his laugh, he doesn't guffaw any more."[63]

In addition to revealing their anger, writers protested the necessity to hide pain in order to fulfil white fantasies, a message running through Mary Jenness's poem, "The Negro Laughs Back:" "You laugh, and I must hide the wound your laughter cuts in me"; similarly, Clarissa Scott Delany bitterly describes the false front she is forced to present in "The Mask" where she emphasizes the distance from self this imposes by referring to herself in the third person: "So detached and cool she is, no notion e'er betrays the secret life within her soul, the anguish of her days."[64]

When read in this context, the love poetry takes on added significance for in it the poet reveals her pain, her human capacity to be vulnerable and suffer deep disappointment. She possesses the gift of laughter, but it is clear that sadness has shaped her as much as joy, that suffering is a big part of her life. The heartbreak over unrequited love that runs through this poetry is an affirmation of humanity in the face of injunctions to play a role. It also asserts that the personal realm of the poet need not be uplifting in order to be a proper subject for public verse. Her feelings are worthy of poetic expression in and of themselves. This claiming of the despondent self represented an important departure from nineteenth century Afro-American poetry which, according to Joan Sherman, followed that era's conception of art as something that should inspire and instruct.[65] It was therefore incumbent on the poet to be optimistic and end poems on a forward looking note. Insisting on the full range of human emotions for their province, poets of the twenties expanded the boundaries of acceptable subjects to include despair and woeful yearning after something dearly lost.

The right, indeed the necessity, to recognize anguish as a consequence of being fully alive is a theme often struck in this poetry of the heart. Refusing to take the safer yet diminshing path of a life without dreams or large emotional risks, the poet proclaims her suffering to be a growth-producing factor in her quest for vitality. Helene Johnson, for example, defines fulfillment as a willingness to endure pain in the passionate pursuit of meaningful experience: "Ah, life, to let your stabbing beauty pierce me ... to grapple with you, loving you too fiercely, and to die bleeding — consummate with Life."[66] Reflecting on a failed love affair, the speaker in Georgia Douglas Johnson's poem, "Afterglow," also affirms the value of opening oneself to hurt: "I smile across the backward way and pledge anew, my vow: For every glancing, golden gleam, I offer, gladly, Pain; and I would give a thousand worlds, to live it all again."[67] Here, emotional transport, whether toward joy or sorrow, is heralded as a lifeforce that brings the poet into contact with her humanity and the world around her. It is both her route to self-actualization as she is willing to encounter life directly, without masks, and her announcement that she is multi-dimensional, a woman of sensitivity and warmth.

Another aspect of Renaissance love poetry that simultaneously went beyond nineteenth century conventions and resisted contemporary stereotypes was the introduction of erotic passionate imagery. Mae Cowdrey mourns a lost lover by explicitly recalling scenes from their lovemaking: "No more the feel of your hand on my breast ... no more the lush sweetness of your lips."[68] In "Ecstacy," Virginia Houston similarly reminisces about a passion no longer hers: "I remember only the ecstacy of soft lips covering mine dragging my soul through my mouth."[69] Jessie Fauset holds close the memory of a fleeting kiss that nevertheless wrung from her. "a sharp caught cry."[70] Kathleen Tannkersley Young's poem, "Hunger," compares her lover's body to "dark wine" that she lifts to her "trembling lips," and Eda Lou Walton bids hers to "lower your lips and let them rest against the anguish of my breast."[71]

In some poems, passion for women too emerges, consistent with the woman-identification found in the nature poetry. Mae Cowdrey's "Insatiate" captures the urgent desire for sensual experience that appears in much of the period's poetry when she admits that even if her lover were exquisite as jewels, "if her lips were rubies red," she would still not be able to satisfy her appetite for pleasure.[72] Angelina Weld Grimké displays a similar urgency as she breathlessly describes a lover's kiss: "Yearning, yearning, languor, surrender; your mouth, and madness, madness, tremulous, ... flaming."[73] She longs explicitly for union with a woman in "A Mona Lisa," alluding to her intense hunger: "I should like to creep through the long brown grasses that are your lashes; I should like to poise on the very brink of the leaf-brown pools that are your shadowed eyes ... I should like to sink down and down and down ... and deeply drown."[74] Finally, "Rainy Season Love Song" celebrates the speaker's passionate encounter with a woman in the rain: "Into my hands she cometh, and the lightening of my desire flashes and leaps about her ... its warm electricity in you pulses wherever I may touch ... The thunder rumbles about us, and I feel its triumphant note as your warm arms steel around me; and I kiss your dusky throat."[75]

The highlighting of sensual passion was a legacy from what Henry May calls the Rebellion, a prewar movement away from Victorianism that, among other things, celebrated spontaneous free expression and release of the body from unnatural confinement.[76] At the same time, it constituted a reclaiming of Black women's sexuality, either denied by desexed images of the plantation mammy or debased in lewd portraits of the "primitive" African. To bring their bodies into public view under their own terms was a liberating act that allowed women the freedom to experience themselves as sentient complex beings.

This poetry has been criticized for its excess emotionality and sentimentality.[77] Much of it is to modern readers embarrassingly dramatic, almost Victorian in its melodramatic gestures and coy allusions to lovers. At the same time, it was important that poets venture into the forbidden territory of erotic passion and explore the world of sensation and spontaneous feeling. In doing so, they were insisting on the right to be human and resisting a society that worshipped machines, architects, engineers but seemed to have no room for love or understanding. If they had a tendency to go to extremes, it was in reaction to what they saw as an unfeeling culture primarily concerned with things and capable of wounding them casually, unthinkingly. Voicing their pain was one step toward authenticity as was celebrating their moments of ecstacy.

Contemporary criticism of the Harlem Renaissance provides a starting point for understanding neglect of women's poetry. When measured against the historical role Renaissance artists claimed for themselves, i.e. creators of a New Afro-American sensibility, the failures in much of their work become apparent. Nathan Huggins, for example, considers Claude McKay and Countée Cullen flawed poets because they embraced a European artistic tradition at odds with the heart of their own experience. Crippled by their notion that art should be more universal than a focus on race alone allowed and unable or unwilling to depart from traditional structures, they ironically fell short of the greatness they sought.[78] Saunders Redding also faults Cullen for adhering to verse modeled after nineteenth century romantic lyricists and concludes he contributed little to Afro-American literature, standing aloof as he did from the revolutionary currents flowing past him.[79] Finally, in his discussion of Renaissance novelists, Addison Gayle Jr. concludes that, while Black writers left a legacy of questioning rebellion, they were not able to develop fully their vision because they were insufficiently independent of white culture.[80]

Known primarily for their lyrical and pastoral verse, women too have been seen as imitating European traditions and devising little that was useful in the creation of a Black aesthetic. Hampered by devotion to a theory of art not their own, so the consensus goes, whatever talent some of these women was snuffed out by conformity to inappropriate poetic models.

I think it is valid to recognize the limitations of artists who overtly tried to develop an indigenous literary canon and who were at the same time constrained by historical conditions militating against radically new visions. There were many ways in which Renaissance poets failed to provide the kind of legacy which they saw themselves creating. Yet, although much of women's poetry is sing-song, clichéd, and awkward, there is a body of work that has held up over time, that speaks with a modern voice and artfully expresses messages of substance. Anne Spencer, Mae Cowdery, Angelina Weld Grimké, Gwendolyn Bennett, and Helene Johnson produced poems of high aesthetic quality and their best pieces inspire careful examination. That their poetic strategies did not often include departure from conventional metaphors and models ought not distract us from the coherent rebellious messages in their verse.

Jean Wagner has drawn a parallel between the attitudes displayed by second and third generation Afro-Americans freed from slavery and those of descendents of immigrants: the second generation tends to reject markers of ethnic identity while the third embraces them.[81] His explanation for the emergence of a generation reclaiming its cultural heritage in the 1920's helps clarify the strain in women's poetry that is divorced from overt identification with the people and focused on subjects traditionally used by Anglo-Saxon male poets. The most influential women — Anne Spencer, Angelina Weld Grimké, Alice Dunbar Nelson, Georgia Douglas Johnson, Jessie

Fauset — were all members of the second generation to experience emancipation and all wrote private poetry.[82] That they should turn away from folk or urban Afro-American expression is perhaps not surprising using Wagner's model.

Yet this kind of analysis cannot account fully for the vast amount of nature and love poetry produced by Black women during the Renaissance, for younger poets like Gwendolyn Bennett and Helene Johnson, while they did move into the new idiom being created by Langston Hughes, followed as well the direction of the older poets. Erlene Stetson asserts that one defining aspect of Black women's poetry is that the writer's quest for identity takes place within a personal landscape.[83] In this sense, then, Renaissance poets remained within a female rather than a white tradition as they explored their inner selves, intimate relations with lovers, and private connections to the natural world in an effort to make themselves visible. They found congenial poetic models in the imagists and English romantics because these forms allowed them access to a core self from which the dominant culture kept them alienated. Communing with nature in spontaneous, associative ways or unself-consciously exploring the intensity of their most initimate connections with people produced a vocabulary for describing the unborn self soon to burst upon the world.[84] It was a markedly female, as well as middle-class, strategy for claiming an authentic Afro-American worldview.

This period witnessed the most significant flowering of Black women's writing until the 1960's and, as such, requires extensive critical attention. Moreover, the poetry with which women came to be identified provided a number of key bridges: from nineteenth century oratorical and sentimental verse to a modern sensibility, from white art to Afro-American, and from the male-dominated New Negro movement to female experience. Despite the gaps, theirs are among the first voices that sound familiar to us and that anticipate contemporary issues. Women poets of the Harlem Renaissance went beyond their predecessors to find a form that spoke to their special needs as Afro-Americans with a new outlook and as modern women of strength, vision, and passion.

Notes

1. Critics disagree on the starting date of the Harlem Renaissance but most agree it was over by the end of 1931. I have elected to study the poetry from 1920 through 1931 as it was not until 1924 that large numbers of poems were published by women and 1920 provides a neat beginning for a comprehensive view of the decade. Only a small amount of fiction was written by Black women during the Renaissance. Six novels were produced, four by Jessie Fauset and two by Nella Larsen, and around fifty short stories were published in *Opportunity* and *The Crisis*. Women's poetry was published in these important periodicals and also by A. Philip Randolph's socialist journal, *The Messenger*, and Marcus Garvey's *Negro World*. For a discussion of the latter, see Tony Martin *Literary Garveyism: Garvey, Black Arts and the Harlem Renaissance* (Massachusetts: Majority Press, 1983), p. 50-88.

2. Sterling Brown *Negro Poetry and Drama* (Washington D.C.: Assocs. in Negro Fold Education, 1937) p. 62 and 65.

3. James Weldon Johnson *The Book of American Negro Poetry* (N.Y.: Harcourt, Brace and World, 1959 © 1922) p. 243 and 205.

4. Margaret Perry *Silence to the Drums: A Survey of the Literature of the Harlem Renaissance* (Westport, CT: Greenwood Press 1976) p. 153; Margaret Just Butcher *The Negro in American Culture* (N.Y.: Alfred A. Knopf 1973)p. 123. Studies that omit women altogether include Saunders Redding *To Make A Poet Black* (Chapel Hill: Univ. of North Carolina Press 1939); Blyden Jackson and Louis Rubin *Black Poetry in America* (Baton Rouge: Louisiana State Univ. Press 1974); Jean Wagner *Black Poets of the United States* (Urbana: Univ. of Illinois Press 1973); Arthur P. Davis *From the Dark Tower* (Washington DC: Howard Univ. Press, 1974) discusses fiction writers but no women poets; Michael Cooke *Afro-American Literature in the Twentieth Century* (New Haven: Yale Univ. Press 1984) mentions only Larsen and Hurston; Arthur P. Davis and Saunders Redding *Cavalcade: Negro American Writing from 1760 to the Present* (Boston: Houghton Mifflin 1971) includes two women poets, Frances E.W. Harper and Anne Spencer; Wallace Thurman "Negro Poets and Their Poetry" in Addison Gayle, Jr. ed. *Black Expression* (N.Y.: City College of New York 1969).

5. Arthur P. Davis and Michael Peplow *The New Negro Renaissance* (N.Y.: Harper and Row 1975) place poems by Fauset, Spencer, Grimké, and Georgia Johnson under the category "Raceless Literature." Richard Barksdale and Kenneth Kinnamon *Black Writers of America: A Comprehensive Anthology* (N.Y.: Macmillan Co. 1972).

6. Brown, 1937, p. 65 and 74.

7. "Poem" in Countée Cullen *Caroling Dusk* (N.Y.: Harper and Row 1955 © 1927) p. 218.

8. *Ibid.*, p. 160.

9. *Ibid.*, p. 157; "Sonnet to a Negro in Harlem" p. 217.

10. This conclusion is based on a reading of all the poetry appearing by women in these two periodicals for the years in question.

11. Omitting names whose gender was not clearly marked, e.g. first names omitted in favour of initials, a total of 347 poems appears by men in both journals from 1925 through 1931 and 277 by women. The numbers are even for *The Crisis* where Jessie Fauset was literary editor until March 1927.

12. Exceptions to this trend are Davis and Peplow, 1975, who include poems by women under the category "Race Pride." Arna Bontemps *American Negro Poetry*

(N.Y.: Hill and Wange 1963) anthologizes many poems concerning race by women; Nathan Huggins *Voices from the Harlem Renaissance* (N.Y.: Oxford Univ. Press 1976) is another anthology with poetry of this kind; William Adams, Peter Conn, Barry Slepian *Afro-American Literature* (Boston: Houghton Mifflin 1970) reprints racial poetry by Bennett, Helene Johnson, and Frances Harper.

13. There is a chapter on Spencer's political poetry in the excellent study J. Lee Greene *Time's Unfading Garden: Anne Spencer's Life and Poetry* (Baton Rouge: Louisianna State Univ. Press 1977) Chapter 8.

14. "Courier," *The Crisis* (November 1926) p. 29.

15. Newsome's poem is "Morning Light" in Cullen, 1955, p. 55.

16. See, for example, Gwendolyn Bennett's "Nocturne" *The Crisis* (November 1923) p. 20 and Helene Johnson's "Summer Matures" in Cullen, 1955, p. 217.

17. Quoted in Carolyn Sylvander *Jessie Redmon Fauset, Black American Writer* (Troy, N.Y.: The Whitson Pub. Co. 1981) p. 83.

18. Cullen, 1955, p. 47.

19. Butcher, 1973, p. 123.

20. Erlene Stetson *Black Sister: Poetry by Black American Women, 1746-1980* (Bloomington: Indiana Univ. Press 1981) p. xvii.

21. Nathan Huggins *The Harlem Renaissance* (N.Y.: Oxford Univ. Press 1971) p. 188.

22. Gregory Holmes Singleton provides a demographic chart demonstrating the urban origins of Renaissance writers in "Birth, Rebirth, and the 'New Negro' of the 1920s" *Phylon* XLIII No. 1 (March 1982): 29-45. Of the women for whom place of birth is known, Georgia Douglas Johnson was born in Atlanta, Jessie Fauset and Effie Lee Newsome in Philadephia, Alice Dunbar Nelson in New Orleans, Angelina Weld Grimké and Helene Johnson in Boston, Lucy Ariel Williams in Mobile, Alabama. Those born in rural areas include Gwendolyn Bennett, Giddings, Texas; Clarissa Scott Delaney, Tuskegee Institute, Alabama; and Blanche Taylor Dickinson, a Kentucky farm. Anne Spencer was born somewhere in Virginia.

23. Helene Johnson and Jessie Fauset lived in New York City at this time. Gwendolyn Bennett spent the early 1920's in New York, then moved to Washington D.C. in 1924. Angelina Weld Grimké, Georgia Douglas Johnson, and Clarissa Scott Delaney were all in Washington D.C. during the years of the Renaissance. Blanche Taylor Dickinson was in Sewickley, Pennsylvania, Effie Lee Newsome in Wilberforce, Ohio, Lucy Ariel Williams in Oberlin, Ohio, Anne Spencer spent her entire adult life in Lynchburg, Virginia. Aquah Laluah, a.k.a. Gladys May Casely Hayford, lived in Sierra Leone, the African Gold Coast.

24. Ruth G. Dixon "Epitome" *The Crisis* (October 1930) p. 342. Gilbert Osofsky discusses the objectifying aspects of white interest in the "New Negro" in *Harlem: The Making of a Ghetto: Negro New York, 1890-1930* (N.Y.: Harper and Row 1963) p. 183.

25. Henry F. May *The End of American Innocence: A Study of the First Years of Our Own Time, 1912-1917* (N.Y.: Alfred A. Knopf 1959) p. 361.

26. Malcolm Cowley *Exile's Return: A Literary Odyssey of the 1920's* (N.Y.: Viking Press 1951).

27. May, 1959, p. 347; Paula Giddings *When and Where I Enter: The Impact of Black Women on Race and Sex in America* (N.Y.: William Morrow and Co. 1984) p. 145. The NAACP reported eighty-one lynchings in 1919 and sixty in 1920 *The Crisis* (February 1921) p. 160.

28. Bessie Mayle "Skylines" *The Crisis* (May 1930) p. 163.

29. *The Crisis* (November 1929) p. 378.
30. "Substitution" in Cullen, 1955, p. 48.
31. "The Wind Blows" *Opportunity* (November 1929) p. 299.
32. "The River" *The Crisis* (March 1930) p. 93.
33. "Desire" *The Crisis* (June 1928) p. 196.
34. *The Crisis* (March 1923) p. 204.
35. Lillian Byrnes *The Crisis* (August 1930) p. 273. Many of the women poets were teachers, for example, Alice Dunbar Nelson, Allison Davis, Angelina Weld Grimké, Lucy Ariel Williams, Georgia Douglas Johnson, Jessie Fauset, Clarissa Scott Delaney, Blanche Taylor Dickinson, Aquah Laluah, and Gwendolyn Bennett. Bennett was the only one to teach at a university (she was a professor at Howard University).
36. *The Crisis* (March 1929) p. 85.
37. "Moon Death" *Opportunity* (February 1931) p. 51.
38. *Opportunity* (April 1925) p. 100.
39. "Snow in October" in Cullen, 1955, p. 40.
40. Frances M. Frost, *The Crisis* (May 1929) p. 160.
41. Cullen, 1955 p. 40.
42. *Opportunity* (November 1923) p. 343.
43. *Opportunity* (May 1925) p. 147.
44. "Portraiture" *The Crisis* (June 1931) p. 199.
45. "What Do I Care for Morning" in Cullen, 1955, p. 216.
46. Bessie Mayle, "Poems," *The Crisis* (May 1930) p. 163.
47. *Opportunity* (May 1926) p. 152.
48. Esther Popel, "Night Comes Walking," *The Crisis* (August 1929) p. 249.
49. "Last Night" *The Crisis* (February 1929) p. 50.
50. "To A Dark Dancer" *The Crisis* (January 1928) p. 14.
51. "Longings" *The Crisis* (December 1927) p. 337.
52. "Stars in Alabama" *The Crisis* (January 1928) p. 14.
53. "Wants" *The Crisis* (November 1928) p. 372.
54. *The Crisis* (May 1925) p. 15.
55. Verna Bright *The Crisis* (March 1929) p. 85.
56. "To An Icicle" in Cullen, 1955, p. 110.
57. *Ibid.*, p. 223.
58. "Sonnet" *Ibid.*, p. 160.
59. Bontemps, 1963, p. 19.
60. *Survey Graphic* (March 1, 1925) p. 661.
61. Huggins, 1971. Chapter 6; Osofsky, 1963, p. 184.
62. "Black Faces" *Opportunity* (Octoer 1929) p. 320.
63. Grace P. White, "Sambo — Passing," *The Crisis* (July 1927) p. 158.
64. Jenness's poem is in *Opportunity* (August 1928) p. 233; Delaney's appears in Robert Kerlin *Negro Poets and Their Poems* (Washington D.C.: Associate Publishers 1923) p. 279.
65. Joan Sherman *Invisible Poets: Afro-Americans of the Nineteenth Century* (Urbana: Univ. of Illinois Press 1974) p. xxi.
66. "Fulfillment" *Opportunity* (June 1926) p. 194.
67. *The Crisis* (March 1920) p. 266.
68. "Farewell" *The Crisis* (February 1929) p. 50
69. *Ibid.*
70. "Fragment" in Cullen, 1955, p. 70.

71. Young's poem is in *Opportunity* (June 1928)   p. 168; Walton's is "A Kiss Requested" *The Crisis* (October 1927) p. 265.
72. This poem appears in Mae Cowdrey's anthology *We Lift Our Voices* (Philadelphia: Alpress 1936) p. 57. This is one of the few anthologies to be published by a woman poet from the Renaissance period. Others include three by Georgia Douglas Johnson *The Heart of a Woman* (Boston: The Cornhill Co. 1918), *Bronze* (Boston: B.J. Brimmer Co. 1922), and *An Autumn Love Cycle* (N.Y.: H. Vinal Ltd. 1928); and a later one by Lucy Ariel Williams *Shape Them Into Dreams: Poems* (N.Y.: Exposition Press 1955).
73. "El Beso" in Kerlin, 1923, p. 154.
74. Cullen, 1955, p. 42. Gloria T. Hull has done ground-breaking research on Black lesbian poets of the Renaissance. See "Under the Days:' The Buried Life and Poetry of Angelina Weld Grimké" *Conditions: Five* Vol. II No. 2 (Autumn 1979): 17-25; and *Give Us Each Day* (N.Y.: Random House 1983), an edited diary by Alice Dunbar Nelson.
75. Gladys Casely Hayford (a.k.a. Aquah Laluah) in Cullen, 1955, p. 198.
76. May, 1959, p. 249.
77. Perry, 1976, p. 153.
78. Huggins, 1971, pp. 161-214.
79. J. Saunders Redding "The New Negro Poet in the Twenties" in Donald Gibson ed. *Modern Black Poets* (Englewood Cliffs: Prentice-Hall 1973).
80. Addison Gayle, Jr. *The Way of the New World: The Black Novel in America* (Garden City, N.Y.: Anchor Press 1975) p. 5, 95, 107.
81. Wagner. 1973, p. 165. Robert Bone also adheres to this model in *The Negro Novel in America* (New Haven: Yale Univ. Press 1958) p. 56.
82. Spencer was born in 1882, Grimké in 1880, Nelson in 1875, Johnson in 1886, and Fauset in 1882.
83. Stetson, 1981, p. xxii.
84. The theme of birthing a new self was a key one for Renaissance writers according to Gregory Singleton "Rebirth," 1982.

American Studies in Scandinavia, Vol. 19, 1987: 01-12

The Harlem Renaissance and the American Twenties

By Carl Pedersen

University of Copenhagen

The Harlem Renaissance, which symbolized the emergence of the Afro-American on the American cultural scene, and the American twenties, as preceived by the writers of the so-called Lost Generation, are usually treated as worlds apart. Indeed, while the white writers of the twenties seemed to have lost their identity, Afro-American writers in Harlem were celebrating an affirmation of racial identity and cultural roots. Paradoxically, the awakening of black consciousness coincided with the development of Harlem as a modern ghetto, while the spiritual dislocation of white intellectuals unfolded in an atmosphere of material prosperity.

In order to evaluate this period without succumbing to the temptation of neat categorization, I intend to examine the concerns of white and black writers in the postwar era in the context of the transformation of America from a rural, small-town nation to an industrialized urban society. In twentieth century Western literature, the encounter with the urban landscape provided an appropriate symbol for the malaise of modern man. The city seemed to take on a life of its own, and was perceived as a controlling force.

Petersburg is the title as well as the main protagonist of the Russian symbolist poet Andrei Bely's novel written between 1911 and 1913. Viewing fragmentation as the bane of modern urban man, Bely conceived his novel as a diatribe against the pervasive urge to separate and divide. The main focus of *Petersburg* is the eternal question of Russian national identity: the supposedly irreconcilable schism between the irrational East and the rational West, which impeded the quest for an authentic and integral selfhood. The chaotic nature of urban existence in Petersburg, which Dostoevsky called "the most fantastic and intentional city in the world," was for Bely a symbol of the entropy of modernity. Similarly, in his magnum opus from the 1930's, aptly titled *The Man Without Qualities,* the Austrian novelist Robert Musil charted the disintegration of the human spirit in an impersonal urban landscape,

1

and emphasized that his description of Vienna could apply to any modern city.

In the United States, the antecedent of postwar disorientation can be traced further back than World War I, to the profound demographic and social transformation of American society beginning shortly after the Civil War and reaching its zenith in the decades immediately preceding and following the turn of the century. The main contours of this transformation were almost complete by the end of World War I. The 1920 census revealed that, for the first time in American history, more people lived in cities than in the country and towns combined.[1] Whether they came from the farmlands of the Midwest, the rural communities of the South, or the villages and towns of Eastern and Southern Europe, the new inhabitants of American cities experienced not only physical dislocation, but cultural discontinuity. Faced with the imposing reality of an omnipotent urbanism, many newcomers retreated to the solace and community of a common group culture only to find it beset with disintegration and internecine conflict. An inevitable dispute arose between those who would embrace this urbanized America wholeheartedly and without reserve, and those who believed that such a drastic step implied a loss of identity and cultural impotence.

Furthermore, the mass migration and emigration from a rural to an urban environment undergoing rapid technological progress and a massive institutionalization of the corporate economy underscored the fundamental disequilibrium between economic modernization coupled with creeping secularization on the one hand, and the relative social backwardness of many of the new city dwellers on the other. This "cultural lag," as one commentator in the twenties, William Ogburn, called it, affected not only the sense of selfhood, but the perception of national identity. Repelled by the apparent vacuity of American civilization in the twenties, many intellectuals blamed the anachronistic residues of New England Puritanism and provincial ethics. The conflict of twentieth century America between what Warren Susman calls "an older culture, often loosely labeled Puritan-republican, producer-capitalist culture, and a newly emerging culture of abundance," was reflected in the opposition of the provincial perception of America embodied in the small towns to the alien, decadent influences of the cities.[2] Populated by immigrants and blacks, intellectuals espousing European socialistic ideologies of class conflict and proletarian revolution, and the new captains of industry and advertising promoting godless materialism, the cities represented the epitome of evil to the prophets of provincialism. Nativist sentiment generated a blacklash against modern urban society in

2

the Red Scare, the Palmer raids and the subsequent deportation of radical elements, racism and the resurgence of the Ku Klux Klan, religious fundamentalism, and Prohibition.

However, the urban experience offered no secure refuge from this provincial broadside. Fragmentation and anonymity precluded any unified comprehension of the complexities of an urbanized society. The unreality of the city substituted loss of autonomy and aimlessness for national self-interest, the fulcrum of Progressive ideology. The aesthetics of intellectuals and writers in the twenties was shaped by their disillusionment with the war and the nature of postwar American society, their lack of direction, and seeming loss of control over events directly affecting them. In seeking a sense of authenticity to combat the diffuseness of their visual environment, they embarked on a quixotic search for a usable past.

The notion of a usable past was first formulated by Van Wyck Brooks in 1918 in an attempt to uncover the roots of American culture and to bridge the yawning chasm he saw between contemplation and action, idealism and the real, and highbrow and lowbrow aesthetics. I would like to explore how black and white writers responded to the changes in American society outlined above in light of the confrontation with and subsequent alienation from urbanism, and the quest for a usable past to make sense of the entropy they experienced around them.

A pervasive feeling of fragmentaion and unreality, alienation from the provincial past and the urban present, was reflected in the concerns of American writers in the twenties. Although T.S. Eliot took London as his model for *The Waste Land,* he, like Musil, believed that his bleak description of emotional sterility and death in life applied to every modern city. The spiritual chaos of Eliot's urban vision struck a chord in many writers, notably Hemingway in *The Sun Also Rises* and in his concept of *nada,* and Fitzgerald, who in *The Great Gatsby* mentioned the waste land by name in his description of a desolate valley of ashes appended by a "compact Main Street" which was "contiguous to absolutely nothing."[3]

John Dos Passos's novel of New York from 1925, *Manhattan Transfer,* also owes a dept to the structure and metaphor of Eliot's poem. The fragmentary structure of *Manhattan Transfer* signifies the existential confusion of the time and the inadequacy of traditional aesthetic forms in expressing this confusion. The impersonality and absence of love in *The Waste Land* is echoed in Dos Passos's novel. His characters become reified and suffer the loss of compassion and genuine feeling. Like Eliot, Dos Passos makes a moral judgment on the malaise of modern urban

3

man by employing fragmentary impressions and symbols of degeneration and regeneration such as fire and water abstracted from their total context, thus underscoring the dissolution of human values in an institutionalized environment.

The city acted as a controlling force, but any assertion of independence from this control could lead to the total disintegration of the personality. By admitting his own confusion, Jimmy Herf, one of the main protagonists of the novel, feels as if he is succumbing to the disorientation of urban existence. He declares at one point: "The trouble with me is I cant decide what I want most, so my motion is circular, helpless, and confoundedly discouraging."[4]

The imposing architecture of urbanism not only separated the city dweller from his immediate environment, but servered his already tenuous link with the past. Desire and hope remain unfulfilled, and the city can only be tolerated when its constricting physical contours are invisible to perception.

"I think that this city is full of people wanting inconceivable things... Look at it."

"It's all right when you cant see it. There's no artistic sense, no beautiful buildings, no old-time air, that's what's the matter with it."[5]

The one-dimensionality of many of Dos Passos's characters expresses the dangers of conditioning by impersonal dehumanizing structures with a realization that without these structures, only a void remains. Futility and aimlessness are the inevitable result of this loss of self: Genuine human values are subverted by a relentless pursuit of material success. In the figure of Ellen Thatcher, Dos Passos underscores the despair of emotional sterility: Ellen is incapable of real love, has an abortion (for Dos Passos the very negation of life), and ends up as a "procelain figure under a bellglass."

At the end of the novel, Jimmy Herf realizes that he cannot survive in such an environment and decides to leave New York. His decision is conscious, but nevertheless negative: he has no idea of where he is going and sums up his experience by observing: "I'm beginning to learn a few of the things I don't want."[6]

The perception that the modern city lacks the "old-time air" anticipates Dos Passos' usable past in his monumental trilogy USA. His vision of a pristine, innocent America in Camera Eye 49 of The Big Money, "a world unfenced," had been distorted by modern urban society. Fitzgerald's past in The Great Gatsby resembles that of Dos Passos: the "green breast of the new world," a majestic and wonderous sight full of hope

4

and promise. Such retrogressive concepts of a usable past seemed doomed to disuse. Furthermore, the visions of Pilgrims landing at Plymouth Rock and Dutch sailors beholding the lush magnificence of the Eastern shores of a new found land by definition excluded the Afro-Americans, whose descendents came to America in shackles. The recoil of writers like Dos Passos and Fitzgerald from the confrontation with the modern metropolis led to a tacit acceptance of the premises of the provincial idea of an America free from the evil of urbanism and the noxious influences of alien races and ethnic groups.

In *The Great Gatsby*, the perception of the past becomes for Jay Gatsby the only possible future, a dream which can be repeated at will. Fitzgerald's novel offers a succinct illustration of Brooks' dichotomy between the idealistic world of theory and the pragmatic world of action in the characters of Gatsby, who has no conception of reality, and Tom Buchanan, who is obsessed with the pursuit of money. However, Tom is also beset by a vague premonition of doom heralded by the ascent of foreign ethnic groups and races concentrated in the cities.

> "Civilization's going to pieces," broke out Tom violently. "I've gotten to be a terrible pessimist about things. Have you read *The Rise of the Coloured Empires* by this man Goddard?"
> "Why, no," I answered, rather surprised by his tone.
> "Well, it's a fine book, and everybody ought to read it. The idea is if we don't look out the white race will be utterly submerged. It's all scientific stuff; it's been proved."
> ..."This fellow has worked out the whole thing. It's up to us, who are the dominant race, to watch out or these other races will have control of things."[7]

Tom is, of course, referring to Lothrop Stoddard's *The Rising Tide of Color* from 1920, which, along with Madison Grant's *The Passing of the Great Race* from 1916, marked the resurgence of the idea of the innate superiority of whites, based on the theory that mental traits are determined by race. Interestingly enough, Stoddard considered colonial America as a land rich in racial promise, which was betrayed by the influx of blacks, who had "no historic pasts" and by immigration from Southern and Eastern Europe. The concentration of "swarming, prolific aliens" in urban areas was leading America down the road to "racial bankruptcy and the collapse of civilization."[8]

Naturally, the blacks who had migrated from the South or immigrated from the West Indies to Northern industrial centers did not see themselves as a threat to "civilization." One of the features of the Harlem Renaissance was an abiding faith in the resilience of racial consciousness and community against the inroads of a hostile white culture.

5

However, at the same time that Afro-American intellectuals were promoting the image of Harlem as a black Mecca, there was a recognition that the movement northward had separated blacks from the traditional bonds of rural community.

In the introduction to the famous anthology *The New Negro* published in 1925, Alain Locke designated the emerging Afro-American awareness of national identity and self-determination as an urban phenomenon, comparing it to the postwar rise of nationalism in Europe. The city provided an enclosed arena of contact between disparate elements forced together by social proscription and racial prejudice. Locke felt, however, that the negative aspects of this development were outweighed by the Afro-American quest for identity.

> (The) movement of the Negro becomes more and more a mass movement toward the larger and the more democratic chance – in the Negro's case a deliberate flight not only from countryside to city, but from medieval America to modern... Hitherto, it must be admitted that American Negroes have been a race more in name than in fact, or to be exact, more in sentiment than in experience. The chief bond between them has been that of a common condition rather than a common consciousness; a problem in common rather than a life in common. In Harlem, Negro life is seizing upon its first chances for group expression and self-determination... Harlem has the same role to play for the New Negro as Dublin has had for the New Ireland or Prague for the New Czechoslovakia.[9]

The racial community of Harlem was perceived by many writers as an enclave of forced confinement, a curious anomaly in the arid, geometric sterility of white Manhattan. Thus blacks experienced a dual displacement from their rural past and their surrounding urban environment. Constantly confronted with two cities, one dominant and the other emergent, many blacks existed on two levels of experience. In her novel *Quicksand* from 1928, Nella Larsen describes Helga Crane's encounter with the two cities:

> But, while the continuously gorgeous panorama of Harlem fascinated her, thrilled her, the sober mad rush of white New York failed entirely to stir her. Like thousands of other Harlem dwellers, she patronized its shops, its theaters, its art galleries, and its restaurants, and reads its papers, without considering herself a part of the monster. And she was satisfied, unenvious. For her this Harlem was enough. Of that white world, so distant, so near, she asked only indifference.

Afro-Americans were thus continually compelled to respond to the social isolation of their own group and an alien culture they could feel, but could never be a part of. The quest for a usable past was conducted with the realization that there could be no return to the rural community of the South. As a social movement, the Harlem Renaissance reflected the

6

encounter of the uprooted Southern and West Indian black with the constrictions of ghetto urbanism. Jean Toomer acknowledged that this encounter would become an irrevocable part of Afro-American identity, but nevertheless believed that Afro-American literature could not survive unless it was imbedded in the soil, "soil in the sense the Russians know it."[11] His seminal work from 1922, *Cane*, was at once a paean and an epitaph to the rich cultural heritage of the agrarian past. Asked why he did not write a sequel to *Cane*, Toomer replied with regret:

> With Negroes also the trend was towards the small town and then towards the city – and industry and commerce and machines. The folk-spirit was walking in to die on the modern desert. That spirit was so beautiful. Its death was so tragic. Just this seemed to sum life for me. And this was the feeling I put into "Cane." was a swansong. It was a song of an end. And why no one has seen and felt that, why people have expected me to write a second and a third and a fourth book like "Cane," is one of the queer misunderstandings of my life.[12]

Exempted from the colonial pastoralism of Dos Passos and Fitzgerald, black writers were forced to appropriate Brooks' notion of a usable past by recasting it. Following Dos Passos, Afro-American writers became "architects of history" in attempting to make sense of the transition from a traditional to an urban environment. Although the recoil from the hostile atmosphere of the city and the search for selfhood resembled the pattern formulated by white writers, young Afro-American authors such as Wallace Thurman, Langston Hughes, and Claude McKay felt that slavish imitation of white existential concerns would divorce them from their own experience.

Claude McKay's first novel, *Home to Harlem*, published in 1928, voices many of the dilemmas of Afro-American intellectuals, while also expressing the general mood of the times found in Hemingway and Dos Passos. Like them, McKay offers a moral judgment on modern society. He proposes a historical past (which is further elaborated in his later two novels, *Banjo* and *Banana Bottom*) as an alternative to the spiritual disorientation of urban life. Critics like W.E.B. DuBois failed to discern this moral dimension and accused McKay of pandering to the white vogue of "primitivism" (in itself a response to the loss of self in urban America). This criticism can be seen as an Afro-American corollary to the distinction between high and low culture formulated by Brooks. Denying the social realities of the black urban experience condemned Afro-American literature to aesthetic sterility and servitude to white values. McKay and Hughes believed that the effort of "the Nordicized Negro intelligentsia' to willfully suppress literary portrayals of lower class black life was tantamount to cultural emasculation. As Hughes observed

7

in his famous article from 1926, "The Negro Artist and the Racial Mountain:"

> (T)he low-down folks, the so-called common element, and they are the majority... furnish a wealth of colorful, distinctive material for any artist because they still hold their own individuality in the face of American standardizations.[13]

However, McKay realized that the pernicious influence of American standardization had seeped into Harlem and was robbing the Afro-American of the cultural content, if not the form, of his racial identity. The carbaret scenes in *Home to Harlem* which so offended DuBois can be compared to the night life of Paris in Hemingway's *The Sun Also Rises*. The physical abandon of blacks reveling to the syncopated rhythm of jazz, however essential to the black spirit, was divorced from an organic connection with cultural roots. A hollow shell remained, marred by violence and hate, a showcase for whites titillated by the exoticism of it all.

Despite the absence of an intricate plot, *Home to Harlem* is not as loosely conceived as it appears to be. The opening pages recount Jake Brown's homecoming from World War I, after having deserted from the army because of his disillusionment with the "white folks' war." In Harlem, he picks up a prostitute. For the rest of the novel, Jake tries to find the prostitute Felice (i.e. happiness) once again. When he finally meets her again, he realizes he can no longer stay in Harlem. Like Jimmy Herf and Nick Carraway, he leaves New York at the end of the novel. As if to underscore the permanence of the migration of American blacks from a rural to an urban environment, Jake does not return to the South, but leaves with Felice for Chicago.

In Jake, McKay portrays the rural black whose moral attitude has been shaped by experience. His fierce sense of independence and integrity put him at odds with those who have succumbed to white values of greed, corruptibility, and violence. Jake's first meeting with Felice is not tainted by money, and McKay inevitably associates money with moral corruption and spiritual hollowness, as does Dos Passos in *Manhattan Transfer* with characters like Congo Jake and George Baldwin. Jake refuses to become a "sweetman" like his friend Zeddy and insists on working even when Congo Rose takes him under her wing. His relationship with Rose symbolizes his relationship with Harlem, and he escapes from her by getting work with a railroad company. "Jake had taken the job on the railroad just to break the hold that Harlem had upon him."[14] Harlem has become like Congo Rose to Jake: fascinating, sensual, but at the same time a controlling force about to rob him of his identity.

8

In the second part of the novel, Jake meets Ray, a restless, troubled Haitian intellectual, who is acutely aware of the disparity between his white education and the search for authentic black roots. The reconciliation between thought and life, which Brooks had attempted to find, could not be mediated in traditional American terms. Instead, Ray looks to Russian literature, as did Toomer, as a model for Afro-American aesthetics. "Only the Russians of the late era seemed to stand up like giants in the new... Here were the elements that the grand carnage swept over and touched not. The soil of life saved their roots from the fire."[15] Furthermore, Ray has a vision of a past unlike Toomer's swan song of the South, Dos Passos's Jeffersonian storybook democracy or Fitzgerald's Long Island. He imparts this vision of his native island to Jake:

> (Jake) learned that the universal spirit of the French Revolution had reached and lifted up the slaves far away in that remote island; that Black Hayti's independence was more dramatic and picturesque than the United States' independence and that it was a strange, almost unimaginable eruption of the beautiful ideas of the "Liberté, Egalité, Fraternité" of Mankind, that shook the foundations of that romantic era.
>
> Jake felt like one passing through a dream, vivid in rich, varied colors. It was revelation beautiful his mind. That brief account of an island of savage black people, who fought for collective liberty and was struggling to create a culture of their own. A romance of his race, just down there by Panama. How strange![16]

Thus white writers like Dos Passos and Fitzgerald reacted to the urban waste land by harkening back to a virgin past of open space and unbounded promise. Toward the end of *The Big Money*, the subjective character of the Camera Eye has perceived an image of an unblemished past at Plymouth, Massachusetts:

> this is where the immigrants landed... on the beach that belonged to no one between the ocean that belonged to no one and the enormous forest that belonged to no one that stretched over the hills where the deertracks were up the green rivervalleys where the redskins grew their tall corn in patches forever into the incredible west.[17]

Alienated from modernity, these writers found no other recourse than to embrace the very provincial vision of an innocent American they had tried to escape from. They had rediscovered a history that was already lost.

At first glance, it might appear that Afro-American writers like McKay, Toomer, and Hughes were following white writers in recoiling from modern urbanism and searching for a usable past. As I have attempted to show, there was indeed a similar pattern of response to the profound transformations of American society. However, the expression of this

9

response was markedly different. Unlike the past of Dos Passos and Fitzgerald, the Afro-American past had been repudiated and suppressed by the dominant culture, and black writers saw it as their task to resuscitate this past. In doing so, they became genuine architects of history. Furthermore, Toomer recognized the demise of the Southern past even while reviving its cultural heritage. However, he realized that without the revival of the roots of the Afro-American experience, blacks would not be able to survive the encounter with the urbanized white world.

McKay's Haiti can likewise not be dismissed as an Afro-American parallel to Plymouth Rock. His past was more a revelation than a repetition, an expanding vision instead of a restraining one. Haiti was an example of the liberation of black culture from the bonds of white civilization. As Tom Buchanan feared, the twentith century witnessed the rise of the colored races, who were imposing their history and cultural roots on the white world, expanding the image of the past and informing the exigencies of the present.

In his last novel, *Banana Bottom*, McKay embarked on a literary return to his native land, Jamaica, and resolved the conflict between thought and life in the context of Jamaican cultural history. Bita Plant, a black girl from the mountains of Jamaica, is educated in England and chooses to return to her native village, and becomes the recipient and the fulfillment of an historical promise arising out of the inevitable conflicts of post-Emancipation Jamaica. The triumph of Bita Plant is the synthesis of her experience, the incorporation of her intellectual upbringing into the fact of her black heritage.

McKay's past was thus not only "new" in the sense that'it had previously been ignored or distorted. It was dynamic because it speaks directly to the paramount concerns of Afro-American culture. At the same time however, McKay's vision remained pastoral, promoting a conscious movement away from the city to the land (or the soil). For McKay, this vision was still very much alive and formed the basis for the further development of a vibrant and universal black culture.

Both white and black writers failed to provide any viable solution for the disorientation and alienation of modern urban man. However, Afro-American writers were uncovering a past and creating history, while white writers clung desparately to the illusion of a lost past which only distorted their preception of the present. Thus although the Harlem Renaissance and the American twenties unfolded as a response to the cultural confusion of and alienation from twentieth century urban society, and looked to the past to make sense of the present, these two histo-

10

rical moments remained separate. Instead of regarding the transformation of American society as a totality of interconnected processes, the reaction of the intellectual community to modernization reinforced the divisions and confusion it attempted to oppose.

NOTES

1. Loren Baritz, ed., *The Culture of the Twenties* (Indianapolis: Bobbs-Merrill Company, 1970) pp. xxiii-xxiv.
2. Warren I. Susman, *Culture as History. The Transformation of American Society in the Twentieth Century* (New York: Pantheon, 1984) p. xx.
3. F. Scott Fitzgerald, *The Great Gatsby* (Harmondsworth: Penguin, 1985) p. 27.
4. John Dos Passos, *Manhattan Transfer* (Boston: Houghton Mifflin, n.d.) p. 176. For Dos Passos's indebtedness to Eliot, see E.D. Lowry's article *"Manhattan Transfer: Dos Passos's Wasterland"* from 1963, reprinted in Andrew Hook, ed., *Dos Passos. A. Collection of Critical Essays* (Englewood Cliffs, N.J.: Prentice-Hall, 1974) pp. 53-61.
5. Dos Passos, op.cit., p. 262.
6. Ibid., p. 360.
7. Fitzgerald, op.cit., p. 18.
8. Lothrop Stoddard, *The Rising Tide of Color* (New York, 1920) pp. 91, 262-263, 302-303.
9. Alain Locke, ed., *The New Negro* (New York: Atheneum, 1983) pp. 6, 7.
10. Nella Larsen, *Quicksand* (New Brunswick, NJ: Rutgers Unicversity Press, 1986) p. 45.
11. Quoted in Alain Locke, ed., op.cit., p. 51.
12. Darwin T. Turner, ed., *The Wayward and the Seeking. A Collection of Writings by Jean Toomer* (Washington, D.C.: Howard University Press, 1982) p. 123.
13. Langston Hughes, "The Negro Artist and the Racial Mountain," reprinted in Francis L. Broderick and August Meier, eds., *Negro Protest Thought in the Twentieth Century* (Indianapolis: Bobbs-Merrill Company, 1965) pp. 93-94.
14. Claude McKay, *Home to Harlem* (New York: Harper and Bros., 1928) p. 125.
15. Ibid., p. 228
16. Ibid., pp. 131, 134.
17. John Dos Passos, *The Big Money* in *USA* (New York: The Modern Library, 1937) p. 435.

11

WITH 'BANJO' BY MY BED : BLACK FRENCH WRITERS
READING CLAUDE McKAY

by

BRIDGET JONES

Every historian of Negritude points to the role of Claude McKay when looking at the influences which converged in Paris between the Wars, and gave birth to a dynamic new ideology for black writers.[1] Cessaire, Damas and Senghor have all paid tribute to McKay, and a wealth of lesser figures refer to him, re-echoing various images and ideas.

It should be straightforward enough to date French translations of McKay's novels, and the poems and key passages from *Banjo* which were featured in little magazines, but real questions of influence also depend on personal affinities and are seldom easy to establish. A nostalgic haze has made everything Black prewar quite Beautiful, and every Left Bank drinking hole and *bal negre* a high old time. Marcer Cook, who was there, has warned us not to confuse 'influence with coincidence'.[2] A diverse group of writers, American, Caribbean, African, were affirming black pride and rediscovering a shared heritage. They promoted distinctive gifts of 'rhythm' and 'soul', a collective spirit, conscious that in the struggle against past and present exploitation based on race, culture had a role to play. Once World War II scattered most of the students and artists concerned, national divergences became clearer, but again in the 1950s Paris became a centre, and McKay found reads among a new generation of students from Africa and the Caribbean.

Claude McKay spent relatively little time continuously in Paris, and though proud of the success of *Banjo*[3], may well have been aware until much later that it had achieved the status of a cult novel or manifesto. He needed the kind of appreciation which provided daily bread. Material needs kept his feet on the ground, and it is this grasp of reality, combined with an extraordinary receptivity to all shades of emotional and sensual experience, which underlies McKay's appeal, and still makes his response to the black Francophone world worth reading. His sophisticated insight into French colonial attitudes owed much to his Jamaican origins (it was up at Jekyll's home at Mavis Bank that he had first begun to study French) but in Europe he was, and still is, more often identified as an American.

Some key links in the chain of transmission from Harlem Renaissance to Negritude have been identified: the sociable Martinican sisters, Paulette and Jane Nardal, who held regular gatherings to welcome back writers and scholars. McKay was responsible for first bringing along Alain Locke,[4] and the French Guianese writer, Goncourt prize-winner and colonial administrator, Rene Maran. *Les continents*, which Maran co-edited with Prince Kojo Tovalou, carried an article by Locke citing McKay's poetry in 1924,[5] and when the Nardal sisters produced their bilingual *Revue du Monde noir* (1930-32), they printed two poems in full with translation. In a final article on the 'Awakening of Racial Consciousness' Paulette Nardal invoked the work of McKay and Langston Hughes, pointing out how black American writers were expressing themselves without the inferiority complex that inhibited their brothers in the Caribbean.

Until his novel made an impact, McKay typically figured among poets of the Harlem Renaissance, linked with Langston Hughes, Countee Cullen, Jean Tommer, *et al* as a critic of white racism and exploitation. The ironical 'Spring in Hew Hampshire', or the stoical pride of 'The White House', which Senghor frequently quoted,[6] supported this view. While the Harlem poets were mainly known through anthologies, particularly Alain Locke's rich source-book *The New Negro* (1925), and in translation, it was thematic similarities which emerged: the celebration of black music and dance, protest poetry dealing with segregation and violence, as for example in McKay's *'Negro Dancers'*

> For them the dance is the true joy of life (...)
> And yet they are outcasts of the earth,
> A race oppressed and scorned by ruling man

In contrast, *Banjo* dealt with race relations within France and the French colonies, speaking directly and critically to the successful, those scholarship-holders, privileged and often light-skinned, who frequent the Parisian *salons*. As a West Indian, McKay was never tempted to reason in terms of a simplified black/white dichotomy.

It seems as if the translation of *Banjo* circulated informally before publication in book form by Rieder (1931), as Marcer Cook writes of the sensation it created one year after appearing in the U.S. (1929). An extract from the beginning of Chapter XVI was featured in the militant student pamphlet, *Legitime defense* (1932), no doubt attracting additional attention. It is worth lingering over the content of the passage selected. It is scarcely a discussion, more a harangue by Ray, the black Haitian writer and alter ego of the author (cf. also *Home to Harlem*), addressing a 'Negro student from Martinique'. The fellow displays all the prejudices of the insecure mulatto, despising the Senegalese (a blanket term for West Africans) as savages, but proud of that reactionary white Creole, Napoleon's Empress Josephine. Ray takes him to task as one of the lost blacks, brainwashed by their education. He reminds him that the true racial renaissance will be achieved by 'getting down to our native roots and building up from our own people'. Though sarcastic about 'mixed-bloods', Ray suggests a range of cultural resources: Irish and Russian literature, Gandhi's philosophy, indigenous African languages. the return to roots is not to be exclusive or blinkered but will draw nourishment from many sources, guided by faith in the vigour and potential of the proletariat. The radical nature of this challenge can hardly be exaggerated. Despite May 1968 and endemic student protest, French intellectual discourse remains hierarchical and elitist in its assumptions, the slippery glass pyramid of the Louvre its fitting symbol. With his Caribbean sensitivity to class and colour, McKay is trying to invert the structure, to show his readers that the coloniser's myth of cultural superiority has been used to divide *Antillais* from *Africans*, inciting them to jostle up the ladder to the purest French, the lightest skin, the most perfect assimilation into, if not rebirth in the likeness of, the Parisian archetype. He is well aware of the political usefulness for France of using Caribbean administrators in African colonies who do not identify with the "subject" races. Ray's sermon to the alienated student is charged with McKay's own distrust for chauvinistic French culture and his generous idealism. However, it should not be assumed that it was only as a novel of ideas that *Banjo* made an impact. The joyful scenes celebrating music and dance: 'Ho! Secouez Qa!', helped legitimate the equation 'I am black therefore I dance'. the sketches of the Old Port of Marseille, the solidarity of its poor blacks (shown for example at Bugsy's funeral, p. 260), the scrapes, the moral values (Latnah) became as much of a classic warm-hearted portrait of this cosmopolitan milieu as did Marcel Pagnol's 'Marius' trilogy for the native French.

Of the three founding fathers of the Negritude movement, Leopold Sedar Senghor, the doyen, frequently quoted McKay. A typical example would be his concluding quotation from *Banjo* to an audience at the Dakar Foyer France-Senegal in 1937, reminding them that an authentic culture must be constructed from their African roots: quite a revolutionary message in that place and time.[7] In this earlier period he used McKay and Harlem poets as evidence of the potential or a consciously black literature, and has not failed since, in typical schoolmasterly style, to acknowledge what negritude owed to Afro-American sources. His own poetic expression draws on images current in the work of several poets featured in the *New Negro* anthology, including the antithesis between the harsh mineral technology of white civilisation and the vitality and warmth of black spirituality. A Senghor poem like 'A New York', a favourite of Edward Kamau Brathwaite,[8] may well owe something to McKay's vision of the hostile power of the

American city.

Cesaire too absorbed this climate of ideas, with its key metaphoric polarities and emphatic assertions of the black man's privileged harmony with the natural world. But equally he perceived that the claim for a specific black cultural birthright must be accompanied by the demand for equal respect and equal rights. After composing a research paper on the 'Theme of the South in the Negro-American literature of the United States' in his final year at the Ecole Normale Superieure, he developed his ideas in a much more significant context, *Tropiques*, a literary magazine he and Rene Menil founded in Martinique during the Occupation of the island by pro-Nazi forces. By describing the role of the black American poet in fighting white oppression, he could issue a coded summons to Martinican intellectuals to identify with their own humiliated people instead of yearning after Parisian recognition.[9] Cesaire also praised *Banjo* for creating a hero out of the 'ordinary Negro (...) drawn seriously and passionately', a contribution to the project of replacing ludicrous stereotypes of the "exotic" with authentic portraits of black experience.[10]

Nevertheless, however, much Senghor and Cesaire admired the poetry of McKay and others, and drew inspiration from *Banjo*, the influence appears to have been more theoretical than personal. their outstanding academic successes and leadership roles tended to bring them increasingly into contact with French social and political elites, whereas Leon Damas remained a more marginal figure, closer in temperament and life-style to McKay. In his formative pre-war years, Damas moved between worlds belonging to none, and when his family cut off his funds, knew a hand-to-mouth existence in Paris of dead-end jobs relieved by wild sprees.

Damas used some lines from McKay's poem 'To The White Fiends' as epigraph for his *Pigments* (1937), presenting forcefully his poetic persona as '... hot jazz, the collections of the Museum of Ethnography and the Negro writers (Claude Mactay (sic), Langston Hughes and Alain Locke) have taught him the role and mission of his race'.[12]

Several concerns important to McKay surface in Damas's poetry: his best-known poem, the dramatic monologue, 'Hoquet' (Hiccup), sums up a world of colour discrimination in its punch line,[13] recalling McKay's suspicious scorn for 'yaller niggers' who divide the race by their class pretensions. We can surely read a clear allusion to McKay in the little boy's demand for a banjo instead of piano lessons, especially as the hero of one of Damas's rewritten folktales in *Veillees noires* is 'Cockroach-Guitar', a vagabond musician much in demand for his irresistible rhythms. The title of another early poem, 'Solde', picks up McKay's image of 'reach-me-down' Negro education: 'When the whites move out, we move in and take possession of the old dead stuff.'[14] Damas wittily develops from mockery of alien formal clothes and behaviour to a harsh critique of the hypocritical and violently repressive 'civilisation' whose accomplice he must become in the nàme of assimilation. The emblematic figure of the truant, the wandering bad boy, haunts Damas's writing, a self-image in several of the *Pigments*, and strong in the boozy extended poem, *Black-Label*. Damas shares the rueful lucidity of McKay's hero Barclay in the story, 'Truant': a restless yearning for 'eternal inquietude', even at the expense of home and security, but linked, as in McKay, to the demoralising 'great tradition of black servitude' which deprived most black breadwinners of worthwhile employment. the analogy might be pursued: both writers became permanent exiles, exploring life through people and diverse places, rather than committing themselves to one community, leaving a strongly self-centred body of work which yet gave a sense of promise not wholly fulfilled. Both viewed with sharp insight and pungent observation the social and psychological absurdities of racist thinking.

In poetic form Damas gave an important place to rhythm, more in the manner of Langston Hughes than McKay, but he was alone among the first generation of Negritude writers in writing poetry that was direct, slangy, accessible to the ordinary reader, better performed than read on the page. He took his poetic cues from the blues poets, but the prose of *Banjo* was also liberating, in the risks taken with jazz effects, free-wheeling textual excitement not correctness and good taste.

McKay was jubilant to see a bookseller's window full of copies of *Banjo* on the Avenue de l'Opera, and it is undoubtedly this work which has been most influential in the Francophone world. Read as a source book for arguments against assimilation, as a plea for mutual respect between blacks from Africa and the diaspora, or simply as a rueful warm-hearted 'story without a plot', its impact extended well beyond the trio of founders of Negritude.

Especially in the postwar period, when the Societe Africaine de Culture organised lectures and two seminal congresses, when *Presence africaine* began publication, McKay was again an obvious point of reference. For example, Guy Trirolien (1917-1988), a Guadeloupean writer whose gentle talent was always ready to absorb the candences of others, summons up strength by this association:

> My voice
> the voice of Cesaire and McKay
> of Robeson and Guillen
> will be stronger than your pride
> higher than your skyscrapers
> for it springs from the dark womb of suffering
> America[15]

The collection, *Balles d'or* (1961), explores typical Negritude topics in poems like 'Satchmo', 'Amerique', 'Black Beauty', though probably Senghor was to some extent an intermediary (they were together in a German Stalag after the fall of France in 1940). Tirolien himself later worked as an administrator in Africa, and in *Feuilles vivantes au matin* (1977) comments with perceptive tolerance on social situations: racial dogmatism has become for him a source of wasted potential, and he spent his last years sagely in his native Marie-Galante.[16]

Joseph Zobel, now widely known through Euzhan Palcy's appealing film version of his semi-autobiographical novel, *La Rue Cases-Negres*, also belongs to the generation influenced by McKay. though his hero Jose becomes a scholarship boy at the prestigious Lycee Schoelcher, he is by no means co-opted into the Martinican ruling class, and spends his evenings with the chauffeur Carmen, newly literate thanks to his young friend and a passionate reader: 'He liked Balzac, Gorki, Tolstoy ... But the day I had him read *Banjo*, by Claude McKay, he was beside himself with joy'.[17] The less well-known sequel to *La rue Cases-Negres*, initially entitled *La fete a Paris* (1953), and slightly revised as *Quand la neige aura fondu* shows an influence from *Banjo*. Zobel takes care to stage-manage debates between blacks of different origins, and reacts against the ignorant scorn many West Indians displayed towards Africans. A scene where Jose comes face to face with the first real African he has met betrays a touchingly clumsy idolatry: 'Ousmane Diop, standing in his dressing-gown of garnet-red with yellow edging, had the hieratic beauty of a totem in the centre of the village'.[18] Zobel conveys a sense of Paris as a focal meeting point for blacks but his characters remain wooden, pegs on which to hang attitudes to race. As is unfortunately the way with sequels, he fails to recapture the intensely felt world of *La rue Cases-Negres*.

Among other novels composed by black students in Paris in the 1950's, in what Merle Hodge calls the "Banjo cycle"[19], there is Ousmane Soce's *Mirages de Paris* (1955). Soce highlights the obligatory presence of a copy of *Banjo* on the bookshelf of every conscious black student at this time. But the author and film-maker who commands most interest was largely self-taught, the Senegales Sembene Ousmane, whose prestige in French-speaking Africa today is comparable to that of Soyinka or Ngugi. His first novel, *Le Docker noir*[20], set in Marseille, powerfully summons up the spirit of McKay: the hero Diaw Falla is a docker immersed in the black community of the port, yet striving to become a writer. Uncompromising in its concern to articulate a protest against exploitation of black by white (Diaw's book on black history is published as her own by a white writer, the brutal conditions for dock labour are detailed), the novel by no means condones inter-ethnic hostility and patriarchal oppression of black by black. Diaw, condemned to hard labour for life, becomes an exemplary sacrifice to a colonial power whose justice is corrupted by racism. Stiffer and more sombre than *Banjo*, at times melodramatic, this novel returns to McKay's 'Ditch' to comment on the interlock-ing economic and ideological system through which colonialism denies humanity to its victims. Sembene Ousmane has increasingly used the medium of film in order to reach a wide public, but this early novel, published at his own expense and full of echoes of his reading (Zola and Camus as well as McKay) already shows his stature: a rare blend of dignified critical thinking and warmth of response.

The example of Sembene Ousmane incites the critic to daydream - alive today Claude McKay would surely have developed his interest in film beyond script reading and crowd scenes for Rex Ingram - *Banjo* as a great jazz movie? Bita Plant walking again through the luxuriant green of Banana Bottom?

McKay's strength was his receptivity, to mood and moment, to writing from many different sources, to the diversity as well as to the vital solidarities of the black world. If he influenced many of those who has passed through the French educational system, it may be because he evaluated with a keen mind its strengths and weaknesses. His letters to William Bradley suggest a critical distance. Paris served him as a port of call on the way from Moscow to North Africa, from Brittany or Spain, it was never the lodestar of all intellectual activity. He relished the mordant wit of Voltaire, the work of Gide and Maupassant, but saw the limitations of a literary culture which required subservience to its norms of refinement, which, even while proclaiming Revolutionary ideals, sought to impose its own intellectual mould. Not for him the straitjacket of the professional Francophone.

A word finally on the question of translation. so far it has been too easily assumed that on both sides of the Atlantic a unitary discourse labelled McKay was received and proved a stimulating influence. The most alert of current critics warn us against such simplifications. Michael Dash has shown how a Haitian translator like Rene Piquion selectively heightened the impact of Harlem poets, including McKay, in accordance with his own emphatically black agenda.[21] Similarly Michael Fabre points to the unmistakeable shift of emphasis involved when for example McKay's 'people' is translated as 'classe ouvriere' (working class), and the homespun 'folks' politicised to 'the people'.[22] Whether translators or readers and whatever our first language, we are all reconstructing a personal version of Claude McKay. It is certain that *Banjo* had a powerful appeal for blacks resisting French assimilation, but, like all McKay's best work, it also speaks to any reader trying to find the 'spiritual passion and pride to be his human self in an inhumanly alien world'.[23]

NOTES AND REFERENCES

1.   See for example Lilyan Kesteloot **Les escrivains noirs de langue francaise**, Brussels: Universite Libre, 1965, especially Chapter V. Available in translation Temple U.P. 1974. The author collected valuable testimony on the enduring impact of **Banjo** (interviews c. 1959). Also, more simplistically, Julio Finn **Voices of Negritude**, London: Quartet Books, 1988.

2.   Mercer Cook 'Some Literary Contacts: African, West Indian, Afro-American' in Lloyd Brown ed. **The Black Writer in Africa and The Americas**, Los Angeles: Hennessy & Ingalls, 1973, p. 119.

3.   See **A Long Way From Home**, New York: Harcourt Brace, 1970, Chapter VI, but note Wayne Cooper's view that 'Even as late as 1937, he probably had little idea of the influence he had exerted upon the development of black French literature'.

4.   Wayne F. Cooper **Claude McKay**, Louisiana State U.P., 1987, p. 215.

5.   For all the contacts and publications in this period Michael Fabre's **La Rive noire: De Harlem a la Seine** (Paris: Lieu Commun, 1985) is an invaluable guide. Chapter IV deals with McKay, the 'well-informed visitor'.

6.   See Eloise Briere 'Senghor et l'Amerique' in **Sud**, 17e an, 1987, papers of L.S. Senghor Colloque, Cerisy, p. 325.

7.   Text of the lecture in L.S. Senghor **Liberte I: Negritude et Humanisme**, Paris: Seuil, 1964.

8.   L.S. Senghor **Poemes**, Paris: Seuil, 1973, pp. 113-5. Brathwaite made a point of introducing the work of Negritude poets to Caribbean students in the 1960s.

9.   Kesteloot, p. 225.

10.   Kesteloot, p. 80 ff. based on **Tropiques**, 1941.

11.   Extracted with an extra syllable on 'Afric' which mangles the metre. Cf. **Selected Poems**, p. 38.

12.   **Esprit**, 2e an, Nos. 23-4, 1934, p. 705. Note Christophe Dailly 'Leon Damas et al Negro-Renaissance, **Presence africaine**, No. 112 (1979).

13.   On this poem see R. Burton 'My Mother Who Fathered Me: "Hoquet" by Leon Damas', **Journal of West Indian Literature**, Vol. 4, No. 1, January 1990, pp. 14-27.

14.   **Home to Harlem**, New York: harper Brothers, 1928, p. 243.

15.   'Amerique', **Balles d'or**, Paris: Presence africaine, 1977, p. 69.

16.   **Guy Tirolien, de Marie-Galante a une poetique afro-antillaise**, Paris: Editions Caribeennes/GEREF, 1990 (interviews ed. M. Tetu).

17.   Quoted from the translation published as **Black Shack Alley**, London: Heinemann, 1980, p. 167.

18.   Passage as translated in Merle Hodge's seminar paper 'Novels on the French Caribbean Intellectual in France', Mona, 1975.

19.**Ibid**, p. 11.

20.   Paris: Presence africaine, 1973 (first published Editions Debresse, 1956). Available in translation as **Black Docker**, Heinemann.

21.   J. Michael Dash **Haiti and the United States: National Stereotypes and the Literary Imagination**, London: Macmillan, 1988, p. 67.

22.   Fabre **Rive noire**, p. 110.

23.   **Banjo**, p. 322.

HARLEM: ENTRANCE AND INITIATION

Christopher Mulvey

King Alfred's College, England

The epic event of twentieth century black America is the Great Migration which remade the American North as much as it remade the American South. Three major routes out of the South were established in the decade between 1910 and 1920 when blacks began moving along the Atlantic Seaboard towards Boston, up the Mississippi towards Chicago and Detroit, and out to the West towards California. This simple but huge pattern accounted for the present population distribution of black Americans making them in the twentieth century an urban people. The "magnitude of this migration" was represented by the statistics from *The Report of the National Advisory Commission on Civil Disorders* (the *Kerner Report*) which reported in 1968 that in the half century since 1910 there had been an internal migration of nearly five million people.[1]

"In the very process of being transplanted the Negro is being transformed," Alain Locke wrote in 1925 in *The New Negro*.[2] And Locke rejected the demographic and statistical explanation of the "New Negro" which was to become the kernel of the *Kerner Report*.

> The tide of Negro migration, northward and city-ward, is not to be fully explained as a blind flood started by the demands of war industry coupled with the shutting off of foreign migration, or by the pressure of poor crops coupled with increased social terrorism in certain sections of the South and Southwest.[3]

"The American Negro has the great advantage," said James Baldwin in 1962, "of having never believed that collection of myths to which white Americans cling: that their ancestors were all freedom-loving heroes, that they were born in the greatest country the world has ever seen, or that Americans are invincible in battle and wise in peace."[4] But the American Negro, the American black, did not escape quite as completely as Baldwin believed the pervasive influence of the dominant culture. If blacks did not share with whites the myth "that their ancestors were all freedom-loving heroes," Alain

94

Locke nonetheless preferred in 1925 to explain the great migration in terms of the mythology which had interpreted movement towards New York for at least a hundred, perhaps two hundred, years. "The wash and rush of this human tide on the beach line of the northern city centers is to be explained primarily in terms of a new vision of opportunity, of social and economic freedom, of a spirit to seize, even in the face of an extortionate and heavy toll, a chance for the improvement of conditions. With each successive wave of it, the movement of the Negro becomes more and more a mass movement toward the larger and the more democratic chance."[5] The Negroes had not moved towards America as towards freedom, they had come in chains, but they were moving North, they were moving towards New York as other American people had moved across the Atlantic towards a vision of opportunity, of freedom, of democratic chance.

There was a tension here between the mythologically-enhancing reading of the city of New York as a place which spoke of opportunity, freedom, and democracy and the demographically-reductive reading of the city as a place which spoke of statistics, politics and economics. People did not want their own experience to be aggregated in mass patterns which reduced their actual or apparent self-determination. Some preferred the aggrandizement of individual endeavour which myth permitted but math denied. To do this, Locke availed himself of the images of the New Man and the New Dawn, co-opting De Crevecoeur's New American Man so that he became Alain Locke's New Negro.

The prize, as opposed to the price, for this imagery was the splendid intoxication, the oceanic stimulus, the visionary excitement with which *The New Negro* was filled. The myth pattern of New Man and New Dawn needed completion by image of the New Land, a City on a Hill, to which the renewed people would flock. Again Alain Locke was ready to complete the formulation. "Take Harlem as an instance of this," he wrote, speaking in fact of the modern but it would do well as an instance of the New Land: "Here in Manhattan is not merely the largest Negro community in the world, but the first concentration in history of so many diverse elements of Negro life."[6] Locke celebrated the diversity of the New Negro, coming as he was to come, from North and South, from city, town and village, from Africa, the Caribbean and America, and in doing so, Locke echoed the celebration of the diverse origins of the eighteenth-century New American man. The celebration of the fusing of these diverse elements in the "the laboratory of a great race-welding,"[7] as he put it, updated with a modernist image and co-opted for

95

a black readership one of the most powerful myths of nineteenth-century white America, that it was the melting pot of races.

There was a clash here between myth and ideology, consciousness and politics, plainly stated at the end of Locke's celebration of Harlem as the laboratory of a great race-welding. "Without pretense to their political significance, Harlem has the same role to play for the New Negro as Dublin has had for the New Ireland or Prague for the New Czechoslovakia." The rejection of a claim to political significance for Harlem was one with Locke's mythologising of the Great Migration as something with origins beyond those of politics and economics. But this left Harlem nonetheless with a crucial role to serve in the forging of the consciousness of the New Negro in the smithies of the souls of all those poets, artists, and musicians who made Locke's Renaissance, who became his literati, who set the pattern for writing about Harlem through the 1930s and through the 1940s.

This art mythologized the migrants' arrival in Harlem as the moment when the New Negro was born out of the Old; it was the moment that stirred the emergence of the new consciousness. Economics determined that it should be New York City which provided the locus for texts which celebrated this apotheosis of the migrant as well as the immigrant, the one to become the New Negro, the other to become the New American Man. But in this black version of the myth it was the South which equalled the Old World and Harlem which equalled the New. It was a classic motif of the American literary tradition (though its starting points need not be limited to American originals). Locke was not inventing his pattern; he was reflecting it. Exactly what Harlem meant for the migrant hero was represented by Rudolph Fisher in a short story, "The City of Refuge" in *The Atlantic Monthly* of February 1925. This was included later in the same year in Alain Locke's *The New Negro* in a selection of short stories introduced by Locke under the general title: "Negro Youth Speaks."

The hero of "The City of Refuge," King Solomon Gillis, takes the train from North Carolina to New York's Penn Terminal and the subway from Penn Terminal to Harlem to the 135th Street stop:

The moment of rebirth, renewal and resurrection was clearly pointed. From the hellish heat of the subway, the hero, a king, was delivered from his suffocating imprisonment. "Jonah emerging from the whale." He came into the New World as a man awakening in the New Dawn: "Clean air, blue sky, bright sunlight."[8]

96

The major theme of this rhetorical structure was that of the world populated by the hero's own kind, "Negroes at every turn..... Negroes predominantly, overwhelmingly everywhere." It was important in fact that there was "here and there a white face;" that emphasised for Gillis and the reader that the Negro predominated. The predomination of the Negro made for the New World. Gillis had known that this was the Harlem reality before he had left North Carolina because he had read "occasional 'colored' newspapers from New York: newspapers that mentioned Negroes without comment, but always spoke of a white person as 'So-and-so, white.' That was the point. In Harlem, black was white."[9] By the act of travelling from Waxhaw, North Carolina to Harlem, New York, King Solomon Gillis had accomplished the revolutionary act of transforming the world, turning authority on its head, making black white. Seeing with distinctly mythical vision, as who would not who had just been delivered from a whale, but seeing without distinctly political vision, King Solomon Gillis saw a world in which the black man had power:

> For there stood a handsome, brass-buttoned giant directing the heaviest traffic Gillis had ever seen; halting unnumbered tons of automobiles and trucks and wagons and pushcarts and streetcars; holding them at bay with one hand while he swept similar tons peremptorily on with the other; ruling the wide crossing with supreme self-assurance; and he, too, was a Negro![10]

The moment of gaping amazement was not only one of renewal and rebirth; Rudolph Fisher sees his hero as ambiguously placed at the entrance of a new life. Gillis was not only to be initiated into the mysteries of black consciousness; he was also to become the victim of black betrayal. But his first reflections, at the point "'where you find all the jay birds when they first hit Harlem - at the subway entrance," as one of the less-recently arrived inhabitants put it, was that he had experienced resurrection. "'Done died an' woke up in Heaven,' thought King Solomon, watching, fascinated."[11] Harlem as Heaven was a repeated motif of this literature and it brought with it the corollary of Harlem as Hell. The apocalyptic and demonic imagery alternated: Harlem was opposed to the Old World of the White South against which it could be seen to be a Heaven; Harlem was opposed to the Old World of the Black South against which Harlem could be seen to be a Hell. Harlem

97

was by this comparison a horrifying version of the New World of the North. This hellishness of Harlem was reinforced by the very fact that the heroic New Negro would be betrayed by his own kind; King Solomon Gillis was being sized up and set up even as he stood at the entrance to Harlem by one Mouse Uggams from his home town.

New York City was for the rural innocent a foreign land and the black hero shared in this configuration with all the heroes who landed on America's shores to make their name and win their fame. Arrival overland obscured this dimension of the pattern and for this reason, Langston Hughes's account of his arrival in Harlem following a boat journey from Mexico drew the analogy between the patterns of migrant and immigrant arrival very clearly and pointed up how other black writers focused their emotional attention on Harlem not on New York City. Gillis in "City of Refuge" and Jake in *Home to Harlem* passed through white New York; it was part of the journey not part of the arrival. Langston Hughes's particular journey, following the grief and anxieties of his reluctant sojourn in Mexico at his father's bidding, made him as excited as any traveller by the sea approach to New York:

> But, boy! At last! New York was pretty, rising out of the bay in the sunset - the thrill of those towers of Manhattan with their million golden eyes, growing slowly taller and taller above the green water, until they looked as if they could almost touch the sky! Then Brooklyn Brldge, gigantic in the dusk! Then the necklaces of lights, glowing everywhere around us, as we docked on the Brooklyn side. All this made me feel it was better to come to New York than to any other city in the world.[12]

Langston Hughes arrived in New York harbour in the evening of Sunday, September 4, 1921.[13] He had to take a room in a hotel off Times Square that first night. It was not until the Monday morning that he displaced the great immigrant scene of New York Bay from the ship rail with the great migrant scene of Harlem from the subway entrance at 135th Street. The initiating event of 1921 was recreated as a centre piece of Hughes's autobiography of 1940, *The Big Sea*:

> Like the bullfights, I can never put on paper the thrill of that underground ride to Harlem. I had never been in a subway before and it fascinated me - the noise, the speed, the green lights ahead. At every

98

station I kept watching for the sign: 135TH STREET. When I saw it, I held my breath. . . .

I went up the steps and out into the bright September sunlight. Harlem! I stood there, dropped my bags, took a deep breath and felt happy again. I registered at the Y.[14]

The *locus classicus* of the Harlem entrance and initiation was Ralph Ellison's representation of the trope in *Invisible Man*. Ralph Ellison crafted this novel in the 1940s out of his autobiographical material of the 1930s. He created the great migrant text which contained in its title the full political negation of the mythological positivism which would make the New Negro the New American Man, fulfilling the promise of James Weldon Johnson, Alain Locke and the Negro Literati. Ellison's hero was eventually to go unseen altogether in a world which was blind to colour. But before the political reality overwhelmed the mythical vision, Ellison let the pattern have full play.

All the elements were present, the terrifying subway ride, the delivery into Harlem, the world of black people, black women serving behind counters, black policemen directing white traffic, the directions to the Men's House where the hero would first room. The moment of gaping amazement was one of enlightenment and the Harlem hero was never closer to Heaven than at the moment when the unrealised potentialities of his race were presented to him. The Invisible Man stood as wide-eyed as King Solomon Gillis. The Invisible Man's emergence from the subway matched that of Langston Hughes's own emergence from the subway at 135th Street when he had stood in 1921 and taken "a deep breath and felt happy again."

The new world of Harlem represented for the hero of the black text exactly what the New World has always represented in the American text, a land of plenty. The hero was a Dick Whittington making his way from childhood poverty to adult wealth in the capital city where he would find the streets paved with gold. In white stories, the poor boy had every chance of becoming Lord Mayor; in black stories, the chances were not so good. Like the Invisible Man, every black hero carried with him a letter of introduction which would close the doors of the land of opportunity. "I had seen the letter," the Invisible Man said, "and it had practically ordered me killed. By slow degrees."[15] The white hero might carry a deathletter in his pocket, even a Dick Whittington, certainly a Hamlet, but the white hero for the very reason that he was a hero could hand it on to someone else; the black hero could not and for this very reason he became heroic for the black writer. The deathletter

99

was of course concealed only from the naive hero newly emerging from the underworld, underground, the subway. He carried his *todesbrief* not only in a closely-enveloped message secure in his briefcase but in the openly-displayed message exposed in his colour.

The hero was to be kept running and the hero en route to Harlem was typically a hero in flight to Harlem as the title of Rudolph Fisher's story, "The City of Refuge" made plain. "Back in North Carolina Gillis had shot a white man and, with the aid of prayer and an automobile, probably escaped a lynching...; and so he had come to Harlem.... The land of plenty was more than that now: it was also the city of refuge."[16] Harlem became then an alternative to the prison and death represented by the old country of the South. Defying the white man, killing the white man was the heroic crime, and even the well-meaning Invisible Man came close to giving his whiteman a heart attack. Here was the distinction to be made between the mythical and the ideological meanings of that city. If it were read in the mythic mode then the hero swelled with every kind of glorious but delusory fulfilment. It was a land of plenty, land of freedom, city of refuge, a black kingdom. If it were read ideologically, then hero did not allow his mind to be dazzled by the image of a black policemen or a black shop girl and recognised that he still carried his deathletter about with him wherever he went.

Exactly what was going on here in terms of texts and the canon was again described in the preface to *Native Son* that Wright wrote in Harlem in 1940. He claimed to be engaged in a process which both fulfilled and transformed the Great Tradition established by Nathaniel Hawthorne and he did so by taking the pattern of the American hero and rewriting the story for Bigger Thomas in all his guises.

Let me give examples [says Wright] of how I developed the dim negative of Bigger. I met white writers who talked of their responses, who told me how whites reacted to this lurid American scene. And, as they talked, I'd translate what they said in terms of Bigger's life. But what was more important still, I read their novels. Here, for the first time, I found ways and techniques of gauging meaningfully the effects of American civilization upon the personalities of people. I took these techniques, these ways of seeing and feeling, and twisted them, bent them, adapted them until they became my ways of apprehending the locked-in life of the Black Belt areas. This association with white writers was the life preserver of my hope to depict Negro life in fiction, for my race

100

possessed no fictional works dealing with such problems, had no background in such sharp and critical testing of experience, no novels that went with a deep and fearless will down to the dark roots of life.[17]

The significance for Wright of the writing in the 1930s and the publishing in 1940 of *Native Son* was that it represented a first of a special kind. He began a literature which took the black proletarian as the heroic figure and representative of the black people. He wrote in defiance not only of the white bourgeoisie but perhaps more passionately in defiance of all "the Negro doctors, lawyers, dentists, bankers, school teachers, social workers, and business men" whom Wright knew were engaged in a denial of the Bigger figure in black life. *Native Son* was also to be a first because it took the literature of the great American tradition and transformed it. This point was an important one for Wright. He did not claim in his Harlem preface that *Native Son* was a completely new kind of literature; he was an activist who wished to appropriate the American canon by making black white. "In Harlem," as Fisher put it, "black was white."

> Early American writers, Henry James and Nathaniel Hawthorne, [Richard Wright wrote in the preface to *Native Son*] complained bitterly about the bleakness and flatness of the American scene. But I think that if they were alive, they'd feel at home in modern America. True, we have no great church in America; our national traditions are still of such a sort that we are not wont to brag of them; and we have no army that's above the level of mercenary fighters; we have no group acceptable to the whole of our country upholding certain human values; we have no rich symbols, no colorful rituals. We have only a money-grubbing, industrial civilization. But we do have in the Negro the embodiment of a past tragic enough to appease the spiritual hunger of even a James; and we have in the oppression of the Negro a shadow athwart our national life dense and heavy enough to satisfy even the gloomy broodings of a Hawthorne. And if Poe were alive, he would not have to invent horror, horror would invent him.[18]

The echoes of Henry James's infamous denunciation of American culture in his life of Nathaniel Hawthorne suggested that the twentieth-century black artist exiled within his own country felt an alienation from mainstream

101

American culture like that the nineteenth-century white artist felt in foreign exile.

New England had imprisoned Henry James's imagination and he could not achieve artistic liberation until he escaped to the Old World which was for James a New World. Dixie, as Wright called it, was a prison and the black artist like the black hero in flight to Chicago's South Side or to New York's Harlem had to escape this prison before he could sing. The link of artist, exile and imagination established by Alain Locke and identified by him with James Joyce and the new Dublin was endorsed by these texts in powerful fashion. Wright moved North to Chicago and from Chicago to New York and, as it were, in the same spiritual direction from New York to Paris. James Baldwin moved in the same trajectory except that starting in Wright's North, his first move was to Paris.

Locke had drawn the black reader's attention to the New Dublin and it is difficult not to see an analogy between these black artists and their movement towards Paris and that of many white artists in earlier decades. Wright certainly framed this in the pattern of the American Dream and in this passage he explicitly referred to his childhood reading of "my Horatio Alger stories, my pulp stories, and.... my Get-Rich-Quick Wallingford series." The artist, even one so socially aware as Wright, saw the pattern of his life in terms of his art. While Wright was not subscribing in *Black Boy* to any ordinary version of the American Dream, "I had sense enough," he wrote, "not to hope to get rich,"[19] he was subscribing to Alain Locke's enunciation in *The New Negro* that the black was choosing to go north. Opportunity, freedom and democratic chance seems even more a thing chosen in the case of the black artist. "Yet I felt that I had to go somewhere and do something to redeem my being alive." The authenticity of the individual's experience of his own reality should not be denied but the reality of the black's going north was just as well expressed in a scene which James Weldon Johnson recalled from Jacksonville, Florida, during the First World War. After the government and the big industrial concerns had started to send "hundreds, perhaps thousands, of labor agents into the South who recruited Negroes by wholesale," he wrote

I sat one day and watched the stream of migrants passing to take the train. For hours they passed steadily, carrying flimsy suit cases, new and shiny, rusty old ones, bursting at the seams, boxes and bundles and impedimenta of all sorts, including banjos, guitars, birds in cages and

102

what not. Similar scenes were being enacted in cities and towns all over the region. The first wave of the great exodus of Negroes from the South was on. Great numbers of these migrants headed for New York or eventually got there, and naturally the majority went up into Harlem.[20]

Naturally they went to Harlem, he said, and if it were not in fact a fact of nature but very much one of economics and demography, it might as well have been a fact of nature for the millions caught up in the exodus. They took banjos with them and guitars and singing birds and they took jazz musicians with them and poets and novelists. It was a motif at once out of key and in tune with America's "Song of Myself." It defined one limit of the American's limitless self-ambition and worked to produce new texts from the old canon.

REFERENCES

[1] *Kerner Report, Report of the National Advisory Commission on Civil Disorders*, New York: Dutton, 1968, p.240.

[2] Alain Locke, ed., *The New Negro*, New York: Atheneum, 1975, p.6.

[3] Locke, *The New Negro*, p.6.

[4] James Baldwin, *The Fire Next Time*, New York: Dell, 1969, p.136.

[5] Alain Locke in Richard Barksdale and Keneth Kinnamon, *Black Writers of America: A Comprehensive Anthology*, New York: Macmillan, 1972, p.576.

[6] Locke in Barksdale, p. 576.

[7] Locke in Barksdale, p. 577.

[8] Rudolph Fisher in Locke, *The New Negro*, p.57.

[9] *Ibid.*, p. 58.

[10] *Ibid.*, pp. 58-59.

[11] *Ibid.*, p. 59.

[12] Langston Hughes, *The Big Sea: An Autobiography*, New York: Hill and Wang, 1977, p.80.

103

[13] Arnold Rampersad, *The Life of Langston Hughes*, Vol.1: 1902 - 1941, *I, Too, Sing America*, New York: Oxford Univ. Press, 1986, p.50.

[14] Hughes, p. 81

[15] Ralph Ellison, *Invisible Man*, Harmondsworth: Penguin, 1982, p.159.

[16] Fisher in Barksdale, p.591.

[17] Richard Wright, *Native Son*, London: Jonathan Cape, 1970, p.X.

[18] Wright, *Son*, p.VIII.

[19] Richard Wright, *Black Boy: A Record of Childhood and Youth*, London: Longman, 1977, p.148.

[20] James Weldon Johnson in Locke, p.305.

104

A Vision of Black Culture in Two Novels by Claude McKay

Manfred Wolf

University of Helsinki - San Francisco State University

Is there a way of life, a mode of being, a culture, that is black? How has this been regarded by black writers? The question is asked evermore these days with the ideal of ethnic and cultural diversity spreading in the U.S. But it has been asked frequently before, among others by such writers as Claude McKay, a major figure in the Harlem Renaissance of the Twenties. McKay's novels, poems and essays focus less on the plight of blacks than on their manner of living and their way of thinking and being. Two novels especially, *Home to Harlem* (1928)[1] and *Banjo* (1929)[2] do so.

The subtitle of *Banjo* is "A Story without a Plot," and this is an accurate description, for it as well as McKay's earlier *Home to Harlem* mainly show scenes from a way of life and pictures of a state of being. While both books are clearly works of fiction, they are also highly evocative debates about blacks and whites, joy and bitterness, spontaneity and restraint, naturalness and civilization. McKay, a Jamaican who moved to the United States in 1912 at the age of twenty-one, became well-known at that time in the Twenties when, as Langston Hughes put it, "the Negro was in vogue," and whites went to Harlem in numbers to listen to jazz, to watch black people dance, to go to parties, and to meet black intellectuals. *Home to Harlem* is an episodic narrative about a young man's enthusiastic return to that time and place from Europe, while *Banjo,* equally episodic, is set among black drifters on the waterfront of Marseilles. Both works dare to ask what it is about the black way of life that so startlingly differs from the white. And *Banjo* actually offers an answer: blacks live more freely, more immediately, more whole-heartedly than whites.

---

[1] Boston: Northeastern University Press, 1987. Original Public. Harper & Brothers, 1928.
[2] New York: Harcourt Brace Jovanovich (A Harvest/HBJ Book), 1957. Original Public. Harper & Brothers, 1929.

That seems a cliche, and when said by whites about blacks a rather insulting one at that. To say that black people have "natural rhythm," for instance, has long been regarded as the ultimate put-down. Yet the narrator of *Banjo* says: "Chinese and Arab men are awkward in modern dances. They have nothing of the natural animal grace and rhythm of Negroes jazzing" (166). The difference would seem to be that when whites say such things, they feel that blacks can't do much of anything else and that they are "primitive" or "uncivilized," but when McKay says it, and when many black writers continuing into the present say it, they allege that the black way of life is in fact a rejection of civilization, that is, of the white brand of civilization which has somehow conquered the world. Black writers tend to depict a willed rebellion, a conscious choice; far from failing to be white, black people have chosen to be black, favoring a more expressive style and a fuller vitality.

In these two novels this vital mode of being is shown, explained, discussed, analyzed. In *Home to Harlem* one thing that makes such a way of life possible is the cultivated ability to forget, the graceful talent to turn hardship and squalor into music; while in *Banjo* it is the capacity for friendship and the shared pleasure in talk for its own sake. Moreover, despite the wide spectrum of black opinion in the latter novel—on subjects ranging from the Back to Africa movement to the way whites should be treated—all endorse this way of being: the thoughtful intellectual as well as the carefree banjo player engage in the dance-like talk and affirm the spontaneity and sexuality of the "earth-loving race."

The question of a specifically black way of life can be framed generally because McKay's books say what black writers, past and present, have frequently said. In an otherwise bitter essay written during the angry Sixties, LeRoi Jones wrote: "The legitimate cultural tradition of the Negro in Harlem (and America) is one of wild happiness, usually at some black man's own invention—of speech, of dress, of gait, the sudden twist of a musical phrase, the warmness or hurt of someone's voice."[3] Jones' remark about happiness is surprising in an essay about the miseries of Harlem and yet typical, for its view of the black experience is commonplace: to give one fairly recent example, the black psychologist Joseph White in his *The Psychology of Blacks* says flatly, perhaps too flatly, that "a quality of spontaneity, openness to feelings, and emotional vitality is expressed in the behavior styles of Black folks."[4]

What restrains this emotional vitality and inhibits this natural spontaneity is the behavior of whites and their all-powerful civilization. White civilization has darkened the earth with its oppressive rules, its tight-lipped prohibitions, and its concentration on all that is joyless. An exploitativeness and a sense of

[3] LeRoi Jones, *Home*, (New York: William Morrow, 1966), pp. 92-3.

[4] Joseph White, *The Psychology of Blacks: An Afro-American Perspective* (Englewood Cliffs, N.J.: Prentice-Hall, 1984), p. 4.

superiority; an emotional unresponsiveness; a commercial view of pleasure; morality that condemns rather than affirms; deceit, deception and self-deception—these are the hallmarks of that civilization. "Leave them alone in their vanity and tigerish ambitions to fret in their own hell...."(284), says one character in *Banjo,* and the narrator notes that black people are not the problem of that civilization but its challenge (273).

Such thinking is strikingly close to that of Romanticism, not only in its celebration of the natural human being but also in the concept of the restraints brought about by civilization. These restraints create anguish and turn human beings into slaves. In Romantic literature, such manacles are variously represented, but in one famous depiction, the poet William Blake sketches a pale old man, Urizen, who measures the world with his puny compasses, and hence symbolizes the inner principle that curbs, narrows and limits. It is the basic metaphor of Romanticism and it is central to black literature as well. Possibly the similarity can be explained by the argument that all revolt is Romantic—or that Romanticism is essentially a matter of revolt. And perhaps it can be argued too that the connection between the motif of black revolt against restraint and the Romantic archetype of rebellion against an internalized authority figure is that each presupposes natural human beings who are capable of throwing off the prohibitions that limit them. But whereas Romanticism unveils the struggle towards such liberation, the fiction of Claude McKay, and that of many black writers, reveals the liberation that has already been attained, if indeed those free beings are left alone to pursue their own ends.

And that is where place comes in. Harlem and the Marseilles waterfront are both enclaves in a white world. White rules still dominate even these two places, but they do so in an attenuated form. The Harlem of *Home to Harlem* allows a style of life that the Jazz Age Expatriates found on the Left Bank of Paris. It is wild and orgiastic and free. Labor is performed but soon forgotten. In *Banjo*, Marseilles tolerates a collection of black drifters who scavenge, fight, dance, love, and talk. The Vieux Port is, as one character says, "a jazzing circus some'n' lak Harlem" (299). Both novels demonstrate that these characters have to be taken out of the ordinary, white-dominated circumstances to attain their more natural way of life. Harlem and Marseilles are insulated and somehow out of time. Not that these places are necessarily free from white encroachment—especially in the world of Banjo, the police, the pimps, the greedy shopkeepers, the corrupt officials are ever-near.

For one person in the novel, the rejection of the majority culture is utterly conscious. Ray, the resident intellectual among the beach boys, and clearly the author's alter ego, resorts to middle class methods by writing a beautiful letter to an American consular official urging repatriation for a hapless drifter, and that letter gets immediate results. This way to power is precisely what the black bourgeoisie has used, and in a good many books by black American and Caribbean writers the two ways are played off against each other. But

McKay's fiction rejects that other way; the black bourgeoisie is viewed as merely copying white people, and more important, Ray himself, though he has all the skills available to "succeed," refuses to use them. He feels ambivalent about having written the letter. And he is certain that the irrepressibly life-loving Banjo points the better way. His one concession on this point is that as a writer he also needs the "solitary delight of the spirit, different from and unrelated to the animal joy he felt when in company with the boys..." (260).

"With an intellect standing watch over his native instincts," (164) Ray could not be entirely like the others. But he has no doubt that they know how to live and that he can learn from them. He craves to be like them fully. They "represented more than he ... the irrepressible exuberance and legendary vitality of the black race" (324). The strength he draws is from what they do and how they are: "Never had Ray guessed from Banjo's general manner that he had known any deep sorrow. Yet when he heard him tell Goosey that he had seen his only brother lynched, he was not surprised, he understood, because right there he had revealed the depths of his soul and the soul of his race—the true tropical African Negro. No Victorian-long period of featured grief and sable mourning, no mechanical-pale graveside face, but a luxuriant living-up from it, like the great jungles growing perennially beautiful and green in the yellow blaze of the sun over the long life-breaking tragedy of Africa" (322).

It is the character of Banjo who "in all matters acted instinctively" (164) who is presented as emblematic of what's best in black life. He lives in the moment and he values experience above all. Life is to him a great sensual event. He is not amoral, but he wears his morality lightly. And, as Helen Pyne Timothy has pointed out, "He carries with him the music of Afro-America with his banjo, and it is a music which unites all blacks in moments of complete abandonment and joy."[5] She also remarks perceptively that McKay reminds blacks that they are united by more than color; "their music, their stories, their attitudes can still appeal across national boundaries."[6]

Banjo is not the only one who defines this black way of life. Latnah, his girl-friend, shows one of its main features: she is presented as admirably lacking in jealousy at Banjo's involvement with other women, and while such sexual tolerance may not be exactly commonplace in black culture, at least it's a value McKay seems to think is possible in it. Where Latnah draws the line is Banjo's spending money on white women—in fact, when she suspects him of not being loyal to his people she turns against him. Here too McKay shows that whatever hedonism he values, a fierce black consciousness is not thereby ruled

---

5 Helen Pyne Timothy, "Claude McKay: Individualism and Group Consciousness," *A Celebration of Black and African Writing,* eds. Bruce King and Kolawole Ogungbesan (New York: Oxford University Press, 1976), p. 25.

6 *Ibid.*

out. On the contrary, loyalty to each other, a black communalism, is an organic part of the best black life.

Not only sensuality and generosity and loyalty mark this life, but also creativity. The music of *Home to Harlem* and the talking of *Banjo* are linked to the love of play, of language, of word-spinning. Black language is intent on replacing "rotten-egg stock words" (217 and esp. 321). Words are generated partly to throw off white people—words like ofay, cracker, peckawood, Mr. Charlie—and partly for their own sake. Where white civilization uses language instrumentally, black civilization does so playfully, poetically, for the sheer pleasure in language itself. These new words are like new tunes, or jazz improvisations, and not only are they magical and reflect what McKay calls the "necromancy of language" (321), they also permit a greater freshness of perception and a deeper honesty.

It would be too great a claim to make that this highly idealized way of life has been lived by anyone, anytime, anywhere. But what haunts McKay's books, and those of other black writers, is that Africa before slavery may well have been such a time and place. It is hard to know, of course, but the evidence still clinging to the life of black people is that indeed it may have. And here McKay's books are very much in line with the thinking of scholars writing fifty and sixty years after he did: that black culture was not destroyed with slavery but survived in greater or lesser degree. Certainly the great many Africans in *Banjo*, with their dignity and self-assuredness, underscore the worth of that kinship.

McKay knows that the way of being he sketches is far more easily portrayed than practiced. The enemy is formidable and seductive. In passage after passage, he is deeply pessimistic about the survival of black culture. But he does not doubt its splendor. Like the Romantic poets of past ages, he offers his vision as a challenge, as a corrective, as a possibility for another life than the one that has become too narrow, too cerebral and too mean. The natural man like Banjo is an image of hope, the picture of an opportunity, for those who can see. Naturalness is a state of being, available to those, white and black, who dare to live.

Nor is this an opportunity for the individual only. The majority culture has the chance, as some present-day black intellectuals feel is beginning to happen, of assimilating into itself the best features of black life.

ABOUT US, FOR US, NEAR US: THE IRISH AND HARLEM RENAISSANCES

BRIAN GALLAGHER

THE HARLEM RENAISSANCE of the 1920s, which lasted through the 1930s in a much diminished form, constituted the first widespread movement in Afro-American literary history. For the first time, Black writers, as well as painters, sculptors and musicians, had direct contact with dozens of their fellow artists. Harlem had become the acknowledged "cultural capital" of Black America.[1] In their attempt to comprehend and expand the role Harlem had in this cultural revolution, Black writers often looked beyond national boundaries for models, and one of the most commonly invoked was the Irish Renaissance.[2] "Harlem has the same role to play for the New Negro as Dublin had for the New Ireland," wrote Alain Locke in the introduction to his landmark interpretative anthology, *The New Negro* (1925).[3] While it would be too much to claim that modern Irish writers had a strong influence on the writers of the Harlem Renaissance, it can be said that the paradigm of an oppressed people rising to literary greatness in one short generation did serve as a continuing inspiration and occasional guide for Afro-American writers in the 1920s. Moreover, the situation

1 Fed by the ever-increasing numbers from the "Great Migration" of Blacks from rural South to urban North, New York City by 1920 had replaced Washington, D.C., as the largest Black urban center in the nation. See Gilbert Osofsky, "'Come Out from Among Them': Negro Migration and Settlement, 1890–1914," in *Black History: A Reappraissal* (Garden City, N.Y.: Doubleday Anchor, 1969), pp. 374–86.

2 "Irish Renaissance" is used here in its narrower sense — chiefly the decade 1900–1910 and most significantly the work of Lady Gregory, Synge, and Yeats. A much broader delineation of the period is exemplified by Richard Fallis's recent study, *Irish Renaissance* (Syracuse: Syracuse University Press, 1977), which spans more than half a century, 1885–1940.

3 Rpt. New York: Atheneum, 1970, p. 7.

of the Irish writer around the turn of the century — with respect to *language, heritage* and *cultural institutions* — is remarkably similar to that of the Afro-American writer in the 1920s, a fact which suggests the two literatures, Anglo-Irish and Afro-American, may profitably be looked at in a comparative framework.

The first issue writers in both Renaissances had to face was whether they represented a genuine, and at least partially autonomous, cultural unit within the dominant culture, be it English or white American. "Like Irish writers," says Nathan Huggins in his thoroughgoing study, *Harlem Renaissance*, "the Negro artists had to resolve the question of whether there was a special Negro voice and art."[4] The facts of linguistic history would seem to indicate a basis for a distinct, discernible "voice" in both instances: "Irish English," circa 1900, reflected the phrasings, locutions, idioms and vocabulary survivals of a nation that had been, until but fifty years before, nearly half Gaelic-speaking; "Black English" circa 1920, although it contained certain survivals from various West African languages, derived its special character more from the process of linguistic adaptation and differentiation forced on Blacks in a racist society, that is, as a means of cultural preservation and survival.[5] Both dialects — and here I would state my disagreement with those who see either as separate languages — are characterized by one major verb construction missing in standard English: the Irish tendency, because of its absence in the Irish language, to eschew the perfect tense ("have gone") in favor of a combination of a preposition with the present progressive ("after going"); the Black employment of the "be-durative" to distinguish habitual actions ("He be late") from singular occurrences ("He is late"). Both dialects reflect, perhaps because oppressed groups often have to direct anger inward, stylized patterns of belittlement: from the addition of the diminutive "-een" to names for the ironic use of the most elaborate hyperbole in Irish English; and from derogatory terms like "dicty," for pretentious persons or acts, to the elaborate insult system of the "dirty dozens" in Black English. And both dialects encourage, almost demand, eloquence, particularly of the oratorical variety.

4 1971; rpt. New York: Oxford University Press, 1973, p. 203.

5 The strict concept of a "Black English" is one that has evolved only over the last twenty years, although Afro-American writers in the Renaissance and earlier periods were well aware of the numerous ways in which English as used by most Black Americans differed from English as used by most white Americans.

Of course, neither group of Renaissance writers was interested primarily in the literal transcription of speech patterns, however distinctive. Even John Synge, a thoroughly mimetic writer linguistically, saw his artistic task as a distillation, and not a direct representation, of the "fiery and magnificent, and tender" imagination of "the Irish peasantry" — to create "poetic" works very much in opposition to those by writers like "Ibsen and Zola dealing with reality in joyless and pallid words."[6] When, at the beginning of the Harlem Renaissance, James Weldon Johnson tried to chart a course for Afro-American literature to steer between the "absolutely dead" stereotype of "Negro dialect" and the tepid, acultural use of conventional English, he tellingly invoked the example of what Synge had been able to create through the fresh use of language:

> What the colored poet in the United States needs to do is something like what Synge did for the Irish; he needs to find a form that will express the racial spirit by symbols from within rather than by symbols from without, such as the mere mutilation of English spelling and pronunciation. He needs a form that is freer and larger than dialect, but which will still hold the racial flavor; a form expressing the imagery, the idioms, the peculiar turns of thought, and the distinctive humor and pathos, too, of the Negro, but which will also be capable of voicing the deepest and highest emotions and aspirations, and allow of the widest range of subjects and the widest scope of treatment.[7]

In the preface to his major creative contribution to the Harlem Renaissance, *God's Trombones: Seven Negro Sermons in Verse* (1927), Johnson quoted this passage verbatim as an explanation of what he was trying to achieve in his suite of poems. His verse sermons are meant to represent the particular combination of linguistic, religious, and cultural elements that characterize the noble "old-time preaching" of the ministers Johnson types as "God's trombones": their chromatic cadences:

Weep not, weep not,

6 "Preface," *The Playboy of the Western World*, in *The Complete Plays of John M. Synge* (New York: Vintage Books, 1960), pp. 7, 8. The linguistic compression and nonmimetic intensity for which Synge was striving is indicated by the fact that each act of *Playboy* went through at least seven complete drafts.

7 "Preface to Original Edition" [1922], *The Book of American Negro Poetry*, rev. ed. (1930; rpt. New York: Harcourt, Brace and World, 1930), pp. 41–42.

> She is not dead;
> She's resting in the bosom of Jesus.[8]

their recalls of Biblical phraseology:

> But the boy was stubborn in his head,
> And haughty in his heart,
> And he took his share of his father's goods,
> And went into a far-off country.[9]

their vivid imagery:

> And the sun will go out like a candle in the wind,
> The moon will turn to dripping blood,
> The stars will fall like cinders,
> And the sea will burn like tar.[10]

and their reliance on dramatic repetitions:

> Sinners came a running down to the ark;
> Sinners came a-swimming all round the ark;
> Sinners pleaded and sinners prayed —
> Sinners wept and sinners wailed —
> But Noah'd done barred the door.[11]

Similar reflections of the spoken language and oral tradition abound in the literature of the Irish Renaissance. For instance, the Blind Man in Yeats's *On Baile's Strand* (1903, 1906) speaks in cadenced repetitions: "There had been a fight, a great fight, a tremendous great fight."[12] When Lady Gregory announced her intention to set her cycle of Cuchulain tales in the Kiltartan idiom of her native Galway, she did so in locutions that very much reflected the Irish language from which the tales had passed into English: "I have told the whole story in plain and simple words, in the same way my old nurse Mary Sheridan used to be telling stories from the Irish long ago, and I a child at Roxborough."[13] Naturally, Synge's combination of linguistic

8 "Go Down, Death — A Funeral Sermon," *God's Trombones* (1927; rpt. New York: Penguin Books, 1976), p. 27.

9 "The Prodigal Son," *ibid.*, p. 22.

10 "The Judgment Day," *ibid.*, p. 56.

11 "Noah Built the Ark," *ibid.*, p. 36.

12 William Butler Yeats, *Eleven Plays*, ed. A. Norman Jeffares (New York: Collier Books, 1964), p. 21.

13 Augusta Gregory, "Dedication," *Cuchulain of Muirthemne* (1902; rpt. Gerrards Cross, Buckinghamshire: Colin Smythe, 1973), p. 5.

and cultural elements most closely parallels that in *God's Trombones*, Maurya's lament after Bartley's departure in *Riders to the Sea* comes from much the same kind of vivid, simple folk imagination found in Johnson's "sermons": "He's gone now, God spare us, and we'll not see him again. He's gone now, and when the black night is falling I'll have no son left me in the world."[14]

In *The Weary Blues* (1927), Langston Hughes, the most important young writer to emerge from the Harlem Renaissance, sought a more "secular" solution than Johnson to the problem of inventing a language fully adequate to the nuances of the Afro-American experience. Often he looked to the short lines and repetition patterns that characterize blues and jazz lyrics:

> Weary,
> Weary,
> Trouble, pain.
> Sun's gonna shine
> Somewhere
> Again.
>
> I got a railroad ticket,
> Pack my trunk and ride.
>
> Sing 'em, sister!
>
> Got a railroad ticket,
> Pack my trunk and ride.
> And when I get on the train
> I'll cast my blues aside.[15]

In other poems, Hughes sought to capture the ungrammatical eloquence of the long-suffering: "Well, son, I'll tell you: / Life for me ain't been no crystal stair."[16] Jimmy Farrell, in Synge's *Playboy*, expresses an equally ungrammatical, if somewhat more surreal, vision of life's trials and tribulations: "It's a fright surely. I knew a party was kicked in the head by a red mare, and he went killing horses a great while, till he eat the insides of a clock and died after."[17]

14 *Complete Plays*, p. 87.
15 "Blues Fantasy," *The Weary Blues* (1927; rpt. New York: Alfred A. Knopf, 1931), p. 37.
16 "Mother to Son," *ibid.*, p. 107.
17 *Complete Plays*, p. 57.

THE IRISH AND THE HARLEM RENAISSANCES

18

Conversely, writers in both renascences would sometimes resort to the extremes of lyricism in an attempt to break down traditional genre boundaries and thereby suggest the poetic quality of their "racial" stories. Jean Toomer's *Cane* (1923) mingles poetry and prose, lyrical flight and scrupulous description, in its evocation of Black Southern life. The heroic plays of Yeats's early theater period, too, mix high rhetoric with high emotion, as in Deirdre's insistence on seeing the body of her beloved, murdered Naoise: "For I will see him / All blood-bedabbled and his beauty gone."[18] Later, writers in both groups would reintroduce dialect, in their attempt to explore the symbiotic relationship between imposed and evolved identity, between the comic stereotype and achieved individuation. Zora Neale Hurston's depictions of Black Southern folkways, *Mules and Men* (1936), a collection of folktales, and *Their Eyes Were Watching God* (1937), a novel, in this regard much resemble Sean O'Casey's dissection of Dublin tenement life in plays like *Juno and the Paycock* (1924) and *The Plough and the Stars* (1926).

With regard to the cultural heritage out of which they approached the reality of the present, Irish writers and Black writers faced a similar dilemma, namely, that the dominant culture in large measure refused to recognize that heritage, or at least its validity. Irish writers, starting with Standish O'Grady in the late 1870s, as a consequence began to revive, and update, the body of heroic legend and lore — specifically the cycle of Red Branch tales, centering on Cuchulain and Conchubar, and the later cycle of Fenian tales — which made Ireland the cultural equal, at least in terms of cultural continuity, of any European nation. The image of a lost golden past permeates Yeats's very early narrative poem, "The Wanderings of Oisin" (1889):

> 'Men's hearts of old were drops of flame
> That from the saffron morning came,
> Or drops of silver joy that fell
> Out of the moon's pale twisted shell.'[19]

Yeats's youthful desire to "Sing of old Eire and the ancient ways" —

18 "Deirdre" [1907], *Eleven Plays*, p. 70. It might be noted that Toomer, who became a disciple of Gurdjieff in the late 1920s, shared with Yeats a strong and abiding interest in occult and mystical matters.

19 *The Collected Poems of W. B. Yeats* (New York: Macmillan, 1956), p. 358.

which meant to hymn "A Druid land, a Druid tune!"[20] — eventually gave way to the more valid and viable task of using the ancient legends as frames for the depiction of present historical and personal concerns with abiding human ones— a process exemplified by the cycle of Cuchulain plays Yeats produced over a 35 year span, the last, "The Death of Cuchulain," being, fittingly, written in his final years. The Afro-American writer in the 1920s, unfortunately, did not have so definite a body of heroic lore on which to draw. There were, it is true, scores of heroic tales from the period of slavery, particularly the large number centering around the legendary figure of "High John, the Conqueror," as well as the African-based tales of that archetypal trickster figure, "Brer Rabbit," but such legend was highly compromised both by its origin in slavery, where heroism was exclusively of the resistive kind, and, more significantly, by the white coöptation and sanitization of it in works like Joel Chandler Harris's "Uncle Remus" tales.

What many Black writers opted for instead in the romanticizing 1920s was a vision of the land of origin, Africa, the land from which the original slaves were so rudely torn, as an ancient, fully developed civilization. Claude McKay's "Africa" is typical:

> The sun sought thy dim bed and brought forth light,
> The sciences were sucklings at thy breast;
> When all the world was young in pregnant night
> Thy slaves toiled at thy monumental best.
> Thou ancient treasure-land, thou modern prize,
> New peoples marvel at thy pyramids![21]

Often the image of mythical land is combined with that of present reality in a way which suggests a significant degree of primal racial experience survives in modern Afro-American life, as in the opening lines of Hughes's "Nude Young Dancer": "What jungle tree have you slept under, / Midnight dancer of the jazzy hour?"[22] Sometimes the

20   These lines are found, respectively, in the opening and closing poems of Yeats's 1893 collection, *The Rose* — "To the Rose Upon the Rood of Time" and "To Ireland in the Coming Times." See *Collected Poems*, pp. 31, 50.

21   *Selected Poems of Claude McKay* (New York: Harcourt, Brace and World, 1953), p. 40.

22   *The Weary Blues*, p. 33. Black writers of the 1920s were hardly immune to the influence of so many works by white authors that depicted Negroes as "primitive" and "exotic": O'Neill's *All God's Chillun Got Wings* (1923), DuBose Heyward's *Porgy* (1925),

invocation of the African past is informed more by wish fulfillment than by historical understanding, in a manner resembling Padraic Pearse's somewhat strained attempt to make Cuchulain a living part of modern Irish culture.[23] The opening stanza of the "Proem" in *The Weary Blues* is just such an instance: "I am a Negro: / Black as the night is black, / Black like the depths of my Africa."[24] If Afro-American writers could grow nostalgic over a land from which they were geographically separated, Irish writers could grow equally nostalgic over a land from which they were historically separated. The literal statement of Synge's Deirdre, "it's a lonesome thing to be away from Ireland always,"[25] might also be heard as the symbolic lament of the early Irish Renaissance writers, who saw themselves historically stranded in a tawdry and unheroic present. Kathleen ni Houlihan, that symbol of tragic and suffering Ireland employed by Yeats and others, derives from the same backward looking impulse to turn a history of oppression into a fount of racial wisdom that informs Hughes's "The Negro Speaks of Rivers" — "My soul has grown deep like the rivers"[26] — and Arna Bontemps's "A Black Man Talks of Reaping" — "I have sown beside all waters in my day."[27]

More than occasionally the very writers who celebrated the mythic past would despair over its seeming irrelevance for the present. Yeats's poetic sneer is well known: "Romantic Ireland's dead and gone, / It's with O'Leary in the grave."[28] In "Heritage," Countee Cullen expresses a decided ambivalence towards the "homeland" he readily evoked in a number of other poems:

> Africa? A book one thumbs
> Listlessly, till slumber comes.
>
> One three centuries removed

Carl Van Vetchen's *Nigger Heaven* (1926), and, most demonstrably, Marc Connelly's *The Green Pastures* (1930).

23   As Desmond Ryan put it, Cuchulain was an important member of the staff at St. Enda's, the school Pearse ran. See George Dangerfield, *The Damnable Question: One Hundred and Twenty Years of Anglo-Irish Conflict* (Boston: Little, Brown, 1976), pp. 137–38, for some relevant analysis of Pearse's vision of Cuchulain as an inspiration for political action.

24   *The Weary Blues*, p. 19.

25   *Deirdre of the Sorrows* [1910], *Complete Plays*, p. 248.

26   *The Weary Blues*, p. 51.

27   *Book of American Negro Poetry*, p. 262.

28   "September 1913," *Collected Poems*, p. 106.

From the scenes his father loved,
Spicy grove, cinnamon tree,
What is Africa to me?[29]

Obviously, both groups of writers saw a mythical "national" past as something of a fiction, but a necessary fiction, if a literary and cultural renaissance were not to be stillborn.

The very need to reaffirm a significant racial past, even at the cost of some conscious mythmaking, derived in part from the on-going fight against racial stereotypes propagated by the cultural institutions controlled by the dominant culture: universities, newspapers, book publishing, and, most particularly, the stage. "At first," notes Sterling Brown in *Negro Poetry and Drama* (1937), "like the Irish in English drama, because of a roughly similar social position, the Negro seemed doomed to be the comic relief in plays."[30] Of course, the remarkable success of Yeats, Lady Gregory and others in founding a national theater for Ireland epitomized the early achievement of the Irish Renaissance. Not only did they kill off the "stage Irishman," that happy-go-lucky roarer, they also, in conjunction with the Fay brothers and other Abbey players, fostered a new acting style noteworthy for its combination of poetic intensity and physical quietude. In the mid-1920s, W. E. B. DuBois would outline four principles for a Negro theater movement, principles virtually identical in spirit to those on which the Irish theater movement was based:

> Negro theater must be: I. *About us*. That is, they must have plots which reveal Negro life as it is. II. *By us*. That is, they must be written by Negro authors who understand from birth and continual association just what it means to be a Negro today. III. *For us*. That is, the theatre must cater primarily to Negro audiences and be supported and sustained by their entertainment and approval. IV. *Near us*. The theatre must be in a Negro neighborhood near the mass of ordinary Negro people.[31]

Although it would be three decades before DuBois's plan was realized on any significant scale, the theater it encouraged had much the same counteractive intent Yeats and Lady Gregory expressed in founding a national theater that would "show that Ireland is not the home of

29 *Book of American Negro Poetry*, p. 222–23.
30 Rpt. New York: Atheneum, 1969, p. 103.
31 Quoted, from the July, 1926, *Crisis*, in *Harlem Renaissance*, p. 292.

buffoonery and of easy sentiment, as it has been represented, but the home of an ancient idealism."[32]

Other cultural institutions, most particularly publishing, also remained largely beyond the control of both Irish and Afro-American writers, often to their great disadvantage. Without the help of the dilettante author Carl Van Vetchen, who dabbled in Negro culture, many authors of the Harlem Renaissance would not have gotten a hearing from publishers. Nor was there always a public ready or willing to understand what the "new" Irish or Black author was trying to say about them: the controversy over *Playboy* in America was even worse than in Dublin.

To control cultural institutions ultimately means to control the vision of one's past, to control one's history. In this respect, DuBois's long editorship (1910–34) of the NAACP periodical *The Crisis* was especially significant, for he not only set social situations and racial problems in their national and international contexts, but he also published much of the important Afro-American literature growing out of, and reflecting, those contexts. The continuing value of such a symbiotic relationship between cultural awareness and the literature it fosters is attested to by Lady Gregory's assessment of the significance of the Gaelic League:

> It was a movement for keeping the Irish language a spoken one, with, as a chief end, the preserving of our own nationality. That does not sound like the beginning of a revolution, yet it was one. It was the discovery, the disclosure of the folk-learning, the folk-poetry, the folk-tradition. Our Theatre was caught into that current, and it is that current, as I believe, that has brought it on its triumphant way. It is chiefly known now as a folk-theatre. It has not only the great mass of primitive material and legend to draw on, but it has been made a living thing by the excitement of that discovery.[33]

The literature of both Renaissances is characterized by another, rather more negative, desire for cultural control — namely, the desire to forge some sort of memorial dignity out of the losing, often fatal,

---

32 Augusta Gregory, *Our Irish Theatre* (1913; rpt. New York: Capricorn Books, 1965), p. 9. The words are from a public statement Lady Gregory and Yeats drew up in 1898.
33 *Ibid.*, p. 76.

confrontations with the dominant culture. Yeats's grudging paean to the "heroes" in "Easter 1916" reflects this impulse:

> We know their dream; enough
> To know they dreamed and are dead;
> And what if excess of love
> Bewildered them till they died?
>
> I write it out in a verse —
> MacDonagh and MacBride
> And Connolly and Pearse
> Now and in time to be,
> Wherever green is worn,
> Are changed, changed utterly:
> A terrible beauty is born.[34]

The rallying tone of McKay's antilynching sonnet, "If We Must Die," bespeaks a similar impulse:

> If we must die, let it not be like hogs
> Hunted and penned in an inglorious spot,
> While round us bark the mad and hungry dogs,
> Making their mock at our accursed lot.
> If we must die, O let us nobly die. . . .[35]

The intent here, as in Yeats, is to control, if not the event, at least its tenor and meaning.

The parallel between these two developing literatures holds for works and writers after each Renaissance. For instance, towards the end of *A Portrait*, Stephen Dedalus has, when speaking to an English Jesuit at the university, this revelation of cultural dissociation:

> The language in which we are speaking is his before it is mine. How different are the words *home, Christ, ale, master,* on his lips and on mine! I cannot speak or write these words without unrest of spirit. His language, so familiar and so foreign, will always be for me an acquired speech. I have not made or accepted its words. My voice holds them at bay. My soul frets in the shadow of his language.[36]

34 *Collected Poems*, pp. 179–80.

35 *Selected Poems*, p. 36. It is not without a certain irony that, in one of his most impassioned speeches on the necessity of resisting Nazi tyranny, Winston Churchill quoted this sonnet in full.

36 James Joyce, *A Portrait of the Artist as a Young Man* (1916; rpt. New York: The Viking Press, 1964), p. 189.

THE IRISH AND THE HARLEM RENAISSANCES

24

James Baldwin undergoes a parallel revelation in a remote Swiss village:

> For this village, even were it incomparably more remote and incredibly more primitive, is the West, the West onto which I have been so strangely grafted. These people cannot be, from the point of view of power, strangers anywhere in the world; they have made the modern world, in effect, even if they do not know it. The most illiterate among them is related, in a way that I am not, to Dante, Shakespeare, Michaelangelo, Aeschylus, Da Vinci, Rembrandt, and Racine.[37]

More recently, writers in both groups have dealt significantly with the issue of how to survive, personally and artistically, in a hybrid culture. John Montague's "A Grafted Tongue" typifies a certain bitter fatality about the Irish linguistic, and hence cultural, situation: "To grow / a second tongue, as / harsh a humiliation / as twice to be born."[38] Afro-American writers have tended, though, to be more hopeful, opting either for a vision of the Afro-American experience as a microcosm of the American experience, represented by Ralph Ellison's *Invisible Man*, or for a vision of the Black American experience in a Pan-African nexus, represented by the writers and theorists of the "Black Aesthetic."[39]

One could draw other valid parallels between the Irish Renaissance and the Harlem Renaissance — for instance, that the essentially celebratory spirit of each soon provoked major naturalistic works as counterforces, namely Joyce's *Dubliners* (1914) and Richard Wright's *Native Son* (1940). However, to avoid overemphasizing the congruities of the two literary periods, and the two literatures, both incongruities and outright dissimilarities should be borne in mind. Whereas the Irish Renaissance had from the beginning, in the works of Synge and especially of Yeats, a literature of genius, the Harlem Renaissance reached its apotheosis long after its closure, with *Invisible Man* (1952). And, since 1922, Irish literature has been a national literature in the literal sense, whereas Afro-American literature has, at most, aspired

---

37 "Stranger in the Village," *Notes of a Native Son* (1955; rpt. New York: Bantam Books, 1968), p. 140.

38 *The Faber Book of Irish Verse*, ed. John Montague (London: Faber and Faber, 1974), p. 345.

39 The most important statements, definitions, and examples of this aesthetic are contained in *The Black Aesthetic*, ed. Addison Gayle, Jr. (Garden City, N.Y.: Doubleday Anchor, 1971).

to a cultural nationalism, which some modern Black writers would reject. Still, the valid parallels between modern Irish literature and modern Afro-American literature — parallels which grow out of much the same kind of experience of cultural imperialism — suggest the grouping of the two literatures in at least one alternate theoretical *and* pedagogical framework.[40] At present, Afro-American literature is often placed alongside Irish-American literature in the burgeoning, and necessary, field of "Ethnic Studies." Yet, the Afro-American experience, and the literature reflecting it, is really much closer to the Irish national experience, and the literature reflecting it. Similarly, much Irish literature — especially by writers like O'Casey, Frank O'Connor and Behan — describes an experience, and a world, more like that found in Afro-American literature than in the English literature, under which it is still so regularly subsumed. Since categorizations imply, if not determine, interpretations and valuations, we might do well to keep the parallels between modern Irish literature and modern Afro-American literature in mind, if only as a check against the too rigid schematization of either literature.

—Brown University

40 Having taught courses in both Afro-American literature and Irish literature, as well as having used Black and Irish writers in close conjunction in courses like "Art, Politics and Protest," I can attest to the pedagogical efficacy of viewing the two literatures in conjunction and using one to illuminate the other.

ZORA NEALE HURSTON, THE BLACK WOMAN WRITER IN THE THIRTIES AND FORTIES (PART1); MOSES, MAN OF POWER, MAN OF KNOWLEDGE (PART2).

Luisanna Fodde and Paola Boi, University of Cagliari.

The twenty years we have been called to discuss may be considered as a period of great awakening for Afro-American Literature. Strengthened by the Harlem Renaissance success that brought at last Black Arts to the notion of a wider public, the major black authors being published during the 30s and 40s became selfassured political militants, writing novels or poetry in order to have the "real sufferings" of their own people known and spread. Theirs was a predominantly social and political literature based on naturalistic/realistic principles. Writers such as Richard Wright, Ann Petry, the late Langston Hughes, Ralph Ellison, Gwendolyn Brooks, became the representatives of such a literary school, a serious political way of thinking which brought some of them to enroll in the Comunist Party. Their manifesto was plain and simple: the black artist sought to represent the racism of American society in and through his/her art-form.; ought to describe with precision and crudeness (was not most black people's life in the United States crude, terrible and deeply unhappy?) the life, the sufferings, the horrible conditions of Black-Americans both in the South and the North of the United States.

Zora Neale Hurston, the author we are dedicating this paper to, did not accept such literary philosophy, and therefore cannot be unconditionally placed among her contemporary lot. Robert Hemenway, her most succesful biographer, acutely summerizes this contrast: "...her fiction exhibited the knowledge that the black masses had triumphed over their racist environment, not by becoming and emulating bourgeois values, not by engaging in a sophisticated program of political propaganda, but by trying inward to creating the blues, the folktales, the spiritual, the hyperbolic lie, the ironic joke" [1].

Nonetheless, her major works were published between 1931 and 1939; during the Forties - war and post-war years - she wrote social, anthropological and literary articles for white magazines, and was considered as one of the most representative and well-known black spokespersons of the time.

For these reasons, for having been so publicly present in the cultural scene of the American Forties, so intimate with most major Afro-American writers of the Thirties and Forties, and yet so lonely and pecularly idiosyncratic in her literary and political ideas, she has to be placed somewhere in the distance as

127

to her contemporaries, being different both in a literary sense and in her real life, from all the other authors mentioned above.

Hurston's literary and social career started during the roaring Twenties in New York where, a young woman from the deep deep South, she took part in all cultural meetings, in all parties given by the black and white bourgeoisie for celebrating the discovery of the New Negro.

Almost, if not all Afro-American writers active in the Thirties and Forties, had been influenced, when not present by and in the Harlem Renaissance, the black cultural awakening of the 1920s. We should therefore keep in mind those remarkable years when discussing the Black literature of the Thirties and Forties. Famous writers of the Renaissance like Langston Hughes, Alain Locke, Countee Cullen, Sterling Brown, Arna Bontemps, Jessie Fauset, Nella Larsen, to name but some, continued to be published during the 30s and early 40s; in the Twenties, younger poets and novelists such as Richard Wright, Ralph Ellison, Ann Petry, Margaret Walker were considered as young, promising writers who couldn't be but influenced by that cultural explosion of the Black Arts.

Zora Neale Hurston lays in between these two groups, as she began writing and being published during the Twenties, but reached fame and some success only in the Thirties and Forties - between 1931 and 1949 -. She was one of the most flamboyant, liveliest protagonists of Harlem's social life of the Twenties and probably the greatest Black-American woman writer of the years under discussion.

Before setting off to discover some of Hurston's literary charms, we would like to concentrate this first half of our paper on the social and cultural milieu the Afro-American woman had had to face since the 1920s. As we emphasized before, those years preceding the Depression cannot be disregarded when discussing subsequent Black culture and social life.

The Twenties, up until the Big Crash in 1929, had been a period of enthusiasm and hope even for the black people. A better future seemed possible for the ''inferior race'', especially in the cities, and Harlem in particular, where the New Negro felt himself to be beautiful, ruler of his world, where he was even rich sometimes.

Those blacks who made up the public world, who were the race representatives, those educated blacks, "bourgeois and glamourconscious" [2], had assembled the negro town of New York City where black, especially fair, light-complexioned black, was beautiful.

The black women, having theoretically acquired public respect through the 19th amendment giving them the right to vote, were more self-assured than they had ever been. Specialized black magazines started advertising cosmetics to

128

improve features and lighten complexions. Others, at the same time, assured their readers that "brown skin was not only more beautiful to them but, if the truth be told, more appealing to Whites as well" [3]. It is not surprising to notice that the first Black-American woman millionaire, Madame C.J. Walker, made her fortune by inventing and selling creams and contitioners to straighten and beautify black women's hair [4].

This search for beauty and glamour had also a cultural reason: according to the black opinion-makers of those years, intellectuals like W.E.B. Du Bois, Jessie Fauset, Alain Locke, all of whom contributed to periodicals like The Crisis, Opportunity, The Messenger, it was important for the negro to acquire a racial pride, a belief in the beauty of his/her race, and in the thousand possibilities that a black person now had.

Middle or upper-class, cultivated, sophisticated persons: this was the goal. The philosophy of such "Niggerati", as Zora Neale Hurston came to call her literaty friends, and the years which saw the new cultural and social supremacy of the black people is known under the name of Harlem Renaissance. Black singers, painters, poets and novelists were forming for the first time in the United States a black school of all arts, so to speak, a race mirror into which all blacks could look and hope. As a consequence of all this enthusiasm, black education was growing, especially among women. In 1920, 2 out of every 10 graduates from black colleges were women, and the percentage of black women working was 38.9 as compared to 17.2 of white women [5]. Such figures could not but increase after the Depression years, when the Afro-American woman became the only bread-winner in her household. During the Renaissance, middle and upper-class urban black women would organize cultural teas and parties, and though striving for their cultural and familiar independence, were only supporters and friends of the opinion-making black men. The Harlem Renaissance Manifesto, The New Negro philosophy, had been created by the best black male minds of the time, Alain Locke and Sterling Brown to mention two. The most successful poets were men: Langston Hughes, Arna Bontemps, Claude McKay, Countee Cullen in all their different modes of expression stressed the potentialities and the deepness their black art had reached. They felt that their art ought to interpret the beautiful but uncultivated voice of the black folk, that the black artist "should consciuously strive for a pure rather than propagandistic art, and should base this conscious creation on the unconscious aesthetics manifested by the spirituals, the folk sermons, the folk-tales, the proletariat's artistic forms" [6]. Of the two women writers of the Renaissance, who published their works between the mid 20s and 30s, neither was popular nor relevant to this literary movement. Both Jessie Fauset and Nella Larsen were unable to portray a successful, plausible, creative, emancipated, modern black woman character. Even though an activist in the politics of the Renaissance, literary editor of the N.A.A.C.P. magazine The Crisis Jessie Fauset did not go further than re-describing the plight of the tragic mulatto so much exploited by nineteenth century black writers [7]. Her first three

129

novels, <u>There is Confusion,</u> <u>Plun Bum</u> and <u>The Chinaberry Tree</u>, written between 1924 and 1931 all show that mulatto classism so typical among black middle-class society of the time. Only fair-complexioned women could enter the good society and make good marriages. The security of money and the protection and enstrangement from the other black people that a middle-class, fair husband could give were considered as main goals in a black girl's life.

Fauset's protagonists desire and strive for these goals. "Born to a prominent Philadelphia family in 1885, educated at Cornell,... and the Sorbonne, she believed in emphasizing the ability of blacks to become a part of (upper-class) American society" [8], but did not go further than depicting that "outward" capacity. Her characters are never too deep, never too sensitive. She strenuously believed in the advancement of her race, but was only able to portray the final, easy steps of this advancement, without considering the desperate conditions in which most contemporary black people lived.

She was sophisticated and well-to-do, the tea parties she used to give in her New York apartment were famous and wellattended. Zora Neale Hurston was among her assiduous guests [9]. Her active participation in the black literary circles of the 1920s and 30s aimed to fight preconceptions against black people's intellectual and social potentialities. Nonetheless, her works are mere portraits of upper-class, pretentious, improbable black experience. Only in her last novel, does she seem to admit that during that search for security and happiness the black woman had also to face her identity as a woman and a black person. <u>Comedy, American Style</u>, (1933), presents us with a complex character, if compared to her predecessors; Olivia Cary "is not reconciled with either White or Black community in America, nor has she accepted a 'third race' mulatto status" [10]. Unable to confront with her reality she escapes to Paris, where she will feel as enstranged as before.

With Nella Larsen (1893-1963) we have again an upper-class black woman writer of mixed parents (her mother being Danish) confronting herself with the notion and the consequences of "passing". A fair black person could often easily "pass" for white, and as Barbara Christian notices "ironically, passing is a major theme of the 1920s when race pride was supposedly at a peak" [11]. If cultivated, sophisicated blacks could easily equal whites, what was the point in pretending to belong to the other race? This is one of the most contradictory issues of the Harlem Renaissance.

Nella Larsen had been educated as a white, north-european descendant up until her college years, when she decided to attend Fisk University. The impact with the race she now felt she belonged to was a hard one. She soon left Fisk and attended the University of Copenhagen. Her life was, right from the start, a series of continuous changes, a series of "passings" from Scandinavia to New York, from the black to the white world, and vice versa. She married a Black-American physician, left New York again, got a divorce, came back to the States were she settled as a superintendent nurse until her death. <u>Quicksand</u> (1928), Larsen's most praised novel, reflects these terrible uncertainties, these

130

difficulties in finding her own self, and reality. Helga Crane's life is partly based on the author's. She, as well as Fauset's protagonists, is a well-educated sensitive mulatto who is torn between two realities: the black, bourgeois, sophisticated world that tries to imitate the white one, and that somehow she believes to be incoherent, and the simple rural life where she could be helpful and could overcome her feelings of guiltiness, but which she doesn't belong to.

Everything had been easy in Helga's life: because of her fair features she is automatically treated as a ''lady'', all social doors open to her. She gets used to such treatment and lifestyle but recognizes the hypocrisy of it and keeps on fleeing, in a desperate search for identity.

Nella Larsen, unlike Fauset, creates with her major character Helga Crane, a complex woman who finally confronts with her personal, sometimes even sexual problems, instead of simply adjusting to a decorative and hollow role created by others. ''The urban, sensitive, light-skinned heroine of the Twenties is not free either in conventional, urban, upper-class society or in 'primitive', rural Aamerica. Given her options, she is doomed in Larsen's novels to become a self-centered, oppressed neurotic, or a downtrodden, half-alive peasant'' [12]. Both Larsen's and Fauset's protagonists of their late 1920s novels are too rare to be found in the contemporary black real world; too sophisticated, they had traveled to Europe, had known no poverty, were fair. How could a black girl/reader recognize herself in such women? Their novels, as much as most black literature written during the 19th century, were novels for a white public, happy and ready to read about such good, and -thank God- rare, black people.

Their Eyes Were Watching God (1937), Zora Neale Hurston's novel, gives the first example in the history of Afro-American female literature of a character's complexity and reality. Not only is Janie Stark real, not only is her story realistic, but her inner thoughts and feelings, her relationship with nature and other people are described as perfectly human and natural for a black girl. There is no propaganda in the book, no attempts to present a reality which is hard to believe. Zora Neale Hurston, as most critics agree, managed in that novel to mix some brilliant fiction with her first-hand notions of black folklore[13]. She, contrarily to most intellectuals of the Renaissance, particularly to black women writers, had been educated in the South, had lived among ''the folk'', the unsophisticated, often illiterate blacks of Eatonville, Florida: though of no modest origin, she had always kept in contact with those people who could provide her with first-hand oral folk materials. This fact puts her again in contrast with contemporary writers, especially women. As a black woman intellectual, she was very nonconformist. She travelled a lot on her own up and down the States, did not finish her degree, married twice, never reached financial stability. Something a black woman could rarely experience in the 1930s and 40s. Only very few writers, black or white, could support themselves after and during the Depression. F.D. Roosevelt had to set up a revolutionary Welfare Federal Program, The Writers' Project, to help American intellectuals overcome the crisis. Zora Neale Hurston, Arna Bontemps, Richard Wright,

131

Margaret Walker, Ralph Ellison were among those writers.

Thus, being a writer was not only an adventure for a woman, but also an act of rebellion, even of craziness in the eyes of others. In years where black women stood in lines for hours early in the mornings waiting for a white lady to offer whatever job available, women novelists, poets, even teachers, were regarded as very awkward and strange. Though the percentage of black women graduates was gradually increasing, most of them found lower if not degrading jobs: "The most poignant symbol of the lowered status of all Black women workers was the phenomenon known as the 'slave market' in New York City. Magazines such as The Crisis ran articles about how domestic workers lined up on empty lots in the Bronx each day, regardless of the weather, to wait for prospective employers who bargained for their day's services. The white, often lower-middle-class women who would not be able to afford domestic help in normal circumstances, would ascertain the lowest wage a woman would accept for that day, thereby forcing the Black women to underbid one another" [14].

In this situation, a black woman who wanted to be a writer could only survive through a teaching job, or the Federal Writers Project, or with some wealthy white people's help. Zora Neale Hurston managed to wander throughout the States, to write, do her research thanks to her well-known "god-mother", the many scholarships she obtained and her strenuous character which enabled her to survive with two apples a day on occasion. Most other black women struggling to have their works published during the Depression had to teach and live in terrible conditions; working in the remotest colleges of the South and West, they got the lowest salary on the job-market, were mistreated and fired without notice. Margaret Walker, who won the Yale Younger Poet Award in 1942 for her poem For My People, written in 1937 (the year in which Their Eyes... was published), describes such an experience in her autobiography: "As for myself, my teaching career has been fraught with conflict, insults, humiliations and disappointments. In every case when I have attempted to make a creative contribution and succeeded, I was immediately replaced by a man. I began teaching.... for the handsome sum of $135 a month. I was very happy to get it. I had a masters degree but no teaching experience. They would not have a man for less than $150 to $200 a month". Her next job "paid the grand sum of $200 a month. My mother thought it her duty to grab it before somebody else did. While I was there I never had a stable living situation.... Five places in one school year. I had had it. If I had been a man, none would have dared to move me around like that". In 1949 she was married, had three children, and another job: "My youngest was nine- weeks- old. For nine months everything went well, and they kept saying that they were honored to have me until I moved my family and furniture. When they saw my husband was sick and disabled from the war, that I had three children all under six years of age, .that I was poor and had to work, then they put their foot on my neck..." [15].

Notwithstanding these terrible work conditions, Black-American women

132

kept looking for jobs and founding some. By the time of the War the number of working women had increased to about 18 millions; with the majority of black men being drafted, they were employed in jobs "that had previously been the exclusive domain of men" [16]. Still, discrimination against blacks especially in the defence industry during pre-war and war years was strong and open. The famous 1941 march on Washington caused the approval of the "Executive Order 8802... which forbade discrimination in hiring of workers in the nation's defence industries on the basis of race, creed, color, or national origin" [17]. (For the word sex to be included in such an Order, American women are still waiting and fighting).

Can we say that the black woman had acquired dignity as a member of the working force by the 1940s? There were black women teachers, novelists and poets, very rare examples indeed, there were secretaries, but "Where they were allowed to work, they often had the dirtiest and most taxing jobs. In the steel mills they were assigned to the sintering plants as grinders; in the defense industries they were more often than not in custodial positions. One study revealed that although more Black women than before were employed in industry, in many cases they shifted from private homes to commercial enterprises" [18].

Post-war industrialism witnessed a re-consideration, on the part of the ruling class, of the role lower and upper-middle class black people could play in the growing market. They represented a great buying force that could not be mistreated or menaced by Southern racist extremists. Racial peace was the goal. No more lynchings in the South. "Separate- but-equal" theories were developed and advertised to encourage Blacks to take part in the new capitalistic, consumistic American life.

Though integration and racial peace were far from being obtained, The mid-forties and early fifties saw the participation of many black women full of the enthusiasm and optimism of the time.

In literature, only one relevant novelist emerged in the forties after Zora Neale Hurston, and that was Ann Petry, the subject matter of one paper in this workshop. As we said before, Hurston was at the time one of the most prominent and well-known Black intellectuals in the United States. In a couple of years' time she will face the hardest time of her life, when she will be erroneously charged and imprisoned for non-existent sexual abuse of a boy. The remaining part of her life will be devoted to fight poverty and regain literary fame. But those ten years or so, from 1931 to 1939, in which she published some of the best black literature of the time must not be forgotten. The contents and tone of her short stories, of Their Eyes Were Watching God, of Mules and Men, of Tell My Horse, and of Moses, Man of the Mountain, the use of Black slang, of the folklore, her continuous depiction and evident belief in the beauty and richness of black culture, will be somehow found in the female Black literature to follow.

We already stated that apart from Ann Petry, no major black woman novelist

133

emerged from the late 40s to the early 60s. These years were the literary domain of two great poets, still alive and active, Margaret Walker and Gwendolyn Brooks, whose first collections of poems were published between 1942 and 1949. The early production of these two writers, together with the novels of Ann Petry, cover in Black female literature the remaining years of the two decades under discussion. Margaret Walker, the oldest of the two, published only one collection of poems during the Forties, but won the Yale Younger Poet Award with it. For My People is a collection of conventional, standard poems, about Black life in the South. The "incantatory" tone in works such as the title poem "For My People", or "Southern Song", "Memory", or "Childhood", as critics Long and Collier have defined it [19], has helped them become popular and well-known among Blacks and Whites. Verses like:

"I want my body bathed again by southern suns, my soul reclaimed again from southern land. I want to rest again in southern fields,/ in grass and hay and clover bloom ; to lay my hand again upon/ the clay baked by a southern sun, to touch the rainsoaked earth/ and smell the smell of soil", remind us of some conventional production of the Renaissance like Claude Mc Kay's "If We Must Die", and because of their standard and conventional languaae could be easily mistaken for White. Walker's early poetry was certainly influenced by the philosophy of integretion so common among Black intellectuals of the time. Her work published during the late 1960s, as well as Gwendolyn Brooks'; is more political, more centered and devoted exclusively on and to a Black world.

The poems written by the latter author during the 1940s, on the contrary, concentrate on the Black urban environment, as much as other black writers such as Wright and Petry were doing in the meantime. But unlike Petry and Wright, Gwendolyn Brooks tries to point at the various hidden aspects of the Black life in the slums, at the feelings of men and, particularly, women. In "A Street in Bronzeville" (1945) and "Annie Allen" (1949), her two collections of poems, the second of which made her the first black to receive a Pulitzer Prize for poetry, she concentrates on portraying the ordinary life of her black people; something she will perfectly succeed in with her only novel Maud Martha(1952). Poems like "Kitchenette Building", "When You Have Forgotten Sunday: The Love Story" or "The Mother", give us beautiful, unforgettable verses, in which the black woman is the most frequent protagonist.

We linked Brooks' treatment of the 'ordinary' and the Black environment with Petry's and Wright's fiction. Instead, she differed from them in her celebration of the Black race, of the beauty, humour and irony that could be found among her suffering people, something Margaret Walker did also but in a different way. We might also add that this last characteristic is typical of Zora Neale Hurston's work and that this link, which has a personal as well as literary quality, could represent a good way of closing the introductory part of this paper. Zora Neale Hurston has left an important legacy in Black culture which

134

is by now acknowledged by most contemporary black women writers. As we have tried to point out, she has lived and written duringthree fundamentally important decades for Black literature, for the Black woman and for the Black woman writer. Her work has been influenced by and has influenced that of her contemporaries, moreorless unconsciously maybe, but cannot be disregarded when studying American Women in the 1930's and 40's.

REFERENCES

1   <u>Zora Neale Hurston: A Literary Biography</u>, Urbana: University of Illinois Press, 1977, p. 51.
2   Paula Giddins, ''A Search for Self'' in <u>When and Where I Enter: The Impact of Black Women on Race and Sex in America</u>, New York: Bantam Books, p. 186.
3   Ibid., p. 186
4   Ibid., pn. 187-189
5   Ibid., p. 196 (all information concerning black women's employment rate and education are taken from Giddins' precious book).
6   R. Hemenway, op.cit., p. 50
7   Cfr. Barbara Christian, ''The Rise and Fall of the Proper Mulatta'' in <u>Black Women Novelists: The Development of a Tradition</u>, Westport, Conn.: Greenwood Press, 1980, pp. 41-47, and Sandra O'Neale, ''Race Sex and Self: Aspects of Bildung in Select Novels by Black American Women Novelists'' in <u>MELUS</u>, vol. 9, n. 4, Winter II, 1982, pp. 25-37.
8   P. Giddins, op.cit., p. 190.
9   R. Hemenway, op.cit., p. 23.
10   S. O'Neale, op.cit., p. 29.
11   B. Christian, op.cit., p. 44.
12   Ibid., p. 53.
13   Cfr. B. Christian, op.cit. pp. 56-61 and s.a. <u>Black Feminist Criticism</u>, Pergamon Press, 1985; Alice Walker ''Looking for Zora'' in <u>In Search For our Mother's Garden; Conjure: Black Women, Fiction and Literary Tradition</u> ed. by M.Pryce and H.J. Spillers, Indiana University Press, 1985; S. O'Neale, op.cit., .R. Hemenway, op.cit.
14   P. Giddins, op.cit., p. 204.
15   Quoted by the author in <u>Black Women Writers at Work</u>, ed. by Claudia Tate, New York: Continuum, 1983, pp. 189-191.
16   P. Giddins, op.cit., p. 235.
17   Ibid., p. 237.
18   Ibid., p. 237.
19   <u>Afro-American Writing: An Anthology of Prose and Poetry</u>, Richard A. long and Eugenia W. Collier editors, New York University Press, 1972, p. 519.

135

The CRUSADER Monthly's Black Nationalist Support For The Jazz Age

Ted Vincent[1]

The relationship of political to cultural radicalism continues to be a much debated issue in the Afro-American freedom struggle. A better picture of how these relationships were handled in the past would be helpful. For instance: in the absence of documentation, the attitude toward the "Jazz Age" music revolution on the part of the black radicals of that period has been made without an appraisal of one important segment of the radicals. This segment could be called "the *Crusader* crowd," the contributors to the *Crusader* monthly of 1918-1922, perhaps the most outspoken of the "New Negro" monthlies published in Harlem in those years. Less than half a dozen *Crusader* issues were retained in libraries. Consequently, opinions as to what editor Cyril V. Briggs and others of his "crowd" stood for, on cultural and other issues has been left largely evidence from those people's lives in later years, in different socio/political settings.

Fortunately, a contributor and subscriber to the *Crusader*, J. Ralph Casimir of the island of Dominica, carefully saved a nearly complete set of the magazine. Thanks largely to the careful preservation by the aged West Indian poet and political militant, a complete run of the *Crusader* was published in 1987 by Robert A. Hill, director of the Marcus Garvey Paper's Project at the University of California at Los Angeles. Finally, a long overdue assessment of this magazine and its distinctive socio/political circle is possible. The article which follows here addresses the cultural question by analyzing how the *Crusader* approached jazz and blues - those music forms which at that time were considered by many to be without artistic merit, in bad taste, or, down right immoral.

To understand the *Crusader* is to first know something of Cyril V. Briggs, its editor and founder. He is probably best remembered for his black-only para-military African Blood

63

Brotherhood, which was founded early in 1919 and disolved sometime in 1925. The ABB had a secret membership, a "blood ritual" initia- tion, amd advocated blacks be armed for self-defense and that they keep physic- ally fit through "calesthenics." From its inception in 1919, the ABB grew in the early 1920s to include about 7,000 members in its secret cadres. By the mid-1920s Briggs was moving away from his nationalistic organization to become a prominent black member of the U.S. Communist Party. A bitter falling out with his former ally, Marcus Garvey, excellerated the change.[2]

In effect, Briggs evolved through a militant political nationalism during World War I into a militant marxist. During the transition period of 1918-1921, Briggs's *Crusader* magazine was a sounding board for the social circle of intel- lectuals who didn't fit in the European-focused mold of the "Harlem Renaissance" elite that contributed to the NAACP's *Crisis* monthly and various white-left and bohemian journals. Most of intellectuals who graced the pages of Briggs' *Crusader* also contributed to black nationalist Marcus Garvey's *Negro World*. This was a circle including Hubert H. Harrison, Arthur A. Schomburg, John "Grit" Bruce, T. Thomas Fortune, W. A. Domingo, sports and theatre writer Romeo L. Dougherty, and the poets Lucian B. Watkins, J. Ralph Casimir, Claude McKay, Ben Burrell and Andy Razaf.

The "jazz age" was barely underway when the *Crusader* first appeared in September 1918. What was to become extensive *Crusader* support for jazz and blues was hinted at in that first issue. Displaying an unselfconscious pro-black chauvinism, Briggs urged all to adopt his "Race Catechism" - a pledge declaring loyalty to one's race the most important part of the struggle for freedom. Another early issue carried a tribute to the superiority of black women over all other women, the black woman being not only more beautiful, but also, more "full of life and female vanity." Historical articles on the glory of ancient African civilizations were plentiful in the *Crusader*.[3]

Cyril Valentine Briggs was born in 1888 in St. Kitts, the Virgin Islands. His father was white and his mother a light skinned black. The special intensity in Cyril's pro-black attitude may have been his psychological compensation for the frustration of being a reportedly good looking fellow with a flair for social dancing who had the twin drawbacks of being extremely light complexioned and having a very serious speech

64

impediment. Harry Haywood, a member of Briggs's African Blood Brotherhood, recalled the one time in Briggs's life that he gave an impromptu speech in public. "Briggs had had a falling out with Garvey," Haywood explains, "and Garvey knew how to get back at Cyril - Garvey called him a white man. One day, Cyril was walking past a street corner speaker, a Garveyite, who happened to be blasting Briggs and calling him a white man. Cyril got so mad he forgot his speech problem, mounted the speaker's soap box and waxed eloquent for three hours."[4]

Briggs's reputation for political radicalism was initially established through his editorial columns on the New York *Amsterdam News*, a paper on which he started working in 1913 as a sports and theatre writer. In 1917, when President Woodrow Wilson declared the rights of national minorities in Europe to political "self-determination," Briggs responded in the *Amsterdam News* with an editorial titled "'Security of Life' for Poles and Serbs - Why Not for Colored Americans?" Briggs declared that Black America was certainly as oppressed and exploited as was Poland or Serbia, etc. And he asked, "Is it not time to consider a separate political existence? As one-tenth of the population, backed with many generations of unrequited toil and half a century of contribution, as free men, to American prosperity, we can with reason and justice demand our portion for purposes of self-government and the pursuit of happiness, one-tenth of the territory of continental United States."[5]

In other editorials Briggs ridiculed the idea of Black Americans having to fight for democracy abroad, and in a letter to the New York *Globe*, he raised the call of "African for the Africans." Early in 1918 Briggs was removed from his job with the *Amsterdam News*.[6]

The *Crusader* was launched in September 1918, with a substantial portion of the funds for publication coming from benefit jazz dances held at the Manhattan Casino. Romeo Dougherty, later to be music and theatre reviewer for Marcus Garvey's press and other papers, described the first of these "Liberty Dances" in the New York *News*. The "enthusiastic audience...nearly overran the Casino" in what Dougherty felt was a strong display of its support for the founding of the *Crusader*, a magazine which Dougherty said "shall have as its purpose, intelligent agitation for a real, true and unvarnished democracy for all the darker peoples of the world."[7]

It was fitting for Briggs to use dance fund raisers for his

65

magazine. Historian Robert Hill notes that Briggs looked back on the World War I period and called it the "Dancing Master period" of his career. Briggs claimed to have been an avid exponent of "the modern dances introduced in that period by the Castles," referring to the famous cabaret dance team of Irene and Vernon Castle, who in addition to promoting ballroom dancing, aided the pioneering jazz band of James Reese Europe. Hill suggests, "It is possible that Briggs might have had a dancing part in the Lafayette Players' production of *The Octoroon* in January 1916. And Hill concludes, "Tall, handsome, and polished, Briggs was, culturally speaking, a protege of the ragtime era as it swept toward its zenith amid the clouds of war."[8]

By war's end ragtime was being surpassed by blues and jazz. From its first issues, the *Crusader* showed a special favoritism to the blues, the "funkier" side of the jazz revolution. Advertisements for blues sheet music, blues records, photographs of blues singers, and articles about blues singers abounded in the CRUSADER during the important formative years for the jazz boom - 1918-to early 1922. This was a period when the rival black monthly on the left, the *Messenger*, had very few record ads for any kind of music, and no articles or pictures about jazz or the blues. When the "integrationist" Socialist Party funded *Messenger* did finally turn attention to the new music, in 1923, the initial articles were strongly critical.[9]

As for the *Crusader* blues and jazz coverage: W. C. Handy received special attention. The first of many glowing articles on Handy appeared in the January 1919 *Crusader*. Handy was congratulated for the success of his blues band and for his work in promoting the new music. The *Crusader* noted that "Mr. Handy intends... to show that these BLUES can be woven into beautiful symphonies and a truly higher art." Other endorsements of the new sounds include the one in the May 1920 issue that reviewed the success of the Pace and Handy sheet music company and noted that orders for the blues were coming "from every country in the civilized globe... These orders show that this 'new' music is appreciated even in Scandinavia, China and Japan."[10]

The idea of "the blues" being a serious "art form" was not widely held, but the *Crusader* made the point in many ways. There was the choice of terminology, "blues artist" over "blues player." And in the *Crusader* the blues had "composers" just as did writers of symphonies. For instance: a *Crusader* piece on

66

the pioneering blues singer Mamie Smith noted that her records came from "the eminent song composer Perry Bradford." Composer Bradford had been making his living playing blues piano in saloons, when he wasn't working as a secretary for vaudeville star Bert Williams.[11]

Originality was the greatest plus for a musician, in the judgement of Cyril Briggs, Romeo Dougherty, Charles Henry and other *Crusader* writers on music. (By way of contrast, Briggs and company rarely mentioned performances of black musicians before British royalty or assorted heads of state, events which received much notice in some politically conservative black weeklies and in the NAACP's monthly, *The Crisis*). One *Crusader* acknowledgement of originality came from its Boston based writer, Charles Henry, who was particularly impressed with an early version of what appears to have been musical "rap." Reviewing the christmas season 1920 run of the musical revue *Strut Yo' Stuff* at Harlem's Lafayette Theatre, Henry pointed out:[12]

> To those who can appreciate originality of treatment plus much new material, "Strutt Yo' Stuff" must stand head and shoulders above most of its competitors in showland. The originality of the Jazz land Scene in which the audience is treated to a rare bit of syncopated dialogue - this alone should put "Strutt Yo' Stuff" at the head of a show business that boasts too little originality.

In a February 1921 review of Mamie Smith's work, Briggs wrote:

> Her songs have the individuality known as BLUES. Gifted with a voice of expressive quality her dramatic songs stir the emotions and revive pleasing sensations. Having a keen perception for the humorous notes in her songs, she adroitly charms the listener with her delightful characterizations.

Photos of blues players carried supportive captions, as in "Lucille Hegamin and her *Blue Flame Syncopators*, an irresistible blues combination..."

Crusader advertising stressed innovation, as in new cooperative real estate firms in Harlem; in the Art Novelty Company's line of goods that included black dolls and engraved photos of Marcus Garvey; and in ads for new music stores. In addition to ads for Handy's sheet music company, editor Briggs also plugged his own Crusader Music Company which promoted politically radical songs, "songs with a purpose," as he called them. The *Crusader* also had a regular column for black per-

67

formers in classical and religious music, and it had a "play of the month" column. Briggs was apparently a close personal friend of Abbie Mitchell, the star female of the Lafayette Players dramatic troupe, who also had an extensive career as a singer on the concert stage and in Broadway musicals, as well as giving performances for Garvey's UNIA.[13]

In addition to *Crusader* endorsements of jazz, blues and black theatre, Cyril Briggs continued his involvement in promoting dances that had helped him initially to launch his magazine. His contributions included being a judge at a music store "blues contest" where a fellow judge was the blues singer Mary Stafford.[14] The *Crusader* writers included, Lester A. Walton, manager of the Lafayette Theatre - the top Harlem Theatre for musicals, vaudeville and serious drama. And the rival Roosevelt theatre was managed by the busy *Crusader* columnist Romeo Dougherty.

The journalistic promotion of the black community was compromised by the need to cater to powerful economic forces (advertisers) who were often less interested in enhancing the community than in exploiting it. Briggs learned something of this the hard way in a brief publishing venture he had two years before the *Crusader*, his short-lived *Colored American Review*. Articles and cartoons in the *Review* strongly argued that it was in the interest of the Harlem community that people buy at stores and shops that were black owned. And Briggs listed black owned establishments, most all of which were, at that time, too small to afford to take an add in a monthly.

The *Colored American Review* lost additional potential advertisers when its theatre and music editor, R. C. Doggett - who actually took over the magazine in its last issues - used a brilliantly informative graph to rate the quality of musical entertainment in Harlem theatres and clubs. The theatre owners in black communities, especially the white owners, didn't want objectivity out of black theatre reviewers. They wanted praise, otherwise the owners would simply refuse to advertise. And the advertising starved black papers, typically, caved in, at least part way. They caved in far enough for Doggett's graph to be the only known example of the black press of the Jazz Age using a rating scale for acts and shows.

Doggett's graph actually was more telling than the usual ratings of one to four stars in today's papers. He evaluated every act presented on the basis of crowd response at

68

"reception" and at "finish." His rather subjective <u>applause-meter</u> was then displayed in a range going from **fair, pleasing, fine, good, big, splendid, great**, to **riot**.

So, among the 73 acts evaluated in the January 1916 issue, the reader could see that Malcolm the juggler at the Lincoln had a "fair" reception and "good" applause at the end; while the Anita Bush comedy act won over an audience with a closing score of "riot" after starting with a relatively low score of "fine." Doggett's chart ran for only the one January 1916 issue in the *Colored American Review*. The magazine had no advertising from Harlem theatres during its brief lifetime. In the *Crusader*, the theatre and music coverage, although occasionally critical of a performance, shied away from blunt grading. The *Crusader* had much theatre advertising.

An integral part of the developing popular culture in black communities was the growing (and then relatively new) sport of basketball. The start of the "Jazz Age" coincided with professional basketball's infancy, when the game rarely could draw a crowd without being combined with a dance, as in the "Saturday Night Basketball Game and Dance." The *Crusader* aggressively promoted the sport, selecting its own "all-star" team, and advertising many a Saturday night social of basketball and dancing. The Manhattan Casino, later known as the Renaissance Casino was the major Harlem pro basketball house. When the game was over and the fans were let on the floor for the dance, the music was usually provided by E. Gladstone Marshall's dance band, assisted by Arnold J. Ford - Ford and Marshall also being known in the community for their leadership with Garvey's UNIA Band.[15]

In one sense, Cyril Briggs "owed one" to basketball. The single most important professional basketball promoter in Black America during the 1920s, 1930s and 1940s was not Abe Saperstein (of comic Globetrotter's fame) but rather Robert L. "Bobby" Douglas, the organizer of the famous Harlem Renaissance Five, the team named after its home court, the Renaissance Casino. Bobby Douglas had the honor of being the very first subscriber to the *Crusader*. Briggs credited Douglas with invaluable assistance in organizing the first fund raising dances for the *Crusader*, which were held at the Casino. Briggs also acknowledged that in the first two months of his magazine's existence Douglas had combed the streets and night spots of New York, and together with two other hard workers, had collected

69

over 500 subscriptions.[16]

In part, this basketball Hall of Famer was just helping a fellow immigrant from St. Kitts. On the other hand, the *Crusader* was specifically launched by those who wanted Briggs to have an outlet for the sensationally militant writing that had gotten him removed from the *Amsterdam News*. Moreover, Douglas seemed zealous enough in the *Crusader* cause to suggest he was a bit of a political as well as a basketball revolutionary. In the mid-1920s Douglas's "Harlem Rens" beat the "Original Celtics" and briefly reigned as professional World Champions. The Rens regained the world title in the 1930s and were voted the professional "Team of the Decade." In 1949, Douglas's aging all-black Rens were in the National Basketball League, the forerunner of today's National Basketball Association - the NBA.[17]

Crusader basketball coverage focused upon the developments <u>within</u> the black community. Although generally supporting the pros, there was an article by Romeo Dougherty calling for amateur community teams to organize for protection against player raids by the pros. Dougherty was later credited with being the founder of the tradition of bringing basketball teams from the Southern black colleges to play games in Harlem.[18]

The attention to the community, found in *Crusader* articles on blues, jazz and basketball, mirrored the focus in other areas. The May 1919 *Crusader*, for example, ridiculed the decision of black actors in dramatic performances at Harlem's Lafayette theatre to paint their faces white when they were performing plays that were set in Europe or some other white setting. Briggs pointed out that since these plays typically involved a drawing room scene, or some other middle-class backdrop, the black actors in white face were saying that one had to be white, or one did not belong in a setting of such refinement and good taste.

Briggs's friend Hubert Harrison made a similar point in a column written for Garvey's *Negro World*, which also reprinted Briggs's *Crusader* piece on white faced black acting.[19] Harrison was one of a number of prominent Garveyites who had a falling out with Marcus Garvey and saw in Briggs and the African Blood Brotherhood an opportunity to break with the UNIA while publically maintaining a black nationalist position rather than appearing to have become an "integrationist." UNIA Assistant President General J. D. Gordon, and the UNIA Chaplain General, Bishop George Alexander McGuire were among the

70

luminaries who drifted into the ABB. Were it not for Briggs's strong pro-black stance on cultural matters he probably would not have gotten these Garveyites. Briggs's marxist politics weren't acceptable to most black nationalists.[20]

The Garveyite renegades in the ABB included important cultural figures. There was poet and song writer Ben Burrell who was co-author of the UNIA Anthem, and there was poet song writer Paul Andrea Razafkeriefo, grandnephew of the Queen of Madagascar. He is better known today as Andy Razaf, libretist for hit songs of Eubie Blake, James P. Johnson, and especially for Fats Waller, for whom Razaf provided the words to so very many enduring hits, including "Aint Misbehavin," "Spoosin," and "Why Am I So Black and Blue."[21]

In the first years of the Garvey movement in New York, Razaf put his talents to work promoting the UNIA, his efforts in this regard including the authorship of the songs "Garvey, Hats Off To Garvey," and "UNIA" - songs he sang to an enthusiastic crowd at New York's Liberty Hall in 1920. The prolific Razaf contributed poetry to the *Negro World, Voice, Challenge, Spokesman,* New York *News*, and *Amsterdam News*, as well as to Briggs *Crusader* - for which Razaf was a staff member through most of 1919.[22]

Razaf's poetry in the vein of "The Fifteenth Regiment," and the anti-police brutality "To Certain Policemen," blended well with other *Crusader* items designed to inspire militant response from readers - such as the cartoon depicting a brutishly large white man clutching at a frail black woman. Razaf's poetic comment on "certain" Harlem policemen is as relevant today as when Razaf wrote it, and is a peom one might not expect from the author of such polite pop balleds as "Memories of You." "To Certain Policemen" addressed the issue of black troops from Harlem then being in Europe fighting the so-called World War for democracy, while back home the black men's women and children were at the mercy of the cops. As published in the *Crusader* of May 1919, the first two verses read:

> Hail to our bully policemen
> The heroes of the town
> Who spend their time abusing
> And knocking Negroes down.
> Who blindly wield their night-sticks
> Spurred on by racial hate
> And thus betray democracy
> Their uniform and state

71

All honor to these policemen
Who ever seek the chance
To thank black men in Harlem
Who's sons have gone to France,
By cursing at their women
While passing on their way
And beating up their children
Engaged in harmless play.

The *Crusader* ceased publication after its January-February 1922 issue. A number of African American monthlies failed around this time, including the politically radical *Promoter, Challenge* and *Voice of The Negro*. No doubt, there had been something of a glut on the magazine market. However, Brigg's failure with the *Crusader* was a special loss. Among other things, there may not have been another "marxist" journal on the planet with the strong support of pop culture that Briggs showed in his support of jazz, blues, basketball, etc.

While the *Crusader* was promoting marxist theory, black self-defense, and explanations of the Russian and Mexican revolutions, it was also promoting black community life, from sports to barber shops, to record stores, theatres and movie houses, and the short lived craze for cooperative apartment house ownership. The *Crusader* also had photo displays of what Briggs felt were the best looking women in Harlem. The Socialist *Messenger* magazine, although published in Harlem as was the *Crusader*, carried very little news or advertising of the community. It appears that Randolph and co-editor Chandler Owen kept their journal going almost entirely with financing from their white-left Socialist Party supporters. Interestingly enough, when Briggs's *Crusader* folded in the spring of 1922 it had just recently lost most of its community advertisers.

Some support had, no doubt, been scared away after the ABB practically bragged in the pages of the *Crusader* about its role in the bloody Tulsa riot of June 1921. The Brotherhood had, allegedly, been responsible for setting up the barricades and providing the military order to the black defense lines at the edge of the Tulsa neighborhood, defense lines which kept white mobs outside for days. Although Tulsa was a noble struggle, the ending was horrifying, with the black citizenry being herded aside by the Oklahoma National Guard while white mobs burned and sacked what was left of the black community.[23]

72

The Tulsa episode no doubt frightened away some of the more mainstream minded advertisers on Briggs's *Crusader*. And Briggs further lost support when he became embroiled in bitter mudslinging with Marcus Garvey over issues of black self-defense and Briggs's belief that blacks should make a political alignment with the Workers (Communist) Party.

After the folding of the *Crusader* Cyril Briggs went until 1927 before getting another editorship, the *Negro Champion*, local organ for the Harlem branch of the Communist Party. Significantly enough, the *Negro Champion* did not relate to jazz, nor to blues, nor to the life of the black community in general. It was almost exclusively an organ of news about "the struggle" of the black masses. Briggs' *Negro Champion* seemed to be edited by a completely different human being than the man who had produced the *Crusader* a few years earlier.

What had happened? In turning from a vision of a Black Internationale to the Red Internationale, it appears that there was a rechannelling of the powerful ego drive that enabled Cyril Briggs to stand in the forefront of "New Negro" black radicalism at the beginning of the Jazz Age. His sense of life's urgency had been focused upon the black community. From that focus he supported the music of that community, and he reached out and brought into the community, the idea of linking forces with outsiders, radicals of other races and countries. The change was that his focus had gone from a social one, as in *Crusader* articles on who were the best looking women in Harlem, to an intellectual focus, an intellectual theory - scientific socialism. Even though he was editor of a Harlem journal, the *Negro Champion*, he was no longer a black militant so much as he was a marxist, and a heady one at that. As has been pointed out in many studies, the scientific intellectuals of the Jazz Age generally took their cues from Thorstein Veblen and other "objective" prudes who considered modern popular culture mere Roman circuses.

While the *Crusader* died, its former staff member of 1919, Andy Razaf, still influenced the music revolution through his lyrics for Waller and other composers. And the *Crusader*'s Romeo Dougherty went on through his work on various black weeklies to earn from *Billboard* magazine the plaudit, "the most widely known Negro writer on sports and playhouses," while the Pittsburgh *Courier* called him the "dean of the East among theatre reviewers," and the *Messenger* called him "the dean of

73

show business writers."[24]

Analysis of the *Crusader* leads to the conclusion that a revision may be needed in the historical view of the attitude of Harlem Renaissance intellectuals and politicians towards the revolutionary jazz and blues developments of that period.

The *Crusader* mix of support for jazz and blues combined with serious discussion of African and Afro-American history seems to stand out in sharp contrast to the standard intrepretation of Renaissance era heavy thinkers' relations to the new music. Historian of the Renaissance Nathan Huggins, for instance, concluded that while the Renaissance was a time when black intellectuals "promoted poetry, prose, painting and music as if their lives depended on it," the intellectuals were unable to endorse jazz, the blues and the dance phenomenas of the period. And music historian Leroy Ostransky notes that while classical music, any "serious" music was worthy of praise, jazz "was not generally considered by the leaders of the Harlem Reniassance as worthy of inclusion in their list of serious achievements.[25]

Perhaps a more accurate view would point out that intellectual activity of the Renaissance/Jazz Age period had two sides. There were those who socialized and became known within circles close to the white left-liberal academic environment, an environment of individuals who, while titilated by African rhythms, etc., tended to personally prefer Brahms or Beethoven. On the other hand, there were others who focused their attention closer to the black community - those around the *Crusader*, for instance. Being short on academic degrees, and published poems in Greenwich village journals, the *Crusader* crowd may not have been "card carrying" members of the intellectual elite. But this is not to say people like Hubert H. Harrison, John "Grit" Bruce, Cyril Briggs and company did not view the world in a systematic manner based on research and reflection. Take theatre and sports writer Romeo Dougherty, for instance. Although his fields of show business and sports are generally considered areas of journalism inhabited by mental lightweights who have a knack for name dropping, Dougherty was a bibliophile who collected a personal library of over 2,000 volumes; and he proudly claimed to have read every one of them.[26]. In addition to all his reading, Dougherty wrote a politically radical novel, *Punta! Revolutionist*, which was serialized in the *Crusader* during 1919.

74

1.

Ted Vincent is employed at Vista College in Berkeley, California. Hi is the author of three books on the period of the Garvey movement, *Keep Cool: African American Politics of the Jazz Age* (African World Press, Fall 1191); *Black Power and the Garvey Movement* (reissued from its 1970 edition by Nzinga Books, Oakland CA, 1988); *Voices of a Black Nation: Political Journalism of the Harlem Renaissance* (reissue from 1972 edition by African World Press 1991).

2. Briggs and A.B.B. in Robert A. Hill "Racial and Radical" introduction to reprint of *The Crusader Monthly* (University of California, 1987) pIX-XXV; Robert A. Hill, editor, *The Marcus Garvey And Universal Negro Improvement Association Papers* (University of California at Los Angeles 1983-1989) vol 1 pp. 521-527; Ted Vincent, *Black Power And The Garvey Movement* (Nzinga, Oakland 1988) pp. 85-96; Tony Martin, *Race First The Ideological And Organizational Struggles Of Marcus Garvey And The Universal Negro Improvement Association* (Greenwood Press, Westport CT 1975) pp. 237-242.

3. see *Crusader* September 1918, Nctober 1919; November 1919.

4. Interview with Harry Haywood June 1966.

5. In Hill, "Racial and Radical" *op.cit.* pp. X-XV.

6. *Ibid.* pp. XIII-XV.

7. *Crusader* September 1918.

8. Hill, "Racial and Radical" *op.cit.* pp. XI.

9. *Messenger* February 1923, May 1923.

10. See also *Crusader* December 1921 on endorsement of jazz from Richard Strauss.

11. *Crusader* February 1921; and see Bradford, *Born With The Blues*, (Oak Books, NY 1965).

12. *Crusader* January 1921.

13. Hill, "Racial and Radical" *op.cit.* p. XI; *Negro World* 9 August 1924.

14. *Crusader* April 1921.

15. *Crusader* September 1918, October 1918, November 1918; on Ford, New York *Age* 11 June 1914, 23 August 1918; Who's Who in Colored America 1927-1928.

16. *Crusader* November 1918

17. See Ted Vincent, *Mudville's Revenge, op.cit.* pp. 251-253, 291, 302.

18. WWCA 1928-1929

75

19.   *Negro World* quoted in *Crusader* April 1921.

20.   Hill, *Garvey Papers, op.cit.* Vol 1 p. 523.

21.   On Razaf, Who's Who Colored America, 1915; Eileen Southern, *Biographical Dictionary of Afro-American Musicians*; Hill, *Garvey Papers, op.cit.* Col 2 pp. 230, 237-238, Vol 5 p. 802; Ed Kirkaby, *Ain't Misbehaving': The Story of Fats Waller* (DaCapa, NY 1966), pp. 77-78; Tom Lord,*Clarence Williams* (Storyville, Chriswell, England 1974) pp. 495, 499-500

22.   Hill, *Garvey Papers, op.cit.* Vol 2 pp. 230, 237-238.

23.   See especially Chicago *Whip* 4 June 1921, 11 June 1921; Chicago *Defender* 11 June 1921; *Billboard* 25 June 1921.

24.   See *Billboard* 6 August 1921; also 9 September 1922; 5 November 1922; Pittsburgh *Courier* 30 April 1927; *Messenger* January 1927.

25.   Nathan Huggins, *Harlem Rennaisance* (Oxford University Press NY 1971) p. 9; Leroy Ostransky, *Jazz City: The Impact of Our Cities On The Development of Jazz* (Prentice-Hall, Englewood NY) p. 190.

26.   See Dougherty obituaries in New York *Age* 16 December 1944; Chicago *Defender* 16 December 1944

Carl Van Vechten, photographed by E.O. Hoppe, n.d. *HRHRC Photography Collection.*

Carl Van Vechten, Blanche Knopf, and the Harlem Renaissance

By Peter Flora

The years between World War I and the Depression witnessed an outpouring of activity by African American actors, musicians, and writers who had gathered in New York. This first concerted, self-conscious artistic movement of African Americans, the "Harlem Renaissance," was met by the genesis of white appreciation for black art and represented the first widespread recognition of the African American as a creative artist. In retrospect, the white patronage of the movement appears to have been in part wrongheaded and condescending, but it was not without its positive aspects. Carl Van Vechten is a good example of an influential patron of the Harlem Renaissance who was enlightened and well-meaning, though at times misguided.

One way in which whites encouraged the Harlem Renaissance was through creating serious works about African Americans, such as Eugene O'Neill's *All God's Chillun Got Wings* (1924), Sherwood Anderson's *Dark Laughter* (1925), and Van Vechten's *Nigger Heaven* (1926). While not without stereotypical portrayals, these works acted as a spur to black writers and created a sympathetic audience for the serious treatment of African American subjects.

Another important manifestation of growing white interest in black culture came from the publishing industry, possibly as a response to the vogue of "primitivism" inspired by Picasso and other artists. In his study of Alfred Knopf, Randolph Lewis suggests that a new breed of publishers, mostly young Jewish men sensitive to prejudice, opened up the literary marketplace for black writers.[1] Lewis points out that before 1920 few major publishers would issue the work of African Americans, but innovators like Alfred Knopf and Harcourt, Brace allowed the writing of the Harlem Renaissance to reach a broad audience. Although Alfred Knopf and his wife Blanche began their publishing firm in 1915 with the intention of specializing in such works as

---

[1] Randolph Robert Lewis, "Prejudice in Publishing: Alfred A. Knopf and American Publishing, 1915-1935" (Master's thesis, The University of Texas at Austin, 1990).

65

translations and cookbooks that were not commonly published by major firms, it was thanks to such innovative publishers as the Knopfs, with their wide-ranging book list, that black authors no longer had to depend on self-publication or small presses with small advertising budgets and limited distribution. Lewis observes that the Knopf firm was only able to print black writing because the books made money, but he contends that Alfred and Blanche Knopf's enthusiasm for African American writers was more than a fad, their promotion more than financial, and that this support continued after the Harlem Renaissance years.

The Knopf patronage was in large part a result of Carl Van Vechten's enthusiasm for black artists and his considerable influence on the Knopfs. Whether considered as boon or bane, Van Vechten was a central figure of the Harlem Renaissance. As a critic of the arts he played an important role in alerting white audiences to the power and beauty of black music and drama, and his novel *Nigger Heaven* (1926), though of dubious merit, called attention to the piquancy and complexity of Harlem society. In addition, Van Vechten's involvement with the Harlem Renaissance as a friend and advisor to several young black writers was truly complex and unique. The letters of Blanche Knopf to Van Vechten, contained in the Knopf archives at The University of Texas at Austin's Harry Ransom Humanities Research Center, provide new insight into the role Van Vechten played in the Harlem Renaissance and make possible a fuller picture of the extent of Van Vechten's power as a patron of black artists.

I.

Carl Van Vechten was born on 17 June 1880 in Cedar Rapids, Iowa, where he received what was at the time an unusually enlightened introduction to multiculturalism. Van Vechten's father, Charles Duane Van Vechten, was a Universalist—one who believed in salvation for all—and he helped found a school for black children and "always addressed Negroes as Mr. and Mrs., even the laundry woman and the man who cut the grass."[2] Through the black yardman Carl Van Vechten met more African Americans, including the singer Carita Day, and when Van Vechten was about ten years old he heard Sissieretta Jones, "Black Patti," and by the turn of the century had encountered many other black entertainers, including Bert Williams. At the University of Chicago, Van Vechten went with his fraternity's black house-keeper to the Quinn Chapel, where he played the piano for services. He also wrote several of his college papers on African American subjects.

[2]Edward Lueders, *Carl Van Vechten* (New York: Twayne, 1965), p. 95. In addition to this work, Bruce Kellner's *Carl Van Vechten and the Irreverent Decades* (Norman, OK: University of Oklahoma Press, 1968) and George Schuyler's profile, "Carl Van Vechten," in *Pylon* 11 (1950): 362-68, provide useful biographical information.

66

Armed with a bachelor's degree in philosophy, Van Vechten left the Midwest in 1903 to commence a storied life of several distinct careers in New York, where the world of Harlem held for him a natural attraction. His love of the bizarre and avant garde as well as his involvement in many different projects earned him a reputation as a dilettante, but his little-known achievements as a critic of the fine arts and a friend and supporter of writers are considerable. Van Vechten's first occupation was as a drama and music critic for the *New York Times* and the *New York Press*, and as a critic he became an early friend and supporter of George Gershwin and was one of the first Americans to praise in print the music of Erik Satie, Richard Strauss, and Igor Stravinsky. Van Vechten also realized early on the value of music created for the ballet and for motion pictures. Alfred Knopf, who had begun publishing his Borzoi books in 1915, recognized Van Vechten's skill as a music critic and published his *Music and Bad Manners* in 1916; in all, Knopf would publish some nineteen titles by Van Vechten.[3] Throughout his life Van Vechten associated with many famous musicians, writers, dramatists, and film stars, and his numerous books and articles on music and drama were innovative and well-received. In 1914 Van Vechten married Fania Marinoff, a famous Russian actress.[4]

In his mid-thirties, with Knopf's blessing, Van Vechten turned to writing fiction. His seven novels, among which *Peter Whiffle* (1922) was the most successful, were largely portraits of the exotic and decadent, and generally sought to capitalize on the fashions of the day. Van Vechten also wrote several books of non-fiction, and his books on cats, *The Tiger in the House* (1920) and *Lords of the Housetops* (1921), proved quite popular. In 1926, shortly after publishing *Nigger Heaven*, Van Vechten came into two inheritances which freed him of financial concerns and his artistic output slackened. Still, as a photographer he pursued his undying enthusiasm for artists and entertainers, capturing images of hundreds of celebrities, from James Weldon Johnson and H.L. Mencken to Sammy Davis, Jr. and Martha Graham. Bruce Kellner points out that Van Vechten's uncanny sense for future stars is revealed in these pictures, for he photographed Chester Himes at age 30, Lena Horne at 21, and by the 1950s he had photographed James Baldwin, Diahann Carroll,

---

[3]G. Schirmer published Van Vechten's first book, *Music After the Great War*, in 1915. Van Vechten then joined Joseph Hergesheimer and H.L. Mencken as the first members of Knopf's Borzoi authors, and these three became lively friends of one another and of Alfred and Blanche Knopf.

[4]Evidence of Van Vechten's remarkable involvement with cultural affairs can be gleaned from his extensive and colorful correspondence. He communicated regularly with such figures as Gertrude Stein, H.L. Mencken, James Branch Cabell, and Ellen Glasgow, as well as the African American writers Langston Hughes, James Weldon Johnson, and many others. He clearly expended a lot of his artistic energy in writing letters, which Bruce Kellner demonstrates with his collection, *Letters of Carl Van Vechten* (New Haven, CT: Yale University Press, 1987).

67

LeRoi Jones, Alvin Ailey, and Harry Belafonte.[5] Van Vechten had his pictures printed on postcards to ensure wide circulation, and he used the photographs as the basis for several collections at colleges, the most important being the "James Weldon Johnson Memorial Collection of Negro Arts and Letters" at Yale University.

While Van Vechten is chiefly remembered today as a minor novelist, his musical, dramatic, and literary insights are impressive and his efforts on behalf of artists should not be underrated. In addition to his shrewd musical predictions, he was one of the first to resurrect interest in Herman Melville, was a promoter of Wallace Stevens, and was an intimate friend and vocal supporter of Gertrude Stein.[6]

Of course, Van Vechten was also one of the first and most committed of a handful of white writers who recognized the artistic potential of African Americans; indeed, it could be said that Van Vechten enjoyed a full career as a patron and agent of Harlem and its black artists. Van Vechten was one of the first whites to champion African American drama and music, such as ragtime, jazz, and the blues, and he praised Paul Robeson and Ethel Waters before they were well known to white audiences. Van Vechten's first professional writing devoted solely to African American subjects appeared long before the Jazz Age and the vogue of primitivism made "slumming" in Harlem a craze. In December of 1913 he enthusiastically wrote pieces on Bert Williams and a Harlem production called "My Friend from Kentucky" for the *New York Press*.[7] In a 1914 *Trend* magazine article Van Vechten urged the formation of a black theater organization, with black actors and black playwrights.

Though Van Vechten was not without prejudice, he voiced an enthusiasm for African American music and drama that appears to have been based solely on his appreciation of their intrinsic beauty, power, and originality. At the same time that Van Vechten played a crucial role in the recognition of African Americans as creative artists during the Harlem Renaissance, he also perceived that black art was beset with shortcomings. For instance, he decried the minstrel tradition, and he saw that whites controlled the conditions in which black artists worked and that African Americans were

[5]Other notable figures photographed by Van Vechten include Sherwood Anderson, Marc Chagall, William Faulkner, F. Scott Fitzgerald, George Gershwin, William Inge, Billie Holiday, Joe Louis, Norman Mailer, Henri Matisse, Henry Miller, Eugene O'Neill, Gertrude Stein, Evelyn Waugh, Tennessee Williams, and Thomas Wolfe.

[6]In *Nigger Heaven*, Van Vechten has the Harlem sophisticate Mary Love quote the poetry of Wallace Stevens and from Stein's short story "Melanctha."

[7]"My Friend From Kentucky" was part of a vaudeville show entitled *The Darktown Follies*, about which Van Vechten wrote in his 1920 book *In the Garret*: "How the darkies danced and sang and cavorted! Real nigger stuff. . . . They're delightful niggers, those inexhaustible Ethiopians, those husky, lanky blacks!" (p. 312). These comments show that Van Vechten was not immune to racial stereotypes. Yet his treatment of African Americans improved considerably during the Harlem Renaissance as he became acquainted with many Blacks, some of whom remained close friends.

68

James Weldon Johnson, photographed in New York on 3 December 1932 by Carl Van Vechten. *HRHRC Photography Collection.* Reproduced by permission of the Carl Van Vechten estate.

trapped within the imaginative limitations and commercial considerations of others. While he publicly deplored these conditions in articles for *Vanity Fair* and *The Crisis*, as an advisor to the Knopf publishing firm Van Vechten himself may have limited black artists.[8]

Like many artists and celebrities of the Jazz Age, Van Vechten admitted to being a heavy tippler during the prohibition era that he termed the "splendid drunken Twenties."[9] His notorious behavior no doubt confirmed for critics of Van Vechten his reputation as a poseur, but his hedonistic tendencies may have had positive results. Van Vechten loved to visit cabarets, but he was also a frequent and lavish entertainer, and his legendary New York parties, for which Gershwin usually played piano, were commonly filled with celebrities. While certainly a means of indulging in his love for drink, music, and other pleasures, Van Vechten's numerous gatherings represented a cultural exchange that was unparalleled at the time: the parties were always fully integrated, and as Langston Hughes relates, they were reported as a matter of course in Harlem's newspapers.[10] Walter White reportedly called Van Vechten's salon the "mid-town office of the N.A.A.C.P."[11] It could be said, then, that during the 1920s Van Vechten's Manhattan apartment was a focal point for the New York literati, just as Gertrude Stein's salon served the American expatriates in Paris. Van Vechten's literary salon provided a congenial and relaxed atmosphere where black and white artists could meet on an equal footing, and by all accounts, Van Vechten's parties were successful in overcoming prejudice. As George Schuyler wrote, "the doyen of the dilettanti made it smart to be interracial."[12]

Still, in spite of Van Vechten's favorable exposure to African Americans in Cedar Rapids and his desire to aid the "New Negro" movement in New York, like many whites much of his attraction was for the exotic, piquant side of Harlem. At times Van Vechten's "know the Negro" campaign with its love of "slumming," particularly as revealed in his novel of Harlem, *Nigger Heaven,*

---

[8]Van Vechten published the following articles on African American subjects: "Countee Cullen: a Note About the Young Negro Poet, Author of *The Shroud of Color*," *Vanity Fair* 24 (June 1925): 62; "The Folksongs of the American Negro," *Vanity Fair* 24 (July 1925): 52, 92; "The Black Blues: Negro Songs of Disappointment in Love: Their Pathos Hardened with Laughter," *Vanity Fair* 24 (August 1925): 57, 86, 92; "All God's Chillun Got Songs," *Theatre Magazine* 42 (August 1925): 24, 63; "Langston Hughes: A Biographical Note," *Vanity Fair* 25 (September 1925): 62; "Prescription for the Nigger Theatre," *Vanity Fair* 25 (October 1925): 46, 92, 98; "Moanin' Wid a Sword in Ma Han'," *Vanity Fair* 25 (February 1926): 61, 100, 102; "The Negro in Art. How Shall He Be Portrayed," *The Crisis* 31 (March 1926): 219.

[9]Kellner, *Carl Van Vechten and the Irreverent Decades*, p. 149.

[10]Langston Hughes, *The Big Sea* (New York: Hill and Wang, 1940), p. 255.

[11]Quoted in Bruce Kellner, "Carl Van Vechten's Black Renaissance," in *The Harlem Renaissance*, ed. Amritjit Singh, William Shiver, and Stanley Brodwin (New York: Garland, 1989), p. 28.

[12]Schuyler, "Carl Van Vechten," *Pylon*, p. 364.

70

greatly harmed Van Vechten's reputation among African Americans, and the furor it aroused has cast a shadow on his contributions to the Harlem Renaissance.

II.

While Van Vechten grew up with a favorable awareness of African American entertainers, his vast acquaintance with African Americans came about mostly through Walter White, whom he met in August of 1924. At the time, Van Vechten was planning a "Negro novel," and asked Alfred Knopf to introduce him to White, whose angry account of the Atlanta riots, *The Fire in the Flint*, had been published by Knopf earlier in the year.[13] White promptly introduced Van Vechten to Harlem's most notable residents,[14] and Van Vechten was thereafter a regular sight in Harlem, as well known as the cabaret celebrities he went to enjoy.[15] In 1925 Van Vechten wrote to Gertrude Stein that he had

> passed practically my whole winter in company with Negroes and have succeeded in getting into most of the important sets. This will not be a novel about Negroes in the South or white contacts or lynchings. It will be about NEGROES, as they live now in the new city of Harlem[. . . .] About 400,000 of them live there now, rich and poor, fast and slow, intellectual and ignorant.[16]

For his other novels the author did not conduct any such elaborate preparations as those indicated to Stein. In spite of its elements of exotic primitivism, Van Vechten's *Nigger Heaven* represents a serious artistic endeavor.

While Van Vechten prevailed upon Knopf to advertise the novel far in advance of publication, "so that the kind of life I am writing about will not come as an actual shock,"[17] he could not be dissuaded from his inflammatory title. Indeed, his own father warned him not to use such a controversial word choice. The elder Van Vechten wrote to his son, "I have myself never spoken of a colored man as a 'nigger.' If you are trying to help the race, as I am assured you are, I think every word you write should be a respectful one towards the black."[18]

[13]Walter White, *The Fire in the Flint* (New York: Knopf, 1924).

[14]Although Van Vechten and White were reportedly close friends, White's autobiography, *A Man Called White* (New York: Viking, 1948), scarcely mentions Van Vechten.

[15]Van Vechten's easy acceptance in Harlem was such that a popular song of the time, "Go Harlem" by Andy Razaf, quipped "Go inspectin' like Van Vechten" (see David Levering Lewis, *When Harlem Was in Vogue* [New York: Knopf, 1981], p. 182).

[16]*Letters*, p. 80.

[17]Ibid., p. 86.

[18]Quoted in Kellner, *Carl Van Vechten and the Irreverent Decades*, pp. 210-11. Carl could not make the same boast as his father, for prior to meeting Walter White, Van Vechten sent White's

71

Van Vechten must have been aware that most African Americans would be offended by his title, and he was careful to explain its meaning in his notes for the novel:

> Nigger Heaven is an American slang expression for the topmost gallery of a theatre, so-called because in certain of the United States, Negroes [. . .] are arbitrarily forced to sit in these cheap seats. The title of this novel derives from the fact that the geographical position of Harlem, the Negro quarter of New York, corresponds to the location of the gallery in a theater.[19]

This explanation is reiterated in the text of the novel when the frustrated, would-be writer Byron declares, "Nigger Heaven! That's what Harlem is. We sit in our places in the gallery of this New York theatre and watch the white world sitting down below in the good seats in the orchestra."[20] However, many of Van Vechten's detractors did not care to read beyond the book's cover and, for those who did, the title certainly affected their reading regardless of the author's intent. Langston Hughes later wrote that African Americans grew angry as soon as they heard of the novel. He explained the sensitive nature of the title in plain terms:

> the word *nigger* to colored people of high and low degree is like a red rag to a bull. Used rightly or wrongly, ironically or seriously, of necessity for the sake of realism, or impishly for the sake of comedy, it doesn't matter. Negroes do not like it in any book or play whatsoever, be the book or play ever so sympathetic in its treatment of the basic problems of the race.[21]

Hence, *Nigger Heaven* caused great resentment in Harlem, with W.E.B. DuBois as the best-known and perhaps most vocal of the novel's detractors. Blacks gathered in libraries to denounce the book, and Van Vechten was hung in effigy on 135th Street.[22] Hughes wrote in an understatement that perhaps "Mr. Van Vechten's title was an unfortunate choice."[23]

Insofar as the title was meant to secure attention so that the white reading public could learn more of the true nature of Harlem, it served its purpose.

The Fire in the Flint to Mabel Dodge Luhan, informing her that the book was "written by a Nigger" (*Letters*, p. 70). Perhaps Van Vechten's meeting with the sophisticated Walter White marked a turning point in his attitude toward African Americans.

[19]Quoted in Lueders, *Carl Van Vechten*, pp. 102-103.

[20]Van Vechten, *Nigger Heaven*, p. 149.

[21]Langston Hughes, *The Big Sea*, pp. 268-69.

[22]Donald Petesch, *A Spy in the Enemy's Country: The Emergence of Modern Black Literature* (Iowa City: IA: University of Iowa Press, 1989), p. 168.

[23]Hughes, *The Big Sea*, p. 270.

72

Dust jacket of Carl Van Vechten's novel, *Nigger Heaven*, published by Knopf in 1926. *HRHRC Collections*.

Yet if the novel was meant to contribute to a racial rapprochement, as Van Vechten claimed, the title was counterproductive, for African Americans found it antagonistic. In the matter of his title Van Vechten's penchant for notoriety got the better of him.[24]

Given such a scandalous title, it is no wonder that Van Vechten's critics found the novel too sensational, and in fact, the sensationalism implicit in the title is forcefully duplicated in the novel's opening scenes. The Scarlett Creeper struts in with chest bared and "display[s] his teeth," and when he goes into a nightclub and meets Ruby, the reader finds that

> Couples were dancing in such close proximity that their bodies melted together as they swayed and rocked to the tormented howling of the brass, the barbaric beating of the drum. Across each woman's back, clasped tight against her shoulder blades, the black hands of her partner were flattened. Blues, smokes, dinges, charcoals, chocolate browns, shines, and jigs.
> Le's hoof, Ruby urged.[25]

The major criticism of Van Vechten's novel is that it concentrates too heavily on Harlem's underside, sensationalizing the people and perpetuating white stereotypes. The novel contains numerous images of people who are merely creatures of appetite. On the other hand, the novel depicts the complexities of Harlem's social structure, and its chief characters, Byron Kasson and Mary Love, are intelligent, educated people—rare indeed for black characters in a 1926 novel. Yet these characters are melodramatic, and their relationships are jejune.

Claude McKay expressed discomfort with this equivocal portrayal of the novel's supposed heroes. In his autobiography, he wrote that

> it puzzled me a little that the author, who is generally regarded as a discoverer and sponsor of promising young Negro writers, gave Lascar, the ruthless Negro prostitute, the victory over Byron, the young Negro writer, whom he left, when the novel ends, in the hands of the police, destined perhaps for the death house in Sing Sing.[26]

---

[24]When Van Vechten tried to help Ronald Firbank get his book *Sorrow in Sunlight* (London: Brentano's Ltd, 1924) published in the United States, he advised Firbank that the novel would create more of a sensation if the title was changed to *Prancing Nigger*. Firbank agreed, and Van Vechten wrote an introduction for the American edition (New York: Brentano's, 1924—see Lueders, p. 53). Clearly, Van Vechten appreciated the commercial value of sensationalism. As a marketing ploy Van Vechten's own title appears to have been a shrewd choice: *Nigger Heaven* went through nine printings in four months.

[25]Van Vechten, *Nigger Heaven*, pp. 12-13.

[26]Claude McKay, *A Long Way From Home* (New York: Lee Furman, 1937), p. 319.

74

The message of the novel's conclusion is indeed troubling, for in the final scene, the black intellectual Byron is rendered impotent by a savage black man. Given Van Vechten's lifelong efforts to encourage and promote African American artists, Byron's frustrations are puzzling, particularly because in Van Vechten's earlier novel, *Peter Whiffle*, the white writer Whiffle succeeds under circumstances quite similar to those faced by Byron in *Nigger Heaven*. Thus, after demonstrating the wide variety of Harlem life and the potential for success among several of its characters, the novel ends on an ambiguous, disturbing note.

Nigger Heaven may have derived from patronizing sympathy on the part of Van Vechten, but he appears to have been motivated by pecuniary reasons as well. The novel was written just before Van Vechten unexpectedly came into a large inheritance, and shortly before the novel's appearance he published "The Negro in Art: How Shall He Be Portrayed?" in *The Crisis*.[27] This piece was ostensibly intended to assert the artist's right to poetic license, but Van Vechten possibly meant it to aid the cause of *Nigger Heaven* as well.[28] Mercenary ambitions aside, there can be no doubt that through his novel Van Vechten helped create a white readership for black writers and popularized Harlem. After the novel's publication there was an increased number of white visitors to upper Manhattan and greater demand from publishers and readers for works with a similar emphasis by black writers. Indeed, Chidi Ikonné states that the "Literary Awakening" of African Americans can be defined by two stages, "the essentially Negro self-possessing and Negro self-expressing period before 1926; the publisher/audience controlled, even if essentially Negro self-exposing, period after 1926."[29] After the publication of *Nigger Heaven*, the range of acceptable subjects for black writers was, according to Ikonné, "compelled by mercenary considerations (of publishers mainly) to be limited to those aspects of Negro life which had proved financially successful."[30]

Nigger Heaven has been widely criticized for adversely affecting the work of black writers who wrote Harlem-centered novels. Claude McKay's *Home to Harlem* (1928), Wallace Thurman's *The Blacker the Berry* (1929) and *Infants*

[27]Carl Van Vechten, "The Negro in Art: How Shall He Be Portrayed?," *The Crisis* 31 (March 1926): 219.

[28]Van Vechten's letter to Alfred Knopf of 20 December 1925, in which he asks Knopf to advertise *Nigger Heaven* well in advance of its appearance, explains that "I have during the past year written countless articles on Negro subjects . . . and I have seen to it that as many outoftowners as possible saw enough of the life themselves so that they would carry some news of it back to where they came from" (*Letters*, p. 87). Van Vechten does not suggest that these "countless articles" were written for humanitarian purposes, but rather to lessen the shock of his own novel, and thus to increase sales. Interestingly, Van Vechten's articles on African American subjects virtually ceased after 1926.

[29]Chidi Ikonné, *From DuBois to Van Vechten: The Early New Negro Literature. 1903-1926* (Westport, CT: Greenwood Press, 1981), p. xi.

[30]Ibid., p. xii.

75

of Spring (1932), and Arna Bontemps's *God Sends Sunday* (1931) are representative of the "Van Vechten Vogue," for these works focus on the sensual and make little attempt to effect racial reforms.[31] Yet while the success of *Nigger Heaven* encouraged later works and perhaps, in a few cases, perverted young black writers, to stress the "Van Vechten Vogue" discredits the many fine writers of the Harlem Renaissance, as well as Van Vechten himself whose other work for African American artists should not go unnoticed. While the merit of Van Vechten's Harlem novel is questionable and its influence exaggerated, his significance for the Harlem Renaissance was not limited to *Nigger Heaven* or his critical writings. Van Vechten affected this movement through other means, both publicly as a host of inter-racial gatherings and as a sponsor of writing contests, and privately as a consultant for the Knopf publishing house.

III.

Some critics identified Langston Hughes as a writer perverted by Van Vechten, a charge which Hughes tried to dispel in his autobiography:

> What Carl Van Vechten did for me was to submit my first book of poems to Alfred A. Knopf, put me in contact with the editors of *Vanity Fair*, who bought my first poems sold to a magazine, caused me to meet many editors and writers who were friendly and helpful to me, encouraged me in my efforts to help publicize the Scottsboro case, cheered me on in the writing of my first short stories, and otherwise aided in making life for me more profitable and entertaining.[32]

Hughes declares that many other black artists would second this testimony, and that to claim "Carl Van Vechten has harmed Negro creative activities is sheer poppycock."[33] The record of Van Vechten's work in the 1920s bears Hughes out. In addition to writing countless articles, introductions, and reviews, Van Vechten encouraged many black artists, loaned them money, and put them in contact with agents and publishers. Certainly, in spite of the sensationalist aspect of *Nigger Heaven*, Van Vechten's interest in African American culture was not superficial. He made seeking recognition for black writers a full-time job in the latter half of the 1920s, which led George

---

[31]Claude McKay, *Home to Harlem* (New York: Harper & Brothers, 1928); Wallace Thurman, *The Blacker the Berry* (New York: Macauley, 1929) and *Infants of Spring* (New York: Macauley, 1932); Arna Bontemps, *God Sends Sunday* (New York: Harcourt, Brace, 1959).
[32]Langston Hughes, *The Big Sea*, p. 272.
[33]Ibid.

76

Schuyler to assert that Van Vechten "has done more than any single person in this country to create the atmosphere of acceptance of the Negro."[34]

It is well known that during the twenties Carl Van Vechten recommended to the Knopf firm that it publish Langston Hughes and James Weldon Johnson, as well as several African American writers such as Rudolph Fisher and Nella Larsen, who, though seldom read today, were important contributors to the Harlem Renaissance. Knopf publicly acknowledged Van Vechten's good advice, and often relied entirely on his judgment in decisions about manuscripts.[35] However, this aspect of Van Vechten's influence on the Harlem Renaissance has been largely ignored. Blanche Knopf handled the firm's affairs with African American writers, and the letters she wrote to Van Vechten soundly demonstrate the great extent of the firm's reliance on him. Indeed, Van Vechten may have affected the state of African American art as strongly in his role as a self-appointed literary critic of black writers as from any other of his many offices.

The Knopfs were remarkably kind and liberal in their dealings with Van Vechten from the beginning of their association, and he soon became intimate with Alfred and Blanche, dedicating *The Music of Spain* (1918) "Pour Blanchette." The Knopfs allowed Van Vechten to write blurbs for his own books,[36] and from the first they humored his insistence on having celebrities such as Charlie Chaplin witness him signing his book contracts with the firm.[37] Soon after the Knopfs introduced Van Vechten to Walter White and observed his enthusiastic embrace of Harlem's literary circle, they placed total confidence in Van Vechten's judgment of African American writers, and he unofficially became their chief advisor on black writing, though under no contract for such work. Blanche Knopf's letters to Van Vechten reveal that she submitted to him several manuscripts by black writers in order to get his opinion on the writing, or she simply asked him if he had heard of a certain writer and wanted to read that writer's manuscript. If Van Vechten was not interested, Blanche did not consider the writer worth the firm's attention either. For instance, on 25 September 1931, Blanche wrote Van Vechten a typical query, asking if he knew one Glen Blodgett of Seattle. Following her quote of a blurb on Blodgett's book she asked, "Do you think you want to look at it in which case I will send it over; otherwise I will reject it."[38] Blanche habitually followed Van Vechten's advice blindly. She was loath to make any

[34]George Schuyler, "Carl Van Vechten," p. 362.

[35]Alfred A. Knopf, "Reminiscences of Hergesheimer, Van Vechten, and Mencken," *Yale University Library Gazette* 24 (April 1950): 151.

[36]"Good Egg," *The New Yorker*, 18 June 1955, p. 18.

[37]Kellner, *The Irreverent Decades*, p. 237.

[38]Unless otherwise noted, the correspondence of Blanche Knopf and Carl Van Vechten quoted in this section is found in the unpublished Knopf archives of the Harry Ransom Humanities Research Center at The University of Texas at Austin.

77

decisions on a manuscript by an African American on her own, but she rarely sounded out anyone else at the firm either. For black writers at Knopf, the buck clearly stopped at Van Vechten.[39]

A letter of 26 June 1931 further reveals Blanche's curious dependence on Van Vechten. She asked him about the poet Haines J. Washington, who had sent Knopf a manuscript entitled "Climb Low, Nigger." She confided, "I want to reject it but not until I know from you whether the name means anything and whether the manuscript might." Van Vechten typed his reply, unfortunately not very informative, up the left margin of Blanche's letter. He advised her that "Climb Low, Nigger" had been published by F.P.A. in the *Conning Tower* and had received a lot of attention, but uncharacteristically, Van Vechten did not offer any other advice for dealing with Washington.

On 19 November 1931, Blanche solicited Van Vechten's opinion on a book proposed by a "Miss Moriarta." Regrettably, Moriarta's outline does not seem to survive, but Van Vechten's response indicates that she wished to present a study of African American art. Blanche's letter again reveals her reliance on "Carlo," for although she did not think the firm likely to publish the work that year, Blanche wrote, "I don't want to discourage her if there is anything in it in your opinion." Van Vechten replied on 23 November that such a book must be done some time, and that Moriarta had a good plan for the work. Strangely, though, he declared that

> there is no one important enough in the field of Negro Art to make a book of this kind important, even if Miss M. were an important writer[. . . .] In other words, you may expect a solid, journalistic book on a subject of no great importance. This is my view, which you will please consider confidential.

On the same day Blanche wrote to thank Van Vechten for his opinion, "which is, God knows, final."

Thus Miss Moriarta slipped into oblivion. Van Vechten's assertion that there was no one important enough in the field of African American art to make her book significant is surprising, given his broad support and admiration of black efforts in music, drama, and literature. Besides, some might think he was mistaken. Prentiss Taylor was a respected artist during the era—Langston Hughes wanted him to illustrate his collection of poems entitled *The Dream Keeper* (1932), though Knopf chose Helen Sewell—and Richard

[39]Indeed, Blanche depended on Van Vechten's advice regarding any work that dealt remotely with African American culture. On 25 September 1933, she asked him about a cookbook of recipes in dialect by Eleanor Purcell, saying "I should like very much to check up with you on it before turning it down." Van Vechten replied on 27 September that if the book was done, the dialect should be preserved: "If people thought they could buy a short cut to old Southern NEGRO cooking they might flock to it."

78

From left to right: Alfred Knopf, Carl Van Vechten, and Texas Guinan at the signing of a Van Vechten contract in 1930. *HRHRC Photography Collection.*

Nugent, Gwendolyn Bennett, Hale Woodruff, Richmond Barthe, and the sculptress Augusta Savage are some of the artists who garnered attention during the Harlem Renaissance. Aaron Douglass was the best-known painter of the Harlem Renaissance, and among other impressive commissions he was employed by Knopf to illustrate the publicity for *Nigger Heaven*.[40] Surely, then, with the tremendous interest in "primitivism" and African American culture that prevailed during the era, Moriarta's book could have been an important and profitable contribution to the Harlem Renaissance, helping further white appreciation for black artistic achievement as well as cultural pride among African Americans. Van Vechten never hesitated to speak his mind concerning music, drama, and literature by African Americans, so the wish that his negative view of black art not be repeated is also surprising. Perhaps, however, Van Vechten was not trying to keep his view of black art a secret, but rather the complex nature of his involvement with the Knopf firm.[41]

An exchange between Blanche Knopf and Van Vechten regarding a manuscript by Taylor Gordon demonstrates the care taken by the two to maintain secrecy concerning his contributions as a critic for the Knopf firm. In a letter of 11 December 1931, Blanche manifests her usual hesitation to act before hearing Carl's opinion, informing him that a Mr. Abbott of the firm did not like Gordon's manuscript, but that "I would like you to take a squint at it without Taylor's ever knowing it of course, if you will, as it may have hidden assets that we are not catching and I do not want to turn down Taylor too lightly."[42] Van Vechten complied with this request, writing on 17 December that the book amused him and "may be a book of genius, like Ulysses," but that Knopf need not bother with it. He asked, "Please do not implicate me in this transaction," although he already had Blanche's word that she would not. Van

[40]Charles Scruggs argues in "Crab Antics and Jacob's Ladder" (in *The Harlem Renaissance Re-examined*, ed. Victor Kramer [New York: AMS Press, 1987], pp. 149-181) that Douglass's drawings reveal him to have been the most perceptive reader of *Nigger Heaven*, for his sketches succinctly depict the complexity of the Harlem community and its separateness from the white world.

[41]A letter to Gertrude Stein shows Van Vechten's concern that his complex relationship with Knopf not be known. He tried admirably to place Stein's *The Making of Americans* with an American publisher. Knopf would not commit to it, and when Horace Liveright expressed interest Van Vechten quickly brought the manuscript to him. Liveright rejected it, and Van Vechten wrote Stein that she had better ask for the volumes back, because if he did, "it would look as if I were getting them back for Knopf" (*The Letters of Gertrude Stein and Carl Van Vechten*, ed. Edward Burns [New York: Columbia University Press, 1986], p. 100). Van Vechten evidently did not want to be known as an agent for Knopf.

[42]Blanche used Gordon's first name, for she knew that he was a friend of Van Vechten's. Indeed, in his autobiography, *Born to Be* (New York: Covici, Friede, 1929), Gordon calls Van Vechten "the Abraham Lincoln of negro art" and reports that when trying to establish himself as a singer he chanced to sing one afternoon for Van Vechten. Gordon averred that "that afternoon led to all our success" (p. 186).

80

Vechten's willingness to assist Knopf covertly at the risk of harming the career of a friend suggests that for all Van Vechten's efforts on behalf of his black friends, his conduct in those relationships may have been equivocal.[43]

Because Van Vechten introduced Langston Hughes to the Knopf firm, it is not surprising that Blanche would look to Carl for her questions on Hughes's manuscripts, and he was happy to assist her. On 24 March 1933, Blanche informed Van Vechten that a new book of poems by Hughes had just come in and she wondered whether he would look at it "immediately." A year later she asked Van Vechten to comment again on the same group of poems, probably revised by Hughes in the meanwhile, for Van Vechten told Hughes that he liked the poems even less than he had the previous year.[44] In a letter postmarked 12 March 1934, Van Vechten wrote Blanche his thoughts in a firmer manner. He called the revolutionary collection rather bad as poetry, more revolutionary than poetic, and he went on to suggest that Hughes had gone as far as he could go as a poet. Such radical sentiment should be expressed in magazines, Van Vechten maintained, for no one would want to buy such a book. However, Van Vechten stressed that Hughes should not be allowed to take the book elsewhere, that Knopf should publish the book if Hughes insisted.

Of course, as a friend to both Hughes and the Knopfs, Van Vechten did not want to see their association end. Yet the tone of this letter is remarkable, for it sounds like more than mere advice—indeed, Van Vechten's exacting directions make it sound like he was in charge. Blanche submissively followed his precise instructions, and even showed Van Vechten her letter to Hughes to make sure it was all right. She wrote, "I would like you to see this before it goes. If it is okay with you will you just drop it in the post box for me? If not, will you let me know." Thus Blanche rejected the collection, telling Hughes that his volume of poems was not as good a book of poetry as his earlier ones.[45]

Blanche followed Van Vechten's instructions in this and other matters devoutly. Randolph Lewis demonstrates that Hughes's poetic freedom was limited by the Knopfs; the letters from Blanche to Hughes's first white champion, Van Vechten, demonstrate that Van Vechten was in part responsible for the alienation Hughes experienced with the firm. Indeed, Van Vechten was involved in every decision the Knopfs ever made on Langston

[43]*Letters*, p. 137.

[44]The condescending nature of Van Vechten's friendship can be seen in the "Foreword" he wrote for Gordon's *Born to Be*; though Gordon was 32 when he met Van Vechten and 36 at the time of the book's publication, Van Vechten refers to him as "the boy." In a 1932 letter to Blanche Knopf, Van Vechten likewise uses this derogatory name for Hughes, though Hughes was also in his thirties.

[45]Kellner notes that some of these poems were published in 1938 by the International Workers' Organization as *A New Song*, while others appeared posthumously in *Good Morning, Revolution* (see *Letters*, p. 138 n.6).

81

Hughes, and Blanche sought Van Vechten's assistance with every other African American writer the firm encountered.[46] Thus his role with Knopf, though carefully guarded, clearly went beyond a merely advisory position, and comprises an important aspect of Van Vechten's extensive involvement with black artists.

IV.

Hisao Kishimoto writes that Van Vechten demonstrated a "steady, unswerving belief that prejudice must be eliminated."[47] Van Vechten's involvement with African Americans may have been "steady," but his contributions to the Harlem Renaissance appear to have been a mixed blessing. In addition to the much-discussed sensationalism of *Nigger Heaven*, the correspondence between Van Vechten and Blanche Knopf demonstrates that he played a key role in repressing what might have proven to be an important examination of African American artists during the Harlem Renaissance. Furthermore, due to his free rein with Knopf, Van Vechten was influential in promoting or curbing the careers of several aspiring black writers. Just as Van Vechten seems to have had a mixture of both magnanimous and scandalous intentions for *Nigger Heaven* and his parties, so it is with the question of his work for the Harlem Renaissance on the whole. Yet while his character sometimes got in the way of his work for the movement, for the most part his intentions appear to have been noble. Of course, judging the racial attitudes of an earlier time is a thorny business, but it appears that Van Vechten's interest in and admiration for black artists was lifelong and genuine, and his ceaseless efforts on behalf of African Americans are all the more impressive since so many had disparaged his Harlem novel. While Van Vechten made some questionable decisions, of which his correspondence with Blanche Knopf provides evidence, he seems to have grown in his relationship with African Americans, respecting and appreciating their culture increasingly over the years.

Through his relationship with the Knopf firm, Van Vechten exerted a crucial influence on black writers of the 1920s and beyond. The fact that he voluntarily though secretly did so much work for the Knopfs indicates that he relished his role as a molding force of the movement. He summed up his relationship to the Harlem Renaissance in a letter to Alfred Knopf in 1962:

---

[46]The extent of Blanche's reliance on Van Vechten is truly extraordinary; a note Van Vechten wrote to his wife indicates that this reliance went beyond professional affairs to include emotional needs, for he told Fania that Blanche had divulged to him intimate details of her marriage. (*Letters*, p. 75).

[47]Hisao Kishimoto, *Carl Van Vechten: The Man and His Role in the Harlem Renaissance* (Tokyo: Seibido, 1983), p. 40.

82

You started something when you published a book by Walter White.
Then you introduced me to Walter & HE introduced me to James
Weldon Johnson, Langston Hughes and ever so many more and I
eventually wrote Nigger Heaven. Well what we started has eventually progressed to James Baldwin, John A. Williams, and JOHN
OLIVER KILLENS. . . . The Negro has at last learned to say what
is really on his mind . . . and I am proud that you and I started a
movement that has become so lusty."

Many critics would be uncomfortable with this self-congratulatory report, for
while some enlightened whites like Knopf and Van Vechten improved the
chances for African Americans to reach a wide audience, it was the creative
efforts of the artists that ultimately made up the Harlem Renaissance. Still,
through his many articles, photographs, and parties Van Vechten left an
impressive record of enterprise in furthering the visibility and esteem of
African American artistic culture in the United States, and his work for Knopf
represents an important, if little-known, aspect of this enterprise.

⁴⁸*Letters*, p. 288.

83

PATRONAGE AND THE HARLEM RENAISSANCE: YOU GET WHAT YOU PAY FOR

By Ralph D. Story

The New Negro is not to me a group of writers centered in Harlem during the second half of the twenties. Most of the writers were not Harlemites; much of the best writing was not about Harlem, which was the show-window, the cashier's till, but no more Negro America than New York is America.
— Sterling Brown (1955)[1]

Why was it that the Renaissance of literature, which began among Negroes ten years ago, has never taken real and lasting root? It was because it was a transplanted and exotic thing. It was a literature written for the benefit of white people and at the behest of white readers, and started out privately from the white point of view. It never had a real Negro constituency, and it did not grow out of the inmost heart and frank experiences of Negroes; on such an artificial basis no real literature can grow. — W. E. B. Du Bois (1933)[2]

Very few writers have had to confront the issue of patron-artist relations as did Langston Hughes (1902-1967) at the end of the Harlem Renaissance (HR). The preceding commentary of Brown and Du Bois, two of the most eminent black scholars ever, and Hughes' particular case reveal that he was faced with more than just a personal decision. His choice to disassociate himself from his patron, Charlotte Osgood Mason, would also have psychological, cultural, racial, and political implications for generations of black writers. Indeed, Hughes, as many other black American writers have discovered, essentially could have threatened his career by severing his ties with this rich white widow who liked to be referred to as "Godmother" by the artists she sponsored. Thus, despite the existence of nu-

---

[1] Sterling Brown, *Southern Road* (Boston: Beacon, 1974), p. xxxiv.

[2] W. E. B. Du Bois, "The Negro College," in *A Reader*, ed. Meyer Weinberg (New York: Harper, 1970), p. 181.

merous celebratory critiques of the HR, and despite the glossing over of the role of patronage during the era of the "New Negro," it is impossible to say that the art produced by black Americans between 1920 and 1932 would have ever made it into print without the support of rich whites. Their motives for providing such support, however, were varied, and their desire to control the art and the artists was extremely heavy-handed. They wanted to make sure that they "got what they paid for." As Hughes' biographer, Faith Berry, makes clear, Charlotte Osgood Mason had specific ideas about black folk and black art: ". . . she subscribed to his [her deceased husband, Dr. Rufus Osgood Mason's] beliefs that the most magnificent manifestations of the spiritual were found in "primitive" "child races."[3]

Mason, starting in the summer of 1927, would eventually subsidize Langston Hughes for three years. She felt that of all the HR writers, Hughes possessed the most natural gift and could delineate her wishes about primitivism through his art. But their relationship proved to be extremely constraining for Hughes; Mason required strict obedience. She requested, for instance, that Hughes write her almost daily. She also "chose the books he read, the music he listened to, and the plays he saw."[4] In fact, Mason would soon ask Hughes to answer only *her* letters, pressure him to change the title of his novel, try to select a composer for one of his earliest plays, and take Zora Neale Hurston's side against him in their infamous dispute over their collaborative theatrical work, *Mule Bone*.[5] When Hughes finally realized the price he was paying for Mason's financial and maternalistic support and ended their relationship in 1930, Mason predicted his downfall:

She lectured him on the limitations of his talent, reminded him

[3] Faith Berry, *Langston Hughes: Before and Beyond Harlem* (Westport, Conn.: Lawrence Hill, 1983), p. 87.

[4] Ibid., p. 92.

[5] Ibid., p. 102.

of all the things she had done for him. But for her he would never have written his novel. But for her his foster brother would not have had the privilege of attending a New England school. She predicted that, lacking her support, Hughes would fall. . . . The unpleasant goodbye was traumatic for Hughes and irrevocable for both concerned.[6]

The Hughes-Mason relationship was merely one of many similar artist-patron associations that marked the second phase of the HR: a phase during which Harlem was "in" and rich whites, for a variety of not too altruistic reasons, flocked to Harlem to participate in the Harlem nightlife. The underwriting of black art, however, was just as much a matter of Lost Generation sentiment for things primitive and "natural" (which was fading from American life as a result of industrialization) as it was an open acknowledgement of black creativity. As David Levering Lewis contends in his informative and entertaining *When Harlem Was in Vogue* (1981), patronage was widespread but rarely if ever admitted:

> White capital and influence were crucial, and the white presence, at least in the early years, hovered over the New Negro world of art and literature like a benevolent censor, politely but pervasively setting the outer limits of its creative boundaries.[7]

Another HR writer who had patrons, but of a different sort, was the Jamaican-born Claude McKay (1889-1947).

Unlike Hughes, McKay's linkages and associations to and with whites were with those of "the left," principally Max Eastman, then editor of the radical periodical *The Liberator*. McKay made his way to New York after his "vagabond" days in other parts of the United States. He had an affection for his leftist colleagues and friends while simultaneously he was alienated from the New Negro group just as much for his age as his Jamaican and radical roots:

> I was an older man and not regarded as a member of the renais-

---

[6] Ibid., p. 107.

[7] David Levering Lewis, *When Harlem Was in Vogue* (New York: Knopf, 1981), p. 98.

sance, but more as a forerunner. Indeed, some of them [those abroad in Paris during McKay's sojourn there] had aired their resentment of my intrusion from abroad into the renaissance set-up.[8]

In his autobiography, *A Long Way from Home* (1937), McKay did not really describe or allude to patronage as a separate issue or critique those most responsible for giving him the opportunities to display his work. He generally had very warm words for most of his associates during the era; he characterized whatever rifts he had with those at *The Liberator* as artistic differences or a clash of personalities, e.g., his disagreements with Michael Gold over which pieces should go into the magazine.[9] Instead, he leveled his sharpest criticism at the HR writers for what he considered their mistaken ideas about the New Negro renaissance:

> The Negroes were under the delusion that when a lady from Park Avenue [Mason lived on Park Ave.] or from Fifth Avenue, or a titled European, became interested in Negro art and invited Negro artists to her home, that was a token of Negroes breaking into upper-class white society. I don't think that it ever occurred to them that perhaps such white individuals were searching for a social and artistic significance in Negro art which they could not find in their own society.[10]

McKay's assertion is obviously a reference to Mason and Hughes; yet it also underscores his accurate and less sentimental understanding of what patrons wanted from black art and artists. But McKay also had an association, despite his failure to mention it, with the patron Mason:

> McKay, another "precious child," was one of Locke's . . . stiffest challenges. . . . But after a few months of righteous silence, he and Locke were corresponding again, for McKay was always careful not to break irrevocably with people who could help him. As for Godmother, the poet accepted her checks gratefully and wrote adoringly, thanking her for news clippings and renewed magazine subscriptions, and in return penning vivid descriptions

[8] Claude McKay, *A Long Way from Home* (New York: Harcourt, 1970), p. 321.

[9] Ibid., pp. 50-56.

[10] Ibid., p. 321.

of "primitive" life in North Africa.[11]

One of the most interesting comments McKay makes on the Harlem artists is his revelation of intense competition between HR writers for the leading role in the New Negro play. In essence, the Awakening writers were engaged in a battle for ascendancy to a separate and elevated status as *the* black writer most respected by white patrons, critics, editors and publishers; they sought the designation of "best" of the brightest:

> Also, among the Negro artists there was much of that Uncle Tom attitude which works like Satan against the idea of a co-herent and purposeful Negro group. Each one wanted to be the first Negro, the one Negro, and the only Negro *for the whites* instead of for their group. Because an unusual number of them were receiving grants to do creative work, they actually and naively believed that Negro artists as a group would always be treated differently from white artists and be protected by pow-erful white patrons.[12]

McKay's last point about "protection" seems just as much a political critique as an aesthetic one. For early in McKay's career, as a result of his most famous poem, "If We Must Die," as well as his associations with Communists, Marxists and black nationalists (he wrote articles for Marcus Garvey's *Negro World*), he was branded "bitter" and a black radical.[13] Consequently, his relations with whites were more politically dangerous and radical than those of his pro-integrationist HR counterparts. But McKay would discover, as did Richard Wright some twenty years later, that the American Communist Party was supportive of black artists only if those artists parroted the party line in their public speeches and their work:

> He returned to Paris ill and with the American Communists

[11] Lewis, pp. 153-54.

[12] McKay, p. 322.

[13] See U. S. Congress, Senate, 66th Congress, 1st Session, Senate Document No. 153 (Washington, D.C.: U.S. Government Printing Office, 1919) for a discussion of the work of McKay and other HR writers the Congress classified as "Radical" and "Seditious."

hostile toward him for refusing to join their ranks and submit to party discipline.[14]

A larger issue, however, as it pertains to white patronage—and I am saying that radical whites and the Communist Party in the U.S. constituted a support group, a patron group, and publication outlets for black writers—is that neither shared ideological beliefs nor aesthetic sensibilities would alter the patron(s)' desire to have the artist re-create what they viewed as important about the black experience. For the HR writers and painters, once they agreed to a patron-artist relationship—especially a financial one—it seemed to obligate them to produce a certain kind of product that would meet the patron(s)' approval. Hence, it is difficult to imagine just what kind of art might have been produced had not the artists been under such covert pressure to please their supporters. The best example of this transactional arrangement was the contract which Charlotte Osgood Mason had her lawyer create for Zora Neale Hurston, whom she subsidized for five years. Only a portion of it is provided below:

> This agreement made and entered into this 1st day of December, 1927, by and between Charlotte L. Mason, of New York City, first party, and Zora Hurston, of the same place, second party:
>
> *WITNESSETH*:
>
> Whereas said first party, Charlotte L. Mason is desirous of obtaining and compiling certain data relating to the music, folklore, poetry, voodoo, conjure, manifestations of art, and kindred matters existing among American Negroes but is unable because of the pressure of other matters to undertake the collection of this information in person. . . .[15]

Although Zora Neale Hurston would be able to create without worrying about finances, the actual Afro-American artifacts which could have been used to produce her art would, ultimately, belong to Mason. Such artifacts could have en-

[14] McKay, p. xiv.
[15] Berry, p. 90.

ded up in a proposed museum for Afro-American art that
Mason's procurer for the arts, Alain Locke, worked on creating during the latter years of the HR.

In his role as Mason's procurer of black art no HR figure
is more representative of patron-middleman-artist relations
that the ubiquitous Locke. He had the dubious role of carrying out Mason's wishes regarding the most well-known
writers and artists of the era: Langston Hughes, Zora Neale
Hurston, Claude McKay, and the painter/illustrator Aaron
Douglas. Operating in the shadows of Du Bois and Charles
S. Johnson (who was singularly responsible for bringing together quite a few artists and publishers via his *Opportunity* magazine awards banquets),[16] Locke was able to carry
out his personal vision of *The New Negro* (1925) with financial support that, at least for a time, seemed unlimited.
As Mason's steerer he was responsible for direct communications to the artists which not only fulfilled Mason's
wishes but his own aesthetic ideas as well:

> Locke's bondage to Charlotte Mason, despite patronizing lec-
> tures and occasional acts of rank tyranny, was more apparent
> than real. He walked a tightrope between obsequious accomoda-
> tion to the old lady and nervous fidelity to his own beliefs, dis-
> sembling masterfully and taking the cash. His strategem was to
> use Mason's money to prove how like well-bred, intelligent
> whites, well-bred, intelligent Afro-Americans were.[17]

In fact, more than occasionally, Locke functioned as a kind
of "spy" for Mason on those artists who had defected from
the Mason camp, such as Langston Hughes. Years after
Hughes severed his ties with Mason, Locke was still report-
ing regularly to his Godmother on Hughes' work and activities with some of his correspondence personally vindictive
and cruel:

> Locke, still harboring deep resentment for Hughes and pereni-
> ally expressing it in letters to Godmother, had even harsher
> words for *The Ways of White Folks* (1934) in his correspon-

[16] Lewis, p. 95.

[17] Ibid., p. 154.

dence to her. . . . Forever eager to turn up anything he could to give Langston a verbal flogging, that March (1934) he had sent Godmother a clipping of Hughes's caustic essay "Would You Fight for the U.S. in the Next War?"—with a note attached: "The latest blast from Langston—in which his megolamania grows to ridiculous proportions—Aesop's Frog."[18]

Fortunately for Zora Neale Hurston, Locke's support was, typically, unwavering; quite possibly though, he supported Hurston because her loyalty to their mutual benefactor was unquestionable. Note Locke's support of Hurston in the *Mule Bone* incident as well as his disparagement of Arthur Spingarn (of the NAACP and Hughes' lawyer in the case):

> I don't think I should write the Cleveland people [the Jelliffes, founders of Karamu House]—but just send Z[ora]'s introduction, showing absolute confidence in her. . . . Moreover, Locke's willingness to embrace the doctrinaire anti-Semitism of Mrs. Mason would have added to the poet's disillusionment and disappointment with the critic-professor (and Rhodes Scholar) he had once trusted as a friend. Locke's remark to her—"it shows what you say about jews"—was meant to cast an aspersion on Arthur Spingarn, whom the professor resented for wiring him that Langston had justifiable rights to *Mule Bone*.[19]

Although Locke and McKay interacted with one another cordially in public, they engaged in a rather protracted disagreement over Locke's alteration of McKay's poem "White House." Locke made it plural, changing it to "White Houses," and in the process this enraged McKay:

> I wrote him saying that the idea that my poem had reference to the official residence of the President of the United States was ridiculous. . . . It changed the whole symbolic intent and meaning of the poem. . . . But Dr. Locke high-handedly used his substitute title of "White Houses" in all the editions of his anthology.[20]

Just as Locke had secured the services of Hughes, Hurston, and McKay for Mason, he would also get the painter Aaron Douglas on Mason's payroll:

[18] Berry, p. 205.

[19] Ibid., p. 116.

[20] McKay, p. 314.

Painting murals at a Harlem club, Aaron Douglas remembered
being ordered down from his scaffolding after his repeated re-
fusals to appear at 399 Park Avenue compelled Godmother to
motor to Harlem. To his later regret, Douglas became a retainer
in Mason's court, frequently compelled to delay and even with-
draw from major commissions offending his patron's sense of
what was "proper Negro art"—until, at last, Douglas fled to
Merion, Pennsylvania, on a fellowship at the New Barnes
Foundation.[21]

Locke's manner and extremely refined and sophisticated
appearance, as well as his impeccable academic credentials,
clearly overshadowed his behind-the-scenes role as a mid-
dleman between black artists and his patron/Godmother. In
retrospect, Locke's roving ambassadorship of the HR obscured the most obvious, yet far-reaching, historical precedent for his true role—procurer of the black arts. For
Locke's relationship to Mason is clearly similar to those
"anonymous *sensali*" who worked on behalf of the Medici
family in fifteenth- and sixteenth-century Florence, Italy.
Indeed, if Mason perceived herself as a twentieth-century
financial and spiritual Medici for obscure yet soon-to-be-fa-
mous black essayists, poets, novelists, folklorists, and painters, then certainly Locke, who is sometimes credited with
coining the term "Renaissance," saw himself as a twentieth-
century Paolo del Sera. Locke, like del Sera, was both *dilettante* and *professori* and acquired numerous works of art
on behalf of Mason as did del Sera for Leopoldo de Medici.[22] Locke was also noted for his "good taste and incisive
understanding of the local art market," a characterization
identical to del Sera's.[23] If there was to be a Renaissance,
Locke probably reasoned that someone would have to be
the courtier and courier to secure its financial and aesthetic
underpinnings. He seemed, for reasons of upbringing, personality, and his simultaneous beliefs in racial integration

[21] Lewis, p. 152.

[22] See Edward L. Goldberg, *Patterns in Late Medici Art Patronage* (Princeton,
N.J.: Princeton Univ. Press, 1983).

[23] Ibid., p. 57.

and the significance of folk art, to be ideally suited for the job. Nonetheless, just as the Medicis have come to be known as rather infamous owners of art and artists, so too would figures like Mason. In typical *quid pro quo* fashion she wanted to play, like other white patrons of black arts and artists, a major role in the creation of black art and not just be a monetary nursemaid for its growth:

> Nor was the Negro artist assumed to be the final judge of truth and relevant statement. The patron—as best illustrated by Van Vechten—was a teacher, guide and judge; his search for authentic Negro voices was dictated by his own needs. . . . But white guidance and encouragement probably prevented those few men and women of real talent from wrestling with their senses and plodding through to those statements which the thrust of their lives and experience would force them to make. Whatever other burdens Negro artists carried, this arrangement stigmatized Negro poetry and prose of the 1920s as being an artistic effort that was trying to be like something other than itself.[24]

One of the more significant means, beyond the Locke-Mason connection, for artists and patrons to come together for mutual benefit during the HR were the *Opportunity* awards banquets. Ironically though, many of those who did in fact win awards but who did not have the financial ties to white patrons beyond the banquets achieved their place in the limelight only during the HR and plunged—literally like shooting stars—into obscurity when the Great Depression had a firm grip on the country. Writers like Joseph Cotter, Jr., Warren MacDonald, John Matheus and Frank Horne, all *Opportunity* awards winners, for instance, are rarely even mentioned in the chronicles of the HR or its lists of literary figures. Eventually, after 1933, the "Urban League would mount one more annual literary gala before concluding that the money and interest to sustain the tradition were lacking."[25]

To be sure, those artists who were able to cultivate sepa-

---

[24] Nathan Huggins, *Harlem Renaissance* (New York: Oxford Univ. Press, 1971), pp. 128-29.

[25] Lewis, p. 294.

rate ties to individual white patrons were obviously better off when the interest of large numbers of whites in black art faded after the stock market crash of 1929. It could also be said, however, that any folk art which is not sustained and/or supported by the folk it purportedly represents and is instead bought and paid for by significant others is inevitably and inherently doomed to failure. It is not surprising that we know so much about Hughes, McKay, and Hurston and so little about Horne and Matheus. At any rate there are clearly some lessons which can be learned from the failure of the Harlem Renaissance to sustain itself.

A primary point would obviously be the need for art and artists to be independent and autonomous if their work is to be inspirational and truly representative. Moreover, as this pertains to black people, if they want believable imagery of themselves and consider those images to be important, and if they desire art about themselves that is uplifting and seeks to deliver the "truth," then they have to be willing to pay for it, institutionalize it, and support its creators. Yet, some of the tensions between black creative artists and their older black intellectual peers were sparked by the issue of artistic freedom and whether the black art they created did more harm than good for the black masses. Ironically, however, the black middle class, the group most desirous of black artists creating "uplift" fiction depicting refined and "successful" blacks in the HR, was too small in number and lacked the financial clout to support the black artists and art produced in the 1920s. Then, as now, without this group's support—the group most able to create, financially sustain, and promote black publishing institutions and creative outlets—the black artist is forced to go to the dominant culture for the publication of her/his work and the recognition and visibility that accrues from such critically recognized endeavors. Thus, white patronage of black art during the Harlem Renaissance was crucial if the art were to ever be exposed. Nonetheless, such aesthetic and commercial support from either left or right political circles and/or individuals inherently makes it difficult for artists to be truly free to create. It is clear today, as it has been throughout the twentieth century, that black writers need black publishers of books and periodicals if their art is to be honest and uplifting for their people.

University of Michigan
Ann Arbor, Michigan

Onita Estes-Hicks

JEAN TOOMER AND THE POLITICS AND POETICS OF NATIONAL IDENTITY

J EAN TOOMER'S PLACE IN THE WORLD of letters rests on *Cane,* the author's profound statement on the quest for African-American identity. Published in 1923, *Cane* was composed during a year of intense creativity which followed Toomer's three-month stay in Sparta, Georgia in 1921, during which time he served as Acting Principal in an industrial and agricultural school. As had happened to Du Bois in rural Tennessee, in backwards, poverty-ridden, oppressive Georgia, Toomer touched base with the deep roots of Black culture under conditions which recalled the slave past. The writer celebrated that return to the foundations of Black life in *Cane,* charting his own adventures on southern soil, contrasting the conditions of Blacks in the North, and positing cultural / geographical tradeoffs in search of a whole, healthy Black identity. Compressed yet exhaustive, *Cane* would be the author's main creative statement on African-American identity. That splendid work justly merits the acclaim it received at the time of its publication and the place it now occupies in the literary canon. An experimenter in life and in letters, *Cane*'s author realized that *Cane* need not and could not be duplicated; he next focused his energies on mastering the poetics of national identity, a project which had captivated his imagination during his apprentice years. Little attention has been given to this aspect of Jean Toomer's literary and personal life, although the author's earliest excursions into writing centered on the challenges of national identity or what he called "the new world soul." Additionally, Toomer intermittently wrestled with the composition of a work on national identity for over fifteen years, ultimately achieving a sterling measure of success in his magnum opus, "Blue Meridian," published in 1936.

Even before he began composing *Cane,* the Washingtonian explored the poetics of national identity in a poem entitled "The First American." This Whitmanesque fragment assayed the possibility and process of constructing an inclusive national character by merging the best racial characteristics of America's three racial groupings—Black, Red, White. This achievement would eventuate in "The First American"—a being free of the conditions of class and color, moving American nationality from theory to fact, from ideality to actuality.

Toomer's deep interest in the question of national identity stemmed not only from his own multi-racial heritage, but also from his early life in turn-of-the-century Washington, D.C., where he was reared among a significant mulatto population, some of whom—such as the Grimkes—maintained family ties across the color line.[1] Toomer's grandfather, Reconstruction politician, P. B. S. Pinchback, was himself the offspring of a long and stable Black-White relationship between a wealthy southern planter, Major William Pinchback, and his emancipated slave-mistress, Eliza Benton Stewart, a woman of Indian, Caucasian, and African descent. The Pinchbacks maintained ties for over eighteen years in two different states. They had eight children, two of whom, P. B. S. Pinchback and Napoleon, were sent by the father to Gilmore Academy, a private school in Cincinnati, famed for educating the mixed children of wealthy white men and African-American women. In addition to the Pinchbacks Jean Toomer's racial lineage consisted of other Black-White families, a condition which prompted his concern with national identity. Caucasian in appearance, Nathan Toomer, the writer's father, lived on both sides of the color line, while listed alternately as Black and mulatto in census data. Prior to marrying Nina Pinchback, Jean's mother, Nathan had been married to Amanda Dickson of Augusta, Georgia. The latter was the "natural" daughter of one of the wealthiest white men in the South, David Dickson, who claimed Amanda as his child in a deathbed confession, leaving her the major portion of his considerable wealth. Following the breakup of the Nathan Toomer-Nina Pinchback marriage, Nina's second husband was Archibald Combes, of New Jersey's famed and historic mulatto colony, Gouldtown, which had been settled by the descendants of a seventeenth-century African named Gold or Gould and the granddaughter of the Englishman Walt Fenwick, founder of southwestern New Jersey and friend of William Penn.[2] Either by the clerk's perception or by their own statements, both Archibald and Nina were listed as "white" on their marriage certificate.

[1] For additional information on black-white family relations see James Hugo Johnston, *Race Relations in Virginia and Miscegenation in the South* (Amherst, Mass.: University of Massachusetts Press, 1970), especially chapter Nine, "The White Man and His Negro Relations"; Carter G. Woodson, "The Beginnings of Miscegenation of Whites and Blacks," *Journal of Negro History,* 3 (1919); Caroline Day, *A Study of Some Negro-White Families in the United States* (Cambridge, Mass.: Peabody Museum, Harvard University, 1932); William Steward and Theophilus Steward, *Gouldtown, A Remarkable Settlement of Ancient Date* (Philadelphia: Lippincott, 1913); Joel Williamson, *New People: Miscegenation and Mulattoes in the United States* (Glencoe, Ill.: The Free Press, 1980).

[2] Steward and Steward, *Gouldtown.*

Toomer's complex racial background left him sceptical of racial labels and suspicious of a social system which designated people who were palpably "white" as "black." Like Richard Wright, who similarly could not understand why a woman of his grandmother's "white" complexion was labeled "colored," Toomer early in his life began seeing through the social construction of reality.[3] Race, Toomer was convinced, was a cultural, not a biological issue. Like many light-skinned Washingtonians of his time, Jean Toomer lived on both sides of the color line, as he so chose, exploiting his own biology to subvert the caprices of color. In Washington "functional passing"—to obtain jobs, to attend educational institutions, to secure entrance to entertainment facilities—had been raised to a fine art. Jean knew many Washingtonians who passed during the day to maintain jobs and who rode "uptown to the respite of a Negro home" at the end of the day, the situation faced by Vera, the central character in the author's short story "Withered Skin of Berries."[4] Mary Church Terrell, a friend of the Pinchbacks, whose daughters grew up with young Jean, reported that her daughters often utilized their white skin to purchase tickets for their "darker brothers."[5] Questions about race and nationality never came up at the University of Wisconsin. But before going off to college, the student had prepared himself to adopt the strategy of "functional passing," a resource which Gunner Myrdal noted was historically called upon by numerous light-skinned students in pre-integration America to avoid the added tensions of racial problems in university life.[6] In New York in the twenties, Toomer, Gorham Munson recalled, gained luncheon accommodations for Charles Johnson and Alain Locke by a functional pass. Moving easily across the color line, the writer, like Lear and Cordelia, regarded himself as one of "God's spies," garnering data on the human condition as race distorted it. Like another famous Shakesperian character, Jean Toomer often felt "what fools these mortals be." Seeing beyond race, he felt the nation and saw it off balance and off guard and culled his own sense of nation and national identity from hardcore experience.

Toomer's interest in national identity was further intensified by contemporary debates on American nationality. The depiction of national character framed "the battle of the books" which took place during the early years of the

[3] *Black Boy* (New York: Harper and Row, 1966 [1945]).
[4] Written in 1922, "Withered Skin of Berries" was published in *The Wayward and the Seeking: A Collection of Writings by Jean Toomer,* Darwin Turner, ed. (Washington, D.C.: Howard University Press, 1980).
[5] Mary Church Terrell, *A Colored Woman in a White World* (Washington, D.C.: Ransdall Inc. Publishing Co., 1940).
[6] Gunnar Myrdal, *An American Dilemma* (New York: Harper & Brothers, 1944), 65.

century. The moderns—heralded by Van Wyck Brooks, Randolph Bourne, and Waldo Frank—called for a "deprovincialization of the arts" and for a literature which reflected a more inclusive national character. The younger generation of writers, spurred on by the heavy waves of immigration which changed the face of America, succeeded in moving American letters from its New England base, making way for the depiction of other regions and other cultures. Deeply immersed in the social and cultural criticism of the period, the apprentice writer quickly perceived that the literary broadening of national identity should and must include the presence of the African-American. Having embarked on an intense reading program in contemporary criticism in 1921, Toomer became electrified by a passage from Waldo Frank's *Our America,* a highly influential manifesto which pleaded the modern's cause. Published in 1919, *Our America* examined the historical roots of American culture and included an analysis of the Native American and Jewish presence, Frank's attempt to expand the base of national character. An avowed cultural pluralist, Frank, who called himself "mystical," challenged writers to develop a "historical / anthropological" approach to American culture and character, one that would capture the unity-in-plurality that time and the mingling of cultures had produced in this country:

> Some day some one who is fitted for the task will take the subject matter of this Chapter and make a book of it. He will study the cultures of the German, the Latin, the Celt, The Slav, the Anglo-Saxon and the African on the American continent: plot their reactions one upon the other, and their disappearance as integral worlds in the vast puddling of our pioneering life.

Toomer was immensely impressed by *Our America's* brief put pioneering inclusion of the African presence as part of America's "buried cultures," and later used the concept of "buried cultures" in "Withered Skin of Berries," written in 1922. His own racial background included (among others) French, Indian, Anglo-Saxon and African, and he warmed to the recognition of complexity and diversity that an anthropological approach to American life promised. While sensing a radical breakthrough in Frank's brief acknowledgement of the African ethos, Toomer had been disappointed that the New Yorker had not matched his chapter-long discussions of Indian, Puritan, and Pioneer with a like chapter on the American Negro. "I missed your not having included the Negro in *Our America,*" he chastened Frank. "I have often wondered about it."[7]

[7] Letter to Waldo Frank, March 24, 1922. Waldo Frank Papers, University of Pennsylvania.

Frank welcomed the letter from Toomer and saw a veritable cultural goldmine in Toomer's complex background. "My own life," Toomer explained, "has been about equally divided between the two racial groups." The introductory letter continued:

> And the family, for the most part . . . has lived between the two worlds, now dipping into the Negro, now into the white. Some few are definitely white; others definitely colored. I alone have stood for a synthesis in the matters of mind and spirit analogous, perhaps, to the actual fact of at least six blood minglings.

"You're the sort of like one doesn't forget," Frank responded, encouraging further correspondence from the serious young Washington writer.[8] Toomer, Frank realized, was the-thing-in-itself—a walking symbol of the multi-cultural world which the moderns theorized they sought. Frank himself requested Toomer's assistance on a projected—but never completed—revision of *Our America*, which was to include the chapter on the American Negro. But Frank had in fact already abandoned the *Our America* "program"—a fact which Jean would not realize for another two years.

Frank's "buried cultures" passage was to serve as intellectual objective correlative for Toomer, giving programmatic shape and real-world substance to the complex of radical and subversive ideas with which the yet-unpublished-writer struggled. Invigorated by the encouragement of Frank, now a forgotten presence in American letters, but then a controversial and celebrated presence, Toomer appointed himself heir apparent to the "buried cultures" theme, which both personally and professionally struck a responsive chord, promising the possibility from moving Mixed America from underground to foreground. For him the double-consciousness produced by the national and the ethnic promised a *too*-ness. Unlike Du Bois and other members of the "tortured tenth," who regarded their twoness as a painful burden, Toomer, who had come under Dostoevski's influence, saw the heightening of consciousness caused by racial / social diversity as an exhilarating experience—the fortunate fate of modern man. He shared Hegel's view of America as the staging ground for a new world order and further intuited that the national-ethnic crucible would produce the futuristic, universal man. On these convictions, from his Washington base, the author plunged into the debates on national identity, positive that he spoke from a unique perspective. He engaged the New York writers in long, epistolary discussions on creativity and culture. By the time he had completed *Cane*,

[8] Jean Toomer Collection, Fisk University.

portions of which were published in the little magazines of the period, Toomer had an avid following awaiting him in New York.

In May of 1923, Toomer moved to New York, having notified his publisher Horace Liveright of two projects, the most serious of which focused on a novel on national identity. Correspondence with Frank, Munson, and other members of the Village coterie lead him to believe that he was entering a community of like-minded artists, committed to his vision. In New York, he soon discovered that the literary avant garde to whose program he had attached himself had become the descending wing of the modern movement. The program outlined in *Our America* had been abandoned by Frank himself, who was soon to leave America for Europe, convinced that he had won the battles but had lost the war. Of the Village writers only the desperate Hart Crane remained faithful to the cause of national identity, sharing notes and plans with Toomer on the ambitious project which became *The Bridge,* published only in 1930. Surveying his prospects from close encounters with literary New York, the newcomer soon realized that he was caught in a genuine crisis of literary development. He had exhausted the ethnic theme in *Cane;* moreover, he had deep doubts about the incipient Harlem Renaissance, whose sensationalism was at war with Toomer's seriousness. Yet the climate did not seem supportive of his national identity project.

Toomer's adjustments to literary New York and to life in Greenwich Village where he settled became immensely complicated by the love which erupted between him and psychologist Margaret Naumberg, the wife of Waldo Frank. Frank agreed to release Naumberg from a loveless marriage and voiced understanding of the Toomer-Naumburg love, but then turned hostile to Toomer, creating an underground climate of gossip and suspicion for which Frank was notorious. Toomer, new to the literary intrigue and malice of New York, became un-nerved by the behavior of Frank, trying on a number of occasions to bring Frank to terms with their disintegrating relationship. Toomer continued to struggle valiantly from May 1923 to January of 1924 with the national identity project, determined to find the "new world soul" in soul-less New York. He sketched out "notes for a novel," and wrote an exploratory essay which summarized the achievements of the moderns, clearing the way for a modern creative synthesis such as he envisioned accomplishing in those "notes." But the times were out of joint. In addition to the break with Frank, who had secured the contract for *Cane* and had written its "Foreword," Toomer next found himself in an agon with his publisher over the advertising strategy for *Cane,* a dispute which touched deeply the question of Toomer's identity.

In August of 1923, while vacationing in Ellenville, New York, where he had gone to seek respite from Frank's hostility and from the fallout which attended the collapse of the Village literary front, Toomer turned his hand to composing an autobiographical sketch, requested by Liveright for inclusion in review copies of *Cane.* The ensuing controversy concerning the material proved to be a traumatic form of experiential learning for Jean, forcing him to see that a wide gap existed between him and his presumably avant-garde publisher. More significantly, this Liveright incident began undermining Toomer's faith in art as he needed to practice it. In advance of the request for an autobiographical sketch, Liveright had taken out an ad in *The New York Times,* which appeared on August 19th, publicizing *Cane* as "a book about Negroes by a Negro." In an early instance of "blacksploitation," the publisher had determined to use the racial line as the authenticating principle of *Cane* in his advertising program. Toomer had been distressed when Frank chose to "feature Negro" in *Cane's* "Foreword," having preferred that his book appear without racial identification, as Chesnutt's works initially had been sent forth. However, both Liveright and Frank had commercial considerations in mind and felt the racial identification would help sales of *Cane* and of Frank's new novel, *Holiday.* Their advertising strategy encompassed the simultaneous release of two books on the Black South, with the "Foreword" to one book written by the author of the other. In seeking the sketch from Toomer, Liveright, whose intensive use of advertising was innovative in a publishing world slow to conceive of books as commodities, conjectured the autobiographical enclosure as part of his advertising strategy.

Toomer welcomed the chance to present his life to the public and seized the occasion as an opportunity to advance the persona he wished to create for the "new world soul" book to which he was deeply committed. With these ideas in mind, Jean prepared a submission following his 1922 letter to *The Liberator,* cataloguing the various racial lines in his background. In response, Village poet, Isidore Schneider, who worked in Liveright's publicity department, thanked his fellow-writer for the prompt cooperation and indicated satisfaction with the contents, although not the length, of the piece:

> Thanks for acting so promptly and helpfully on my suggestion for a story on your career. What you have is, of course, too full for general newspaper use, but I think it can be excerpted to make a very acceptable piece. To the Associated Negro Press it is going complete, and I am in hopes of having it given equal prominence in some of the magazines.[9]

[9] *Ibid.*

Schneider additionally inquired about the novel-in-progress, the work which relied on the persona Toomer had developed in the copy sent for reviews. "Your account of your plans interested me personally, very much," the immigrant writer advised the disciple of Whitman, "and if we can get together again I should like to hear more about your new book."

Having received Schneider's gracious acceptance of the material, Toomer was angry and confused by a subsequent letter from Horace Liveright, redirecting the focus of the article. Promising that review copies were to be put in the mail that week, the entrepreneur-publisher returned the copy. The tone of Liveright's letter betrays that businessman's exasperation with the complexity of Toomer's life; the contents, the publisher's intent to reduce a multi-racial background to one-dimensional ethnicity:

> I'm returning this to you because I want to make a few suggestions. In the first place, I think it is at least one page too long. Second, I feel that right at the very start there should be a definite note sounded about your colored blood. To me this is the real human interest of your story and I don't see why you should dodge it. Of course it is difficult to say where this would be published. My own idea would be to have a little pamphlet made of it right away and inserted in the review books as they go out. Will you let me know what you think of this plan?[10]

Toomer took a few days to let the publisher know what he thought of his plans, sorting out the various feelings the letter generated. His response—detailed and complex—reveals the concerns of a serious man resisting the falsification of his life's history. Moreover, close scrutiny of the incident in the context of that crucial summer shows a committed artist grappling with a creeping and unnerving understanding of the extent to which extra-literary motives could distort and control the contours of his artistic career. His September 5th return letter to Liveright began:

> Your letter of August 29th on hand. First I want to make a general statement from which detailed statements will follow. My racial composition and my position in the world are realities which I alone may determine. Just what these are, I sketched in for you that day I had lunch with you. As a unit in the social milieu, I expect and demand acceptance of myself on their basis. I do not expect to be told what I should consider myself to be.[11]

[10] *Ibid.*
[11] *Ibid.*

Toomer then took umbrage at Liveright's dishonorably accusing him of dodging the racial issue:

> Nor do I expect you as my publisher, and I hope as my friend, to either directly or indirectly state that this basis contains any element of dodging. In fact, if my relationship with you is to be what I'd like it to be, I must insist that you never use such a word, such a thought again.

The September letter then drew a fine line between the author's inviolable rights as a human being and his obligation to the promotion strategy of a commercial publishing house:

> As a B and L author, I make the distinction between my fundamental position and the position which your publicity department may wish to establish for me in order that *Cane* reach as large a public as possible. In this connection, I've told you, I have told Messrs. Tobey and Schneider to make use of whatever factors you wish.

Eschewing that role which Leslie Fiedler years later brilliantly characterized as "the pimp of the particular," the poet of Washington established independence from the publisher's intentional use of racial exploitation:

> Feature Negro if you wish, but do not expect me to feature it in advertisements for you. For myself, I have sufficiently featured Negro in *Cane*.

Toomer's letter concluded on a promise to "go over the sketch and revise it as near as possible in accordance with your wishes." But he insisted that the publisher honor the distinction between advertising and reviewing. It was acceptable that Liveright devise advertising copy along racial lines if he so chose. Toomer felt convinced that the community of reviewer-writers would see his multi-racial background as an interesting and needed addition to the contemporary art scene and wanted to impart that information to them.

Records indicate that the disputed pamphlet did in fact accompany review copies of *Cane*, although a sample has not been located.[12] The heated exchange alerted Toomer that his own publisher opposed the literary persona that was the genius and genesis of the national identity novel. Moreover, Toomer sensed the hand of Waldo Frank at work behind the desired contents of the sketch. Frank, Toomer recalled, had insisted on racially characterizing the author of *Cane* in that work's "Foreword," and had written Jean of Liveright's plans to get his assistance in "creating a Negro market for *Holiday*."[13] Toomer's anger

[12] Interview, Victor Schmalzer, Norton/Liveright Publishing Company.
[13] Toomer Collection.

toward both Frank and Liveright was intensified by the two men's participation in a 1922 trip to South Carolina, where Frank, with Toomer's assistance, had successfuly "passed for Negro," in order to get material for *Holiday*. That trip had provided ample measure of the ambiguity of race in America and had given both Frank and the publisher grounds upon which to develop a more humane and sophisticated approach to the complexity of Toomer's racial background. Additionally, Jean was galled by the arrogance and duplicity of the two men, who, while proclaiming themselves high priests of art, were, in practice, subjecting the Washingtonian's embryonic career to the whims of segregation and discrimination. To identify him as a Negro writer in pre-integration America was to throw him and his art to the caprices of a yet deeply racist society, an act Toomer would perhaps have expected and accepted of men of less pretense. In the context of that crucial midseason, the new writer needed the imaginative act of grace which, in sexist England, had given Mary Ann Evans space to produce the masterpieces of George Eliot. In contrast, under pressure of their perceived interests, Frank and Liveright ignored Toomer's precarious position, remaining insensitive to the implications of their actions on the newcomer's mind, life, and art. That behavior created an environment of anxiety and doubt which seriously affected Jean's attitude toward his work. Moreover, the incident dramatically forced a yet-insular mind to see that the author and the publisher of *Our America* had but a verbal commitment to the national identity question, the pursuit of which was leading Toomer into an existential void. "No one there spoke to my condition," the poet later wrote of that period, using the lamentable language of George Fox to capture the void of that barren season.[14] So that winter, Toomer began deconstructing the poet in himself, deciding, like Fitzgerald's Basil Duke, that since he could not be the type of artist he needed to be, he would then become nothing but a man.

Toomer had fallen prey to that winter's discontent when G. I. Gurdjieff, Director and Founder of the Institute for the Harmonious Development of Man arrived in New York from France towards the end of 1923. Entering in the wake of the collapse of the avant garde, Gurdjieff, who called himself Beelzebub, found a host of dejected souls and weary bodies languishing in their broken tower, seeking refuge from the backlash which the bourgeoisie inflicted on the aesthetic movement that notorious winter. Toomer warmed to the possibilities of the Institute upon reading the Prospectus distributed in trendy bookstores and other radical / liberal thoroughfares. While ignorant of the

---

[14] *Ibid.*

Institute's founder, the poet knew that Gurdjieff had been the mentor of Ouspensky, whose *Tertium Organum* had animated late night discussions in the Village upon his arrival in the Spring. Ouspensky proclaimed the existence of a higher race of men / women and held self-development as the beauty of existence. Gurdjieff's Prospectus, not only affirmed humankind's potential for development, but, more compelling to Toomer, the Institute proposed a path, a method to synchronize belief and practice. With a deep-felt need for a community of like-minded folk and his conviction that he had come to an end, Toomer responded to the Institute's call. Accompanied by Naumburg, who also shared his excitement, Jean attended the Demonstration given by Gurdjieff and his pupils at Webster Hall.

Responses to the Webster Hall demonstrations revealed Toomer's need for a community bound together by values—such as the talented tenth environment against which he had rebelled but whose claim on him would remain indelible. The Washington of his youth and the Pinchback household had engendered models of masculine mastery, and in the Gurdjieff of that performance there loomed the flickerings of Pinchback of Bacon Street, whose values and supreme self-sufficiency Toomer yet respected, although he had rejected the grandfather's way. These memories and longings, operating in conscious and subliminal forms, haunted the writer, who contrasted the world of art as he had discovered its operations in New York with the aspirations he had levied against the art enterprise. Later he wrote:

> With an intensity of experience such as I have seldom known I distilled the essence of the literary and art world I came in contact with. With the result that I saw with unmistakable clarity the truth that neither art nor literature were doing for men and women who engaged in them what was most necessary in life . . . namely providing them with a constructive and whole way of thinking.

Severing the pain and the confusion of that cruel midseason, on July 19, Toomer abandoned his quest for the new world soul and sailed to Fontainebleau to scale the magic mountain of the Institute for the Harmonious Development of Man. An unpublished poem from that period, here entitled "That Cruel Midseason," preserves that metaphoric moment and also contains the misgivings which the anguished poet in Toomer registered against the actions of the man:

> My will has ever been a pliant thing
> To loss of leaves,
> Knowing new leaves would come,

Knowing, in a mind superior to mine,
The purpose of it all;
Now some blight has struck
And will would hold,
Hold leaves against withering.
What cruel mid-season is this,
(No ecstasy of ferment)
That the sun upon my roots is torture.
Leaves fall,
A sound scratches against the hollow winds,
It is my call for soil to cover me.[15]

The writer remained in the Gurdjieff experience for a decade—from 1924 to 1934. In short time he had become second in command in the Gurdjieff work in this country, leading workshops on self-development, raising funds to help maintain the Institute, writing. He himself developed a loyal group of supporters and devoted himself to his groups. In between the demands of the Gurdjieff work he completed a number of manuscripts, all of which were hastily composed and never published. Yet the aborted 1924 project on national identity continued to haunt him. Toomer saw clearly—as Harold Cruse was later to argue persuasively—that the national identity question was at the soul of a genuine American cultural movement.[16] In his own way, Toomer substituted the Gurdjieff experience for the national identity project. In fact, his decade-long commitment to Gurdjieff is best understood as a desperate attempt to environ himself in a context which kept alive his faith in universalism upon which the national identity project rested. Returning to the ideas of 1924 intermittently, he finally completed "Blue Meridian," a poem on national identity.

Published under the title "Brown River, Smile," a short version of "Blue Meridian" first appeared in *Pagany*, in 1932, during Toomer's marriage to the writer, Marjorie Latimer.[17] Some form of the poem had been completed as early as summer of 1931, when Jean used the existing sections as title poem for a volume which he sent to Harper. Following Harper's rejection, Toomer received another expression of regrets from Harrison Smith, which found 1932 "bad times for poetry."[18] But Kreymborg *et al.* introduced "Blue Meridian" to

[15] *Ibid.*
[16] *The Crisis of the Negro Intellectual* (New York: William Morrow, 1967).
[17] Toomer and American writer, Marjorie Latimer, married in 1931; she died in childbirth in 1932.
[18] Toomer Collection.

the public, carrying the poem in a version which ran over 700 lines in their 1936 annual, *The American Caravan.* Publication of this marvelous poem marked the end of a fifteen-year-old preoccupation with the "new world soul myth" whose themes had first invaded and captivated young Toomer's imagination in 1921. The poem has the energy and force of a long-incubated expression and carries the inevitability and conviction of a poetic idea whose time has come. Written in free verse, in stanzas of varying lengths, "Blue Meridian" rightly claims a place in that woefully short collection of democratic vistas which contains *Leaves of Grass* and "The Bridge." Having neither the bulkiness of *Leaves* nor the obscurity of parts of "The Bridge," Toomer's new world soul epic too celebrates an American civic aesthetic. "Blue Meridian" advocates as it creates a vision of America free of the bitterness occasioned by unfair social divisions in class, color, race, and sex. Understanding the power of ideas to create a just society, Toomer also lamented the fragmentation of knowledge in American life and foresaw the rebellion against the academy which the sixties brought. Indeed, the major themes of "Blue Meridian" read like a blueprint for the widespread social rebellion of the sixties, as *Cane's* ethnic passage made its theme a bible for young African-Americans during the same period.

Like *Cane,* "Blue Meridian" too is about a process of becoming. The earlier work had charted the modernization of the African-American personality, developing an ideal personality over a three-part structure from thesis through antithesis to synthesis. Utilizing a similar structure, "Blue Meridian" works out the coming-into-being of the omni-American, contrasting the worlds of black, red, and white America, eventuating in a new world of the blue man, or the man of the color purple. The lengthy first and second sections of the poem repeat, recapitulate, and fulfill each other, reaching a new synthesis in the short, culminating, third "meridian." Each section or meridian begins with a three-line stanza which describes a meridian, first conceived as divided halves in the "Black Meridian" and "White Meridian" sections, finally seen as one magnificent whole in the transformation brought about as black and white meridians form the new blue meridian. The lines of the introductory stanzas suggest the process of completion from separation and division to wholeness and perfection which this paean to democracy achieves. The first division addresses "Black Meridian, black light"; the second, "White Meridian, white light," both brought together when black and white combine to form "Blue Meridian, banded light." Toomer designates the "light" of each meridian as the "I of earth and of mankind," calling on the primordial source of life / light / energy. In Toomer's myth of genesis, the light of humankind was initially one life force, as the gods of "Blue Meridian" originally came from one "root religion." In its Wordsworthian falling away, human society broke the wholeness of the life circle, consigning humanity to separate existences seen as half meridians, imprisoning life in categories of race and nationality, abandoning the universal spark which represented wholeness. Neither black nor white meridian can reach a higher point of existence until they partake of each other's nature, by accepting that *tertium quid* which will propel a new fusion, a stronger and higher strain of being because it shares all of nature's bounty and inherits all of culture's gifts.

The evolutionary image and processes of change and accommodation, loss, gain, and ultimate fulfillment dominate "Blue Meridian." Following Whitman, Toomer sees all the humankind as part of one long march dating back to Adam. Again echoing Whitman, Jean insists that every strata of humankind has played some part in determining the current stock:

> We—priest, clown, scientist, technician,
> Artist, rascal, worker, lazybones,
> This is the whole—
> Individuals and people,
> This is the whole that stood with Adam
> And has come down to us.

Building from the "new Adam" myth of the Puritans, Jean heralds America as the land of the new Adam, but insists that that being has yet to fulfill itself; the great promise of American personality must be moved from ideality to reality. The American—conceived as the ultimate development of historical man—yet bears the mandate to become that being worthy of the munificence of contemporary America, this rich legacy captured in references to the splendid geography and natural resources of the country:

> Thou great fields, waving thy growths across the world,
> Couldst thou find the seed which started thee?
> Can you remember the first great hand to sow?
> Have you memory of His intention?
>
> Great plains, and thou, mountains,
> And thou, stately trees, and thou,
> America, sleeping and producing with the seasons.

While nature's bounty provided the material conditions which made America the staging ground for a new world vision, the inhabitants were not "spirit-selected" to fulfill the country's destiny, but rather came by the accidents of fate:

> When the spirit of mankind conceived
> A New World in America, and dreamed
> The human structure rising from this base,
> The land was as a vacant house to new inhabitants,
> A vacuum compelled by Nature to be filled.
> Spirit could not wait to time select,
> Weighing in wisdom each piece,
> Fitting each right thing into each right place,
> But had to act, trusting the vision of the possible,
> Had to bring vast life to this vast plot,
> Drawing, in waves of inhabitation,
> All the peoples of the earth.

Toomer describes the three main waves of inhabitants and the contribution each made to the American continent, beginning with the European influx:

> The old people—
> The great European races sent wave after wave
> That washed the forests, the earth's rich loam,
> Grew towns with seeds of giant cities,
> Made roads, laid silver rails.

Africa's gifts to the "vision of the possible" came in the form of forced labor and compensatory song:

> The great African races sent a single wave
> And singing riplets to sorrow in red fields,
> Sing a swan song, to break rocks
> And immortalize a hiding water boy.

"Blue Meridian" celebrates the magnificence of the "great red race," the final major racial group constituting the omni-American:

> The great red race was here,
> In a land of flaming earth and torrent-rains,
> Of red sea-plains and majestic mesas,

As each group had a major role to play in building the country, each helped undermine the historic mission of the new world. The Europeans, led by greed and the desire to be dominant, lost spiritual motivations and "perished displaced by machines." These "dear defectives" or civilized barbarians created a world of chaos. In the wake of rampant industrialization and commercialization America became unlivable, alien to human needs, echoing the end foreshadowed in Revelations:

> They say that near the end

> It was a chaos of crying men and hard women,
> A city of goddamn and Jehovah
> Baptized in finance
> Without benefit of saints.

The African, too, shares responsibility for stunting the American plan. As the European has been fixed in a group image of master, the African remained frozen in its slave personality, even after the period of slavery had ended. They insisted, Toomer insists, on "keeping the watermelon," the author's highly inventive metaphor for perpetuating a destructive stereotype, remaining the dialectical other of the European, moaning and groaning of its fate as an oppressed class, rather than effecting a new self:

> But we must keep keep keep
>   The watermelon—
> He moaned, O Lord, Lord,
> This bale will break me—
> But we must keep keep keep
>   the watermelon.

The native American had lost its glory and splendor, its culture trivialized in the descent from the purple hill to pueblo, where that spirit "Sank into the sacred earth." Indians, too, fixed on symbols of group narcissism: "The ghosts of buffalos / A lone eagle feather, An untamed Navajo." Frozen by their commitment to their "dear defective" selves, all divisions of America cannot grow beyond their present level, leaving the country united by geography, but unjoined in spirit:

> And thus we are—
> Gathered by the snatch of accident,
> Selected with the speed of fate,
> The alien and the belonging,
> All belonging now,
> Not yet made one and aged.

"Blue Meridian" then proclaims the need for an American civic aesthetic which will cultivate and harmonize one nation out of its many people.

As in *Cane,* in "Blue Meridian" Toomer's evolutionary perspective centers in humanism—in the death of the old gods and the empowerment of man. Each of the old gods perished in the new world, their demise presaging the rise of humanism:

> The old gods, led by an inverted Christ,
> A shaved Moses, a blanched Lemur,

And a moulting Thunderbird,
Withdrew into the distance and died,
Their dust and seed drifting down
To fertilize the seven regions of America.

Toomer's new God will spring as a "faceless deity"— safe from the claims of group narcissism, able to herald a multi-cultural / multiracial people:

We are waiting for a new God,
For revelation in our day,
For growth towards faceless Deity.

The poet calls upon the great primordial forces of nature to generate that energy which, in turn, will generate the new world soul:

O thou Radiant Incorporeal
The I of earth and of mankind, hurl
Down these seaboards, across this continent,
The thousand-rayed discus of thy mind,
And blend our bodies to one flesh,
And blend this body to mankind.

While the inspiration and force will come from the world spirit, each American in submission to the new world spirit, creates and sustains the new American, partakes of a "civic Holy Communion":

It is a new America
To be spiritualized by each new American
To be taken as a golden grain
And lifted, as the wheat of our bodies,
To matter uniquely man.
We are waiting for a new people,
For the joining of men to men
And man to God.

The second half of "Blue Meridian" is devoted to the second division of America—the white meridian, those "who have power" but "are less than we should be." Toomer depicts inhabitants of the white meridian as power-driven and insular, cut off from their best selves, power without wisdom. Group narcissism marks their habits of control and exclusion. In a series of imperatives, the poet appeals to white meridians to "Let go" of the destructive hold which has categorized, divided, separated and alienated humankind. "Unlock the races" the poet implores. "Open this pod by outgrowing it. Free men from this prison and this shrinkage." Toomer sees sexism stemming from the same forces of control and power that created racism and orders:

> Free the sexes
> From the penalties and proscriptions
> That allegedly are laid on us
> Because we are male or female.

Class divisions too must become part of the past in the new America:

> Unlock the classes
> Emerge from these pockets;
> I am, we are, simply of the human class.

Understanding that the field of knowledge helps create and sustain false consciousness, Toomer laments the specializations which have imprisoned truth:

> Expand the fields, the specializations,
> The limitations of occupations,
> The definitions of what we are
> That gain fractions and lose wholes—
> I am of the field of being.
> We are beings.

Religion too must be liberated from the sects and schisms that divide rather than unite:

> Open the religions, the exclusive creeds,
> Those tight parodies of God's intentions;
> There is a Root religion
> And we are of it, whose force transforms,
> Whose way progressively reveals
> The shining terraces of one reality.

The new America will celebrate emancipated humankind, which then casts a "rainbow to heaven":

> Uncase, unpod whatever blocks, until,
> Having realized pure consciousness of being,
> Knowing that we are beings
> Co-existing with others in an inhabited universe,
> We will be free to use rightly with reason
> Our own and other human functions—
> Free men, whole men, men connected
> With one another and with Deity.

By developing its highest potential, the new American reaches its own divinity:

> This new God we have—

> Man at last triumphant over not-man,
> Being born above anti-being,
> And in this being, and everywhere,
> The god who is, the God we seek.

The "White Meridian" section of the poem fulfills the "Black Meridian" part, by accommodating the cultural tradeoffs which must be achieved for group harmony and social cohesion to exist. In this section, the insular inhabitants of the White Meridian give up privileges based on group identity and take their chances in the world as individuals, people at large in the universe, true to self rather than to group identity:

> The old peoples—
> The great European races sent wave after wave
> That washed the forests, the earth's right loam,
> Grew towns with the seeds of giant cities,
> Made roads, laid silver rails,
> Factoried superb machines,
> Died, and came alive again
> To demonstrate the worth of individuals
> The purpose of the commonwealth.

The descendants of the Africans also experience a death-in-life; they overcome their slave psychology and come to know that all labor—even forced toil—is sacred:

> Love does not brand as slave or peon
> Any man, but feels his hands,
> His touch upon his work.

Dying to group identity, the African emerges as an individual in the new world:

> And welcomes death that liberates
> The poet, American among Americans,
> Man at large among men.

The death of group identity among "the great red race" will help sustain the banded new world soul:

> And pueblo, priest, and Shalakos
> Sank into the sacred earth
> To resurrect—
> To project into this conscious world
> An example of the organic;
> To enact a mystery among facts—

"Blue Meridian" posits the necessity of perpetual cultural tradeoffs, in patterns of accommodation and adjustments, in the interest of a higher humanity:

> Islanders, newly come upon the continents,
> If to live against annihilation,
> Must outgrow themselves and their old places,
> Disintegrate tribal integrators,
> And fix, as their center of gravity,
> As their compelling ideal
> The symbol of Universal Man—
> Must outgrow clan and class, color,
> Nationalism, creed, all the fetishes
> Of the arrested and dismembered,
> And find a larger truth in larger hearts,
> Less the continents shrink to islands,
> Less human destiny abort
> And man, bristling against himself, explode.

Section Three of "Blue Meridian" presents the "high way of the third," the path of "The man of blue or purple." Toomer sees the blue man or the man of the color purple reconciling "yes and no." This higher order of being has been "Struggling for birth through ages." The autobiographical poem contained within "Blue Meridian" charts Toomer's own progress and struggles for birth at a higher level and offers his life as a "reconciling force," his own being as a "generator of symbols, Source of a new force." The autobiographical poem presents the poet as a companion of the cosmos, working against "Anti-cosmic outlaws" for the brotherhood of man:

> Driven by what the cosmos has put in me
> Let me then affirm to those, the mazed,
> Who like myself have seen self-streaks,
> Who too have felt the sear
> And would rather suffer it than pass it on—
> We are made to grow, and by growing attain,
> Rising in new birth to live in love.

The references to "self-streaks" and to "the sear" point to Toomer's troubles with Frank and with Liveright and the battle over the personality of the poet in 1924. The poem reflects on the *Cane* days, and depicts the poet's peak experiences during the splendor of the spring in 1923:

> I held a fair position as men rate things,
> Even enviable—
> I could taste flavors in a grain of sand,
> My eyes saw loveliness.

Toomer then records his yet-lingering surprise concerning the failure of the brotherhood of art. As he sought highest ground and took the "highway to heaven," the brotherhood sought to undo him:

> Curious, then, that I, of all people,
> In the month of the nasty mouth,
> Should have found myself caught
> In a backbay leased by public and private scavengers:

Toomer's criticism of the failure of the New York art scene reflects his decision in 1924 to give up the personality of the poet and his break with the moderns, who falsely claimed themselves "the brotherhood of art":

> The brotherhood of man cannot be realized
> By stunted men, nor by those dismembered,
> Closed in themselves, but off from the mainstream
> And therefore frustrated and bent to live in hate;
> Exiles can but gang against themselves and earth,
> Suffering the wrong turn as it works out
> With even stronger compulsion towards catastrophe.
> We who would transform ex-I to I
> And move from outlaw to I AM,
> May know by sacred testimony—
> There is a right turn,
> A struggle through purgatories of many names,
> A rising to one's real being
> Wherein one finds oneself linked with
> The real beings of other men, and in God;
> The kingdom exists, and is to be entered.

The poet pinpoints the personality of Margaret Naumburg as a redeeming agent in his life:

> I met a woman—
> Much that I am I owe to her,
> For she was going where I was going.
> We together,
> And a buried being was called to life,
> A beauty and a power, a revelation
> Of what life is for, and why we are;

The autobiographical poem records the separation of poet and psychologist— "I and she pushed we apart, We divided us."

Following the chronology of Toomer's life, the autobiographical excursus addresses Marjorie Latimer, her essence captured in memories of the midwest

where she and Toomer met and of the southwest where they had their honeymoon:

> Sweetheart of the lake!
> Marvel of the prairies with starry eyes!
> Angel child! Princess of earth!
> Girl of the mesas and the great red plains!
> Star of the sky! Joy of the sun!
> Pride of the eagle! Beloved of the thunderbird!

Moving through the loss of loves, Toomer then accepts the loss of celebrity as
the price paid for his fidelity to the new world soul:

> My life is given to have
> Realized in our consciousness,
> Actualized in life without celebrity,
> This real: wisdom, empowered: men growing
> From womb to birth, from birth to rebirth,
> Up arcs of brightness to the resplendent source.

The poem comes to an end with the poet as the new world soul realized,
triumphant, praising his America:

> No split spirit can divide
> No dead soul can undermine thee,
> Thou, great coasts and harbors,
> Mountains, lakes, and plains,
> Thou are the majestic base
> Of Cathedral people;
> America,
> The seed which has started thee has grown.

Through sympathetic identification and powers of imagination of the poet, the
new meridian gains life, banded by the poet:

> Blue Meridian, banded-light,
> Dynamic atom-aggregate,
> Awakes upon the earth;
> In his left hand he holds elevated rock,
> In his right hand he holds lifted branches,
> He dances the dance of the Blue Meridian
> And dervishes with the seven regions of America, and all the world.

"Blue Meridian" was to be to Toomer's maturity what *Cane* had been to his
youthful experiences. Both works issued from the compulsions of the writer's
internal development. And as *Cane* exhausted and fulfilled Toomer's obsession

with the rites of ethnicity, "Blue Meridian" absorbed and expressed the creative energies and personal fidelities attached to the new world soul myth. The publication of "Blue Meridian" brought Jean Toomer immense joy and cathartic release. His personal sense of achievement compensated for the virtual silence which greeted his marvelous poem. The greatest interest in "Blue Meridian" came from a University of Pennsylvania composer, Carl McDonald, who sought permission to set the work to music for the University's Choral Society; however, the Director was unable to raise funds for a commission and abandoned that project, leaving the work which expressed Toomer's deepest poetic convictions without an audience. The neglect of this major poem confirmed the wisdom of having aborted that project back in 1924; then, as in 1936, a harmonizing inclusive civic aesthetic did not have a public in America. Toomer's success in completing the poem brought his life full-circle and effectively marked the end of his quest for fulfillment as a secular, creative writer.

MARCUS GARVEY AND THE HARLEM RENAISSANCE

John Runcie

During the 1920s Afro-American history was dominated by two developments. Black intellectuals, who believed that a display of cultural achievements by black writers and artists would foster pride within the black community and win respect and other more tangible benefits from white America, launched the Harlem Renaissance. Meanwhile, Marcus Garvey organized and led a very different type of movement. His Universal Negro Improvement Association attracted a large following, especially among the black masses of the urban north. Both these movements contributed to the idea of the "New Negro" which flourished during the 1920s. They seemed to have much in common in their attitudes to race pride and the African past and yet the relationship between them was frequently characterized by mutual hostility or indifference.

Antagonism towards black intellectuals was certainly a recurring theme in Garvey's speeches and writings during the 1920s. In the early years of the decade his attacks were not directed at the Harlem Renaissance as such but at intellectuals in general and at such individuals as W.E.B. DuBois and James Weldon Johnson in particular. DuBois and Johnson incurred Garvey's enmity because they were among his principal rivals for leadership within the black community; their status as important figures in the Renaissance movement was largely coincidental. However, though it may not have been deliberate, Garvey's criticism of these "rogues and vagabonds" effectively contradicted one of the central tenets of the Renaissance—that cultural achievement would pave the way for black social and political equality.[1]   In a speech delivered during July 1924 at Liberty Hall in New York, Garvey scorned the idea that "the solution of the race problem depends upon our development in music, in art, in literature . . . and in poetry." [2] Over a year earlier in the course of a U.N.I.A. meeting in Carnegie Hall, Garvey had identified himself with a quite different set of priorities. "You talk about music and art and literature, as such men like DuBois and Weldon Johnson take pride in doing. A nation was not founded first of all on literature or on writing books, it is first founded upon the effort of real workers."[3]   Clearly sensitive to the charge that his

John Runcie is a lecturer in the Department of History at the University of Leicester, England.

Afro-Americans in New York Life and History (July 1986)
P.O. Box 1663
Buffalo, New York 14216

followers were "rude, ignorant and illiterate",   Garvey argued that "Philosophy and the ability to write books were not going to bring to the Negro the recognition for which he was looking."[5]   Instead he emphasized the value of the practical knowledge and skills of the ordinary worker which could be translated into industrial and commercial progress for the black race. "They call us the common people," Garvey sneered, "They say we are illiterate. Let us see if they can live without the so-called illiterates."[6]   On another occasion he stressed that "when we can provide employment for ourselves, when we can feed ourselves, then we can . . . find time to indulge in the fine arts."[7]

By the late 1920s Garvey's criticisms of the Harlem Renaissance had changed direction and become more specific.   His skeptical dismissal of intellectuals in general and his particular dislike of the older upper-middle class elitist wing of the Renaissance gave way to a virulent attack on the movement's younger, more radical writers, who sought to exploit the folk culture of the black lower class and the primitive exotica of the black experience.

The publication in 1928 of Claude McKay's controversial novel *Home to Harlem* furnished Garvey with the occasion for an attack on this trend, but his bitter comments were clearly directed at the Harlem Renaissance movement and not just at McKay. In a front page *Negro World* editorial Garvey contended that "It is my duty to bring to your attention this week a grave evil that afflicts us as a people at this time. Our race, within recent years, has developed a new group of writers who have been prostituting their intelligence, under the direction of the white man, to bring out and show up the worse (sic) traits of our people. . . . They have been writing books, novels and poems under the advice of white publishers, to portray to the world the looseness, laxity and immorality that are peculiar to our group. . . ."[8]

There was nothing particularly original in Garvey's remarks. Many other blacks had attacked this trend in the race's literature from a variety of political and cultural perspectives. Writers like Claude McKay and Langston Hughes had been widely criticized for pandering to depraved white tastes, succumbing to the demands of white publishers, and publicizing everything that was coarse, brutal and grotesque in the lives of the superstitious, illiterate dregs of black society.[9]   Garvey's criticisms were inaccurate and uninformed as well as unoriginal. To link the short story writer Eric Walrond with Claude McKay was perhaps not inappropriate, but to include DuBois, Johnson and Walter White in the same group of writers suggests that Garvey had personal rivalries and political propaganda in mind, as much as objective literary criticism. The work of writers like Hughes and McKay did not always conform to the "high art" expectations of this older generation and indeed DuBois had been just as critical of the direction of the Harlem Renaissance as Garvey. However, none of this detracts from the significance of Garvey's position. In the space of four years he had progressed from an unfocused tirade against all black intellectuals to a much more specific attack on some of the principal luminaries of the Harlem Renaissance in which he denounced them as "literary prostitutes" and demanded a boycott of their works. [10]

Garvey's hostility to the intellectuals of the Harlem Renaissance is more easily described than explained. It was the product of a complex combination of circumstances and influences. One would, for example, hardly have expected Garvey to endorse a movement whose very existence was so dependent on the approval and support of white patrons, publishers, critics and readers.

White involvement in the Harlem Renaissance was complemented by the support, encouragement and publicity given to the movement by such black magazines as the *Crisis*, *Opportunity*, and the *Messenger*. These were the mouthpieces of organizations and individuals who were vying with Garvey for influence in the black community and who were critical of his policies and his personality. Support for the Renaissance by magazines whose editors dismissed Garvey as a "monumental monkey," an "unquestioned fool and ignoramus," "the most dangerous enemy of the Negro race in America and in the world," was unlikely to dispose Garvey favorably towards it. [11] It was also partly as a result of their connection with these magazines and the organizations they represented that some of the Renaissance intellectuals identified the movement with the kind of integrationist interracial philosophy which was incompatible with Garvey's separatist black nationalism. This in turn helps to explain why the writers of the Renaissance, whose work appeared so frequently in other black publications, rarely submitted any material to the *Negro World*.

Another vital clue to Garvey's apparent anti-intellectualism lies in the dramatic contrast between his comparatively deprived educational background and the high level of formal education enjoyed by virtually all the participants in the Harlem Renaissance. The educational attainments of the Renaissance artists were remarkable by any standards. By those applicable to the black community in the 1920s their record was positively astonishing. DuBois and Alain Locke both held Ph.D.s from Harvard University. Countee Cullen and Sterling Brown had earned their Master's degree from the same university. James Weldon Johnson, John Matheus, Zora Neal Hurston and Jessie Fauset had also completed their M.A.; while Rudolph Fisher held both an M.A. from Brown University and an M.D. from Howard. Most of the others had completed their first degree and many of them had spent some time as graduate students. Someone like George Schuyler who never attended any university or college was a rare exception to this characteristic pattern.

Garvey enjoyed none of these advantages. Most of his formal education was acquired at an elementary school in Jamaica which he was forced to leave at the age of fourteen as a result of his father's financial difficulties. Garvey's enemies frequently contended that the U.N.I.A. attracted only ignorant and illiterate blacks and they did not allow Garvey to forget his own educational deficiencies. DuBois, in particular, placed considerable emphasis on this fact. Garvey, he contended, was ". . . a poor black boy . . . He received little training in the Church of England grammar school . . . he had no chance for a university education. . . . Garvey had no grasp of high education and a very hazy idea of the technic of civilization."[12]

Garvey reacted to this situation in a number of fairly predictable ways. He claimed to be better educated than he was;[13] he evolved a pretentious pseudo-intellectual style of speaking and writing; he frequently addressed his audiences wearing the cap and gown of the academic, and he invented degrees as well as impressive-sounding titles for himself. Garvey's attempts to compensate for the inadequacies of his formal education also led him to question the value of this kind of training. In his *Philosophy and Opinions* he wrote, "Many a man was educated outside the school room." "Develop your mind," he argued, "and you become as great and full of knowledge as the other fellow without even entering the class room."[14] Education according to Garvey was "not so much the school that one has passed through, but the use one makes of that which he has learned."[15] Garvey did not approve of the use which many of the Harlem Renaissance intellectuals were making of their many formal qualifications. His attack on them was another form of compensation for his own shortcomings and those of his followers.

Color prejudice further widened the gulf between Garvey and the Negro intellectuals. Garvey viewed the American racial situation from a West Indian perspective and insisted on dismissing light-skinned mulattoes as a separate and hostile caste. He repeatedly denounced racial amalgamation and called for "pride and purity of race."[16] Hitherto, light-skinned Negroes had enjoyed certain advantages in America and there was a disproportionate number of them in the better educated upper strata of Afro-American society. This fact is at least partially reflected in the membership of the Harlem Renaissance. The point should not be exaggerated. The physical appearance of Claude McKay, Wallace Thurman, and Countee Cullen could hardly have offended Garvey's inverted racial prejudices. However, the fact remains that the movement did attract a significant percentage of light-skinned Negroes. Langston Hughes had so much white blood in him that native Africans did not even recognize him as a negro.[17] Nella Larsen had a Danish mother. The appropriately named Walter White was blond-haired, blue-eyed and could very easily have passed for white. Jean Toomer was a very pale-skinned mulatto who twice married white women, and for whom color was so unimportant that he once declared, "I am of no particular race. I am of the human race."[18] Finally, two of the leading figures in the Renaissance, DuBois and Weldon Johnson clearly belonged to the mulatto group.

Garvey exploited the possibilities of this situation. He dismissed Walter White as someone "whom we can hardly tell from a Southern gentleman . . . ,"[19] and referred scathingly to DuBois as "This unfortunate mulatto," "this near white or colored man."[20]. According to Garvey, DuBois represented a group that hates the Negro blood in its veins . . ."[21] This was a charge which was clearly inapplicable to many of the extremely race-conscious Renaissance artists, but for reasons of ignorance or expediency Garvey showed no understanding of the complexities of this movement. Without any attempt to distinguish between one artist and another he accused all the authors and poets of the Renaissance of being unworthy of their race and of feeling no pride in their color. Instead, said Garvey, "they are prostituting their intelligence and ability as authors and writers against their race for the satisfaction of white people."[22]

Garvey's hostility towards the Harlem Renaissance was reciprocated in full. To the more politically involved members of the movement Garvey represented a threat to their leadership which had to be met, and they responded with a stream of critical essays, articles and editorials. Many of the important figures in the Renaissance were not politically active. Their lives and their correspondence were often dominated by literary and cultural concerns and reveal little interest in Garvey or his Universal Negro Improvement Association. However, Garvey was too important a figure to be ignored even by the most a-political of writers. He provided a rich source of subject matter for light-hearted satire as well as for serious analysis. The Renaissance reaction to Garvey was expressed in novels by Countee Cullen, Claude McKay and George Schuyler, in essay and short story form by Zora Neal Hurston, Rudolph Fisher and Eric Walrond, and in Wallace Thurman's unpublished play "Jeremiah the Magnificent," just as effectively as in the critical analyses of W.E.B. DuBois and James Weldon Johnson.

The intellectuals of the Harlem Renaissance attacked Garvey in many different ways and on many different levels. His aims and objectives, his policies and programmes were all subjected to critical scrutiny. Assessments of Garvey's character and personality and references to his physical appearance were particularly abusive. In his satirical novel *Black No More*, George Schuyler depicts Santop Licorice, head of the Back to Africa Society, and clearly a fictional version of Garvey, as "250 pounds, five-feet-six inches of black blubber."[23] Schuyler's description of the real-life Garvey in his autobiography as "a short, smooth, black, pig-eyed, corpulent West Indian," was scarcely less offensive.[24] Garvey, according to Schuyler, was an "ignorant mountebank," a rabble rouser and a megalomaniac who in many respects "anticipated Hitler."[25] These views were shared to a greater or lesser degree by many other members of the Renaissance. DuBois, himself the subject of so much of Garvey's contempt, retaliated by describing his tormentor as "A little, fat black man, ugly, but with intelligent eyes and big head."[26] In DuBois' eyes Garvey was a dangerous demagogue, "dictatorial, domineering, inordinately vain and very suspicious." DuBois also referred to Garvey's penchant for "bombast and exaggeration," identified an element of paranoia in his behavior and dismissed him as "either a lunatic or a traitor."[27] To Wallace Thurman, Garvey was in certain respects like "a primitive child, arrogant, egotistical and lacking any real mental depth."[28] Claude McKay was less restrained. He described Garvey as a "West Indian charlatan" who cowed his audiences with "his huge ugly bulk," and who "wasn't worth no more than the good boot in his bahind that he don got."[29]

Garvey's success in the early 1920s owed much to his realization that policies had to be supplemented by the colorful pageantry of massive parades, gaudy uniforms, marching bands, banners, ostentatious titles and "court receptions." This dimension of Garveyism attracted mass support to the U.N.I.A. It also attracted the attention of several members of the Harlem Renaissance. Claude McKay referred to Garvey's activities as a form of "stupendous vaudeville",[30] while James Weldon Johnson saw them as "the apotheosis of the ridiculous."[31] Even the normally sober DuBois saw the humor in the knighting of U.N.I.A. members at a specially organized reception. "A casual observer," he said of the ceremony, "might have mistaken it for the . . . rehearsal of a new comic opera . . ."[32] Characteristically, George Schuyler went further. His satirical "Shafts and Darts" column in the *Messenger* frequently poked fun at Garvey. To Schuyler, Garvey was a suitable candidate for the "Nobel Mirth Prize. Certainly no man or woman living today has contributed more to the mirth of the world than the little octoroon admiral. He has outdistanced Falstaff, Don Quixote and Bert Williams in the production of guffaws."[33]

This resort to humor in dealing with everything that was most ostentatious and pretentious in Garvey's behavior is also apparent in some of the literature of the Renaissance. In his only novel, *One Way to Heaven*, Countee Cullen gently mocks the elevation of an undistinguished elocution teacher to the rank of Duchess of Uganda in Garvey's self-created nobility.[34] The much more abrasive Zora Neal Hurston dealt less gently with Garvey's conceited arrogance in an unpublished essay titled appropriately, "The Emperor Effaces Himself." Using the language of exaggerated irony, Hurston argued that "Self-effacement was typical of Mr. Garvey and his organization. He would have no fuss nor bluster—a few thousand pennants strung across the street overhead, eight or nine bands, a regiment or two, a few floats, a dozen or so titled officials and he was ready for his annual parade." [35] Hurston also directed her irony at Garvey's weakness for bestowing the most grandiloquent-sounding titles on himself. Garvey, she suggested, granted titles to others "till it hurt them to carry all that he gave them. . . . For himself he kept almost nothing. He was merely Managing Editor of the Negro World, President of the Black Star Steamship and Navigation Line, President-General of the Universal Negro Improvement Association, Supreme Ruler of the Sublime Order of the Nile, Provisional President of Africa and Commander in Chief of the African Legions." [36]

Garvey was attacked in a similar vein in the unpublished satirical play "Jeremiah the Magnificient," co-authored by the white writer William Jourdan Rapp and the important Harlem Renaissance figure, Wallace Thurman. The central character in the play, Jeremiah Saunders, is very obviously based on Garvey and nowhere is this more apparent than when the authors describe their hero's exaggerated sense of his own importance. Jeremiah strikes poses before a mirror and practices his oratory with such modest statements as "The Jews had their Moses, the Italians their Caesar, the French their Joan of Arc, the Americans their George Washington . . . the Russians their Lenin, and now the black man has Jeremiah." [37] Jeremiah also shared with Garvey a weakness for ostentatious and colorful costumes. He addresses his followers wearing "a purple robe lined with red and trimmed with imitation ermine." [38] In his lavisly furnished private office the walls "are literally covered with flag draped full length pictures of Jeremiah in his various costumes of state; one in an emporor's robes, another in an admiral's regalia, another in a general's outfit, and another in a religious habilment worthy of a high priest." [39] It was left to Claude McKay to deflate Garvey's pretentions completely and to see the man from an altogether different perspective. The hero of McKay's novel, *Banjo*, says of Garvey, "I guess he thought . . . that he was Moses or Napoleon or Frederick Douglass, but he was nothing but a fool, big-mouf nigger." [40]

Treating Garvey as a buffoon, as someone to be mocked and ridiculed, was one way of reacting to the excesses of the man and his organization, but Garvey was a source of concern and embarassment as well as of amusement to the Renaissance intellectuals. Eric Walrond grasped the fact that Garvey's use of pageantry, of colorful parades, and impressive-sounding titles was enabling him to manipulate increasing numbers of the repressed black proletariat, by bringing an element of excitement into their otherwise drab lives. [41] Both Cullen and Johnson saw sinister implications behind the

creation of Garvey's nobility. If he ever fulfilled his African
ambitions, the government he would establish there would be based
upon the hereditary class distinctions which he had experienced as a
colonial in the British West Indies and far removed from the
democratic republican system favored in America.[42] Finally, to the
more conservative wing of the Renaissance in particular, Garvey's
antics were intolerable. He threatened their power and status in the
black community, and at a time when they were seeking to prove
something to white society through their artistic achievements,
Garvey's excesses seemed likely to confirm many of the
contemptuous white prejudices and stereotypes about blacks. At one
point in Thurman and Rapp's play, Jeremiah is visited by a group of
leaders of other black organizations. One of the characters, clearly
based on DuBois, expressed precisely these anxieties when he
complained that "We feel that your organization is a detriment to the
whole race. It holds the Negro up to ridicule. Because of you, the
world is laughing at us."[43]

Many people were also laughing at Garvey's numerous ambitious
business ventures. The idea of promoting economic self-sufficiency
among Afro-Americans was an important part of the U.N.I.A.
programme. Garvey contended that businesses owned and operated
by the black community would create more employment for blacks
and free them from white domination and exploitation. With these
aims in mind he established U.N.I.A. factories, stores, laundries and
restaurants. The organization also operated its own hotel, newspaper
and university. The piece de resistance in Garvey's programme of
economic nationalism was his steamship company, the Black Star
Line, which it was envisaged would promote trade between the
colored people of the world and carry U.N.I.A members back to
Africa. Garvey's failures were as spectacular as his ambitions and
attracted the attention of the Renaissance satirists. Wallace
Thurman was of the opinion that the history of the S.S. Yarmouth,
Garvey's first purchase, had "a Gilbertian flavor which makes it one
of the major maritime comedies."[44] George Schuyler lamented the
fact that Gilbert and Sullivan were no longer alive "to do justice to
the U.N.I.A. fleet."[45] In 1924, when Garvey revived his commercial
ambitions in the form of the Black Cross Line, Schuyler noted the fact
in the *Messenger*. "Marcus Garvey is again entering the scrap iron
business. The Black Cross Line is to succeed the wharf-hugging Black
Star Line of joke book fame. Merely for the sake of accuracy, we
suggest that the adjective 'Double' be used in the new name instead
of 'Black'."[46] Several years later Schuyler reviewed Garvey's
various business ventures and concluded that "The result was and is a
tragic farce highly amusing to the gods."[47]

Schuyler was not alone in his perception that there was tragedy as
well as farce inherent in the failure of Garvey's business and

commercial enterprises. Other members of the Harlem Renaissance condemned Garvey for his complete lack of business sense, for failing to keep proper accounts, for paying exorbitant salaries and expense accounts and for indulging in impractical and wild schemes. Eric Walrond accused Garvey of being incompetent and dishonest, and contended that in business affairs he was no more than "a hopeless nincompoop."[48] Garvey's inexperience was also evident in his unfortunate choice of assistants. He alienated many able blacks and in Thurman's opinion, "perversely placed himself in the hands of a few sycophants, who eventually played Judas to his Messiah."[49] Garvey had squandered money as well as opportunities. He was guilty, according to Claude McKay, of "wasting the wealth of the Negro masses."[50] This wastefulness was especially galling to someone like DuBois, who was interested in leadership as well as art and whose efforts failed to attract the same kind of support as Garvey's, and were dependent on white philanthropy. DuBois was astute enough to recognize the feasibility of some of Garvey's schemes but this simply made their failure even more intolerable. To someone as image-conscious as DuBois, Garvey's business failures seemed as damaging to black prospects as his other extravagent indulgences.[51]

Africa was another bone of contention between Garvey and the intellectuals of the Harlem Renaissance. Garvey argued that America was a white man's country and that Afro-Americans should seek to establish an independent nation in Africa, their ancestral homeland. To many of the period's black intellectuals Garvey's ideas on African redemption, his creation of the U.N.I.A.'s African Legion, and his pretentious styling of himself as "Provisional President of Africa," constituted another of his wild fantasies. During the 1920s many black creative artists were interested in and influenced by their African heritage. They extolled Africa's culture and its contribution to civilization and this sensitivity to their racial past was reflected in their poetry, novels, essays and graphic art. Africa was important in more immediate ways. Unlike Garvey, George Schuyler, W.E.B. DuBois and Langston Hughes all visited Africa and were much moved by the experience. However, the intellectuals of the Renaissance was primarily interested in the aesthetic meaning of Africa and in the idea of Africa as a symbol of primitivism, and this kind of interest, which was in any case not shared by all the Renaissance writers, was far removed from the back-to-Africa activities of Marcus Garvey. This central part of the U.N.I.A. program was criticized by many different members of the Renaissance for a wide variety of reasons.

Claude McKay, for example, emphasized just how naive and ill-informed Garvey's understanding of the African situation really was. "He talks of Africa as if it were a little island in the Caribbean Sea. Ignoring all geographical and political divisions, he gives his followers the idea that that vast continent of diverse tribes consists of a large homogenous nation of natives struggling for freedom and waiting for the Western Negroes to come and help them drive out the European exploiters."[52] Some of McKay's points were taken up by George Schuyler and Wallace Thurman. Schuyler pointed out that the whites who controlled most of Africa would prevent any large scale immigration of American or West Indian Negroes, and that there was no reason to anticipate that native Africans would be any more enthusiastic about it. According to Schuyler, "The experience of the American Negro colonists in Liberia who have had to fight off the natives for almost a century proves that."[53] Thurman also had something to say about the Liberian situation. He made the point that Abyssinia and Liberia were the only independent states in Africa. The former excluded foreign blacks and the latter "was too much in debt to America and American financiers to risk incurring their displeasure by becoming a colonization center for empire building Garveyites."[54] The failure of Garvey's negotiations with the Liberian government partly affirmed the accuracy of Thurman's analysis.

Events also confirmed that Afro-Americans were no more interested in emigrating to Africa than the native Africans were in having them there. Garvey's African vision received as little popular support as its various nineteenth century incarnations. Rudolph Fisher got to the root of this problem in his short story, "Ringtail," in which a group of West Indians living in Harlem discuss the merits of African emigration. One of them argues the U.N.I.A. line of America as a white man's country and Garvey as the "Moses of his people," but the response of one of the others, a naturalized American, is more convincing. "'Back to Africa!' snorted Payner. . . . I stay right here! . . How de hell I'm goin' back where I never been?"[55] This same point runs through much of the literature of the Renaissance. James Weldon Johnson emphasized that despite their African origins black Americans "were as much American as anyone in the nation."[56] Langston Hughes shared this sense of an American identity. Despite the African activism which runs through much of Hughes' early poetry, despite his image of himself as "Black like the depths of my Africa,"[57] and despite his long-standing interest in Africa, he recognized that he was fundamentally American. The tom-toms of the jungle might beat in Hughes' blood but as he conceded in his autobiography, "I was only an American Negro—who loved the surface of Africa and the rhythms of Africa—but I was not Africa. I was Chicago and Kansas City and Broadway and Harlem."[58] This kind of self-knowledge was hardly likely to breed enthusiasm for Garvey's programme of repatriation to the African motherland. Instead it led more typically to the attitude assumed by one of the characters in Nella Larson's novel, *Passing*, who rejected the idea of emigration on the grounds that "She was an American. She grew from this soil, and she would not be uprooted."[59] In typically pungent fashion George Schuyler underlined this fundamental weakness in the Garveyite program, "Africa for the Africans is all right, but we are not, and have not been for 300 years Africans."[60]

With the exception of West Indians like Claude McKay and Eric Walrond the Renaissance writers all shared a sense of their identity as Americans and from this stemmed a commitment to priorities quite different from Garvey's. DuBois spoke even for the politically inarticulate members of the renaissance when he emphasized that "the battle of Negro rights is to be fought right here in America. . . we must unite to fight lynching and 'Jim Crow' cars, to settle our status in the courts, to put our children in school and maintain our free ballot. . . . Africa needs her children, but she needs them triumphant, victorious, and not as poverty-stricken and cowering refugees."[61]

W.E.B. DuBois had his own particular reasons for opposing Garvey's African policies. Of all the intellectuals identified with the Harlem Renaissance he was the one most interested in Africa. DuBois' interest was not confined to the complex history and sophisticated cultures of Africa. He was also a leading figure in the Pan-African movement during the 1920s. Pan-Africanism shared with Garveyism an interest in the idea of redeeming Africa for the African people but it hoped to accomplish this through the efforts of black leaders on an international basis. The idea of international cooperation working for gradual reforms which would lead to independence and self-determination for the countries of Africa was incompatible with the separatist fantasies of the Provisional President of Africa. It annoyed DuBois that the U.N.I.A. attracted much more support than the Pan-African movement, and that foreigners sometimes confused the two. He felt that Pan-Africanism had been "seriously harmed by the tragedy and comedy of Marcus Garvey."[62] In this area as in others, DuBois was clearly embarrassed by Garvey's behaviour and by the impracticability of his schemes.

Garvey's African policies have to be seen in the context of his belief in the importance of racial solidarity and his exaltation of everything black. This emphasis on race and color, and Garvey's West Indian way of viewing these matters were further sources of annoyance to some of the Renaissance intellectuals. For someone with socialist sympathies, like Claude McKay in the early 1920s, Garvey's emphasis on race rather than class stood in the way of cooperation between black and white workers in their struggle against the capitalist system. McKay complained that Garvey had "never urged Negroes to organize in industrial unions."[63] From a totally different conservative, middle-class, perspective George Schuyler made a similar point when he argued that racial differences between blacks and whites were less important than cultural and class differences which cut across racial boundaries. According to Schuyler, blacks and whites in America shared a common culture and a common language and consequently "the Aframerican is just a lamp-blacked Anglo-Saxon." [64] When Garvey's preoccupations with racial purity and black separatism led him into dealings with the Ku Klux Klan, Schuyler used similar terminology to express a distaste which was shared by other black intellectuals. He dismissed the Garveyites as "nothing more than lamp-blacked Ku Klux Klansmen, leading their followers astray with absurd doctrines of fanatical racialism. . . ." [65]

The fact that Garvey and many of his supporters in America were West Indian was a further source of annoyance. The level of black West Indian migration to America was high in the early 1920s and this generated various nativist prejudices and resentments among the Afro-American group. Without in any way identifying himself with these feelings, Rudolph Fisher described them in one of his short stories. Having expressed the hope that Garvey would take all the West Indian "monkey-chasers" back to Africa with him, one of Fisher's characters justifies this hope on the grounds that the foreigners are "too damn conceited. They're too agressive. They talk funny. They look funny. . . . An' there's too many of 'em here." [66] There is no evidence that the intellectuals of the Harlem Renaissance ever held prejudices quite as blatant as this, but many of them valued their American identity, and their descriptions of Garvey as a "West Indian Charlatan," a "black, pig-eyed, corpulent West Indian from Jamaica," and a "West Indian agitator," suggest that his foreign birth contributed to their hostility towards him.[67] This was certainly true in the case of Johnson and DuBois both of whom resented Garvey's influence and dwelt on the fact that he was not an American citizen, and that his followers, in DuBois' words were "the lowest type of Negroes, mostly from the Indies." [68]

The enmity between Marcus Garvey and the intellectuals of the Harlem Renaissance was deep rooted and mutual, but it was far from absolute. To interpret the relationship between the two purely in terms of their hostility and indifference towards each other fails to recognize the complexity and subtlety of the situation. To some members of the Renaissance, Garvey was more than simply a figure of fun, a source of embarrassment or a target for criticism. Garvey was equally ambivalent in his attitudes to culture and his opinions of intelllectuals.

Garvey's scathing comments on black intellectuals must be off-set by the clear understanding of the potential importance of this group to the success of the U.N.I.A., which he and other members of his organization occasionally displayed. In October 1924, for example, the *Negro World* carried "An appeal to the Intelligentsia" on its front page. "I appeal," wrote Garvey, "to the higher intelligence as well as to the illiterate groups of our race. We must work together . . . for the higher development of the entire race."[69] The reasoning behind this appeal is clear enough. When it suited him to do so Garvey sang the praises of the illiterate common people and the ordinary workers but he understood with T. Thomas Fortune, the editor of the *Negro World* from 1923 until 1928, that "No movement that amounts to anything can get anywhere without intelligent leadership."[70]

In the light of these opinions it is not surprising to find that in its heyday the U.N.I.A. attracted a diverse group of individuals who clearly qualify as members of the black intelligentsia, and who in some instances had important connections with the Harlem Renaissance.

This group included such people as William Ferris who held Masters degrees from both Yale and Harvard, who served for a year as Assistant President General of the U.N.I.A. and who was literary editor of the *Negro World* from 1919 to 1923. During this same period the paper was edited by the orator and lecturer, Hubert Harrison, described by one of his contemporaries as "perhaps the foremost Afro-American intellect of his time."[71] Also identified with the *Negro World* and hence with Garvey were T. Thomas Fortune who edited the paper from 1923-1928, and the essayist, short story writer and important Harlem Renaissance figure, Eric Walrond, who was one of the paper's associate editors from 1921-1923. The most committed of Garvey's supporters among the black intellectuals was the journalist, historian and co-founder of the Negro Society for Historical Research, John E. Bruce. Other black intellectuals of the period enjoyed a much looser relationship with the Garvey movement. Without actually joining the U.N.I.A. respected figures like Carter G. Woodson, Joel Rogers, and Arthur Schomburg contributed to the *Negro World* and lectured to meetings of Garvey followers.

The implications of this situation should not be exaggerated. For all their qualities people like Bruce and Harrison had enjoyed little formal education. They and the mildly eccentric Ferris were not part of the intellectual mainstream represented by the Harlem Renaissance. Renaissance writers who did have something to do with Garvey, like Eric Walrond, who wrote short stories and book reviews as well as editorials for the *Negro World*, Claude McKay who contributed a series of articles to the *Negro World* in 1919, and Zora Neal Hurston, three of whose earliest peoms were published in successive April 1922 editions of the paper, were motivated by considerations other than a belief in Garveyism. McKay admitted this when he noted that by 1920 "I had stopped writing for the *Negro World* because it had not paid for contributions."[72] For Hurston the *Negro World* offered an opportunity to have some of her poems published. There is no evidence that she was interested in or influenced by Garvey's ideas and in different circumstances she was perfectly willing to ridicule the man and his movement. Walrond's involvement with Garveyism went deeper and lasted longer but in the end he too displayed a similar lack of commitment and consistency. He joined the ranks of Garvey's critics and within a year of leaving the *Negro World* had become business manager of *Opportunity*, the magazine issued by the Urban League, which was a rival organization to the U.N.I.A.

However, the fact remains that men of intelligence did participate in Garvey's movement in a variety of different ways, and this in turn meant that Garvey and the Harlem Renaissance were not two totally unrelated phenomena. Someone like Eric Walrond provided an obvious link between the two movements, but the roles of John Bruce and Arthur Schomburg were more durable and more important. The papers of these two men reveal the extent of their involvement with the activities and personalities of the Renaissance.

The example of John Bruce is particularly interesting. This important figure in the U.N.I.A. was a member of the prestigious American Negro Academy which included such prominent Renaissance intellectuals as DuBois and James Weldon Johnson and was presided over by the pro-Garvey Arthur Schomburg. He was also on friendly terms with Alain Locke, the patron-saint of the Renaissance.[73] In addition, although Bruce was not a profound thinker or a highly educated man, this one-time slave and self-taught journalist was a person of sufficient intelligence and culture to collect African art objects and to turn his hand to the writing of essays, pamphlets, plays, short-stories, poetry, song lyrics and even music. Activities of this kind by the most pro-Garvey of black intellectuals indicate that the movement's attitude to black culture was as ambivalent as its attitude to black intellectuals .

This ambivalence is certainly reflected in Garvey's own writings. When it suited him to do so Garvey attacked intellectuals and dismissed the idea that art, literature and music could be as important in the solving of black problems as industrial and commercial strength. On other occasions, however, his priorities were rather different. In a speech delivered in Washington in 1923, Garvey emphasized that unless Negroes evolved their own education system, philosophy, civilization and culture they would remain "mental slaves." "You must first emancipate your mind," he contended, "and then only can you emancipate your bodies."[74] Garvey developed this theme in other speeches and in his articles and editorials. He argued that all the world's ethnic groups had developed their own cultures and that the Negro should do likewise,[75] and he resorted to ideas reminiscent of those used by the theorists of the Harlem Renaissance when he expressed the belief that cultural achievement would encourage respect for the black man. According to Garvey, "The Negro will have to build his own government, industry, art, science, literature and culture, before the world will stop to consider him."[76]

Garvey's nationalism embraced economics and politics as well as culture and as such it went far beyond anything contemplated by even the more radical members of the Renaissance. But whatever his social, political and economic objectives, Garvey shared with the Renaissance intellectuals some understanding of the importance of creating a rich black culture. This concern was apparent, for example, in the program of Garvey's 4th International Convention, held in the summer of 1924, which included discussion of "The promotion of an independent Negro literature and culture."[77] Some of the means used to promote culture by the U.N.I.A. during this period cast further light on the interrelationship between Garvey and the Harlem Renaissance. The *Negro World* had pioneered the idea of encouraging black writers by inviting them to participate in a literary competition which it sponsored in December, 1921. This idea had subsequently been developed with such success by magazines like *Opportunity* and *Crisis* that The *Negro World* revived the practice and sponsored its own "Great Literary Contests" in 1926 and 1927.[78]

The outcome of these various attitudes, objectives and incentives was predictable enough. There was a significant cultural dimension to the activities of the Garvey movement. The U.N.I.A. contained its own artists, essayists, dramatists and poets, just as it evolved its own musicians, choirs, bands and orchestras. U.N.I.A. meetings in Liberty Hall and in all the local divisions were invariably preceded by a musical program. Theatrical evenings and poetry readings were fairly common. Garvey himself emulated John Bruce and wrote plays, song lyrics and poetry. Much of Garvey's literary output was published in the *Negro World*, which frequently offered its readers a remarkable selection of book reviews, short stories and poems alongside accounts of U.N.I.A. activities and reproductions of Garvey's speeches.

These cultural activities helped to reduce the distance between Garvey and the Harlem Renaissance, but they also reveal how different the two movements really were. Culture in the context of the U.N.I.A. was frequently quite different in content, quality and motivation from the efforts of the Renaissance. Artists like Professor Packer Ramsey, "the celebrated Basso-profunda," and Miss Carolina Reed, the "song bird of the East," could captivate audiences in New York's Liberty Hall,[79] but it is unlikely that they would have been as well received by more discerning audiences as were Roland Hayes or Marian Anderson. Similarly, although the Renaissance produced more than its share of inferior, derivative literature, its artists rarely sank to the depths of cultural ineptitude regularly reached by contributors to the *Negro World*. It is hardly surprising that Ethel Trew Dunlap, "the poetess-laurente" of African redemption, appears in no anthologies of Afro-American poetry from this period, though her efforts were superior to those of many others including Garvey himself. Garvey in his *Poetic Meditations* and in lengthy works like *The Tragedy of White Injustice* vacillated between the bombastic pretention which characterized so many of his speeches and a kind of banal saccharine naivete. Thomas Fortune could claim that Garvey was "a poet of high order,"[80] but his wife showed more insight when she conceded that "he never learned versification."[81] This fact was everywhere apparent in Garvey's poetry, for example in a poem like "Loves Morning Star," which contained the immortal lines

> I've waited patiently for you,
> And now you come to make me glad
> I shall be ever good and true
> And be the dearest sweetest dad.[82]

The motives underlying Garvey's encouragement of cultural activities were fairly complex. They were both similar to and quite different from the purposes of the Harlem Renaissance. Both groups shared a common interest in fostering race pride among blacks through artistic achievement and by glorifying African history and culture. Garvey's motives also coincided with those of at least a faction of the Renaissance in one other respect. Although their objectives were totally different, Garvey shared with the elitist conservatives of the Renaissance the belief that art could prove the black man's worth and further his cause. As he put it on one occasion, "let us build up a culture of our own, and then the whole world will fall down in appreciation and respect before the black man."[83] This objective required a certain kind of art, and the Renaissance conservatives would certainly have endorsed the suggestion that the best way to educate white public opinion was by promoting "such songs, plays, paintings, motion pictures and literature as will fully interpret the true ideals and aspirations of the Negro."[84] Garvey had similar considerations in mind in 1928 when he attacked Claude McKay's *Home to Harlem* for its misrepresentation of black life, and insisted that "We must encourage our own black authors . . . who are loyal to their race, who feel proud to be black. . . ." These were the people who would "advance our race through healthy and decent literature."[85] There was more than a little irony in the fact that Garvey's position on these matters should have aligned him with his arch-enemy DuBois in opposition to those Renaissance writers who were seeking to explore the culture and life-style of the black proletariat, so well represented in Garvey's own movement.

The element of irony and confusion in the relationship between Garvey and the Harlem Renaissance was reinforced by another part of Garvey's cultural philosophy—his belief that culture should reach and influence a mass audience. This belief differentiated Garvey from the bourgeois elitists of the Renaissance who were committed to the concept of "high" culture, and took him closer to artists like Claude McKay and especially Langston Hughes. Hughes was certainly active in trying to take his poetry to a larger black audience by means of poetry readings and by making available special cheap editions of his poems, which he claimed on one occasion "sold like reefers on 131st Street."[86] However, on the subject of culture and the black masses the priorities of Garvey and Hughes were quite different. Hughes was primarily interested in utilizing and legitimizing in his poetry the language and folk culture of the black ghetto, and in providing blacks with an alternative to the middle-class consciousness which permeated so much of the Renaissance. Garvey was primarily interested in capturing and manipulating a mass audience in the interests of the U.N.I.A. This objective was not immediately reconcilable with Garvey's hopes of advancing the race by artistic achievement, but he overcame this problem skillfully. Garvey's bid for respect combined with his British West Indian background to encourage the kind of art which strove to be impeccably "decent," Europeanized and middle-class. This is reflected, for example, in Garvey's own poetry, and in the kind of music invariably performed at U.N.I.A. functions. There was little trace of the colloquial speech, or of the jazz and blues, so dear to Langston Hughes. At the same time, however, Garvey catered to the masses by exploiting a different more popular kind of culture, in the form of mass meetings, political rhetoric, colorful parades, marching bands, banners, uniforms and impressive-sounding titles.

One final motive remains to be considered. It can be discerned in much of the cultural activity of the U.N.I.A. and it is totally absent in the work of the Harlem Renaissance. It was the degree to which art was deliberately used as propaganda on behalf of Marcus Garvey and his organization. The propaganda value of U.N.I.A. pageantry is obvious enough, but the manipulation of culture went much further than this. When the *Negro World* urged its readers to "Read Good Books During the Vacation," it was Garvey's *Philosophy and Opinions* which was recommended.[87] When the *Negro World* sponsored its "Great Literary Contest" in 1926 it stipulated that all entries were to be essays on the subject of "Why I Am A Garveyite," and when the winning entries were subsequently published in the paper they all emphasized Garvey's important role in arousing race pride and race consciousness.[88] The 1927 contest offered more choice. Entrants were to select what they felt to be the most forceful passage from Garvey's *Philosophy and Opinions*, and to explain their choice.[89] In similar vein, songs were sung in praise of Garvey at U.N.I.A. meetings and he was defended and applauded in poems and plays written by U.N.I.A. members. John Bruce's work was typical in this respect. In his short play *Soundings*, one of the characters describes Garvey as "one of the common people. . . . He is honest, brave hearted and true blue to his race. . . ."[90]

No member of the Harlem Renaissance ever expressed sentiments of this kind. Neither the ambivalence of Garvey's attitudes towards intellectuals and black culture, nor the cultural activities of the U.N.I.A.'s own intellectuals and artists were enough to resolve the considerable differences and mutual hostility between the two movements. However, the cultural dimension of Garveyism, plus the limited interests and objectives which it shared with the Renaissance, did have some influence on the relationship between the two. Occasionally the abuse which they hurled at each other was qualified by an element of mutual recognition and respect.

Though he modified his views on the role of intellectuals in the struggle for black liberation Garvey himself never retracted his criticisms of the Renaissance writers. However, the *Negro World*, his mouthpiece, publicized poetry readings, lectures and other events involving Renaissance artists, and it recorded the triumphs of people like Roland Hayes and Countee Cullen.[91] The paper's editor, T. Thomas Fortune, praised the Renaissance in general terms and singled out Walter White's novel *The Fire in the Flint* for special mention as "a masterpiece. . . . an epoch-making novel."[92] Garvey's friend John Bruce found occasion to commend the work of Claude McKay, James Weldon Johnson and in particular of W.E.B. DuBois, whom he described in 1921 as "unquestionably the greatest living Negro scholar today in America."[93] Even Garvey's wife joined in with an enthusiastic description of Langston Hughes as "a keen student of Garveyism"[94] following the publication of his 1926 article, "The Negro Artist and the Racial Mountain," which insisted that Negroes should produce an identifiably black art. The following week Mrs. Garvey's women's page in the *Negro World* included one of Hughes' poems.

No journal associated with the Harlem Renaissance ever published any of Garvey's poems. But if the people involved in the Renaissance were not prepared to recognize Garvey as a fellow artist and intellectual, some of them were at least able to identify his strengths as well as his weaknesses and one or two of the most discerning realized how important he was for the Renaissance itself.

Even Garvey's most bitter critics occasionally paid him compliments. George Schuyler described him as a "charismatic character," and Claude McKay conceded that he possessed "a very energetic and quick-witted mind."[95] Both of them recognized Garvey's abilities as propagandist, orator and organizer, and so too did men like James Weldon Johnson and W.E.B. DuBois who admired and envied the great influence which Garvey enjoyed among the black masses. In 1920 DuBois referred to Garvey's "tremendous vision" and "great dynamic force," and even some years later when the relationship between the two men was one of almost unrelieved hostility he conceded that his enemy's "plan to unite Negrodom by a line of steamships was a brilliant suggestion and Garvey's only original contribution to the race problem.[96]   Alain Locke also recognized the significant implications of Garvey's African policy. He emphasized how important and potentially constructive it was that Garvey had "stirred the race mind to the depths with the idea of large-scale cooperation between the variously separated branches of the Negro peoples." The Garvey movement in Locke's view had served to arouse a serious interest in Africa among American and West Indian Negroes and had effectively "built bridges of communication for the future."[97]

Alain Locke was also a perceptive enough observer of the Afro-American scene during the 1920s to grasp the fact that for some of the period's artists these "bridges of communication" were related parts of the phenomenon which he identified as the "New Negro." Although he never mentioned Garvey by name, Locke clearly had him in mind when in his analysis of the background to the Renaissance he emphasized the importance of the current upsurge of race-pride, race-consciousness and race-solidarity in the black community. "The younger generation," Locke wrote, "is vibrant with a new psychology; the new spirit is awake in the masses."[98]

What Locke had implied about the relationship between Garvey and the Harlem Renaissance was much more forcefully stated by Wallace Thurman. Thurman had been among the most articulate of Garvey's Renaissance critics and had condemned most aspects of the U.N.I.A. leader's personality and policies. One of the characters in Thurman's novel *Infants of the Spring* describes Garvey as "a great man with obvious limitations,"[99] and although Thurman himself found the limitations much more obvious than the greatness he was objective enough to recognize the importance of Garvey's role. For Thurman, Garvey's "one great contribution to the American Negro" was his insistence that Negroes should reject white standards and be "proud of their black skins, thick features, and kinky hair."[100]It was precisely this issue which formed the core of Thurman's novel *The Blacker the Berry* in which the central character Emma Lou Brown suffers much pain and humiliation until she comes to terms with her color. Thus Thurman drew on his own experience as an artist as well as on his familiarity with the work of his contemporaries when he summed up the relationship between Garvey and the Harlem Renaissance in this way: "Garvey did much to awaken 'race consciousness' among Negroes . . . The alleged Negro renaissance which has been responsible for the great number of suddenly articulate Negro poets, novelists, etc. (sic), owes much to Garvey and to his movement. He laid its foundation and aroused the need for its inception."[101]

NOTES

1 Amy Jaques Garvey, ed., **The Philosophy and Opinions of Marcus Garvey** (London, 1967), II, p. 123.

2 **Negro World,** July 12, 1924, p. 3.

3 **Ibid.**, March 3, 1923, p. 7.

4 **Ibid.**

5 **Ibid.**, March 17, 1923, p. 3.

6 **Ibid.**, August 23, 1924, p. 1.

7 **Ibid.**, September 27, 1924, p. 1.

8 **Ibid.**, September 29, 1928, p. 1.

9 For the views of Arthur Schomburg see the **Philadelphia Tribune,** March 15, 1928. William Ferris attacked McKay and Hughes in the **Pittsburgh Courier,** March 31, 1928. DuBois criticized McKay in language similar to Garvey's in **Crisis,** 35 (June 1928), 202.

10 **Negro World,** September 29, 1928, p. 1.

11 These quotations are from A. Philip Randolph, **Messenger,** V (January 1923), 561; W.E.B. DuBois, **Crisis,** 28 (May 1924), 8; and Charles S. Johnson, **Opportunity,** 1 (August 1923), 232.

12 W.E.B. DuBois, "Back to Africa," **Century Magazine,** 105 (February 1923), 540-41.

13 This issue is discussed in Edmund David Cronon, **Black Moses: The Story of Marcus Garvey and the Universal Negro Improvement Association** (Madison, Wisc., 1955), pp. 7-8.

14 Amy Jacques Garvey, **Philosophy and Opinions,** I, pp. 15-16.

15 **Ibid.**, II, p. 318.

16 **Ibid.**, I, p. 17.

17 Langston Hughes, **The Big Sea** (New York, 1963), p. 11.

18 Cited in Margaret Perry, **Silence to the Drums. A Survey of the Literature of the Harlem Renaissance** (Westport, Conn., and London, 1976), p. 32.

19 Amy Jacques Garvey, **Philosophy and Opinions,** II, p. 59.

20 **Ibid.**, II, pp. 310, 84.

21 **Ibid.**, II, p. 57.

22 **Negro World,** 29 September 1928, p. 1.

23 George S. Schuyler, **Black No More** (New York and London, 1971), p. 103.

24 Geogre S. Schuyler, **Black and Conservative: The Autobiography of George S. Schuyler** (New Rochelle, N.Y., 1966), p. 120.

25 Information from Schuyler's "Views and Reviews" column in the **Pittsburgh Courier** contained in the George Schuyler section of the Schomburg Collection Clipping File, New York Public Library. Schuyler, **Black and Conservative,** p. 120. The term megalomaniac was also applied to Garvey by Eric Walrond. See Walrond, "The New Negro Faces America," **Current History,** XVII (February 1923), 787.

26 Cited in Tony Martin, **Race First: The Ideological and Organizational Struggles of Marcus Garvey and the Universal Negro Improvement Association** (Westport, Conn., and London, 1976), p.297.

27 **Crisis,** 21 (December 1920), 58, 60; 24 (September 1922), 214; 28 (May 1924), 8.

28 Wallace Thurman, "Marcus Garvey," pp. 11-12. This undated and presumably unpublished article is in the Thurman Collection, Box I, Folder 15, The Beinecke Rare Book and Manuscript Library, Yale University.

29 Claude McKay, **A Long Way From Home** (New York, 1969), p. 354. See also McKay, **Banjo** (New York, 1957), p. 76.

30 Claude McKay in **The Liberator,** 5 (April 1922), 9.

31 James Weldon Johnson in his "Views and Reviews" column in the **New York Age**, August 19, 1922.

32 W.E.B. DuBois, "Back to Africa," **Century Magazine**, 105 (February, 1923), 539.

33 George S. Schuyler in **Messenger** VI, (July 1924), 213.

34 Countee Cullen, **One Way to Heaven** (New York and London, 1932), p. 190.

35 Zora Neale Hurston, "The Emperor Effaces Himself," p. 1. A typed carbon of this incomplete and presumably unpublished essay is in the Hurston Collection, Box I, Folder 16, The Beinecke Rare Book and Manuscript Library, Yale University.

36 **Ibid.**, p. 3.

37 Wallace Thurman and William Jordan Rapp, **Jeremiah the Magnificent**, Act I, p. 36. A Microfilm of the typescript of this unpublished play is in the Schomburg Collection, New York Public Library.

38 **Ibid.**, Act I, p. 10.

39 **Ibid.**, Act II, p. 1.

40 McKay, **Banjo**, p. 77.

41 Eric Walrond, "Imperator Africanus. Marcus Garvey: Menace or Promise," **The Independent**, 114 (January 1925), 9.

42 Cullen, **One Way to Heaven**, p. 191. James Weldon Johnson, **New York Age**, August 19, 1922.

43 Thurman and Rapp, **Jeremiah**, Act II, p. 30.

44 Thurman, "Marcus Garvey," p. 6.

45 **Messenger**, VI (February 1924), 41.

46 **Messenger**, VI (May 1924), 138.

47 **Pittsburgh Courier**, August 10, 1929.

48 Walrond, "Imperator Africanus," 10.

49 Thurman, "Marcus Garvey," p. 11.

50 McKay to James Weldon Johnson, Marseille, April 30, 1928, James Weldon Johnson Correspondence, Series I, Folder 308, The Beinecke Rare Book and Manuscript Library, Yale University.

51 W.E.B. DuBois, "Marcus Garvey and the NAACP," **Crisis**, 35 (February 1928), 51. See also **Crisis**, 22 (May 1921), 8.

52 Claude McKay in **The Liberator**, 5 (April 1922), 9.

53 George S. Schuyler, "A Negro Looks Ahead," **American Mercury** (February 1930), 214.

54 Wallace Thurman, "Marcus Garvey," p. 1.

55 Rudolph Fisher, "Ringtail," **Atlantic Monthly**, 135 (May 1925), 657.

56 Cited in Eugene Levy, **James Weldon Johnson. Black Leader, Black Voice** (Chicago and London, 1973), p. 231.

57 From Hughes' poem "Negro," **Crisis**, 23 (January 1922), 113.

58 Hughes, **The Big Sea**, p. 325.

59 Nella Larsen, **Passing** (New York and London, 1971), p. 178.

60 **Pittsburgh Courier**, January 7, 1928. Essentially the same point was made by Wallace Thurman in his article, "Nephews of Uncle Remus," **The Independent**, 119 (September 1927), 297. See also his novel, **Infants of the Spring** (Freeport, N.Y., 1972), pp. 234-241.

61 **Crisis**, 22 (May 1921), 8. In fairness to Garvey, it should be mentioned that he proposed to be selective in his choice of those members of his organization who were to go back to Africa. He emphasized that his program was one of African redemption rather than "Back to Africa" and argued that "we do not want all the Negroes in Africa. Some are no good here and naturally will be no good there." Garvey clearly saw the need in Africa for scientists, engineers, doctors, teachers and businessmen, but he also talked, less selectively, of repatriating "hundreds of thousands" of men and women. See Amy Jacques Garvey **Philosophy and Opinions**, II, p. 122, **Negro World**, January 12, 1924, p. 1,

and January 19, 1924, p. 1.

62 **Crisis**, 27 (November 1923), 9.

63 **The Liberator**, 5 (April 1922), 9. See also Wayne F. Cooper, ed., **The Passion of Claude McKay. Selected Poetry and Prose, 1912 -1948** (New York, 1973), pp. 15, 53.

64 George S. Schuyler, "A Negro Looks Ahead," **American Mercury** (February, 1930), 217.

65 **Pittsburgh Courier**, July 23, 1927.

66 Fisher, "Ringtail," 656-57.

67 See above, p. 11. Also, DuBois, cited in Tony Martin, **Race First**, 295.

68 Cited in **Ibid.**, p.287. See also pp. 276, 299.

69 **Negro World**, October 25, 1924, p. 1.

70 **Ibid.**, April 27, 1928, p. 4.

71 Joel Rogers, **World's Great Men of Color** (New York, 1972), II, p. 432.

72 McKay, **A Long Way From Home**, p. 87.

73 John E. Bruce Papers, Bruce 430, Schomburg Collection, New York Public Library.

74 **Negro World**, April 28, 1923, p.10.

75 **Ibid.**, July 17, 1926, p. 1.

76 Amy Jacques Garvey, **Philosophy and Opinions**, II, p. 24. See also **Negro World**, January 26, 1924, p. 3.

77 **Negro World**, June 7, 1924, p. 1.

78 **Ibid.**, December 17, 1921, August 28, 1926, February 5, 1927.

79 **Ibid.**, March 3, 1923, p. 3; March 7, 1925, p. 5.

80 **Ibid.**, October 22, 1927, p. 4.

81 Amy Jacques Garvey, **Garvey and Garveyism** (London, 1970), p. 168.

82 Marcus Garvey, **Selections from the Poetic Meditations of Marcus Garvey** (New York, 1927), p. 20.

83 **Negro World**, April 28, 1923, p. 1.

84 **Ibid.**, August 23, 1924, p. 20.

85 **Ibid.**, September 29, 1928, p. 1.

86 Hughes to Carl Van Vecten, February 17, 1932, Carl Van Vecten Correspondence, Beinecke Rare Book and Manuscript Library, Yale University.

87 **Negro World**, September 4, 1926, p. 9.

88 **Ibid.**, August 28, 1926, p. 5, January 8, 1927, p. 3.

89 **Ibid.**, February 5, 1927, p. 5.

90 Bruce Papers, B 9-87.

91 See, for example, **Negro World**, March 31, 1923; April 7, 1923; October 6, 1923; December 1, 1923; December 15, 1923, p. 6; November 22, 1924, p. 4; December 13, 1924, p. 4.

92 **Ibid.**, October 4, 1924, p. 4; November 22, 1924, p. 4.

93 Bruce Papers, B5 3-5.

94 **Negro World**, July 10, 1926, p. 5.

95 Schuyler, **Black Conservative**, p. 120. McKay in **The Liberator**, 5 (April 1922), 8.

96 **Crisis**, 21 (December, 1920) 58, Ibid., 24 (September, 1922), 210.

97 Alain Locke, "Apropos of Africa," **Opportunity**, 2 (February 1924), 37-38.

98 Alain Locke, **The New Negro. An Interpretation** (New York and London, 1968), pp. 3, 7, 8.

99 Thurman, **Infants of the Spring**, p. 219.

100 Thurman, "Marcus Garvey," p. 2.

101 **Ibid.**, pp. 11-12.

ALAIN LOCKE AND WALTER WHITE: THEIR STRUGGLE

FOR CONTROL OF THE HARLEM RENAISSANCE

CHARLES W. SCRUGGS

For a long time, it was fashionable to believe that the Harlem Renaissance was no more than a puff of smoke in a brightly-lit Harlem cabaret. The music was real; the cabarets were real; the white people slumming in Harlem were real; but the literary movement was not. "It was all," as Abraham Chapman has ironically said, "a figment of the Negro imagination."[1] Today we have no trouble accepting the reality of the Harlem Renaissance, but we have also come to accept views about it which are only half-true. We are told, for instance, that the Harlem Renaissance failed because of the dictatorial policies of white publishers, the meddling of white patrons, and the corrupt tastes of the white public. In other words, the black intellectuals themselves had very little to do with governing their own destinies.[2] In this paper, I wish to argue that two black writers of the 1920s were very much in control of their destinies to the point that they actually challenged one another for the leadership of the Harlem Renaissance. Furthermore, in following the literary careers of Alain Locke and Walter White during this period, we are in a position to see that both the patronage system and the publishing situation were far more complicated than we have previously imagined.

Between 1923 and 1926, the crucial early years of the Harlem Renaissance, Alain Locke and Walter White were each building a separate base of political power. Although Walter White is more commonly identified with his later role as Executive Secretary of the NAACP, his unpublished correspondence in the 1920s shows that he frequently came into conflict with Alain Locke over matters involving personal ambition. There was never an open declaration of war between White and Locke, but the unpublished correspondence of both reveals an uneasy tension between them. White was hostile to Locke because he felt that Locke had betrayed him, and Locke, in turn, was suspicious of White's motives vis-à-vis the Harlem Renaissance.[3]

"Charmy" Patterson at the Umbra Workshop (1963)

91

Walter White had two qualities which Americans generally admire: perseverance and ingenuity. In six short years (1918-1924), he had gone from an obscure insurance salesman in Atlanta, Georgia, to become the Assistant Secretary of the NAACP and the author of a popular novel. Published by Alfred Knopf in 1924, *The Fire in the Flint* marked the beginning of White's literary career.

White's entrance into the literary world is indicative of his enterprising personality. When H. L. Mencken's famous essay "The Sahara of the Bozart" appeared in *Prejudices II* (1920), White was responsive to Mencken's theme that the South had become a cultural desert after the Civil War. He wrote Mencken in praise of the essay, and Mencken encouraged White to write a novel about his own racial experiences in Georgia. [4] Following Mencken's advice, White wrote *The Fire in the Flint* in twelve days during the Summer of 1922, but a problem immediately arose over publication. Doran and Company accepted the manuscript but then had second thoughts. White desperately wanted the novel published by Doran, but the publishing house had changed its mind, for both aesthetic and non-aesthetic reasons. [5]

White's cleverness can be seen in the way that he manipulated Mencken into believing that Doran was guilty of great moral cowardice. Knowing Mencken's "prejudices," White told Mencken that Doran had refused to publish his manuscript because it had feared the novel's "effect on the South." [6] White said nothing, of course, about Doran's aesthetic objections. Naturally the novel's fate now took on a new significance for Mencken. Convinced that once again the South was responsible for suppressing the truth, Mencken sent the manuscript to Knopf with a strong recommendation, and the novel was accepted in December, 1923. [7]

The Fire in the Flint enjoyed a modest success, and White exploited its popularity by cultivating people in high places. Being both charming and shrewd, he made friendships with well-known authors, editors, publishers, and literary critics. Within a short time, he was on intimate terms with Alfred Knopf, Horace Liveright, Sinclair Lewis, Carl Van Vechten, Carl Van Doren, Heywood Broun, and others.

As his circle of famous acquaintances widened, Walter White saw an opportunity to benefit the black writers of the 1920s. In 1924, for instance, he took Countee Cullen's poetry to Horace Liveright, and when that venture failed, he went to Harper Brothers, and he singlehandedly convinced them to publish Cullen's first book (*Color*). In the eyes of black writers, he became a symbol of worldly wisdom. Langston Hughes, Rudolph Fisher, and Claude McKay eagerly sought his help, for Walter White knew how to get a book published and he knew how to sell that book once it was published. [8]

Because Renaissance writers admired White's *savoir-faire* and because White saw himself as their friend at court, he began to entertain thoughts of becoming a spokesman for the Harlem Renaissance. In

1925 and 1926, he penned several critical pieces which defined the movement's goals and accomplishments. Between March and July of 1926, he wrote a literary column in *The Pittsburgh Courier* called "The Spotlight," in which he sought to introduce the Harlem Renaissance to the black public. Given White's pragmatic cast of mind, it is not surprising that he ran into conflict with the academic Alain Locke.

A Rhodes scholar, a Harvard Ph.D., a student at Oxford University and the University of Berlin, and, in the early 1920s, a professor of philosophy at Howard University — Alain Locke had more patience than White and waited to have greatness thrust upon him. It came at the hands of Charles S. Johnson, editor of the newly-created *Opportunity* magazine. In June, 1923, Johnson asked Locke if he would like to serve "as a special foreign correspondent" for *Opportunity*. [9] Locke responded by writing an article called "The Colonial Literature of France," in which he praised René Maran, author of the prize-winning *Batouala*, for breaking new ground. In his novel, Maran had depicted the life of the African native "in and for itself" without any special pleading. Locke thought that the Afro-American writer could learn a lesson from the African novelist. The true artist, Locke suggested, should take a "purely aesthetic approach" to his material: "art for its own sake combined with that stark cult of veracity — the truth, whether it hurts or not." [10]

Impressed by Locke's views, Charles S. Johnson told Locke about a group of young writers who had been meeting under his direction. On March 4, 1924, Johnson wrote Locke to ask him if he would be a "sort of Master of Ceremonies" at a dinner party, scheduled for March 21, 1924, "to mark the growing self-consciousness of this newer school of writers." Notables from the white literary world, Johnson added, would also be invited. Johnson made it clear, three days later, that this Opportunity Dinner (as it came to be called) would also give official sanction to Locke's role as " 'Dean' of this younger group." [11]

An episode which followed the Opportunity Dinner, however, brought Locke and White into opposition for the first time and was to establish the tension between them which characterized their communication with one another for nearly a decade. The episode itself must be described in the larger context of each man's relationship with Alfred C. Barnes, a white collector of African art.

In the early months of 1924, both Walter White and Alain Locke had been engaged in researching the impact of Negro art on Western Civilization, and during this time, the two men exchanged letters concerning their discoveries. [12] As early as December, 1923, White had written Carl Van Doren to tell him about an essay he had been working on, "in which," he said, "I am trying to show that, artistically, the world would probably be much further advanced if Negroes had been the masters and whites the slaves in the South." [13] He hoped to publish this article in Mencken's *American Mercury*, for he thought its ironic premise would appeal to the castigator of American humbug. [14] When the Opportunity Dinner was held in

March, Alain Locke, knowing of White's projected article, seated White next to Alfred C. Barnes. [15]

At this memorable dinner, both White and Locke gave speeches about the new literary movement, but White also used this opportunity to ask questions of Barnes, in the hopes that Barnes's immense learning might prove useful. He informed Barnes that he had spent the last six months "running down information on the influence of primitive African art on Modern art," and asked if Barnes would criticize his essay, which he enclosed. [16]

Barnes was not one to mince words. He red-penciled White's article and returned it. Not satisfied that he had done all he could to discourage White, he also included a copy of an article he had written on African art, which had not yet been submitted to a journal, and a letter he had written to Charles S. Johnson outlining a program whereby Negro art in America could be advanced by Afro-American intellectuals. On the same day he wrote White (March 25), he complained to Locke that "if babes like him [White] are to be entrusted with the presentation of negro essentials to an educated public, I fear the cause will be a hard one to push to its right end. I saw the other night that he was a lightweight but his manuscript has revealed a cheapness which I hardly suspected." On March 28, Barnes again wrote Locke and called White a "personal pusher."

Meanwhile, White simply ignored Barnes's scathing criticism of his article, and he blithely asked Barnes on March 26 if he could use "one or two quotations from your letter [to Charles S. Johnson] and your article ['The Temple']." Barnes answered him quite cautiously on March 27: He was not sure how much White could borrow from " 'The Temple,' without detracting from its value as an original communication soon to be published (I hope)." He told White that he had given "The Temple" to Charles S. Johnson, asking him to send it to The American Mercury.

In actual fact, Johnson had sent two articles by Barnes to Mencken, the one dealing with native African art ("The Temple") and another with American Negro art. Barnes expected Mencken to publish both, but, to his astonishment, Mencken published neither. On April 7, Charles S. Johnson wrote Barnes that Mencken had rejected "The Temple" and the essay on American Negro art. It seemed that Mencken wanted to confine his magazine to American themes for the first year, and that—here was the shock—White was evidently doing the only essay on Negro art for The American Mercury. Mencken, said Johnson, "is apparently under the delusion that White's article is going to discuss primitive Negro art"; that is, in addition to American Negro art.

Barnes was furious. He was convinced that White was going to steal his ideas. On the same day he received Johnson's bad news, he wrote an angry letter to White asking for the return of "The Temple." He then complained to Mencken about White, but Mencken seemed genuinely confused by Barnes's letter. Mencken said that he knew White well and was "delighted to discover your interest in him and his work." This feigned innocence, as it seemed to the

waspish Barnes, made the art critic angrier still. He wrote Mencken a letter on April 10 he could not possibly misunderstand. He told Mencken that he had never given White permission to use "his documents," that White had never returned them, "and has ignored my request to return them." He desired that his "wishes" be respected, but if Mencken insisted on publishing White's article, said an embittered Barnes, "as a son-of-a-bitch you are a thoroughbred." No one knows Mencken's response to this letter, but it is possible to conjecture that both Johnson and Locke supported Barnes against White: White's article was never published, anywhere. Furthermore, Johnson published "The Temple" in Opportunity (May, 1924), and Locke later published Barnes's "Negro Art and America" in The Survey Graphic, a white magazine which devoted one issue (March, 1925), edited by Locke, to a "Special Negro Number." This "Number" was later to become the well-known anthology The New Negro.

Although White had been guilty of overweening ambition (and possibly plagiarism), Locke made a special effort to placate White. He told White that he planned to reprint an essay which White had written— called "Color Lines"—in The New Negro. Now Locke had recently published this essay, which analyzed color prejudice within the race, in the March, 1925, issue of The Survey Graphic, but between March and the forthcoming winter publication of The New Negro, the white anthropologist Melville Herskovits had written an article on the same subject as White's for the October issue of The American Mercury. Locke diplomatically suggested to White that he incorporate Herskovits's new information into his own essay, and he sent White a copy of Herskovits's article. [17] White's response to this ploy indicates that he had not forgiven Locke for siding with Barnes. He was angry that the writing of another white "authority" was given precedence over his own work, and on June 3, 1925, he bluntly rejected Locke's "suggestion":

I have read his article and, frankly, I don't see that there is anything in it which would improve my Survey article. As a matter of fact, every one of us who is colored knows more instinctively about color lines within the race than almost any white man can ever know. You will forgive my frankness, I am sure, when I am dogmatic enough to say that I have never yet met a white person who thoroughly understood the psychology of race prejudice within the Negro race. [18]

He concluded by telling Locke that he could either take the article as it was, or leave it out of the anthology altogether.

There was yet another reason for White's seeming indifference to the fate of this article in The New Negro. It was White who had suggested creating the anthology in the first place, and he wanted to edit it himself. In March, 1925, he had telephoned Lewis Baer of the publishing firm of Albert and Charles Boni when the "Special Negro Number" appeared on the newsstands. He told Baer over the phone that he would like to transform this "Special Negro Number" into a book. The next day, White had second thoughts. He wrote

93

Baer and told him that he would still like to be the editor of this book but that there were "difficulties." He admitted that "Alain Locke . . . is the man more largely responsible for the number than any other individual," and that he would not take the job of editor unless Locke agreed to it. "If these difficulties can be overcome," he added, "then we can be in a position to talk more definitely." [19] Although White had seriously considered stealing another man's work, his conscience finally overcame his anger and ambition. It is to his credit that he saw the "difficulties."

It is also a remarkable historical irony that White was responsible for the publication of *The New Negro*. Albert and Charles Boni agreed that Locke should be consulted about being the anthology's editor, [20] and naturally he accepted the job. Again, Fortune seemed to smile upon Locke; *The New Negro* became the artistic manifesto of the Harlem Renaissance and made Locke famous. When a second Opportunity Dinner was held on May 1, 1925, Alain Locke was again Master of Ceremonies. Significantly, Walter White did not attend. [21]

II

Alain Locke's public triumphs, however, were not an accurate indication of his political power. One reason for White's audacity in writing Baer was that five days earlier he had persuaded Harper Brothers to accept Countee Cullen's first book of poetry. It is here that White's superior resources were apparent: He knew important people. During the early years of the 1920s, both White and Locke had seen Cullen as the bright new Harlem poet, and both tried to be his mentor and patron. Cullen's desertion of Locke in favor of White demonstrates the inherent weakness in Locke's role as Renaissance spokesman. In the 1920s, black writers wanted to be published by prestigious white firms, and Locke was in no position to help them.

As a student at New York University in 1922, Cullen sought to become a Rhodes scholar. Locke was, as Cullen said in his first letter to him, "our race's sole representative." [22] They spent the Christmas holidays together, confessed their private lives to one another, and soon became fast friends. Cullen encouraged Locke (January 12, 1923) to "continue to manifest such laudable interest in the aspiring youth of the race. We need it more than we need money. It is a cause worthy of any man's devotion, but so many of our men whose names have meaning now cannot realize their duty to those who come after them. I am thankful to you." The thirty-six-year-old Locke soon began to take a paternal interest in Cullen's literary career, and the nineteen-year-old Cullen soon began to depend upon Locke for advice and spiritual support.

Since he was not an athlete, Cullen felt that publishing a book of his poems would help him with the Rhodes Scholarship judges. He asked Locke on February 20, 1923, if he had "any influence with publishers." That Locke had little influence with publishers caused hardly a ripple in the father-son relationship which was developing throughout 1923.

In May, 1923, Cullen received a sympathetic letter from Horace Liveright (of Boni and Liveright) and immediately wrote to Locke about it. Liveright had told Cullen that if "you could give us a volume of poems . . . as good as 'To a Brown Boy' and 'King Arthur to Guinevere,' . . . I would publish it." Lamenting that he had not "enough material of that calibre," he told Locke that "perhaps by September" he would. A few days later, on June 8, 1923, he thanked Locke for continuing to stand by him: "I am sincerely grateful to you, and I wish more race men were concerned with the younger fellows."

At the beginning of 1924, Cullen began to be lionized by important people, and his poems were being accepted by white journals. An impressionable Cullen met the popular imagist poet Witter Bynner, who "treated me," he said to Locke on January 7, "as if he had known me all his life." On January 13, he informed Locke that Oswald Villard, editor of *The Nation*, promised to recommend him for the Rhodes Scholarship and had taken a poem ("The Wise") for his magazine. During 1924, Cullen was also to have poems accepted by *American Mercury, Century Magazine, Bookman*, and *Harper's*. He was beginning to get a reputation.

Cullen had asked Witter Bynner to write an introduction to his book of poems if and when they were published. He was both pleased and troubled when Bynner agreed to do the introduction, as there had been a tacit understanding between Locke and Cullen that Locke himself was to write the introduction. Since he had not told Locke about Bynner's introduction, an anxious Cullen wrote Locke on March 24: He had asked Bynner, he said, because "I thought his name would avail much. . . . You can appreciate my dilemma, and I am relying on you to help me extricate myself. I would much prefer you to do the introduction, unless you think there would be more point to one outside the race. Be thinking it over; you know my faith in your judgment." By throwing the decision on Locke, Cullen was trying to escape facing the fact that he really wanted the better-known Bynner to do the introduction.

Locke's response was fair-minded, but his tone was that of a man who had suffered disappointment. He was leaving the decision up to Cullen: "I appreciate your attitude, but I have no suggestion to offer as long as Bynner has a mind to keep the agreement." He said that he would want to know, however, which way Cullen decided. Locke was at that time writing an article on "The Younger Generation," and if Cullen chose him, he would "hold back some things from the article" for the introduction. Locke also warned Cullen that he "should by all means see his [Bynner's] preface before deciding." [23] In short, Locke did not let Cullen escape the responsibility of choice, and from this time on, tension existed between the two men whenever Cullen's literary future was discussed.

In the second half of 1924, Locke was busy working on his *Survey Graphic* project. Cullen had promised Locke poems for the "Special Negro Number," but as the established magazines began to accept his work, he asked Locke to return some of them. At first Cullen had

94

been quite generous. He told Locke on July 1, "As to the poems you want for the Survey—you may use them all except 'To a Brown Boy,' for it was published last November in the *Bookman*." But as the year wore on, more and more poems seemed committed to white magazines. Cullen's letter to Locke on October 17 suggests that Locke was becoming desperate: "You need never beg for any of my work that you desire to use; whatever I have is going for the asking." But after this avowal of good faith, Cullen added, " 'Fruit of the Flower' I can't send you; you know it was taken by *Harper's*." Then three days later Cullen had to apologize again: "Please don't think me utterly irresponsible, but I just received a letter from *Harper's* saying that they had accepted six Epigraphs from a group which I sent them over two months ago and which I thought had been lost. . . . Please don't be disgusted with me."

No doubt Locke *was* disgusted with Cullen at this point, especially since his behavior had been erratic on more than one occasion in 1924. Cullen had come running back to Locke when Witter Bynner decided that Cullen did not have enough good poems for a book. A contrite Cullen had tried to make amends: "I have decided that it is imperative that you do my introduction. It is folly for me to consider allowing anyone else to do it." When *Color* was finally published, it included no introduction; and the fact is significant. By 1925 Locke and Cullen's friendship had greatly deteriorated.

The rupture came in December, 1924. On October 27, Cullen had told Locke that *The Survey Graphic* could have his poem "Heritage" but only if "they are willing to pay fifty dollars for it, and only then because of my desire to see nothing lacking that I can supply in a venture fostered by *you*." Cullen's motives were not simply mercenary; there was some snobbery here as well. After keeping such good company, he felt that he was lowering himself by publishing his best poem in a "Special Negro Number." He halfway hoped that *The Survey Graphic* would refuse to pay the money, so that "Heritage" could be published in a prestigious white magazine.

On December 20, Cullen wrote Locke that he needed the money badly and that he would contact the editor of *The Survey Graphic* unless they sent it to him: "For me to go to Mr. Kellogg does not seem in the best taste, but I shall be forced to do that unless I hear from him by Wednesday morning." Then without waiting for Locke's answer, Cullen phoned Mr. Kellogg and got the fifty dollars. He wrote Locke immediately (December 23), asking him not to "be angry about it."

Locke did not answer Cullen's letter for several days. For him, the incident involved more than bad taste; it put the whole *Survey Graphic* project in jeopardy. Not hearing from Locke, Cullen started to worry (January 6): "I am beginning to fear that you are angry with me, and I am deeply concerned over your silence. Am I to lose another friend over a trifle?" Locke apparently wrote Cullen and told him that their relationship was over, for Cullen wrote to Locke on January 19: "Should you persist in your determination, at any rate the break

will not be mutual. I still consider myself your friend."

Locke soon relented and forgave Cullen, but their friendship was never the same, and it was further impaired by the ubiquitous Walter White. Cullen had met White in 1924, and White—as indefatigable as ever—immediately began to seek a publisher for Cullen's book. He sought advice from Carl Van Doren and tried to convince Horace Liveright that publishing Cullen would be a worthwhile financial venture. It is characteristic of Walter White that he was not satisfied just to place Cullen's book with Harper Brothers. He began an enthusiastic advertising campaign for *Color* before it was even published. [24]

Thus White supplanted Locke as Cullen's mentor. On May 27, 1925, Cullen told Locke that since "your coming is uncertain," he would ask Walter White to be Master of Ceremonies at the reception for his book. Later, in January, 1926, Cullen asked White to write an introduction (concerning "the general trend of modern Negro verse") to a special issue of the Mexican literary journal *Palms* which Cullen was editing. [25] This time, White, not Locke, was to introduce the New Negro.

III

In different ways, Alain Locke and Walter White imposed their wills on the writers they helped. Locke wanted to fit the aesthetic energies of the Harlem Renaissance into his preconceived plan. In addition to Cullen's desertion of Locke for practical reasons, the growing coolness between the two men can be traced to Cullen's apostasy from Locke's credo for black literature. Locke urged the black writer to express his racial self and the "folk-spirit" of his race; whereas Cullen, after the publication of *Color*, was trying to escape the nets of race and the label of black poet. [26] As we shall see, Locke's rigid views had also caused him to lose the trust of Claude McKay. On the other hand, Walter White wanted to be the movement's administrator. He saw himself as a traffic cop directing black writers to their various destinations. He did not especially care (as Locke did) what these destinations were, but he *did* become angry when black writers did not follow his advice as to how to get there. Claude McKay was one writer who refused to listen to Walter White and who paid for it.

Claude McKay had always remained on the periphery of the Renaissance, partly because of his strongly individualistic personality, but also because of his self-exile in France. As an outsider, he had some perceptive insights into what was going wrong with the Harlem Renaissance, and some of his criticism applies to Locke and White, both of whom did in fact betray him.

In 1924, McKay was working on a first novel entitled *Color Scheme*. White's connection with this novel is complex, but he is partly responsible for its never being published. White had written McKay in November, 1924, that he had heard about McKay's novel from Locke and that he wanted to know more about it. Locke had described *Color Scheme* in his usual abstract manner, said White, "which did not amount to much

95

when boiled down to words of less than two syllables.'' He urged McKay to show the novel to Sinclair Lewis, who was also living in France. Lewis, he told McKay, had gone over *The Fire in the Flint* ''page by page, line by line.'' [27]

In subsequent correspondence, White kept reminding McKay to submit his novel for publication as soon as possible. ''The Negro artist is really in the ascendancy right now,'' he said in May, 1925. He urged McKay to send *Color Scheme* to a new firm, Viking Press. The owners were ''two young, enthusiastic and intelligent men. . . . If you want me to, I will put you in touch with them.'' [28]

McKay answered White in June, 1925. He told White that he had sent his novel to Arthur Schomburg and that White could get the manuscript from him. Expecting White to help him with a publisher as he had promised, McKay then explained that he wanted an established firm like Knopf, or Boni and Liveright, or Harcourt Brace. Having failed those, he agreed, ''I should try Viking.'' [29]

On July 8, 1925, White wrote McKay, expressing mild disapproval. He said that he had no ''quarrel with Knopf,'' but that a new firm like Viking would advertise a book more than would an old firm, ''and in this day of modern salesmanship, a book stands practically no chance unless it is pushed and pushed hard. However, it is your novel and yours is the final decision to be made.'' [30] Although McKay had indicated that he was willing to try other publishers if he failed with Knopf, White appears to have been offended that his original advice had not been taken. Schomburg proceeded to send McKay's manuscript to Knopf, and McKay innocently thought that White, in accord with the early promise, would help him get it published there. As it turned out, White had not spoken to anyone at Knopf; he had washed his hands of the whole matter.

Like McKay, Schomburg thought that White was encouraging Knopf to publish *Color Scheme*. When Knopf rejected the novel, the manuscript was sent to Schomburg on July 22, and Schomburg immediately wrote to White on July 24. Knopf objected, he said, to certain ''candid references'' in *Color Scheme*. He asked if White wanted to submit the manuscript to another publisher. [31]

McKay heard the bad news from Schomburg. Schomburg also enclosed a letter he had received from White (July 23), deploring McKay's choice of Knopf. An angry and troubled McKay immediately wrote White to explain once again the reason for his wanting Knopf. An old firm, he said, had no trouble selling its books. By this time he did not care who published *Color Scheme*; he just wanted ''some firm that will pay me something down on the M.S.'' [32]

A few days later in August, McKay wrote White another letter, apologizing for the tone of the previous one. He had been angry, he said, because the Knopf readers had kept his book for so long. He had heard that ''your friend Carl Van Vechten is doing a novel on Harlem Negro life and I don't want him to get in ahead of me because he would hurt my chances, being a white man and a popular novelist known to all the gaudy crop

of bleating reviewers.'' [33] Puzzled by the rejection, Claude McKay still knew nothing of White's indifference to the fate of *Color Scheme*. [34] One has to wonder whether White's sense of obligation to his friend Carl Van Vechten was influencing him at the time. Van Vechten was already a Knopf author, and *Nigger Heaven*, the Harlem novel, turned out to be as racy a manuscript as one could find in the 1920s. Did White deliberately refrain from talking to Knopf about *Color Scheme* because of his friendship with Van Vechten, and did the publishing house reject *Color Scheme* because it was waiting for Van Vechten to finish *Nigger Heaven*? If so, the politics of the Harlem Renaissance are murky indeed.

The intrigue was further complicated by a letter White received in August from Sinclair Lewis. Lewis had read *Color Scheme* and did not like it. White accepted this opinion without question. He immediately wrote his friend Oppenheimer at Viking, who was still waiting to see the manuscript: ''I wanted to give you some new information I got from Sinclair Lewis about the McKay novel.'' [35] Although this letter to Oppenheimer did not indicate the precise nature of that ''information,'' Gracie Lewis's biography of her husband does. Sinclair Lewis had delicately urged McKay ''to scrap the whole thing.'' [36]

A day after his letter to Oppenheimer, White wrote Schomburg. He was at a loss over what to do, since McKay did not want his novel published by Viking: ''When I first spoke to the Viking Press I think I could have gotten it by there, but now I do not think they would be so interested in it.'' [37] For some reason he did not tell Schomburg that Sinclair Lewis had not liked *Color Scheme* or that he had communicated Lewis's opinion to Viking. White encouraged Schomburg to send the manuscript to Harcourt Brace, but it does not appear to have been sent there.

On August 28, White finally answered McKay's three letters. He defended Knopf's rejection of *Color Scheme*: ''I am quite sure that in that case there was no element of color prejudice or conservatism.'' He recommended Harcourt as a logical choice because it ''has had nothing by a colored writer on its list since [James Weldon] Johnson's Anthology.'' [38] A despondent and beaten McKay replied on September 7 that he ''didn't give a whoop what publisher took the M.S.'' [39] By the beginning of the new year, he had resigned himself to the idea that *Color Scheme* would never be published. ''I have made up my mind to the fact,'' he told Alain Locke, ''that the book must be bad, so I must do another.'' [40]

No one is likely ever to know how ''bad'' the novel was—the manuscript of *Color Scheme* has never been located. McKay might have destroyed it in despair. In any event, a partial answer is given by this episode to a question which critics often ask: Why did McKay wait until 1928 to publish his first novel (*Home to Harlem*)? Whatever excuses might be found for White's loss of interest in securing a publisher for McKay's novel, he was certainly guilty of intellectual timidity: He refused to challenge the opinion of Sinclair Lewis. He probably did not know himself why he dumped McKay's novel.

He may have wanted to keep the prestige of being the only black novelist published by Knopf at that time. If so, there is a special irony here, for White had made an appeal to H. L. Mencken similar to that which McKay had made to him. When White had been looking for a publisher for *The Fire in the Flint* after Doran had rejected his manuscript, he had told Mencken that he wanted an established firm like Knopf to assure his book of having the widest possible reading audience. But whatever White's motivation for ignoring his tacit promise to McKay, part of it appears to have been a desire to please his impressive friends, Van Vechten and Lewis.

White eventually gave up his literary career and his interest in the Harlem Renaissance for a different political arena. In 1931, he replaced James Weldon Johnson as Executive Secretary of the NAACP. Only a year before White's retirement from the Harlem literary scene, Claude McKay—still not knowing of White's part in his first novel's fate—wrote an ironically perceptive letter to Mrs. Osgood Mason, a white patron:

> The Negro renaissance movement in America seems a hopeless mess to me. . . . If I were in touch with any of the young aspiring Negro artists I'd advise them to get as far away as possible from it. I read the writings of the so-called leaders and I got a good drift of the whole thing from some of its members in Paris last summer. They are all no doubt terribly insincere. They have no real idea of what they want to do—what they can get in an artistic form from this life of the Negro. They were much more interested in the opinions of a few white persons of *authority*—even though these were lacking in the fine esthetic spirit of appreciation. [41]

Claude McKay probably had others in mind besides White, but his portrait of the Renaissance "leaders" brings home a striking truth about White's character. His greatest virtue, his toughminded pragmatism, was also his greatest flaw. He knew how to manipulate white people in the world of action, but as a Renaissance leader he was hesitant to act in the world of ideas. Having advertised the young literary movement to his powerful white friends, he also tied himself to their shirttails, and he sometimes forgot where his real loyalties lay. Blinded by the glitter of his own personal success, he never really caught sight of the fact that a renaissance means a rebirth of ideas as well as the recognition of its artists in the literary columns of fashionable magazines.

In his dealings with Alain Locke, McKay found further cause for his disaffection for the Harlem Renaissance. McKay had submitted, at Locke's request, several poems for the "Special Negro Number" of *The Survey Graphic*. Locke found one poem, "Mulatto," too "strong" for this white journal. McKay was furious that the poem was excised, and he complained to Locke that "Mulatto" was "not stronger than 'If We Must Die' which *The Liberator* first published. I guess if *The Liberator* had not set that example not a Negro publication would have enough of the 'guts' you mention to publish it! It isn't *The Survey* that hasn't guts enough. It is *you*." For taking "such a weak line,"

McKay called Locke "a dyed-in-the-wool pussy-footing professor." [42]

Locke was to incur McKay's wrath once again, for Locke had meddled with another McKay poem in the "Special Negro Number." Not content with deleting "Mulatto," he also changed the title of "The White House" to "White Houses." As McKay was to complain to Locke several years later, the change of title made him appear "as a ridiculous, angry person hankering after the unattainable fleshpots of the whites." [43] Locke simply refused to recognize McKay's rights as an author, and he continued to publish the poem as "White Houses" in *The New Negro* and *Four Negro Poets* (1927). And Locke was to take more liberty with McKay's poetry. He published "Negro Dancers" in *The New Negro* without asking McKay's permission. [44]

By 1927, McKay had lost his patience with Locke's high-handed ways. After McKay had discovered that Locke had anthologized his poetry in *Four Negro Poets*, again without asking, McKay told Locke that he no longer wanted to be included in any of Locke's work. Locke wrote him back and lamented that "the movement suffers," and implied that McKay's recalcitrant behavior was somehow responsible for the decline. McKay responded with candid criticism of Locke and the Harlem Renaissance: "The 'movement suffers,' you write. I won't comment on that except to say that perhaps the movement would suffer less, if the individuals who pretend they are leading it displayed a little more intellectual solidarity and disinterestedness." [45] This last jab no doubt hurt, for McKay pinpointed exactly the egotism of which we have seen examples.

Nevertheless, Claude McKay was wrong about Locke's reasons for doctoring his poems. Locke was neither a coward nor a toady. Locke simply found that some of Claude McKay's poems did not fit his own aesthetic program for the Harlem Renaissance. "Negro Dancers" *did* fit his philosophical schema because it illustrated the search for African roots which, Locke believed, should be a primal concern of all black writers. But both "Mulatto" and "The White House" were too inflammatory for the kind of cultural pluralism Locke espoused. He could tolerate "protest" poetry but not the kind McKay wrote, for McKay—being the outsider that he was—sometimes thumbed his nose at society altogether. Locke wanted individualism, but only the kind which was finally a part of the whole. For Locke, the Negro was to celebrate his racial past and glorify his own culture but always with an eye toward being incorporated into the American tossed salad. McKay's romantic individualism was simply too anarchic to deal with.

Being a "pussy-footing professor," then, was not one of Locke's faults. Rather, he tended to feel that it was *his* Renaissance, that he was its sole proprietor. His wealthy white patron, Mrs. Osgood Mason, encouraged him to take this view. Locke had met her in 1927, and at age eighty-four she discovered the presence of the Negro in American culture. (In the previous decade she had been fascinated by the plight of the American Indian.) She was willing to help

97

financially those writers who belonged to Locke's coterie, but Mrs. Mason's money was a mixed blessing. On the one hand, Locke did have something tangible to offer black writers for once. Langston Hughes, Zora Neale Hurston, Claude McKay, and Rudolph Fisher were all brought into Mrs. Mason's fold on Locke's recommendation; her money gave Locke the kind of respect that was ordinarily reserved for the more practical Walter White. On the other hand, "Godmother" (as she was affectionately called) could be a demanding governess. In his autobiography *The Big Sea*, Langston Hughes documents her attempts to force him to write and feel like a "primitive." Hughes finally broke from her, because he could not give her the African poetry she wanted [46]; but Locke, in letter after letter, seemed to yield to her dictatorial opinions. Her attitude was, in fact, a caricature of his own aesthetic platform for the Harlem Renaissance, [47] which probably explains why he found it so hard to reject her.

"Godmother's" influence upon Locke was finally pernicious. Under her guidance, Locke became petty and intolerant, and he no doubt drove away many of the younger writers. When he wrote to "Godmother," the urbanity of his public statements disappeared. He became uncharitable to writers he felt had betrayed him or had not written as he wanted them to. Wallace Thurman was a "traitor" (for writing *Harlem*); James Weldon Johnson was "profiteering" (from editing a second anthology of Negro poetry); Zora Hurston had been "disloyal"; and Arthur Fauset, because he married, "will be of no use to us now for some years." [48] As the group around Locke and "Godmother" slowly dissolved, Locke told her on January 13, 1935, that he had composed an article called "Why the Negro Renaissance Failed." He said that "the deaths of Fisher and Thurman and the bankruptcy of L[angston] H[ughes] and Cullen make a good text." [49] The article was never published, and it is doubtful that he ever intended to publish it. He probably wrote it to placate "Godmother," who was bitter at the apostasy of so many.

Locke too was bitter, but in his public statements he never lost hope for the Renaissance. In his critical articles for *Opportunity*, he often noted its ebbs and flows, and he sometimes tallied its wins and losses. [50] He affectionately referred to it as "Our Little Renaissance" in *Ebony and Topaz*, calling for black writers to give it an infusion of "Florentine urbanity," as if he were the prince of a small city-state in Italy. [51] He called for a "Reformation" when things were not going right in the 1930s and begged the writers not to abandon the Renaissance, almost as if he feared that its downfall would be his as well. [52]

If Walter White and Alain Locke had worked together during the 1920s, they might have complemented one another, for each man had some quality which the other lacked. Walter White's virtues were his common sense and his inexhaustible energy, but he never possessed Locke's commitment to the life of the mind. On the other hand, Locke did not have White's passion for the marketplace. A professor of philosophy, Locke lived in the world of ideas. The aesthetic discussions in *The New Negro* existed on one plane and the city of Harlem—where people endured from day to day—existed on another. Locke spoke eloquently of the exalted aims of the Harlem Renaissance and of the commitment of the black writer to the highest ideals of Art, but it was often Walter White who kept the efforts of the black writer from being stillborn. The fact that these two men never got along in the 1920s is perhaps symbolic: The Harlem Renaissance failed not because of racism in America but because its own energies were never integrated.

NOTES

[1] Abraham Chapman, "The Harlem Renaissance in Literary History," *CLA Journal*, 11 (1967), 38.

[2] Two books which express this attitude with incisiveness are Harold Cruse's *The Crisis of the Negro Intellectual* (New York: Morrow, 1967) and Nathan Huggins's *Harlem Renaissance* (New York: Oxford Univ. Press, 1971). Cruse offers an economic explanation for the Renaissance's ultimate failure. Denied real financial self-sufficiency, the black bourgeoisie was "unwilling and unable" to serve as patrons to its young artists. Many of these artists found white patrons, but in so doing, they gave up their right to direct their own Renaissance (pp. 35, 38). Huggins takes a psychological approach to the question of the Renaissance's audience; he insists that the black artist of the Harlem Renaissance could not tell the truth about black life because he met resistance from a white audience which had come to depend upon stereotypes of the Negro for its own self-definition (see his especially interesting chapter "Personae: White/Black Faces—Black Masks").

[3] Previous critics of Walter White's connection with the Harlem Renaissance have assumed that White worked in harmony with Locke (see Charles F. Cooney, "Walter White and the Harlem Renaissance," *Journal of Negro History*, 57 [1972], 231-40; Edward E. Waldron, "Walter White and the Harlem Renaissance," *CLA Journal*, 16 [1973], 438-57, and *Walter White and the Harlem Renaissance* [Port Washington, NY: Kennikat, 1978]). In writing this article, I have made extensive use of both the NAACP files at the Library of Congress (hereafter cited as *LC*) and the Alain Locke collection at Howard University. The correct citation for letters to and from Locke is Alain Locke Papers, Manuscript Division, The Moorland-Spingarn Research Center, Howard University—hereafter cited as *M-S Center*.

[4] Letter from Walter White to H. L. Mencken, 22 Nov. 1920, *LC*. Also, see Walter White's autobiography *A Man Called White* (New York: Viking, 1948), p. 65. *The Fire in the Flint* illustrates almost point by point Mencken's attack on Southern culture, and in a letter to Eugene Saxton, who represented the publishing house of Doran and Company, White defended his novel's thesis by referring specifically to "The Sahara of the Bozart" (see letter from Walter White to Eugene Saxton, 19 Aug. 1923, *LC*).

[5] Doran's motives for rejecting White's manuscript are not easy to discover. There is truth to White's allegation that Irvin Cobb, a popular Southern humorist, had objected to the novel's attack on the South and had urged Doran not to publish it (see *Walter White and the Harlem Renaissance*, p. 57; see also David Levering Lewis, "The Politics of Art: The New Negro, 1920-1935," in *Prospects: An Annual of American Cultural Studies*, ed. Jack Salzman, No. 3 [New York: Franklyn, 1977], p. 245). However, Doran did have a legitimate complaint concerning White's artistry. As Doran's representative Eugene Saxton told White: "Practically speaking, there is nobody in court but the attorney for the prosecution" (letter from Eugene Saxton to Walter White, 16 Aug. 1923, *LC*). White himself admitted the "justice" of Saxton's criticism, and he pleaded with the publishing house to reconsider its decision (see letter from Walter White to Eugene Saxton, 23 Aug. 1923, *LC*).

[6] See letter from Walter White to H. L. Mencken, 5 Oct. 1923, *LC*.

[7] Later, whenever White told the story of how his novel came to be published, he pictured himself as a black David taking on the great publishing house of Doran, the Goliath who represented the philistine South. He boasted that he had withdrawn his novel from Doran because he would not be coerced into revising it. See letter from Walter White to Robert Kerlin, 26 Dec. 1923, *LC*: "I informed

98

350

them [Doran] that I would destroy my manuscript before I would submit to emasculation." Also, see *A Man Called White*, pp. 65-67. In truth, he had told Eugene Saxton that he would revise his manuscript along the lines of Doran's criticism (see letter from Walter White to Eugene Saxton, 23 Aug. 1923, *LC*).

Scholars have accepted White's view of the circumstances leading to his novel's publication. Waldron sees the entire episode with Doran as a parable for the difficulties which the black writer faced in the early 1920s (see *Walter White and the Harlem Renaissance*, p. 47; see also Charles F. Cooney, "Mencken's Midwifery," *Menckeniana*, 43 [Fall 1972], 1-4). What the episode actually illustrates is that a street-wise black writer knew how to use white liberal sympathies to his own advantage.

8 See *Walter White and the Harlem Renaissance*, pp. 113-56.

9 Letter from Charles S. Johnson to Alain Locke, 29 June 1923, *M-S Center*.

10 Alain Locke, "The Colonial Literature of France," *Opportunity*, 1 (1923), 331-35.

11 Letter from Charles S. Johnson to Alain Locke, 4 Mar. 1924, *M-S* Center; letter from Charles S. Johnson to Alain Locke, 7 Mar. 1924, *M-S Center*.

12 Undated letter from Alain Locke to Walter White, *LC*; letter from Walter White to Alain Locke, 28 Jan. 1924, *LC*.

13 Letter from Walter White to Carl Van Doren, 14 Dec. 1923, *LC*.

14 Letter from Walter White to H. L. Mencken, 22 Dec. 1923, *LC*. White predicted to Mencken that the article would "bring down on my head the maledictions of all the professional confederates."

15 Locke had met Barnes in Europe. Since the feisty art collector wanted to meet the leading Afro-American intellectuals when he returned to the United States, he contacted Locke at Howard. Locke told Barnes about Charles S. Johnson's literary group, and Barnes asked Locke if he could join "the people you say you are assembling next week in New York" (letter from Alfred C. Barnes to Alain Locke, 11 Mar. 1924, *M-S Center*). He soon became quite friendly with the *Opportunity* intellectuals, and as he was the foremost authority in America on African art, he was invited to the Opportunity Dinner.

16 Letter from Walter White to Alfred C. Barnes, 24 Mar. 1924, *M-S Center*. The correspondence concerning the entire Barnes episode is conveniently placed in a single folder, and that folder can be found within the other Alain Locke correspondence. I have given the dates of these letters within the text, but I have not footnoted them individually.

17 Undated letter from Alain Locke to Walter White (probably late May 1925), *LC*.

18 Letter from Walter White to Alain Locke, 3 June 1925, *LC*.

19 Letter from Walter White to Lewis Baer, 11 Mar. 1925, *LC*.

20 Letter from Lewis Baer to Walter White, 18 Mar. 1925, *LC*.

21 See letter from Walter White to Langston Hughes, 27 May 1925, *LC*. White told Hughes that he had planned to attend the Opportunity Dinner, but that he had previously committed himself to an engagement in Trenton which he "had made some weeks ago and forgot."

22 Letter from Countee Cullen to Alain Locke, 24 Sept. 1922, *M-S Center*. The letters between Locke and Cullen are in a single folder. I have placed the dates of these letters within the text.

23 Undated letter from Alain Locke to Countee Cullen, Countee Cullen Papers, Amistad Research Center, Dillard University, New Orleans, Louisiana.

24 *Walter White and the Harlem Renaissance*, pp. 149-50, 155.

25 Letter from Countee Cullen to Walter White, 16 Jan. 1926, *LC*.

26 See Cullen's review of Hughes's *The Weary Blues*, "Poet on Poet," *Opportunity* 4 (1926), 74; see also "Forward," in *Caroling Dusk*, ed. Countee Cullen (New York: Harper, 1927), p. xii. In 1927 Cullen reviewed Locke's *Four Negro Poets* and attacked Locke's generalization "that Negro poets feel themselves more strongly obligated to their race than to their own degree of personal talent" (see "The Dark Tower," *Opportunity*, 5 [1927], 210).

27 Letter from Walter White to Claude McKay, 6 Nov. 1924, *LC*.

28 Letter from Walter White to Claude McKay, 20 May 1925, *LC*.

29 Letter from Claude McKay to Walter White, 15 June 1925, *LC*.

30 Letter from Walter White to Claude McKay, 8 July 1925, *LC*.

31 Letter from Arthur Schomburg to Walter White, 24 July 1925, *LC*. From this point on, information about the manuscript's whereabouts is confusing. McKay thought that it had been sent to White, but White evidently never received it. The manuscript was

eventually returned to McKay but long after there was any hope for its publication. See letter from Claude McKay to Walter White, 7 Sept. 1925, *LC*; also see letter from Claude McKay to Arthur Schomburg, 1 Aug. 1926, The Schomburg Center for Research in Black Culture.

32 Letter from Claude McKay to Walter White, 1 Aug. 1925, *LC*.

33 Letter from Claude McKay to Walter White, 4 Aug. 1925, *LC*.

34 McKay did consider the possibility that White had betrayed him with Knopf because he disapproved of the obscene passages in *Color Scheme*. "I wonder," he asked Schomburg, "if it is a mere coincidence that Bloch [Knopf's editor] sent back the M.S. to you on the 22nd of July and Walter wrote to you on the 23rd? Did you think of that?" (letter from Claude McKay to Arthur Schomburg, 3 Aug. 1925, The Schomburg Center for Research in Black Culture).

35 Letter from Walter White to George Oppenheimer, 26 Aug. 1925, *LC*.

36 Grace Hegger Lewis, *With Love from Gracie: Sinclair Lewis, 1912-1925* (New York: Harcourt Brace, 1951), p. 291. Mrs. Lewis mistakenly refers to *Color Scheme* as an "autobiography."

37 Letter from Walter White to Arthur Schomburg, 27 Aug. 1925, *LC*.

38 Letter from Walter White to Claude McKay, 28 Aug. 1925, *LC*. On the basis of this letter, McKay thought White would put in a good word for him at Harcourt. He wrote White in October: "You haven't written since your August letter whether you did try Harcourt and what was their decision. Did you?" (letter from Claude McKay to Walter White, 15 Oct. 1925, *LC*). We do not know White's answer, but it is clear from the other correspondence that White gave all responsibility for *Color Scheme* to Schomburg.

39 Letter from Claude McKay to Walter White, 7 Sept. 1925, *LC*.

40 Letter from Claude McCay to Alain Locke, 2 Jan. 1926, *M-S Center*.

41 Letter from Claude McKay to Mrs. Osgood Mason, 13 Feb. 1930, *M-S Center*.

42 Letter from Claude McKay to Alain Locke, 7 Oct. 1924, *M-S Center*.

43 Letter from Claude McKay to Alain Locke, 18 Apr. 1927, *M-S Center*.

44 Letter from Claude McKay to Alain Locke, 1 Aug. 1926, *M-S Center*. McKay told Locke that he had not wanted "Negro Dancers" published in *The New Negro* because it had belonged to an earlier poetic period in his life. This letter is published in Wayne F. Cooper's *The Passion of Claude McKay* (New York: Schocken, 1973), pp. 143-44.

45 Letter from Claude McKay to Alain locke, 4 June 1927, *M-S Center*.

46 Langston Hughes, *The Big Sea* (1940; rpt. New York: Hill & Wang, 1968), pp. 324-26.

47 "Godmother" wanted Negro writers to express their African heritage, and she was hostile toward Negro writers who expressed themes common to Western civilization. For an amusing account of "Godmother's" relationship to the Harlem Renaissance writers, see David Levering Lewis, pp. 257-58.

48 Letter from Alain Locke to Mrs. Osgood Mason, 26 Feb. 1929, *M-S Center*; letter from Alain Locke to Mrs. Osgood Mason, 25 Feb. 1931, *M-S Center*; letter from Alain Locke to Mrs. Osgood Mason, 10 Mar. 1931, *M-S Center*.

49 Letter from Alain Locke to Mrs. Osgood Mason, 13 Jan. 1935, *M-S Center*. Locke felt that Hughes had ruined himself as an artist when Hughes embraced the radical politics of the 1930s.

50 His first "Retrospective Review," which appeared in Jan. 1929, examined Negro literature of the previous year (1928). These reviews continued throughout the 1930s, and in them Locke could never quite decide whether the Renaissance was progressing or retrenching.

51 Alain Locke, "Our Little Renaissance," in *Ebony and Topaz*, ed. Charles S. Johnson (New York: Opportunity, 1927), p. 117.

52 See Alain Locke, "A Year of Grace," *Opportunity*, 9 (1931), 51. Locke probably got this idea of a necessary "Reformation" from Mencken (see *Ebony and Topaz*, p. 117; see also Alain Locke, "The Negro: New or Newer," *Opportunity*, 17 [1939], 4). Locke argued that the generation of black writers in the 1930s was not a counter-movement but a "matured phase of the movement of the 20s." For a more detailed view of Locke's relationship to the 1930s, see James Young, *Black Writers of the Thirties* (Baton Rouge: Louisiana State Univ. Press, 1973), pp. 141-49.

99

GENDER AND AMBITION: ZORA NEALE HURSTON IN THE HARLEM RENAISSANCE

by Ralph D. Story

In the literary world the "battle" between the sexes for publicity, publications and position is a conflict rooted historically in the dynamics of race, class and gender as they have existed and continue to exist in the United States.

It is thus enlightening and intriguing to illustrate and examine the antecedents of the contemporary situation by way of the literary skirmishes and aesthetic debates between Zora Neale Hurston (1901-1960) and two of her well-known contemporaries, Langston Hughes (1902-1967) and Richard Wright (1908-1960) beginning in the Harlem Renaissance (hereafter referred to as HR).

Although many of the more recent in-depth analyses of the Harlem Renaissance contain contrasting points of view on quite a few issues, most of the accounts and descriptions of Hurston as a person during the era are relatively consistent.[1] Yet relative judgement in the case of Hurston seems to be determined by the gender of the scholar or writer; black male scholars hold one view of her and black female writers hold another.

The typical, and male, rendering of Hurston during the HR can be seen in Langston Hughes' autobiography, *The Big Sea* (1940). In this work she is depicted as a joke-telling, uproariously funny woman who went out of her way to ingratiate herself with influential, rich whites—her purpose being to receive material rewards and financial sponsorship to further her literary career.

Yet very few of the scholars who hold such views of her are willing to concede that such a characterization tells us little about her abilities as a writer. Implicitly, the HR Hurston "character" (some would say caricature) seems to be more important than the characters which people her fiction and folklore, most of which was not published during the HR but

instead in the 1930s.[2]

In sharp contrast to the views of most HR scholars and the various depictions of the era, the views of contemporary black women writers, and Alice Walker's specifically, are almost exclusively devoted to the lasting importance of Hurston's work. Walker sees Hurston's work as a rare body of literature, "an indication of the quality I feel is most characteristic of Zora's work—a sense of black people as complete, complex, and undiminished human beings. . ."[3]

June Jordan, herself a very great African-American poet, provides a positive analysis of Zora Neale Hurston's Eatonville (Fla.) environment, seeing it as an inspiration for Hurston's fiction in which black folk play, "their own particular selves in a family and community setting that permits relaxation from hunted/warrior postures and that fosters the natural person-postures of courting, jealousy, ambition, dream, sex, work, partying, sorrow, bitterness, celebration and fellowship."[4]

Such complimentary analyses make one wonder just how the work of Hurston the writer fits the HR persona of Hurston, a person who has been disparagingly characterized by an African scholar as a woman "predisposed to identify more with whites (and whose) parents had large quantities of white blood in their veins,"[5] and by scholar David L. Lewis as a "minion" to the white patron Charlotte Osgood Mason.[6]

It is compelling to consider, moreover, that Hurston, who her astute biographer Hemenway acknowledges as "one of the most memorable personages of the period," has been singled out for biting criticism as if she was the only player in the artist-gatekeeper-patron literary game that was, in fact, so much a part of the entire HR. Perhaps condemnation of Hurston's behavior is in part attributable to the scarcity of information on those hard-to-describe but fairly well-known relationships between other black writers, "race" leaders, and their white patrons whom Hurston jokingly labeled "Negrotarians."

As it is, however, the publication of David Lewis' *When Harlem Was In Vogue* (1982), an innovative and primary source of information on the HR, makes it obvious that Hurston was not the only writer "on the take." Indeed, many of the major black HR writers had a benefactor or benefactors: a patronage system which makes the HR seem just as much a matter of interracial connections and networking as it was a matter of black talent in abundance so obvious that the dominant culture's literary world had to acknowledge it through social liaisons and publication opportunities.

It is very surprising that this well-known nexus of interracial relationships had not been adequately addressed prior to Lewis' incisive analysis and commentary. In his close examination, the linkages between major HR black artists, influential black intermediaries, and white philanthropy and/or patronage, are clearly discernible.[6]

Hurston, contrary to popular belief, was not the only HR writer who had clear-cut financial ties to a white patron—Charlotte Osgood Mason. Langston Hughes, Claude McKay, Aaron Douglas and Alain Locke were all recepients of Osgood's financial and moral support. Hughes, in particular, was emotionally traumatized by his break with Mason after three years of relatively heavy-handed if not generous guidance (since Mason preferred to have "her artists" address her as "Godmother.")

It shouldn't be surprising to contemporary readers that the second phase of the HR, as part and parcel of the more visible forays of rich whites who flocked to Harlem to have a good time, was distinguishable as the era of widespread white support of black creative intellectuals. Joel Spingarn, one of the founders and supporters of the NAACP, had discernible linkages to Harcourt Brace Publishing Company which published the works of Claude McKay and James Weldon Johnson;

Alfred Knopf, a personal friend of Carl Van Vechten and an associate of Walter White, a writer and longtime secretary of the NAACP, was the publisher for both Hughes and White.

Horace Liveright (of Boni and Liveright publishers) was one of the notable publishers in attendance at the Opportunity Awards banquets. His company published Jean Toomer, Jessie Faucet and Alain Locke. Charles S. Johnson and Locke were the managers of the Rosewald and Harmon Funds respectively—funds which were responsible (beyond literary support for artists) for building YMCAs in the black community and the funding of Tuskeegee Institute and other traditional black colleges' endowments.[7]

In a scenario such as that indicated by the associations described above, Zora Neale Hurston's "behavior" seems to be more of a variation on the same theme rather than the conspicuous activities of an individual artist desperately coveting the kind of support which had been extended to black male writers. Lewis' delineation of this broader issue makes her actions all the more understandable and thereby exposes certain characterizations of her as sexist at worst and suspect at best. As Lewis perceives the HR,

> . . .white capital and influence were crucial, and the white presence...hovered over the New Negro world of art and literature like a benevolent censor, politely but pervasively setting the outer limits of its creative boundaries.[8]

Another aspect of the game in which Hurston was a participant was that of the much talked about—but rarely documented—literary infighting for recognition and publication engaged in by struggling artists. In the fishbowl world of that infighting, publicity was precious and each artist was in competition with all others to be seen and heard at book parties and social events where work and play were merged.

It was also at such gatherings that influential patrons would hear the creative work of the writers and choose a rising star (or stars) to sponsor. Hurston, like her male counterparts, was merely acting as any other artist would in a competitive situation. Claude Mckay, an HR participant, made it clear in his autobiography, *A Long Way From Home* (1937), that Hurston was merely one of many who found it necessary to court and covet connections with rich white patrons:

> Also, among the Negro artists there was much of that UncleTom attitude which works like Satan against the idea of a coherent and purposeful Negro group. Each one wanted to be the first Negro, the one Negro, and the only Negro, *for the whites* instead of for their group. Because an unusual number of them were receiving grants to do creative work, they actually and naively believed that Negro artists as a group would always be treated differently from white artists and be protected by powerful white patrons.[9]

Hurston was a player in a game which had many unwritten rules of convention for women—a game any woman at the time would have found impossible to win and especially a black woman writer-intellectual unwilling to discard her rural-southern black folk background.

One rule which she violated was the rule stipulating conventional and conservative public behavior; she smoked in public and consistently and candidly spoke her mind. And despite much retrospective glamor attached to this era, the "Roaring Twenties," despite its rich flapper veneer, was still a decade dominated behaviorally by straightlaced conventions and ideals and particularly so for black women.

One only has to read the works produced during the era by the other well-known black woman editor-novelist-writer, Jessie Faucet, to understand how far afield Hurston truly was from her mostly middleclass (or, if not from that background, certainly aspiring to it) black male contemporaries.[10]

Additionally, within the smaller, private black literary city of the Harlem Renaissance, there was still the need for the artist to prove her/himself deserving of a major publisher to financially support and distribute her/his work. Thus, the task for Hurston as a black woman player in the interracial literary game was to make it: to win in a game dominated at the time by white men who controlled the game, by white spectator-readers who comprised the primary audience, and by black men who functioned as gatekeepers and occasionally as players themselves.

For Hurston was in fierce competition with her own peers when it came to seeking entry at the dominant culture's gates of fame and fortune. *She recognized it for what it was and made no attempt to disguise it;* as a result, those who were unwilling or afraid to expose such widespread accommodation and courting of favors criticized her repeatedly as if her behavior was unusual and revealed a secretritual most others agreed upon privately to keep off the record.[11]

It is much easier to understand Hurston's energetic presence as well as the contrasting behavior and work of Jessie Faucet, who focused her imaginative attention on the black middle class and its "cultured" and Victorian behavior in this context.[12] The eventual conflict between Hurston and one of her best HR friends, Langston Hughes, over the play *Mule Bone* can be perceived as an inevitable clash which began during the HR but was lurking just underneath the surface, obscured by the retrospective glitter of an era which seemed so promising but ended so abruptly.

An even more interesting context in which to place Hurston is as a southern black woman challenging the traditional position of women and exceeding the aesthetic space they had been traditionally provided: She dared to see herself as a writer with talent equal to if not greater than her peers at representing the "folk" orally and in writing. She was, essentially, more "downhome" than all the other Negro artists who "were" the HR and was not afraid to flaunt it.

The controversy and bitter dispute between Hurston and Hughes over *Mule Bone* and especially Hurston's role in the affair contain all the aforementioned elements and tensions. *Mule Bone*, understood in this manner, becomes a compelling drama, a play underwritten by larger societal forces and staged with the traditional conflicts between men and women which are and have been all too universal. In this case, Hurston was an emergent, adlibbing and provocative leading lady.[13]

> "But Tea Cake, it 's too awful out dere. Maybe it's better tuh stay heah in de wet than it is tuh try tuh—" He stunned the argument with half a word. "Fix," he said and fought his way outside. He had seen more than Janie had.

This brief dialogue, an exchange between Janie Crawford and Tea Cake, two lovers whose relationship takes on epic proportions in Hurston's *Their Eyes Were Watching God* (1937), symbolically etches out and foreshadows the aesthetic debate between black female and black male writers. In short, the debate (which is still ongoing but discussed only occasionally) can be reduced to some basic questions.

To what extent are the experiences of black folk —and especially their interaction with whites, typically symbolizing the dominant (and oppressive) culture—important or significant enough to warrant their heavy-handed inclusion and/or subsequently dominant role in most twentieth century fictional depictions of black life? Or, are the day-to-day lives of black folk, interior lives in which whites only occasionally appear and then as mere bit players, more representative of the "core" black experience and hence, more appropriate subject matter for artistic renderings by black writers? [14]

The most fitting response to these queries is that both situational realities deserve literary attention and that black men and black women writers have fictionalized those experiences in their lives which have appeared to be the most compelling, enduring and collectively encompassing. But what happens if those experiences are divergent, and uniquely so, because of gender, i.e., if the perspectives of black women writers were in sharp contrast to those of black male writers as a result of their respective sexes and the realities so intimately linked to their sex-specific experiences? The actual dialogue on this matter would seem to indicate as much. Alice Walker, for instance, has written rather bluntly on the issue:

> It seems to me that black writing has suffered because even black critics have assumed that a book that deals with the relationship between members of a black family—or between a man and a woman—is less important than one that has white people as a primary antagonist. The consequence of this is that many of our books by "major" writers (always male) tell us little about the culture, history, or future, imagination, fantasies, etc., of black people, and a lot about isolated (often improbable) or limited encounters with a nonspecific white world. [15]

Mary Helen Washington, in the course of an essay on Hurston's *Their Eyes Were Watching*

God, has also commented on what might be considered a skewed version of black life rendered by black male writers:

> The black writer sometimes gets his eyes so fixed on the white world and its ways of acting toward us that his vision becomes constricted. He reflects, if he is not careful, but one aspect of his people's experiences: suffering, humiliation, degradation. And he may fail to show that Black people are more than simply reactors, that among ourselves, we have laughter, tears, and loving that are far removed from the white horror out there. [16]

The gist of this debate, even considering Walker's and Washington's comments to be accurate, however, has more to do with the specific focus of the writer at a given point in historical time and space. Black male writers, throughout most of the twentieth century, have seen the macrocosmic issues affecting black folk—justice, equality and respect for the "race"—as being more suitable for fictional recreations of black life because these issues were more important for the vast majority of black folk. This was especially true during the pre-WWII era. Black women writers, however, have generally taken the opposite stance which, loosely translated, says the black community—its women and men in that order—should have always been the central focus for black writers. Thus, the moment Hurston's novel appeared in print black male writers critiqued it negatively.

Their Eyes Were Watching God was reviewed by Richard Wright for *New Masses* shortly after its release. In his critique he accused Hurston of perpetuating stereotypes. [17] Moreover, Sterling Brown and Ralph Ellison shortly thereafter voiced similar misgivings about Hurston's work which they felt consciously or unconsciously avoided the more serious and consequential tensions and issues in black life, i.e., the struggle of blacks against whites to achieve justice, which both deemed as the major task for serious black fiction writers. [18]

Despite such disparaging criticism from such African-American literary giants, the work is a significant, very well-written novel with obvious philosophical and social significance that Wright, Brown and Ellison either dismissed as irrelevant or overlooked when writing their reviews. Indeed, *Their Eyes Were*

Watching God is a novel that exposed philosophical differences between black men and women; equally significant, the reviews of the novel revealed a literary division of labor and hierarchy before there was a concerted and. consistently visible women's movement, which has provided the ideological and literary foreground for the views of black women writers.

To put it in simple terms, black male writers during the 1930s were unwilling to concede their own territorial literary dominance over the most "serious" subject matters—interracial conflicts, the "state"s inadequacies, the fight of black folk against racism and poverty and the recreation of black historical figures in fictional form. Thus, even if a talented black female writer had emerged who wanted to deal with such issues, it would have been extremely difficult for her to convince publishers and/or readers that she was up to the task given the chauvinism and sexism (and not to mention racism) so characteristic of American life in the pre-WWII era. Black male writers, perhaps unconsciously, were also unwilling to perceive the struggle of black women for sexual equality and the perspective brought to bear on that struggle by a great black woman writer as literary territory and as an orientation worthy of detailed delineation in Hurston's novel.

Wright, Brown and Ellison wanted to insist that man's inhumanity to man, in this instance the oppression of black people as a group by those with money and power, makes the possibility of genuine, reciprocal and enduring love remote at best and willful self-delusion at worst. They would have contended that the more serious problems affecting black people are those problems which stemmed from powerlessness and minority status.

It follows in their view then that any writer attempting serious fiction has to address the more encompassing global, political, psychological and material conflicts of a people in the symbolically collective sense. *Their Eyes Were Watching God* was for them a work which they very easily dismissed as minor and of secondary importance given "the struggle of the people" at the time. A black love story which took place in an all-black setting was not suffciently realistic nor artistically sound for all the aforementioned reasons.

Hurston's view, had she articulated it, might have been just the opposite. Black women, more than anything else, have wanted love whereas black men have wanted justice and power; yet neither is guaranteed. She might have also asserted that if one were given the choice, the quest for love and its subsequent attainment by black men and women are ultimately more realizable and necessary for black folk as a *precondition* to their engagement in any protracted, life-threatening struggle.

Hurston, in this imaginary dialogue, symbolizes the woman's perspective and demonstrates that women have had a different set of values than black male writers and this is made clear in their fictional recreations of black life. *Their Eyes Were Watching God* embodies a different value system in that it is clearly a delineation of the quest for love and self-fulfillment by Janie Crawford (the protagonist of the novel).

Black women writers, in addition to their different values, have also had a different set of experiences than black male writers and this is made patently obvious in their fictional recreations of black life, with Hurston's novel being an exceptional case in point. This work begins with this understanding and from the very first page presents the perspectives of men and women which are then substantiated by the work:

> Ships at a distance have every man's wish on board. For some they come with the tide. For others they sail forever on the horizon, never out of sight, never landing until the Watcher turns his eyes away in resignation, his dreams mocked to death by TIME. That is the life of men. Now, women forget all those things they don't want to remember, and remember everything they don't want to forget. The dream is the truth. Then they act and do things accordingly.[19]

By the tale's end Janie Crawford is a fully developed, complex black female character. Indeed, Hurston revised, as Barbara Christian contends, "the previosuly drawn images of the mulatta, (and) the author's rendition of her major characters beautifully revealed the many dimensions of the black woman's soul as well as the restrictions imposed upon her by her own community—that she, like all others, seeks not only security but fulfillment."[20] It is rather refreshing and poignant that Janie's reaction to the death of Tea Cake (her last lover in the novel) is not one of morbid resignation but instead an elevated, heightened consciousness:

> She pulled in her horizon like a great fishnet. Pulled it from around the waist of the world and draped it over her shoulder. So much of life in its meshes. She called in her soul to come and see.[21]

In effect, *Their Eyes Were Watching God*, Hurston's greatest literary accomplishment, established her as one of the great imaginative writer-folklorists in the twentieth century. Her characterization of Janie Crawford, the breath of strongly feminine perspective she gave Janie and her authentic rendering of black folk speech and legend should make it impossible for any African-American scholar to disparage her importance to the African-American and American literary traditions respectively.

Yet, Hurston's non-fiction, excluding the folklore, and particularly her later statements in articles on race are another issue.[22] She reacted bitterly to disparagement and what she considered to be generalizations about race which she resisted. Nevertheless, even on this count contemporary black women writers are more sympathetic and have a more specific understanding of Hurston's tragic life and unappreciated work than do black male writers (with the exception of the late Larry Neal). Barbara Christian, an astute contemporary black female literary critic, sees Hurston's life and work as example and creative precedent:

> One of the first writers to use folk images and speech as well as the insular folk culture, Hurston anticipated future black women writers who would attempt to define themselves as persons within a specific culture rather than primarily through their relationships with whites. Faucet's characters, particularly in *The Chinaberry Tree*, also insulated themselves with a particular class, but Hurston's *Their Eyes Were Watching God* invokes not one class but the total community—its language, images, mores, and prejudices—as its context. In so doing it articulates the Afro-American experience not only as a condition but as a culture.[23]

Christian's view of Hurston as a writer who "anticipated future black women writers" and one who had achieved a consciousness of a distinct black culture is an accurate assessment. For Hurston's work was in many ways culturally nationalistic (as in the late 1960s) and anticipated and surely inspired the literary works of black women writers of the 1970s and 1980s.

Indeed, her work foreshadowed the issues of black women which came to prominence in the early 1970s, specifically the plight of black women as a subject matter in and of itself deserving of literary and scholarly attention. The work of Ntozake Shange, and especially the brilliantly poetic *For Colored Girls Who Have Considered Suicide When the Rainbow Is Enuf* (1975) and the reactions to that work are most comparable to that of Hurston's experiences as a writer for both political and aesthetic reasons. For Shange, like Hurston, has had to withstand some rather ascerbic and pointed criticism from black male writers for her choreopoem. Hopefully, history will not repeat itself and allow Shange's talent and creative power to be appreciated in her lifetime. Zora Neale Hurston was not that fortunate.

FOOTNOTES

1. See Nathan Huggins' *Harlem Renaissance*; Langston Hughes' *The Big Sea*; Arna Bontemps' (Ed.) *The Harlem Renaissance Remembered* ; David Lewis' *When Harlem Was In Vogue*.
2. Zora Neale Hurston was the author of *Jonah's Gourd Vine* (1934), *Mules and Men* (1935), *Their Eyes Were Watching God* (1937), *Tell My Horse* (1938), *Moses, Man of the Mountain* (1939), *Dust Tracks On a Road* (1942) and *Seraph on the Suwanee* (1948) and numerous other anthropological, folklore and "race" articles.
3. Alice Walker's "Introduction" to *Zora Neale Hurston: A Literary Biography*, by Robert Hemenway (Chicago: University of Illinois Press, 1978), p. xii.
4. Hemenway, *Zora Neale Hurston*, p. 12.
5. Chidi Ikonne, *From DuBois to Van Vechten: The Early New Negro Literature, 1903-1926* (Westport, CT: Greenwood Press, 1981), p. 183.
6. David Levering Lewis, *When Harlem Was In Vogue* (New York: Alfred A. Knopf, 1981), p. 151.
7. Ibid., pp. 75-78, 152-153, 50-58, 58-74, 125, 229-230, 277-281, 233-234, 127, 196-197, 143-149, 121-125, 152-155,89-98, 66-67, 59, 99, 151, 262-263, 144-146, 70-71, 78-88. Also see George Kent's "Patterns of the Harlem Renaissance," *The Harlem Renaissance Remembered*, Ed. Arna Bontemps (Dodd Mead & Co.: New York, 1972).
8. Ibid., p. 98.
9. Claude McKay, *A Long Way From Home* (New York.

Harcourt, Brace & World, 1970), p. 322.

10. Jessie Faucet's fiction has been negatively criticized (for the most part justifiably) because of her almost exclusive focus on the black "upper class." Yet, her work in the real world as an editor for *Crisis* and as a literary raconteur has not received the positive attention it deserves.

11. Numerous writers who either lived through the Harlem Renaissance as participants or are considered experts on the era have barely skimmed the surface on the subjects of patrons and patronage during this era. Lewis' work is clearly a threshold investigation of this subject and exposes it in ways never before uncovered.

12. See Barbara Christian's *Black Women Novelists* (Westport, CT: Greenwood Press, 1980) for an excellent discussion of Faucet's work.

13. Hurston and Hughes were friends before and during the play's draft but "lifelong enemies" after its solo completion by Hurston. Subsequent to this conflict, Hurston and Hughes "avoided each other for the rest of their lives" or approximately forty years. It is also significant that Hurston's claim to sole authorship was grounded not only in her belief that the characters and story of *Mule Bone* were essentially hers; she probably believed, and rightfully so, that she was more representative of "the folk" (blacks residing in the rural south) and hence had a more legitimate claim to recreating their lives than Hughes who was essentially a writer who focused his attention on the urban black experience. This "hidden" posture is just underneath the surface in the following excerpt from her correspondence: "Now about the play itself. It was my story from beginning to end. It is my dialogue; my situations. But I am not concerned about that."

14. I am using John Langston Gwaltney's term "core" which he uses to characterize the most representative, germane experiences of "everyday" black people. See John Langston Gwaltney, *Drylongso* (New York: Random House, 1980), p. xxii.

15. John O'Brien, ed., *Interviews with Black Writers* (New York: Liveright, 1973), p. 202.

16. Mary Helen Washington, "Zora Neale Hurston's work," *Black World*, August 1972, pp. 68-75.

17. Richard Wright, "Between Laughter and Tears," *New Masses*, October 6, 1937, pp. 24-25.

18. Ralph Ellison, "Recent Negro Fiction," *New Masses*, August 5, 1941, pp. 22-26.

19. Zora Neale Hurston, *Their Eyes Were Watching God* (Philadelphia: J.E. Lippincott, 1937), p. 1.

20. Christian, p. 47.

21. Hurston, p. 286.

22. One of the more controversial articles by Hurston detailing her positions on blacks and voting is "I Saw Negro Votes Peddled," *American Legion Magazine*, 49 (November 1950), pp. 12-13, 54-57, 59-60.

23. Christian, p. 46.

WORKS CITED

Berry, Faith. *Langston Hughes: Before and Beyond Harlem.* Westport, CT: Lawrence Hill & Co., 1983

Bontemps, Arna. *The Harlem Renaissance Remembered.* New York: Dodd Mead & Co., 1972.

Brown, Sterling. "The New Negro In Literature." *The New Negro Thirty Years Afterwards.* Ed. Rayford Logan. Washington D.C.: Howard University Press, 1955.

Christian, Barbara. *Black Women Novelists.* Westport, CT: Greenwood Press, 1980.

Ellison, Ralph. "Recent Negro Fiction." *New Masses.* August 5, 1941.

Faucet, Jessie. *The Chinaberry Tree.* New York: Stokes, 1933.

Gwaltney, John Langston. *Drylongso.* New York: Random House, 1980.

Hansberry, Lorraine. *A Raisin In the Sun.* New York: Random House, 1959.

Hemenway, Robert. *Zora Neale Hurston: A Literary Biography.* Chicago, Ill: University of Illinois Press, 1978.

Huggins, Nathan. *Harlem Renaissance.* New York: Oxford University Press, 1971.

Hughes, Langston. *The Big Sea.* New York: Alfred A. Knopf, 1940.

_____. *The Weary Blues.* New York: Alfred A. Knopf, 1926.

Hurston, Zora Neale. *Moses, Man of the Mountain.* Philadelphia: J.E. Lippincott, 1939.

_____. *Their Eyes Were Watching God.* Philadelphia: J.E. Lippincott, 1937.

_____. "I Saw Negro Votes Peddled." *American Legion Magazine*, Vol. 49., November 1950.

Ikonne, Chidi. *From DuBois to Van Vechten: The Early New Negro Literature, 1903 - 1926.* Westport, CT: Greenwood Press, 1981.

Lewis, David Levering. *When Harlem Was In Vogue.* New York: Alfred A. Knopf, 1981.

McKay, Claude. *A Long Way From Home.* New York: Harcourt, Brace & World, 1970.

O'Brien, John. Ed. *Interviews with Black Writers.* New York: Liveright, 1971.

Shange, Ntozake. *For Colored Girls Who Have Considered Suicide When The Rainbow Is Enuf.* New York: Bantam Books, 1977.

Walker, Alice. "In Search of Zora Neale Hurston." *Ms.* Vol. III, No. 9, March 1975.

Washington, Mary Helen. "Zora Neale Hurston's Work." *Black World.* August 1972.

Wright, Richard. "Between Laughter and Tears." *New Masses.* October 6, 1937.

THREE NOTES TOWARD A CULTURAL DEFINITION OF THE HARLEM RENAISSANCE

By Gerald Early

There has certainly been no reluctance on the part of scholars and writers these days to discuss the significance of the Harlem Renaissance and, thus, there has been no shortage of commentary—good, bad, and indifferent—on this fabulous era when blacks, particularly black artists, attained a peculiarly ambiguous and not altogether untroubling presence in American popular and highbrow cultures. It is not my purpose in this short essay to quarrel with my colleagues about anything they may have said; I am in fact far too grateful for their labors to harbor any desire to provoke contentions. I would simply like to make a few observations, a few points that may have fallen in the cracks, unnoticed and unconsidered, about the Harlem Renaissance that, I hope, will amplify or clarify points that have already been made in far more elaborate and intellectually rehearsed ways.

Doubtless, our fascination with the Harlem Renaissance is, in part, explained because this period coincides with the social/historical era known as the American 1920s—Prohibition, primitivism, the new poetry (Eliot, Pound, H.D., Hart Crane, William Carlos Williams, imagism, Langston Hughes), the new criticism (Allen Tate and the Fugitives), the new cinema (Charlie Chaplin, Sergei Eisenstein, Fritz Lang, F. W. Murnau, the coming of sound), and all that.

Although scholars often speak of the mood of discontent and despair caused by the failed idealism of World War I that induced, paradoxically, both the hedonism and backwater reactionism of the twenties, it must not be forgotten that between 1913 and 1920—a dramatically short time for such far-ranging revision in the national law to occur—four amendments of major social and political importance were added to the Constitution: the federal income tax and direct election of senators in 1913; Prohibition in 1919; and women's right to vote in 1920. These amendments indicate as much as anything a society in flux, trying to redefine its relation to its government. Thus, the twenties may have still been something like the twenties we have come to know even without the catastrophe of an imperialistic European-dominated war. The war may simply have intensified the feeling of dislocation.

The conflation of the white 1920s and the black 1920s is probably intellectually valid, but one must be wary that the very glamor that makes the 1920s interesting is the very element of the period that may partially obscure our understanding of black artists during this time. Doubtless, however, the complexities of glamor—profane, perverted, or strange eminence—and the development of the African-American artist, a subject that David L. Lewis explored compellingly in his *When Harlem Was in Vogue*, merits further meditation. But if glamor is an important facet in understanding the

Callaloo 14.1 (1991) 136–149

creative black mind of the twenties, so is the idea of honor for a people who had been
so denied the possibilities of expressing it while experiencing a debasement that aug-
mented the honor of their oppressors. Something like the concept of honor had to be
on James Weldon Johnson's mind, for instance, when he wrote in the preface of his
1922 anthology, *The Book of American Negro Poetry*, calling for racial uplift through the
creation of art: "No people that has produced great literature and art has ever been
looked upon by the world as distinctly inferior." Put another way, as this era, the
Harlem Renaissance, gave us the cultural paradigms for seeing blacks and black expression in relation to modern American popular culture, it might be time to recast
our concerns and consider this epistemological question: What is the meaning of some
mythologies of American popular and high cultures and how has black expression
played a role in our understanding of both that expression and those mythologies?
Here are three observations.

Observation I: The Piano and the Rent Party

> But a ritual is not just a pattern of meaning: it is also a
> form of social interaction.
>
> —Clifford Geertz, *The Interpretation of Cultures*

> I know it's cold outside
> Come on in, I'll keep you satisfied
> All you got to do is move
> Everybody feel the groove
> It ain't nothing but a party
> It ain't nothing but a house party
>
> —The Show Stoppers' 1967 hit, "Ain't Nothing but a House Party"

It is commonly and quite correctly thought that the development of jazz music by
the African-American led to the creation of two glamor-solo instruments, two instruments of masculine sexual myth in American popular music: the saxophone and the
electric guitar. But jazz music, in the days of its development before the technological
innovations of recordings and radio and thus in the days before its stylizations became
both a manipulation and a subservience to the electronic distortion of mass reproduction, the piano—old-fashioned in comparison to both the sax and the electric guitar, both of which were to most twentieth-century, Eurocentric traditionalists, new-
fangled inventions of bad taste; burdensome to move; requiring constant tuning to be
truly suitable to the professional; yet commonly available in every home in the days
of selling music by the sheet instead of by the compact disc—was, in effect, the quintessential jazz instrument, the synergistic link between European and African musics.
Ragtime, the precursor of jazz, was a piano music and, as James Weldon Johnson's

137

1912 novel, *The Autobiography of an Ex-Colored Man,* written at the height of the ragtime craze, makes clear, the ragtime piano player was something of a charismatic, glamor figure. A significant stylization of jazz was to grow out of ragtime piano and blossom in Harlem.

Listening to Fats Waller's "The Joint is Jumping," his famous tune composed and recorded in 1937, when Waller was about thirty-three years old (later made into a short feature in 1941 which was shown in black theaters between full-length movies) there are some immediate conclusions we can come to about the Harlem Renaissance if we assume for a moment that Waller's tune is an epistemological gloss and unabashed celebration of the twenties, the years when he himself developed his own style and began to make his name as a musician.

First, the tune is in the style of Harlem stride piano, a derivative of ragtime and a forerunning component to black big band swing music. This style of music, whose major practitioners included Waller's mentor, James P. Johnson, was developed between 1913 and 1922. This means that by 1922 when, according to most scholars, the Harlem Renaissance had already begun, there was already a distinctive artform associated with Harlem, a school of art, if you will. This style of playing was largely developed at Harlem rent parties, as well as at cellars and small clubs, common venues of young pre- and post–World War I black musicians such as Waller as well as Johnson, Willie "The Lion" Smith, Lucky Roberts, Jack the Bear, and an especially inept but willing Duke Ellington.

It must be remembered that Ellington, along with Fletcher Henderson, had to be taught jazz music and stride piano when they arrived in New York by accomplished New Orleans and New York players and, further, the establishment of the Henderson and Ellington bands was nothing more than extending the tradition of the urban black big band established back in 1910 by James Reese Europe, with his 125-piece Carnegie Hall band and his radical formation of New York black musicians into the Clef Club. Had not Europe been murdered by a disgruntled drummer in 1919, he would have been at least as influential a band leader as Ellington and Henderson and possibly even a greater one. One reason that Europe is not more noted is because his music was produced before the days of rampant recording and radio and thus much of it is unpreserved, although Europe was commemorated in the 1943 black musical film, *Stormy Weather.* Europe, offspring of two musical parents, produced a highly arranged, complex band music that required broad musical knowledge and compositional skills. Obviously, he could play the piano as such music could only be composed on that instrument.

Once again, it must be noted that the roots of black musical art were well established in New York before the Great Migration of 1915 and before the Harlem Renaissance. It was during the twenties that a great deal of interest in creating symphonic, composed jazz was expressed by both blacks and whites. It is true that white musicians Paul Whiteman and Vincent Lopez gave concerts of "serious" jazz music in European art music halls in New York in the mid-1920s. But it must be recalled that James Reese Europe preceded them by at least ten years and that James P. Johnson and his student, Fats Waller, gave such a concert in the late 1920s. If jazz was to become a more formally composed, arranged, "symphonic" music, then it goes without saying that the piano would be the central instrument to effect such a transition. Finally, among the most influential, epochal jazz recordings made before 1930 are, for black musicians, James P. Johnson's "Carolina Shout" and, for white musicians, cornetist Bix Beiderbecke's "In a Mist," both piano solos.

Accepting some possible implications of the establishment of this school of art leads to the second and third points to be learned from Fats Waller's music or, more precisely, from the lyrics to Waller's song. "The Joint is Jumping" is a quite humorous and delightful song about a Harlem rent party, common enough before the twenties (a point that needs to be emphasized as many think that rent parties were largely a result of the economic necessity of the thirties), but a virtual institution from the 1920s on. But rent parties were more than places where this type of playing developed. They were particular and interesting sociological realities. Rent parties tell us that Harlem in the 1920s already had within its boundaries the makings of the ghetto it was to become. Rent parties may have been a kind of exoticism for slumming whites of the day or a certain fashionable vogue for some blacks, like Langston Hughes, but they were more often cultural symptoms of the massive overcrowding and extreme poverty of many of the people who lived in Harlem. The Harlem Renaissance is the story of the creation of a national black cultural community but the rent parties tell us that blacks did not control or influence loans for mortgages, rent policies, small businesses, banking practices in general; in short, they did not control nearly any economic aspect of the community they wished to create. This is why the Harlem Renaissance failed and Harlem became a ghetto. And it is for this reason of economic powerlessness that the Harlem Renaissance focused so much of its hope and aspirations on the creation of black art.

But the jazz piano and the rent party also tell us of the irrepressible human urge for integrative and functional art that transcends the conditions under which it is made while in fact satirically and even joyously celebrating those conditions. The rent party was and was not a symptom of an anomic community. The very fact that the rent party existed was recognition that anomic disintegration threatened the new black urban dweller but in the very structure that abetted his disintegration, the apartment house, the tenement, the African-American invented a way to overcome the degradation of his restrictive life. The rent party was not a response to economic necessity pure and simple, but to the economic and spiritual dislocation of urban life.

Observation II: Fighting and Dying

> You are of no interest to them, the swine, except when
> you're bleeding.
>
> —Louis-Ferdinand Celine, *Journey to the End of the Night*

From all indications, two of the most famous blacks in the 1920s were Battling Siki and Tiger Flowers. Neither is listed in the otherwise very fine reference book, *The*

Harlem Renaissance: A Historical Dictionary for the Era, edited by Bruce Kellner; yet the death of each man—Siki in 1925 and Flowers in 1927—was major news in the *New York Times*. Siki's murder in Harlem on December 15, 1925 was a major news story on page 3 of the *Times* on December 16, with follow-up stories on his funeral over the next few days and an opinion piece on Siki in the Sunday *Times*, December 20. Theodore "Tiger" Flowers's death on November 16, 1927 was a major news story on page 21 of the *Times* on November 17, with a follow-up story on his funeral in the November 22 issue of the *Times*. The only other black person of the era whose death received greater coverage in the white press was singer/dancer Florence Mills, who died of appendicitis a few weeks before Flowers passed away.

Obviously, Flowers and Siki were black men who made some considerable impact on the culture at large to have their deaths so prominently reported in the major white papers at a time when blacks, alive or dead, rarely made news for whites and when even noted black leaders such as James Weldon Johnson and W. E. B. Du Bois were unknown names to the average white. While Siki and Tiger Flowers are names only ardent sport enthusiasts would recognize today, they were probably better known to the average white, particularly the average white male, of the 1920s than any black leader with the possible exception of Marcus Garvey. They were understandably better known than any black writer, artist, or intellectual. Siki, a West African, and Flowers, a former shipyard worker and Baptist deacon from Georgia, were champion prizefighters.

Siki briefly held the light-heavyweight championship of the world when, in Paris, in 1922, he defeated George Carpentier—the daring Apollo and war hero of the French, beloved of Bernard Shaw (quite a boxing enthusiast himself) and middle-class American white women when he fought and lost to heavyweight champion Jack Dempsey in 1921 in the first million-dollar-gate fight—in six rounds in what proved to be one of the most controversial bouts in the history of boxing. (That Siki himself was, in truth, French and also a war hero was a fact that seemed lost on the French as it was on nearly every western white when Siki, in their eyes a mere backward colonial, won the fight. There was a great deal of fear, as Jeffrey Sammons details in his book, *Beyond the Ring: The Role of Boxing in American Society*, for what sort of restlessness this bout might provoke among the natives.) Siki, a wild carousing sort of fellow, was shot to death under mysterious circumstances one night in New York's Hell's Kitchen.

Flowers became the first black to become middleweight champion when he defeated the Pittsburgh Windmill, Harry Greb, on points in both February and August of 1926. He lost the title in December 1926 to Mickey "Toy Bulldog" Walker on a highly questionable referee's decision. He was campaigning to take on Walker again when, in November 1927, he decided to undergo a minor operation to have scar tissue removed from his right eye. He never regained consciousness after he succumbed to the ether, dying, ironically, in a way almost identical to Harry Greb, who underwent surgery to remove scar tissue from his nose and eye a year earlier. (Greb—a relentless and dirty fighter, noted for smashing Gene Tunney to bits the first time they fought and for having sexual intercourse with female elevator operators between floors while they were on duty—died in October 1926.)

140

There are two points of comparison that need to be made here regarding how the two boxers were alike according to the perception of the white public. The *New York Times* wrote this about Flowers, "The clownish champion . . . disregards all accepted boxing procedure for a style which is now peculiarly his own . . ."; and this about Siki: ". . . and his unusual antics in the ring won the fancy of his French fans. With virtually no knowledge of ring science he displayed a willingness to take punches and mix it that made him popular instantly." So they were both unschooled, undisciplined fighters who did not know technique or craftsmanship. It is difficult to know if either man was terribly accomplished as a boxer. However, a few facts should be kept in mind: first, black fighters were often forced to "carry" inferior white fighters and, in many instances, allow the white fighter to win. Black fighters were certainly often restrained from knocking out many, if any, of their white opponents during this time. To "carry" an opponent and still create the illusion of a creditable, competitive fight for the audience is no easy task and certainly required a great deal of technical skill. Both Siki and Flowers had to "carry" inferior white opponents or fight in fixed fights against whites during their careers. Indeed, Siki's fight against Carpentier was a fixed match that Carpentier was supposed to win quite easily. Second, after the explosive nearly cataclysmic career of the first black heavyweight, Jack Johnson (1908–1915), black fighters found it difficult to fight for a championship in any division, let alone for the heavyweight title. Dempsey, for instance, would not let Harry Wills, the leading black heavyweight contender of the 1920s, fight for the title, largely on the basis of several trumped-up reasons, although Dempsey's then-wife, Estelle Taylor, a minor actress, seemed more publicly honest, as she frankly stated that she did not want "to see the nigger fight for the title." "I don't like niggers," she continued. This prejudice meant that blacks who were to be popular fighters or to gain even a remote chance at the title had to present a certain, nonthreatening personality, as did Tiger Flowers. Finally, because Jack Johnson was such a technically accomplished fighter and because of the bitter taste he left on the collective palette of the American male sporting public, black fighters may have found it advantageous to adopt a more clumsy, less schooled appearance of fighting.

(The long-standing idea that the black possessed no sense of craft, that the idea of method was alien to his nature was combated in two ways through the literature of the Harlem Renaissance: in poetry, where the idea of craft and method becomes both transparent conceit and the cultural politics of the mastery of intelligibility, two distinct black schools arose: the Countee Cullen antivernacular, mastery of traditional forms approach and the Langston Hughes, Sterling Brown, James Weldon Johnson school of reconstructed dialect and the operating belief that black expression was inherently and undeniably craftsmanship and discipline. Claude McKay, as poet, worked in both schools.)

Siki and Flowers were different, seemingly, in that the white public saw Siki as a jungle boy, a buffoon, a child, a savage; his manager called him "a gorilla. He has the gorilla's tricks and the gorilla's manners. He's just a bit crazy, judged by human standards." Flowers, however, a southern black, was deeply religious, praying before each of his fights. His boxing nickname was the Deacon. He was known outside the ring to be a gentle and forebearing man. Even in the ring, according to one story, Flowers

141

kept his religious demeanor. The second time he fought the kicking, gouging, butting, thumbing Harry Greb, sometime during a clinch when Greb, trying mightily to push Flowers's eye out, cursed in frustration, Flowers supposedly said: "Mister Greb, put my eye out if you want, but please don't take the name of the Lord in vain." He was also, obviously, very respectful of whites. He called all white men Mister. At his funeral, then heavyweight champion Gene Tunney said, "When I think of Flowers, Kipling's line on Gunga Din keeps running in my ears: 'He's white, clean white, inside.' That's my tribute to a great fighter and a real man!" The measure of according Flowers honor came at the expense of the very quiddity of his humanity.

In essence, the differences of both men collapse; they are simply forms of black primitives. At least this was how they were perceived by the white public: one an African savage destroyed by his encounter with civilization, the other an African-American southern "darky," a veritable Uncle Tom replete with the standard religious fervor. They were, indeed, the old images of the Negro or, specifically, the old images of the Negro male. That they would be among the most famous, the most glamorous blacks of the era, participating in the most glamorized sport of the time, noteworthy blacks in the era when primitivism reigned, is significant and problematizes our understanding of the so-called New Negro who was supposed to represent something new and more assertive in post–World War I American culture. During the 1920s, with the growth of modern mass media and the shaping of modern mass society, the Negro male, as an icon, still found himself in a cultural *cul-de-sac*. He could not escape the myth of his origins that insisted that he represented a debased pastoral ideal: a noble, if demented, savage. In effect, in the age of modernity, the image of these two fighters suggests that black males could not escape the persistent cultural assertion that they could never be modern, that they could never evolve, that they could never obtain honor. Black intellectuals saw two specific remedies to the problem of the modern world and the "unchanging nature" of the Negro: First, that blacks should leave the South and become an urban people and, second, that the image of Africa as "the dark continent" should be renovated and repoliticized as evangelical, race vision. Of all black intellectuals, it was Countee Cullen, whose attraction to certain aspects of this dilemma was a driving force in the early years of his career, who was to radically revise the Christ myth into something like a new racial myth of honor.

Observation III: Countee Cullen

In poem after poem, Cullen states or implies that the
Negro in America is a perpetual alien.

—Arthur P. Davis, "The Alien-and-Exile Theme
in Countee Cullen's Racial Poems"

Countee Cullen was born in 1903 but probably not in New York City as many have commonly believed and as he himself began to propagandize around the time of the publication of his anthology, *Caroling Dusk*, in 1927. But he apparently spent a good deal of his youth and adolescence in New York, perhaps from 1910 on, perhaps even earlier. As one of the stars of the Harlem Renaissance, indeed, as *the* star of the era during the twenties, it might make Cullen a more intelligible figure and it certainly might make much of his major poetry more intelligible if we uncover the forces that created him.

In his childhood, well before 1915, there existed in New York, as was noted in the first section of this essay, a thriving black music, from stage performance and theatrical productions to rent parties, a music that was both commercially attractive and exerted the influence of its own sense of tradition. Cullen was always deeply attracted to music generally, as is evidenced by the number of times he consented to have his poems adapted by composers or the number of times he collaborated with them. He was especially attracted, despite his misgivings about it, to jazz music and to theatrical music as well. (He was working with Arna Bontemps and Harold Arlen on the musical adaptation of Bontemps's novel, *God Sends Sunday*, when he died in 1946.) He enjoyed dancing and especially liked black religious singing. What distinguishes him from Langston Hughes, who was also deeply attracted to music, is that Cullen grew up in the most significant center for the creation and selling of popular music, especially black popular music, in the United States and Hughes did not. (Perhaps the distinction is not much of a difference when one considers how much Cullen's very late poems such as "Apostrophe for the Land" or "Christ Natus Est" or many of the poems in Cullen's children's books resemble, like Hughes's blues poems, undisguised song lyrics.) This love of music is especially understandable when one recalls that Cullen spent a significant portion of his youth in a black church.

Moreover, Cullen grew up in a time when African-Americans were trying to create a great, model urban community for the first time in their history, in the very center of the most important English-speaking cultural center in the United States. And one of the groups most influential in this regard was black ministers. Ironically, for African-Americans, the only way to fashion a great secular community like Harlem was through the leadership of black churches. Cullen was adopted and reared by a minister. Frederick A. Cullen, along with Adam Clayton Powell, Jr., and Reverdy Ransom, had already established important black missions in New York well before 1915. Knowing that black churches have historically been the cornerstone of stability and leadership for black American communities, the fact that these important black ministers were already established in New York before the Migration and before the start of the Renaissance explains a significant observation: namely, that the foundation for mainstream leadership of blacks in Harlem was already in place before the community itself began. The southern blacks did not bring a cadre of their leadership with them (although Father Divine was an important black religious leader who came from the South to New York City in 1915). The leadership, by and large, was already waiting for the immigrants and it was in part that that leadership existed that attracted blacks. For instance, the Rev. Reverdy Ransom, editor of the influential *AME Church Review*, was giving speeches as early as 1909 exhorting blacks to leave the South. Adam Clayton Powell was a nationally known pastor before the war and Frederick Cullen was already doing important work with black youth in the Tenderloin area before the great rush of blacks materialized.

Unlike virtually any of the other younger writers of the Harlem Renaissance, Countee Cullen was intimately shaped, forged if you will, by the compulsive historical, political, and social values and stresses that were to make themselves intelligible in the realization of the Renaissance. For what is the meaning of the formation of Harlem and the self-conscious creation of the Renaissance? Understanding that the politics of this formidable and independent black community would be both, contrarily yet complementarily, nationalistic and assimilationist, the conclusions are these: first, blacks wished to create a national myth of migration to freedom; second, that true group cohesion and solidarity necessary for true coalition building and bloc politics were made possible for urban blacks through churches; third, once again, that the essential dimension of expression in the Harlem Renaissance was neither religion (which symbolized the force of the Negro's past as the slave who endured) nor politics (which symbolized the Negro's present as quasi-participatory American citizen) but art (which symbolized the Negro's future as the new westerner, the innovative imaginative force in the Western world). Cullen, as a lyric poet, was, in some vital ways, the quintessential Renaissance figure and its most representative writer. Indeed, to be a lyric poet made him the most charismatic and most glamorous kind of writer and one of the very few black crossover literary heroes between highbrow white culture and black American popular culture before 1930.

What Cullen symbolized as the Renaissance's chief poet was not merely the spontaneous coming together of migrating blacks. The Renaissance was the culmination of a series of social, political, and artistic forces which resulted in, for the first time, the articulate, self-conscious mobilization and politicization of African-American culture in the industrialized world. What must be remembered about the Harlem Renaissance is not the number of books that were produced by black writers—relatively few as the late Nathan Huggins, Harold Cruse, and others have pointed out—but the sense that a school of literature was being produced and that there was a necessity more clearly recognized by black political leaders of the era than by black leaders of any other time in the history of black Americans that great literature must be produced before blacks could achieve a fully realized culture in the western world. NAACP Field Secretary, novelist, poet, songwriter, diplomat, and essayist James Weldon Johnson made this clear in the lengthy preface to his anthology, *The Book of American Negro Poetry*. (To be sure, black writers of the 1930s thought they shared a common task but the idea of a national black literature or a great racial literature was not to become a real topic again until the 1960s and it was, after the 1920s, never a topic or a part of the national agenda for any black leader or politician.) The literary and aesthetic aims of the Renaissance seem particularly nationalistic while also seeming acceptably assimilationist. It was the obvious tension in these aims which was inherent in the twoness of being a black American that gave much of Cullen's best poetry its force and relevancy.

Countee Cullen launched his career with such extraordinary success and in the midst of such extraordinary anticipation that between 1925, the year his first book of poems, *Color*, was published, and 1929, the year of his third collection, *The Black Christ and Other Poems,* his fifth book overall, he went from an intense and hopeful popularity to largely being suspected of being an overhyped failure. And this change in critical attitude was not just with white reviewers and supporters of Cullen's work; black readers began to wonder as well. And the disastrous marriage to Yolande Du Bois, daughter of W. E. B. Du Bois, in 1928, which made Cullen such a laughingstock in some black newspapers (going on his honeymoon with his best man and longtime friend, Harold Jackman, was played up prominently in the gossipy black press), publicly hinting at his homosexuality did not help his reputation in certain conservative black circles. Yet I contend that it was really the publication of *The Black Christ,* the poem itself as well as most of the work in the collection (written while Cullen was abroad on a Guggenheim), that permanently ended any hope that Cullen may have had in sustaining his career as a major American poet or a major African-American poet. For many readers, the single poem, "The Black Christ," is the worst poem Cullen ever wrote or at least, doubtless, the worst long poem he ever wrote, and with its sometimes amazingly clumsy diction, faulty rhymes, and occasionally unsure measures, the case made against the work is not without substance. Coming as it did at the end of the decade and having been written while the poet was in France, thus, giving the poem something of retrospective quality in its examination of the American race scene, it may be fruitful to briefly look at this poem (it is not my intention to give a full reading of it here), as perhaps one of the few exemplary poems of its time and one of the most telling assessments of the Renaissance mind itself.

The poem's dedication is itself unusual and disturbing: "Hopefully dedicated to White America." Cullen had never before dedicated a poem to an abstraction. Usually his dedications were extremely personal as tributes, appreciations, or remembrances to friends, important figures in the promotion of his career, or historical or literary figures for whom he felt some sort of affinity. Superficially considered, the dedication for "The Black Christ" must have instantly made white reviewers wary of what they felt, quite rightly, to be a polemical and political poem. Many black readers may have felt just as uneasy. When the decade of the twenties opened, Hubert H. Harrison's *When Africa Awakes,* published in 1920, suggested through its title alone that the expectation of liberation for blacks in America was through the awakening of an Afro-centric consciousness. By 1929, the best and most celebrated literary hope for black America was suggesting that this expectation of liberation was through an awakening of the consciousness of white America, a seemingly direct repudiation of Harrison's nationalist beliefs and, indeed, of any nationalist claims that the Renaissance may have fostered. It has always been difficult for the oppressed to know whether they should act as physicians for themselves or as physicians for those who oppress them. In any case, whatever Cullen might be suggesting about making an appeal to or an accusation against the white mind, the very use of the term, "white America," implies a distinction and an alienation or, more precisely, a distinction that is a form of alienation and, of course, it implies the existence of a "black America" or a black national conception.

The simplest way to understand "The Black Christ" is to understand how it manipulates the idea of reversal. If we have a "white America" in the dedication that implies the existence of a black one, so we have in the title the implication of a white Christ, the existence of which, in a world where color is political, makes Christian

145

theology a dubious if not impossible doctrine for the black American believer. The theological concern of the poem is not a search for a historically valid or a historically revealed Jesus (in short, a historically resurrected black Jesus) but rather the reworking of the ahistorical Christ so that the meaning of his sacrifice becomes politically rejuvenated for American blacks.

> How Calvary in Palestine,
> Extending down to me and mine,
> Was but the first leaf in a line
> Of trees on which a Man should swing
> World without end, in suffering
> For all men's healing, let me sing.

All persecutions are historically collapsed into the paradigm persecution, so, in effect, all salvation history, ironically, becomes universal through the particularization of some temporal politics of oppression that makes salvation both necessary and inevitably desired. In effect, Cullen accuses the white reader of misunderstanding the very nature of Christian theology by mislocating it historically. Christian theology is never in the past; it is always in the present, always being re-acted out. Christian theology is never truly a transcendent vision except in understanding that it is being constantly played out in local politics. This is the philosophic foundation of Liberation theology, a contemporary Christian doctrine, especially attractive to many black Christians, that is the outgrowth of the late nineteenth- and early twentieth-centuries' social gospel, a form of Christian social activism that influenced a good many New York ministers, both black and white, when Cullen was a child, including his adopted father. Knowing this, it is now clear why Cullen would have such preoccupations. Thus, for Cullen, the universal is the particular, an aesthetic and political stance of some strategic significance for a black writer, a member of an artistic community usually accused of being insufficiently universal or being too localized in its concerns.

"The Black Christ" is built on two superimposed triads—suggestive of course of the Christian Trinity (the unity in multiplicity idea that is central to Christianity and which was also central to Cullen's philosophical creed). The first triad is that of the atheistic narrator whose conversion to Christianity is one portion of the central theme of the poem; Jim, his brother, the Black Christ figure who seems equally atheistic at times and whose transfiguration is the other portion of the central theme; and their mother, a black Christian woman in the traditional sense that most whites and many blacks have come to understand stereotypical black Christian belief. Here is the classic black family paradigm, the absent black father, the alienated sons, the enduring mother whose values of survival and whose unquestioned faith are challenged and mocked. The second triad, an exact reversal of the first, not the image of uneasy domesticity but of the disruptive tribal politics of enforcing the social humiliation of an unquestioned taboo, is Jim, the rebel; his white victimized girlfriend; and the white man whom Jim kills when Jim's white girlfriend is insulted. It is of course the classic social triad of sexual competition and the dramaturgy of lynching in America that is symbolized by Jim, the white woman, and the jealous white male. The whites remain

146

shadowy and unrealized throughout the poem, acting with the kind of compulsive impersonality that characterizes the same modern industrialized society that "murders spring," which is, poetic diction, why the white man is killed. The blacks are the only true presences. It is not Jim's victimization that links the triads but his rebellion against both the black mother and the oppressive white male authority figure. Paradoxically, in keeping with the grid of reversals that Cullen has established, Jim's rebellion against the mother only serves in the end to reinforce the validity and messianic power of the mother's faith (Cullen has no wish to subvert traditional black Christianity) while wholly displacing the power of white authority despite the fact that Jim is lynched and his rebellion crushed through an arbitrary exercise of that power.

This last point is only fully understood when we see that the poem turns on the concept of honor, which in a pathologically timocractic, male-dominated, oppressive regime (the American South, for example, at the time the poem was written) is precisely the reason why the oppressed male is killed if he violates the taboo of not having a sexual interest in the oppressor's women. In "The Black Christ" it is the black male, Jim, who defends the honor of the white woman by killing the white man who insulted her, for the defense of her honor is, in truth, the defense of his own. At the root of the self-determinism of the professed nationalism of the oppressed is the honor which the so-called honor of the oppressor denies him. With the rebellion and sacrifice of Jim being conflated in one large assertion of acting in honor of one's own selfhood, his transfiguration is thus the symbolization of the black Christian faith. In short, Jim's quest for honor, and his dying for the honor, not the sins, of his race, are what makes both his resurrection and his politicization of Christianity intelligible. It is what, in the conversion that comes at the end of the poem, makes Christianity a believable, workable, noble theology for the narrator and for all the blacks he represents. But Cullen is too much of a traditional black Christian or has too much respect for the type of Christian both his adoptive parents are ultimately to have Jim die only for the earthly honor of disobedience and rebellion, so the poem must also turn on Jim's resurrection ending the narrator's disbelief and thus suggesting that Jim died for his brother's nonbelief or that Jim's death only has meaning because it ended his brother's atheism. Otherwise, Jim's death might seem too much the result of the tragic flaw, hubris.

> Now god be praised that a door should creak,
> And that a rusty hinge should shriek.
> Of all sweet sounds that I may hear
> Of lute or lyre of dulcimer,
> None ever shall assail my ear
> Sweet as the sound of a grating door
> I had thought closed forevermore.
> Out of my deep-ploughed agony,
> I turned to see a door swing free;
> The very door he once came through
> To death, now framed for us anew
> His vital self, his and no other's
> Live body of the dead, my brother's.

147

Like one who dreams within a dream,
Hand at my throat, lest I should scream,
I moved with hopeful, doubting pace
To meet the dead man face to face.

"Bear witness now until His grace";
I heard my mother's mounting word,
"Behold the glory of the Lord,
His unimpeachable high seal.
Cry mercy now before Him; kneel,
And let your heart's conversion swell
The wonder of His miracle."

But the tension that exists between Jim as sacrificial victim and Jim as rebel is precisely the tension that exists earlier in the poem when the mother in her long speech provides several different meanings for the word "dirt."

The very odor of the loam
Fetters me here to this, my home
The whitest lady in the town
Yonder trailing a silken gown
Is less kin to this dirt than I.
Rich mistresses with proud heads high
This dirt and I are one to them;
Of lovely garments we supply;
But I and the dirt see just as high
As any lady cantering by.
Why should I cut this bond, my son,
This tie too taut to be undone?
This ground and I are we not one?

To the eyes of the haughty whites, the blackness of the mother's skin signifies not only her actual dirtiness, her physical uncleanliness ("The Negro always stinks," so the slave master would say) but the state of the mother's soul, the dirt of her sin which can only be washed white by the blood of the lamb. But here Cullen does not have the mother desire cleanliness through the traditional Christian white-washing. The mother's faith is buried in the dirt. For Cullen, this tension signifies the tension of his Christian and his pagan inclinations for the mother's beliefs become perilously close to making Christianity seem the very thing that its doctrines vehemently repudiate: a nature religion. But Cullen cleverly conflates the idea of Christianity being a quasi-nature religion while suggesting that it is a religion that is opposed to class and status (the use of garments as an image is telling not only in the strictly Christian context of Christ's garments being available for all to touch but in the specific social context of black women, most of whom worked as laundresses in white homes, cleaning the dirt from whites). Cullen thus makes traditional black Christian belief honorable without

148

really violating the tenets of the religion itself. This is why, in the end, the poem celebrates the victory of the mother's theology. She is, after all, the only person in the poem with a theology.

But these are the inherent tensions for a black believer that attract Cullen to the Christ myth and for Cullen is precisely the tension that makes Christianity a compelling force in the black imagination. Personal honor and group honor is tied inextricably to individual and group salvation and to the ultimate faith that salvation history is the unfolding of an intelligible theodicy that signifies that justice is not simply divine but natural and inevitable.

That the ambivalent quest for honor by the oppressed is one of the major themes of the Renaissance is perhaps a subject that has never been fully considered before. The fact that it has never been fully considered may be one reason that "The Black Christ" and Countee Cullen's entire career have been misunderstood and unappreciated.

Masks and Masquerade: The Iconography of the Harlem Renaissance

PATTI CAPEL SWARTZ

IN SOME PLACES the autumn of 1924 may have been an unremarkable season. In Harlem, it was like a foretaste of paradise. "A blue haze descended at night and with it strings of fairy lights on broad avenues" (Lewis, *Vogue*, 103). Arna Bontemps's description of Harlem provides an appropriate backdrop for a world of magic and masquerade. The Harlem of the twenties was such a world—a mecca for black artists and performers and their supporters, and for white as well as black audiences. The Harlem of the twenties created a space in which African-American artists had an unparalleled environment for creativity, an environment in which both production and artistry were controlled by the "actor."

The use of the term actor to designate the artists working in all areas of production—art, theatre, music, writing—implies control. The idea of control of production is vital to understanding the artistic creations of Harlem. The concept of artistic control also helps to reclaim the importance of what happened in Harlem, that world so often described as "almost heaven." In his forward to *Black Magic* Ossie Davis writes:

> Langston [Hughes] reminds us that our singing, our dancing, our music, our humor, our stories, our "entertainment"—spirituals, jazz, the blues, rap—was, and still is all too often, the one place where we have a chance to set standards and make definitions . . . the one thing about us that could never be fully explained or explained away . . . an island of self-sufficiency set

in a sea of almost universal doubt. Our art, to us, was always, and still is, a form of self-assertion, a form of struggle, a repository of self-esteem that racism, Jim Crow, and the Ku Klux Klan could never beat out of us—the only authentic history that black folks have in America, because we made it ourselves.

Harlem brought together a large group of African-American artists in one location. Close to white culture, 1920s Harlem allowed a community of artists the freedom to maintain control of artistic production. The Harlem Renaissance has often been accused of failure. Central to any examination of the success or failure of this movement is who controlled production. In Harlem, it was the artist who controlled the audience and the gaze. Neither a failed economy that affected whites and blacks alike, or the later relative submersion (except for musical forms) by the white mainstream of the production of the Renaissance could change that tradition of reversal of artist control.

In an examination of control, several aspects of African-American culture are important, but two seem vital. Both concern African-Americans as marginal to a white society that has controlled or attempted to control them. One has to do with the idea of carnival, and the power reversals that carnival creates; the other concerns the idea of speaking from behind a mask.

In Arna Bontemps's description of Harlem—a "blue haze" and "fairy lights"—a feeling of a special space eluding time is created, the atmosphere often connected with carnival. The iconography of the Harlem Renaissance is akin to that of the masque or carnival—of perceptions and reversals, of expectations about the performer, and of a reversal of societal positions in that the normally marginalized person or group gains control. The idea of the mask, the masque, and the masquerade—what Russian literary theorist Bakhtin would describe as Carnival— illuminates the phenomenon of Harlem during the 1920s in fascinating ways and provides additional credence to

Ossie Davis's statement of control from a performative view. It also creates a different view of spectators, of a white audience which becomes marginalized, losing ownership of the gaze rather than performing its usual function of marginalizing those others performing for it.

Examples of social reversals in instances of carnival appear in a long tradition of literary works—in Jonson's *Bartholomew Fair*, for instance, or in Hawthorne's description of carnival in his *The Marble Faun*. Annual examples of reversals through carnival occur in the festivals of Mardi Gras in New Orleans or Carnival in Rio de Janeiro. In each, the carnival atmosphere creates a new freedom of action and permits new interactions and power reversals to occur; a suspension of the everyday, the creation of a mythic world with mythic performers peopling it—performers like Florence Mills, Bill Robinson, "Duke" Ellington, or the "Empress of the Blues," Bessie Smith.

In Harlem, a normally marginalized group of African-American artists and performers gained control and became the locus of power that expressed and created a space of another kind, a space freed from convention and sometimes laced with exoticism and a return to primitive motifs.

For the African-American, a return to the primitive was a search for or a return to roots. For the white audience the primitive implied exoticism and the African-American artist embodied an "exotic other," an escape from "civilization." This white audience was alienated from "civilization" by the horrors of trench warfare and gas and by an increasingly mechanistic industrial society with its accompanying machine-age iconography. Popular conceptions of Einstein's theories of relativity had shaken not only scientific circles with a restructuring of physical bases, but they appeared in popular magazine articles and were transferred to the social and philosophical worlds as well, causing a shifting relativity in interpersonal and individual relationships. This white audience also accepted the new psychological theories of Freud that presented the subconscious or the "id" as a repository of primitive and sexual desires wishing escape. Harlem, with its music and often primitive iconography, seemed a perfect escape for the tensions of modern life; an escape to the primitive with the promise of a freer sexuality to an audience whose paid guides took them on a safari to the clubs. This look to the "primitive other" was a circumstance the Harlem artist often used advantageously, turning the mask on the visitor and thus maintaining control of the production of art.

Masks have been essential to African-Americans. From the time of their importation as slaves, African-Americans have had to devise strategies for physical, emotional, and cultural survival. Any examination of the production of works in Harlem and the role of the artist or actor must take this history into account and examine two kinds of discourse or expression that arose out of "wearing the mask." The concept of the Signifying Monkey is vital to a discussion of masks and masquerade.

The Signifying Monkey is rooted in African folklore. The story was carried in stories from Africa to the United States, and it survived slavery. In fact, the idea of a signifying trickster became a survival technique for the African-American living in a white world. The Signifying Monkey was given new forms in slave tales, in both the Br'er Rabbit stories collected by white Joel Chandler Harris, and in African-American Charles Chestnutt's *Conjure Woman* stories. The Signifying Monkey is able to best a larger, more powerful creature through a quickness of wit and a false appearance of reality or desire. Through this ability, although appearing oppressed, the Signifying Monkey—or person—is often able to change circumstances and best the oppressor. Signifying's history extends through performances in Harlem to present-day rap and discourse in which the meaning of words often varies from the dictionary or "white" meaning. Signifying implies speaking from behind a mask to those who will not understand, and implies a complicit understanding of the wearing of the mask from those who do understand.

In his book, *Modernism and the Harlem Renaissance*, Houston Baker, Jr., speaks of the masks used in two kinds of discourse or signifying traditionally used by African-American writers and speakers. The first is the mask assumed, as Baker says Booker T. Washington assumed it, within the "form" or a discourse of race that satisfied white assumptions about racial stereotypes. Baker contends that in his speeches and appeals for funds, Washington was careful to frame his discourse within the stereotypical expectations of a white audience, then to go beyond those stereotypes to attain his goals. The context in which Washington acted was one that Baker says had slavery as a beginning historical precedent, even though the signifying that it implies reaches back to African roots. This discourse, however, looks no further for its images than those images of slavery—of blacks as childlike, often without ambition or "white" morals, "needing" white guidance and support for survival. It is from this tradition that the white conception of the African-American embodied in the minstrel show character or in the characters familiar to the white audience that were created in both the book and the play *Uncle Tom's Cabin*, a white northern woman's conception of the Negro, appeared and grew.

In representational iconography that was created in the Harlem Renaissance, this mask can be seen in some of the work of painter Palmer Hayden. David Driskell writes:

> Hayden saw no reason to refrain from borrowing from the popular images of Blacks by White artists. He often exaggerated Black features, stylizing eyes, noses, lips, and ears, and making the

heads of many of his subjects look bald and rounded in form. But he insisted that he was not poking fun at Black people. (132)

Hayden was interested in folklore and felt his images were creating a visual representation of that folklore. Because of a lack of critical acceptance, however, he was often placed in a position of defending his work. Hayden actually repainted his autobiographical *The Janitor Who Paints*. The "Black man wearing a beret" and the "beautiful young black woman holding a child" cover the original painting in which "the janitor looks like a caricature of a Black person" and "the beautiful black woman and her lovely newborn are a minstrel-faced mammy and a grinnin' child" (Campbell, 33). In her introduction to *Harlem Renaissance: Art of Black America* Mary Campbell writes:

> Hayden's deliberately self-effacing interpretation of his efforts as an artist, his insistence on portraying Blacks with the masks of the minstrels—that is, as performers for a White audience—and his ingratiating reference to the benevolence of his liberators, are probably honest . . . portrayals of Hayden's very real feelings about his efforts at making art. As such, they are poles apart from Meta Fuller's aristocratic defiance and political sophistication or Aaron Douglas's epic perspective on the history and origins of the African-American. (33)

Meta Fuller's work and that of Aaron Douglas better fit the second mask, or "veil," of which Baker writes, that of deformation (essentially de-formation), in which the act of speech or performance goes beyond, or de-forms expectations in a return to an ancient trope of form—in this case a return to African and primitive motifs. This de-formation creates a space in which new forms and tropes, based on transformations of older ones, are possible. Through the use of de-formation, many diverse sounds, images, and voices are possible. A polyphonic present that includes many past forms, ways of being, or ways of seeing can be created: For example, the return to primitive motifs in the painting of Aaron Douglas goes beyond the historical fact of slavery as the beginning point of his imagistic discourse, returning rather to African roots and to a long history that did not begin with, but included and survived, slavery. Douglas's flat, hard-edged style that harkens back to African motifs probably reached its greatest achievement in his thirties' mural "Aspects of Negro Life," a work that contains much reference not only to the history of the slave and to African roots, but also to the trope of music.

These divergent discourses, both Washington's style and DuBois's vision, have relationships to music. The musical form of jazz is transformative in the same sense as any other discourse for the melodies of jazz can be traced through combinations of syncopated marching bands, ragtime, blues, and spirituals—transformations of those African melodies imported with persons sold as slaves. Through the use of one or the other of these forms of discourse, a freed world is provided to the audience. The form used extends from that of the expectations of a white audience (or a black audience enjoying the actors'—and their own—ability to signify on the more powerful white world) to an interest in determining a past and rootedness through the tracing of roots and culture through slavery to African sources. The reversal, or the control that the performer holds, is contained in the private joke of the performers who act from behind this mask and in the vision of the black audience which is a party to the signifying being done. The signifying is not revealed to those outside. Performance, then, occurs to a greater or lesser degree as a masque depending on spectators' understanding and expectations.

Genevieve Fabre cites a historical precedent for such masquerade and reversal in her *Drumbeats, Masks and Metaphor*:

> From the time they boarded ships for the passage to the New World, slaves provided shows for the entertainment of whites. . . . From their very first appearances, these shows took

on a subversive character. Similar in form to African ceremonies
or festivals, they were clearly occasions to perpetuate certain customs and to preserve the cultural heritage. . . . Mimed songs
that had all the appearance of praising whites actually satirized
them. Slaves were thus able to express their dissatisfaction and
unhappiness without risking punishment for their insolence. (4)

The issue of control raised by Fabre is vital, as is the
issue of an African-American standard for judging African-
American art. In *Black Theatre: Premise and Presentation*, Carlton and Barbara Molette state:

> There is presently a great deal of concern that many Afro-Amer-
> ican concepts or aesthetics are so totally a product of white op-
> pression that we ought not to glorify them. Some have taken the
> position that we should consciously reject traditional Afro-Amer-
> ican art that is clearly connected to oppression. (43)

The Molettes however, feel that art must reflect the cultural experience of the maker and of the audience for
that art. They stress the importance of who is in control
of the form and production of art. In speaking of Black
theatre they say:

> Although the style of the language and other such surface char-
> acteristics may have changed through the years, there is no in-
> dication that the intended functions of Black theatre for Black
> audiences have changed concurrently. The combined use of dou-
> ble meaning and comic irony as a contributor to survival within
> an environment of systematic oppression appears to be a recurring
> function, as does the galvanizing of existing anti-slavery sentiment.
> (35)

> Whenever a Black comic hero succeeds in controlling his destiny
> while exhibiting wit and comic irony, Black audiences seem to
> be willing to accept some accompanying racial cliches. So, as
> heroes in plays by Black playwrights are encountered, a key ques-
> tion must constantly be raised: Who is really in control? (113)

The question of control in theatre might best be looked
at through a musical review that appealed strongly to
both black and white audiences. "Shuffle Along," the first
all-black musical play of the twenties to be seen on Broadway, appealed to both black and white audiences although

it was conceived for black theatre. Written, directed, and acted by African-Americans, "Shuffle Along" was described as an "explosion" of energy, singing and dancing on stage. The plot was concerned with the campaign for mayor of one virtuous and one not-so-virtuous pair of candidates. Both black and white audiences loved the show. Stanley Green says "white audiences were happy to travel a bit north of the theatre district to enjoy the show's earthy humor, fast pacing, spirited dancing, and infectious rhythms" (1921 np).

We, looking back, are taken aback by the pictures of this production which show black actors in blackface. While familiar with Al Jolson's state renditions of black, minstrel-like characters in such plays as "Bombo" and "Sinbad," or his rendition of "Mammy," sung from his knees in the movie "The Jazz Singer," we do not expect to see black actors performing in blackface for a black audience. Yet the use of such a mask descends from the tradition of minstrel show where stereotypical portrayals of African-Americans were performed for white audiences and from which blacks were often barred as audience. As we do not expect Palmer Hayden's hidden janitor who paints, we do not expect such interpretations from black actors. Yet "Shuffle Along" had wide appeal for black audiences as well as white ones—for white audiences not only because of the power and energy of the performances, but also because expectations of black stereotypes were reinforced. The appeal for black audiences was because of excellence and energy of the performances and *the signifying irony* that bonded performers and audience members.

"Shuffle Along" as a musical revue differed from the Eugene O'Neill play that opened the white stage to black actors and that created white interest in Africa-American culture and theatre—the drama "The Emperor Jones." O'Neill's character Brutus Jones, while a fine psychological portrait of a disintegrating man, is a portrait of a black man whose descent and spiritual collapse is directly related to the misuse of power; a concept that many black critics call a Eurocentric rather than an Afrocentric view of the psyche. O'Neill's creation, then, is seen by many black critics as a white creation for a white audience. Loften Mitchell in his book *Black Drama* says that, during the twenties revival of the play in Harlem, when Jules Bledsoe, the actor who played Brutus Jones, ran fearfully through the jungle "negroes shouted from the audience: 'Man, you come on outa that jungle! This is Harlem!' " (84).

Despite excellent stock companies, the cost of tickets and the production of plays like "The Emperor Jones" or "In Abraham's Bosom" by white authors and a failure to speak to the daily life of African-Americans caused a decline in black theatre. Mitchell says "It was . . . easy for people to turn from the lies and fairy tales placed on the American stage to those manufactured by Hollywood, especially since the latter were considerably less expensive" (84). Although black film companies were developed in Harlem, the stranglehold of Hollywood distribution made their continued existence problematic because of production costs and the limited revenues that could be gained without wide distribution. Images of blacks in Hollywood films were stereotypical and created for white audience expectations. The stereotypes of lazy, stupid, shiftless black male characters in the early silent films of "Rastas" and "Sambo," the later roles of Stepin Fetchit, the easily frightened, gullible black, or the singing mammy were the images that Hollywood projected for many years. Black audiences often had to create reversals in order to identify with movies. In Hollywood film, the locus of control was certainly not with the African-American performer engaging with an African-American audience. In *Black Magic* Langston Hughes and Milton

Meltzer indicate the extent of Hollywood stereotyping, the lack of control of the black artist or writer, and the failure to recognize the potential of a black audience.

If film characters were stereotyped, the characters created by African-American writers during the Harlem Renaissance were not. Writing had a wide range. Claude McKay's *Home to Harlem*, a celebration of primitive sexuality and sensuality that caused W.E.B. DuBois to say that he felt he needed to take a bath (Lewis, "Harlem," 72) explored a world of sex, clubs, and music that was entirely black. Like the artist Douglas, McKay was concerned with a primitive motif, but with a very different outlook and outcome, one greatly concerned with sexual prowess.

While McKay was criticized for the blatant sexuality of *Home to Harlem*, the Harlem community felt that white writer and critic, Carl Von Vechten, an avid supporter of the Harlem Renaissance and frequent visitor not only to clubs but to house parties as well, had betrayed them with the sexual portraits that made up his book about Harlem, *Nigger Heaven*.

In contrast, Nella Larsen's fiction explores the African-American middle class world and examines the constructs of race in *Passing*, and in *Quicksand* the Mulatto's place in society. Larsen's protagonist, Helga Crane, is divided in her feeling about Harlem, at first feeling it is home, then feeling later that Harlem is a world from which she must escape. She is not comfortable in either the black or the white world, and is destroyed as a result of her search for identity.

In Larsen's, McKay's, and Von Vechten's books, clubs, music and dancing are all important parts of Harlem life. It was, after all, primarily the music, musical artists, and new dance forms that attracted white audiences to the more "sexually free and primitive" Harlem. The influence of musical forms on literature may, however, be seen most clearly in the poetry of Sterling Brown and Langston Hughes. Brown celebrates Blues singer Ma Rainey as well as the Blues form from which jazz developed. Kathy J. Ogren, in her essay "Controversial Sounds: Jazz Performance as Theme and Language in the Harlem Renaissance" says "Hughes equates the effect of the performance atmosphere with that of the Garden of Eden and of ancient Africa" in "Jazzonia" (172). She says Hughes's 1920s poems are his "own blues and jazz performances" (174).

The clubs *were* music, and music more than any other expression survived the slave voyages form Africa, slavery, emancipation, segregation, and the Jim Crow laws. Transformations of musical forms and the interpretations given by musicians are perhaps the most outstanding heritage of the Harlem Renaissance. Music not only informed the other art productions of the time, but more than art, theatre, film or writing, music has been the transformative trope that created the most cultural and artistic appreciation for black artists.

Jazz, the musical drawing card of Harlem, was not unknown to the white population. World War I disseminated and popularized jazz. When James Reese Europe enlisted in the army and was asked to form a musical regiment, he presented concerts in the States before debarkation for Europe and left the trenches to play in Paris, taking France and Europe by storm with the innovative musical techniques that Europe described as innately black. Europe said:

> I have come back from France more firmly convinced than ever that negroes should write negro music. We have our own racial feeling and if we try to copy whites we will make bad copies. . . . Our musicians do their best work when using negro material. (Southern, 225)

In the jazz clubs of Harlem, the musician ruled. The world of Harlem, that pre-taste of paradise, was greatest for the musician. As Doctor Clayton wrote in "Angels in

Harlem," Harlem was the place where brown-skinned angels in the form of blues singers, worldly angels, helped to find a way for an exchange of culture in an increasingly changing and transformative world. He wrote:

> I know Harlem can't be Heaven 'cause New York is right down here on earth,
> But it's headquarters for brownskin angels from everywhere else in this world. . . .
> I know blues singers don't go to Heaven 'cause Gabriel bawls 'em out,
> But all the good ones go to Harlem and help them angles beat it out. (Oliver, 77)

Those angels of the blues and jazz musicians helped to carry the poetry, writing, music and art of Harlem far beyond its geographic boundaries as well as beyond the relational boundaries of time, leaving us not only with a memory of a nostalgic past, but with a tradition that continues to grow and change, and transform.

BIBLIOGRAPHY

Baker, Houston A. Jr. *Modernism and the Harlem Renaissance*. Chicago: University of Chicago, 1987.

Bakhtin, Mikhail M. "From the Prehistory of Novelistic Discourse." *The Dialogic Imagination: Four Essays by M. M. Bakhtin*. Ed. by Michael Holquist. Trans. by Caryl Emerson and Michael Holquist. Austin: University of Texas, 1981.

Brown, Sterling. "Ma Rainey." Houston A. Baker, Jr. *Modernism and the Harlem Renaissance*. Chicago: University of Chicago, 1987.

Campbell, Mary Schmidt. "Introduction." *Harlem Renaissance: Art of Black America*. Charles Meirs, ed. New York: Abrams, 1987.

Clayton, Doctor. "Angels in Harlem." Paul Oliver. *Aspects of the Blues Tradition*. New York: Oak, 1970.

Davis, Ossie. "Forward." Langston Hughes and Milton Meltzer. *Black Magic: A Pictorial History of the African American in the Performing Arts*. New York: DeCapo, 1990.

Driskell, David C. "The Flowering of the Harlem Renaissance: The Art of Aaron Douglas, Meta Warwick Fuller, Palmer Hayden, and William H. Johnson." *Harlem Renaissance: Art of Black America*. Ed. by Charles Meirs. New York: Abrams, 1987.

Fabre, Genevieve. *Drumbeats Masks and Metaphor: Contemporary Afro-American Theatre*. Trans. by Melvin Dixon. Cambridge: Harvard, 1983.

Green, Stanley. *Broadway Musicals, Show by Show*. Milwaukee: Leonard, 1990.

Hughes, Langston and Milton Meltzer. *Black Magic: A Pictorial History of the African-American in the Performing Arts*. New York: DeCapo, 1990.

Larsen, Nella. *Quicksand* and *Passing*. New Brunswick: Rutgers, 1986.

Lewis, David Levering. "Harlem My Home." *Harlem Renaissance: Art of Black America*. Ed. by Charles Meirs. New York: Abrams, 1987.

_____. *When Harlem Was in Vogue*. New York: Knopf, 1981.

McKay, Claude. *Home to Harlem*. Boston: Northeastern University, 1987.

Mitchell, Loften. *Black Drama: The Story of the American Negro in the Theatre*. New York: Hawthorn, 1967.

Molette, Carlton W. and Barbara J. Molette. *Black Theatre: Premise and Presentation*. Bristol: Wyndham Hall, 1986.

Ogren, Kathy J. "Controversial Sounds: Jazz Performance as Theme and Language in the Harlem Renaissance." *The Harlem Renaissance: revaluations*. Eds. Amritjit Singh, William S. Shiver, and Stanley Brodwin. Hofstra: Garland, 1989.

Oliver, Paul. *Aspects of the Blues Tradition*. New York: Oak, 1970.

Southern, Eileen. *Readings in Black American Music*. New York: Norton, 1971.

Stowe, Harriet Beecher. *Uncle Tom's Cabin or, Life Among the Lowly*. New York: Penguin, 1981.

BLACK POETS, WHITE PATRONS:

By Faith Berry

THE HARLEM RENAISSANCE YEARS OF LANGSTON HUGHES

Editor's Note: This narrative is adapted from Faith Berry's forthcoming biography of Langston Hughes, BEFORE AND BEYOND HARLEM. The contents are condensed from a chapter focusing on Hughes's life and work during the period 1926-1930.

Langston Hughes, who was a frequent contributor to *The Crisis* until his death in May, 1967, published his first major poem——"The Negro Speaks of Rivers"——in the magazine in 1921.

Hughes's enrollment as a freshman at Lincoln University in February, 1926, coincided almost exactly with his twenty-fourth birthday and the publication of his first volume of poetry, *The Weary Blues*. He had no difficulty accepting the fact that he was nearly six years older than most of his classmates, but at a time when the Harlem Renaissance was beginning to peak, it was not easy to meet the demands made upon a new and immediately popular poet.

With the publication of his book, invitations for poetry readings poured in. The critical reception of *The Weary Blues* highlighted his spring and summer. Reviews in *The New York Times, New York Herald Tribune, Washington Post, Boston Transcript, New Orleans Picayune, The Independent, World Tomorrow, The New Republic,* and *Palms* were laudatory.

Black critics generally were somewhat less complimentary. Indeed, some of them heartily disliked the "jazz poems," which comprised the first section of the book. Hughes's friend and fellow poet, Countee Cullen, wrote in the February (1926) issue of *Opportunity* that he considered the "jazz poems as interlopers in the company of the truly beautiful poems in other sections of the book," and he took exception to some of the poems in other sections on racial rather than aesthetic grounds. There can be little doubt that Hughes was referring to Cullen and responding to Cullen's criticism when he wrote, a few months later, in a piece entitled "The Negro Artist and the Racial Mountain" for *The Nation:*

"One of the most promising of the young Negro poets said to me once, 'I want to be a poet—not a Negro poet,' meaning, 'I want to write like a white poet'; meaning, subconsciously, 'I would like to be a white poet'; meaning behind that 'I would like to be white.' And I was sorry the young man said that, for no great poet has ever been afraid of being himself. . . ."

The Nation essay, which became a declaration of motives and intentions for some of the younger artists and writers in the New Negro movement, was bought and published by the magazine in June, 1926. This provided enough money for his trainfare to New York, but Hughes lingered at Lincoln awhile longer. Apparently work on what turned out to be his autobiographical first novel, *Not Without Laughter,* was going too well just then to be interrupted. He wrote to Alain Locke: "I'm doing 10 to 20 pages a day now and rather enjoy it." When he did go to New York later in June, he took a room in a house on 137th Street, in the heart of Harlem, where another aspiring young black writer, Wallace Thurman, also lived.

Thurman, a native of Salt Lake City and a graduate of the University of Southern California, had moved to New York the year before. Brilliant, restive, and facile, his superior talents later landed him a job with the Macaulay publishing company — the first black to be hired in an editorial capacity by a major firm. Later, too—largely due to Thurman's personality and his bohemian life-style—his home became a favorite gathering place for both white and black artists and writers. He had not yet written his scurrilous novel, *Infants of the Spring,* which would fictionalize so many characters of the Harlem Renaissance, including himself (as a character named Raymond). But already he had the setting for his "Niggeratti Manor," which he would make famous as the fictional center for numerous fictionalized artists. In reality, it was 267 West 136th Street, a Harlem rooming house as well known for its all-night parties as for its enlightened intellectual discussions. Formerly a tenement, it had been bought by a black businesswoman, Yolanthe Sydney, who converted it into living quarters for impecunious writers and artists who often gathered there. She herself would be fictionalized in Thurman's novel (as Euphoria Blake), and he would be even less kind in his portrayal of her than he would be of Hughes, disguised as a poet named Tony Crews in *Infants of the Spring:*

"As time passed, others came in. Tony Crews, smiling and self-effacing, a mischievous boy, grateful for the chance to slip away from the backwoods college he attended. Raymond had never been able to analyze this young poet. His work was interesting and unusual. It was also spotty. Spasmodically he gave promise of developing into a first-rate poet. Already he had published two volumes, prematurely, Raymond thought. Both had been excessively praised by whites and universally damned by Negroes. Considering the nature of his work this was to be expected. The only unknown quantity was the poet himself. Would he or would he not fulfill the promise exemplified in some of his work? Raymond had no way of knowing and even an intimate friendship with Tony himself had failed to enlighten him. For Tony was the most close-mouthed and cagey individual Raymond had ever known when it came to personal matters. He fended off every attempt to probe into his inner self and did this with such an unconscious and naive air that the prober soon came to one of two conclusions: Either Tony had no depth whatsoever, or else he was too deep for plumbing by ordinary mortals."

Hughes never let Thurman come too close, and the latter always resented it, but when *Infants of the Spring* was published, Hughes must have recognized himself as "Tony," along with their contemporaries Thurman satirized, including Countee Cullen as DeWitt Clinton, Rudolph Fisher as Dr. Manfred Trout, Eric Waldron as Cedric Williams, Zora Neale Hurston as Sweetie May Carr, Alain Locke as Dr. A.L. Parkes, and Harold John (Bunny) Stephanson as Stephen Jorgenson, who in real life was one of Thurman's white lovers.

Hughes's relationship with Thurman began and continued amicably. Later some of their mutual acquaintances would accept Thurman's boast that his association with Hughes was more than just friendly. But those who knew them both knew better. One who did was Bruce Nugent.

279

A struggling artist (who gave himself the pen name Richard Bruce), he had met Hughes in Washington, where they became good friends. Encouraged to join the Harlem Renaissance crowd in New York, Bruce lived with Thurman (at 267 West 136th Street) and later said of him: "Wallie had a fascination for people that only the devil could have—an almost diabolical power. Langston was the opposite; he couldn't touch anyone without making them better. He brought out the good in everyone . . . he was not corrupted. He had the toughness of absolute goodness, which Wallie never had."

In the summer of 1926, Thurman worked as managing editor of *The Messenger*, a "radical" black magazine, and in his spare time organized a circle of friends and acquaintances that included Hughes, painter Aaron Douglas, and writers Zora Neale Hurston, Gwendolyn Bennett, and Bruce Nugent to plan a black quarterly of the arts. They chose to call the quarterly *Fire*, "the idea being," Hughes later wrote in *The Big Sea*, "that it would burn up a lot of the old, dead conventional Negro-white ideas of the past, *epater le bourgeois*, into a realization of the existence of the younger Nego writers and artists and provide us with an outlet for publication not available in the limited pages of the small magazines then existing." The first issue was scheduled for the fall of 1926. Meanwhile, Hughes was still contributing to "small maga-zines" such as *Opportunity*, where five of his poems were accepted for the October issue, with illust-rations by Aaron Douglas. He also tried writing lyrics for a projected revue, "O Blues!" featuring black American folk music, but in the end production plans fell through. With a com-poser named Ford Dabney, he also experimented that year with the libretto for a short dramatic musical entitled "Leaves," which also went nowhere.

The golden days of the Har-lem Renaissance were some-times clouded with disappoint-ment and failure. *Fire*, the quar-terly to which Hughes, Thur-man and other organizers had contributed much time and tal-ent, was a critical fiasco, when the first and only number was issued in November, 1926. Ex-cept for a short favorable review that month in *The Bookman*, the journal went unnoticed by most of the white periodicals, and the black press, except for *Opportun-ity*, condemned it bluntly and vigorously. Alain Locke, how-ever, writing in the *The Survey* nine months after the quarterly appeared, was more sympathe-tic.

The sale of *Fire* was very dis-appointing, Stacks of the issue were stored. In an irony like no other, a fire reportedly de-stroyed them, leaving the spon-sors with a printer's debt of more than $1,000.

But a letter attributed to Hughes and allegedly sent to Wallace Thurman tells a differ-ent story:

. . .FIRE!!! which I now hear wasn't burnt up at all in any-body's cellar but is in the possession of Service Bell . . . FIRE that I thought was in smoke, but which is now a la casa de Service Bell, after Locke said that you said they all got burnt up at 267 [West 136th Street].

"Service Bell" was the actual, though somewhat curious, name of a black actor-singer who lived briefly in the infamous bohe-mian apartment house at 267 West 136th Street. When Bell moved out, it was said he took with him the unsold copies of FIRE, and stored them in a basement elsewhere in Harlem. Though none of the FIRE con-tributors could ever prove it, the rumor persisted. Hughes pur-portedly complained to Thur-man:

. . . Service Bell . . . therefore holds the whole younger gen-eration in his grasp, and in 2650 when we're the prey of research experts . . . his heirs will receive a tremendous sum for the lot, all first and last editions of original copies containing source material on the whole Negro Renais-sance. . . .

But Thurman and the group decided to let the fire die down. So many heated arguments had spread about *Fire* that they thought another would only fan the flame of critics. Enough was enough.

Langston Hughes had armed himself against the adverse criti-cal reaction to *Fire*. In his essay, "The Negro Artist and the Ra-cial Mountain," some months before, he had written, "We younger Negro artists who create now intend to express our individual dark-skinned selves without fear or shame. If white people are pleased we are glad. If they are not, it doesn't matter . . . If colored people are pleased we are glad. If they are not, their displeasure doesn't matter either."

If this was his conviction and his abiding creed—and his subsequent writings suggest that it truly was—it served him when his second volume of verse, *Fine Clothes to the Jew,* was published in 1927. The volume displeased most black critics for some of the same reasons *Fire* had done, and some white critics found it easy to restrain their enthusiasm.

During that spring, Hughes made frequent weekend visits to New York where he often joined Alain Locke, who made the trip from Washington. The latter, pleased with the success of *The New Negro,* then in its second printing, had recently edited another volume, *Four Negro Poets,* in which Hughes was represented by twenty-one poems. Eleven of his poems were also anthologized that year in *Caroling Dusk* by his friend Countee Cullen, and three more appeared in *Portraits in Color,* edited by Mary White Ovington. Things "Negro" were the vogue, and many wealthy whites, especially in New York City, followed the vogue. One of these, Mrs. Charlotte Mason, was particularly attracted to the work of

Professor Locke and his young poet friend. An influential arts patron, she was the wealthy widow of a noted surgeon and acknowledged authority in the field of parapsychology and therapeutic hypnotism. Having married in her early thirties, she had been the second wife of Dr. Rufus Osgood Mason, who,

Poet Langston Hughes (second from left), 45th Spingarn Medalist, with (l-r) Arthur B. Spingarn, Roy Wilkins and University of Minnesota Vice President Malcolm Willey, following Spingarn Award ceremony on the college campus during the NAACP 51st Annual Convention, June 26, 1960.

nearly twice her age, had died in 1903. She still shared the views her husband had expressed in such monographs as "Telepathy and the Subliminal Self," and "Hypnotism and Suggestion in Therapeutics, Education and Reform," and she subscribed to his belief that the most significant manifestations of the spiritual were found in "primitive," "child races," such as Indians and peoples of African descent, whose creative energies, Mrs. Mason believed, had their source in the unconscious. As Hughes wrote later, "Concern-

ing Negroes, she felt that they were America's great link with the primitive . . . that there was mystery and mysticism and spontaneous harmony in their souls . . . that we had a deep well of the spirit within us and that we should keep it pure and deep."

Mrs. Mason's money and influence seem to have hypnotized Locke, who, like a courtier before a queen, presented to her at her Park Avenue apartment, the most promising artists and writers of the Harlem Renaissance, including Hughes, Zora Neale Hurston and Aaron Douglas. Locke's postulate in the introductory essay of *The New Negro* that Negroes must free themselves from the patronizing and philanthropy of whites was one he ignored when it came to Mrs. Mason. He based his agreements with her upon his own that one must encourage young black artists to stress African origins in

281

393

their work. It was this side of the professor, however, that Wallace Thurman in *Infants of the Spring* later satirized, disguising Locke in the character of Dr. Parkes whose message to Harlem Renaissance writers and artists was: "Let me suggest your going back to your African roots, and cultivating a healthy paganism based on African traditions." Nevertheless, among the artists and writers Locke presented to Mrs. Mason, Hughes was one of those who most impressed her, whose talent she wanted to "protect," and whose "great link with the primitive" (according to her beliefs) she wanted to remain strong.

On his part, Hughes found Mrs. Mason "instantly one of the most delightful women I had ever met, witty and charming, kind and sympathetic, very old and white-haired, [she was then in her seventies but amazingly modern in her ideas, in her knowledge of books and the theater, of Harlem, and of everything then taking place in the world." Hughes was ultimately to outlive this "very old and white-haired" woman by only twenty-one years. But beginning in the spring of 1927, and for three and a half years thereafter, she was to be his principal patron and to fasten a grip upon him that only the gradual reassertion of his personal and creative integrity permitted him to break.

Mrs. Mason, who was childless, requested her young proteges to call her "Godmother," and stipulated that she not be revealed as their benefactress.

And her request that he write her several times a week, about everything he was doing, he found rather flattering—at least at the time. Only very slowly did Hughes begin to realize that some of her requests, such as writing letters to her (unmentioned in his autobiography), were in the nature of demands. She chose the books he read, the music he listened to, and paid his admission to the plays he saw. Though he later declared in *The Big Sea,* that all he needed to do was say "when and where I wished to go and my patron's secretary would have tickets for me," the truth is that he went where Mrs. Mason chose, and she frequently went with him. And Hughes was responsive to the subtle manner she had of directing him. "She has her victrola now," he wrote Locke, "and a great collection of records, all of Paul Robeson, I believe, and almost all the best blues. She loves the 'Soft Pedal' and even the 'Yellow Dog.' And they sound marvelous on her machine."

The young poet had accepted her as a surrogate mother, whose interest in him was entirely unselfish and altogether motivated by maternal love. Moreover, employing her usual shrewdness and the facade of anonymity, she agreed to send Hughes's foster brother, Gwyn, to school in Springfield, Massachusetts, where he would board with a black family.

With no financial worries, Hughes was content during those months of 1928. Consist-

ent to the pattern of not writing when he did not feel blue, he wrote little, and it was ultimately to lead to a weakening of his relationship with his patron, who demanded to see *everything* he wrote. New novels by black authors who aroused much talk in Harlem literary circles were all published that year: *Quicksand* by Nella Larsen, *Plum Bun* by Jessie Fauset, *Walls of Jericho* by Rudolph Fisher, and *Home to Harlem* by Claude McKay. Hughes's own novel, *Not Without Laughter,* was to be quite different from any that he had read, and he settled down to drafting it in June in the Lincoln dormitory, where he remained most of the summer.

For his senior year project in sociology, he decided to do a study of the Lincoln campus—its academic goals and standards, its social atmosphere, and its student-faculty relations. The twenty-six-page paper that resulted passionately deplored the fact that sixty-three percent of Lincoln juniors and seniors preferred an all-white faculty. He attacked the (unstated) policy of not employing black scholarprofessors such as Charles S. Johnson, Charles H. Wesley and Alain Locke. He lashed out at a faculty-student relationship that was confined to classroom contact. The paper created a furor at Lincoln and elsewhere. Yet there was one strange, incongruous note to Hughes' Lincoln survey paper: the Foreword. That Foreword is strikingly similar to the Introduction of *The Indians' Book,* written by a white author, Natalie Curtis Burlin, who was influenced and subsidized by Charlotte Mason, who also encouraged her to produce *Negro Folk Songs* and *Song and Tales from the Dark Continent.*

Moreover, Hughes himself indirectly hints that his patron influenced the writing of the Foreword, which he reproduces in *The Big Sea* with the following note:

After I had finished my survey, I added a kind of poetic foreword . . . A poetic foreword has no place in a sociological survey, but, nevertheless, I put it there as a kind of extra flourish.

The Foreword reads:

In the primitive world, where people live closer to the earth and much nearer to the stars, every inner and outer act combines to form the single harmony, life. Not just the tribal lore then, but every movement of life becomes a part of their education. They do not, as many civilized people do, neglect the truth of the physical for the sake of the mind. Nor do they teach with speech alone, but rather with all the acts of life. There are no books, so the barrier between words and reality is not so great as with us. The earth is right under their feet. The stars are never far away. The strength of the surest dream is the strength of the primitive world.

His apologetic tone is revealing. The Foreword, in the context of the study-survey itself, is preposterous. But not until later did he fully perceive that this was a subtle instance in which his patron manipulated him against his will. His poems during the following months were increasingly political—"Advertisement for the Waldorf Astoria," "Negro Servant," "Black Seed," "Merry Christmas," and "Pride"—all of them social protest verses which must have hit her where it hurt.

It was her view that the expression of political opinions should be left to white people, like herself. Her own political opinions, however, never extended much beyond holding forth during drawing-room conversation. She never joined the NAACP. She did not even hire black servants. The "advancement" she was most interested in for Afro-Americans was limited to her belief in an image of cultural exoticism and in supporting black artists whom she thought would foster it. And her insistence that she see everything Hughes wrote did not help matters on either side. Hughes's displeasure with this demand resulted in the writing of one poem which he never showed her and did not publish until nine years later—"Poet to Patron":

What right has anyone to say
That I
Must throw out pieces of my heart
for pay?

For bread that helps to make
My heart beat true,
I must sell myself
To you?

A factory shift's better,

A week's meagre pay,
Than a perfumed note asking
What poems today?

Hughes' pride and his developing social consciousness brought about the final break with his patron, which came on a wintry day in late 1930—one year after the stock market crash had plummeted the nation into economic depression. "I asked to be released from any further obligations to her, and that she give me no more money, but simply let me retain her friendship," he wrote later. Somewhat naively, he had believed the latter entirely possible, never realizing that her interest did not extend beyond any relationship in which she could exert control over him. "There must have been only the one thread binding us together," he confessed later. "When that thread broke, it was the end."

But not only was his relation to his patron and her financial support at an end. With the onslaught of the economic depression, the Harlem Renaissance was at an end too. As Hughes wrote later, "some Harlemites thought the millenium had come," with the onset of the Renaissance. "They thought the race problem had been solved through Art . . . I don't know what made any Negroes think that—except that they were mostly intellectuals doing the thinking. The ordinary Negroes hadn't heard of the Negro Renaissance."

The break with his patron, coinciding with the close of the *(Continued on Page 306)*

Black Poets, White Patrons

(Continued from Page 283)

Renaissance, was a blessing, although in terrifying disguise. His early career was over; he could move in a significant new direction unencumbered by the past. The jazz and blues poems he had written—so appropriate to the Jazz Age—were no longer a literary concern. He had already made a new beginning as an international poet and signalized it in the December, 1930, issue of *New Masses,* with a poem, "Merry Christmas"—about a world his patron had preferred he ignore:

> Merry Christmas, China
> From gunboats in the river,
> Ten-inch shells for Christmas
> gifts
> And peace on earth forever.
>
> Merry Christmas, India,
> To Gandhi in his cell,
> From righteous Christian
> England,
> Ring out, bright Christmas
> bell!
>
> Ring Merry Christmas, Africa,
> From Cairo to the Cape!
> Ring Hallelujah! Praise the
> Lord!
> (For murder and for rape.)
>
> Ring Merry Christmas, Haiti!

> (And drown the voodoo
> drums—
> We'll rob you to the Christmas
> hymns
> Until the next Christ comes.)
>
> Ring Merry Christmas, Cuba!
> (While Yankee domination
> Keeps a nice fat president
> In a little half-starved nation.)
>
> And due to you down-and-
> outers,
> ("Due to economic laws")
> Oh, eat, drink and be merry
> With a bread-line Santa
> Claus—
> While all the world hails
> Christmas
> While all the church bells
> sway!
> While better still, the Chris-
> tian guns
> Proclaim this joyous day! . . . .

The political voice of Langston Hughes was now beginning to speak loud and clear.

From an unpublished biography, Langston Hughes: Before and Beyond Harlem, *by Faith Berry, excerpted for prepublication in* The Crisis. *Copyright © by Faith Berry. Ms. Berry compiled and edited the anthology,* Good Morning Revolution: Uncollected Social Protest Writings By Langston Hughes, *published in 1973.*

396

Two Black Poets and Their Legacy

By **HENRY F. WINSLOW**, Sr.

ARNA BONTEMPS-LANGSTON HUGHES LETTERS, 1925-1967. Selected and Edited by Charles H. Nichols. New York: Dodd, Mead & Company. 1980. 529 pp., with index. $17.95.

THE correspondence between Arna Bontemps and Langston Hughes, edited with prologue and epilogue by Brown University Professor Charles H. Nichols and covering a forty-two year period, is doubtless the most significant publishing event of its kind since the emergence of *William Johnson's Natchez* (1951), the diary of the free, antebellum landowner-barber with which the Louisiana State University Press inaugurated its "Source Studies in Southern History." (Historians W. R. Hogan and E. A. Davis, who edited the diary, later summarized the essentials of the Johnson matter in *The Barber of Natchez*, 1954.)

For students and scholars of history and imaginative literature, moreover, and for all of us honestly concerned with the role of authentic Americana in shaping and sustaining the humanist tradition, this correspondence between two sober souls of poetic perceptiveness and balanced judgment is indispensable. Who, then, were poets "Arna" and "Lang" (as they addressed each other), and what is their legacy?

Of the two, Lang was far and away the more widely known, and, indeed, traveled, what with his dearest friend and collaborator being early and solidly based in family life (six children, eventually) and his work as librarian at Fisk University. That they were as alike as Siamese twins is no wonder:

MR. WINSLOW, author, literary critic and New York City resident, is at work on a biography of Richard Wright.

their "quarterings," as Voltaire jeeringly inflected the word, revoked the value of every fiat in the dense and spurious glossary of apartheidolatry. In the grand branches of Lang's genealogical tree were a French merchant, a Cherokee Indian, a Jewish slave trader, an Old Dominion State planter who boasted a bloodline flowing from Cavalier-royalist poet Francis Quarles (1592-1644) and a Scotch liquor distiller.

The jazz and blues rhythm folk poet's father, James Nathaniel Hughes, read law, only to be turned away when he attempted to take the bar examination in Oklahoma, whereupon he went bitterly into expatriation—south to Mexico. Hence the color bar broke the Hughes family unit, and it was a break from which neither the mother (with one year of college training and nothing open for her except domestic service or kitchen work), Carrie Langston, nor her precocious and sensitive son would ever fully recover. In due time they followed the father, but the mother could not adjust to a stern husband and a strange setting; and the father, fiercely proud and obsessed with the drive to make money, literally hated the racist social tyranny that locked him out of law practice in the South. To make matters worse, the senior Hughes reacted so vindictively he scorned blacks who endured the humiliations attendant upon their status, his wife Carrie among them. So, with her young lad and often without him (Lang was reared partly by his grandmother and aunts), she moved from place to place: from Missouri, where Lang was born in Joplin on the first of

365

February, 1902, to Kansas, Illinois, Pennsylvania and Ohio. She remarried, bore a second son (Kit) and eventually died of cancer in a Cleveland hospital, four years after her first husband's death in 1934. The elder Hughes did fund the education of his son, but he left the property he had accumulated to a trio of quaint, kindly Catholic spinsters who cared for him during a lengthy illness.

When he was nineteen, Lang was in Mexico living with his father, teaching English and reading Cervantes in Spanish. He was back again a dozen years later to hear his father's will read. These experiences he tapped vividly in writing the first part of his two-volume autobiography (*The Big Sea*, 1940, and *I Wonder As I Wander*, 1956) and creating Jesse B. Semple, or "Simple," one of the most amiable folk creations in the annals of literature. The Arna-Lang letters reveal that the Simple pieces, launched in 1943 in a column he wrote for the *Chicago Defender*, earned for their creator only $25 weekly until Arna (always urging him on and pinpointing his works of permanent value) suggested he ask for an increase—to $35. In the lead essay he wrote in a series (*The Harlem Renaissance Remembered*, 1972), Arna indicated that during his formative years Lang was in a dilemma between a possessive father and a possessive dam; indeed, Lang had spelled out the turmoil and pain in *The Big Sea*.

James Hughes had designs for his son's education. He preferred one of the famous universities overseas but settled for engineering at Columbia; Lang disliked both, and eventually went down to Lincoln at Oxford (Pa.). There, nearing graduation as a senior, he and two other students polled the upperclassmen on the fitness and feasibility of Lincoln's lily-white faculty and teachers. Fifty-one years ago the poll showed that the majority of these middle-class gentlemen in the making not only liked things as they were (overall), but three of the 127 did not like *blacks*, or other blacks! (See Horace Mann Bond, *Education for Freedom: A History of Lincoln University, Pennsylvania*, 1976, p. 281.) Upon his death (on May 22, 1967, in mid-Manhattan's Polyclinic Hospital) Lang's library went to his alma mater and is currently shelved in a special room in the $3 million Langston Hughes Memorial Library (1972) on the Lincoln University campus.

Dr. Nichols points to what he concludes to be "The paradox of Hughes's sense of identity...," and finds him "reticent about his genuine feelings, his experiences of love and sex, his candid estimate of his contemporaries." This suggests the questions of why the poet chose to go it alone and where he got the blues.

There is sufficient evidence in the overall pattern of his travels to indicate what he was not: he shook off a "chicken hawk" when as a young adult he was in Chicago and duly recorded the incident in *Not Without Laughter* (1930), his autobiographical novel. Of James Baldwin's *Go Tell It on the Mountain* (1953), he noted in an extended comment (letter to Arna dated February 18, 1953) that it is "muddy and pretty and poetic and exalted without being exalting." More tersely, he said simply, "But it ain't my meat. I wish he had collabo-

rated with Zora," meaning Zora Neale Hurston (1901-1960, the celebrated novelist and folklorist of Florida origin.

Stranded in Paris during the first of his overseas wanderings, he shared a bedroom with a similarly stranded Russian ballerina, who was the first to get a job and who befriended and fed him until he likewise found work. Thereafter, he fell in love with Mary, the mulatto daughter of a black Nigerian business man and an English woman. But her father, then based in London, had programmed her for someone "in His Majesty's service," and dispatched a doctor to rescue his darling. Knowing fathers, rivers and the world of reality (particularly the way of marginal man in pursuit of a writing career), he countered her proposal that they elope with, "What would we live on?"

In the letter to Lang dated 18 July '52, Arna agreed that Joyce had been held off long enough and that Simple should take a wife. Lang comes through these communications as a kind of uncle to Arna's and Alberta's children and an intimate soul brother to the couple. Hence it is not by accident that the fictional Mrs. Johnson appearing in the Simple series is a strong and steady bridge: Mrs. Bontemps was not a woman outside the relationship between the two poets, but a model of muliebrity at front and center; she usually read Lang's letters to Arna over the phone before he came home from work. This family-unit togetherness extended to the children, about whose welfare the best friend of the Bontemps' often inquired.

1958—Mrs. Lillie M. Jackson, Kivie Kaplan, Dr. Martin Luther King and Mrs. Memphis T. Garrison at the 49th Annual Convention in Cleveland.

IN the American South and heartland of the first quarter of the twentieth-century the blues came down with the winter weather. They fell hard upon the homeless and ill-sheltered dispossessed by the politics and economics of exclusion. And when the thaw and rains of spring flooded the plains and river valleys (the Ohio, Mississippi and their tributaries particularly), these unfortunates were doubly distressed; tragically adrift; decimated by flu and tuberculosis; ravaged by that most terrible of twisters, the tornado; heartbroken; and terrified by the vogue of lynching and the victimizing penalties of Jim Crow oppression. Against these sundering forces the hapless thousands of blacks, having come into no gift of 160 acres merely for staking it out, had only their humanity to sustain them. So they lyricised their sufferings and the brief snatches of laughter punctuating them; the result was folksong, the

366

spirituals and the blues. In a tremulous and plaintive tenor, Blind Lemon Jefferson recorded the blues of travel:

> I'm just sitting here wondering
>> Can a matchbox hold my clothes;
> I ain't got so many clothes,
>> But I got so far to go.

The mournful wail of Victoria Spivey spelled out the effect of the prevalent terminal disability of the era:

> TB's all right to have, if yo' friends didn't treat
> yuh so low down,
> Ask 'em for a favor, an' they'll even stop coming
> around.

The ill-fated, troubled and tempestuous daughter of a Baptist minister, destined to become the greatest of blues singers, Bessie Smith Gee (1894-1937), cried out from the lowly depths of her world;

> When it rains five days, and the sky turns dark as night,
> Then trouble's taking place in the lowlands at night.

Or, again, on a thing she knew too well:

> There's two things got me puzzled, there's two things
> I don't understand:
> That's a mannish-acting woman, and a skipping, twisting
> woman-acting man.

These blues and others like them came up the rivers, roads and railways with the black exodus from Dixie. Lovers of folk music among country blades and plowmen, small-town and big-city settlers picked up the tunes from recordings and sang and whistled them as they moved about over dirt roads or cinder paths, through nights and days. Langston Hughes heard them (once most clearly when he listened to Bessie's voice floating upon the air in Macon, Georgia) and responded to their basic beauty, or, as he put it in one of his definitions of jazz, "the eternal tom-tom beating of the Negro soul."

Writing of how blacks become alienated from themselves in the most significant of his many essays, "The Negro Artist and the Racial Mountain" (1926), indeed, a blueprint for black artists, he registered his unalterable apreciation of the folk and their resources. To be sure, he was duly sympathetic and understanding towards "the Nordicized Negro intelligentsia," but seeing more for having a genuine poet's depth of vision and integrity, he pinpointed his preference: "But then there are the low-down folks, the so-called common element, and they are the majority—may the Lord be praised!" Knowing then what he would later confirm during his senior year at Lincoln, he defined the black's situation as it relates to his art: "He is never taught to see that beauty. He is taught rather not to see it, or if he does, to be ashamed of it when it is not according to Caucasian patterns." Four years after his death and one year before Arna and others began to set the matter of the Harlem Renaissance in focus, black intellectual historian Nathan Irvin Huggins gave his version of the period and his opinion of Lang's contribution: "Langston Hughes avoided the Scylla of formalism only to founder in the Charybdis of folk art." (See Huggins' *Harlem Renaissance*, 1971, p. 277.)

ARNA Wendell Bontemps was born ten months and twelve days after Lang (on October 13, 1902) in Alexandria, Louisiana. His father, a stone mason whose religious temperament led him to the pulpit of the Seventh-Day Adventist Church, moved his family west to Los Angeles when Arna was three, and in due time sent him for further education far up into northern California to Pacific Union College (out from Santa Rosa at Angwin). The sire's advice to his son was not to go up there acting "colored." Arna glowed when his teacher of English composition chose a paper the student had written as an example to his class; it prefigured the straightforward clarity and poetic flow of language that would mark Bontemps' works until the end of his days (at Fisk on June 4, 1973). It is significant to note that when Arna took his bachelor's degree at Pacific Union in the spring of 1924, the faculty employment *quota* for blacks educated in northern, quality institutions was *no quota!* He turned, therefore, to the post office, as did another omnivorous reader of southern origin, Richard Wright. Hence he soon found himself among other blacks squirrel-caged and learning the *scheme*. With easy access to the open shelves of the main library in the City of Angels, his reading and writing urge won over his efficiency in filing mail, whereupon he hit upon a use for the mails which got one of his first poems published in *The Crisis* (for August, 1924).

The bluestocking serving under Du Bois as literary editor of *The Crisis* in 1924 was Jessie R. Fauset (1884-1961). It was she who three years earlier recognized in Lang's "The Negro Speaks of Rivers" a talent to be considered. The poem was appropriately dedicated "To W.E.B. Du Bois," the Old Man of Great Barrington who was himself born on the Housatanic. Miss Fauset was an Ivy League (Cornell) Phi Beta Kappa with roots in an old Philadelphia family. She had lived in Paris, attained a translator's fluency with French and decided against rendering Rene Maran's *Batouala* (1922) in English; indeed, Jessie Fauset "belonged," particularly to that inner circle of "the talented tenth" which endeared her to the guiding lights of the Harlem Renaissance and the middle-class black clerisy. (See David Levering Lewis, "Dr. Johnson's Friends," *The Massachusetts Review*, Autumn, 1979.) Hence when the 21-year-old postal clerk-poet received from Miss Fauset a copy of *The Crisis* with his poem in it, he thereupon resigned his job in Los Angeles and headed east to Harlem. By that time, moreover, he had discovered Jean Toomer, Claude McKay and Countee Cullen, as well as Hughes. His Harlem experience from its beginnings was surprisingly and doubly rewarding. Led by a newly made friend to the parsonage door of "Mother Salem" (A.M.E.), he was mistaken for Lang by the Rev. Frederick A. Cullen, pastor at Salem and foster father of young Countee, on hand to correct the error and later to direct Arna to the meeting place of luminaries in the constellation of Renaissance figures. Indeed,

> Bliss was it in that dawn to be alive,
> But to be young was very heaven!

Arna arrived in Harlem with the winter season of late 1924

367

and when Lang was coming home from his first trip to Europe. Hence within a few days Countee Cullen notified the Angelino that the cynosure of the black literati would be welcomed home at a party "a few blocks above 135th Street on Edgecombe Avenue," as Arna recorded it in his essay, "The Awakening: A Memoir." After the party, Arna and two or three others walked with Lang back to the Harlem YMCA. During the exchange, Arna revealed that he had not read Lang's "Suicide's Note," at which Lang promised to send him a copy of the poem from Washington, D.C., his next stop and where his mother then lived. The receipt of the poem in early 1925 marked the beginning of their correspondence and collaboration. There had, indeed, been a time in Lang's life when he was "half in love with easeful death," and some six years afterwards he published among other poetries one that stands among the very best in the elegiac tradition:

> Dear lovely Death
> That taketh all things under wing—
> Never to kill—
> Only to change
> Into some other thing....
> Dear lovely Death,
> Change is thy other name.

THERE seems never to have been a time in the life of Bontemps when he did not know who, what and why he was. Everything he asked either for or from the world he lived in was straight and clean and clear. Thus it is logical that he would fall in love with a mother type he found among his students when he began to teach (as did Professor Nichols thirty years ago at Hampton Institute with the Mildred Thompson Nichols to whom this volume of selected letters is dedicated). Equally understandable are the subject matters and thrust of his several books: the Gabriel Prosser rebellion attempt of 1800 in Virginia (*Black Thunder*, 1936), the life of Federick Douglass (*Free at Last*, 1971), a fictionalized account of the Fisk Jubilee Singers (*Chariot in the Sky*, 1951), and like materials germane to the knowledge and intellectual growth of the young and open-minded. Before Bontemps turned from writing poetry to the poetic prose in which he eulogized worthies, he aptly summarized the rose-fingered dawn of consciousness in the Harlem where he launched his career:

> We are not come to wage a strife
>   With swords upon this hill;
> It is not wise to waste the life
>   Against a stubborn will.
> Yet would we die as some have done:
>   Beating a way for the rising sun.

Young Bontemps knew quite well that a revolution was under way and that it was cultural.

It is important to indicate, particularly to the generation that knows not genesis, that "There were giants in the earth in those days...." For whatever the shortcomings of the Harlem Renaissance, its major voices spoke for themselves and earned a hearing. Three publications in particular provided their platform. In addition to *The Crisis*, there was the National Urban League's *Opportunity*, piloted by sociologist Charles S. Johnson, in time to be installed as the first black president of Fisk University; and there was *The Messenger*, founded in 1917 by A. Philip Randolph and Chandler Owen and speaking out at the top of its independent, sassy, left-wing tone in 1925. Lang published in all three organs, appearing in *The Messenger* as an emerging short story writer.

The Johnson whom Bontemps cited as steering head of "The Daybreakers" awakening (See Patrick J. Gilpin, "Charles S. Johnson: Entrepreneur of the Harlem Renaissance," in *The Harlem Renaissance Remembered*) was the son of a Baptist minister. Born in Bristol, Virginia, in 1895, he had worked with and under Park at the University of Chicago and played a key role in drafting the voluminous report on the Chicago race riot of July 27-August 2, 1919, published as *The Negro in Chicago: A Study of Race Relations and a Race Riot* (1922) by the University of Chicago Press. In New York City by 1921 to work as director of research and investigator for the Urban League, he argued for an organ of communication. Hence *Opportunity*.

Du Bois throughout his long, effective and stormy career singularly vindicated the must value of a free and responsible press vehicle for minority development and protection. His independent temperament and learned courage established and sustained him, what with the fact that his chosen mission was the relief of the black man's estate. Beyond the works for which he is best known to the general public of informed Americans, *The Souls of Black Folk* (1903) and the posthumously published autobiography (1966) there stands the classic

1957—Dr. John A. Morsell, Walter Reuther and Herbert Hill at the 48th Annual Convention in Detroit.

1958—President Arthur B. Spingarn and Mrs. Daisy Lampkin, member of the NAACP Board, at the 49th Annual Convention.

Black Reconstruction in America, 1860-1880 (1935), and at its heart Chapter VIII "Transubstantiation of a Poor White," an eighty-seven page profile of President Andrew Johnson and the world he lived in which is the most penetrating account of a political tragedy in the long and lamentable annals of the American historical experience.

A. Philip Randolph (1889-1979), again the son of a black preacher (A.M.E.), was in 1926 challenged to take up the cause of 15,000 poorly paid and apathetically exploited Pullman Porters, whereupon he moved from his role as editor of *The Messenger* into labor organization. Thereafter and over a period of forty-odd embattled years he at once established himself as one of the all-time greats among labor leaders and blacks. It was his main achievement that Morehouse College scholar-economist Brailsford R. Brazeal worked into a dissertation (at Columbia University) and later developed into a book (*The Brotherhood of Sleeping Car Porters*, 1946); the man himself intellectual journalist Jervis Anderson treated in *A. Philip Randolph: A Biographical Portrait* (1973), a study serialized in *The New Yorker*; and Lincoln University historian Philip S. Foner singled him out for special mention in *Organized Labor and The Black Worker, 1619-1973*, (1974), a meticulously documented and thorough assessment of the black worker in America. So it was in the lengthening shadows of these older, distinguished contemporaries that Arna and Lang elected to render a true account of their collaboration and times in letters, lyrics and poetic prose. They shared the vision Du Bois conceived during his formative years in the Berkshire Hills and uttered in rounded cadence when Arna and Lang were suckling babes:

I have seen a land right merry with the sun, where children sing, and rolling hills lie like passioned women wanton with harvest. And there in the King's Highway sat and sits a figure veiled and bowed, by which the traveller's footsteps hasten as they go. On the tainted air broods fear. Three centuries' thought has been the raising and unveiling of that bowed human heart, and now

behold a century new for the duty and the deed....

PROFESSOR Nichols has selected from roughly 2300 letters overall the 500 he judged "most interesting and significant." They are arranged in three groups, 1925-1940, 1941-1958 and 1960-1967, and followed by a chronology on the authors, staggered, and another citing events in Afro-American affairs during the period 1900-1973. It is noteworthy that of the 53 letters in the first part, 37 are from Arna to Lang, 15 from Lang to Arna and the other a joint communication to James W. Washington, dated July 21, 1940, and demanding a reply, compensation and credit for work they did in behalf of the American Negro Exposition he managed from his base in Chicago (the matter was *Cavalcade of the Negro Theatre*).

In terms of content these letters may be read as a revision of much that is standard in the American learning experience, and particularly what is offered through college and high school curricula. Perhaps the most important thing about Arna and Lang is that neither the New Critics, so-called (that closed circle of self-styled Fugitives and Agrarians who while day was breaking in Harlem conjured up a private language for their preferences and followers), nor the old tradition defined their parameters. They sang no odes to the Confederate dead or their nostalgic cause. In the introduction to the last of his anthologies, *American Negro Poetry* (1974), Bontemps, noting that "Negroes take to poetry as they do to music," and that "Most Negro poets in the United States remain near enough to their folk origin to prefer a certain simplicity of expression," questioned the wisdom of Countee Cullen's displeasure at being called a "Negro" poet instead of a poet. Cullen worshipped Keats and brought off a lachrymose imitation of his English master, indeed, "a sick eagle looking at the sky." But the white owls called no tunes for the nightingales who looked to blues and Louis Armstrong for their consciousness, and to Gabriel Prosser and Frederick Douglass as models to set before the young. Indeed, the tune they internalized Bessie recorded and passed on in "Sorrowful Blues":

I'm goin' to tell you, daddy, like the Chinaman told the Jew,
If you don't lika me, me sure don't lika you.

It is regrettable that neither Arna nor Lang lived to read Alex Haley's *Roots*, forward as it should be read and in terms of what "Chicken" George represents to generations tethered to the "tragic mulatto" concept, that contradiction in the eyes of beholders to whom mixed ethnic strains from Douglass to Andre Watts are yet invisible as types; and again, in terms of the meaning of Tom Lea, like Prosser a blacksmith, and the one who built the wagons for the migration from North Carolina to Hope, Tennessee.

The list of literary notables about which Lang and Arna exchanged opinions and made significant moments in this correspondence runs from South African poet-novelist-

369

journalist Peter Abrahams to the Wrights, Bruce McMarion Wright, the poet (*From The Shaken Tower*, 1947), well known and highly respected as a judge in Manhattan, as well as the famous novelist and his first and second wives, Dhima Meadman, the ballerina and Ellen Poplar, the mother of Richard Wright's two daughters (Julia and Rachael) and his widow. The calculated build-up of writers on the South African scene like Alan Paton, Nadine Gordimer and Athol Fugard (dramatist) has obscured the primacy of interpretations Abrahams and Alex La Guma bring to matters in their native Soweto and Capetown, respectively. *The Path of Thunder* and *Cry, the Beloved Country* were published during the same year, but it was Paton's novel which majority critics promoted into a best seller, a movie, and what people who determine high school classroom materials want American students to know about the grim realities in the land of apartheid.

During his first visit to this country in the winter of 1955-56, Abrahams, having written himself into considerable repute with the publication of *Tell Freedom* (1954), was warmly hosted at a party given in Langston's residence at 20 East 127th Street. Like Arna, the South African "colored" had in his formative years found his way to the library and black writers in America, and by the time of his visit Arna was in a position to welcome him to the Fisk campus. By the mid-fifties, moreover, a Big Four whose province among other things was the wretched of the Third World earth (Ralph Ellison, Chester Himes, Ann Petry and Richard Wright) were firmly established by the sheer merit of their works if not everywhere recognized. And there was an authentic dean of literary criticism among black writers: J. Saunders Redding. Redding had paid his dues writing a column for the *Norfolk Journal and Guide*, book reviews for the Baltimore-based *Afro-American*, a remarkably honest and brilliant autobiographical travelogue, *No Day of Triumph* (1942), and a sharply focused portrait of a black academic handkerchief head, *Stranger and Alone* (1950), his sole venture into fiction. Hence their several references to Redding (ten) reflect their respect for him as an authority. Similarly, Horace Cayton, for many years a columnist for the *Pittsburgh Courier* and co-author (with anthropologist St. Clair Drake) of *Black Metropolis* (1945), yet the best of studies of ghetto lifeways in urban America, is frequently mentioned, what with both Arna and Lang knowing him intimately.

In a letter Arna wrote from Chicago, dated November 4, 1942, we see reflected their mutual concern about being drafted into the Army: "Horace is taking his expected call rather hard, it seems to me. Drunk more than usual. And at unaccustomed hours of the day. He says it is because Irma is in the WACs. I think his own military prospects figure in it."

A ripple of rich and healthy humor runs like an underground stream through these letters as it does in all of the authentic writing by Afro-American literary artists of genuine talent. Nothing is more characteristic of Ellison than the Aristophanic tone; Willard Motley's *Let Noon Be Fair* (1966), for all that it is about majority group lifestyles, is leavened with salty mirth;

the essence of the comic spirit comes to life in the key characters of Ann Petry and Toni Morrison; Chester Himes, John Oliver Killens, John A. Williams and the Richard Wright of *Lawd Today* (1963) particularly (as I indicated in reviewing it for the St. Louis *Post-Dispatch*), literally throb with an inimitable laughter and bluesy lyricism. Hence in a P.S. to his letter dated June 20, 1944, Langston tells his friend that "Lightning struck the Hotel Theresa yesterday—knocking various unmarried folks out of bed. It did not, unfortunately, strike the switchboard." And what could be the humorous gem of the entire exchange has a serious context. In his letter of November 15, 1961, Arna reported an affair of high tension and hairline tragedy on the Fisk campus. The wife of a playboy medical student at Meharry showed suddenly at Fisk to confirm news that her mate was spreading joy with other women at her expense, what with the fact that she was funding his training and he was involved with one black and another white coed on campus. Unable to reach him for confrontation and the kill, she reported him to the White Citizens Council.

Arna and Lang alike were always sensitive to matters involving cross-pollination and institutionalized hypocrisy about this basic American and human proclivity and diversion. Instead, *Montage of a Dream Deferred* (1951) included "Mellow," Lang's mildly mocking tribute to the ways of some black and white folk:

> Into the laps
> of black celebrities
> white girls fall
> like pale plums from a tree
> behind a high tension wall
> wired for killing
> which makes it
> more thrilling.

He thought well enough of it to include it among his *Selected Poems* (1959).

IN April 30, 1946, Arna wrote Lang for information for an article in *Ebony* and got a response written two days later. It provides an outline of the folk poet's life and peculiar traits. Anger made him ill; he gave away as many books as he sold and never had any money to speak of; he was not mechanical; liked to eat; was once arrested for defying Jim Crow in Havana; was once reported to be engaged to Elsie Roxborough, the niece of Joe Louis' manager, but never married; and his friends ranged from Mrs. Mary McLeod Bethune to novelist Ernest Hemingway. Seventeen years later he wrote Arna that he was making his will and asked what he wanted. On the very next day (in the letter dated 8 March '65), Arna answered:

> . . . since we have both marched across the frontiers of sixty, I might say that, God willing, and should you wish it, I'd be mighty proud to edit and properly introduce your *Complete Poems*, and I would hope the copyright picture would be clear enough so that no publisher could

monkey-wrench such a project. I have also in mind, as you know, a biography, and it would help if this could be properly authorized.

Of the wealth of commentary and roughly ten biographies of Langston Hughes, the one we find most rewarding for being deeply searched is *Langston Hughes: An Introduction to the Poetry*, by Jemie Onwuckekwa, one of a half dozen Twentieth Century Poetry Series and published by the Columbia University Press (1976). Currently (or then) associate professor of English and Afro-American literature at the University of Minnesota, the East Nigerian educated at Columbia and Harvard has rendered in the second chapter of his study an interpretation of Lang's blues which may well be beyond what Arna himself would have done had he lived or been able to fulfill his dream and promise. To be sure, Arna had the blues, but not as did Lang and Bessie. Richard Wright had the blues, as Ralph Ellison has indicated, what with being at once musician and lyrical novelist, but not in the same way Lang had them. The blues bring John A. Williams through at his best in *Sissie* and *Night Song*. And they make Mamie Powther (the grand ingredient in Ann Petry's *The Narrows*) one of the truly memorable creations in the literature of liberated woman:

Trouble sits at my front door
Can't shut him out any more
And I'm lonesome—lonesome.

It is tempting to say of Arna and Lang that they got it all together in probing and presenting the dimensions of the black experience. Arna was of a decidedly religious temperament, given the Seventh-Day Adventist atmosphere of his early years. Lang's *Tambourines To Glory* (1958), a novel, and the hilarious short story, "Rock Church, Rock," reveal his acquaintance with the inner ferment of the *gospel* spirit in black church circles; and "Big Meeting," the most pointed and perhaps the best of his short sketches, shows how well he understood the eloquence and subtlety of "the black and unknown bards of long ago" in the revival fervor of the camp meeting. But the more thoughtful and disciplined pulpiteers on the order of Adam Clayton Powell, Jr., Martin Luther King, Jr., indeed, the leaders who preached and marched and kept the church doors open for planning and organizing to obtain "the things which belong unto our peace," are not represented in the works of Lang.

They were both fond of the theatre, as literary beings would logically be; but the kind of funding required for launching plays was not available during their time and is not available now. *St. Louis Woman* (1946), the joint venture of Bontemps and Cullen, drew scornful comments; and Lang's *Little Ham* (1934) and *Mulatto* (1935) cut too deeply into the soft underside of subtle racist roguery and power-rape miscegenation to be tolerated by American culture barons; Ketti Frings' adaptation of Richard Wright's *The Long Dream* (1960) and playwright

Richard Wesley's *The Mighty Gents* (1978) were alike hooted off the Broadway stage (the Ambassador Theatre, in fact) for revealing the role and ruthlessness of the power-structure pimp in ghetto racketeering. Lang often referred to the theatre he dearly loved as a "worriation."

The last letter from Lang to Arna was written (on the basis of Dr. Nichols' selections) from the Hotel Wellington on Manhattan's Seventh Avenue at 55th Street, roughly six blocks from the hospital where he would die exactly a month later. He referred to Milton Meltzer's biography, the clearest and closest account of Langston the working poet, then in its second draft. He was here because he found it impossible to work at 20 East 127th Street, and was planning a trip to Europe during the summer season to follow. The last letter from Arna to Lang is dated May 1, 1967. It dealt with the problems of publishing and updating their works and the matter of furnishing educational materials for junior high schools. The conventional close from Arna was "Best ever"; from Lang, "Sincerely."

It was Arna who opened the correspondence and Arna who closed it. During the six years he lived beyond the death of his friend he continued to make solid contributions to the literature of the black experience from campus bases (as professor of English at the University of Illinois, Chicago Circle, and professor and curator of the James Weldon Johnson Collection in the Beinecke at Yale). He edited *Great Slave Narratives* (1969) with an introduction which tapped events in his personal experience which challenged him to explore black history. His teachers had given him "to understand that the only meaningful history of the Negro in the United States (possibly even in the world) began with the Emancipation Proclamation of 1863." Two years later appeared *Free at Last: The Life of Frederick Douglass;* the biography balances the man and his mission, and fills in Douglass' European honeymoon tour with his second wife, Helen Pitts, at which point Edmund Fuller's *Star Pointed North* (1946), now out of print but available in two copies in the Langston Hughes Library at Lincoln, comes to a dead stop. Bontemps' version ends as did he and his friend: "And so was buried the once furious slave, the intrepid giant whom Thomas Wentworth Higginson called 'the imperial Douglass,' born of a rage to live, spent by struggle, but free at last."

The culling and editing of this correspondence must have been a tedious and monumental task for Dr. Nichols; indeed, he may well have had one or two other scholars equally knowledgeable about the time and events covered to write either the prologue or epilogue (a seasoned and proven literary historian such as Blyden Jackson at Chapel Hill or Darwin Turner at Iowa State) and identify for readers of the younger generation some of the names currently insignificant. But set against the value of having this record of the past from the best sources, these reservations are mere quibbles. ■

Flower-Dust and Springtime:
Harlem Renaissance Women

by Sharon Dean and Erlene Stetson

Zora Neale Hurston

Four distinctly female voices arose out of the Harlem Renaissance (1919-1931): Georgia Douglas Johnson, Anne Spencer, Nella Larsen, and Zora Neale Hurston. The first two, as poets, and the last two, as novelists, provided a range of images for the black woman that defied her stereotypes. As Paule Marshall contends in her contribution to **Freedomways'** Spring, 1966 symposium on "The Negro Woman in Literature," the black woman

has in a sense been strung up on two poles and left hanging. At one end of the pole, there is the "nigger wench" — sensual, primitive, pleasure-seeking, immoral, the siren, the sinner.... And at the other end of pole, we find that larger than life figure, the Negro matriarch, who dominates so much fiction — strong, but humble, devoted, devoutly religious, patient — a paragon of patience, if you will — wise beyond all wisdom,

the saint, the mammy, the great wet nurse of the society, and the country deep within the recesses of its psyche longs to return to her ample breasts. (p. 20)

These four women did not so much deny that these figures exist, as they attempted to bridge their polarities by expressing the complexities that make for rich and credible characters in literature.

As he so often did with similarly polar realities in black experience, W.E.B. DuBois gave the black woman's "double consciousness" an ideological dimension. "The Damnation of Women," an essay published in 1920 (in **Darkwater: Voices from Within the Veil**) develops the thesis that "All womanhood is hampered today because the world on which it is emerging is a world that tries to worship both virgins and mothers and in the end despises motherhood and despoils virgins." (p. 164) He suggests, instead, that the world make a choice — between the "free woman and the white wraith of the prostitute. Today it wavers between the prostitute and the nun." (p. 165) But for black womanhood in particular DuBois demands worship, for "the world must heed these daughters of sorrow, from the primal black All-Mother of men down through the ghostly throng of mighty womanhood, who walked in the mysterious dawn of Asia and Africa." (p. 165) But when we add to this African honoring of the "mother-idea" Elise Johnson McDougald's sense of "The Task of Negro Womanhood," we have a fair idea of the two new poles from which many New Negro women found themselves hanging. McDougald sees the "Negro woman of today," not in Africa but in Harlem, where

more than anywhere else, the Negro woman is free from the cruder handicaps of primitive household hardships and the grosser forms of sex and race subjugation. Here, she has considerable opportunity to measure her powers in the intellectual and industrial fields of the great city.(1)

Johnson, Spencer, Larsen, and Hurston attempt in their works, with varying degrees of success, to mediate between these expectations.

In 1918, when William Stanley Braithwaite wrote the introduction to Georgia Douglas Johnson's first volume of poems, **The Heart of a Woman**, he emphasized for how short a time (less than fifty years) women had been speaking or acting with a sense of freedom. He went on to say:

Sadness is a kind of felicity with woman, paradoxical as it may seem; and it is so because through this inexplicable felicity they touched, intuitionally caress reality ....Mrs. Johnson creates just that reality of woman's heart and experience with astonishing raptures. It is a kind of privilege to know so much about the secrets of woman's nature, a privilege all the more to be cherished when given...with such exquisite utterance, with such lyric sensibility.(2)

As Braithwaite's comments indicate, Mrs. Johnson's "Heart of a Woman" poem clearly speaks from within "that veiled Melancholy" of DuBois's "daughters of sorrow."

The heart of a woman falls back with the night,
And enters some alien cage in its plight,
And tries to forget it has dreamed of the stars
While it breaks, breaks, breaks on the sheltering bars.

And in her poem "Pent" she implores:

Break! break!! ye flood-gates of my tears
All pent in agony,
Rain, rain! upon my scorching soul
And flood it as the sea!!

The most frequently used word in the volume (as in these two poems) is "break." It carries a multiplicity of meanings that go beyond the conventionality of the poems' surface. The speaker repeatedly associates the "breaking" with confinement, repressed emotions, broken dreams, and the imposition of one will upon another as in "The Measure," where a man and woman (unmistakably man and wife, as befits Mrs. Johnson's sense of decorum) have a brief battle of wills:

Fierce is the conflict — the battle of eyes,
Sure and unerring, the wordless replies,
Challenges flash from their ambushing caves —
Men, by their glances, are masters or slaves.

Unexpectedly, paired with the above poem is "Smothered Fires":

A woman with a burning flame
Deep covered through the years
With ashes. Ah! she hid it deep,
And smothered it with tears.

Sometimes a baleful light would rise
From out the dusky bed,

And then the woman hushed it quick
To slumber on, as dead.

At last the weary war was done
The tapers were alight,
And with a sigh of victory
She breathed a soft — good-night!

We have here a renunciation of passion and a redirection of that passion into the "Tears and Kisses" of marriage, which seem slight compared to the tempests just associated with the woman's wrestling with her heart:

There are tears sweet, refreshing like dewdrops
that rise,
There are tears far too deep for the lakes of the
eyes.
There are kisses like thistledown, fitfully sped,
There are kisses that live in the hearts of the
dead.

As with the poems about the marriage bed, "Tears and Kisses" takes on irony when read with the poem with which it is paired: a poem that discusses the husband's death — the subject of at least five poems in this small volume — in openly sensual terms:

Alone! yes, evermore alone — isolate each his
way,
Though hand is echoing to hand vain sophistries
of clay,
Within that veiled, mystic place where bides the
inmost soul,
No twain shall pass while tides shall wax, nor
changing seasons roll.

Enisled, apart our pilgrimage, despite the arms

that twine,
Despite the fusing kiss that wields the magic
charm of wine,
Despite the interplay of sigh, the surge of
sympathy,
We tread in solitude remote, the trail of destiny!

Or is this, instead, as its title "Isolation" implies, simply a parting of ways? This kind of ambiguity gives depth to her poetry, but the critics are content with quoting this single line of her work: "I want to die while you love me."(3) W.E.B. DuBois wrote the Foreword to Mrs. Johnson's 1922 volume, **Bronze**.(4) He starts by mentioning her blackness, which Braithwaite had failed to do, and which she, herself, had played down in the first volume: "Her work is simple, sometimes trite, but it is singularly sincere and true, and as a revelation of the soul struggle of the women of a race, it is invaluable." (p. 7) Although DuBois' comments hint at a certain critical reservation about the artistic worth of her poems, he clearly is in sympathy with her new tact. She is no longer merely engaged in what Braithwaite labels as "the task of documenting the feminine heart;" she is now a bronze mother, "Her heart sandalling [her son's] feet."

This collection is unabashedly maternal, and surprisingly aggressive. Instead of the "Illusions" of the earlier poems, we have "Calling Dreams," wherein the speaker asserts "The right to make my dreams come true/I ask, nay, I demand of life." (p. 23) **Bronze** displays an advance in her technique and in her "rending of the veil." The romantic sensibility that Ronald Primeau sees as definitive in her work, stressing "the creative role of dreams not in running away from difficulties but in helping man to experience them more fully and overcome them," is muted.(5) If not defiance, at least there is rebuke in the poem about "The Cross" of racial prejudice:

All day the world's mad mocking strife,
The venomed prick of probing knife,
The baleful, subtle leer of scorn
That rims the world from morn to morn,
While reptile-visions writhe and creep
Into the very arms of sleep
To quench the fitful burnished gleams:
A crucifixion in my dreams!

But the poem that follows, if of another "cross" — the mulatto or "half-caste." Cedric Dover contends that Mrs. Johnson "is definitely of" the Harlem Renaissance, "but equally definitely not in it."(6)

Her first volume, **The Heart of a Woman** (1918), echoes Sara Teasdale and shows real sensibility, but contains no hint of the ferment which, a little later, inspired Claude McKay's moving sonnets of protest, his evocative explorations of the Harlem scene, and his exquisite lyrics of nostalgia....
Mrs. Johnson's second book, **Bronze** (1922), reflects these departures from the poesy of the comfortable villa in the manner indicated in its title. The subject is still the heart of a woman, but now it is the heart of a colored woman aware of her social problem and the potentiality of the so-called hybrid. (pp. 633-4)

Dover argues that "The Importance of Georgia Douglas Johnson" (the article's title) lies in her poems facing and resolving "the psychological and social complications of being a near-white, while retaining enough traces of the 'tragic mulatto' feeling to stress the merit of her conquest..., she is the first and still the most prolific poet of the 'half-caste.' " (p. 635) It is this element of the "tragic mulatto" that connects her with so many women writers of the period, Nella Larsen in particular. She includes her poems about the mulatto in a section called "Shadow," along with poems about prejudice and "The Passing of the Ex-Slave." In her hands the "near-white" of "The Octoroon" has

> One drop of midnight in the dawn of life's pulsating stream
> Marks her an alien from her kind, a shade amid its gleam;
> Forever more her step she bends insular, strange,
>   apart —
> And none can read the riddle of her wildly warring heart.

She seems to indicate that the octoroon's "kind" is the white race. She states this more openly in the next poem, "Aliens," and pronounces the familiar fate upon all those who "lie, the fretted fabric of a dual dynasty":

> A single drop, a sable strain debars them from their
>   own, —
> The others — fold them furtively, but God! they are
>   alone,
> Blown by the fickle winds of fate far from the travelled
>   mart
> To die, when they have quite consumed the morsel of
>   their heart. . . .

It is interesting that Mrs. Johnson reserves such racial ambivalences for her female characters, her only female characters that do not appear as mothers-to-sons. The only other mention of a female is in reference to "My daughters, unhaloed, unhonored, undone, [who] feed the/lust of a dominant land." But this bitter accusation is made in the voice of a runaway male slave who is explaining to his Southern master his reasons for fleeing the South.

The essential mood of Georgia Douglas Johnson's poems is tragic: her tragic heroine, the mother; her tragic scapegoat, the mulatto. Sterling Brown accurately describes the poems as "generally autumnal in tone."(7) In contrast, Nella Larsen's Quicksand unfolds under the alternating sun and rain of Spring and Summer. These are not the seasons of tragedy, but of rising expectations and their fulfillment. From the outset, Nella Larsen is intent upon redirecting the tragic mulatto stereotype Sterling Brown describes in "A Century of Negro Portraiture in American Literature":

> The mulatto, or quadroon, or octoroon heroine has been a favorite for a long time; in books by white authors the whole desire of her life is to find a white lover; then balked by the dictates of her society, she sinks to a tragic end. In our century, Negro authors have turned the story around; not after restless searching, she finds peace only after returning to her own people. In both cases, however, the mulatto man or woman is presented as a lost, unhappy, woebegone abstraction. (p. 570)

The "traditional" mulatto is close to those in Mrs. Johnson's poems. Yet she, as will Nella Larsen, has "turned the story around." In "Cosmopolite" she redefines the mulatto. For her this cross-cultural being is a psychological reality, an angle of vision. It is DuBois' "double consciousness" made feminine:

> A product of the interplay
> Of traveled hearts.
> Estranged, yet not estranged, I stand
> All comprehending;
> From my estate
> I view earth's frail dilemma;
> Scion of fused strength am I,
> All understanding,
> Not this or that
> Contains me.

Mrs. G.D. Johnson

She "turns around" the initially negative connotations of the first line, "Not wholly this or that." Her mulatto sounds God-like in Her prescience, in Her paradoxical nature, and in Her denial of boundaries. She is freedom. More importantly, this God-like creature is also "free" of race.

Nella Larsen's heroine Helga Crane, in Quicksand (1928), says toward the middle of the book: "there were moments when it was as if she were shut up, boxed with hundreds of her race, closed up with that something in the racial character which had always been, to her, inexplicable, alien."(8) To rephrase DuBois, there are two souls warring in one light body. Helga it appears, desires the freedom from race attained by Mrs. Johnson's mulatto. However, as the story develops, it becomes clear that what is "alien" to her being and "boxing" in her attempts at self-definition — that from which she would be free — is not her blackness, but the white contagion of sexual prudery and social respectability. As Hortense E. Thornton has remarked, "because of society's taboos," Helga "has repressed a significant part of her being. Helga's inability to allow herself authentic sexual expression assumes a significant role in her tragic dilemma at the novel's end."(9) The dilemma is heightened by her apparent ability to "pass," her cosmopolitan background, being the daughter of a Danish mother and black father (a gambler who deserts both mother and daughter to return to America), her education and intelligence, and her success in the working world as a college English teacher. George Kent has argued that "despite the fact that her novels Quicksand and Passing deal with some light-skinned characters who pass for white, the author's real interest was to test the characters of blacks whose cultural circumstances provided a high level of choices."(10)

The reader of **Quicksand** is immediately conscious of Helga's "restless searching" as she moves with increasing rapidity from Naxos to Chicago to Harlem to Copenhagen to New York again, and finally to a small town in rural Alabama. But the movement is not outward; it is inward and downward. Each new place indicates a state of mind, a psychological reality that Larsen cues perfectly in the narrative by associating atmospheric setting and time with Helga's emotional and mental state at the beginning of each chapter. The first chapter opens with the novel's most crucial scene, presenting all the major images at their point of fullness and balance. Their dissolution will reflect Helga's gradual degradation:

> Helga Crane sat alone in her room, which at that hour, eight in the evening, was in soft gloom. Only a single reading lamp, dimmed by a great black and red shade, made a pool of light on the blue Chinese carpet, on the bright covers of the books which she had taken down from their long shelves, on the white pages of the opened one selected, on the shining brass bowl crowded with many-colored nasturtiums beside her on the low table, and on the oriental silk that covered the stool at her slim feet. It was a comfortable room, furnished with rare and intensely personal taste, flooded with Southern sun in the day, but shadowy just then with the drawn curtains and single shaded light. Large, too. So large that the spot where Helga sat was a small oasis in a desert of darkness. And eerily quiet.

Anyone returning to this passage after reading the entire novel, cannot fail to recognize the quicksand motif in its benign form as an "oasis in a desert of darkness." There is no mistaking the intense individuality of the room's objects, their orderly placement around the central object, Helga, the vivid colors and smooth textures of the brass bowl, Chinese silk, Chinese blue carpet, and red and black shade. The "downward spiral" of Helga's "motivations and conflicts," as Hortense Thornton phrases the narrative movement of the novel, is a steady movement away from rooms decorated with her own taste and love for color, toward ever smaller rooms filled with other people's things.(11) In Chicago, her first stop after leaving Naxos, to request a loan from her mother's brother, Uncle Peter, Helga is turned away at his door by his new wife who, quite literally, refuses to recognize Helga as her husband's niece, thus setting up the contrast between Naxos, where she was always observed, and Chicago, where she is invisible. But more importantly, Helga is, in effect, orphaned from this point on, so that her search is as much for a place to be at home in, as it is for a self to be at ease with.

Her small room in Chicago is as unclaimed as she is in its "stark neatness." Her first job is with a " 'race woman'," Mrs. Hayes-Rore, organizer of the black YWCA,(12) for whom Helga will serve as speech-editor. On the day that Helga learns she will accompany Mrs. Hayes-Rore to New York, she decides to seek a job there. "With her decision she felt reborn. She began happily to paint the furniture in vivid colors. The world had changed to silver...." Once in New York, and intent on staying, Mrs. Hayes-Rore arranges for Helga to live with a distant relative in Harlem, Anne Gray, a widow, as are all of the novel's important female characters (Mrs. Hayes-Rore, Helga's mother, Mrs. Dahl), and to whom, like the others, a large sum of money has been left, providing her with the kind of economic independence and freedom of movement Helga wants. Helga likes her elegant furnishings. They were "in complete accord with what she designated as her 'aesthetic sense.' " Anne fills her home

Nella Larsen

with things instead of people and she unmistakably is a member of Harlem's black aristocracy. Her rooms are large, as Helga describes her own room in Naxos, and contain some of the same kinds of things: long shelves of books, gay colors, smooth textures, and above all, a profusion of oriental objects. The latter recall DuBois's statement, in "The Damnation of Women," celebrating the "harmony" of East and West but pointing to something missing in Anne's rooms: "The Father and his worship is Asia; Europe is the precocious, self-centered, forward-striving child; but the land of the Mother is and was Africa."(13) But there is nothing in these rooms to remind us of the mother, much less of Africa, and these are not the sorts of objects one would want around even one "forward-striving child." The irrelevance of the room and of Anne's social class, with its carefully acquired lustre of culture based on material objects, makes a mockery of DuBois's injunction that "The world wants healthy babies and intelligent workers" (p. 164). In the initial description of Helga's room, her "oasis," in the Naxos desert, Larsen was careful to give it a passional, spiritual center that is entirely missing from Anne's museum-like rooms. Precisely in the middle of that description are the "brass bowl crowded with many-colored nasturtiums" and her "slim feet," both subtle sexual reminders of the self she discovers beneath her surface, barely more distant from her than are these objects in the room.(14)

Thus it is not long before the things in Anne's house begin to close in on Helga. To her "rescue" comes a letter from

Uncle Peter with $5,000 and advice to visit her Aunt Katrina in Denmark, and not to do what her mother had done — marry a black man. Helga resents her dependence on a man's money. Nevertheless, the money represents freedom to Helga at this point.

In Copenhagen Frau Dahl, as her name suggests, treats and dresses Helga like an exotic doll "in shining black taffeta with...bizarre trimmings of purple and cerise,...long earrings and two great bracelets." Clothes, as did the furniture in Harlem, begin to operate like quicksand: the greater her effort to elude them, the more deeply is she pulled down. Her sedate, Old World room is choked with clothes:

> There were batik dresses in which mingled indigo, orange, green, vermillion, and black; dress of velvet and chiffon in screaming colors...a leopard skin coat, a glittering opera-cape. There were turban-like hats of metallic silks, feathers and furs,...a nauseous Eastern perfume, shoes with dangerously high heels.

The scene's "screaming" sexuality stands in contrast to the quiet sensuality of Helga's room in Naxos. This is Europe's idea of the exotic-erotic black woman, and Helga is "incited to inflame attention and admiration. She was dressed for it, subtly schooled for it. And after a little while she gave herself up wholly to the fascinating business of being seen, gaped at, desired."

Eventually, Frau Dahl selects Axel Olsen, a well-known artist doing a portrait of Helga, as a likely husband. Olsen's marriage proposal follows her refusal to become his mistress:

> "Very commendable, my Helga — and wise. Now you have your reward. Now I offer you marriage."
> "Thanks," she answered, "thanks, awfully."

Her restraint forces him to reveal the real reason for the marriage: he needs it for his work; she will be his muse. "It may be that with you, Helga, for wife, I will become great. Immortal. Who knows?...I make of myself a present to you. For love."

This exchange prepares us for the novel's climax, the unveiling of Olsen's portrait of Helga, which, he says, represents the contradiction in her nature:

> You have the warm impulsive nature of the women of Africa, but, my lovely, you have, I fear, the soul of a prostitute. You sell yourself to the highest bidder.

But the portrait represents nothing so much as a white male fantasy. In Helga it revives a nearly racial memory of slavery and of the black woman's degradation at the hands of white slave owners. She responds with a new sense of her blackness and her independence. She refuses to be owned, and rejects him on racial grounds: "But you see, Herr Olsen, I'm not for sale. Not to you. Not to any white man. I don't care at all to be owned." Nevertheless, the portrait disturbs Helga. Olsen's final comment on it does reveal some real insight: "though I don't understand you entirely, in a way I do too.... I think that my picture of you is, after all, the true Helga Crane. Therefore — a tragedy." Nathan Huggins has suggested that Helga is here finally brought face to face with the sensuality and "primitive nature" she has repressed thus far. The portrait reveals "the key to her acceptance by the painter as well as her Danish relatives. He senses a tiger, an animal within her which he wants to possess — to ravish and to be ravished — through marriage if necessary."(15)

The portrait represents the final male vision of her Helga is willing to accept. Throughout the novel images of eyes and seeing have reinforced the idea that Helga has seen herself as men have chosen to see her. When she returns to America for Anne's wedding to Dr. Anderson, he tells her: "You haven't changed. You're still seeking for something." His shadowy gray eyes and their puzzling gaze have always made Helga uncomfortable. They seem to operate as mirrors for her own submerged sexuality. He alone of the male characters does not project an image upon her; instead, what she sees is her own reflected confusion over her divided nature: "And another vision, too, came haunting Helga Crane: level gray eyes set down in a brown face which stared out at her, coolly, quizzically, disturbingly. And she was not happy."

But the Helga back from abroad is no longer so confused. When Dr. Anderson, drunk from the wedding celebration, pursues, embraces, and kisses Helga, the shadowy man becomes the object of her fully emerged sensuality. His clumsy and conventional apology for this lapse, weeks after it had occurred, causes feelings in Helga of "ridicule and self-loathing, this knowledge that she had deluded herself." The images of suffocation and enclosure reassert themselves and the pull of the quicksand is felt again: " 'I can't stay in this room any longer. I must get out or I'll choke.' Her self-knowledge had increased her anguish." To get herself out of her "mental quagmire," she wanders out into the streets of Harlem and into a storefront church's revival meeting. The racial memory aroused in Copenhagen makes her feel that the songs she heard "she was conscious of having heard years ago — hundreds of years it seemed." The past she identifies with is made both black and female by Larsen's construction of the scene: the congregation appears to be wholly female, except for a "fattish yellow man with huge outstanding ears and long, nervous hands." With the women's songs and moaning the meeting takes on "an almost Bacchic vehemence" to which she finally gives herself: "The thing became real. A miraculous calm came upon her. Life seemed to expand, and to become very easy. Helga Crane felt within her a supreme aspiration toward the regaining of simple happiness. Unwilling to forego any longer the need to express her sexuality, she marries the "rattish yellow" Mr. Pleasant Green; flaunting society's taboos, she admits that she bears the days in anticipation of the nights: "And night came at the end of every day. Emotional, palpitating, amorous, all that was living in her sprang like rank weeds at the tingling thought of night, with a vitality so strong that it devoured all shoots of reason."

With this sexual release come the confinements of successive pregnancies, ill health, and loss of self, the latter imaged in Helga's room in this rural Alabama town:

> Helga, looking about in helpless dismay and sick disgust at the disorder around her, the permanent assembly of partly emptied medicine bottles on the clock-shelf, the perpetual array of drying baby clothes on the chairbacks, the constant debris of broken toys on the floor, the unceasing litter of half-dead flowers on the table, dragged in by the toddling twins from the forlorn garden, failed to blame [Mr. Green] for the thoughtless selfishness of his absences.

She refuses to place the blame on anyone for "the quagmire in which she had engulfed herself." Yet it is clearly a man's world, whether in Naxos, Harlem, Copenhagen, or Alabama. It is not coincidental that the final role victimizing her is that of motherhood, with DuBois's veil of romantic suffering and Mrs. Johnson's mask of heroic sacrifice removed. Helga's only refuge within marriage is madness, itself a survival strategy:

> She mustn't, she thought to herself, get well too fast. Since it seemed she was going to get well. In bed she

could think, could have a certain amount of quiet. Of aloneness.

Madness allows Helga an escape from her husband's sexual demands. She can retreat to her newly found "oasis": "somewhere in that delightful borderland on the edge of unconsciousness, an enchanted and blissful place where peace and incredible quiet encompassed her." The day arrives when she is found out by her nurse:

> The truth was that she had been back for some hours. Purposely she had lain silent and still, wanting to linger forever in that serene haven, that effortless calm where nothing was expected of her. There she could watch the figures of the past drift by.... It was a refreshingly delicious immersion in the past. But it was finished now. It was over.

Madness sustains both rebellion and submission, the psychic hell of unfulfilled sexual wholeness amid the conflicting claims of motherhood, wifehood and womanhood.

Taken together, Anne Spencer and Zora Neale Hurston serve as counterposes to Georgia Douglas Johnson and Nella Larsen. Spencer and Hurston move away from the tragic toward the affirmative. This is not to say that their interests differ from Johnson's and Larsen's. On the contrary, the issue of women's dreams as opposed to male fantasies persists, as does the issue of sexuality. In the work of both Spencer and Hurston "race consciousness" seems to be defined as affirmation of racial faith. Above all, in their concern with the psychology of black women they create a sense of their autonomy, their desire to be self-defined. Spencer's and Hurston's female characters, unlike Johnson's and Larsen's, possess from the start an uncanny sense of who they are.

Anne Spencer is generally regarded by critics of the Harlem Renaissance to be the most sophisticated of its women poets. Unlike Georgia Douglas Johnson and the lyric poets, she expresses her protest with irony, sometimes with anger, but never with humility. In her dramatic monologues she often uses a male persona, particularly in poems that deal with women.

A partial explanation may be found in her remarks prefacing the poems collected in **Caroling Dusk**:

> Mother Nature, February, forty-five years ago forced me on the stage that I, in turn, might assume the role of lonely child, happy wife, perplexed mother — and, so far, a twice resentful grandmother...I have no academic honors, nor lodge regalia.... I write about some of the things I love. But have no civilized articulation for the things I hate. I proudly love being a Negro woman — it's so involved and interesting. We are the PROBLEM — the great national game of TABOO.(16)

Her last line is the cue to her often complex use of narrators. It links her to Nella Larsen's concern over the black woman's objectification, that she can be both the totem and taboo Larsen represented by the mulatto figure of Helga Crane. Spencer is particularly averse to the kinds of dehumanizing "worships" that cluster around the black woman, including the romanticizing of the mother. But Spencer marks a break with Larsen and Johnson in her avoidance of the mulatto as theme or persona. She has, in a sense, unified the division that figure represents in the larger issue of "TABOO." Her concern is to expose this "national game" played by the black woman's antagonists: white men, white women, and black men. "Innocence" summarizes several of the oppositions in her poetry, one of the dominant ones being innocence and experience:

> She tripped and fell against a star,
> A lady we all have known;
> Just what the villagers lusted for
> To claim her one of their own....

Spencer repeatedly associates black love and physical desire with the star, since it illumines the blackness of the woman's skin. In this poem the first four stanzas describe a "Lady's" first yielding to love, her first indiscretion — an act that linking her with the "we" in the poem, who have themselves "lusted" after her, anxious that she too should join their guilty assembly:

> Fallen but once the lower felt she,
> So turned her face and died, —
> With never a hounding fool to see
> 'Twas a star-lance in her side!

Apparently she has died for love. But there is some mocking of her, as the line "So turned her face and died" sounds very like the line from "Barbara Allen." The crucial line is "Fallen but once the lower felt she," because it implies that she has sacrificed herself to the community's totem of virginity, rather than become their other necessary idol, the Fallen Woman. In this case DuBois's insight in "The Damnation of Women" has found poetic expression. We think Anne Spencer is concerned in a number of her poems with exposing DuBois's paradox that "the world...tries to worship both virgins and mothers and in the end despises motherhood and despoils virgins." "At the Carnival" deals with this same tension between innocence and corruption, employing the figure of the "Gay little Girl-of-the-Diving-Tank," who images for the male speaker and others their desires and their redemption:

> Gay little Girl-of-the-Diving-Tank,
> I desire a name for you,
> Nice, as a right glove fits;
> For, you — amid the malodorous
> Mechanics of this unlovely thing,
> Are darling of spirit and form.

The first stage in her objectification is the speaker's desire to "name" her as he sees her, "as a right glove fits" — tight and inescapable. Since the speaker is a chauffeur, we can assume that the mention of the "right glove" is intentional, and designed to imply the element of safety for a man in being able to put a name to, possess, a woman:

> I know you — a glance, and what you are
> Sits-by-the-fire in my heart.
> My Limousine-Lady knows you, or
> Why does the slant-envy of her eye mark
> Your straight air and radiant inclusive smile?

Deeper into his fantasies he feels he "knows" her, and we have a hint of the fantasy with which he is associating her: "Sits-by-the-fire in my heart" has a domestic ring to it, as though she were tending the "hearth," rather than the passionate flames of desire. The Limousine-Lady, whom he has also made mechanical, is consumed with an unwilling envy of her antithesis in this fully human form:

> Guilt pins a fig leaf; Innocence is its own adorning.
> The bull-necked man knows you — this first time
> His itching flesh sees form divine and vibrant health,

and "Hands like, how like, brown lilies sweet," engulf him, too: "As once in her fire-lit heart I felt the furies Beating, beating." In "Before the Feast of Shushan," Spencer's Persian King is angered that he cannot command love as he com-

410

mands submission. He points to the maze of differences between the way men and women love:

And I am hard to force the petals wide;
And you are fast to suffer and be sad.

...

Have him 'maze how you say love is sacrament;
How says Vashti, love is both bread and wine;
How to the altar may not come to break and drink,
Hulky flesh nor fleshly spirit!

But he does not ask Vashti to explain her own desires. Instead he asserts his male prerogative and sums up the fears and intimidations and injuries of all women:

I, thy King, teach you and leave you, when I list.
No Woman in all Persia sets out strange action
To confuse Persia's lord —
Love is but desire and thy purpose fulfillment;
I, thy King, so say!

Almost as a companion to the situation above, "Letter to My Sister" warns against either "defying the gods/...with the tongue's thin tip," or "mincing timidly,/...or kneel or pray,/Be kind, or sweat agony drops/Or lay your quick body over your feeble young." The woman's only recourse to male oppression is to "Lock your heart, then quietly,/And lest they peer within,/Light no lamp when dark comes down/Raise no shade for sun." Spencer is primarily interested in exploring the ways in which black women, and probably most women, can be manipulated and denied their own avenues of expression if subject to their own desires — and the desires of men to have their real-life women act out their fantasies.

Janie Woods, the heroine of Zora Neale Hurston's **Their Eyes Were Watching God**, is subjected not only to various male definitions, but to her Nanny's dream of marriage. As June Jordan remarks, Janie seeks "Black-love," and the freedom to define her own boundaries. She is also bent on denying the old folk saying that "de nigger woman is de mule uh de world," as her Nanny sees it. Janie rebels first of all against male definitions, and finally against all outer-imposed definitions. Her story presents the other side of Helga's dilemma and creates a black heroine who takes on the heroic attributes of Hurston's favorite male hero, High John D'Conquer. In addition, Janie's wanderings return her to her beginnings, where she becomes the bearer of her own experiences, transformed into a folk experience — she returns with a feminine hero tale. Unlike the previous women writers, however, Janie will achieve heroic stature because of her relations with men, making of sexuality a positive force for self-revelation, rather than a means for suffocating her individuality.

After hearing Janie talk of self-discovery, her friend Phoeby declares, "Ah done growed ten feet higher from jus' listenin' tuh you, Janie. Ah ain't satisfied wid maself no mo!" Janie is a black woman who lives according to her own dreams and ideals. And her search is always for an independent identity. The narrative frame for the story, Janie's relating the saga to her friend Phoeby, presents a picture of one more experienced woman passing on her thoughts and emotions to one less experienced. Janie — reared by the myth of marriage as the only route of expression and satisfaction for a woman, wonders, "Did marriage compel love like the sun the day?" She finds in her youthful marriage to Logan Killicks that certainly it does not. Feeling, however, that the myth is true even if her specific case has not worked out, she marries Joe Starks, who captivates her by his confidence and dynamism; but this time she is smothered by a man's possessiveness. Realizing that Joe was "building a high chair for her to sit in and overlook the world," Janie begins to understand herself and her own need for an active, participating life; she realizes that Starks crushes any possibility of self-development: "You done lived wid me twenty years and you don't know me at all...Mah own mind had tuh be squeezed and crowded out tuh make room for yours in me."

After Joe's death, Janie meets, loves, and marries Tea Cake, a playful and passionate man who helps Janie's "great tree" of life to bloom. His death, when she is forced to shoot him as he is about to shoot her in the delirium of rabies, is carefully constructed to force her independence from men. His death leaves her content, however, with the memory of a life fully lived: "Ah done been tuh de horizon and back and now Ah kin set heah in mah house and live by comparisons." This is in contrast to Nanny, whose name Lethe indicates the rich folk background she has forgotten when she asserts that black people are "like branches without roots." Janie refuses to belong to her grandmother's kind who "loved to deal in scraps."

These four women of the Harlem Renaissance, in their rich and complex works, seem to be balancing the dilemma of self and world, the tasks of Negro Womanhood and the adventure of sexuality. Each of the women wants to avoid Nanny's description of herself as "Ah'm a cracked plate," but each also bears witness to Janie's desire for a life with "flower-dust and springtime sprinkled over everything." Finally, Georgia Douglas Johnson, Nella Larsen, Anne Spencer, and Zora Neale Hurston desire for their protagonists what Janie says she got from living with Tea Cake: "Ah been a delegate to de big 'ssociation of life." But each of these writers sought to place their heroine's chances in a slightly different arena of choice, and thus present the range of expectations, strategies, failures and triumphs open to black women in literature written by black women.

1. Gerda Lerner, **Black Women in White America** (New York: Vintage Books, 1973), 169.
2. (New York: Books for Libraries, 1918), ix. All subsequent quotations from the text will be indicated by page number in the body of the paper.
3. Frequently linked to what male critics have termed the sapphic love cult. The poem invariably appears in the headnotes to selections of her poems, or in any summary discussion of her work, such as in Benjamin Brawley's Negro **Genius**.
4. (New York: Books for Libraries Press). All subsequent quotations from the text will be indicated by page number in the body of the paper.
5. "Frank Horne and the Second Echelon Poets of the Harlem Renaissance," **The Harlem Renaissance Remembered**, Arna Bontemps ed. (New York: Dodd, Mead & Co., 1972), 265.
6. "The Importance of Georgia Douglas Johnson," **The Crisis**, 59 (December 1952), 633. Mr. Dover, himself a Eurasian. wrote the period's "text" on the mulatto called **The Half-Caste**, which was lavishly praised by DuBois.
7. **The Negro in Fiction, Poetry and Drama** (New York: Atheneum, 1969), 62.
8. Larsen, 120-21. All subsequent quotations from both novels will be indicated by page number in the body of the paper.
9. "Sexism as Quagmire: Nella Larsen's Quicksand," CLA **Journal** (March 24, 1973), 288.
10. **Blackness and the Adventure of Western Culture** (Chicago: Third World Press, 1972), 29.
11. Thornton, 293.
12. Larsen may have modeled Mrs. Hayes-Rore after Eva Bowles, the fiery and persistent first "colored secretary" of the YWCA, who travelled across the country speaking for interracial clubs for women and girls.
13. DuBois, 166.

14. We will encounter these passionate red, yellow, and orange flowers, with their funnel-like flower and shield-shaped leaves — frequently associated with Africa and Egypt in the graphics of the Renaissance period — in the openly sexual poem by Anne Spencer entitled: "Lines to a Nasturtium (A Lover Muses)."

15. Nathan Irvin Huggins, **The Harlem Renaissance** (New York: Oxford University Press, 1971), 158. Huggins is one of the few critics who have given Larsen a fairly close reading. He states that she "came as close as any to treating human motivation with complexity and sophistication" (p. 236). This kind of reevaluation is needed to offset the kind of flippant shorthand criticism of Arthur P. Davis, who describes Helga as "mixed-up...complex...who, unable to seduce the one man she really wants,...impulsively marries a peasant-like preacher and becomes a hopeless, drab, child-bearing wife of a boorish minister in a small Southern town" (p. 96).

16. Countee Cullen ed. (New York: Harper & Bros., 1927), 47. Unless otherwise indicated, all subsequent quotations will refer to this text.

GEORGIA DOUGLAS JOHNSON AND MAY MILLER: FORGOTTEN PLAYWRIGHTS OF THE NEW NEGRO RENAISSANCE

By Jeanne-Marie A. Miller

In the United States of the 1920s and the early 1930s, almost every facet of the lives of blacks was circumscribed by both tradition and laws that bound them in an inferior position. The century-old practice of influencing the readers' perception of blacks through the use of degrading and destructive stereotypes was continued in the works of some white authors. The American theatre also perpetuated these negative images, particularly that of the buffoon, the low comic, and the minstrel, a one-dimensional character who was designed to provoke laughter and who was never to be considered seriously. While the minstrel show in its original form was no longer in vogue, the comic black or stage darky lived on in other theatrical forms. Though the tradition was changing slowly with the discovery of folk material as a suitable subject for drama, in the hands of those attempting to sculpt plays about a people whom they scarcely knew, much was left untold in their depictions of the black

experience. Thus white American playwrights, such as Eugene O'Neill and Dorothy and DuBose Heyward, who were
rising to fame using these new materials, not only employed
negative black stereotypes but reflected a distorted view of
black life as in a broken mirror.[1] A valuable outcome of
these playwrights' works, however, was their suggesting the
many possibilities of this new material.

Spanning this same period was the New Negro Renaissance, the black literary and artistic movement known also
as the Harlem Renaissance. Since the creative foundations
had been laid before the 1920s, the productivity of this period must be viewed as part of a continuum. What *was* new,
however, was the attention being paid to a body of literature that in the past had been largely ignored; thus strategic to the literary activity of blacks and spurring it on were
the increased opportunities for publishing. A multipronged
movement, the New Negro Renaissance explored a broad
range of black life—from the rural and urban folk, including the so-called "high livers" of Harlem, to the "respectable" black middle class, whose values paralleled those of its
white counterpart. Langston Hughes, then a young, promising writer, boldly and succinctly declared the movement's
independence and expressed its mood when he wrote that
both the "beautiful" and the "ugly" of black life would be

---

[1] While O'Neill's *The Emperor Jones* (1920) and the Heywards' *Porgy* (1927)
have some characters who are marked departures from the traditional comic relief
figures prevalent in American drama up to that time, these playwrights continued
to employ features commonly associated with the manner in which blacks were
portrayed in literature. Although *The Emperor Jones*, for example, deals with the
tragedy of the disintegration of a human soul, the major character's speech has
remnants of the language of black minstrelsy. In *Porgy*, which centers on Porgy,
the crippled beggar, and his tender love for Crown's Bess, the playwrights contribute to the gallery of negative black stereotypes the characters Crown, a brutish
black man; Bess, a black woman with tainted morals; and Sporting Life, a demonic black man who preys on the weaknesses of others. For an excellent discussion of the early stereotypic treatment of blacks in American literature, see Sterling A. Brown, "Negro Character as Seen by White Authors," *The Journal of
Negro Education*, 2 (April 1933), 179-203.

expressed in the literature of the period.[2] Inherent in this statement was the promise of an expanded angle of vision of blacks, one more closely akin to their real lives, and a cessation of their past monotonous depiction in literature.

In realizing their potential as authors, black writers, as a rule, turned to short stories, novels, and poetry as the preferred literary genres. Perhaps because the mainstream American theatre had kept its doors shut tightly, with few exceptions, to black playwrights and, historically, to most truthful portrayals of black life, black writers chose forms that did not require the often difficult-to-obtain apprenticeships in a theatrical arena, stewardships essential to playwrights learning their craft. Of importance to the development of black playwrights were the Negro Little Theatre Movement, with its emphasis on nonprofit theatre, which came into existence around 1925, and the later proliferation of drama groups and departments in black colleges and universities, a movement spearheaded and nourished by Randolph Edmonds, a black professor of drama.[3] Not to be overlooked were the literary contests sponsored by the journalistic organs of the National Association for the Advancement of Colored People and the Urban League, *The Crisis* and *Opportunity* magazines, respectively. The purposes of these contests were to encourage blacks to write about themselves and to eradicate the overworked synthetic images that were dominant in much of the literature.[4] Together these activities encouraged the writing of drama.

Two playwrights who wrote significant dramatic works during this period and whose contributions to the develop-

[2] "The Negro Artist and the Racial Mountain," *The Black Aesthetic*, ed. Addison Gayle, Jr. (Garden City, New York: Doubleday, 1971), pp. 175-81. Hughes' article was published originally in *The Nation*, 122 (June 23, 1926), 692-94.

[3] See Randolph Edmonds, "Black Drama in the American Theatre: 1700-1970," in *The American Theatre: A Sum of Its Parts* (New York: Samuel French, Inc., 1971), pp. 419-20.

[4] See Editorial, *Opportunity*, 2 (September 1924), 258, and Mark Seyboldt, "Play-Writing," *The Crisis*, 29 (February 1925), 165.

ment of black American drama have been long neglected
are Georgia Douglas Johnson and May Miller. The artistic
fires that flamed the spirit of the New Negro Renaissance in
Harlem also sparked creative talents in other localities, including the nation's capital, which was the adopted home of
Johnson[5] and the birthplace of Miller.[6]

Several of Johnson's and Miller's plays focus on folk
characters and culture, one of the literary emphases of the
Renaissance.[7] Though writers during this period were not
the first of their race to realize the value of black folk material, their use of it contributed significantly to the development of black American literature. Unlike Paul Laurence

[5] Born in 1886 in Atlanta, Georgia, Georgia Douglas Johnson moved with her
husband to Washington, D.C., when President William Howard Taft appointed
him Recorder of Deeds in 1909. Johnson was comfortable in her new environment
with its abundance of resources, like the Library of Congress, which fed her intellectual appetite, and a good educational system, which would benefit her two sons.
The Johnson home became a famous gathering place for black intellectuals and
artists, including Waring Cuney, Sterling Brown, Jean Toomer, Alice Dunbar-Nel-
son, Alain Locke, Langston Hughes, James Weldon Johnson, W. E. B. Du Bois,
Owen Dodson, and May Miller. The Oberlin Conservatory-trained Johnson gave
up her first choice of a career as a composer and turned to writing. She was both a
poet and a playwright. Among her books of poetry are *The Heart of a Woman
and Other Poems* (1918), *Bronze: A Book of Verse* (1922), *An Autumn Love Cycle*
(1928), and *Share My World* (1962). Johnson died in 1966 in Washington, D.C.

[6] May Miller [Sullivan], daughter of Kelly Miller, a well-known educator, was
born in 1899 in Washington, D.C. She was an honors graduate of Howard University in 1920 and continued her studies at American and Columbia Universities.
Miller contributed plays to *Plays and Pageants from the Life of the Negro* (1930),
edited by Willis Richardson, and *Negro History in Thirteen Plays* (1935), which
she coedited with Richardson. In the middle 1940s she abandoned playwriting after retiring for health reasons from the Baltimore Public Schools. She stated that
after retirement she no longer had the built-in support system of her school's art,
music, and physical education departments. In addition, she had lost an important
platform on which to mount her dramatic works. From that time to the present,
she has concentrated on writing poetry. Her books of poetry include *Into the
Clearing* (1959), *Poems* (1962), *Not That Far* (1973), *The Clearing and Beyond*
(1974), *Dust of Uncertain Journey* (1975), *Halfway to the Sun* (1981), and *The
Ransomed Wait* (1983). She is one of three poets of *Lyrics of Three Women*
(1964).

[7] Wherever the term *Renaissance* appears in this essay, it is referring to the
New Negro Renaissance.

Dunbar and his contemporaries, who earlier had written in the dialect tradition mainly about humorous events, good times, and the sentimental aspects of black life, these new writers approached folk life differently. They treated the various aspects of this life—the trivial as well as the serious, the comic as well as the tragic. Black intellectuals, like Montgomery Gregory and Alain Locke, recognized that black American drama also could be enriched by folk material.[8]

One of the finest plays of the Renaissance is Johnson's short one-act folk tragedy entitled *Plumes*, which won first prize in the 1927 *Opportunity* play contest.[9] The setting of the play is a poor cottage in the South, and the controlling element is the power of the superstitious beliefs of its black folk characters. Charity Brown, the central character, is faced with a dilemma when she must choose between a physician's advice about her young daughter's recovering from an illness and that offered by Tildy, a friend, who prophesies by reading coffee grounds in a cup. "Coffee ground don't lie," Charity is told. In a culture where ailments are treated by the folk themselves with herb teas, broths, and other homemade brews, there is a general distrust of the unknowns of medical science. In an environment where the minute details of life take on prophetic meaning, the funeral procession that passes just outside the cabin lends credence to the prediction of the child's death.

[8] See Alain Locke, Introduction, "The Drama of Negro Life," *Plays of Negro Life: A Source-Book of Native American Drama,* ed. Alain Locke and Montgomery Gregory (1927; rpt. Westport, Conn.: Negro Universities Press, 1970), pp. [i-vi], and Montgomery Gregory, "The Drama of Negro Life," *Anthology of the American Negro in the Theatre: A Critical Approach*, ed. Lindsay Patterson (New York: Publisher's Co., Inc., 1969), pp. 25-30. Gregory's article was written in 1925.

[9] *Opportunity*, 5 (July 1927), 200-01, 217-18. *Plumes* also was published in 1927 in New York by Samuel French. In addition, it may be found in *Plays of Negro Life*, ed. Locke and Gregory, pp. 287-99, and in *The New Negro Renaissance: An Anthology*, ed. Michael W. Peplow and Arthur P. Davis (New York: Holt, 1975), pp. 314-22.

Obsessed with the desire to give her daughter a "decent" burial, with horses wearing plumes, for the manner of the ritual is indicative of one's feelings about the deceased, Charity pauses, for the projected funeral and the suggested operation cost exactly the same. While she hesitates, the child dies.

Johnson's *The Starting Point* (n.d.), while not a folk play, contains folk ingredients as do most of this playwright's dramatic pieces. Focusing on the internal problems of a black family in Charleston, South Carolina, the play treats the sacrificial love of a parent.[10] A young man, who is supposed to be studying in a medical school in another city, has forsaken his education and succumbed to the attractions of the easier and more lucrative life of a gambler. When his illegal numbers business runs into trouble with the law, he returns to his parents' home with his blues-singing wife. The father, who once rejoiced that, unlike him, his son will not have to "set at a white man's door . . . fetching and carrying all his life," in the end relinquishes his menial job to him so that the younger man can have a new beginning.

In Johnson's *Blue Blood* (1926), two mothers, one with her roots in folk soil and the other, a member of the middle class, bury their social differences in order to solve a painful dilemma.[11] On the wedding day of their children it is discovered that the potential bride and groom are actually brother and sister, children of the same immoral white father. The two mothers, with the aid of a young man who has always loved the bride-to-be, join together to prevent the occurrence of an incestuous marriage.

The centerpiece of May Miller's *Riding the Goat* (1929) is the conflict between an older, less-educated generation

---

[10] TS, James Weldon Johnson Collection, Yale University Library.

[11] *Fifty More Contemporary One-Act Plays*, ed. Frank Shay (New York: D. Appleton-Century, 1938), pp. 297-304. *Blue Blood* won honorable mention in the Second Literary Contest sponsored by *Opportunity*.

who cherishes such activities as belonging to a lodge and the better-educated younger group whose values and interests differ.[12] This play, an important contribution to Renaissance drama, takes place in a community of draymen in Baltimore, Maryland. Ant Hetty, a folk figure and a representative member of this society, is Miller's most memorable character.

Setting the mood for the action that follows, Ant Hetty sings "Such a Meetin's Goin' Be Here To-night" as she irons the white dress that she will proudly wear to view the lodge parade that evening. Lodges instill pride, provide social interaction, and give meaning and beauty to otherwise drab lives. Some lodges even provide such needed services as offering insurance against sickness and death in addition to aiding widows and orphans. Embodying this community's attitudes and beliefs, Ant Hetty, in vivid images, states the important role the lodge played in her late husband's funeral—the shining swords, the waving plumes, the candle-ringed coffin, and, most of all, the turnout of the members.

In contrast to Ant Hetty, Dr. William Carter, the fiancé of the old woman's granddaughter Ruth, vaguely disguises his contempt for the lodge, of which he unfortunately was elected the grand exalted ruler after he began his medical practice in this little community. He is especially intolerant of this evening's parade. When he intimates that rain may prevent the event, Ant Hetty counters with her own folk barometer. Last night's moon did not have a ring around it, and the parts of her body that always ache when rain is imminent are free of pain. Aware of the doctor's attitude toward the lodge, she tells him that a woman would value his lodge position. She relates the tale of a woman who, hidden from view, observed the initiation rites at one of her husband's lodge meetings. When she was discovered, she

---

[12] *Plays and Pageants from the Life of the Negro*, ed. Willis Richardson (Washington, D.C.: Associated Publishers, 1930), pp. 141-76.

was given the choice of joining the lodge (riding the goat) or dying. She, of course, rode the goat. This tale foreshadows Ruth's courageous action later in the drama.

When even Ruth cannot persuade her fiancé to march in the parade, in his absence she secretly dons his regalia, including the mask, and marches in his place. Although she shares his attitude toward lodges, she recognizes their importance to the black community and is confident that he will lose that community's support and respect if his true feelings are ever discovered. She takes a leadership role in preserving her fiancé's medical practice, but, more importantly, prevents the community from being deprived of his superior medical service.s

Other plays in which Miller uses folk materials are *The Cuss'd Thing* (1926), which received honorable mention in the second *Opportunity* Literary Contest, and *Scratches* (1929). In *The Cuss'd Thing* a naturally gifted but uneducated musician forfeits his dream of playing music professionally when his pregnant wife, who believes that playing music in a theatre is against God's will, suffers a miscarriage.[13] In *Scratches* urban folk types of the pool-room school, though living harsh lives bordering on tragedy, show compassion for one another.[14]

While many of Johnson's and Miller's plays dramatized the internal life of the black community, in other works these highly perceptive and socially concerned women reacted to the external forces that affected the lives of blacks, such as the violent manifestations of hostility that continued in the new century. Of these, none was more barbaric than lynching. Between the beginning of the twentieth century and World War I, more than a thousand blacks had been lynched, and this illegal system of punishment did not cease even when black uniformed men returned home after

---

[13] The typescript of this unpublished play is in the possession of the playwright.

[14] The typescript of this play is in the possession of the playwright. *Scratches* was published in *The Carolina Magazine*, 59 (April 1929).

having helped to fight and win the war against fascism in Europe.[15]

Lynching is treated in three of Johnson's plays—*A Sunday Morning in the South* (ca. 1925), *Safe* (n.d.), and *Blue-Eyed Black Boy* (n.d.). In *A Sunday Morning in the South*, a protest play, the grandson of an elderly black woman is murdered by a bloodthirsty mob after he is arrested for the alleged rape of a white girl.[16] Irony pervades this play, for the grandmother respected the law and her grandson wished to study it in order to change the laws and make the weak ones stronger. The brutal action occurs on a peaceful Sunday morning with hymns emanating from a nearby church in the background. This Christian music underscores the brutality of the crime; the innocence of the victim who believed in both Christ and democracy; and the hypocrisy of the murderers, whose behavior conflicts with one of the major tenets of Christianity—brotherhood. In *Safe* (n.d.), set in 1893 in a Southern town, a helpless seventeen-year-old black boy's cries for his mother before he is lynched so affect a black woman who is giving birth to a son that she strangles the infant to protect him from a future mob.[17] In *Blue-Eyed Black Boy* a lynching is averted when the mother of the would-be victim, who supposedly "brushed against a white woman on the street," sends a message in code to the governor of the state, informing him that the young man is his son.[18]

Miller's only play about lynching, *Nails and Thorns* (1933), won the second prize in a Southern University Contest.[19] In this work two mothers, one black and the other

---

[15] John Hope Franklin, *From Slavery to Freedom: A History of Negro Americans*, 5th ed. (New York: Knopf, 1980), pp. 313-14, 346.

[16] *Black Theater, U.S.A.: Forty-Five Plays by Black Americans, 1847-1974*, ed. James V. Hatch and Ted Shine (New York: The Free Press, 1974), pp. 211-17.

[17] Federal Theatre Project Script Collection, the Research Center for the Federal Theatre Project, George Mason University.

[18] Ibid.

[19] The typescript of this unpublished play is in the possession of the playwright.

white, are psychologically tortured by the hysteria gripping their small Southern town because of the impending lynching of a black man. The black mother, who hides her young sons to protect them, expresses deep concern about their future in such a society. The white mother, distressed over the quality of life that all the young will inherit if this disaster is permitted to occur, rushes out into the street with her infant in her arms in a futile attempt to halt the frenzied mob. Error and evil, however, triumph in this destructive environment.

In their exploration of the whole black life, some Renaissance writers turned their attention to recovering the black past. Black history, despite being saturated with the oppression of black people, also has courageous and glorious moments. Black history plays, which are informational for their audiences and link the present to the past for blacks, were written during this literary movement. Carter G. Woodson, a black Harvard-trained historian who believed that black life was the *real* drama in America and could best be interpreted by blacks themselves, encouraged the writing and publication of black-authored plays, which included historical works.[20] Johnson and Miller were among the contributors.

In two historical dramas, *William and Ellen Craft* (1935) and *Frederick Douglass* (1935), Johnson concentrates on events leading up to this famous trio's escapes from slavery.[21] Escapes to freedom by slaves were often spectacular, heroic, and dangerous, and few were more daring and dramatic than that of William and Ellen Craft. As a slave, William had some freedom of movement, for he was a skilled cabinetmaker who was hired out for wages that were paid

---

[20] Introduction, *Negro History in Thirteen Plays*, ed. Willis Richardson and May Miller (Washington, D.C.: Associated Publishers, 1935), p. iii.

[21] *William and Ellen Craft* and *Frederick Douglass* were published in *Negro History in Thirteen Plays*, pp. 163-86 and pp. 143-62, respectively. In the history plays of Johnson and Miller, the playwrights use their prerogative to handle material freely.

to his master. Ellen, on the other hand, was a favorite house slave whose near-white complexion had been both a curse and a boon to her in this slavery environment. Because she was often mistaken for one of her first mistress's children, she was given by this woman as a wedding present to her daughter. It is Ellen's fair complexion, however, that facilitates her and her husband's goal of freedom, for it enables her to dress in male clothing and pose as a white man while William accompanies her as a slave. In this guise they engineer a brilliant escape from bondage. William, who used to accompany his young master by train to Philadelphia and was taught by him to read, write, and do arithmetic,[22] is well rehearsed in the role that he must play. He teaches his wife how to walk "biggity" like a white man. Since she cannot write, she will pretend to have rheumatism. William assures Ellen that he will walk *behind* her in the light but *with* her in the dark.

Similar to the Crafts' escape being intensified because of the threat of Ellen's being sold, the date of the planned escape of Frederick Douglass (in the play of the same name) must be changed when he is apprised that he will be returned to the Eastern Shore in Maryland from Baltimore, where he is living a comparatively free life as a slave.[23] The play is set in the home of Ann, a free black, whom Douglass has come to court and to instruct in arithmetic and reading. Once in the North and married, he and Ann plan to work together to help their people. Elements of folk culture are

[22] Johnson uses dramatic license here as neither Ellen nor William Craft could read and write when they escaped from bondage. See "Running a Thousand Miles for Freedom" by William Craft in *Black Women in Nineteenth-Century American Life: Their Words, Their Thoughts, Their Feelings*, ed. Bert James Loewenberg and Ruth Bogin (University Park: Pennsylvania State Univ. Press, 1976), pp. 104-23.

[23] Frederick Douglass' successful escape was motivated by his overwhelming desire to be free. His master's practice of collecting the wages that he had been hired out to earn only intensified his wish. See Douglass' *Narrative of the Life of Frederick Douglass: An American Slave* (1845; rpt. Garden City, New York: Doubleday, 1963), pp. 93-105.

essential to the plot, for a character pretending to read Ann's brother's tea leaves must convince the brother that his dead mother wishes him to relinquish the travel pass that will ensure Douglass' escape to freedom. Train whistles in the background lend a sense of urgency to the plot.

In Miller's historical plays with American settings, incidents in the lives of the black heroines Sojourner Truth and Harriet Tubman are explored. As a former slave named Isabella, Sojourner Truth knew firsthand the cruelties of bondage. As a free woman she felt compelled to wander and spread the word of a God of love. Miller's play is set on the grounds of a camp meeting in Northampton, Massachusetts, where Sojourner hopes to talk to those present about her personal religious experience.[24] Before she is granted permission to participate, she stops a group of reckless white youths from setting fire to the tents on the camp site. They are spellbound as she speaks to them about God and her past experiences in a language filled with witticism and imagery. In *Harriet Tubman* a young slave woman plays a crucial but dangerous role in the escape of a group of slaves under Harriet's leadership.[25]

Miller's *Christophe's Daughters* (1935) captures a moment of Haitian history, specifically the final hours of the reign of Henry Christophe in 1820.[26] The play's concentration is on Christophe's daughters, who, under great stress during this rebellion against their father, display dignity and courage. Though offered safety, they choose to remain with him to the end. One daughter's human feelings surface, however, when she declares her love for life and reveals her wish not to be captured by the enemy.

Africa was a popular literary subject for some Renaissance writers, although in many instances this continent served as a symbol. It was often an idealized Africa, un-

---

[24] *Negro History in Thirteen Plays*, pp. 313-33.

[25] Ibid., pp. 265-88.

[26] Ibid., pp. 241-64.

touched by corrupt Western civilization, a place where blacks in America once had been free, happy, and noble. This perception of Africa was idyllic and mythic rather than realistic. A group of Miller's plays may be classified as her African plays. It is the African setting that unifies them, for each play develops its own dramatic idea.

Graven Images (1929), a mythological play set in Hazeroth, Egypt, in 1490 B.C., was written to enable black children to have a better image of themselves.[27] Eliezer, a son of Moses and his Ethiopian wife and a target of prejudice because of his dark complexion, maneuvers to replace a golden bull that the children are worshipping in a game. He succeeds in teaching them that he, too, is a child created in God's image and thus belongs to the human race. In the background are the pageantry of the chanting elders as they enter and leave the tabernacle, and there is a secondary conflict between Miriam and the people whom she has tried to persuade against Moses.

The plays set in Sub-Saharan Africa were written at a time when knowledge about this vast area was scant compared to the vast and complex body of information now available. Two of Miller's plays, imbued with an aura of romanticism, recall the greatness of the past and the superiority of the uncontaminated African culture, a Rousseau-like ideal. The African Sudan is the setting for *Samory* (1935), a play that takes its name from the African warrior who successfully leads his army against the French colonialists.[28] In the exposition some features about the greatness of ancient African civilization are supplied by an objective French soldier who is waiting with others to waylay the dreaded warrior.

Moving Caravans (n.d.) contrasts cultures through two of its characters: an educated African diplomat who is com-

[27] *Plays and Pageants from the Life of the Negro*, pp. 109-37. This play has been published also in *Black Theater, U.S.A.*, pp. 353-59.

[28] *Negro History in Thirteen Plays*, pp. 289-311.

fortable with Western civilization and his brooding adopted son from the hills, who, after experiencing some of the contradictions of this new culture, elects to return to his people.[29] In the prologue, a dancer symbolizing civilization beckons to the young man who, at first, is seeking "enlightenment"; later, one symbolizing the hills from which he fled recalls him.

The final play in this group, *The Bog Guide* (1925), awarded a third prize in the *Opportunity* Literary Contest, has as its focal point the tragedy of racial prejudice that encompasses two worlds.[30] Jealousy has driven Rupert Masters, an Englishmen, to reveal the mixed racial blood of his rival to the woman whom they both love. When this revelation causes the rival to be rejected by the woman, the dispossessed lover leaves England in search of a place, a utopia, without prejudice. In Africa he falls in love with a dancer, who conceives his child. When the drama opens, Masters has come to Africa to seek forgiveness, only to learn that the man whom he wronged is now dead along with the African mother of his child. Only the child, a daughter, who is to guide Masters over the bog, survives. She speaks a strange poetic language, which she learned from her father, and remembers well his teachings, as she leads Masters, a symbol of prejudice, to the quagmire where they both perish. The racial prejudice of two groups of people, one white and the other black, has caused her parents to live in painful isolation. In the play neither group is absolved of its wrong.

For the past half century the plays of May Miller and Georgia Douglas Johnson, with few exceptions, have been lying dormant between the covers of early editions of magazines and seminal, often neglected collections of black American drama.[31] In some cases, unpublished scripts have

---

[29] The typescript of this unpublished play is in the possession of the playwright.

[30] The typescript of this unpublished play is in the possession of the playwright.

[31] As cited earlier, in 1974 Miller's *Graven Images* and Johnson's *A Sunday*

been in the playwrights' possession or scattered in research libraries. During the time when these plays were produced, the productions, out of necessity, were confined, in the main, to the stages of the then-segregated black churches, secondary schools, institutions of higher education, and community theatres. Over a period of time, during which a multiplicity of overshadowing events occurred—the fighting of a second global war followed by a series of smaller ones and the intensification of the battle for human rights—these little dramas slipped from memory and were forgotten.

A reexamination of Miller's and Johnson's plays, however, reveals that through their miniature genres, all one-act plays, these two playwrights made worthwhile contributions to the development of black American drama, especially during the New Negro Renaissance. As participants in the proliferation of black artistic expression, they added to the writing of black self-portraiture, and in their best plays they replaced synthetic renderings and negative stereotypes of their people in American drama with realistic interpretations and recordings of the black experience told from a black perspective.

Pride in their race is apparent as Miller and Johnson set out to explore in dramatic form the diversity of their people. Their mythological and historical plays, some written with children in mind and designed to teach and inspire, link the past to the present and dramatize with quietude the heroism of their protagonists. In their folk plays, especially, they have created authentic black characters with human conflicts and natural speech. As the skies over America darkened from the inhumanity and irrationality of the horrendous lynchings of blacks in this then not-so-old century, both women, though Miller's is the gentler hand, dramatized some of the injustices of the American system.

Morning in the South were published in *Black Theatre, U.S.A.* In 1975 Johnson's *Plumes* was published in *The New Negro Renaissance: An Anthology.*

A harsh situation sometimes triggers an equally as severe response from their protagonists. Their plays on lynching are in the best tradition of protest plays, with the action or situation articulating the statement. Women in many of their plays not only take control of their own lives but move boldly to eradicate injustice and to quicken freedom for their people. In tackling moral issues, in highlighting "the great discrepancy between the American social creed and the American social practice."[32] Miller and Johnson contributed to the morality of American society.

The structure of their plays and the settings are uncomplicated, a spareness that permits the plots to appear in bas-relief. Their use of language is, more often than not, realistic and convincing, and dialect, when used, is never forced. While Miller's range of material is greater than Johnson's and she experiments more freely, at times incorporating dance and music in her plays, Johnson's approach to much of her material is more intense. However, their plays are not without flaws, simplicity and brevity being the norm.

Nevertheless, the plays of these two women were among the best written by black playwrights during the 1920s and the early 1930s, and their works serve as important transitions between the older extant black-authored plays—such as William Wells Brown's *The Escape* (1858) and Angelina Weld Grimké's *Rachel* (1916)—and the later works of black playwrights, some of whom gained recognition and won accolades. Miller's and Johnson's short protest plays against lynching, for example, were forerunners of later full-length works by other black playwrights who continued to denounce the oppression and injustice, in whatever form, inflicted upon blacks. Among these plays are Theodore Ward's *Big White Fog* (1937), William Branch's *A Medal for Willie* (1951), Loften Mitchell's *A Land Beyond the*

[32] Alain Locke, "The New Negro," in *The New Negro*, ed. Alain Locke (1925; rpt. New York: Atheneum, 1969), 1969), p. 13.

River (1957), and James Baldwin's *Blues for Mr. Charlie* (1964). Miller's early focus on Africa was expanded by Hall Johnson in his contemporaneous *Run, Little Chillun* (1933), a folk drama whose concern was orthodox religion and paganism. Later Lorraine Hansberry, in *A Raisin in the Sun* (1959), used the character Asagai, a Nigerian student, to help reforge the broken link between black Americans and their ancestral land as did Joseph Walker in *A River Niger* (1972) with the character Ann, a black South African nurse. The trend of dramatizing incidents from the lives of black historical figures was continued in such plays as Branch's *In Splendid Error* (1954), Clifford Mason's *Gabriel* (1968), N. R. Davidson's *El Hajj Malik* (1968), Charles Fuller's *The Rise* (1968), and Phillip Hayes Dean's *Paul Robeson* (1978). The theme of miscegenation that was treated in several plays by Johnson was employed by Langston Hughes in *Mulatto* (1935) and during the 1960s by Adrienne Kennedy in her imagistic and complex one-act plays, *Funnyhouse of a Negro* (1964) and *The Owl Answers* (1969). Toward midcentury, folk plays with Southern settings shifted to the North and the characters became the urban folk in the plays of Langston Hughes and Ed Bullins. And the voices of women, dominant in the plays of Miller and Johnson, gained an even greater range in the works of Lorraine Hansberry, Alice Childress, J. E. Franklin, Sonia Sanchez, and Ntozake Shange.

One can only conjecture the kinds of dramas that may have been written by May Miller and Georgia Douglas Johnson if they had continued to write plays and to develop and expand in their craft. Although poetry beckoned to them and to that genre to which they turned their attention and their creative energies, their contributions to the development of black American drama should not be forgotten. Much of the material that they chose to dramatize during the period in which they wrote plays was in startling contrast to that of most white playwrights whose works about blacks were being mounted on the professional stage. When

Miller and Johnson held up their mirror to black life, the reflections were recognizable by black audiences. The black experience was the subject of their dramas, and they penetrated that experience and wrote of it from the depths of their souls and the contours of their imagination.

Howard University
  Washington, D.C.

ARNOLD RAMPERSAD

The Origins of Poetry in Langston Hughes

IN HIS STUDY *The Life of the Poet: Beginning and Ending Poetic Careers* (1981) Lawrence Lipking asks three main questions, one of which concerns me here in the case of Langston Hughes: "How does an aspiring author of verses become a poet?" In the case of John Keats, for example, how did the poet arrive at "On First Looking Into Chapman's Homer," that great leap in creative ability in which Keats, sweeping from the legend of "the realms of gold" toward modern history, "catches sight not of someone else's dream but of his own reality? He stares at his future, and surmises that he may be a poet. The sense of possibility is thrilling, the moment truly awesome. Keats has discovered Keats." Or in the well-known words of Keats himself: "The Genius of Poetry must work out its own salvation in a man: It cannot be matured by law & precept, but by sensation & watchfulness in itself—That which is creative must create itself."

Can one ask a similar question about the origins of poetry in Langston Hughes, who in June 1921, at the age of nineteen, began a celebrated career when he published his own landmark poem "The Negro Speaks of Rivers" in W.E.B. Du Bois' *Crisis* magazine? Like Keats before "Chapman's Homer," Hughes had written poems before "The Negro Speaks of Rivers." Much of the poetry before "Rivers" is available for examination, since Hughes published steadily in the monthly magazine of his high school in Cleveland, Ohio. Certain aspects of this verse are noteworthy. It has nothing to do with race; it is dominated by images of the poet not as a teenager but as a little child; and, in Hughes's junior year, he published his first poem in free verse, one that showed the clear influence of Walt Whitman for the first (but not the last) time. Revealing an increase in skill, Hughes's early poetry nevertheless gives no sign of a major poetic talent in the making. At some point in his development, however, something happened to Hughes that was as mysterious

695

and as wonderful, in its own way, as the miracle that overtook John Keats after the watchful night spent with his friend Charles Cowden Clarke and a copy of Chapman's translation. With "The Negro Speaks of Rivers" the creativity in Langston Hughes, hitherto essentially unexpressed, suddenly created itself.

In writing thus about Hughes, are we taking him too seriously? With a few exceptions, literary critics have resisted offering even a modestly complicated theory concerning his creativity. His relentless affability and charm, his deep, open love of the black masses, his devotion to their folk forms, and his insistence on writing poetry that they could understand, all have contributed to the notion that Langston Hughes was intellectually and emotionally shallow. One wonders, then, at the source of the creative energy that drove him from 1921 to 1967 to write so many poems, novels, short stories, plays, operas, popular histories, children's books, and assorted other work. As a poet, Hughes virtually reinvented Afro-American poetry with his pioneering use of the blues and other folk forms; as Howard Mumford Jones marveled in a 1927 review, Hughes added the verse form of the blues to poetry in English (a form that continues to attract the best black poets, including Michael Harper, Sherley Anne Williams, and Raymond Patterson). One wonders, too, in his aspect as a poet, why this apparently happy, apparently shallow man defined his creativity in terms of unhappiness. "I felt bad for the next three or four years," he would write in *The Big Sea* about the period beginning more or less with the publication of "The Negro Speaks of Rivers," "and those were the years when I wrote most of my poetry. (For my best poems were all written when I felt the worst. When I was happy, I didn't write anything.)"

Hughes actively promoted the image of geniality to which I have alluded. Wanting and needing to be loved, he scrubbed and polished his personality until there was no abrasive side, no jagged edge that might wound another human being. Publicly and privately, his manner belied the commonly held belief that creativity and madness are allied, that neuroses and a degree of malevolence are the fair price of art. His autobiographies, *The Big Sea* (1940) and *I Wonder As I Wander* (1956), made no enemies; to many readers, Hughes's mastery of that form consists in his ability to cross its chill deep by paddling nonchalantly on its surface. And yet in two places, no doubt deliberately, Hughes allows the reader a glimpse of inner turmoil. Both appear in the earlier book, *The Big Sea*. Both involve personal and emotional conflicts so intense that they led to physical illness. Because of their extreme rarity, as well as their strategic location in the context of his creativity, these passages

696

deserve close scrutiny if we hope to glimpse the roots of Hughes's originality as a poet.

The first of these two illnesses took place in the summer of 1919, when Hughes (at seventeen) saw his father for the first time in a dozen years. In 1903, James Hughes had gone to Mexico, where he would become a prosperous property owner. In a lonely, impoverished, passed-around childhood in the Midwest, his son had fantasized about the man "as a kind of strong, bronze cowboy, in a big Mexican hat, going back and forth from his business in the city to his ranch in the mountains, free—in a land where there were no white folks to draw the color line, and no tenements with rent always due—just mountains and cacti: Mexico!" Elated to be invited suddenly to Mexico in 1919 at the end of his junior year in high school, Langston left the United States with high hopes for his visit.

The summer was a disaster. James Hughes proved to be an unfeeling, domineering, and materialistic man, scornful of Indians and blacks (he was himself black) and the poor in general, and contemptuous of his son's gentler pace and artistic temperament. One day, Langston could take no more: "Suddenly my stomach began to turn over and over. And I could not swallow another mouthful. Waves of heat engulfed me. My eyes burned. My body shook. I wanted more than anything on earth to hit my father, but instead I got up from the table and went back to bed. The bed went round and round and the room turned dark. Anger clotted in every vein, and my tongue tasted like dry blood." But the boy, ill for a long time, never confessed the true cause of his affliction. Having been moved to Mexico City, he declined to help his doctors: "I never told them . . . that I was sick because I hated my father." He recovered only when it was time to return to the United States.

Hughes's second major illness came eleven years later. By this time he had finished high school, returned to Mexico to live with his father for a year, attended Columbia University for one year (supported grudgingly by James Hughes), dropped out of school, and served as a messman on voyages to Africa and to Europe, where he spent several months in 1924 as a dishwasher. All the while, however, Hughes was publishing poetry in a variety of places, especially in important black journals. This activity culminated in books of verse published in 1926 (*The Weary Blues*) and 1927 (*Fine Clothes to the Jew*) that established him, with Countee Cullen, as one of two major black poets of the decade. In 1929, he graduated after three and a half years at black Lincoln University, Pennsylvania. In 1930, Hughes published his first novel, *Not Without Laughter.*

697

This book had been virtually dragged out of him by his patron of the preceding three years, "Godmother" (as she wished to be called), an old, white, very generous but eccentric woman who ruled Hughes with a benevolent despotism inspired by her volatile beliefs in African spirituality, folk culture, mental telepathy, and the potential of his genius. But the result of her largesse was a paradox: the more comfortable he grew, the less Hughes was inclined to create. Estranged by his apparent languor, his patron finally seized on an episode of conflict to banish him once and for all. Hughes was devastated. Surviving drafts of his letters to "Godmother" reveal him deep in self-abasement before a woman with whom he was clearly in love. Ten years later, he confessed in *The Big Sea*: "I cannot write here about that last half-hour in the big bright drawing-room high above Park Avenue . . . because when I think about it, even now, something happens in the pit of my stomach that makes me ill. That beautiful room . . . suddenly became like a trap closing in, faster and faster, the room darker and darker, until the light went out with a sudden crash in the dark, and everything became like . . . that morning in Mexico when I suddenly hated my father.

"I was violently and physically ill, with my stomach turning over and over. . . . And there was no rationalizing anything. I couldn't." For several months, according to my research (Hughes erroneously presents a far briefer time frame in *The Big Sea*), he waited in excruciating hope for a reconciliation. As in Mexico, he wasted time and money on doctors without revealing to them the source of his chronic illness (which one very ingenious Harlem physician diagnosed as a Japanese tapeworm). Rather than break his silence, Hughes even agreed to have his tonsils removed. Gradually it became clear that reconciliation was impossible. Winning a prize of four hundred dollars for his novel, Hughes fled to seclusion in hot, remote Haiti. When his money ran out some months later, he returned home, healed at last but badly scarred.

Although they occurred more than a decade apart, the two illnesses were similar. Both showed a normally placid Hughes driven into deep rage by an opponent, a rage which he was unable to ventilate because the easy expression of personal anger and indignation was anathema to him. In both cases, he developed physical symptoms of hyperventilation and, eventually, anemia. More importantly, both were triggered in a period of relatively low poetic creativity (as when he was still a juvenile poet) or outright poetic inactivity (as with his patron). In each instance, Hughes had become satisfied with this low creativity or inactivity. At both times, a certain powerful figure, first his father, then "Godmother," had opposed his right to be content. His father had opposed any poetic

698

activity at all; "Godmother" had opposed his right to enjoy the poetical state without true poetical action, or writing. In other words, a powerful will presented itself in forceful opposition to what was, in one sense, a vacuum of expressive will on Hughes's part. (Needless to say, the *apparent* absence of will in an individual can easily be a token of the presence of a very powerful will.) The result on both occasions, which was extraordinary, was first Hughes's endurance of, then his violent rebellion against, a force of will that challenged his deepest vision of the poetic life.

I use the term "will" knowing that to many people it is an obsolete concept, in spite of the revival of interest in Otto Rank, or continuing critiques of Freud's use of the term as, for example, Harold Bloom's excellent essay "Freud's Concepts of Defense and the Poetic Will." But I am referring here mainly, though not exclusively, to the will as a function of consciousness, as in the case of "Godmother's" will, or that of Hughes's father, or—far less demonstrably—Hughes's own volition. And what do I mean by Hughes's "vision of the poetic life"? I refer to what one might call unshaped or amorphous poetic consciousness, poetry not concretized or written down, but the crucial element (when combined with poetic "material") out of which written or oral poetry is made. In an old-fashioned but still significant way, the poet Richard Eberhart has written of "Will and Psyche in Poetry" (in Don Cameron Allen's *The Moment of Poetry*, 1962). Poems of the will value the body, activity, struggle, and the things of this world; poems of the psyche endorse spirit, "an uncontaminated grace," and the "elusive, passive, imaginative quality" of the world beyond this world. A poem of will, such as Marvell's "To His Coy Mistress," might involve a man calling a woman to bed; for an exemplary poem of psyche, Eberhart chose Poe's "To Helen," where desire leads directly away from sexuality toward spirit.

The notorious placidity of surface in Hughes, as I see it, bespeaks the extent to which he was a poet who preferred his poems unwritten—a poet, like his great mentor Walt Whitman, who saw his life itself as a poem greater than any poem he could possibly write. Hughes's greatest poetical instinct was to preserve his unformed or dormant poetic consciousness as the highest form of poetry. Such an instinct may suggest infantilism; one remembers Freud's unfortunate words about the link between creative writing and daydreaming. Infantilism would be wrong as an explanation. But, in Hughes's case, I suspect, the instinct had something to do with the youthfulness of the self he clearly regarded as his authentic, or most cherished self. Placidity of surface, anxiety to

699

please and to be loved, apparent asexuality (the most consistent conclusion—rather than that of homosexuality, for which there is no evidence—about his libido among people who knew him well), and the compulsion against concretized or written poetry reflect a sense of self as prepubescent, or apubescent; in other words, a sense of self as an eternal child. At some level, Hughes saw himself ideally as a child—a dreamy genius child, a perfect child, a princely child, a loving child, even a mothering and maternal child—but first and foremost as a child (almost never is he the destructively rebellious child, in spite of his radical poetry).

It must be stressed that such a sense of self, although it modulates art (as does every other factor of comparable importance), is by no means an inherent handicap to a creative person. In any event, Hughes teetered between a sense of confidence (a sense of being loved by a particular person to whom he was emotionally mortgaged) and a rival, harrowing sense, born in his own childhood, of abandonment and despair. The latter was closer to the origins of his poetry. Release Hughes as an artist from the stabilizing social context and he flies almost immediately toward themes of nihilism and death. For example, take his poem "Border Line":

> I used to wonder
> About living and dying—
> I think the difference lies
> Between tears and crying.
>
> I used to wonder
> About here and there—
> I think the distance
> Is nowhere.

Or "Genuis Child":

> *. . . Nobody loves a genius child.*
>
> Can you love an eagle,
> Tame or wild?
>
> Wild or tame,
> Can you love a monster
> Of frightening name?
>
> *Nobody loves a genius child.*

700

Kill him—and let his soul run wild!

Or "End":

> There are
> No clocks on the wall,
> And no time,
> No shadows that move
> From dawn to dusk
> Across the floor.
>
> There is neither light
> Nor dark
> Outside the door.
>
> *There is no door!*

In Hughes's writing, there is precious little middle ground between such verse and that for which he is far better known (and deservedly so), the poems steeped in race and other social concerns. Nature as flora and fauna bored the man who preferred Harlem in hot summer to the cool New England woods, as he once joked, because "I prefer wild people to wild animals." Hughes understood wherein his salvation rested.

This bleakness, almost always ignored in critical treatments of Hughes, evolved out of the saturation of his dormant poetical consciousness by the powerful will toward death stimulated in him by his loneliness as a child. But Hughes did not surrender passively to the force of his father and "Godmother" when they turned against him. These attacks, in fact, elicited in him a massive retaliatory display of willfulness, at first (while he was ill) as uncontrolled and uncontrollable as the right to the passive poetic consciousness it defended. The invocation of will in such massive degree could easily have remained as toxic as it was while he was sick with his silent rage. Only the modification of will, a compromise between passive poetic consciousness and the purposefulness needed to defend that consciousness, could prevent the consummation of poetry (amorphous or concrete) by rage. And only an appeal to a third force that was neither Hughes nor his enemy could allow him to fashion a balance between will and his unformed poetical consciousness.

Both in the experience with his father in Mexico and in the struggle with "Godmother," the third force was represented by the black race. Hughes's attitude to the black masses is too complicated to detail here. But my argument depends on the crucial understanding that Hughes

701

was virtually unique among major black writers not so much because of the considerable depth of his love of black people, but because of *the depth of his psychological dependence on them.* Hughes became dependent because of a relatively complicated set of circumstances in his youth, when he was reared by his poor but very proud grandmother, the aged, wrinkled, and laconic Mary Langston, whose first husband had died at Harpers Ferry with John Brown. But Mary Langston's zeal to defend the rights of her race was offset for her grandson by her personal remoteness both from him and the race, and by the severity of her pride —a pride compounded by her very light skin, her Indian rather than predominantly African features, her Oberlin education, and her high-toned religion, which all kept her distant from the black masses. She did not attend black churches, did not sing black spirituals (much less the blues); she spoke in a clipped manner, rather than a folksy drawl, and she detested popular culture—as Hughes spelled out partially in *The Big Sea*, but more completely in an unpublished portrait prepared in 1943.

What Mary Langston offered in the abstract, however, was made wonderfully concrete to young Hughes by two persons with whom he lived from time to time (when his grandmother was forced to rent out her house, and after she died) and whom he described in an Arcadian paragraph in *The Big Sea*—"Uncle" and "Auntie" Reed. "Uncle" James Reed, who dug ditches for the city, smoked his pipe and stayed home on Sundays. "Auntie" Reed (later Mrs. Mary J. Reed Campbell) took Langston to St. Luke's A.M.E. church (a church apparently not good enough for his grandmother) and taught the Sunday School there in which the boy was the brightest star. Through the childless Reeds, who clearly adored the boy, he learned how to love the race, its church ways and folk ways, and its dreams and aspirations, of which the handsome, scrubbed, light brown boy, the grandson of "Colonel" Charles Langston (whose brother John Mercer Langston had served in the U.S. Congress and as an ambassador of the U.S.) was the shining embodiment. And it was a lie he told to the Reeds (that Jesus had come to Hughes at a revival meeting, after "Auntie" Reed had prayed that this would happen) that led to the major trauma of his childhood, as related in *The Big Sea*—a long weeping into the night (the second to last time he cried, Hughes wrote) because he had waited for Jesus, who had never come, then had lied to the people who loved him most. In *The Big Sea* Hughes would admit to hating his father; he would partly ridicule his mother; he would admit that he did not cry when his grandmother died. The Reeds, however, were different: "For me, there have never been any better people in the world. I loved them very much."

702

438

In his bitter struggles with his mother and "Godmother," Hughes turned to the black race for direction. But one needs to remember that this appeal in itself hardly gave Hughes distinction as a poet; what made Hughes distinct was the highly original manner in which he internalized the Afro-American racial dilemma and expressed it in poems such as "When Sue Wears Red," "The Negro Speaks of Rivers," "Mother to Son," "Dream Variations," and "The Weary Blues," poems of Hughes's young manhood on which his career would rest. Of these, the most important was "The Negro Speaks of Rivers."

> I've known rivers.
> I've known rivers ancient as the world and older
>   than the flow of human blood in human veins.
>
> My soul has grown deep like the rivers.
>
> I bathed in the Euphrates when dawns were young.
> I built my hut near the Congo and it lulled me to sleep.
> I looked upon the Nile and raised the pyramids above it.
> I heard the singing of the Mississippi when Abe Lincoln
>   went down to New Orleans, and I've seen its muddy
>   bosom turn all golden in the sunset.
>
> I've known rivers:
> Ancient, dusky rivers.
>
> My soul has grown deep like the rivers.

Here, the persona moves steadily from dimly starred personal memory ("I've known rivers") toward a rendezvous with modern history (Lincoln going down the Mississippi and seeing the horror of slavery that, according to legend, would make him one day free the slaves). The death wish, benign but suffusing, of its images of rivers older than human blood, of souls grown as deep as these rivers, gives way steadily to an altering, ennobling vision whose final effect gleams in the evocation of the Mississippi's "muddy bosom" turning at last "all golden in the sunset." Personal anguish has been alchemized by the poet into a gracious meditation on his race, whose despised ("muddy") culture and history, irradiated by the poet's vision, changes within the poem from mud into gold. This is a classic example of the essential process of creativity in Hughes.

The poem came to him, according to Hughes (accurately, it seems clear) about ten months after his Mexican illness, when he was riding a train from Cleveland to Mexico to rejoin his father. The time was sun-

703

down, the place the Mississippi outside St. Louis. "All day on the train I had been thinking of my father," he would write in *The Big Sea*. "Now it was just sunset and we crossed the Mississippi, slowly, over a long bridge. I looked out of the window of the Pullman at the great muddy river flowing down toward the heart of the South, and I began to think what that river, the old Mississippi, had meant to Negroes in the past—how to be sold down the river was the worst fate that could overtake a slave in bondage. Then I remembered reading how Abraham Lincoln had made a trip down the Mississippi on a raft, and how he had seen slavery at its worst, and had decided within himself that it should be removed from American life. Then I began to think of other rivers in our past—the Congo, and the Niger, and the Nile in Africa—and the thought came to me: 'I've known rivers,' and I put it down on the back of an envelope I had in my pocket, and within the space of ten or fifteen minutes, as the train gathered speed in the dusk, I had written this poem."

Here, starting with anguish over his father, Hughes discovered the compressed ritual of passivity, challenge, turmoil, and transcendence he would probably have to re-create, doubtless in variant forms, during the great poetic trysts of his life. Even after he became a successful, published poet, the basic process remained the same, because his psychology remained largely the same even though he had become technically expert. In his second major illness, caused by his patron "Godmother," Hughes wrote poetry as he struggled for a transcendence that would be long in coming. The nature of that interim poetry is telling. When he sent some poems to a friend for a little book to be printed privately, she noticed at once that many spoke of death—"Dear lovely Death/That taketh all things under wing—/Never to kill. . . ." She called the booklet *Dear Lovely Death*. In "Afro-American Fragment," unlike in "The Negro Speaks of Rivers," Africa is seen plaintively:

> . . . Subdued and time-lost
> Are the drums—and yet
> Through some vast mist of race
> There comes this song
> I do not understand,
> This song of atavistic land,
> Of bitter yearnings lost
> Without a place—
> So long,
> So far away
> Is Africa's
> Dark face.

704

But when Hughes returned home, scarred but healed, after months in seclusion in Haiti, he no longer thought of loss and death. Instead, he plunged directly into the life of the black masses with a seven-month tour of the South in which he read his poetry in their churches and schools. Then he set out for the Soviet Union, where he would spend more than a year. Hughes then reached the zenith of his revolutionary ardor with poems (or verse) such as "Good Morning Revolution," "Goodbye Christ," and "Put One More 'S' in the USA."

"Good Morning Revolution," for example, and "The Negro Speaks of Rivers" are very different poems. The former is the polar opposite of the poetry of nihilism; the latter blends aspects of existential gloom with the life-affirming spirit of the black race. Together, the poems illustrate the wide range of possibility in the mixture of will and passivity which characterizes Hughes's art (although one can argue that "Good Morning Revolution"—by far the lesser poem—marks an overreaction of will, and thus is not truly representative of Hughes's poetic temperament in that it contains no element of passivity). But the creative process has remained the same. The right to amorphous poetic consciousness is challenged. The will is aroused in defense of that consciousness. Illness (an extreme version of Wallace Stevens' "blessed rage for order"?) marks the struggle of will against opposing will. The long-endured illness, in silence, gradually allows the mutual fertilization of will and poetic consciousness that is needed for concrete art. Illness ends when that ratio is achieved or perceived, and writing begins. Creativity, in Keats's term, has created itself. A poet, or a poem, is born.

To some extent, this process is nothing more than Wordsworth's definition of poetry as the final recollection "in tranquility" (a phrase often underplayed or even ignored in quoting Wordsworth's definition) of emotion that had once spontaneously overflowed. What is different, of course, is that Wordsworth (and Keats and Stevens) did not have to contend with race as a factor in his creativity. For many writers, perhaps even most, race is a distracting, demoralizing force. Hughes's genius, or his good fortune, consisted in his ability to accommodate race harmoniously within the scheme of creativity common to all major poets, and to turn it from an anomaly into an intimate advantage.

705

AFRICAN-AMERICAN WOMEN ARTISTS: AN HISTORICAL PERSPECTIVE

Arna Alexander Bontemps and Jacqueline Fonvielle-Bontemps

Black women, by virtue of their statistical presence and economic importance in the New World, but more importantly by virtue of the character of their struggle to endure the unendurable—the way she nurtured and reared her children, supported her family, maintained and sustained her own sense of worth and well-being—were undeniably essential to the utlimate survival of the Black community. It follows, therefore, that Black women—through the intellectual and aesthetic choices they made and the traditions they helped preserve—played a vital role in developing those meaningful forms of self-expression by which Black people in America have managed to survive two-and-a-half centuries of chattel slavery and nearly half a millenium of racial oppression.

But what are the specifics of her contributions to that culture? And what was the nature of the intellectual process through which she sought self-realization and self-respect both for herself and for those she loved? Unfortunately, the answers to these questions are sadly lacking, due to the dearth of scholarly research devoted specifically to the history of Black women's cultural contributions in America. This essay will examine the experiences and artistic expressions of African-American women from the early nineteenth century through the Harlem Renaissance. It was from a small group of relatively privileged African-Americans that the first Black women to paint or sculpt in a western tradition achieved public prominence in America.

THE BEGINNINGS: EDMONIA LEWIS

Edmonia Lewis, like most other American sculptors of her time, was not a great artist—there are too many unresolved, conflicting impulses in her work, and her technical proficiency, though solid and promising, was never fulfilled—yet she is nevertheless an important figure in the history of American and African-American art. It is not clear where she was born—either near Albany, New York, or in an Ohio town (Greenhigh) that no longer exists—or when she was born—either in 1843 or 1845.[1] She said, however, that her mother was a Chippewa Indian and her father was a Black man and a gentleman's servant. Thus, as a female American of African and Native American descent, she was subject to a myriad of possible socio-economic, intellectual and cultural influences.

For Edmonia Lewis, as for a growing number of free Black people in the North, the profound transitions that were occurring in American society in the middle decades of the nineteenth century meant that she was able to receive a formal education. In 1859 she entered the preparatory department of Oberlin College in Oberlin, Ohio. Founded in 1832, the college was a direct outgrowth of the sort of reform-minded Protestant, evangelical revivalism that motivated many of the nation's most fervent abolitionists and crusaders for other human rights causes in the first half of the nineteenth century. It is not entirely clear how she managed to go to Oberlin—either on an "abolitionist scholarship" or because of the assistance of a "thrifty brother" who lived in California—but it is certain that she did attend the school from 1859 to 1863, and that she followed the prescribed literary course while there. The significant feature of Edmonia's intellectual and academic life at Oberlin, however, was not that she followed the prescribed liberal arts curriculum or that she was an average, above, or below average student, but that her interest in the fine arts began to develop. It is not clear to what extent she was influenced by the crafts traditions of her Ojibwa ancestors, but her background in that regard was fairly extensive. She made moccasins as her mother did, and it is possible that she had also been influenced by her exposure to other Ojibwa crafts. One of her statues, for instance, is of an *Old Indian Arrow Maker and His Daughter.* The daughter is making moccasins and the father is making arrows.

Regardless of the possible source of her artistic inspiration, she had, by September 9, 1862, produced at least one pencil drawing of a sculpted figure, sculpted in the neo-classical tradition that prevailed in America for the first three-quarters of the nineteenth century.[2] This fact, coupled with those relating to the possible Ojibwa influences on her artistic development, are significant because most scholars, until fairly recently, assumed that Edmonia's artistic inclinations were entirely untapped before she arrived in Boston in 1863 and was exposed to the monumental statuary there.

Edmonia Lewis, though generally thought to have followed Reason's pattern, never sculpted a Black figure, though many of her statues dealt with racial or sexual repression as a theme. She glorified abolition as a movement and individual abolitionists, but not Black people. More than 250 Black students attended Oberlin prior to the Civil War, but her friends were all white. Her father lived until she was a teenager, but all

Arna Alexander Bontemps is a writer and historian who teaches at Hampton University. He is editor of The Hampton Review and writes art criticism on a regular basis for The Virginia-Pilot newspaper in Norfolk, Virginia. A former editor at Ebony Magazine, he is the author of numerous articles and book reviews about African-American literature and art history. Jacqueline Fonvielle-Bontemps is an educator, artist, and art historian. She is an Associate Professor of art education and art history and chairperson of the Department of Art at Hampton University. She is the director and curator of Choosing: An Exhibit of Changing Perspectives in Modern Art and Art Criticism by Black Americans 1925-1985, and Forever Free: Art by African-American Women, 1862-1980.

her memories are of her mother and her mother's people. When she found herself in deep trouble—accused of poisoning two of her closest friends—the Black community in Oberlin pronounced her guilty in advance of her trial because, her Black lawyer recalled, "of all her easy and rather unusual social relations with the whites." Irate local whites attacked and nearly killed her before her trial, undoubtedly because she was Black, but the people who comforted, consoled and tried to protect her were the white liberals (and Blacks like her lawyer who shared their ideals), whose spirit and commitment to religious revival and social reform were the foundations on which Oberlin was built. And it was to those friends that Edmonia gave her trust and affection, and it was into their world that she fled when her life at Oberlin was finally over—after she was accused and acquitted, the following year, of stealing brushes and paints from a local art teacher. A decade later, however, Edmonia recalled rather matter-of-factly that "after I finished what little schooling I had in Ohio, I thought I would go to Boston and learn a little music. I went."[3]

Fortunately, when she left Oberlin, she was given a letter of introduction and recommendation to the radical abolitionist leader William Lloyd Garrison, and he in turn was willing to make it possible for her to meet and study under Edmund Brackett, a local sculptor. Within a year she opened her own studio and by January of 1865, she had received enough encouragement and support for her work to go to Rome where she immediately began to study and attempt original sculpture. According to all accounts of her life and career, she was so impressed by the statuary she encountered in Boston, especially a life-sized statue of Benjamin Franklin by Horatio Greenough, that she decided she would rather study sculpture than music.

The two works that made her career in Boston (both done in 1864) were a medallion of the head of John Brown, of which she sold several copies, and a bust of Colonel Shaw. The Colonel, as leader of the 54th Massachusetts Regiment, had achieved a degree of immortality, along with 247 of his men, at the siege of Fort Wagner on Morris Island, South Carolina, July 18, 1863. Lewis sold nearly 100 plaster replicas of the Colonel's bust, and his family bought the original. The money she earned from the sale of these works and the recognition and interest they inspired among her circle of friends and their associates in Boston made it possible and desirable for her to go to Rome in 1865. There she quickly joined, or was absorbed into, what Henry James called "a white marmorean flock," by which he meant "that strange sisterhood of American 'lady sculptors' who at one time settled upon the seven hills (of Rome)."[4] The "marmorean flock" gathered around Harriet Hosmer—"the best known sculptor of her generation"—and Charlotte Cushman, an actress to whom most of the leading women sculptors in Rome were devoted.[5] Hosmer, in fact, sailed to Rome with Cushman in 1852.

Male American sculptors had begun to go to Italy for inspiration and training as early as 1825, when Horatio Greenough made the journey. Hiram Powers, one of the best known sculptors of the 19th century, also settled in Florence in 1837. Both men, as did all other academically oriented American sculptors of that era, male or female, inherited or adopted the European tradition of neo-classicism as exemplified in the works of Antonio Canova and Bertel Thorvaldsen.

When Lewis arrived in 1865, "Charlotte took her up as a personal project," because, she said, she "has more than anybody else to fight." Both Hosmer and Cushman were devoted feminists with abolitionist sympathies. Most of Edmonia's friends and associates at Oberlin and afterward were similarly disposed. Her pencil drawing in 1862 was, in fact, a gift for Clara Steele Norton, an ardent feminist, and the drawing itself may have had a meaning related to their shared commitment to the feminist movement of their day. In Boston, Garrison and Henry Wadsworth Longfellow and others like them, came generously to her aide; in Rome it was Cushman and Hosmer and William Wetmore Story, a "lawyer turned poet and sculptor" and "the doge of the New England expatriates in Rome."[6] To such people, women sculptors were looked upon as heroes, not social deviants or misfits, and Black female sculptors seemed especially blessed. Thus Edmonia was inspired to give her loyalty to these supporters and friends, just as she did to her Indian relatives and ancestors. Her loyalties, however, did not extend very far toward her father's people; her work, in fact suggests that she sought to avoid the central fact of her life. Yet in doing so she reflected one of the strongest impulses in Black art: the compelling and compulsive urge to declare one's humanity in individual rather than racial terms.

Whatever its motivation, however, her work is full of social commentary about the central human rights issues of her day and it is marked by a degree of naturalism—often too emotional and sentimental—that distinguishes it stylistically from that of many of her contemporaries. In this respect she, like John Adams Ward, must be credited for having helped lead the way toward greater realism in her field, though technically she remained a neo-classicist. She was a relatively prolific sculptor during the first decade or so of her artistic career. There was very little by way of thematic originality in her work, even her best and most skillfully rendered pieces, but she did manage on occasion to transcend the hackneyed themes and subject matter that dominated American sculpture during most of the nineteenth century and to realize a degree of emotional sensibility and interpretive insight that was lacking in the work of lesser artists.

Illustrative of her creative potential was, perhaps, her most controversial work, *The Death of Cleopatra*, which was exhibited during the 1876 Centennial Exposition in Philadelphia. The only description of the work emphasized its realistic depiction of the effects of death, which the observer suggested indicated a lack of taste on the part of the artist. Little is known of Edmonia's life, either professionally or privately, after this date. Consequently, it has been generally assumed that she was unable to respond to the changing artistic tastes of the late nineteenth century.[7] This, however, is an unlikely suggestion considering her stylistic history as a sculptor and considering the modest nature of the changes in American sculpture prior to World War I. A more telling factor, undoubtedly, was the decline of interest, among white liberals, in racial issues, reform movements, and the careers of Black, Ojibwa, female sculptors.

THE TORTUROUS TRANSITION:
BLACK ART IN THE LATE NINETEENTH AND
EARLY TWENTIETH CENTURIES

Edmonia's sincerity of expression and realistic approach to art was vindicated in the work of subsequent American sculptors, including her sister sculptors, May Howard Jackson and Meta Vaux Warrick Fuller, both of whom were born in Philadelphia in 1877. It is interesting to note, though the comparison is seldom made, that Fuller's early work picks up where Edmonia's left off in 1876, with the vivid depiction of sombre and macabre subject matter. It is equally suggestive to note that the eras that followed, known as the Gilded Age and the Progressive era in American history, are known to Black Americans as an age of betrayal or the nadir of Black life, a time of retrenchment and fear, of "compromise. . .compliance and conformity," "of legalized segregation and disfranchisement," of cultural isolation and continued social and economic discrimination.[8]

Caught in the backlash of a nation turned topsy-turvy by the twin forces of modernism—urban and industrial growth—Black Americans sought to defend and protect themselves by stressing the ideas of self-reliance and self-help. In such an atmosphere, as during the long nightmare of slavery, art based or strongly rooted in the Black Folk Tradition flourished and matured, but the fine arts suffered, due largely to the lack of interest in, or the patronizing and condescending attitude white intellectuals had toward Black life and the creative capacity of Black people.

May Howard Jackson "was one of the first Black sculptors to reject popular European tastes and to deliberately use America's racial problems as a thematic source of their art."[9] Born in Philadelphia, as was Henry Ossawa Tanner, the most distinguished Black painter of this era, and Fuller, she studied at Professor J. Liberty-Tadd's art school and the Pennsylvania Academy of Fine Arts. Described as having been "temperamental, withdrawn," and reclusive, her professional life was apparently quite tragic.[10] It would, of course, be interesting to know the full dimensions of her tragedy, but its general outline is an all-too-familiar story. The rebuffs she received in her attempts to study art, for example, were faced by all Black artists then, as well as by most white women artists, although they were somewhat more privileged in this regard than Blacks.[11] Similarly, the lack of exhibition outlets was a major obstacle to the development of Black artists throughout the nineteenth and early twentieth centuries and continues to be one of the most significant impediments to the growth and maturity of Black Art in America. Prior to the end of World War I, state fairs and other such expositions were practically the only places Black artists had to publicly display their art.[12]

Most students of Jackson's art have acknowledged her extraordinary talent as a modeller; they generally allow as well that she frequently achieved a degree of lyrical expressiveness that imbued her work with a distinctiveness worthy of special merit. At the same time, however, critics have tended to dismiss her as a sculptor of "forthright portraits of forthright men," an apt but incomplete assessment. A more telling criticism was that her art exhibited "no great origniality. . .and (that) she made no noteworthy departure from the American pictorial tradition in sculpture as exemplified in the cognate styles

of St. Gaudens and Charles Grafly." Of course, the same judgement could have been applied to many other very fine American sculptors of Jackson's era, although that fact alone does not exempt her from criticism. Indeed, she, perhaps more than anyone else, was aware of her artistic limitations, of how much more she could have achieved if given the opportunity and encouragement. Within those limitations, the most important of which were psychological and thus perhaps unappreciated by her, she achieved an admirable level of technical proficiency and creative expressiveness. Her portrait busts were often very strong yet sensitive character studies, which is what she obviously intended them to be, facts acknowledged by the *Washington Star's* art critic in 1913 and again in 1916.[13] Moreover, she sculpted several groups that strongly suggested that she was capable of realizing more ambitious and complex thematic conceptions, as for example her *Mulatto Mother and Her Child*. More importantly, perhaps, her *Head of a Negro Child* established a sensitive and intensely humanistic approach to the portrayal of Black folk types that Black sculptors have followed and refined ever since, a preoccupation that some Black art critics and historians privately regret but a compelling and entirely understandable one nonetheless. Portraiture, after all, was the most direct means available to those Black artists who wanted to respond to the demeaning and distorted images of Black life and character that white America has nourished so carefully for nearly four centuries, a racist tradition that gathered renewed intensity in the quarter of a century preceding World War I.

Jackson's intense racial pride represented a central feature of a growing Black reaction to the sort of unrestrained racial injustice and bigotry that had gained legal sanction in post-Reconstruction America. Fuller's career, however, is perhaps more expressive of the full breadth and development of that reaction than Jackson's. Unlike Jackson, who was unable to continue her studies after graduating from the Pennsylvania School of Industrial Art in 1897 and the Philadelphia College of Industrial Art in 1898, she studied at the Ecole des Beaux Arts in 1899 and at the Academie Colarrossi from 1899 to 1902. On her return to America, she entered the Pennsylvania Academy of Fine Arts (1903), graduating four years later in 1907.[14]

Both women apparently "married well," Jackson to a mathematics professor and high school principal,[15] and Fuller to a distinguished Black physician.[16] Both apparently came from similar socio-economic backgrounds and faced the same sorts of color-caste prejudices that tormented so many other near-white Black women in post-Reconstruction America. Thus as archetypes they may have very well reflected strong undercurrents of self-hatred and personal guilt symptomatic of a kind of racial schizophrenia and motivated by a powerful, perhaps, irrational, assimilationist dream. As individual artists, however, they were considerably more complex, representing most of the main currents of Black intellectual life prior to the first world war. Indeed, Samella Lewis has suggested that as a transitional figure in the history of Black art, "Warrick expressed ideals that are more in accord with the Black Renaissance of the generation that followed hers than with the prevailing artistic views of her own period."[17]

Thematically, Fuller's work does not seem to exhibit the same clearly articulated social focus as that by Jackson, but Fuller's work was so much more extensive and diverse than

445

Jackson's that such comparisons are meaningless. Her career, in fact, has been generally divided into two very distinct phases: "the romantic and the social." Stylistically, she was an impressionist in the manner of the great French master, Auguste Rodin. Porter noted, however, that she also reflected Edmonia Lewis' desire to evoke a sense of "emotional realism or romanticism."[18] Her early work has been termed "macabre and gruesome" because it dealt with powerful subject matter—themes of death, war, despair, and human anguish. Her subsequent sculpture, however, "demonstrated a social interest and included sentimental ethnic pieces such as *Water Boy.*"[19]

The source of her early thematic concerns, according to Fuller's friend Velma J. Hoover, "was her racial experience," her rejection, first, by white society in general, and later by the American art world, which disdained her work even though it had been acclaimed in Paris. "At the turn of the century in the United States," Hoover explained, "most Black persons were afraid to publicly verbalize the pain, sorrow, and despair of the Black experience, and a woman was seldom expected to voice any opinion at all. Meta Fuller found creative expression of these feelings through her sculpture, and her works were 'powerful' because she was expressing very real pain, sorrow and despair."[20]

In another context, Fuller explained that she "acquired her bent for horrors" from ghost stories her brother and her grandfather used to tell her when she was a child: "Ghost stories and that characteristic type of Negro folklore which is never separated from the fearful, the weirdly superstitious." Oddly, she said, the stories did not frighten her as they were intended to; instead she was fascinated by them. "Maybe some faint vibrations in my spiritual self," she speculated, "carried along through the blood of generations from the wilds of Africa, where my great-great grandmother was captured into slavery—maybe this, too, had something to do with my predilections. Anyway, the horror bent came naturally."

Marked by such a promising beginning, Fuller's subsequent career is often viewed with varying degrees of regret. Her thematic focus was somewhat narrowed yet at the same time her work became more socially relevant. Stylistically, she reverted to a more conventional orientation, that is, as conventional as her extraordinary imagination would allow. Hoover suggested that part of the explanation for this transition in her approach to art was due to the great sense of disappointment she felt when American critics did not accept her art with the same warmth and enthusiasm as had Parisian observers. Also in 1910 much of her early work was destroyed by fire, thereby greatly adding to her general sense of frustration. Thus, Hoover argued, Fuller accommodated herself to expected norms regarding the role of women and Blacks in pre-World War I society. Her creative genius, Hoover explained, was "restricted to expressions of helpful religious fantasy, instead of depicting the reality of life." In 1909 she married Dr. Solomon Fuller and they moved to Framingham, Massachusetts, where she bore three sons and "her work turned more and more to portraiture and traditional themes, thereby losing the qualities which had caused Rodin to describe it as 'powerful.' "[21]

This assessment may be too extreme, though clearly relevant, for it was through the latter phase of her career that Fuller makes her most forceful commitment to the social needs and concerns of Black people, and it is through that concern that post-war artists take their lead. Moreover, the shift in her approach to art was not as complete and definite as Hoover suggests. She continued to be one of the most imaginative Black artists of her generation, and she never entirely relinquished her "bent for horrors." For example, in 1937 she not only sculpted *Richard B. Harrison as De Lawd*, an example of "the sculptural monumentality she often achieved," but she also created *The Talking Skull*, which reflected her earlier stylistic and thematic concerns. In either case, Fuller's work, like Jackson's, prefigured a greater preoccupation with ethnic or racial themes and images and a more direct and forceful approach to social issues by African-American artists. By contrast, the work of contemporary Black painters, most of whom were men, tended to avoid such themes and issues. Annie E. Walker, one of the very few Black women to receive recognition as a painter during the prewar era,[22] strongly reflected this trend.

Born in Alabama in 1855, she studied at the Cooper Union (1892-1895) and was admitted to the Art School of the Corcoran Gallery in Washington, D.C., on the basis of her work, though she was later refused admittance because of her color and despite the protests of leaders such as Frederick Douglass. At the Cooper Union she studied under Eakins, the quintessential American realist, and John Henry Twachtman, a leading American impressionist who represented an effort by some American artists to combine "visual realism and esthetic sensitivity" in their work. She received her diploma in drawing and portrait painting from the Union and earned enough money while there to study in Paris at the Academie Julien in 1896. More conventional, stylistically, than Tanner, who followed Eakins' example in the use of subtle control of light but who moved ahead of him in the direction of Van Gogh as a colorist, she rejected the admonition of her gifted mentor to explore the American scene for appropriate artistic themes; nor did she or any of her immediate African-American contemporaries follow the lead of The Eight, founders of the so-called Ash Can School of American art, to plumb the depths of American society for meaningful subject matter, which is not to say that Eakins, Homer, Thomas Hovenden, Eastman Johnson, the Eight and other American artists, who had begun to develop "the Negro subject and theme as a fresh and fascinating new province of native American material," did not have a significant and lasting influence on the subsequent development of Black Art in America.[23]

THE HARLEM RENAISSANCE

Among Black painters, the transition from the sort of social perspective reflected in the work of Tanner and Walker to that which characterized the age of the New Negro, an age inspired by a "new sense of self and race"—the age of Anne Spencer and Gwendolyn Bennett, of Florence Mills and Josephine Baker, of A'Lelia Walker and Mary McLeod Bethune, of Ethel Waters and Bessie Smith, Nella Larsen and Zora Neale Hurston—can be conveniently observed in the career of Laura Wheeler Waring, who, notwithstanding Walker's promise, was the first African-American to establish herself as a major painter in Black America. She was a truly fine and prolific artist, but unfortunately, she is known almost exclusively for her portraiture, when, in fact, she was equally productive as a painter of still lifes, landscapes and genre scenes. She also sculpted at least two figures in clay—"A Dance in the Round" (1935) and "Nude in Relief" (1937). Oil was her preferred medium, but she also produced numerous watercolors, one of which ("Heirlooms") won a highly competitive prize at the New York Watercolor Club exhibit in 1917.[24]

Born in Hartford, Connecticut, in 1887, she entered the Pennsylvania Academy of Fine Arts in 1906. In 1914 she was awarded the Cresson Traveling Scholarship as a reward for her work as a student illustrator at the Academy, and between 1924 and 1925 she studied at La Grande Chaumiere in Paris. Stylistically, she evolved, accordingly to Professor Porter, from an early preoccupation with chromatic modulations of color and an almost voracious appetite for the planar painting of value. The distinctive nature of her work, however, does not come from its stylistic influences, which reflect a conscious and studied preference for the programmatic European approach to impressionism as opposed to the less self-conscious American attitude, but from the personal perspective she brought to her work, the visual impact of "her scrupulous objectivity," and the corresponding warmth and affection with which she regarded her subjects. Thus, she frequently reflected an expressionistic impulse in her art. Her interest in Black subjects and themes, meanwhile, accurately reflected the prevailing intellectual sentiment among Black artists during the Harlem Renaissance, as well as the general trend in American realism established during the first decade of the twentieth century by The Eight.

Like Douglas, who spent most of his post-Renaissance career teaching art at Fisk University, Waring spent nearly all of her adult life, beginning in 1917, doing the same thing at Cheyney State College near Philadelphia. Both artists shared many other artistic inclinations in common. They were both obsessed with matters of technique and fascinated by the craft of painting, due undoubtedly to the rigorous nature of their training both in America and in Paris, and as a consequence of their long careers as art teachers. Both experimented with other, more modern approaches to their art, but they remained primarily devoted to impressionism; and therein lay the crux of their dilemma as Black artists in a swiftly changing art world.

Both recognized a need and felt a responsibility to explore native themes more fully in their art and to try and realize the aesthetic implications of African art and the African past for Black Art in general; indeed, few Black artists have ever been more dedicated to such aims than was Douglas, and the corpus of Waring's work suggests that she possessed a similar sensitivity. Neither Douglas nor Waring apparently had any difficulty in accepting the idea of a socially relevant art, or in Douglas' case, an art inspired by African rather than European aesthetic traditions. Their continued commitment to impressionism, however, suggests that they were reluctant at the same time to abandon the aesthetic idealism that Black artists had traditionally associated with European traditions in the fine arts. Such reservations, though implied and obscure, caused both artists to become increasingly isolated from the mainstream of Black Art following the decline of the Renaissance; and although both have continued to be admired as pioneers in their field they have been grossly underrecognized in terms of their overall commitment to technical excellence, the constancy with which they sought to pursue their art, their humanistic approach to Black life as an artistic theme and the enormously important transitional role they played in the evolution of modern Black Art.

No other Black woman achieved the distinction that Waring did as a painter during the Renaissance. Vivian Schuyler Key, from New York City, received the Amy E. Spingarn Award as a promising young painter/illustrator in 1927. She exhibited in the Harmon Foundation exhibits in 1930 and 1931 and she continues to paint and sculpt today, but economic pressures and domestic responsibilities have kept her from pursuing her art with the necessary intensity and concentration that continued development requires. Thus, she has only recently begun to realize the extraordinary promise she displayed in paintings such as "Study in Yellow" (oil, 1931). Indeed, the technical skill and imaginative design of "God Bless the Child That's Got His Own" (oil, 1976)—a tribute to Billie Holiday—shows clearly that she is an artist who deserves greater recognition and encouragement.

Thus, the Renaissance belonged to Waring, Fuller, and Jackson, and to two young sculptors—Nancy Elizabeth Prophet and Augusta Savage.

Prophet was born in Warrick, Rhode Island, on March 19, 1890. Her mother was Black, or, as she described herself, a "mixed negro," and her father, a city employee, was a Narragansett Indian.[25] It is doubtful that they would have been able to help or encourage her artistic aspirations if they had wanted to but thinking such dreams impractical they sought to discourage or distract her ambitions; thus Prophet had not only to struggle against obvious economic and racial disadvantages but against the will of her parents and their friends. Without hesitation, however, she set herself against these considerable odds, paying her own tuition to the Rhode Island School of Design from which she graduated in 1918. She also managed to save enough money to pay her own way to Paris in 1922. There she studied at the École des Beaux Arts, exhibited in the Salon d'Automn (1924, 1927) and the Salon des Artists Francaise (1929), received warm and even glowing reviews in the Paris press, and was befriended by Henry Ossawa Tanner. She remained in France for a full decade, returning to America once or twice to exhibit her work. The poet, Countee Cullen, met her in Tanner's studio in 1930, and described her as a well-focused young artist, happy in her surroundings and content with her life.

She swept into the studio, he wrote, with unequalled eclat, wearing "a flowing black cape and a broad, black felt hat." Apparently, he said, she did not live or work in luxury, describing her studio on rue Broca as being set "deep back in a passage that conjured up a picture of vanished dreams, but she seemed to be at peace with herself, content with the direction of her life and her art . . ."[26] He also said that while in Paris she kept herself well-informed regarding cultural affairs in Black America, and that she maintained a strong sense of racial pride and identity. Her work, however, does not appear to be self-consciously racial as was Jackson's. She died, her passing little noted, in 1960, the same year in which Cedric Dover reported in his book, *American Negro Art*, that she had declined inclusion on the basis that she was "not a negro."[28] Her career, meanwhile, had declined much earlier. She taught art at Spelman College and Atlanta University for a number of years, beginning in 1934, but after 1939 her work was apparently not exhibited again during her lifetime.

Augusta Savage's life was equally troubled and difficult, but her response to adversity was much different than Prophet's. Both were strong, determined and ambitious women, but whereas Prophet lived a very private, lonely and reclusive life, Savage lived a more public and socially active existence, often marching ahead of others in the struggle to combat racism and bigotry in American society and in the modern art world as well: as when she was denied an opportunity to study in Paris in 1922 because program officials feared the reaction of southern students;[28] or when she sought and received a $1,500 grant from the Carnegie Foundation during the early days of the Depression to open her studio classes to any Harlem youngster who wanted to study with her; or when she led other Black artists in their efforts to partipate more fully in the WPA art projects; or when she organized The Vanguard, a club designed to "develop among black artists an awareness of the issues and a solidarity in their struggles"; or when she helped to organize the Harlem Artists Guild of which she became the second president.[29]

Her work does not possess a singular aesthetic personality in the way that Prophet's does, but Prophet did not possess Savage's greater skill at characterization. More importantly, perhaps, she was a gifted and inspirational teacher. Indeed, she discovered or helped to train a number of the best known and most talented Black artists of the past half century, including painters Norman Lewis, Ernest Crichlow, Jacob Lawrence, and sculptor William Artis. Thus her significance in African-American art history is manifold. In addition to the intrinsic merit of her art, she established a tradition of cultural leadership as an educator, administrator, organizer and promoter of Black Art and Black artists that persists today in the work of such women as Samella Lewis and Margaret Burroughs.

Born in Green Cove Springs, Florida, on February 29, 1892, her artistic interests developed at an early age, as did her teaching career and her fighting spirit.[30] Like Prophet, but for different reasons, her parents—Edward and Cornelia Fells—did not encourage her artistic interests. Her father, who was a carpenter and an itinerant Methodist minister with little other than his intense religious faith to sustain him and his large family (including 14 children of which Augusta was the seventh), even opposed and tried to suppress her early enthusiasm for sculpting or modelling clay images of small animals, especially ducks. He thought that they were somehow "graven images" and thus sacrilegious. She finally won him over at the age of fifteen with an "eighteen-inch statue of the Virgin Mary," which she modelled from clay she "begged" from a small pottery factory in West Palm Beach. Thereafter, her life-long struggle to break free of other sorts of narrow-mindedness and to pursue her artistic interests vacillated wildly between glorious moments of triumph and failure, between periods of bouyancy and sombre despair. In West Palm Beach, for instance, she managed to earn nearly $175 at a local fair in which she displayed some of her sculpture, but when she tried to use the money to establish herself as a sculptor, seeking commissions to do busts of prominent Black people in Jacksonville, she lost most of that money and with it her dream of founding an art center there.

Thus she arrived in New York City in 1920 with $4.60. Miraculously, however, she managed to enroll at the Cooper Union, but within three months she had to quit school and go to work. Later she was able to return to the Union and continue her studies on a working scholarship, but she nonetheless spent most of the Renaissance living from hand to mouth, clerking, working in laundries, and ironing. Meanwhile, her determination to persevere and her undeniable talent impressed many prominent people in Harlem and through their help she managed to survive the whirlwind of difficulties that plagued her progress throughout the Renaissance and the Depression. In 1922, for example, friends and well-wishers helped her get commissions to sculpt busts of Dr. Du Bois and Marcus Garvey, splendid portraits in the noble tradition of May Howard Jackson. Similarly, in 1923, the Harlem community rallied to her aide when she was denied a fellowship to study in France, an award she was granted on merit but which the white American selection committee withdrew when it discovered that she was Black. The international controversy that ensued made her a hero of sorts in Harlem, but she was branded a "trouble-maker" downtown. "No one knows," her biographers wrote, "how many times she was excluded from exhibits, galleries, and museums on this score."

And so it went throughout the Renaissance. In 1925, Dr. Du Bois managed to secure a scholarship for her to study at the Royal Academy of Fine Arts in Rome but she could not raise enough money to pay her traveling expenses. And thus she was forced to continue to work in factories and laundries until 1929, when, through the efforts of John E. Nail and Eugene Kinckle Jones of the National Urban League, she was granted a Julius Rosenwald Fellowship to study in Europe for two years.

In Paris she studied under Felix Beuneteaux at La Grande Chaumiere. Later she was able to study with Charles Despiau. Both experiences evidently helped refine, though not control, her considerable technical facility, thereby allowing her to explore a greater range of themes in her art, including an unsuccessful atavistic impulse (e.g., "African Savage" and "The Tom Tom"). Her major works, in addition to her portrait busts, include "The Abstract Madonna," "Envy," "A Woman of Martinique," and "Lift Every Voice," a "Sculptural interpretation of American Negro Music," commissioned by the New York World's Fair in 1939 and destroyed by bulldozers at the end of the Fair because she could not afford to have it cast in metal and the Fair did not offer to do so. Through photographs, however, it became her most famous as well as her last major work. She died on March 27, 1962, nearly two decades after she entered a long period of virtual retirement as an artist and a teacher.

CONCLUSION

In the interim—that is, during the two decades following the end of the Renaissance—May Howard Jackson died (1931), Meta Fuller entered a long period of semi-retirement, Prophet faded from prominence and Laura Wheeler Waring began a valiant struggle to continue her career despite the pain she suffered from a recurring illness. The nascent careers of nearly twenty other Black female artists, initially highlighted by the Harmon Foundation exhibits, flared and then quickly dissolved. Indeed, in many ways, the Great Depression appeared to mark the demise of the "New Negro," especially the "New Negro Woman," who dreamed of becoming a painter or sculptor.

Certainly, among the masses of Black people in America the glow of the Renaissance was quickly dimmed. The Renaissance, in fact, had served to obscure a pattern of urban decay that had been spreading throughout northern Black communities since the late nineteenth century. Meanwhile the shockwaves of economic depression that rocked Wall Street in 1929 greatly exasperated Black America's traditional economic woes during the fabled Renaissance. Indeed, by 1926 thousands of Black people who had found jobs in northern industries before World War I "were on the turf" where they were joined by nearly a million other unemployed Black men and women before the decade was over. Forty-eight thousand of the pre-World War I industrial workers who were fired during the "Jazz Age" were Black women. Moreover, the competition for domestic work intensified during the Depression, thereby threatening the livelihood of nearly a million more Black women and lowering the benefits for all.

In a broad cultural sense, however, the Depression did not so much mark the demise of the Renaissance as it signified a profound shift in emphasis and perception among Black artists. Clearly, the Depression shattered a great many naive racial illusions, but the Renaissance was more than an illusion, more than a fad that suddenly lost its appeal among a fashion-conscious intellectual elite. Nonetheless, it very definitely had its voguish dimension. Fed by the romantic racialism of certain white Americans and the racial chauvinism of many Black Americans, the Renaissance of myth and legend was, simultaneously, abandoned by its panic strickened white patrons and admirers and rejected by Black artists and intellectuals, who had become embittered by the condescending nature of white interests in Black Culture and who had grown disillusioned by the realization that their cultural achievements had not materially improved the life of most Black Americans or significantly altered the nature of race relations in American society.

Over the next several decades, Black women continued to demonstrate their ability to forge a world of their own in which they were able to give greater reign to their need for self-expression based on freely chosen aesthetic preferences. Obviously the work of contemporary Black women artists, like the age in which they live, is too fluid and diverse to summarize here; nor is it possible to predict what directions art by Black women in America will take in the future. It is clear, however, that the role of Black women in the development of Black Art has increased rather than diminished in recent years and that more and more their vision of Black reality will shape the visual imagery of Black life in America. She has also begun to reveal more and more of herself in her art, thereby increasing its complexity and meaning, its power to captivate and inspire—to disturb and challenge—all of us.

NOTES

[1] The most reliable biographical information on Lewis is in James A. Porter's entry on her in *Notable American Women, 1667-1950* (Cambridge, Mass.: Belknap Press, 1971), 397-98. This essay says she was born near Albany, N.Y., in 1845; Eleanor M. Tufts, "Edmonia Lewis, Afro-Indian Neo-Classicist," *Art in America* (July-August, 1974), 64-70, reported that Lewis was born in Greenheigh, Ohio, in 1843.

[2] Marcia Goldberg and W.E. Bigglestone, "A Wedding Gift of 1862," *Oberlin Alumni Magazine* (January-February, 1977), p. 11

[3] Phillip M. Montesano, "The Mystery of the San Jose Statues," *Urban West* (March-April 1968), p. 25.

[4] William H. Gerdts, *The White, Marmorean Flock: Nineteenth Century American Women Neo-Classical Sculptors* (New York: Merchants Press, 1972), p. 1.

[5] *Ibid.*; p. 5.

[6] Cedric Dover, *American Negro Art* (New York: Graphic Society, 1960), p. 28.

[7] Tufts, "Edmonia Lewis," pp. 71-72.

[8] Arna Bontemps, *Free at Last: The Life of Frederick Douglass* (New York: Dodd, Mead & Company, 1971), pp. 278-79; Saunders Redding, *The Lonesome Road: The Story of the Negro's Past in America* (Garden City, New York: Doubleday & Company, Inc., 1958), p. 150.

[9] Samella Lewis, *Art: African American* (New York: Harcourt, Brace Jovanovich, Inc., 1978), p. 52; Alain Locke, *Negro Art: Past and Present* (New York: Arno Press, 1969), p. 30.

[10] *The Crisis*, September, 1927, p. 231.

[11] The enormous obstacles faced by women artists in America are detailed and interpreted in Ann Sutherland Harris and Linda Nochlin, *Women Artists: 1550-1950* (an exhibition catalogue published by Alfred A. Knopf, 1978), pp. 50-67; and in Germaine Greer's article, "Repression of Women Artists: Why are there so few great female painters?" *The Atlantic* (September, 1979), pp. 68-77.

[12] Writing in his *Two Centuries of Black American Art*, p. 78, about the decades between 1930 and 1950, Professor David Driskell made a perceptive point that is as applicable today as it was in Jackson's era: "No viable aesthetic," he said, "was developed among black artists . . . because black leaders and intellectuals did not take the artists nor their art seriously." See also Romare Bearden's article, "The Negro Artist's Dilemma," in *Critique: A Review of Contemporary Art*, edited by David Lashak (November, 1946), pp. 16-22.

[13] Dover, *American Negro Art*, p. 29; James A. Porter, *Modern Negro Art* (New York: Arno Press and the New York Times, 1969, 1942), pp. 92-93; The *Crisis*, July 1916, p. 115.

[14] Benjamin Brawley, "Meta Warrick Fuller," *The Southern Workman* (January, 1918), pp. 25-26.

[15] Samella Lewis, *Art: African American*, p. 78; *The Crisis*, June, 1912, p. 67.

[16] Born in Monrovia, Liberia (1872), Dr. Fuller was a neuropathologist, who became "the first Black psychiatrist in the world"; Velma J. Hoover, "Meta Vaux Warrick Fuller: Her Life and Art," *Negro History Bulletin* (March/April, 1977), p. 679.

[17] Lewis, *Art: African American*, p. 55.

[18] Porter, *Modern Negro Art*, p. 77.

[19] Elsa Honig Fine, *The Afro-American Artist: A Search for Identity* (New York: Hacker Art Books, 1982), p. 75.

[20] Hoover, "Meta Vaux Warrick Fuller," p. 679.

[21] *Ibid.*

[22] Lowery Sims, "19th Century Black Women Artists," *Easy: The Black Arts Magazine* (January, 1978), p. 32, and Porter, *Modern Negro Art*, pp. 78-79; also lists Pauline Powell of Oakland, California, and Fannie Hicks of Louisville, Kentucky, as gifted painters during this era.

[23] Alain Locke, *The Negro in Art: A Pictorial Record of the Negro Artist and of the Negro Theme in Art* (New York: Harker Art Books, Inc., 1940, 1969, 1971), pp. 9-10. See also his discussion of this topic in *Negro Art: Past and Present*, Chapter 6.

[24] *The Crisis*, February, 1917, p. 189.

[25] Leslie King Hammond, "Prophet, Nancy Elizabeth," in the exhibition catalogue, *Four From Providence: Black Artists in the Rhode Island Social Landscape* (Providence, R.I.: a joint project of Rhode Island College and The Rhode Island Black Heritage Society, 1978), p. 9.

[26] Countee Cullen, "Elizabeth Prophet: Sculptress," *Opportunity* (July, 1930), p. 205.

[27] Dover, *American Negro Art*, p. 56.

[28] *Opportunity*, June, 1923, p. 25.

[29] Romare Bearden and Harry Henderson, *Six Black Masters of American Art* (Garden City, New York: Doubleday & Company, Inc. 1972), pp. 95-96.

[30] *Ibid.*, pp. 76-77.

ZORA NEALE HURSTON AND ALICE WALKER:
A Spiritual Kinship

Alma S. Freeman

Zora Neale Hurston, born in Florida near the turn of the twentieth century, was, for thirty years, the most prolific Black woman writer in the United States. Alice Walker, born in Georgia some forty years later, is one of the most prolific Black women writers in America today. Not only do both women stand as exemplary representatives of the achievement of the American Black woman as writer, but their fiction reveals a strong spiritual kinship. Though separated by place and by time, these two Black women writers, inevitably it seems, were drawn together, and Zora Hurston became an important influence in Alice Walker's life.

Zora Neale Hurston died in 1960. Alice Walker was not to encounter Zora Hurston and her work until the late 1960's. At this time, Alice was working with the Civil Rights Movement and collecting folklore stories in Mississippi. She was also "writing a story that required accurate material on voodoo practices among rural southern Blacks of the thirties," and she was finding the available resources, written primarily by "white, racist anthropologists and folklorists of the period," disappointing and insulting.[1] Then she discovered *Mules and Men*, Zora Hurston's book recounting her folklore expeditions in the South and relating the stories she had found there. Direct influences from *Mules and Men* can be seen in Alice Walker's short story "The Revenge of Hannah Kemhuss,"[2] a story obviously based on an incident that happened to Alice's mother in the thirties during the Depression.[3] Like Alice's mother, Hannah in the story receives a box of clothes from a relative who lives in the North. She wears one of the dresses from the box into town to get food which is being distributed by the Red Cross. When Hannah presents her voucher, she is shamed and humiliated by a young white woman who refuses to give her food because she is so finely dressed. Unlike Alice's mother, who got the food she needed from a neighbor, Hannah endures extreme suffering as a result of the incident. Her husband deserts her; one by one her children starve to death, and she gradually becomes a broken woman, mutilated both in spirit and body. Finally, when she is awaiting death, Hannah, driven by years of pain and remorse, visits the local rootworker to seek revenge on "the little moppet." Into this story-line, Alice Walker weaves material on voodoo practices from Zora Hurston's book of folklore. For instance, the central character of the story, an apprentice in the rootworking trade, quotes a "curse prayer" used and taught by rootworkers, and she indicates that she "recited it straight from Zora Neale Hurston's book, *Mules and Men*," while engaging in a voodoo ritual with Hannah Kemhuss. Moreover, Alice Walker dedicates the story "In grateful memory of Zora Neale Hurston."[4]

In *Mules and Men*, Alice Walker not only found the authentic folklore material that she needed for her own writing, but she also perceived a spiritual sister to whom she became intensely devoted. The following statements recorded in the Foreword of Robert Hemenway's biography of Zora Neale Hurston reflect

the essence of Alice's commitment to Zora Hurston and her work:

Condemned to a deserted island for life, with an allotment of ten books to see me through, I would choose, unhesitatingly, two of Zora's: *Mules and Men*, because I would need to be able to pass on to younger generations the life of American blacks as legend and myth, and *Their Eyes Were Watching God*, because I would want to enjoy myself while identifying with the black heroine, Janie Crawford, as she acted out many roles in a variety of settings, and functioned (with spectacular results!) in romantic and sensual love. There is no other book more important to me than this one.[5]

By 1979, Alice Walker had read *Their Eyes Were Watching God* about eleven times, and she declared, "It speaks to me as no other novel, past or present, has ever done...There is enough self-love in that one book–love of community, culture, traditions–to restore a world. Or create a new one."[6] Alice Walker was so inspired by Hurston's *Their Eyes Were Watching God* that she wrote the following poem entitled "Janie Crawford" which appears in her book of poems *Good Night Willie Lee, I'll See You in the Morning*:

I love the way Janie Crawford
left her husbands the one who wanted
to change her into a mule
and the other who tried to interest her
in becoming a queen
a woman unless she submits is neither a mule
nor a queen
though like a mule she may suffer
and like a queen pace
the floor[7]

Zora Neale Hurston exerted such a strong influence in Alice Walker's life that Alice set out to bring back into public attention the work, for many years out of print, of the woman whom she had grown to admire, respect, and revere–a sister artist who "followed her own road, believed in her gods, pursued her own dreams, and refused to separate herself from the 'common' people."[8] Feeling a strong spiritual kinship with her sister writer, Alice Walker, posing as a niece, traveled to Fort Pierce, Florida, found the segregated cemetery there, and placed a tombstone, proclaiming "a genius of the South," to honor Zora Hurston's unmarked grave. Another of Alice Walker's lasting tributes to Zora Neale Hurston is embodied in *I Love Myself When I Am Laughing...: A Zora Neale Hurston Reader* which Alice edited and dedicated to "Zora Neale Hurston...wherever she is now in the universe with the good wishes and love of all those who have glimpsed her heart through her work."[9] Alice Walker is one who has truly glimpsed the heart of Zora Neale Hurston. From her first short story collection *In Love and Trouble: Stories of Black Women* to her latest novel *The Color Purple*, Ms. Walker, in her own fiction, is keeping alive, extending, and expanding the vital literary tradition that Zora Neale Hurston established in *Their Eyes Were Watching God*—a tradition which

Alma S. Freeman is Professor of English and Acting Dean of University College at Alabama State University in Montgomery, Alabama.

embodies a strong dedication to unveiling the *soul* of the Black woman.

A comparison of three of Alice Walker's Black women characters with Zora Neale Hurston's Janie Crawford underscores the bond of kinship that exists between Zora's and Alice's exploration of the experiences of the Black woman in the United States. Such a comparison also reveals the author's powerful and poignant portrayal of what it feels like, inside, to be a Black woman struggling to become an autonomous, well-integrated "self" in a society in which her options are severely limited. These four women begin their lives imprisoned by roles and by images and notions of womanhood that conflict directly with their history and with their own vigorous concept of themselves as Black women. Initially, for instance, they find themselves locked in loveless, unfulfilling marriages from which they appear to have no escape and which stifle their dreams, their creativity, and their desire for growth and freedom. Such a situation engenders in these characters a tension that forces them to make personal choices concerning their development as whole human beings. Fighting against both racial and sexual oppression, they choose either a life of continued subservience, anguish, and pain, or they opt to become growing, emergent women who seek to take control of their own lives.

In Hurston's *Their Eyes Were Watching God*,[10] the sixteen-year-old Janie Crawford, against her own adamant protests, is forced, by her relentless grandmother, to marry Logan Killicks, a hard-working man who is much older than Janie but who owns property and has a degree of status in the comnuinity. The grandmother's motivation is clear. She wants to protect Janie from being sexually exploited, as she and Janie's mother have been, by men both Black and white. She also wants to see the dreams she had for herself and for her own daughter realized. Janie's grandmother has internalized the values of white society, which define "what a woman oughta be and do." Denied the opportunity to fulfill the woman's traditional role, she wants this for Janie–the security, protection, respectability, and the material possessions that a good provider like Logan Killicks can give. Dependent on whites all of her life for mere survival, the grandmother wishes to break this dependency for Janie. But she simply transfers it to the man she forces Janie to marry and sets in motion another cycle of dependency for Janie. Janie soon becomes convinced that Logan cannot give her the sweetness, beauty, and adventure she desires in marriage. And she leaves him for Jody Starks, a fast-talking, ambitious man who promises her love and excitement. Jody carries Janie to a newly founded all-Black community in Florida where he becomes a "big voice" and where he places her on a "pedestal," and, like Logan, treats her as property. Janie finds fulfillment only when Jody dies and she leaves the town with Tea Cake, a younger man and a free spirit, who loves and respects her for the person that she is.

Roselily, the central character of the first story in Alice Walker's collection *In Love and Trouble*,[11] faces a kind of entrapment similar to Janie's. Young, Black, and poor, living in the rural South, the mother of four children, all by a different man, Roselily marries a Muslim man in order to escape a brutal life of labor in a sewing plant. She stands during her marriage ceremony weighed down with images of quicksand, ropes, chains, and handcuffs. As Janie sees her blossoming, fruit-bearing pear tree—her symbol of life, fertility, and freedom—

"desecrated" by her grandmother, so Roselily thinks of flowers choked to death; she feels like a rat cornered. Even the veil she wears reminds her of a kind of servitude that she longs to be free of. It is the same kind to which Janie Crawford is subjected. All Logan wants Janie to be is his maid, his cook, and a laborer on his farm; all Jody wants her to be is "Mrs. Mayor Starks" whose "place is in de home" and the humble clerk in his store. The religion of the man whom Roselily is marrying requires, like Jody demands of Janie, that she wear her hair covered, that she separate herself from the men, and that she take her place in the home. But this is Roselily's only chance to be respectable, to achieve status and prestige, and to provide a better life for her children. Despite her misgivings, her feelings of entrapment, she marries the man, and she will go to live in Chicago, have more children regardless of her wishes, and *endure.*

Alice Walker's Myrna in "Really, *Doesn't* Crime Pay?",[12] another story from *In Love and Trouble*, also endures, despite her aspirations to be a writer. Like Janie during her marriage to Jody, Myrna is placed on a pedestal by her hardworking husband, Ruel. And she aspires to be the perfect wife and lady—keeping house, cooking meals, painting her face, polishing her fingernails, visiting the shopping center daily buying hats she would not dream of wearing, dresses already headed for the Goodwill, and shoes that will mold and mildew in her closet. Then she meets Mordecai Rich who praises her for her intelligence and creativity. Mordecai is an aspiring writer, "a vagabond, scribbling down impressions of the South, from no solid place, going to none." As Jody Starks and Tea Cake do for Janie, Mordecai promises Myrna love and excitement. She gives herself to him completely. Not only do they engage in passionate love-making, but Myrna shares with Mordecai her interest in writing and the volumes of stories that she has drafted but has kept hidden from Ruel. Unlike Janie, however, Myrna does not leave with Mordecai, instead, one day, he suddenly disappears. And later, Myrna reads one of her stories in a magazine, "filled out and switched about," authored by Mordecai Rich. Thereafter, she suffers a nervous breakdown, attempts to kill Ruel with a chain saw, and spends some time in a mental institution.

Unlike Roselily, Myrna does, in her own way, fight against her entrapment. Myrna's most important act of rebellion, her only sense of freedom, rests in taking the Pill. Ruel desperately wants a child, and he struggles very hard to make Myrna conceive. She consents to his every wish. She even visits the doctor at Ruel's request to see about "speeding up the conception of the child." But she never tells Ruel that she "religiously" takes the Pill, and this engenders in her a feeling of triumph over him, a sense of independent choice. At the end of the story, Myrna exults in her deceptively won freedom:

> It is the only spot of humor in my entire day, when I am gulping that little yellow tablet and washing it down with soda pop or tea. ...When he is quite, quite tired of me I will tell him how long I've relied on the security of the Pill.[13]

Meridian Hill, the central character of Alice Walker's novel *Meridian*,[14] begins her life, like Janie, Roselily, and Myrna, as a woman with few choices. Meridian, however, bears a special relationship to Janie Crawford because, unlike Roselily and Myrna, Janie and Meridian become women who make options for themselves, who finally choose a life of their own. In Janie's story and in Meridian's story, we see Black women developing a consciousness, an awareness, which allows them to arrive at a deepened sense of self and to grow stronger by speaking from and for that self. They thus are able to take control of their own destiny. Both Janie and Meridian then are involved in a quest for identity. Each woman struggles to affirm the "self" which she knows exists beneath the false images imposed upon her because she is Black and female. Janie's search is deeply personal, her vision intensely romantic. She seeks and finally finds a sense of fulfillment through fusion with another "self." Meridian, however, possesses a deeply social and moral vision. Her story emanates from a broader social and political context than does Janie's. As Mary Helen Washington notes, Meridian "evolves from a woman trapped by racial and sexual oppression to revolutionary figure, effecting action and strategy to bring freedom to herself and other poor disenfranchised Blacks in the South."[15]

Against her wishes, the teenaged Meridian, like the sixteen-year-old Janie, is forced into an unfulfilling marriage. Meridian becomes pregnant; she reluctantly marries Eddie, the father of her child, and makes an effort at being a "proper" wife and mother. Finding this role confining and intolerable, she harbors thoughts of killing her child; then she contemplates suicide rather than harm her own baby. Finally, her marriage ends, and she gives her child away believing she is saving both lives. From this point, Meridian moves through college and the Civil Rights Movement into a revolutionary group where she discovers that she cannot kill for the Revolution. Her spirit broken, she begins a sort of physical degeneration. She loses her hair, dons a cap and dungarees, lives alone in small rooms in small southern towns trying to find her own health while she helps the Black people in these towns find power. She is followed by Truman Held, a man whom she sincerely loves but whom she must finally reject in an effort to get a hold of her own life.

Like Janie Crawford, Meridian Hill leaves the men in her life to search for fulfillment as a human being. While Janie abandons Logan and the memory of Jody, journeys to the horizon with Tea Cake, and finds a satisfying love, Meridian leaves Eddie and Truman, turns inward, and travels back through many generations to free herself. She identifies with her mother's great-grandmother, a slave but also an artist who became famous and bought her freedom by painting lasting decorations on barns. She remembers her father's grandmother, the mystical and high-spirited Feather Mae, and she, like Feather Mae, experiences an ecstatic communion with the past atop the Sacred Serpent, an Indian burial mound. At college Meridian learns about the slave woman and story-teller Louvinie and the Sojourner. She also expresses deep sensitivity for her own mother who, through suffering and sacrifice, fulfilled her dreams of becoming a school teacher. Such an anchor in her ancestral past gives Meridian a sense of strength and continuity, a knowledge of herself as a creative human being, which helps to fortify and to free her from a need for dependence on another person in her quest for identity.

Through the total range of her experiences, Meridian creates a new self—an androgynous self; she is transformed, as sym-bolized by the wasting illness from which she recovers and returns "to the world cleansed of sickness." Meridian's androgynous quality, expressed in physically androgynous features, is communicated through a passage near the end of the novel when she visits a prison and the inmates ask, "Who was that person? That man/woman person with a shaved part in close-cut hair? A man's blunt face and thighs, a woman's breast?[16] Here, Meridian appears as a symbol of one who has creatively united the masculine and feminine opposites and achieved a state of unconscious wholeness. As she leaves Truman for the last time, he recognizes the change in her:

> What he *felt* was that something in her was exactly the same as she had always been and as he had, finally, succeeded in knowing her. That was the part he might now sense but could not see. He would never see "his" Meridian again. The new part had grown out of the old, though, and that was reassuring. This part of her, new, sure and ready, even eager, for the world, he knew he must meet again and recognize for its true value at some future time.[17]

Janie Crawford does not reach the androgynous state that Meridian achieves. Janie longs for it, as symbolized by her mystical experience of the pear tree, an androgynous symbol with roots sinking into the feminine earth and branches stretching forth to the masculine sky. For Janie, the tree represents a loving harmony between the masculine and feminine forces of nature, a union which she desires to attain. Throughout her story, she seeks this unity, this wholeness. But she relies first on Logan and Jody and then on Tea Cake rather than searching within herself to realize it. Finally, she kills Tea Cake in self-defense and thereby frees herself. Through this symbolic act, Janie breaks the cycle of dependency set in motion by her grandmother. Janie ends her story alone, settling down in her own private room, at peace with herself, wrapped in loving memories of Tea Cake. But her experience of happiness is still tied to him. Significantly neither Zora nor Alice endorses isolation as a way of life, but each of their protagonists finds it necessary to be alone in order to achieve insight and growth. At the end of the novel, Janie, alone in her room, is prepared to embark upon the inward voyage that Meridian undertakes. We might even say that Meridian Hill finishes the struggle that Janie Crawford begins, for the end of *Their Eyes Were Watching God* marks the beginning of another story, a story which Alice Walker takes up and completes in Meridian. Thus, Alice Walker further reveals her strong dedication to accomplishing the task to which Zora Neale Hurston, her sister writer, had earlier devoted her creative energy.

"A people must define itself" writes Ralph Ellison in *Shadow and Act.*[18] It is thus the duty of the American Black woman to dispel the myths and burst the stereotypes surrounding her character, personality, and experience. Zora Neale Hurston and Alice Walker are two of the several Black women writers who have sought to fulfill this task. In their literary works, we hear the Black woman speak. She speaks in a loud voice—with power and with fervor, but always with compassion and grace—as she defines, affirms, and preserves in literature the essential humanity of her own group.

NOTES

[1]Robert Hemenway, *Zora Neale Hurston: A Literary Biography* (Urbana, Illinois: University of Illinois Press, 1977), p. xi.

[2]Alice Walker, *In Love and Trouble: Stories of Black Women* (New York: Harcourt, Brace, Jovanovich, 1973), pp. 60-80.

[3]This story is recorded in Alice Walker's essay "The Black Writer and the Southern Experience," *New South*, 25 (Fall, 1970), pp. 23-24.

[4]Walker, *In Love and Trouble*, pp. 72, 60.

[5]Hemenway, p. xiii.

[6]Alice Walker, ed., *I Love Myself When I'm Laughing . . . : A Zora Neale Hurston Reader* (Old Westbury, New York: The Feminist Press, 1979), p. 2.

[7]Alice Walker, *Good Night Willie Lee, I'll See You in the Morning* (New York: Dial Press, 1979), p. 18.

[8]Hemenway, pp. xvii-xviii.

[9]Walker, *I Love Myself When I'm Laughing*, p. 4.

[10]Zora Neale Hurston, *Their Eyes Were Watching God* (Greenwich, Conn.: Fawcett, 1969).

[11]Walker, *In Love and Trouble*, pp. 3-9. For the interpretation of "Roselily" which follows, see Mary Helen Washington's "An Essay on Alice Walker" in *Sturdy Black Bridges: Visions of Black Women in Literature*, eds. Roseann Bell, Bettye Parker, and Beverly Guy-Sheftall (Garden City, New York: Anchor Press/Doubleday, 1979), pp. 139-140.

[12]*Ibid.*, pp. 10-23

[13]*Ibid.*, p. 23

[14]Alice Walker, *Meridian* (New York: Pocket Books, 1977).

[15]Washington, "An Essay on Alice Walker," p. 148.

[16]Walker, *Meridian*, p. 211.

[17]*Ibid.*, p. 219

[18]Ralph Ellison, *Shadow and Act* (New York: New American Library, 1964), p. 60.

Gwendolyn Brooks's *A Street in Bronzeville*, The Harlem Renaissance and the Mythologies of Black Women

Gary Smith

When Gwendolyn Brooks published her first collection of poetry *A Street in Bronzeville* (1945) with Harper and Brothers, she already enjoyed a substantial reputation in the literary circles of Chicago. Nearly a decade earlier, her mother Keziah Brooks, had arranged meetings between her daughter and James Weldon Johnson and Langston Hughes, two of the most distinguished Black writers of America's Harlem Renaissance. Determined to mold Gwendolyn into a *lady Paul Laurence Dunbar*, Mrs. Brooks proffered poems for the famous writers to read. While Johnson's advice to the young poet was abrupt, eventually he exerted an incisive influence on her later work. In a letter and a marginal note included on the returned poems, addressed to her on 30 August 1937, Johnson praised Brooks's obvious talent and pointed her in the direction of Modernist poetry:

> My dear Miss Brooks: I have read the poems you sent me last. Of them I especially liked *Reunion* and *Myself*. *Reunion* is very good, and *Myself* is good. You should, by all means, continue you[r] study and work. I shall always be glad to give you any assistance that I can. Sincerely yours. James Weldon Johnson.
>
> . . .
>
> Dear Miss Brooks — You have an unquestionable talent and feeling for poetry. Continue to write — at the same time, study carefully the work of the best modern poets — not to imitate them, but to help cultivate the highest possible standards of self-criticism. Sincerely, James Weldon Johnson.[1]

Of course, the irony in Johnson's advice, addressed as it is to the future *lady* Dunbar, is that he actually began his own career by conspicuously imitating Dunbar's dialect poems, *Lyrics of a Lowly Life*; yet he encourages Brooks to study the work of the "best Modern poets." He was, perhaps, reacting to the latent elements of modernism already found in her poetry; but the effect was to turn Brooks momentarily away

455

from the Black aesthetic of Hughes's *Weary Blues* (1926) and Countee
Cullen's *Color* (1925) toward the Modernist aesthetics of T. S. Eliot, Ezra
Pound, and e. e. cummings. It is interesting to note, however, that, even
though Johnson's second letter admonishes Brooks to study the Modernist poets, he cautions her "not to imitate them," but to read them
with the intent of cultivating the "highest possible standards of self-
criticism." Flattered by the older poet's attention and advice, Brooks
embarked upon a serious attempt to absorb as much Modernist poetry
as she could carry from the public library.

If Johnson played the part of literary mentor, Brooks's relationship
with Hughes was more personal, warmer, and longer lasting. She was
already on familiar terms with *Weary Blues*, so their first meeting was
particularly inspirational. Brooks showed Hughes a packet of her poems, and he praised her talent and encouraged her to continue to write.
Years later, after Brooks's reputation was firmly established by a Pulitzer
Prize for *Annie Allen* (1949), her relationship with Hughes blossomed
into mutual admiration. Hughes dedicated his collection of short stories,
Something in Common (1933), to her. While Hughes's poetic style had an
immeasurable influence on Brooks's poetry, she also respected his personal values and lifestyle. As she noted in her autobiography, Hughes
was her idol:

> Langston Hughes! The words and deeds of Langston Hughes were
> rooted in kindness, and in pride. His point of departure was always a clear
> pride in his race. Race pride may be craft, art, or a music that combines the
> best of jazz and hymn. Langston frolicked and chanted to the measure of
> his own race-reverence.
>
> He was an easy man. You could rest in his company. No one possessed a
> more serious understanding of life's immensities. No one was firmer in
> recognition of the horrors man imposes upon man, in hardy insistence on
> reckonings. But when those who knew him remember him the memory
> inevitably will include laughter of an unusually warm and tender kind. The
> wise man, he knew, will take some juice out of this one life that is his gift.
>
> Mightily did he use the street. He found its multiple heart, its tastes,
> smells, alarms, formulas, flowers, garbage and convulsions. He brought
> them all to his table-top. He crushed them to a writing paste. He himself
> became the pen. (*Report,* pp. 70–71)

In other words, while Johnson encouraged Brooks to find "standards
for self-criticism" in Modernism, Hughes underscored the value of cultivating the ground upon which she stood. In Hughes, in both the poet
and man, Brooks found standards for living: he was a model of witty
candor and friendly unpretentiousness and, most importantly, a literary

success. Hughes convinced Brooks that a Black poet need not travel outside the realm of his own experiences to create a poetic vision and write successful poetry. Unlike the Modernist Eliot who gathered much of his poetic material from the drawingrooms and salons of London, Hughes found his material in the coldwater flats and backstreets of Harlem. And Brooks, as is self-evident in nearly all her poetry, learned Hughes's example by heart.

II

The critical reception of *A Street in Bronzeville* contained, in embryo, many of the central issues in the scholarly debate that continues to engage Brooks's poetry. As in the following quotation from *The New York Times Book Review*, most reviewers were able to recognize Brooks's versatility and craft as a poet:

> If the idiom is colloquial, the language is universal. Brooks commands both the colloquial and more austere rhythms. She can vary manner and tone. In form, she demonstrates a wide range: quatrains, free verse, ballads, and sonnets — all appropriately controlled. The longer line suits her better than the short, but she is not verbose. In some of the sonnets, she uses an abruptness of address that is highly individual.[2]

Yet, while noting her stylistic successes, not many critics fully understood her achievement in her first book. This difficulty was not only characteristic of critics who examined the formal aspects of prosody in her work, but also of critics who addressed themselves to the social realism in her poetry. Moreover, what Brooks gained at the hands of critics who focused on her technique, she lost to critics who chose to emphasize the exotic, Negro features of the book, as the following quote illustrates:

> *A Street in Bronzeville* ranges from blues ballads and funeral chants to verse in high humor. With both clarity and insight, it mirrors the impressions of life in an urban Negro community. The best poem is "The Sundays of Satin-Legs Smith," a poignant and hour-by-hour page out of a zoot-suiter's life. A subtle change of pace proves Brooks' facility in a variety of poetic forms.[3]

The poems in *A Street in Bronzeville* actually served notice that Brooks had learned her craft well enough to combine successfully themes and styles from both the Harlem Renaissance and Modernist poetry. She even achieves some of her more interesting effects in the book by parodying the two traditions. She juggles the pessimism of Modernist poetry with the general optimism of the Harlem Renaissance. Three of her more notable achievements, "kitchenette building," "the mother," and "Sundays of Satin-Legs Smith," are parodic challenges to T. S. Eliot's dispirited anti-hero J. Alfred Prufrock. "[K]itchenette building"[4] begins with Eliot-like emphasis on the dry infertility of modern life: "We are things of dry hours and the involuntary plan." The poem concludes with the humored optimism that "Since Number 5 is out of the bathroom / we think of lukewarm water, we hope to get in it." Another example is the alienated, seemingly disaffected narrator of "the mother" (*Street*, p. 4) who laments the loss of her children but with the resurgent, hopeful voice that closes the poem: "Believe me, I loved you all." Finally a comparison could be made between the elaborate, self-assertive manner with which Satin-legs Smith dresses himself for his largely purposeless Sunday outing and the tentative efforts of his counterpart, J. Alfred Prufrock.

Because of the affinities *A Street in Bronzeville* shares with Modernist poetry and the Harlem Renaissance, Brooks was initiated not only into the vanguard of American literature, but also into what had been the inner circle of Harlem writers. Two of the Renaissance's leading poets, Claude McKay and Countee Cullen, addressed letters to her to mark the publication of *A Street in Bronzeville*. McKay welcomed her into a dubious but potentially rewarding career:

> I want to congratulate you again on the publication of 'A Street in Bronzeville' [sic] and welcome you among the band of hard working poets who do have something to say. It is a pretty rough road we have to travel, but I suppose much compensation is derived from the joy of being able to sing. Yours sincerely, Claude McKay. (October 10, 1945.) (*Report*, p. 201)

Cullen pinpointed her dual place in American literature:

> I have just finished reading 'A Street in Bronzeville' [sic] and want you to know that I enjoyed it thoroughly. There can be no doubt that you are a poet, a good one, with every indication of becoming a better. I am glad to be able to say 'welcome' to you to that too small group of Negro poets, and to the larger group of American ones. No one can deny you your place there. (August 24, 1945.) (*Report*, p. 201)

The immediate interest in these letters is how both poets touch upon the nerve ends of the critical debate that surrounded *A Street in Bronzeville*. For McKay, while Brooks has "something to say," she can also "sing"; and for Cullen, she belongs not only to the minority of Negro poets, but also to the majority of American ones. Nonetheless, the critical question for both poets might well have been Brooks's relationship to the Harlem Renaissance. What had she absorbed of the important tenets of the Black aesthetic as expressed during the New Negro Movement? And how had she addressed herself, as a poet, to the literary movement's assertion of the folk and African culture, and its promotion of the arts as the agent to define racial integrity and to fuse racial harmony?[5]

Aside from its historical importance, the Harlem Renaissance — as a literary movement — is rather difficult to define. There is, for example, no fixed or generally agreed upon date or event that serves as a point of origin for the movement. One might easily assign this date to the publication of McKay's poems *Harlem Shadows* (1922), Alaine Locke's anthology *The New Negro* (1925), or Cullen's anthology *Caroling Dusk* (1927). Likewise, the general description of the movement as a Harlem Renaissance is often questioned, since most of the major writers, with the notable exceptions of Hughes and Cullen, actually did not live and work in Harlem. Finally, many of the themes and literary conventions defy definition in terms of what was and what was not a New Negro poet. Nonetheless, there was a common ground of purpose and meaning in the works of the individual writers that permits a broad definition of the spirit and intent of the Harlem Renaissance. Indeed, the New Negro poets expressed a deep pride in being Black; they found reasons for this pride in ethnic identity and heritage; and they shared a common faith in the fine arts as a means of defining and reinforcing racial pride. But in the literal expression of these artistic impulses, the poets were either romantics or realists and, quite often within a single poem, both. The realistic impulse, as defined best in the poems of McKay's *Harlem Shadows*, was a sober reflection upon Blacks as second class citizens, segregated from the mainstream of American socio-economic life, and largely unable to realize the wealth and opportunity that America promised. The romantic impulse, on the other hand, as defined in the poems of Sterling Browns's *Southern Road* (1932), often found these unrealized dreams in the collective strength and will of the folk masses. In comparing the poems in *A Street in Bronzeville* with various poems from the Renaissance, it becomes apparent that Brooks agrees, for the most part, with their prescriptions for the New Negro. Yet the unique contributions she brings to bear upon this tradition are extensive: 1) the biting ironies of intraracial discrimination, 2) the devaluation of love in heterosexual relationships between Blacks, and 3) the primacy of suffering in the lives of poor Black women.

III

The first clue that *A Street in Bronzeville* was, at the time of its publication, unlike any other book of poems by a Black American is its insistent emphasis on demystifying romantic love between Black men and women. The "old marrieds" (*Street*, p. 1), the first couple encountered on the walking tour of Bronzeville, are nothing like the youthful archetype that the Renaissance poets often portrayed:

> But in the crowding darkness not a word did they say.
> Though the pretty-coated birds had piped so lightly all the day.
> And he had seen the lovers in the little side-streets.
> And she had heard the morning stories clogged with sweets.
> It was quite a time for loving. It was midnight. It was May.
> But in the crowding darkness not a word did they say.

In this short, introductory poem, Brooks, in a manner reminiscent of Eliot's alienated *Waste Land* characters, looks not toward a glorified African past or limitless future, but rather at a stifled present. Her old lovers ponder not an image of their racial past or some symbolized possibility of self-renewal, but rather the overwhelming question of what to do in the here-and-now. Moreover, their world, circumscribed by the incantatory line that opens and closes the poem, "But in the crowding darkness not a word did they say," is one that is distinctly at odds with their lives. They move timidly through the crowded darkness of their neighborhood largely ignorant of the season, "May," the lateness of the hour, "midnight," and a particular *raison d'etre*, "a time for loving." Their attention, we infer, centers upon the implicit need to escape any peril that might consume what remains of their lives. The tempered optimism in the poem, as the title indicates, is the fact that they are "old-marrieds": a social designation that suggests the longevity of their lives and the solidity of their marital bond in what is, otherwise, an ephemeral world of change. Indeed, as the prefatory poem in *A Street in Bronzeville*, the "old marrieds," on the whole, debunks one of the prevalent motifs of Harlem Renaissance poetry: its general optimism about the future.

As much as the Harlem Renaissance was noted for its optimism, an important corollary motif was that of ethnic or racial pride. This pride — often thought a reaction to the minstrel stereotypes in the Dunbar tradition — usually focused with romantic idealization upon the Black woman. A casual streetwalker in Hughes's poem, "When Sue Wears Red,"[6] for example, is magically transformed into an Egyptian queen:

> When Susanna Jones wears red
> Her face is like an ancient cameo
> Turned brown by the ages.

> Come with a blast of trumpets,
>   Jesus!
>
> When Susanna Jones wears red
> A queen from some time-dead Egyptian night
> Walks once again.

Similarly, six of the first seven poems in Cullen's first published work, *Color* (1925), celebrate the romanticized virtues of Black women. The second poem in the volume, "A Song of Praise,"[7] is particularly note-worthy in its treatment of the theme:

> You have not heard my love's dark throat,
>   Slow-fluting like a reed,
> Release the perfect golden note
>   She caged there for my need.
> Her walk is like the replica
>   Of some barbaric dance
> Wherein the soul of Africa
>   Is winged with arrogance.

In the same manner, McKay's sonnet, "The Harlem Dancer,"[8] extolls the misunderstood virtue of a cabaret dancer:

> Applauding youths laughed with young prostitutes
> And watched her perfect, half-clothed body sway;
> Her voice was like the sound of blended flutes
> Blown by black players upon a picnic day.
> She sang and danced on gracefully and calm,
> The light gauze hanging loose about her form;
> To me she seemed a proudly-swaying palm
> Grown lovelier for passing through a storm.

In *A Street in Bronzeville*, this romantic impulse for idealizing the Black woman runs headlong into the biting ironies of intraracial discrimination.[9] In poem after poem in *A Street in Bronzeville*, within the well-observed caste lines of skin color, the consequences of dark pigmentation are revealed in drastic terms. One of the more popular of these poems, "The Ballad of Chocolate Mabbie" (*Street*, p. 12), explores the tragic ordeal of Mabbie, the Black female heroine, who is victimized by her dark skin and her "saucily bold" lover, Willie Boone:

> It was Mabbie without the grammar school gates.
> And Mabbie was all of seven.
> And Mabbie was cut from a chocolate bar.
> And Mabbie thought life was heaven.

Mabbie's life, of course, is one of unrelieved monotony; her social contacts are limited to those who, like her, are dark skinned, rather than "lemon-hued" or light skinned. But as Brooks makes clear, the larger tragedy of Mabbie's life is the human potential that is squandered:

> Oh, warm is the waiting for joys, my dears!
> And it cannot be too long.
> O, pity the little poor chocolate lips
> That carry the bubble of song!

But if Mabbie is Brooks's parodic victim of romantic love, her counterpart in "Ballad of Pearl May Lee" (*Street*, pp. 42–45) realizes a measure of sweet revenge. In outline, Brooks's poem is reminiscent of Cullen's *The Ballad of the Brown Girl* (1927).[10] There are, however, several important differences. The first is the poem's narrative structure: Pearl May Lee is betrayed in her love for a Black man who "couldn't abide dark meat," who subsequently makes love to a white girl and is lynched for his crime of passion, whereas Cullen's "Brown Girl" is betrayed in her love for a white man, Lord Thomas, who violates explicit social taboo by marrying her rather than Fair London, a white girl. Moreover, Cullen's poem, "a ballad retold," is traditional in its approach to the ballad form:

> Oh, this is the tale the grandams tell
> In the land where the grass is blue,
> And some there are who say 'tis false,
> And some that hold it true.

Brooks's ballad, on the other hand, dispenses with the rhetorical invocation of the traditional ballad and begins *in medias res*:

> Then off they took you, off to the jail,
> A hundred hooting after.
> And you should have heard me at my house.
> I cut my lungs with my laughter,
>   Laughter,
>   Laughter.
> I cut my lungs with my laughter.

This mocking tone is sustained throughout the poem, even as Sammy, Pearl May Lee's lover, is lynched:

> You paid for your dinner, Sammy boy,
> And you didn't pay with money.
> You paid with your hide and my heart, Sammy
> boy,

> For your taste of pink and white honey,
>> Honey,
>> Honey,
> For your taste of pink and white honey.

Here, one possible motif in the poem is the price that Pearl May Lee pays for her measure of sweet revenge: the diminution of her own capacity to express love and compassion for another — however ill-fated — human being. But the element of realism that Brooks injects into her ballad by showing Pearl May Lee's mocking detachment from her lover's fate is a conscious effort to devalue the romantic idealization of Black love. Furthermore, Pearl May Lee's macabre humor undermines the racial pride and harmony that was an important tenet in the Renaissance prescription for the New Negro. And, lastly, Pearl May Lee's predicament belies the social myth of the Black woman as *objective correlative* of the Renaissance's romanticism.

In another poem that uses the Blues tradition as its thematic structure, Brooks takes the reader backstage, inside the dressing room of Mame, "The Queen of the Blues" (*Street*, pp. 38–41). As the central figure in the poem, Mame is similar to Sterling Brown's Ma Rainey, "Mother of the Blues":[11]

> When Ma Rainey
> Comes to town,
> Folks from anyplace
> Miles aroun'
> From Cape Girardeau,
> Poplar Bluff,
> Flocks in to hear
> Ma do her stuff.

But where Ma Rainey is realized as a mythic goddess within Black folk culture, Mame is shown to be the double victim of sexual and racial exploitation. Her social role is that of a less-than-willing performer:

> Mame was singing
> At the Midnight Club.
> And the place was red
> With blues.
> She could shake her body
> Across the floor.
> For what did she have
> To lose?

The question of loss in the poem becomes a chilling, moral refrain: "For what did she have / To lose?" This question is literally answered by the other losses in Mame's private life: her mother, father, relatives, and children. Indeed, unlike the celebrated public performances of Ma Rainey that transformed private griefs into public theatre:

> O Ma Rainey,
> Sing yo' song;
> Now you's back
> Whah you belong,
> Git way inside us,
> Keep us strong. . . .

Mame sings primarily to exorcise herself of the frustrations of unrequited love and intraracial discrimination:

> I loved my daddy.
> But what did my daddy
> Do?
> I loved my daddy.
> But what did my daddy
> Do?
> Found him a brown-skin chicken
> What's gonna be
> Black and blue.

Nonetheless, Mame's problem, as the "Queen of the Blues," might well be her lack of conformity within the Blues tradition. Her questioning rebuke of her profession suggests misplaced values: "But when has a man / Tipped his hat to me?" The most obvious answer, as more than one critic of the poem has suggested, is that the pinches and slaps Mame receives are part of the time-honored rituals of a Blues performance.[12] But as a Black woman whose frustrated life compares with Mabbie and Pearl May Lee, Mame is authentic. Her complaint is not about her demeaning social role as a nightclub performer who is paid to flesh-out the dreams and sexual aspirations of her largely male audience, but more substantially about her dignity as a human being. The real price Mame pays is the loss of her female identity. What she laments is the blurred distinction between her stagelife as a romantic prop and her real life as a Black woman.

IV

To be sure, the Harlem Renaissance poets were not solely romantic in their portrayal of Black women; there was, within their poetry, an equally strong impulse towards realism. In "Harlem Shadows" (*HS*, p. 22), for example, McKay shows the seamier side of Harlem nightlife, wherein "little dark girls" prowl the streets as prostitutes:

> I hear the halting footsteps of a lass
>   In Negro Harlem when the night lets fall
> Its veil. I see the shapes of girls who pass
>   To bend and barter at desire's call.
> Ah, little dark girls who in slippered feet
> Go prowling through the night from street to street!

And Sterling Brown, although he is less dramatic than McKay in his poem "Bessie" (*SR*, p. 41), nonetheless recognizes the realistic underside of urban life for Black women:

> Who will know Bessie now of these who loved her;
>   Who of her gawky pals could recognize
> Bess in this woman, gaunt of flesh and painted,
>   Despair deep bitten in her soft brown eyes?
>
> Would the lads who walked with her in dusk-cooled byways
>   Know Bessie now should they meet her again?
> Would knowing men of Fifth St. think that Bessie ever
>   Was happy-hearted, brave-eyed as she was then?

For Hughes, too, the Black woman in "Young Prostitute" (*WB*, p. 34) is described not as an Egyptian cameo, but rather as a "withered flower":

> Her dark brown face
> Is like a withered flower
> On a broken stem.
> Those kind come cheap in Harlem
> So they say.

In each of the above poems, the impulse toward romantic idealism of Black women gives way to critical realism; the mythic disguises that mask the harsh realities of social and economic deprivations are stripped away, and poor Black women are revealed as the most likely victims of racism within American society.

For Brooks, unlike the Renaissance poets, the victimization of poor Black women becomes not simply a minor chord but a predominant theme of *A Street in Bronzeville*. Few, if any, of her female characters are able to free themselves from the web of poverty and racism that threatens to strangle their lives. The Black heroine in "obituary for a living lady" (*Street*, p. 16) was "decently wild / As a child," but as a victim of society's hypocritical, puritan standards, she "fell in love with a man who didn't know / That even if she wouldn't let him touch her breasts she / was still worth his hours." In another example of the complex life-choices confronting Brooks's women, the two sisters of "Sadie and Maude" (*Street*, p. 14) must choose between death-in-life and life-in-death.[13] Maude, who went to college, becomes a "thin brown mouse," presumably resigned to spinsterhood, "living all alone / In this old house," while Sadie who "scraped life / With a fine-tooth comb" bears two illegitimate children and dies, leaving as a heritage for her children her "fine-tooth comb." What is noticeable in the lives of these Black women is a mutual identity that is inextricably linked with race and poverty.

For Hattie Scott, Brooks's protagonist in a series of vignettes that chronicle the life of a Black domestic worker (*Street*, pp. 33–37), the struggle to assert a female identity begins with the first poem, "the end of day." Hattie's life, measured by the sun's rising and setting, is described as a ceaseless cycle of menial tasks. The second poem in the series, "the date," details Hattie's attempt to free herself from the drudgery of domestic work:

> Whatcha mean talkin' about cleanin' silver?
> It's eight o'clock now, you fool.
> I'm leavin'. Got somethin' interestin' on my mind.
> Don't mean night school.

Hattie's "date" in the third poem, an appointment "at the hairdresser's," turns out to be a rather farcical attempt to have her hair done in an "upsweep" with "humpteen baby curls." Like Sadie's comb, Hattie's "upsweep" becomes symbolic of her persistent efforts to assert a positive identity. The reader senses, though, that her cosmetic changes, like her previous efforts with "Madam C. J. Walker" and "Poro Grower" (two hairdressers that promise instant beauty), will end in marginal success. Indeed, in the poem that follows, "when I die," Hattie imagines her funeral as a solitary affair attended by "one lone short man / Dressed all shabbily."

The final poem in the series, "the battle," ends not on a note of personal triumph for Hattie, but rather resignation and defeat. Hattie's neighbor and spiritual counterpart, Moe Belle Jackson, is routinely beaten by her husband:

> Moe Belle Jackson's husband
> Whipped her good last night.
> Her landlady told my ma they had
> A knock-down-drag-out fight.

Hattie's perception of the beating is charged with the anger and indignation of a *secret sharer* who, perhaps, realizes her own life in Moe Belle's
predicament:

> I like to think
> Of how I'd of took a knife
> And slashed all the quickenin'
> Out of his lowly life.

Nonetheless, in what is surely one of the finest examples of macabre
humor in Brooks's poetry, Hattie combines psychological insight and
laconic understatement in her final musings about Moe Belle's fate:

> But if I know Moe Belle,
> Most like, she shed a tear,
> And this mornin' it was probably,
> "More grits, dear?"

Brooks's relationship with the Harlem Renaissance poets, as *A Street
in Bronzeville* ably demonstrates, was hardly imitative. As one of the
important links with the Black poetic tradition of the 1920s and 1930s,
she enlarged the element of realism that was an important part of the
Renaissance world-view. Although her poetry is often conditioned by
the optimism that was also a legacy of the period, Brooks rejects outright
their romantic prescriptions for the lives of Black women. And in this
regard, she serves as a vital link with the Black Arts Movement of the
1960s that, while it witnessed the flowering of Black women as poets and
social activists as well as the rise of Black feminist aesthetics in the 1970s,
brought about a curious revival of romanticism in the Renaissance
mode.

However, since the publication of *A Street in Bronzeville*, Brooks has
not eschewed the traditional roles and values of Black women in American society; on the contrary, in her subsequent works, *Annie Allen*
(1949), *The Bean Eaters* (1960), and *In The Mecca* (1968), she has been
remarkably consistent in identifying the root cause of intraracial problems within the Black community as white racism and its pervasive
socio-economic effects.[14] Furthermore, as one of the chief voices of the
Black Arts Movement, she has developed a social vision, in such works
as *Riot* (1969), *Family Pictures* (1970), and *Beckonings* (1975), that describes
Black women and men as equally integral parts of the struggle for social
and economic justice.

Southern Illinois

Notes

1. Gwendolyn Brooks, *Report From Part I* (Detroit: Broadside Press, 1972), p. 202. All subsequent references to this source will be cited parenthetically in the text as *Report*.
2. Rolfe Humphrise, "Bronzeville," *New York Times Book Review*, 4 November 1945, p. 14.
3. "Songs and Funeral Chants," *Chicago Daily News*, 22 August 1945, p. 16.
4. Gwendolyn Brooks, *A Street in Bronzeville* (New York: Harper and Brothers, 1945), p. 2. All subsequent references to this source will be cited parenthetically in the text as *Street*.
5. See Nathan I. Huggins, *Harlem Renaissançe* (Oxford: Oxford University Press, 1971), p. 65.
6. Langston Hughes, "When Sue Wears Red," *The Weary Blues* (New York: Alfred A. Knopf, 1926), p. 66. All subsequent references to this source will be cited parenthetically in the text as *WB*.
7. Countee Cullen, "A Song of Praise," *Color* (New York: Harper and Brothers, 1925), p. 4. All subsequent references to this source will be cited parenthetically in the text as *Color*.
8. Claude McKay, "The Harlem Dancer," *Harlem Shadows* (New York: Harcourt, Brace and Company, 1922), p. 42. All subsequent references to this source will be cited parenthetically in the text as *HS*.
9. See Arthur P. Davis, "The Black-and-Tan Motif in the Poetry of Gwendolyn Brooks," *CLA Journal*, 6 (December, 1962), 90–97.
10. Countee Cullen, *The Ballad of the Brown Girl* (New York: Harper and Brothers, 1927), p. 1.
11. Sterling Brown, "Ma Rainey," *Southern Road* (Boston: Beacon Press, 1974), pp. 62–64. All subsequent references to this source will be cited parenthetically in the text as *SR*.
12. See George E. Kent, "The Poetry of Gwendolyn Brooks," *Blackness and the Adventure of Western Culture* (Chicago: Third World Press, 1972), p. 120.
13. See Harry B. Shaw, *Gwendolyn Brooks* (Boston: Twayne Publishers, 1980), p. 70.
14. See William Hansell, "Gwendolyn Brooks' *In the Mecca*: A Rebirth into Blackness," *Negro American Literature Forum*, 8 (Summer, 1974), 199–207.

Jean Toomer and the "New Negroes" of Washington

GEORGE B. HUTCHINSON
University of Tennessee, Knoxville

Up to now, scholars have neglected important evidence of the nature and extent of Jean Toomer's contact with black authors associated with the "New Negro" renaissance prior to and during the composition of *Cane*. Thus one of the chief students of his work has written recently that "he made no efforts to connect himself to a black tradition in letters, and his interactions with contemporary black artists were, at best, minimal and individualized. He acknowledged no black writers as having had an impact on him, and no one black read, criticized, or made suggestions about *Cane* while it was in progress."[1] Similarly, in their recent biography of Toomer, by far the most complete available, Cynthia Earl Kerman and Richard Eldridge suggest that only in 1922 (after his acquaintance with Waldo Frank) did Toomer become "an occasional visitor to the home of Alain Locke. . . . It was at Locke's home that Jean met some of the bright young [African-American] authors."[2] However, correspondence in the Alain Locke collection at the Moorland-Spingarn Research Center at Howard University proves that, in fact, Toomer knew Alain Locke at least as early as 1919, that he participated in the "literary evenings" (which were originally *Toomer's* idea) at Georgia Douglas Johnson's home between 1920 and 1922, and

---

[1] Nellie McKay, "Jean Toomer in His Time: An Introduction," in *Jean Toomer: A Critical Evaluation* (Washington: Howard Univ. Press, 1988), p. 10. The research for this article was pursued as part of a larger project entitled "American Cultural Nationalism and the Harlem Renaissance," which was funded in 1989–90 by a National Endowment for the Humanities fellowship. I would like to thank Esme E. Bhan, Research Associate at the Moorland-Spingarn Research Center, for generously aiding my research.

[2] *The Lives of Jean Toomer: A Hunger for Wholeness* (Baton Rouge: Louisiana State Univ. Press, 1987), pp. 91–92. Throughout their generally outstanding biography, Kerman and Eldridge make no reference to materials in the Alain Locke Papers at the Moorland-Spingarn Research Center of Howard University. Nellie Y. McKay's *Jean Toomer, Artist* (Chapel Hill: Univ. of Carolina Press, 1984) also neglects this source, as have the many other works on Toomer's life and art.

American Literature, Volume 63, Number 4, December 1991. Copyright © 1991 by Duke University Press. CCC 0002-9831/91/$1.50.

that, indeed, he attempted to sway the participants in her salon
to his own views of the "American" race by leading a series of
study sessions concerned with the topic. It appears that these
sessions had an important impact on Georgia Douglas Johnson's
own volume of 1922, *Bronze*. Moreover, it seems highly likely
that, in fact, Toomer read portions of *Cane* before the group.

The correspondence that supports these contentions has thus
far escaped the notice of Toomer scholars, who have not consulted the Alain Locke papers.[3] The first evidence of Toomer's
connection with Locke is a simple note addressed to Locke,
dated 11 November 1919, asking if it would be convenient for
Toomer to visit the Howard University professor on the thir-
teenth. Clearly, Toomer had known Locke previously, although
they were probably not on close terms. In another note of
24 December 1920 Toomer writes that he would like to stop by
and "chat," and sends Christmas greetings to Locke's mother,
which would indicate that the two men were by then rather well
acquainted with each other.

Four months earlier, on 20 August 1920, Georgia Douglas
Johnson, in writing to thank Locke for his "magnificent review"
of her book *The Heart of a Woman and Other Poems* (1918),
went on to mention that "Jean Toomer is here, could you bring
your mother over Saturday evening to my home. I think Mary
Burrill [a black playwright] will be there. Mr. Toomer wishes
to show us his books also. He says that he has some very good
finds." Clearly, Toomer was at least occasionally spending evenings at Johnson's home and sharing his reading during this
period shortly following his first involvement with the New
York intellectuals. Moreover, as the letter implies, he had been
involved with the Washington group even before he met Lola

[3] A neglected but important article on the literary circle led by Georgia Douglas
Johnson does make brief reference to this correspondence and connects Toomer with
Johnson and Locke. See Ronald M. Johnson, "Those Who Stayed: Washington Black
Writers of the 1920s," *Records of the Columbia Historical Society*, 50 (1980), 484–99.
Concerning the Washington group, see also Jeffrey C. Stewart, "Alain Locke and Georgia Douglas Johnson, Washington Patrons of Afro-American Modernism," *Washington
Studies*, 12 (July 1986), 37–44. Throughout my article, passages from the correspondence
in the Alain Locke Papers are quoted with permission of the Moorland-Spingarn Research Center, Howard University. The correspondence from this collection, which has
yet to be catalogued, will be identified within my text by date and the name of Locke's
correspondent.

Ridge, Waldo Frank, and company: "He has met some of the very delightful writers of New York and has improved immensely. Also I wish you would hear his two little gems." As this letter is dated over a year before Toomer would journey to Sparta, Georgia, his "gems" probably do not include pieces published in *Cane*, but one cannot dismiss the possibility out of hand. Certainly, the evidence proves that Toomer was sharing his writing with the chief circle of black writers in Washington three years before the publication of *Cane* and over a year and a half before he was in regular correspondence with Waldo Frank. It hints, further, at the possibility of a longstanding acquaintance for which evidence is slim probably for the simple reason that he had no reason to correspond with people living in his own city.

In the fall and winter of 1920–21, Toomer was meeting with the Washington group at Georgia Douglas Johnson's home and introducing them to his ideas, the books he had been reading, and some of the work he himself had written. Indeed, these evenings surely constitute the autobiographical basis for scenes in his posthumously published play, *Natalie Mann*, which involves— among other things—the conflict between one of Toomer's hero/prophets of the "new race" (Nathan Merilh) and a group of repressed, bourgeois "Negro" intellectuals.[4] Merilh and his lover, Mertis Newbolt, ultimately leave Washington and settle into an apartment in New York City, where they are involved with a multi-ethnic group of left-wing writers and intellectuals partially resembling the circle with which Toomer himself associated. None of the characters in either Washington or New York seems individually drawn from a person Toomer knew in those places, and the representation of the Washington circle makes it out to be more repressive and imitative of white culture than was Johnson's group. The characters in the play, for example, are ashamed of the spirituals. Nonetheless, the theme that African-American intellectuals must emerge from a double "crust" of American "Puritanism" and excessive racial self-defensiveness— which merely exacerbates their self-inhibitions—is one that ap-

[4] *Natalie Mann*, in *The Wayward and the Seeking: A Collection of Writings by Jean Toomer*, ed. Darwin Turner (Washington: Howard Univ. Press, 1980), pp. 243–325.

pears in Toomer's manuscripts of the period and that he clearly considered applicable to the Washington intelligentsia.[5]

On 26 January 1921, some eight months before he would go to Sparta, Georgia, Toomer wrote Alain Locke that he had held two meetings at Johnson's home of a group "whose central purpose is an historical study of slavery and the Negro, emphasizing the great economic and cultural forces which have largely determined them. The aim is twofold, first, to arrive at a sound and just criticism of the actual place and condition of the mixed-blood group in this country, and, second, to formulate an ideal that will be both workable and inclusive."[6] In taking on the topic of "miscegenation," Toomer was going to the heart of one of the most taboo topics in American culture generally, apparently striving to help his friends break out of their "crust" to achieve an "inclusive" vision. The terms match those Nathan Merilh uses to describe his own philosophy in *Natalie Mann*. The phrasing leaves it unclear as to whether Toomer considers the "mixed-blood group" to *be* the Negro group or a group no longer identical with the Negro group. It is worth pointing out, however, that Johnson herself, like perhaps most of those who met at her home, was quite light-skinned and knew of considerable "miscegenation" in her family background. Moreover, both she and Toomer could remember a period in which racial definition in Washington society was less rigid, less distinctly bifurcated

[5] See, in particular, "The Negro Emergent," box 51, folder 1114; untitled ms., box 48, folder 1010; and letter to Mae Wright, 4 August 1922, box 9, folder 283, all in the Jean Toomer Papers, Collection of American Literature, Beinecke Rare Book and Manuscript Library, Yale University, and quoted with permission of the Yale University Library. Of Georgia Douglas Johnson herself, Toomer wrote to John McClure, "Too much poetic jargon, too many inhibitions check the flow of what I think to be real (if slender) lyric gift." Letter of 6 October 1922, in Jean Toomer Papers, box 7, folder 22.

[6] Alain Locke Papers. The members of this group included Mary Burrill (the black playwright), Georgia Douglas Johnson, a Miss Scott of Howard University, Mary Craft, E. C. Williams, and Henry Kennedy (Toomer's longtime friend). This may well have represented the beginning of the weekly "conversations" at Johnson's home that would take place regularly for a decade. Gloria T. Hull quotes Johnson as saying the evenings were Toomer's idea. However, because the first public mention of them does not appear until October 1926 (in Gwendolyn Bennett's "Ebony Flute" column for *Crisis* magazine), Hull implies that they began in the mid-twenties. At this point Toomer had been out of contact with the Washington artists and intellectuals for nearly three years. If the weekly conversations were Toomer's idea, they would surely have started between 1920 and 1922 when Toomer was in Washington and in regular contact with Johnson, Locke, and their friends. See Hull, *Color, Sex, and Poetry: Three Women Writers of the Harlem Renaissance* (Bloomington: Indiana Univ. Press, 1987), p. 165.

into "black" and "white" worlds, than it had become by 1920, the last year in which the "mulatto" designation was included in the U. S. census. A short generation or two earlier, the "mulatto elite" had not been so closely identified with the black masses as they were during the twenties, and liaisons between whites and "mulattoes," including marriage, were more prevalent and openly acknowledged than they would be by 1915.[7] One of the great ironies of Toomer's career is that he matured during the very period in which black as well as white Americans became most insistent upon maintaining "racial integrity."

Some evidence of the nature of the "ideals" to which Toomer attempted to lead the study-group members can be found in Georgia Douglas Johnson's own work of this period. Toomer mentions in his letter to Locke that "as a natural outgrowth" of the meetings "should come the reading of original efforts." Surely it was at this time that Johnson herself wrote the poems of the "new race" which constitute the central section, "Exaltation," in her volume of 1922, *Bronze* (Boston: B. J. Brimmer). "Cosmopolite" is worth quoting in full:

> Not wholly this or that,
> But wrought
> Of alien bloods am I,
> A product of the interplay
> Of traveled hearts.
> Estranged, yet not estranged, I stand
> All comprehending;
> From my estate
> I view earth's frail dilemma;
> Scion of fused strength am I,
> All understanding,
> Nor this nor that
> Contains me. (P. 59)

This poem conveys a very different concept of the "mulatto" than that of, say, Langston Hughes—whose "tragic mulatto" would be not a "fused" and all-comprehending child of "traveled hearts," "scion" of an "estate" transcending the color line,

---

[7] For a fascinating discussion of the gradual rigidification of the black/white racial dualism in the United States, see Joel Williamson, *New People: Miscegenation and Mulattoes in the United States* (New York: Free Press, 1980), pp. 61–139.

but rather a self-divided, disinherited, homeless soul conceived in heartless lust and identified as "neither white nor black" (as opposed to *both* white *and* black).[8]

Indeed, an integral biracial identity rarely appears as a viable possibility in American literature. According to Judith Berzon, the options open to fictional "mulattoes" are restricted to their becoming African-American race leaders, " 'passing,' adopting a white middle-class image and value system, or succumbing to despair."[9] Even in African-American fiction since the Harlem Renaissance, typically the "mulatto" character either is destroyed (or spiritually diminished) by inner conflicts caused by his/her alienated condition in a racially bifurcated society, or he/she becomes "whole" by becoming wholly "black." The idea of biracial persons achieving healthy identities by embracing their multiple ancestry has been virtually unthinkable to both writers and critics; such persons are truly the invisible men and women of our racial ideology, and pose the most radical challenge to racialist discourse.[10] Toomer and Johnson offer rare retorts to conventional encodings of the "mulatto" (for whom we still have no generally accepted, non-pejorative name). Both confronted the challenge of arriving at tropes which would combat the negative and "tragic" imagery. In "Fusion," Johnson would use the "river" image that appealed to Toomer as a metaphor for the fact of racial intermingling:

> How deftly does the gardener blend
> This rose and that
> To bud a new creation,
> More gorgeous and more beautiful
> Than any parent portion,
> And so,
> I trace within my warring blood
> The tributary sources,
> They potently commingle
> And sweep
> With new-born forces! (*Bronze*, p. 60)

[8] See especially Hughes's poems "Cross," in *The Weary Blues* (New York: Knopf, 1926), p. 52; and "Mulatto," in *Fine Clothes to the Jew* (New York: Knopf, 1927), pp. 71–72.

[9] *Neither White Nor Black* (New York: New York Univ. Press, 1978), p. 14.

[10] For a provocative discussion of this issue, see especially Werner Sollors, " 'Never Was Born': The Mulatto, an American Tragedy?" *Massachusetts Review*, 27 (1986), 293–316.

Although Johnson makes use of the traditional trope of "warring blood," she feels the internal conflict as the prelude to a potent synthesis. Her phrasing, moreover, directly contradicts the concept, once common in Southern white racial ideology, that "mulattoes" could not reproduce with each other beyond two or three generations. "Highly ephemeral persons," "effete . . . both biologically and, ultimately, culturally," according to a pervasive mythology, they were destined to disappear since they could reproduce only by "back-crossing" with blacks or whites.[11] This is hardly the view that Johnson conveys in what is arguably the climactic section of her carefully organized volume. In "Perspective" (also part of the "Exaltation" section of *Bronze*), the speaker takes comfort in the thought that she is "a dark forerunner of a race burgeoning" (p. 61); clearly this refers not to the great Negro race whose forerunners date back many centuries, but to a *new* "race."

Johnson seems, at least provisionally, to have adopted some of Toomer's views about the new American people. Indeed, from the early twenties on she would return to related themes throughout her life.[12] Later biracial writers would claim her as a "foremother": "The extent of her influence, of her philosophy of dawn-men born of the fused strength of tributary sources, deserves to be properly recognized. She was the first to give to peoples of mixed origin the pride in themselves that they so badly needed. She was the mother who nourished a whole generation of Eurasians and other 'mixed breeds' like myself," wrote Cedric Dover in 1952.[13] Her poems help support the idea that in his talks with the "New Negro" group that gathered at Johnson's house in the same year he went to Georgia, Toomer presented his developing racial ideology. It was no doubt one of this group who, when Toomer finished reading and explaining his poem "The First American" to him, shook his head and said, "You're white."[14]

---

[11] Williamson, pp. 73, 95. See also Thomas F. Gossett, *Race: The History of an Idea in America* (Dallas: Southern Methodist Univ. Press, 1963); and George Stocking, *Race, Culture, and Evolution* (New York: Free Press, 1968), pp. 48–49. It is interesting to note that images such as these infuse much of the modern scholarship concerning the "disappearances" of Jean Toomer and Nella Larsen.

[12] See Hull, pp. 155–211.

[13] "The Importance of Georgia Douglas Johnson," *Crisis*, 59 (1952), 635.

[14] Toomer, "On Being an American," Jean Toomer Papers, box 15, folder 2. This

Toomer kept up his contact with the Washington circle as
he worked on *Cane*. Indeed, he wrote Locke from Sparta on
8 November 1921, stating that "There is poetry here—and
drama, but the atmosphere for one in my position is almost pro-
hibitory"—suggesting something of the autobiographical facts
behind "Kabnis." Interestingly, in this letter Toomer expresses
his sense that the life of the "Negro" of the South offers a "virgin" field to the writer, yet he does not believe that he can fully
take advantage of it—"for its real exploitation, one would have
to come into it under different circumstances" (presumably, not
as a teacher). Less than three weeks later, he would write Locke
again to say that he would soon be leaving, "both in the interest
of the school (raising funds) and for purposes of my own"—
evidence that he was expected to remain associated with the
school beyond the two months he actually spent teaching there.
He goes on to mention that he will be in Washington for several
days before pushing on for New York, where "several informal
lectures" were supposed to be arranged for him: "And of course
I have material. Want to see you."[15] What this letter proves is
that Toomer was sharing the material that went into *Cane* with
Locke from early on, that he in fact turned to Locke as an advisor and supporter during the crucial period in which his book
was taking shape.

Moreover, he continued to do so. On 1 August 1922 he wrote
to express his appreciation for Locke's criticism of an unspecified
piece which apparently went into *Cane*: "I liked your criticism.
The cocoon *is* both tight and intense." This letter also indicates
that Locke was putting him in touch with one of Locke's own
closest friends and most trusted critics, C. Henry Dickerman:
"Dickerman has not returned the Ms. but there is no hurry.
Little Review has the original."[16] Locke (or "Lockus" as Dickerman addressed him) and "Dickus" were intimate friends from
their years at Philadelphia's Central High School until Dicker-

episode is discussed in Kerman and Eldridge, pp. 80–81. "The First American" was a
poem, no longer extant, that conveyed Toomer's conception of the "new race" coming
into being in the United States, a mixture of all the "older" races, and of which he considered himself the first conscious member. After considerable revision it became "Blue
Meridian."

   [15] Toomer to Locke, 24 November 1921, in Alain Locke correspondence, Moorland-
Spingarn Research Center, Howard University.

   [16] Toomer to Locke, 1 August 1922.

man's early death in 1927.[17] Their letters show an astonishing range of knowledge about literature, from the Greek classics to the full gamut of pre-Raphaelites and early modernists of Europe. That Locke would pass on one of Toomer's sketches—probably "Fern"—to this trusted friend indicates the deep interest and confidence he had in Toomer's work.[18]

Toomer was clearly grateful for whatever advice Locke had to offer, and he asked Boni and Liveright to send this advisor a copy of *Cane* as soon as it came out, agreeing at the same time to give Locke "some sort of play" for a volume Locke was planning in August 1923.[19] Hence, just before the publication of *Cane*, Toomer seems to feel no conflict with Locke or ambivalence about being connected with his project—although we know that at this time Toomer was fully committed to his theory of the "American race" and that he did not consider himself a Negro. On the other hand, Locke certainly considered himself a mentor to Toomer. In an undated, private note located amid the correspondence with Countee Cullen, he refers to Toomer as one of his "spiritual children," consoling himself that if some day he must plead guilty to "corrupting the youth" he can take pride in the artists he had nurtured: "Can a bad tree bring forth good fruit?"

With the publication and public reception of *Cane*, Toomer's connection with Locke—and apparently with the other members of the Washington group—came largely to an end. Yet he did not cut off all contact with "New Negroes" in Harlem. Ethel Ray Nance (Charles S. Johnson's assistant at *Opportunity* magazine) remembered his visiting the Harlem apartment she shared with Regina Anderson in 1924 or 1925, when prominent black writers often dropped by.[20] Moreover, well after *Cane* appeared, black friends such as Dorothy Peterson and Aaron Douglas con-

---

[17] See letters from Dickerman in Alain Locke correspondence, Moorland-Spingarn Research Center, Howard University. Not only had Dickerman, who was white, gone to Harvard with Locke after high school, but both had been Rhodes Scholars together at Oxford. The two men shared intimate confidences about their sexual lives, the literature of homosexuality, and their own literary ambitions.

[18] The reference to the *Little Review* suggests that the unnamed work was "Fern," the only Toomer piece of this period that was published in that magazine.

[19] Toomer to Locke, 17 August 1923.

[20] Ann Allen Shockley, transcript of interview with Mrs. Ethel Ray Nance, 18 November and 23 December 1970, Oral History Collection, Fisk University Library.

tinued to visit him at his home on East 10th Street, according to his second wife.[21] Toomer was not, then, avoiding contact with black artists at this time, although he did not count himself one of them. Neither was he "turning his back" on them; he apparently desired their company. At least for the time being, his actions in this respect remained consistent with those of the pre-*Cane* period. In fact, in 1925, he ran meetings in Harlem attempting to convert black intellectuals to the Gurdjieff system for the "harmonious development of man"—which entailed adopting Toomer's basic racial position.[22] Moreover, following up on an earlier commitment, Toomer would allow Locke to use the play *Balo* in an anthology of "Negro plays" (which he probably did not interpret to mean plays necessarily *by* Negroes, as indeed many Harlem Renaissance writers, including Locke, did not), and Locke would use pieces from *Cane* in *The New Negro* (without Toomer's permission); but in other respects their relationship ended. This is one more indication of the dismay Toomer apparently felt when he was identified as a "Negro writer" after the publication of his book. Perhaps he felt that Locke, along with other friends, had betrayed him in ignoring his long-held convictions concerning the "American race"—convictions he had openly shared with and explicitly articulated for the African-American intelligentsia of Washington, and which perhaps, as David Bradley and Alain Solard have argued, he believed essential to an adequate understanding of *Cane* itself.[23]

---

[21] Ann Allen Shockley, taped interview with Marjorie Content Toomer, 24 October 1970, Oral History Collection, Fisk University Library.

[22] Kerman and Eldridge, pp. 143–44.

[23] Bradley, "Looking Behind *Cane*," *Southern Review*, 21 (1985), 692–93; Solard, "The Impossible Unity: Jean Toomer's 'Kabnis,'" in *Myth and Ideology in American Culture*, ed. Regis Durand (Villeneuve d'Ascq: Univ. de Lille III, 1976), pp. 175–94.

Acknowledgments

Bremer, Sidney H. "Home in Harlem, New York: Lessons from the Harlem Renaissance Writers." *Proceedings of the Modern Language Association* 105, No. 1 (January 1990): 47–56. Reprinted by permission of the Modern Language Association of America. Copyright 1990 by the Modern Language Association. All rights reserved.

Fox-Genovese, Elizabeth. "Myth and History: Discourse of Origins in Zora Neale Hurston and Maya Angelou." *Black American Literature Forum* 24, No. 2 (Summer 1990): 221–35. Reprinted with the permission of Indiana State University, Department of English and the author.

Brigham, Cathy. "The Talking Frame of Zora Neale Hurston's Talking Book: Storytelling as Dialectic in *Their Eyes Were Watching God*." *College Language Association Journal* 37, No. 4 (June 1994): 402–19. Reprinted with the permission of the College Language Association.

Chauhan, P.S. "Rereading Claude McKay." *College Language Association Journal* 34, No. 1 (September 1990): 68–80. Reprinted with the permission of the College Language Association.

Lubiano, Wahneema. "Constructing and Reconstructing Afro-American Texts: The Critic as Ambassador and Referee." *American Literary History* 1, No. 2 (1989): 432–47. Reprinted with the permission of Oxford University Press and the author.

McKay, Nellie. "Black Theater and Drama in the 1920s: Years of Growing Pains." *The Massachusetts Review* 28 (1987): 615–26. Reprinted with the permission of Massachusetts Review, Inc.

Wall, Cheryl A. "Passing for What? Aspects of Identity in Nella Larsen's Novels." *Black American Literature Forum* 20, Nos. 1–2 (1986): 97–111. Reprinted with the permission of Indiana State University, Department of English.

Lauter, Paul. "Race and Gender in the Shaping of the American Literary Canon: A Case Study from the Twenties." *Feminist Studies* 9, No. 3 (Fall 1983): 435–63. Reprinted with the permission of the publisher, Feminist Studies, Inc., c/o Women's Studies Program, University of Maryland, College Park, MD 20742.

480   ACKNOWLEDGMENTS

Baker, Houston A., Jr. "Modernism and the Harlem Renaissance." *American Quarterly*
    39, No. 1 (1987): 84–97. Reprinted with permission of the author and The
    American Studies Association, publisher. Copyright (1987).

Lucky, Crystal J. "The Harlem Renaissance: A Revisionist Approach." *Focus on Robert*
    Graves and His Contemporaries 1, No. 12 (Summer 1991): 25–29. Reprinted
    with the permission of Nene College, Department of English.

Mudimbe-Boyi, Mbulamwanza. "African and Black American Literature: The 'Negro
    Renaissance' and the Genesis of African Literature in French." Translated by
    J. Coates. In Allen F. Davis, ed., *For Better or Worse: The American Influence on*
    the World. (Westport: Greenwood Press, 1981): 157–69. Reprinted with the
    permission of Greenwood Press. All rights reserved.

Honey, Maureen. "Survival and Song: Women Poets of the Harlem Renaissance."
    Women's Studies (Great Britain) 16, Nos. 3–4 (1989): 293–316. Reprinted
    with the permission of Gordon and Breach Science Publishers, Inc.

Pedersen, Carl. "The Harlem Renaissance and the American Twenties." *American Stud-*
    ies in Scandinavia [Norway] 19 (1987): 1–11. Reprinted with the permission
    of the University of Copenhagen.

Jones, Bridget. "With 'Banjo' By My Bed: Black French Writers Reading Claude
    McKay." *Caribbean Quarterly* [Jamaica] 38, No. 1 (March 1992): 32–39. Re-
    printed with the permission of the University of the West Indies, School of
    Continuing Studies.

Mulvey, Christopher. "Harlem: Entrance and Initiation." *European Contributions to*
    American Studies 17: *The Future of American Modernism: Ethnic Writing Between*
    the Wars (1990): 94–104.

Wolf, Manfred. "A Vision of Black Culture in Two Novels by Claude McKay." *Ameri-*
    can Studies in Scandinavia [Denmark] 23, No. 2 (1991): 78–82. Reprinted
    with the permission of the University of Copenhagen.

Gallagher, Brian. "About Us, for Us, Near Us: The Irish and Harlem Renaissances."
    Éire-Ireland: A Journal of Irish Studies 16, No. 4 (Winter 1981): 14–26. Re-
    printed with the permission of the Irish American Cultural Institute.

Fodde, Luisanna and Paola Boi. "Zora Neale Hurston, The Black Woman Writer in
    the Thirties and Forties (Part 1); Moses, Man of Power, Man of Knowledge
    (Part 2)." *European Contributions to American Studies* [Netherlands] 18: *Look-*
    ing Inward–Looking Outward: From the 1930s Through the 1940s (1990):
    127–35.

Vincent, Ted. "The *Crusader* Monthly's Black Nationalist Support for the Jazz Age."
    Afro-Americans in New York Life and History 15, No. 2 (1991): 63–76.
    Reprinted with the permission of the Afro-American Historical Association
    of the Niagara Frontier.

Flora, Peter. "Carl Van Vechten, Blanche Knopf, and the Harlem Renaissance."
    Library Chronicle of the University of Texas at Austin 22, No. 4 (1992): 64–83.
    Reprinted with the permission of the Harry Ransom Humanities Research
    Center, University of Texas, Austin.

Story, Ralph D. "Patronage and the Harlem Renaissance: You Get What You Pay For."
    College Language Association Journal 32, No. 3 (March 1989): 284–95. Re-
    printed with the permission of the College Language Association.

Estes-Hicks, Onita. "Jean Toomer and the Politics and Poetics of National Identity."
    Contributions in Black Studies 7 (1985–1986): 22–44. Reprinted with the per-
    mission of the Five College Black Studies Executive Committee.

Runcie, John. "Marcus Garvey and the Harlem Renaissance." *Afro-Americans in New
    York Life and History* 10, No. 2 (1986): 7–28. Reprinted with the permission
    of the Afro-American Historical Association of the Niagara Frontier.

Scruggs, Charles W. "Alain Locke and Walter White: Their Struggle for Control of the
    Harlem Renaissance." *Black American Literature Forum* 14, No. 3 (1980): 91–
    99. Reprinted with the permission of Indiana State University, Department
    of English.

Story, Ralph D. "Gender and Ambition: Zora Neale Hurston in the Harlem Renaissance."
    The Black Scholar 20, Nos. 3–4 (Summer/Fall 1989): 25–31. Reprinted with
    the permission of the Black Foundation.

Early, Gerald. "Three Notes Toward a Cultural Definition of the Harlem Renaissance."
    Callaloo 14, No. 1 (Winter 1991): 136–49. Reprinted with the permission of
    Johns Hopkins University Press.

Swartz, Patti Capel. "Masks and Masquerade: The Iconography of the Harlem Renais-
    sance." *Midwest Quarterly* 35, No. 1 (Autumn 1993): 49–62. Reprinted by
    permission of *Midwest Quarterly*.

Berry, Faith. "Black Poets, White Patrons: The Harlem Renaissance Years of Langston
    Hughes." *Crisis* 88, No. 6 (July 1981): 278–83, 306. Reprinted with the per-
    mission of the Crisis Publishing Company.

Winslow, Henry F. Sr. "Two Black Poets and Their Legacy." *Crisis* 87, No. 9 (November
    1980): 365–70, 372. Reprinted with the permission of the Crisis Publishing
    Company.

Dean, Sharon and Erlene Stetson. "Flower-Dust and Springtime: Harlem Renaissance
    Women." *The Radical Teacher: A Newsjournal of Socialist Theory and Practice* 18
    (1980): 1–8. Reprinted with the permission of the Boston Women's Teach-
    ers' Group.

Miller, Jeanne-Marie A. "Georgia Douglas Johnson and May Miller: Forgotten Play-
    wrights of the New Negro Renaissance." *College Language Association Journal*
    33, No. 4 (June 1990): 349–66. Reprinted with the permission of the Col-
    lege Language Association.

Rampersad, Arnold. "The Origins of Poetry in Langston Hughes." *Southern Review* 21,
    No. 3 (July 1985): 695–705. Reprinted with the permission of the author.

Bontemps, Arna Alexander and Jacqueline Fonvielle-Bontemps. "African-American
    Women Artists: An Historical Perspective." *Sage: A Scholarly Journal on Black
    Women* 4, No. 1 (Spring 1987): 17–24. Reprinted with the permission of the
    Sage Women's Educational Press, Inc.

Freeman, Alma S. "Zora Neale Hurston and Alice Walker: A Spiritual Kinship." *Sage:
    A Scholarly Journal on Black Women* 2, No. 1 (Spring 1985): 37–40. Reprinted
    with the permission of the Sage Women's Educational Press, Inc.

Smith, Gary. "Gwendolyn Brooks's *A Street in Bronzeville*, the Harlem Renaissance and
    the Mythologies of Black Women." *MELUS* 10, No. 3 (Fall 1983): 33–46.
    Reprinted with the permission of the Society for the Study of the Multi-
    Ethnic Literature of the United States.

Hutchinson, George B. "Jean Toomer and the 'New Negroes' of Washington." *American Literature: A Journal of Literary History, Criticism, and Bibliography* 63, No. 4 (December 1991): 683–92. Reprinted with the permission of Duke University Press.